*The Hermeneutics of the Subject*

# MICHEL FOUCAULT

## The Hermeneutics of the Subject

LECTURES AT THE COLLÈGE DE FRANCE,

1981-82

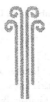

Edited by Frédéric Gros
General Editors: François Ewald and Alessandro Fontana

English Series Editor: Arnold I. Davidson

TRANSLATED BY GRAHAM BURCHELL

Picador
New York

THE HERMENEUTICS OF THE SUBJECT. Copyright © 2001 by Éditions de Seuil/Gallimard. Edition established, under the direction of François Ewald and Alessandro Fontana, by Frédéric Gros. Translation © 2005 by Graham Burchell. Introduction © 2005 by Arnold I. Davidson. All rights reserved. Printed in the United States of America. For information, address Picador, 175 Fifth Avenue, New York, N.Y. 10010.

www.picadorusa.com

Picador® is a U.S. registered trademark and is used by St. Martin's Press under license from Pan Books Limited.

For information on Picador Reading Group Guides, as well as ordering, please contact Picador.
Phone: 646-307-5629
Fax: 212-253-9627
E-mail: readinggroupguides@picadorusa.com

Design by Newgen Imaging Systems (P) Ltd., Chennai, India

Library of Congress Cataloging-in-Publication Data

Foucault, Michel.
    [Herméneutique du sujet. English]
    The hermeneutics of the subject : lectures at the Collège de France, 1981–1982 / Michel Foucault ; edited by Frédéric Gros ; general editors, François Ewald and Alessandro Fontana ; translated by Graham Burchell.
        p. cm.
    Includes bibliographical references and index.
    ISBN 0-312-42570-8
    EAN 978-0-312-42570-8
      1. Self (Philosophy)—History. 2. Philosophy, Ancient. I. Gros, Frédéric. II. Ewald, François. III. Fontana, Alessandro. IV. Title.

B2430.F723H4713 2004
194—dc22                                                                     2004049020

First published in the United States by Palgrave Macmillan

# CONTENTS

**Foreword: François Ewald and Alessandro Fontana**  xiii

**Introduction: Arnold I. Davidson**  xix

**Translator's Note**  xxxi

**one**  6 JANUARY 1982: FIRST HOUR  1
*Reminder of the general problematic: subjectivity and truth.* ~
*New theoretical point of departure: the care of the self.* ~ *Interpretations of the Delphic precept "know yourself."* ~ *Socrates as man of care of the self: analysis of three extracts from* The Apology. ~ *Care of the self as precept of ancient philosophical and moral life.* ~ *Care of the self in the first Christian texts.* ~ *Care of the self as general standpoint, relationship to the self and set of practices.* ~ *Reasons for the modern elimination of care of the self in favor of self-knowledge: modern morality; the Cartesian moment.* ~ *The Gnostic exception.* ~ *Philosophy and spirituality.*

**two**  6 JANUARY 1982: SECOND HOUR  25
*Presence of conflicting requirements of spirituality: science and theology before Descartes; classical and modern philosophy; Marxism and psychoanalysis.* ~ *Analysis of a Lacedaemonian maxim: the care of the self as statutory privilege.* ~ *First analysis of Plato's* Alcibiades. ~ *Alcibiades' political expectations and Socrates'*

CONTENTS

*intervention. ~ The education of Alcibiades compared with that of young Spartans and Persian Princes. ~ Contextualization of the first appearance of the requirement of care of the self in* Alcibiades: *political expectation and pedagogical deficiency; critical age; absence of political knowledge* (savoir). *~ The indeterminate nature of the self and its political implications.*

**three**    13 JANUARY 1982: FIRST HOUR    43

*Contexts of appearance of the Socratic requirement of care of the self: the political ability of young men from good families; the (academic and erotic) limits of Athenian pedagogy; the ignorance of which one is unaware. ~ Practices of transformation of the self in archaic Greece. ~ Preparation for dreaming and testing techniques in Pythagoreanism. ~ Techniques of the self in Plato's* Phaedo. *~ Their importance in Hellenistic philosophy. ~ The question of the being of the self one must take care of in the* Alcibiades. *~ Definition of the self as soul. ~ Definition of the soul as subject of action. ~ The care of the self in relation to dietetics, economics, and erotics. ~ The need for a master of the care.*

**four**    13 JANUARY 1982: SECOND HOUR    65

*Determination of care of the self as self-knowledge in the* Alcibiades: *conflict between the two requirements in Plato's work. ~ The metaphor of the eye: source of vision and divine element. ~ End of the dialogue: the concern for justice. ~ Problems of the dialogue's authenticity and its general relation to Platonism. ~ Care of the self in the* Alcibiades *in its relation to political action, pedagogy, and the erotics of boys. ~ Anticipation in the* Alcibiades *of the fate of care of the self in Platonism. ~ Neo-Platonist descendants of* Alcibiades. *~ The paradox of Platonism.*

**five**    20 JANUARY 1982: FIRST HOUR    81

*The care of the self from* Alcibiades *to the first two centuries* A.D.: *general evolution. ~ Lexical study around the* epimeleia. *~ A constellation of expressions. ~ Generalization of the care of* *the self: principle that it is coextensive with the whole of life.* ~ *Reading of texts: Epicurus, Musonius Rufus, Seneca, Epictetus, Philo of Alexandria, Lucian.* ~ *Ethical consequences of this generalization: care of the self as axis of training and correction; convergence of medical and philosophical activity (common concepts and therapeutic objective).*

**six**    20 JANUARY 1982: SECOND HOUR    107

*The privileged status of old age (positive goal and ideal point of existence).* ~ *Generalization of the principle of care of the self (with universal vocation) and connection with sectarian phenomena.* ~ *Social spectrum involved: from the popular religious milieu to Roman aristocratic networks of friendship.* ~ *Two other examples: Epicurean circles and the* Therapeutae *group.* ~ *Rejection of the paradigm of the law.* ~ *Structural principle of double articulation: universality of appeal and rarity of election.* ~ *The form of salvation.*

**seven**    27 JANUARY 1982: FIRST HOUR    125

*Reminder of the general characteristics of practices of the self in the first and second centuries.* ~ *The question of the Other: three types of mastership in Plato's dialogues.* ~ *Hellenistic and Roman period: the mastership of subjectivation.* ~ *Analysis of* stultitia *in Seneca.* ~ *The figure of the philosopher as master of subjectivation.* ~ *The Hellenic institutional form: the Epicurean school and the Stoic meeting.* ~ *The Roman institutional form: the private counselor of life.*

**eight**    27 JANUARY 1982: SECOND HOUR    149

*The professional philosopher of the first and second centuries and his political choices.* ~ *Euphrates in Pliny's* Letters: *an anti-Cynic.* ~ *Philosophy as social practice outside the school: the example of Seneca.* ~ *The correspondence between Fronto and Marcus Aurelius: systematization of dietetics, economics, and erotics in the guidance of existence.* ~ *Examination of conscience.*

## CONTENTS

**nine**    3 FEBRUARY 1982: FIRST HOUR    169

*Neo-Platonist commentaries on the* Alcibiades: *Proclus and Olympiodorus.* ∼ *The Neo-Platonist separation of the political and the cathartic.* ∼ *Study of the link between care of the self and care for others in Plato: purpose, reciprocity, and essential implication.* ∼ *Situation in the first and second centuries: self-finalization of the self.* ∼ *Consequences: a philosophical art of living according to the principle of conversion; the development of a culture of the self.* ∼ *Religious meaning of the idea of salvation.* ∼ *Meanings of* sōtēria *and of* salus.

**ten**    3 FEBRUARY 1982: SECOND HOUR    187

*Questions from the public concerning subjectivity and truth.* ∼ *Care of the self and care of others: a reversal of relationships.* ∼ *The Epicurean conception of friendship.* ∼ *The Stoic conception of man as a communal being.* ∼ *The false exception of the Prince.*

**eleven**    10 FEBRUARY 1982: FIRST HOUR    205

*Reminder of the double opening up of care of the self with regard to pedagogy and political activity.* ∼ *The metaphors of the self-finalization of the self.* ∼ *The invention of a practical schema: conversion to the self.* ∼ *Platonic* epistrophē *and its relation to conversion to the self.* ∼ *Christian* metanoia *and its relation to conversion to the self.* ∼ *The classical Greek meaning of* metanoia. ∼ *Defense of a third way, between Platonic* epistrophē *and Christian* metanoia. ∼ *Conversion of the gaze: criticism of curiosity.* ∼ *Athletic concentration.*

**twelve**    10 FEBRUARY 1982: SECOND HOUR    229

*General theoretical framework: veridiction and subjectivation.* ∼ *Knowledge* (savoir) *of the world and practice of the self in the Cynics: the example of Demetrius.* ∼ *Description of useful knowledge* (connaissances) *in Demetrius.* ∼ *Ethopoetic knowledge* (savoir). ∼ *Physiological knowledge* (connaissance) *in Epicurus.* ∼ *The* parrhēsia *of Epicurean physiologists.*

**thirteen** 17 FEBRUARY 1982: FIRST HOUR 247

*Conversion to self as successfully accomplished form of care of the self. ∼ The metaphor of navigation. ∼ The pilot's technique as paradigm of governmentality. ∼ The idea of an ethic of return to the self: Christian refusal and abortive attempts of the modern epoch. ∼ Conversion to self without the principle of a knowledge of the self. ∼ Two eclipsing models: Platonic recollection and Christian exegesis. ∼ The hidden model: Hellenistic conversion to self. ∼ Knowledge of the world and self-knowledge in Stoic thought. ∼ The example of Seneca: criticism of culture in Seneca's* Letters to Lucilius; *the movement of the gaze in* Natural Questions.

**fourteen** 17 FEBRUARY 1982: SECOND HOUR 271

*End of the analysis of the preface to the third part of* Natural Questions. *∼ Study of the preface to the first part. ∼ The movement of the knowing soul in Seneca: description; general characteristic; after-effect. ∼ Conclusions: essential implication of knowledge of the self and knowledge (connaissance) of the world; liberating effect of knowledge (savoir) of the world; irreducibility to the Platonic model. ∼ The view from above.*

**fifteen** 24 FEBRUARY 1982: FIRST HOUR 289

*The spiritual modalization of knowledge (savoir) in Marcus Aurelius: the work of analyzing representations; defining and describing; seeing and naming; evaluating and testing; gaining access to the grandeur of the soul. ∼ Examples of spiritual exercises in Epictetus. ∼ Christian exegesis and Stoic analysis of representations. ∼ Return to Marcus Aurelius: exercises of the decomposition of the object in time; exercises of the analysis of the object into its material components; exercises of the reductive description of the object. ∼ Conceptual structure of spiritual knowledge (savoir). ∼ Faust.*

**sixteen** 24 FEBRUARY 1982: SECOND HOUR 315

*Virtue and its relation to* askēsis. *∼ The absence of reference to objective knowledge of the subject in* mathēsis. *∼ The absence of* *reference to law in* askēsis. ~ *Objective and means of* askēsis. ~ *Characterization of the* paraskeuē: *the sage as athlete of the event.* ~ *Content of the* paraskeuē: *discourse-action.* ~ *Mode of being of these discourses: the* prokheiron. ~ Askēsis *as practice of the incorporation of truth-telling in the subject.*

**seventeen 3 MARCH 1982: FIRST HOUR** 331

*Conceptual separation of Christian from philosophical ascesis.* ~ *Practices of subjectivation: the importance of listening exercises.* ~ *The ambiguous nature of listening, between passivity and activity: Plutarch's* Peri tou akouein; *Seneca's letter CVIII; Epictetus' discourse II.23.* ~ *Listening in the absence of* tekhnē. ~ *The ascetic rules of listening: silence; precise non-verbal communication, and general demeanor of the good listener; attention (attachment to the referent of the discourse and subjectivation of the discourse through immediate memorization).*

**eighteen 3 MARCH 1982: SECOND HOUR** 355

*The practical rules of correct listening and its assigned end: meditation.* ~ *The ancient meaning of* meletē/meditatio *as exercise performed by thought on the subject.* ~ *Writing as physical exercise of the incorporation of discourse.* ~ *Correspondence as circle of subjectivation/veridiction.* ~ *The art of speaking in Christian spirituality: the forms of the spiritual director's true discourse; the confession (l'aveu) of the person being directed; telling the truth about oneself as condition of salvation.* ~ *The Greco-Roman practice of guidance: constitution of a subject of truth through the attentive silence of the person being guided; the obligation of* parrhēsia *in the master's discourse.*

**nineteen 10 MARCH 1982: FIRST HOUR** 371

Parrhēsia *as ethical attitude and technical procedure in the master's discourse.* ~ *The adversaries of* parrhēsia: *flattery and*

*rhetoric. ~ The importance of the themes of flattery and
anger in the new system of power. ~ An example: the
preface to the fourth book of Seneca's* Natural Questions
*(exercise of power, relationship to oneself, dangers of
flattery). ~ The Prince's fragile wisdom. ~ The points of
opposition between* parrhēsia *and rhetoric: the division
between truth and lie; the status of technique; the effects
of subjectivation. ~ Positive conceptualization of* parrhēsia:
*the* Peri parrhēsias *of Philodemus.*

**twenty**   10 MARCH 1982: SECOND HOUR   395

*Continuation of the analysis of* parrhēsia: *Galen's*
On the Passions and Errors of the Soul. *~ Characteristics
of* libertas *according to Seneca: refusal of popular and
bombastic eloquence; transparency and rigor; incorporation
of useful discourses; an art of conjecture. ~ Structure of*
libertas: *perfect transmission of thought and the subject's
commitment in his discourse. ~ Pedagogy and psychagogy:
relationship and evolution in Greco-Roman
philosophy and in Christianity.*

**twenty-one**   17 MARCH 1982: FIRST HOUR   413

*Supplementary remarks on the meaning of the Pythagorean
rules of silence. ~ Definition of "ascetics." ~ Appraisal of the
historical ethnology of Greek ascetics. ~ Reminder of the*
Alcibiades: *withdrawal of ascetics into self-knowledge as
mirror of the divine. ~ Ascetics of the first and second
centuries: a double decoupling (with regard to the principle
of self-knowledge and with regard to the principle of recognition
in the divine). ~ Explanation of the Christian fate of Hellenistic
and Roman ascetics: rejection of the gnosis. ~ Life's work. ~
Techniques of existence, exposition of two levels: mental exercise;
training in real life. ~ Exercises of abstinence: the athletic
body in Plato and the hardy body in Musonius Rufus. ~ The
practice of tests and its characteristics.*

**twenty-two** 17 MARCH 1982: SECOND HOUR 437

*Life itself as a test. ~ Seneca's* De Providentia: *the test of existing and its discriminating function. ~ Epictetus and the philosopher-scout. ~ The transfiguration of evils: from old Stoicism to Epictetus. ~ The test in Greek tragedy. ~ Comments on the indifference of the Hellenistic preparation of existence to Christian dogmas on immortality and salvation. ~ The art of living and care of the self: a reversal of relationship. ~ Sign of this reversal: the theme of virginity in the Greek novel.*

**twenty-three** 24 MARCH 1982: FIRST HOUR 453

*Reminder of results of previous lecture. ~ The grasp of self by the self in Plato's* Alcibiades *and in the philosophical texts of the first and second centuries A.D.: comparative study. ~ The three major forms of Western reflexivity: recollection, meditation, and method. ~ The illusion of contemporary Western philosophical historiography. ~ The two meditative series: the test of the content of truth and the test of the subject of truth. ~ The Greek disqualification of projection into the future: the primacy of memory; the ontologico-ethical void of the future. ~ The Stoic exercise of presuming evils as preparation. ~ Gradation of the test of presumption of evils: the possible, the certain, and the imminent. ~ Presumption of evils as sealing off the future and reduction of reality.*

**twenty-four** 24 MARCH 1982: SECOND HOUR 477

*The meditation on death: a sagittal and retrospective gaze. ~ Examination of conscience in Seneca and Epictetus. ~ Philosophical ascesis. ~ Bio-technique, test of the self, objectification of the world: the challenges of Western philosophy.*

Course Summary 491

Course Context: Frédéric Gros 507

Index of Names 551

Index of Notions and Concepts 557

# FOREWORD

MICHEL FOUCAULT TAUGHT AT the Collège de France from January 1971 until his death in June 1984 (with the exception of 1977, when he took a sabbatical year). The title of his chair was "The History of Systems of Thought."

On the proposal of Jules Vuillemin, the chair was created on 30 November 1969 by the general assembly of the professors of the Collège de France and replaced that of "The History of Philosophical Thought" held by Jean Hyppolite until his death. The same assembly elected Michel Foucault to the new chair on 12 April 1970.[1] He was 43 years old.

Michel Foucault's inaugural lecture was delivered on 2 December 1970.[2] Teaching at the Collège de France is governed by particular rules. Professors must provide 26 hours of teaching a year (with the possibility of a maximum of half this total being given in the form of seminars[3]). Each year they must present their original research and this obliges them to change the content of their teaching for each course. Courses and seminars are completely open; no enrollment or qualification is required and the professors do not award any qualifications.[4] In the terminology of the Collège de France, the professors do not have students but only auditors.

Michel Foucault's courses were held every Wednesday from January to March. The huge audience made up of students, teachers, researchers, and the curious, including many who came from outside France, required two amphitheaters of the Collège de France. Foucault often complained about the distance between himself and his "public" and of how few exchanges the course made possible.⁵ He would have liked a seminar in which real collective work could take place and made a number of attempts to bring this about. In the final years he devoted a long period to answering his auditors' questions at the end of each course.

This is how Gérard Petitjean, a journalist from *Le Nouvel Observateur*, described the atmosphere at Foucault's lectures in 1975:

> When Foucault enters the amphitheater, brisk and dynamic like someone who plunges into the water, he steps over bodies to reach his chair, pushes away the cassette recorders so he can put down his papers, removes his jacket, lights a lamp and sets off at full speed. His voice is strong and effective, amplified by loudspeakers that are the only concession to modernism in a hall that is barely lit by light spread from stucco bowls. The hall has three hundred places and there are five hundred people packed together, filling the smallest free space ... There is no oratorical effect. It is clear and terribly effective. There is absolutely no concession to improvisation. Foucault has twelve hours each year to explain in a public course the direction taken by his research in the year just ended. So everything is concentrated and he fills the margins like correspondents who have too much to say for the space available to them. At 7:15 Foucault stops. The students rush towards his desk; not to speak to him, but to stop their cassette recorders. There are no questions. In the pushing and shoving Foucault is alone. Foucault remarks: "It should be possible to discuss what I have put forward. Sometimes, when it has not been a good lecture, it would need very little, just one question, to put everything straight. However, this question never comes. The group effect in France makes any genuine discussion impossible. And as there is no feedback, the course is theatricalized. My relationship with the people there is like that of an actor or an acrobat. And when I have finished speaking, a sensation of total solitude ... ."⁶

Foucault approached his teaching as a researcher: explorations for a future book as well as the opening up of fields of problematization were formulated as an invitation to possible future researchers. This is why the courses at the Collège de France do not duplicate the published books. They are not sketches for the books, even though both books and courses share certain themes. They have their own status. They arise from a specific discursive regime within the set of Foucault's "philosophical activities." In particular, they set out the programme for a genealogy of knowledge/power relations, which are the terms in which he thinks of his work from the beginning of the 1970s, as opposed to the programme of an archeology of discursive formations that previously oriented his work.[7]

The courses also performed a role in contemporary reality. Those who followed his courses were not only held in thrall by the narrative that unfolded week by week and seduced by the rigorous exposition; they also found a perspective on contemporary reality. Michel Foucault's art consisted in using history to cut diagonally through contemporary reality. He could speak of Nietzsche or Aristotle, of expert psychiatric opinion or the Christian pastoral, but those who attended his lectures always took from what he said a perspective on the present and contemporary events. Foucault's specific strength in his courses was the subtle interplay between learned erudition, personal commitment, and work on the event.

⚜

With their development and refinement in the 1970s, cassette recorders quickly invaded Foucault's desk. The courses—and some seminars—have thus been preserved.

This edition is based on the words delivered in public by Foucault. It gives a transcription of these words that is as literal as possible.[8] We would have liked to present it as such. However, the transition from an oral to a written presentation calls for editorial intervention: At the very least it requires the introduction of punctuation and division into paragraphs. Our principle has been always to remain as close as possible to the course actually delivered.

Summaries and repetitions have been removed whenever it seemed to be absolutely necessary. Interrupted sentences have been restored and faulty constructions corrected. Suspension points indicate that the recording is inaudible. When a sentence is obscure, there is a conjectural integration or an addition between square brackets. An asterisk directing the reader to the bottom of the page indicates a significant divergence between the notes used by Foucault and the words actually uttered. Quotations have been checked and references to the texts used are indicated. The critical apparatus is limited to the elucidation of obscure points, the explanation of some allusions, and the clarification of critical points. To make the lectures easier to read, each lecture is preceded by a brief summary that indicates its principal articulations.[9]

The text of the course is followed by the summary published by the *Annuaire du Collège de France*. Foucault usually wrote these in June, some time after the end of the course. It was an opportunity for him to pick out retrospectively the intention and objectives of the course. It constitutes the best introduction to the course.

Each volume ends with a "context" for which the course editors are responsible. It seeks to provide the reader with elements of the biographical, ideological, and political context, situating the course within the published work and providing indications concerning its place within the corpus used in order to facilitate understanding and to avoid misinterpretations that might arise from a neglect of the circumstances in which each course was developed and delivered.

*The Hermeneutics of the Subject*, the course delivered in 1982, is edited by Frédéric Gros.

⚜

A new aspect of Michel Foucault's "œuvre" is published with this edition of the Collège de France courses.

Strictly speaking it is not a matter of unpublished work, since this edition reproduces words uttered publicly by Foucault, excluding the often highly developed written material he used to support his lectures. Daniel Defert possesses Michel Foucault's notes and he is to be warmly thanked for allowing the editors to consult them.

This edition of the Collège de France courses was authorized by Michel Foucault's heirs, who wanted to be able to satisfy the strong demand for their publication, in France as elsewhere, and to do this under indisputably responsible conditions. The editors have tried to be equal to the degree of confidence placed in them.

FRANÇOIS EWALD AND ALESSANDRO FONTANA

1. Michel Foucault concluded a short document drawn up in support of his candidacy with these words: "We should undertake the history of systems of thought." "Titres et travaux," in *Dits et Écrits, 1954-1988*, ed. Daniel Defert and François Ewald (Paris: Gallimard, 1994) vol. 1, p. 846; English translation, "Candidacy Presentation: Collège de France," in *Ethics: Subjectivity and Truth*, ed. Paul Rabinow, *The Essential Works of Michel Foucault, 1954-1984* (New York: The New Press, 1997), vol. 1, p. 9.
2. It was published by Gallimard in May 1971 with the title *L'Ordre du discours*.
3. This was Foucault's practice until the start of the 1980s.
4. Within the framework of the Collège de France.
5. In 1976, in the vain hope of reducing the size of the audience, Michel Foucault changed the time of his course from 17:45 P.M. to 9:00 A.M. Cf. the beginning of the first lecture (7 January 1976) of "*Il faut défendre la société.*" *Cours au Collège de France, 1976* (Paris: Gallimard/Seuil, 1997); English transalation, "*Society Must Be Defended.*" *Lectures at the Collège de France 1975-1976*, translation by David Macey (New York: Picador, 2003).
6. Gérard Petitjean, "Les Grands Prêtres de l'université française," *Le Nouvel Observateur*, 7 April 1975.
7. Cf. especially, "Nietzsche, la généalogie, l'histoire," in *Dits et Écrits*, vol. 2, p. 137. English translation by Donald F. Brouchard and Sherry Simon, "Nietzsche, Genealogy, History," in James Faubion, ed., *Aesthetics, Method, and Epistemology: Essential Works of Foucault 1954-1984*, vol. 2 (New York: The New Press, 1998), pp. 369-92.
8. We have made use of the recordings made by Gilbert Burlet and Jacques Lagrange in particular. These are deposited in the Collège de France and the Institut Mémoires de l'Édition Contemporaine.
9. At the end of the book, the criteria and solutions adopted by the editors of this year's course are set out in the "Course context."

# INTRODUCTION*

## Arnold I. Davidson

NO READER OF FOUCAULT'S books, not even the most attentive, would have been able to anticipate the richness and textual detail of this 1982 course. His last two published books, *L'Usage des plaisirs* and *Le Souci de soi*, both opened up new perspectives on the history of sexuality and elaborated a conception of the history of ethics as a history of forms of moral subjectivation and of those practices of the self intended to support and ensure the constitution of oneself as a moral subject. When placed in the context of *The Hermeneutics of the Subject*, the depth and force of Foucault's final innovations become clearer, more marked, and one sees that his history of ancient sexual practices was framed by a profound knowledge of the entire history of ancient thought.[1] Indeed, *The Hermeneutics of the Subject* was, and remains, the working out of a philosophically new point of access to the history of ancient, and especially Hellenistic, philosophy, a perspective that would be continued and developed in Foucault's final courses at the Collège de France.

Beginning with his very first lecture of January 6, 1982, Foucault aims to unsettle a dominant way of reading the history of ancient philosophy. Rather than isolating the Delphic prescription *gnōthi seauton* (know yourself) as the founding formula of the history of philosophy,

---

*In this introduction, I have chosen to focus on the often overlooked historiographical dimensions of *The Hermeneutics of the Subject*. A discussion of its more properly ethical dimensions would require more space than is available.

I am indebted to the John Simon Guggenheim Memorial Foundation for a fellowship that supported this work.

This introduction is dedicated to the students in my seminar at the University of Chicago who read *The Hermeneutics of the Subject* with me in French in autumn 2002.

Foucault insists, from the background of his interest in the question of the relations between the subject and truth, that the rule "know yourself" should be understood as being formulated in a "kind of subordination" to the precept of the care of the self. It is this *epimeleia heauton* (care of oneself) that provides the general framework and that characterizes the philosophical attitude within which the rule "know yourself" must be placed; thus, this latter precept should be interpreted "as one of the forms, one of the consequences, as a sort of concrete, precise, and particular application of the general rule: You must attend to yourself, you must not forget yourself, you must take care of yourself."[2] Taking Socrates as his point of departure—and emphasizing that he will elaborate this guiding framework of the care of the self not simply with respect to the history of representations, notions, and theories, but from the perspective of the history of practices of subjectivity (or what, strictly speaking and to avoid any misinterpretation, we should call "practices of subjectivation")—Foucault sets forth the historiographical and philosophical stakes of this course, stakes that directly implicate us, our mode of being as modern subjects:

> Throughout the long summer of Hellenistic and Roman thought, the exhortation to care for oneself became so widespread that it became, I think, a truly general cultural phenomenon. What I would like to show you, what I would like to speak about this year, is this history that made this general cultural phenomenon (this exhortation, this general acceptance of the principle that one should take care of oneself) both a general cultural phenomenon peculiar to Hellenistic and Roman society (anyway, to its elite), and at the same time an event in thought. It seems to me that the stake, the challenge for any history of thought, is precisely that of grasping when a cultural phenomenon of a determinate scale actually constitutes within the history of thought a decisive moment that is still significant for our modern mode of being subjects.[3]

Without at all minimizing the comprehensiveness of the scholarly detail of this course, when Foucault speaks of the idea of the care of the self as an "event in thought," we cannot help but hear in these words an invocation of some of the most original dimensions of his own philosophical practice.

Foucault's concern with the notion of event, and his argument that both historians and philosophers have in effect based their principles of intelligibility on practices of "désévénementialisation," has a long history in the development of his work.[4] He incited philosophers and historians to elaborate procedures that would allow them to perceive and think through the singularity of events, and Foucault once remarked that he dreamed of an "histoire événementielle" of philosophy itself. However, the precise expression "an event in thought" is found most explicitly in Foucault's late attempt to conceptualize what it means to "think the historicity itself of forms of experience."[5] If one main goal of Foucault's history of sexuality is to analyze sexuality as "an historically singular form of experience," one fundamental aim of *The Hermeneutics of the Subject* is to analyze the historically different forms of experience of the relation between the subject and truth: "In what historical form do the relations between the 'subject' and 'truth,' elements that do not usually fall within the historian's practice or analysis, take shape in the West?"[6] And the historically specific relation between the care of the self and knowledge of the self will be a crucial axis for understanding the historically and philosophically modifiable connection between the subject and truth. As Foucault says in a late lecture in this course, if we privilege the *gnōthi seauton*, if we consider it in itself and for itself alone, "we are in danger of establishing a false continuity and of installing a factitious history that would display a sort of continuous development of knowledge of the self," and of allowing "an explicit or implicit, but anyway undeveloped theory of the subject" to infiltrate our analysis.[7] If, instead, we follow Foucault's analysis of the connection and interaction between knowledge of the self and care of the self, and we see how in ancient thought "the *epimeleia heauton* is the real support of the imperative 'know yourself,'" then we will "seek the intelligibility and the principle for the analysis of the different forms of knowledge of the self in the different forms of the *epimeleia heauton*."[8] As a consequence, knowledge of the self will "not have the same form or function within this history of the care of the self":

> Which also means that the subject himself, as constituted by the form of reflexivity specific to this or that type of care of the self, will be modified. Consequently, we should not constitute a continuous history of the *gnōthi seauton* whose explicit or implicit postulate would be a general and universal theory of the subject, but should, I think, begin with an analytics of the forms of reflexivity, inasmuch as it is the forms of reflexivity that constitute the subject as such. We will therefore begin with an analytics of the forms of reflexivity, a history of the practices on which they are based, so as to be able to give the old traditional principle of "know yourself" its meaning—its variable, historical, and never universal meaning.[9]

And so Foucault identifies three major forms of reflexivity—memory, meditation, method—and his course as a whole intends to emphasize the specificity of the event in thought constituted by Hellenistic and especially Stoic meditation, an event in thought obscured or effaced by the event of method, what Foucault calls the "Cartesian moment."[10]

Analyzed from the point of view of the history of thought, these events are decisive for understanding the formation, the development, and the transformation of forms of experience—in the present case, of the forms of experience that tie together the subject and truth. And this entire course puts into practice the three general principles that Foucault elsewhere characterizes as the principle of the irreducibility of thought, the principle of the singularity of the history of thought, and the principle of the history of thought as critical activity.[11] We should pose the general questions raised by Foucault about the history of thought within the particular schema of this course:

> What is the price, for philosophy, of a history of thought? What is the effect, in history, of thought and the events that are peculiar to it? How do individual or collective experiences depend on singular forms of thought, that is, on that which constitutes the subject in its relations to truth, to the rule, to itself?[12]

An evident price and effect of this type of analysis is Foucault's recognition of the need to distinguish between "philosophy" and "spirituality," a distinction without which the modern relation between the subject and truth, taken as if universal, would cover over the singularity of the Hellenistic event of meditation and its constitution of the ethical subject of truth. Indeed, from the perspective of the historiography of philosophy, the innovation of this distinction is to allow a decisively new angle of approach to, and a notable reconfiguration of, the significant moments in the history of philosophical thought. Foucault begins as follows:

> We will call, if you like, "philosophy" the form of thought that asks, not of course what is true and what is false, but what determines that there is and can be truth and falsehood and that one can or cannot separate the true and the false. We will call "philosophy" the form of thought that asks what it is that allows the subject to have access to the truth and which attempts to determine the conditions and limits of the subject's access to the truth. If we call this "philosophy," then I think we could call "spirituality" the pursuit, practice, and experience through which the subject carries out the necessary transformations on himself in order to have access to the truth. We will call "spirituality" the set of these pursuits, practices, and experiences, which may be purifications, ascetic exercises, renunciations, conversions of looking, modifications of existence, etcetera, which are not for knowledge but for the subject, for the subject's very being, the price to be paid for access to the truth.[13]

In Foucault's subsequent work this distinction is specifically inflected in the direction of a distinction between a "philosophical analytics of truth in general" (also once called a "formal ontology of truth"), which poses the question of the conditions under which true knowledge is possible, and a "historical ontology of ourselves," one of whose principal questions concerns how we have constituted ourselves as subjects of knowledge and truth.[14] Both sets of distinctions highlight the difference between an analytical and formal inquiry into the conditions under which we can have access to truth and an inquiry into the practices we must undertake to transform ourselves, the necessary work of ourselves on ourselves, in order for us to have access to truth.

According to Foucault, the three most significant characteristics that set apart spirituality from philosophy are (1) spirituality postulates that the subject as such is not capable of having access to truth, and, more specifically, that truth is not given to the subject by a simple act of knowledge founded on his status as subject; (2) in order to have access to truth, the subject has to undergo a conversion or transformation and therefore his very being is at stake; (3) once the subject has access to truth, the effects of spirituality on the subject are such that his very being is fulfilled, transfigured, or saved. And Foucault concludes, from the perspective of spirituality: "In short, I think we can say that in and of itself an act of knowledge could never give access to the truth unless it was prepared, accompanied, doubled, and completed by a certain transformation of the subject; not of the individual, but of the subject himself in his being as subject."[15] Foucault goes on to make the historical claim that throughout Antiquity, in different modalities, "the philosophical question of 'how to have access to the truth' and the practice of spirituality (of the necessary transformations in the very being of the subject which will allow access to the truth) ... were never separate."[16] Thus we can see the significance, as an event in thought, of what Foucault calls the "Cartesian moment." If the notion of the care of the self refers to the set of conditions of spirituality, the Cartesian moment is the event that disqualifies the care of the self and requalifies the *gnōthi seauton*, dissociating a *philosophy* of knowledge from a *spirituality* of the transformation of the subject's very being by his work on himself.[17]

The so-called Cartesian moment allows Foucault to characterize the modern age of the relations between the subject and truth:

> ... we can say that we enter the modern age (I mean, the history of truth enters its modern period) when it is assumed that what gives access to the truth, the condition for the subject's access to the truth, is knowledge (*connaissance*) and knowledge alone... I think the modern age of the history of truth begins when knowledge itself and knowledge alone gives access to the truth. That is to

say, it is when the philosopher (or the scientist, or simply someone who seeks the truth) can recognize the truth and have access to it in himself and through his acts of knowledge alone, without anything else being demanded of him and without his having to alter or change in any way his being as subject.[18]

Even if we leave aside the further details of his analysis, it is nevertheless clear that Foucault understands the "Cartesian moment" not primarily as a chronological moment but as a conceptual moment in the history of thought, the moment in which philosophy is disconnected from spirituality. It is his focus on this pivotal modification in the relations between the subject and truth that allowed Foucault to remark brilliantly, as I remember it, that on this understanding Spinoza is one of the last ancient philosophers and Leibniz one of the first modern philosophers.[19]

Moreover, this historiographical picture of the relation between philosophy and spirituality provides the framework within which Foucault rereads a wide variety of figures in the history of thought, figures whose (otherwise unforeseen) contiguity arises precisely through their attempt, against our modern tradition, to reconnect the questions of philosophy with those of spirituality. As an example, Foucault gives us a brief but stunning interpretation of the figure of Faust, and especially of Goethe's Faust, describing the latter as the "hero" of a world of spiritual knowledge that is disappearing: "What Faust demands from knowledge are spiritual values and effects, which neither philosophy, nor jurisprudence, nor medicine can give him."[20] And when Foucault suggests, in this context, that it would be interesting to write the history of spiritual knowledge and of how this knowledge of spirituality, so prestigious in the Hellenistic period, was "gradually limited, overlaid, and finally effaced" by another mode of knowledge, the knowledge of intellectual cognition alone, we can already find traces of what such a history would look like in other lectures of this course.[21] Thus Foucault can account for the specificity of Jacques Lacan by describing him as the only psychoanalyst since Freud who has tried to make the question of the relation between truth and the subject resurface within psychoanalysis itself:

> ... in terms which are of course absolutely foreign to the historical tradition of this spirituality, whether of Socrates or Gregory of Nyssa and everyone in between, in terms of psychoanalytic knowledge itself, Lacan tried to pose what historically is the specifically spiritual question: that of the price the subject must pay for saying the truth, and of the effect on the subject of the fact that he has said, that he can and has said the truth about himself.[22]

And if the cost of failing to raise these questions is the collapse of psychoanalysis into psychologism (knowledge without the transformations of oneself required by spirituality), one price to be paid as a result of reintroducing these questions might be a certain form of "hermeticism" in which the reading of a text cannot consist in simply becoming aware of its ideas: "Lacan wanted the obscurity of his *Écrits* to be the very complexity of the subject, and wanted the work necessary to understand it to be a work to be carried out on oneself."[23]

In the wake of Foucault's historiographical suggestions, we can also appreciate the singularity of Wittgenstein, with respect to the tradition of analytic philosophy, by recognizing the way in which philosophy and spirituality are linked in his philosophical investigations. If philosophical work "really is more a working on oneself," then we can see why, as Stanley Cavell has definitively put it, Wittgenstein's style of thought "wishes to prevent understanding which is unaccompanied by inner change."[24] From this angle we can also understand why Wittgenstein's thought is so vehemently taken (correctly) as a challenge to the very edifice of the intellectual methods of traditional analytic philosophy. And the accusations of egoism and individual withdrawal that our modernity has lodged against the care of the self have their counterpart in the contemporary charges of narcissism with which Wittgenstein is taxed. Yet Wittgenstein is as rigorously austere in his thought as were the moralities elaborated under the guidance of the ancient care of the self.[25] If, as Foucault remarks, "in Greece, Gide would have been an austere philosopher," Wittgenstein would have been a Stoic.[26]

Returning to the overall perspective of *The Hermeneutics of the Subject*, I want to emphasize that the contrast between spirituality and philosophy should be aligned with a series of contrasts that runs throughout Foucault's writings and that focuses our attention on the way our philosophical tradition has ignored or effaced certain dimensions of our experience. I am thinking of the contrasts between exercise and system and between the singularity of events and architectonic order, both of which appear in Foucault's responses to Jacques Derrida.[27] In the ethical domain, the distinction is to be located in the differences between practices of the self and moral codes of behavior, or between a *tekhnē* and form of life and a corpus of rules.[28] Finally, in "Qu'est-ce que les Lumières?" Foucault distinguishes between an understanding of *Aufklärung* that consists in a commitment to certain theories, elements of doctrine, and accumulated bodies of knowledge and a conception of *Aufklärung* as the "permanent reactivation of an attitude," an *ēthos*, a form of philosophical life.[29] At the moment when Foucault fleshes out the various components of this attitude and specifically when he singles out that feature which he identifies as the "experimental attitude," he has recourse to the notion of *l'épreuve*, the testing of oneself, of one's mode of being and thought, which plays a crucial interpretative role in *The Hermeneutics of the Subject*.[30] He speaks of his concern to put historico-critical reflection to the test of concrete practices and even characterizes the philosophical *ēthos* appropriate to the critical ontology of ourselves "as an historico-practical test of the limits that we can go beyond, and therefore as the work of ourselves on ourselves as free beings."[31] Tests, techniques, practices, exercises, attitudes, events—so many layers of our experience that philosophy has turned away from and that Foucault was able to recover through a style of critical work that is inextricably historical and philosophical. No doubt, he transformed both history and philosophy in the process, but always while operating inside their concerns.

In a promiscuously cited passage of *L'Usage des plaisirs*, Foucault memorably writes:

But what therefore is philosophy today—I mean philosophical activity—if it is not the critical work of thought on itself? And if it does not consist in undertaking to know how and to what extent it would be possible to think differently, instead of legitimating what one already knows?...The "essay"—which one should understand as a modifying test of oneself in the game of truth and not as the simplifying appropriation of others for the purposes of communication—is the living body of philosophy, at least if the latter is still now what it was in the past, that is to say, an "ascesis," an exercise of oneself in thought.[32]

More often than not, the quotation of these remarks regarding the possibility of thinking differently avoids taking seriously the difficulties of exercise, of *askēsis*, of the modifying test of oneself, as if thinking differently were not a matter of slow, sustained, and arduous work. To bring into effect the practice of thinking differently, to modify oneself through the movements of thought, we have to detach ourselves from the already given systems, orders, doctrines, and codes of philosophy; we have to open up a space in thought for exercises, techniques, tests, the transfiguring space of a different attitude, a new *ēthos*, the space of spirituality itself. We have to prepare ourselves to face events in thought, events in our own thought. That is why Foucault's relentless pursuit of knowledge revolves not around the mere acquisition of knowledge, but around the value of losing one's way for the subject of knowledge (*"l'égarement de celui qui connaît"*), a losing one's way which is the price of self-transformation.[33] If we seal ourselves off from this possibility, we will inevitably take up a posture that Foucault found ridiculous—the strident voice of the philosopher-legislator who tells others how to think and what to do. One alternative, Foucault's alternative, was to explore what, *in his own thought*, can be changed by philosophical exercise, exercises that might then permit him to establish "a new and strange relation to himself."[34] An alternative of risks, it goes without saying, but thought without risks is an etiolated substitute for what philosophy can be.

1. For an articulation of the conception of ethics that is in fact common to *L'Usage des plaisirs*, *Le Souci de soi*, and *L'Herméneutique du sujet*, see section 3, "Morale et practique de soi," of the "Introduction" to *L'Usage des plaisirs* (Paris: Gallimard, 1984).
2. This volume, pp. 4-5.
3. Ibid., p. 9.
4. See, for example, Michel Foucault, "Revenir à l'histoire," in *Dits et écrits I, 1954-1975* (Paris: Gallimard, 2001), pp. 1144-48; "Réponse à Jacques Derrida," in *Dits et écrits I*, p. 1163; "Table ronde de 20 mai 1978," in *Dits et écrits II, 1976-1988* (Paris: Gallimard, 2001), pp. 842-44.
5. Michel Foucault, "Préface à l'*Histoire de la sexualité*," in *Dits et écrits II*, p. 1398.
6. Ibid., p. 1397, and this volume, p. 2.
7. This volume, p. 461.
8. Ibid., p. 462.
9. Ibid.
10. Ibid., pp. 460-61. For an earlier description of the practice of meditation, in a very different context, see Michel Foucault, "Mon corps, ce papier, ce feu," in *Dits et écrits I*, pp. 1124-25. Not to be underestimated is Foucault's indication, elsewhere in this course, of the significance of the *event* constituted by confession, by the necessity of telling the truth about oneself, which is central to the specifically Christian hermeneutics of the subject. See, for example, this volume, pp. 363-66. For a more general discussion of the significance of confession, see my introduction to the third part of *Michel Foucault. Philosophie. Anthologie établie et presentée par Arnold I. Davidson et Frédéric Gros* (Paris: Gallimard, 2004).
11. Foucault, "Preface à l'*Histoire de la sexualité*", p. 1399.
12. Ibid., p. 1400.
13. This volume, p. 15 (translation slightly modified).
14. See the two versions of "Qu'est-ce que les Lumières?" in *Dits et écrits II*, especially pp. 1395, 1506-07. For the expression "formal ontology of truth," see "La technologie politique des individus," in *Dits et écrits II*, pp. 1632-33.
15. This volume, pp. 15-16.
16. This volume, p. 17. Foucault's observations here about Aristotle as the exception should not be ignored.
17. This volume, p. 14.
18. This volume, p. 17 (translation slightly modified).
19. For such an interpretation of Spinoza, see Foucault's remarks at the beginning of the second hour of the January 6 lecture.
20. This volume, p. 310.
21. Ibid., pp. 308-9. Foucault's discussion of the relation between spirituality and philosophy is, as he himself told me, the fruit of his encounter with the work of Pierre Hadot on the tradition of spiritual exercises. See my "Préface" to the new enlarged French edition of Pierre Hadot, *Exercices spirituels et philosophie antique* (Paris: Albin Michel, 2002). The differences in the interpretations and uses of this tradition made by Foucault and Hadot have to be reexamined in the light of *The Hermeneutics of the Subject*. For an initial brief attempt to do so, see my "L'etica dell'inquietudine," in *La Repubblica*, April 2, 2004.
22. This volume, p. 30.
23. Michel Foucault, "Lacan, le 'libérateur' de la psychanalyse," in *Dits et écrits II*, p. 1024.
24. Ludwig Wittgenstein, *Culture and Value* (Chicago: University of Chicago Press, 1980) p. 16; Stanley Cavell, "The Availability of Wittgenstein's Later Philosophy," in *Must We Mean What We Say?* (New York: Charles Scribner's Sons, 1969) p. 72.
25. With respect to the charges of egoism and withdrawal, see Foucault's discussion, this volume, pp. 12-13. For an attempt to place Wittgenstein within the tradition of spiritual exercises, see my "Éthique, philosophie et exercices spirituels. De Plotin à Wittgenstein," in *Europe*, October 2004.

26. For Foucault's remark, see "A propos de la généalogie de l'éthique: un aperçu du travail en cours," in *Dits et écrits II*, p. 1435.
27. See Foucault, "Mon corps, ce papier, ce feu," p. 1126, and "Réponse à Jacques Derrida," pp. 1161-63.
28. Foucault, *L'Usage des plaisirs*, especially pp. 41-44, and this volume, pp. 422-25.
29. Foucault, "Qu'est-ce que les Lumières?" pp. 1390, 1396.
30. This volume, see especially the lectures of March 17 and March 24.
31. Foucault, "Qu'est-ce que les Lumières?" p. 1394.
32. Foucault, *L'Usage des plaisirs*, p. 16.
33. Ibid., p. 15.
34. Reading together Ibid., p. 16, and "Préface à l'*Histoire de la Sexualité*," p. 1403.

# TRANSLATOR'S NOTE

IN TRANSLATING FOUCAULT'S QUOTATIONS from Greek and Latin authors my intention has been to stay as close as possible to what Foucault actually says in his lectures. Consequently, I have always translated from Foucault's French sources rather than rely on existing English translations (which often differ significantly from the French). In making my translations I have, however, consulted existing English translations of the Greek and Latin, often, as in the case of Plato, referring to several variants. With a few exceptions—where the editor refers explicitly in the notes to a French or English translation used by Foucault or where only a French or English translation is available—page and/or paragraph numbers refer to the Greek or Latin texts. The works listed below give the titles used in the notes followed by the French translation given by the French editor and the principal English translation consulted. In the case of Plato, individual English translations have not been cited. There are a number of translations available for Plato—the 12 volume *Plato* in the Loeb Classical Library, which contains the Greek, the Hamilton and Cairns edition of *The Collected Dialogues of Plato*, Benjamin Jowett's *The Dialogues of Plato*, the various Penguin translations, and many others.

I would like to take this opportunity to thank Arnold Davidson for his support and assistance in making this translation, and Terry Cullen for invaluable help on a particularly difficult problem.

Cicero, *Tusculan Disputations*
 Cicéron, *Tusculanes*, t.II, translations by J. Humbert, Paris, Les Belles Lettres, 1931;

*Tusculan Disputations*, translations by J.E. King. Cambridge, Mass. and London: William Heinemann and G.P. Putnam's Sons, Loeb Classical Library, 1927.

Diogenes Laertius, *Lives of Eminent Philosophers*
Diogène Laërce, *Vies et Doctrines des philosophes*, translation under direction of M.-O. Goulet-Cazé. Paris: Le Livre de Poche, 1999;
*Lives of Eminent Philosophers*, in two volumes, translations by R. D. Hicks. Cambridge, Mass. and London: Harvard University Press and William Heinemann, Loeb Classical Library, 1925.

Epictetus, *Discourses*
Épictète, *Entretiens*, translations by J. Souilhé. Paris, Les Belles Lettres, 1963;
Epictetus, *The Discourses as Reported by Arrian*, in two volumes, translations by W. A. Oldfather. Cambridge, Mass. and London: Harvard University Press, Loeb Classical Library, 2000.

Epictetus, *The Encheiridion*
Épictète, *Manuel*, translations by É. Brehier, *Les Stoïciens*. Paris: Gallimard, La Pléiade, 1962;
*The Encheiridion*, translations by W.A. Oldfather in Epictetus, *The Discourses as reported by Arian*, vol. II. Cambridge, Mass. and London: Harvard University Press, Loeb Classical Library, 2000.

Epicurus, *Letters, Principal Doctrines, and Vatican Sayings*
Épicure, *Lettres et Maximes*, translations by M. Conche. Villers-sur-Mer: Éd. de Mégare, 1977;
*Letters, Principal Doctrines, and Vatican Sayings*, translations by R. M. Geer. Indianapolis: Bobbs-Merrill, 1964.

Galen, *On the Passions and Errors of the Soul*
Galien, *Traité des passions de l'âme et de ses erreurs*, translations by R. Van der Elst. Paris: Delagrave, 1914;
*On the Passions and Errors of the Soul*, translations by P.W. Harkins. Columbus, Ohio: Ohio State University Press, 1963.

Gregory of Nyssa, *Treatise on Virginity*
 Grégoire de Nysse, *Traité de la virginité*, translations by M. Aubineau. Paris: Éd. du Cerf, 1966;
 Gregory of Nyssa, *Treatise on Virginity*, translations by V.W. Callahan, in *Saint Gregory of Nyssa: Ascetical Works*. Washington, D.C.: Catholic University of America Press, 1966.

Hesiod, *Works and Days*
 Hésiode, *Les Travaux et les Jours*, translations by P. Mazon. Paris: Les Belles Lettres, 1928;
 *Works and Days*, translations by Richmond Lattimore, in *Hesiod*. Ann Arbor: University of Michigan Press, 1959.

Hippocrates, *Ancient Medicine*
 Hippocrate, *L'Ancienne Médecine*, translations by A.-J. Festigière. Paris: Klincksieck, 1948;
 Hippocrates, *Ancient Medicine*, translations by W.H.S. Jones, in W.H.S. Jones, *Philosophy and Medicine in Ancient Greece*. Baltimore: Johns Hopkins University Press, 1946.

Iamblichus, *Life of Pythagoras*
 Jamblique, *Vie de Pythagore*, translations by L. Brisson, A.-P. Segonds. Paris: Les Belles Lettres, 1996;
 Iamblichus (of Chalcis), *Life of Pythagoras*, translations by T. Taylor. London: J. M. Walkins, 1926.

Isocrates, *Busiris*
 Isocrate, *Busiris*, in Isocrates, *Discours*, t.I, translations by G. Mathieu and E. Brémond. Paris, Les Belles Lettres, 1923;
 *Busiris*, in *Isocrates*, vol. III, translations by Larue Van Hook. London and Cambridge, Mass.: William Heineman and Harvard University Press, Loeb Classical Library, 1945.

Marcus Aurelius, *The Correspondence of Marcus Cornelius Fronto with Aurelius Antoninus*
 A. Cassan, *Lettres inédites de Marc Aurèle et de Fronton*. Paris: A. Levavasseur, 1830;

*The Correspondence of Marcus Cornelius Fronto with Aurelius Antoninus*, translations by C.R. Haines. London and New York: Loeb Classical Library, 1919-1920.

Marcus Aurelius, *Meditations*
Marc Aurèle, *Pensées*, translations by A.I. Tannoy. Paris: Les Belles Lettres, 1925;
*The Meditations of Marcus Aurelius Antoninus*, in two volumes, translations by, A.S.L. Farquharson. Oxford: Clarendon Press, 1944.

Methodius of Olympus, *The Banquet*
Méthode d'Olympe, *Le Banquet*, translations by V.-H. Debidour. Paris: Éd. du Cerf, 1963;
*The Banquet of the Ten Virgins*, translations by W.R. Clark, in eds. A. Roberts and J. Donaldson, *Ante-Nicene Christian Library*, vol. 14, *The Writings of Methodius*. Edinburgh T. and T. Clark, 1869.

*Musonius Rufus*
Translations by A.-J. Festugière, in A.-J. Festugière, ed., *Deux prédicateurs dans l'Antiquité, Télès et Musonius*. Paris: Vrin, 1978;
Translations by Cora E. Lutz in Cora E. Lutz, "Musonius Rufus 'The Roman Socrates,'" *Yale Classical Studies*, vol. 10, Cambridge: Cambridge University Press, 1947.

Philo of Alexandria, *On the Contemplative Life*
Philon d'Alexandrie, *De Vita contemplative*, translations by P. Miquel. Paris: Éd. du Cerf, 1963.
*On the Contemplative Life*, in *The Works of Philo*, translations by C.D. Yonge. USA: Hendrickson Publishers, 1993.

Plato, *Alcibiades*
Platon, *Alcibiade*, in *Œuvres complètes*, t.I, translations by M. Croiset. Paris: Les Belles Lettres, 1920.

Plato, *Apology*
*Apologie de Socrate*, translations by M. Croiset, in *Œuvres complètes*, t.I. Paris: Les Belles Lettres, 1920.

Plato, *Charmides*
*Charmide*, translations by A. Croiset, in *Œuvres complètes*, t.II. Paris: Les Belles Lettres, 1921.

Plato, *Cratylus*
*Cratyle*, translations by L. Méridier, in *Œuvres complètes*, t.V-2. Paris: Les Belles Lettres, 1931.

Plato, *Gorgias*
*Gorgias*, translations by A. Croiset in *Œuvres complètes*, t.III-2. Paris: Les Belles Lettres, 1923.

Plato, *The Laws*
*Les Lois*, translations by E. des Places, Paris: Les Belles Lettres, 1968.

Plato, *Meno*
*Ménon*, translations by A. Croiset, *Œuvres complètes*, t.III-2. Paris: Les Belles Lettres, 1923.

Plato, *Phaedo*
*Phédon*, translations by L. Robin, in *Œuvres complètes*, t.IV-1. Paris: Les Belles Lettres, 1926.

Plato, *Phaedrus*
*Phèdre*, translations by L. Robin, in *Œuvres complètes*, t.IV-3. Paris: Les Belles Lettres, 1934.

Plato, *Protagoras*
*Protagoras*, translations by A. Croiset, in *Œuvres completes*, t.III-1. Paris: Les Belles Lettres, 1966.

Plato, *The Republic*
*La République*, translations by E. Chambry, in *Œuvres complètes*, t.IV-3. Paris: Les Belles Lettres, 1926.

Plato, *Symposium*
*Le Banquet*, translations by L. Robin, in *Œuvres complètes*, t.IV-2. Paris: Les Belles Lettres, 1989.

Plato, *Theaetetus*
   *Théétète*, translations by A. Diès, in *Œuvres complètes*, t.VIII-2. Paris: Les Belles Lettres, 1926.

Plato, *Timaeus*
   *Timée*, translations by A. Rivaud, *Œuvres complètes*, t.X. Paris: Les Belles Lettres, 1925.

Plotinus, *The Enneads*
   Plotin, *Ennéades*, translations by E. Bréhier. Paris: Les Belles Lettres, 1924;
   *The Enneads*, translations by Stephen Mackenna. London: Faber and Faber, 1969.

Plutarch, *Advice about Keeping Well*
   Plutarque, *Préceptes de santé*, in *Œuvres morales*, t.II, translations by J. Defradas, J. Hani, and R. Klaerr. Paris: Les Belles Lettres, 1985;
   *Advice on Keeping Well*, in *Plutarch's Moralia*, vol. II, translations by F. C. Babbit. Cambridge, Mass.: and London: Harvard University Press, Loeb Classical Library, 1928.

Plutarch, *On the Control of Anger*
   *Du contrôle de la colère*, in *Œuvres morales*, t.VII-1, translations by J. Dumortier and J. Defradas. Paris: Les Belles Lettres, 1975;
   Plutarch, *On the Control of Anger*, in *Plutarch's Moralia*, vol. VI, translations by W.C. Helmbold. London and Cambridge, Mass: Harvard University Press, Loeb Classical Library, 1939.

Plutarch, *On Curiosity*
   *De la curiosité* in *Œuvres morales*, t.VII-1, translations by J. Dumortier and J. Defradas. Paris: Les Belles Lettres, 1975;
   *On Curiosity* in *Plutarch's Moralia*, vol. VI, translations by W.C. Helmbold. London and Cambridge Mass.: Harvard University Press, Loeb Classical Library, 1939.

Plutarch, *Dinner of the Seven Wise Men*
   *Le Banquet des sept sages*, in *Œuvres morales*, t.II, translations by J. Defradas, J. Hani, and R. Klaerr. Paris: Les Belles Lettres, 1985;

*Dinner of the Seven Wise Men*, in *Plutarch's Moralia*, vol. II, transltions by F. C. Babbit, Cambridge Mass: and London: Harvard University Press and Heinemann, Loeb Classical Library, 1928.

Plutarch, *How to Distinguish the Flatterer from the Friend*
*Comment distinguer le flatteur de l'ami*, in *Œuvres morales*, t.I-2, translations by A. Philippon. Paris: Les Belles Lettres, 1989;
*How to Distinguish the Flatterer from the Friend*, in *Plutarch's Moralia*, vol. I, translations by F.C. Babbit. Cambridge Mass. and London: Harvard University Press and Heinemann, Loeb Classical Library, 1969.

Plutarch, *Isis and Osiris*
*Isis et Osiris*, in *Œuvres morales*, t.V-2, translations by C. Froidefond. Paris: Les Belles Lettres, 1988;
*Isis and Osiris* in *Plutarch's Moralia*, vol. V, translations by F. C. Babbitt. London and Cambridge Mass.: William Heinemann and Harvard University Press, Loeb Classical Library, 1936.

Plutarch, *A Letter of Condolence to Apollonius*
*Consolation à Apollonios*, in *Œuvres morales*, t.II, translations by J. Defradas and R. Klaerr. Paris: Les Belles Lettres, 1985;
*A Letter of Condolence to Apollonius*, in *Plutarch's Moralia*, vol. II, translations by F.C. Babbit. London and Cambridge Mass.: Harvard University Press, Loeb Classical Library, 1928.

Plutarch, *Life of Demosthenes*
*Vie de Démosthène*, in *Vies*, t.XII, translations by R. Flacelière and E. Chambry. Paris: Les Belle Lettres, 1976;
*Life of Demosthenes*, in Plutarch, *Lives*, vol. 5, Dryden translation, corrected and revised by A.H. Clough. London: Macmillan and Co., 1902.

Plutarch, *On Listening*
*Comment écouter*, in *Œuvres morales*, t. I-2, translations by A. Philippon. Paris: Les Belles Lettres, 1989;
*On Listening to Lectures*, in *Plutarch's Moralia*, vol. I, translations by F.C. Babbitt. London and New York: William Heinemann and G.P. Putnam's Sons, Loeb Classical Library, 1928.

Plutarch, *Pericles*
"Périclès", in *Vies*, t.III.2.4, translations by R. Flacelière and E. Chambry. Paris: Les Belles Lettres, 1964;
"Pericles", in *Lives*, vol. 1, Dryden translation, corrected and revised by A.H. Clough. London: Macmillan and Co., 1902.

Plutarch, *Sayings of the Spartans*
*Apophtègmes laconiens*, in *Œuvres morales*, t.III, translations by F. Fuhrmann. Paris: Les Belles Lettres, 1920;
*Sayings of Spartans*, in *Plutarch's Moralia*, vol. III, translations by F.C. Babbit. London and Cambridge, Mass.: Harvard University Press, Loeb Classical Library, 1931.

Plutarch, *Socrates' Daemon*
*Le Démon de Socrate*, in *Œuvres morales*, t.VIII, translations by J. Hani. Paris: Les Belles Lettres, 1980;
*On the Sign of Socrates*, in *Plutarch's Moralia*, vol. VII, translations by P.H. De Lacy and B. Einarson. New York: Putnam's, Loeb Classical Library, 1931.

Plutarch, *On Talkativeness*
*Traité sur le bavardage*, in *Œuvres morales*, t.VII-1, translations by J. Dumortier and J. Defradas. Paris: Les Belles Lettres, 1975;
*Concerning Talkativeness*, in *Plutarch's Moralia*, vol. VI, translations by W. C. Helmbold. London and Cambridge, Mass.: William Heinemann and Harvard University Press, Loeb Classical Library, 1939.

Plutarch, *On Tranquility of Mind*
Fr: *De la tranquillité de l'âme*, in *Œuvres morales*, t.VII-1, translations by J. Dumortier and J. Defradas. Paris: Les Belles Lettres, 1975;
*On Tranquility of Mind*, in *Plutarch's Moralia*, vol. VI, translations by W.C. Helmbold. London and Cambridge, Mass.: Harvard University Press, Loeb Classical Library, 1939.

Porphyry, *Letter to Marcella*
Porphyre, *Lettre à Marcella*, translations by E. des Places. Paris: Les Belles Letttres, 1982;

Porphyry, *To Marcella*, translations by K. O'Brien Wicker. Atlanta: Society of Biblical Literature, 1987.

Quintilian, *Institutio Oratoria*
*Institution oratoire*, translations by J. Cousin. Paris: Collection des universities de France;
*The Institutio Oratoria of Quintillian*, translations by H. E. Butler. London and New York: Heinemann and Putnam's Sons, Loeb Classical Library, 1921-1933.

Seneca, *Letters*
Sénèque, *Lettres à Lucilius*, translations by H. Noblot. Paris: Les Belles Lettres, 1945; (Foucault also refers to the translation of the *Letters* in *Œuvres complètes de Sénèque le philosophe*, éd. M. Nisard, Firmin Didot, 1869);
*The Epistles of Seneca*, 3 vols., translations by Richard M. Gummere. Cambridge, Mass. and London: Harvard University Press, Loeb Classical Library, 1989.

Seneca, *Natural Questions*
*Questions naturelles*, in *Œuvres complètes de Sénèque le philosophe*;
*Natural Questions*, 2 vols., translations by Thomas H. Corcoran. London and Cambridge, Mass.: Heinemann and Harvard University Press, Loeb Classical Library, 1971-1972.

Seneca, *On Anger*
*De la colère*, in *Dialogues*, t.I, translations by A. Bourgery. Paris: Les Belles Lettres, 1922;
*On Anger*, in *Moral Essays*, vol. I, translations by J. W. Basore. London and New York: Heinemann and Putnam's, Loeb Classical Library, 1928.

Seneca, *On Benefits*
*Des bienfaits*, translations by F. Préchac. Paris: Les Belles Lettres, 1927;
*On Benefits*, in *Moral Essays*, vol. III, translations by J.W. Basore. Cambridge, Mass. and London: Harvard University Press, Loeb Classical Library, 1989.

Seneca, *On Providence*
  *De la providence*, in *Dialogues*, t.IV, translations by R. Waltz. Paris: Les Belles Lettres, 1927;
  *On Providence*, in *Moral Essays*, vol. I, translations by J.W. Basore. London and New York: Heinemann and Putnam's, Loeb Classical Library, 1928.

Seneca, *On the Firmness of the Wise Man*
  *La Constance du sage*, in *Dialogues*, t.IV, translations by R. Waltz. Paris: Les Belles Lettres, 1927;
  *To Serenus on the Firmness of the Wise Man*, in *Moral Essays*, vol. I, translations by J.W. Basore. London and New York: Heinemann and Putnam's, Loeb Classical Library, 1928.

Seneca, *On the Happy Life*
  *De la vie heureuse*, in *Dialogues*, t.II, translations by A. Bourgery. Paris: Les Belles Lettres, 1923;
  *On the Happy Life*, in *Moral Essays*, vol. II, translations by J.W. Basore. Cambridge, Mass. and London: Loeb Classical Library, 1979.

Seneca, *On the Shortness of Life*
  *De la brièveté de la vie*, in *Dialogues*, t.II, translations by A. Bourgery. Paris: Les Belles Lettres, 1923;
  *On the Shortness of Life*, in *Moral Essays*, vol. II, translations by J.W. Basore. Cambridge, Mass. and London: Loeb Classical Library, 1979.

Seneca, *On Tranquillity of Mind*
  *De la tranquillité de l'âme*, in *Dialogues*, t.IV, translations by R. Waltz. Paris: Les Belles Lettres, 1927;
  *On Tranquillity of Mind* in *Moral Essays*, vol. II, translations by John W. Basore. Cambridge, Mass. and London: Loeb Classical Library, 1979.

Seneca, *To Helvia, on Consolation*
  *Consolation à Helvia, Consolation à Polybius*, in *Dialogues*, t.III, translations by R. Waltz. Paris: Les Belles Lettres, 1923;

*To Helvia on Consolation* in *Moral Essays*, vol. II, translations by John W. Basore. Cambridge, Mass. and London: Loeb Classical and Library, 1979.

Seneca, *To Marcia, on Consolation*
Consolation à Marcia, translations by E. Regnault, in *Œuvres complètes de Sénèque le philosophey*, éd. M. Nisard: Fismin Didot, 1869.
*To Marcia, On Consolation*, in *Moral Essays*, vol. II, translations by John W. Basore. Cambridge, Mass. and London: Loeb Classical Library, 1979.

Seneca, *To Polybius on Consolation*
*Consolation à Polybius*, in *Dialogues*, t.III, translations by R. Waltz. Paris: Les Belles Lettres, 1923;
*To Polybius on Consolation*, in *Moral Essays, II*, translations by John W. Basore. Cambridge, Mass. and London: Loeb Classical Library, 1979.

Tacitus, *Annals*
Tacite, *Annales*, translations by P. Grimal. Paris: Gallimard, 1990;
*The Annals*, translations by J. Jackson. Cambridge, Mass. and London: William Heinemann and Harvard University Press, Loeb Classical Library, 1937.

Xenophon, *Memorabilia*
Xénophon, *Mémorables*, translations by P. Chambry. Paris: Garnier-Flammarion, 1966;
*Memorabilia*, translations by E. C. Marchant. Cambridge, Mass. and London: Harvard University Press, Loeb Classical Library, 1979.

one

# 6 JANUARY 1982

### First hour

> *Reminder of the general problematic: subjectivity and truth. ∼ New theoretical point of departure: the care of the self. ∼ Interpretations of the Delphic precept "know yourself." ∼ Socrates as man of care of the self: analysis of three extracts from* The Apology. *∼ Care of the self as precept of ancient philosophical and moral life. ∼ Care of the self in the first Christian texts. ∼ Care of the self as general standpoint, relationship to the self and set of practices. ∼ Reasons for the modern elimination of care of the self in favor of self-knowledge: modern morality; the Cartesian moment. ∼ The Gnostic exception. ∼ Philosophy and spirituality.*

THIS YEAR I THOUGHT of trying the following arrangements[1]: I will lecture for two hours, from 9:15 until 11:15, with a short break of a few minutes after an hour to allow you to rest, or to leave if you are bored, and also to give me a bit of a rest. As far as possible I will try nevertheless to vary the two hours. That is to say, in the first hour, or at any rate in one of the two hours, I will give a somewhat more, let's say, theoretical and general exposition, and then, in the other hour, I will present something more like a textual analysis with, of course, all the obstacles and drawbacks of this kind of approach due to the fact that we cannot supply you with the texts and do not know how many of you there will be, etcetera. Still, we can always try. If it does not work we will try to find another method next year, or even this year. Does it bother you much to come at 9:15? No? It's okay? You are more fortunate than me, then.

Last year I tried to get a historical reflection underway on the theme of the relations between subjectivity and truth.[2] To study this problem I took as a privileged example, as a refracting surface if you like, the question of the regimen of sexual behavior and pleasures in Antiquity, the regimen of the *aphrodisia* you recall, as it appeared and was defined in the first two centuries A.D.[3] It seemed to me that one of the interesting dimensions of this regimen was that the basic framework of modern European sexual morality was to be found in this regimen of the *aphrodisia*, rather than in so-called Christian morality, or worse, in so-called Judeo-Christian morality.[4] This year I would like to step back a bit from this precise example, and from the sexual material concerning the *aphrodisia* and sexual behavior, and extract from it the more general terms of the problem of "the subject and truth." More precisely, while I do not want in any way to eliminate or nullify the historical dimension in which I tried to situate this problem of subjectivity/truth relations, I would, however, like to present it in a much more general form. The question I would like to take up this year is this: In what historical form do the relations between the "subject" and "truth," elements that do not usually fall within the historian's practice or analysis, take shape in the West?

So, to start with I would like to take up a notion about which I think I said a few words last year.[5] This is the notion of "care of oneself." This is the best translation I can offer for a very complex, rich, and frequently employed Greek notion which had a long life throughout Greek culture: the notion of *epimeleia heautou*, translated into Latin with, of course, all the flattening of meaning which has so often been denounced or, at any rate, pointed out,[6] as *cura sui*.[7] *Epimeleia heautou* is care of oneself, attending to oneself, being concerned about oneself, etcetera. You will no doubt say that in order to study the relations between the subject and truth it is a bit paradoxical and rather artificial to select this notion of *epimeleia heautou*, to which the historiography of philosophy has not attached much importance hitherto. It is somewhat paradoxical and artificial to select this notion when everyone knows, says, and repeats, and has done so for a long time, that the question of the subject (the question of knowledge of the subject, of the subject's knowledge of himself) was originally posed in a very different expression and a very different precept: the famous Delphic prescription of *gnōthi seauton* ("know yourself").[8] So, when everything in the history of philosophy—and more broadly in the history of Western thought—tells us that the *gnōthi seauton* is undoubtedly the founding expression of the question of the relations between the subject and truth, why choose this apparently rather marginal notion—that of the care of oneself, of *epimeleia heautou*—which is certainly current in Greek thought, but which seems not to have been given any special status? So, in this first hour I would like to spend some time on this question of the relations between the *epimeleia heautou* (care of the self) and the *gnōthi seauton* ("know yourself").

Relying on the work of historians and archeologists, I would like to make this very simple preliminary remark with regard to the "know yourself." We should keep the following in mind: In the glorious and spectacular form in which it was formulated and engraved on the temple stone, the *gnōthi seauton* originally did not have the value it later acquired. You know (and we will have to come back to this) the famous text in which Epictetus says that the precept "*gnōthi seauton*" was inscribed at the center of the human community.[9] In fact it undoubtedly was inscribed in this place, which was a center of Greek life, and later of the human community,[10] but it certainly did not mean "know yourself" in the philosophical sense of the phrase. The phrase did not prescribe self-knowledge, neither as the basis of morality, nor as part of a relationship with the gods. A number of interpretations have been suggested. There is Roscher's old interpretation, put forward in 1901 in an article in *Philologus*,[11] in which he recalled that the Delphic precepts were after all addressed to those who came to consult the god and should be read as kinds of ritual rules and recommendations connected with the act of consultation itself. You know the three precepts. According to Roscher, the precept *mēden agan* ("not too much") certainly does not designate or express a general ethical principle and measure for human conduct. *Mēden agan* ("not too much") means: You who have come to consult, do not ask too many questions, ask only useful questions and those that are necessary. The second precept concerning the *eggu̅ē* (the pledges)[12] would mean precisely this: When you consult the gods, do not make vows and commitments that you will not be able to honor. As for the *gnōthi seauton*, according to Roscher it would mean: When you question the oracle, examine yourself closely and the questions you are going to ask, those you wish to ask, and, since you must restrict yourself to the fewest questions and not ask too many, carefully consider yourself and what you need know. Defradas gives a much more recent interpretation, in 1954, in his book on *Les Thèmes de la propagande delphique*.[13] Defradas proposes a different interpretation, but which also shows, or suggests, that the *gnōthi seauton* is definitely not a principle of self-knowledge. According to Defradas, the three Delphic precepts were general demands for prudence: "not too much" in your requests and hopes and no excess in how you conduct yourself. The "pledges" was a precept warning those consulting against excessive generosity. As for the "know yourself," this was the principle [that] you should always remember that you are only a mortal after all, not a god, and that you should neither presume too much on your strength nor oppose the powers of the deity.

Let us skip this quickly. I want to stress something else which has much more to do with the subject with which I am concerned. Whatever meaning was actually given and attached to the Delphic precept "know yourself" in the cult of Apollo, it seems to me to be a fact that when this Delphic precept, this *gnōthi seauton*, appears in philosophy, in philosophical thought, it is, as we know, around the character of Socrates. Xenophon attests to this in the *Memorabilia*,[14] as does Plato in a number of texts to which we will have to return. Now not always, but often, and in a highly significant way, when this Delphic precept (this *gnōthi seauton*) appears, it is coupled or twinned with the principle of "take care of yourself" (*epimeleia heautou*). I say "coupled," "twinned." In actual fact, it is not entirely a matter of coupling. In some texts, to which we will have to return, there is, rather, a kind of subordination of the expression of the rule "know yourself" to the precept of care of the self. The *gnōthi seauton* ("know yourself") appears, quite clearly and again in a number of significant texts, within the more general framework of the *epimeleia heautou* (care of oneself) as one of the forms, one of the consequences, as a sort of concrete, precise, and particular application of the general rule: You must attend to yourself, you must not forget yourself, you must take care of yourself. The rule "know yourself" appears and is formulated within and at the forefront of this care. Anyway, we should not forget that in Plato's too well-known but still fundamental text, the *Apology*, Socrates appears as the person whose essential, fundamental, and original function, job, and position is to encourage others to attend to themselves, take care of themselves, and not neglect themselves. There are in fact three texts, three passages in the *Apology* that are completely clear and explicit about this.

The first passage is found in 29d of the *Apology*.[15] In this passage, Socrates, defending himself, making a kind of imaginary defense plea before his accusers and judges, answers the following objection. He is reproached with having ended up in a situation of which "he should be ashamed." The accusation, if you like, consists in saying: I am not really sure what evil you have done, but I avow all the same that it is shameful to have led the kind a life that results in you now finding yourself accused before the courts and in danger of being condemned, perhaps condemned to death. Isn't this, in the end, what is shameful, that someone has led a certain life, which while we do not know what it is, is such that he is in danger of being condemned to death by such a judgment? In this passage, Socrates replies that, on the contrary, he is very proud of having led this life and that if ever he was asked to lead a different life he would refuse. So: I am so proud of the life I have led that I would not change it even if you offered to acquit me. Here are Socrates' words: "Athenians, I am grateful to you and love you, but I shall obey God rather than you, and be sure that I will not stop practicing philosophy so long as I have breath and am able to, [exhorting] you and telling whoever I meet what they should do."[16] And what advice would he give if he is not condemned, since he had already given it before he was accused? To those he meets he will say, as he is accustomed to saying: "Dear friend, you are an Athenian, citizen of the greatest city, more famous than any other for its knowledge and might, yet are you not ashamed for devoting all your care (*epimeleisthai*) to increasing your wealth, reputation and honors while not caring for or even considering (*epimelē, phrontizeis*) your reason, truth and the constant improvement of your soul?" Thus Socrates recalls what he has always said and is quite determined to continue to say to those he will meet and stop to question: You care for a whole range of things, for your wealth and your reputation. You do not take care of yourself. He goes on: "And if anyone argues and claims that he does care [for his soul, for truth, for reason; M.F.], don't think that I shall let him go and go on my way. No, I shall question him, examine him and argue with him at length . . ."[17] Whoever I may meet, young or old, stranger or fellow citizen, this is how I shall act, and especially with you my fellow citizens, since you are my kin. For you should understand that this is what the god demands, and I believe that nothing better has befallen this city than my zeal in executing this command."[18] This "command," then, is the command by which the gods have entrusted Socrates with the task of stopping people, young and old, citizens or strangers, and saying to them: Attend to yourselves. This is Socrates' task.

In the second passage, Socrates returns to this theme of the care of the self and says that if the Athenians do in fact condemn him to death then he, Socrates, will not lose a great deal. The Athenians, however, will suffer a very heavy and severe loss.[19] For, he says, there will no longer be anyone to encourage them to care for themselves and their own virtue unless the gods care enough about them to send someone to replace him, someone who will constantly remind them that they must be concerned about themselves.[20]

Finally, in 36b-c, there is the third passage, which concerns the penalty incurred. According to the traditional legal forms,[21] Socrates himself proposes the penalty he will accept if condemned. Here is the text: "What treatment do I deserve, what amends must I make for thinking I had to relinquish a peaceful life and neglect what most people have at heart—wealth, private interest, military office, success in the assembly, magistracies, alliances and political factions; for being convinced that with my scruples I would be lost if I followed such a course; for not wanting to do what was of no advantage either to you or myself; for preferring to do for each particular individual what I declare to be the greatest service, trying to persuade him to care (*epimēletheiē*) less about his property than about himself so as to make himself as excellent and reasonable as possible, to consider less the things of the city than the city itself, in short, to apply these same principles to everything? What have I deserved, I ask, for having conducted myself in this way [and for having encouraged you to attend to yourselves? Not punishment, to be sure, not chastisement, but; M.F.] something good, Athenians, if you want to be just."[22]

I will stop there for the moment. I just wanted to draw your attention to these passages, in which Socrates basically appears as the person who encourages others to care for themselves, and I would like you to note three or four important things. First, this activity of encouraging others to care for themselves is Socrates' activity, but it is an activity entrusted to him by the gods. In acting in this way Socrates does no more than carry out an order, perform a function or occupy a post (he uses the term *taxis*[23]) determined for him by the gods. In this passage you will also have been able to see that it is because the gods care for the Athenians that they sent Socrates, and may possibly send someone else, to encourage them to care for themselves.

Second, you see as well, and this is very clear in the last passage I read to you, that if Socrates cares for others, then this obviously means that he will not care for himself, or at any rate, that in caring for others he will neglect a range of other activities that are generally thought to be self-interested, profitable, and advantageous. So as to be able to care for others, Socrates has neglected his wealth and a number of civic advantages, he has renounced any political career, and he has not sought any office or magistracy. Thus the problem arises of the relation between the "caring for oneself" encouraged by the philosopher, and what caring for himself, or maybe sacrificing himself, must represent for the philosopher, that is to say, the problem, consequently, of the position occupied by the master in this matter of "caring for oneself."

Third, I have not quoted this passage at great length, but it doesn't matter, you can look it up: in this activity of encouraging others to attend to themselves Socrates says that with regard to his fellow citizens his role is that of someone who awakens them.[24] The care of the self will thus be looked upon as the moment of the first awakening. It is situated precisely at the moment the eyes open, when one wakes up and has access to the first light of day. This is the third interesting point in this question of "caring for oneself."

Finally, again at the end of a passage I did not read to you, there is the famous comparison of Socrates and the horsefly, the insect that chases and bites animals, making them restless and run about.[25] The care of oneself is a sort of thorn which must be stuck in men's flesh, driven into their existence, and which is a principle of restlessness and movement, of continuous concern throughout life. So I think this question of the *epimeleia heautou* should be rescued from the prestige of the *gnōthi seauton* that has somewhat overshadowed its importance. In a text, then, which I will try to explain to you a bit more precisely in a moment (the whole of the second part of the famous *Alcibiades*), you will see how the *epimeliea heautou* (the care of the self) is indeed the justificatory framework, ground, and foundation for the imperative "know yourself." So, this notion of *epimeliea heautou* is important in the figure of Socrates, with whom one usually associates, if not exclusively then at least in a privileged fashion, the *gnōthi seauton*. Socrates is, and always will be, the person associated with care of the self. In a series of late texts, in the Stoics, in the Cynics, and especially in Epictetus,[26] you will see that Socrates is always, essentially and fundamentally, the person who stops young men in the street and tells them: "You must care about yourselves."

The third point concerning this notion of *epimeleia heautou* and its connections with the *gnōthi seauton* is that the notion of *epimeleia heautou* did not just accompany, frame, and found the necessity of knowing oneself, and not solely when this necessity appeared in the thought, life, and figure of Socrates. It seems to me that the *epimeleia heautou* (the care of the self and the rule associated with it) remained a fundamental principle for describing the philosophical attitude throughout Greek, Hellenistic, and Roman culture. This notion of the care of the self was, of course, important in Plato. It was important for the Epicureans, since in Epicurus you find the frequently repeated expression: Every man should take care of his soul day and night and throughout his life.[27] For "take care of" Epicurus employs the verb *therapeuein*,[28] which has several meanings: *therapeuein* refers to medical care (a kind of therapy for the soul which we know was important for the Epicureans),²⁹ but *therapeuein* is also the service provided by a servant to his master. You know also that *therapeuein* is related to the duties of worship, to the statutory regular worship rendered to a deity or divine power. The care of the self is crucially important in the Cynics. I refer, for example, to the text cited by Seneca in the first paragraphs of book seven of *De Beneficiis*, in which the Cynic Demetrius, on the basis of a number of principles to which we will have to return because this is very important, explains how it is pointless to concern oneself with speculations about certain natural phenomena (like, for example, the origin of earthquakes, the causes of storms, the reason for twins), and that one should look instead to immediate things concerning oneself and to a number of rules by which one conducts oneself and controls what one does.³⁰ I don't need to tell you that the *epimeleia heautou* is important in the Stoics; it is central in Seneca with the notion of *cura sui*, and it permeates the *Discourses* of Epictetus. Having to care about oneself is not just a condition for gaining access to the philosophical life, in the strict and full sense of the term. You will see, I will try to show you, how generally speaking the principle that one must take care of oneself became the principle of all rational conduct in all forms of active life that would truly conform to the principle of moral rationality. Throughout the long summer of Hellenistic and Roman thought, the exhortation to care for oneself became so widespread that it became, I think, a truly general cultural phenomenon.³¹ What I would like to show you, what I would like to speak about this year, is this history that made this general cultural phenomenon (this exhortation, this general acceptance of the principle that one should take care of oneself) both a general cultural phenomenon peculiar to Hellenistic and Roman society (anyway, to its elite), and at the same time an event in thought.³² It seems to me that the stake, the challenge for any history of thought, is precisely that of grasping when a cultural phenomenon of a determinate scale actually constitutes within the history of thought a decisive moment that is still significant for our modern mode of being subjects.

One word more: If this notion of the care of oneself, which we see emerging quite explicitly and clearly in the figure of Socrates, traversed and permeated ancient philosophy up to the threshold of Christianity, well, you will find this notion of *epimeleia* (of care) again in Christianity, or in what, to a certain extent, constituted its environment and preparation: Alexandrian spirituality. At any rate, you find this notion of *epimeleia* given a particular meaning in Philo (*De Vita contemplative*).[33] You find it in Plotinus, in *Ennead*, II.[34] You find this notion of *epimeleia* also and especially in Christian asceticism: in Methodius of Olympus[35] and Basil of Caesarea.[36] It appears in Gregory of Nyssa: in *The Life of Moses*,[37] in the text on *The Song of Songs*,[38] and in the *Beatitudes*.[39] The notion of care of the self is found especially in Book XIII of *On Virginity*,[40] the title of which is, precisely, "That the care of oneself begins with freedom from marriage."[41] Given that, for Gregory of Nyssa, freedom from marriage (celibacy) is actually the first form, the initial inflection of the ascetic life, the assimilation of the first form of the care of oneself and freedom from marriage reveals the extent to which the care of the self had become a kind of matrix of Christian asceticism. You can see that the notion of *epimeleia heautou* (care of oneself) has a long history extending from the figure of Socrates stopping young people to tell them to take care of themselves up to Christian asceticism making the ascetic life begin with the care of oneself.

It is clear that in the course of this history the notion becomes broader and its meanings are both multiplied and modified. Since the purpose of this year's course will be to elucidate all this (what I am saying now being only a pure schema, a preliminary overview), let's say that within this notion of *epimeleia heautou* we should bear in mind that there is:

- First, the theme of a general standpoint, of a certain way of considering things, of behaving in the world, undertaking actions, and having relations with other people. The *epimeleia heautou* is an attitude towards the self, others, and the world;
- Second, the *epimeleia heautou* is also a certain form of attention, of looking. Being concerned about oneself implies that we look

away from the outside to... I was going to say "inside." Let's leave to one side this word, which you can well imagine raises a host of problems, and just say that we must convert our looking from the outside, from others and the world etc., towards "oneself." The care of the self implies a certain way of attending to what we think and what takes place in our thought. The word *epimeleia* is related to *meletē*, which means both exercise and meditation.[42] Again, all this will have to be elucidated;

- Third, the notion of *epimeleia* does not merely designate this general attitude or this form of attention turned on the self. The *epimeleia* also always designates a number of actions exercised on the self by the self, actions by which one takes responsibility for oneself and by which one changes, purifies, transforms, and transfigures oneself. It involves a series of practices, most of which are exercises that will have a very long destiny in the history of Western culture, philosophy, morality, and spirituality. These are, for example, techniques of meditation,[43] of memorization of the past, of examination of conscience,[44] of checking representations which appear in the mind,[45] and so on.

With this theme of the care of the self, we have then, if you like, an early philosophical formulation, appearing clearly in the fifth century B.C., of a notion which permeates all Greek, Hellenistic, and Roman philosophy, as well as Christian spirituality, up to the fourth and fifth centuries A.D. In short, with this notion of *epimeleia heautou* we have a body of work defining a way of being, a standpoint, forms of reflection, and practices which make it an extremely important phenomenon not just in the history of representations, notions, or theories, but in the history of subjectivity itself or, if you like, in the history of practices of subjectivity. Anyway, as a working hypothesis at least, this one-thousand-year development from the appearance of the first forms of the philosophical attitude in the Greeks to the first forms of Christian asceticism—from the fifth century B.C. to the fifth century A.D.—can be taken up starting from this notion of *epimeleia heautou*. Between the philosophical exercise and Christian asceticism there are a thousand years of transformation and evolution in which the care of the self is undoubtedly one of the main threads or, at any rate, to be more modest, let's say one of the possible main threads.

Even so, before ending these general remarks, I would like to pose the following question: Why did Western thought and philosophy neglect the notion of *epimeleia heautou* (care of the self) in its reconstruction of its own history? How did it come about that we accorded so much privilege, value, and intensity to the "know yourself" and omitted, or at least, left in the shadow, this notion of care of the self that, in actual fact, historically, when we look at the documents and texts, seems to have framed the principle of "know yourself" from the start and to have supported an extremely rich and dense set of notions, practices, ways of being, forms of existence, and so on? Why does the *gnōthi seautou* have this privileged status for us, to the detriment of the care of oneself? Okay, what I will sketch out here are of course hypotheses with many question marks and ellipses.

Just to begin with, entirely superficially and without resolving anything, but as something that we should maybe bear in mind, I think we can say that there is clearly something a bit disturbing for us in this principle of the care of the self. Indeed, going through the texts, the different forms of philosophy and the different forms of exercises and philosophical or spiritual practices, we see the principle of care of the self expressed in a variety of phrases like: "caring for oneself," "taking care of the self," "withdrawing into oneself," "retiring into the self," "finding one's pleasure in oneself," "seeking no other delight but in the self," "remaining in the company of oneself," "being the friend of oneself," "being in one's self as in a fortress," "looking after" or "devoting oneself to oneself," "respecting oneself," etc. Now you are well aware that there is a certain tradition (or rather, several traditions) that dissuades us (us, now, today) from giving any positive value to all these expressions, precepts, and rules, and above all from making them the basis of a morality. All these injunctions to exalt oneself, to devote oneself to oneself, to turn in on oneself, to offer service to oneself, sound to our ears rather like—what? Like a sort of challenge and defiance, a desire for radical ethical change, a sort of moral dandyism, the assertion-challenge of a fixed aesthetic and individual stage.[46] Or else they sound to us like a somewhat melancholy and sad expression of the withdrawal of the individual who is unable to hold on to and keep firmly before his eyes, in his grasp and for himself, a collective morality (that of the city-state, for example), and who, faced with the disintegration of this collective morality, has naught else to do but attend to himself.[47] So, the immediate, initial connotations and overtones of all these expressions direct us away from thinking about these precepts in positive terms. Now, in all of the ancient thought I am talking about, whether it be Socrates or Gregory of Nyssa, "taking care of oneself" always has a positive and never a negative meaning. A further paradox is that this injunction to "take care of oneself" is the basis for the constitution of what have without doubt been the most austere, strict, and restrictive moralities known in the West, moralities which, I repeat, should not be attributed to Christianity (this was the object of last year's course), but rather to the morality of the first centuries B.C. and the first centuries A.D. (Stoic, Cynic and, to a certain extent, Epicurean morality). Thus, we have the paradox of a precept of care of the self which signifies for us either egoism or withdrawal, but which for centuries was rather a positive principle that was the matrix for extremely strict moralities. A further paradox which should be mentioned to explain the way in which this notion of care of the self was somehow overshadowed is that the strict morality and austere rules arising from the principle "take care of yourself" have been taken up again by us: These rules in fact appear, or reappear, either in a Christian morality or in a modern, non-Christian morality. However, they do so in a different context. These austere rules, which are found again identical in their codified structure, appear reacclimatized, transposed, and transferred within a context of a general ethic of non-egoism taking the form either of a Christian obligation of self-renunciation or of a "modern" obligation towards others—whether this be other people, the collectivity, the class, or the fatherland etc. So, Christianity and the modern world has based all these themes and codes of moral strictness on a morality of non-egoism whereas in actual fact they were born within an environment strongly marked by the obligation to take care of oneself. I think this set of paradoxes is one of the reasons why this theme of the care of the self was somewhat neglected and able to disappear from the concerns of historians.

However, I think there is a reason that is much more fundamental than these paradoxes of the history of morality. This pertains to the problem of truth and the history of truth. It seems to me that the more serious reason why this precept of the care of the self has been forgotten, the reason why the place occupied by this principle in ancient culture for nigh on one thousand years has been obliterated, is what I will call—with what I know is a bad, purely conventional phrase—the "Cartesian moment." It seems to me that the "Cartesian moment," again within a lot of inverted commas, functioned in two ways. It came into play in two ways: by philosophically requalifying the *gnōthi seauton* (know yourself), and by discrediting the *epimeleia heautou* (care of the self).

First, the Cartesian moment philosophically requalified the *gnōthi seauton* (know yourself). Actually, and here things are very simple, the Cartesian approach, which can be read quite explicitly in the *Meditations*,[48] placed self-evidence (*l'évidence*) at the origin, the point of departure of the philosophical approach—self-evidence as it appears, that is to say as it is given, as it is actually given to consciousness without any possible doubt [...]\*. The Cartesian approach [therefore] refers to knowledge of the self, as a form of consciousness at least. What's more, by putting the self-evidence of the subject's own existence at the very source of access to being, this knowledge of oneself (no longer in the form of the test of self-evidence, but in the form of the impossibility of doubting my existence as subject) made the "know yourself" into a fundamental means of access to truth. Of course, there is a vast distance between the Socratic *gnōthi seauton* and the Cartesian approach. However, you can see why, from the seventeenth century, starting from this step, the principle of *gnōthi seauton* as founding moment of the philosophical method was acceptable for a number of philosophical approaches or practices. But if the Cartesian approach thus requalified the *gnōthi seauton*, for reasons that are fairly easy to isolate, at the same time—and I want to stress this—it played a major part in discrediting the principle of care of the self and in excluding it from the field of modern philosophical thought.

---

\*Only "whatever the effort..." is audible.

Let's stand back a little to consider this. We will call, if you like, "philosophy" the form of thought that asks, not of course what is true and what is false, but what determines that there is and can be truth and falsehood and whether or not we can separate the true and the false. We will call "philosophy" the form of thought that asks what it is that enables the subject to have access to the truth and which attempts to determine the conditions and limits of the subject's access to the truth. If we call this "philosophy," then I think we could call "spirituality" the search, practice, and experience through which the subject carries out the necessary transformations on himself in order to have access to the truth. We will call "spirituality" then the set of these researches, practices, and experiences, which may be purifications, ascetic exercises, renunciations, conversions of looking, modifications of existence, etc., which are, not for knowledge but for the subject, for the subject's very being, the price to be paid for access to the truth. Let's say that spirituality, as it appears in the West at least, has three characteristics.

Spirituality postulates that the truth is never given to the subject by right. Spirituality postulates that the subject as such does not have right of access to the truth and is not capable of having access to the truth. It postulates that the truth is not given to the subject by a simple act of knowledge (*connaissance*), which would be founded and justified simply by the fact that he is the subject and because he possesses this or that structure of subjectivity. It postulates that for the subject to have right of access to the truth he must be changed, transformed, shifted, and become, to some extent and up to a certain point, other than himself. The truth is only given to the subject at a price that brings the subject's being into play. For as he is, the subject is not capable of truth. I think that this is the simplest but most fundamental formula by which spirituality can be defined. It follows that from this point of view there can be no truth without a conversion or a transformation of the subject. This conversion, this transformation of the subject—and this will be the second major aspect of spirituality—may take place in different forms. Very roughly we can say (and this is again a very schematic survey) that this conversion may take place in the form of a movement that removes the subject from his current status and condition (either an ascending movement of the subject himself, or else a movement by which the truth comes to him and enlightens him). Again, quite conventionally, let us call this movement, in either of its directions, the movement of *erōs* (love). Another major form through which the subject can and must transform himself in order to have access to the truth is a kind of work. This is a work of the self on the self, an elaboration of the self by the self, a progressive transformation of the self by the self for which one takes responsibility in a long labor of ascesis (*askēsis*). *Erōs* and *askēsis* are, I think, the two major forms in Western spirituality for conceptualizing the modalities by which the subject must be transformed in order finally to become capable of truth. This is the second characteristic of spirituality.

Finally, spirituality postulates that once access to the truth has really been opened up, it produces effects that are, of course, the consequence of the spiritual approach taken in order to achieve this, but which at the same time are something quite different and much more: effects which I will call "rebound" (*"de retour"*), effects of the truth on the subject. For spirituality, the truth is not just what is given to the subject, as reward for the act of knowledge as it were, and to fulfill the act of knowledge. The truth enlightens the subject; the truth gives beatitude to the subject; the truth gives the subject tranquility of the soul. In short, in the truth and in access to the truth, there is something that fulfills the subject himself, which fulfills or transfigures his very being. In short, I think we can say that in and of itself an act of knowledge could never give access to the truth unless it was prepared, accompanied, doubled, and completed by a certain transformation of the subject; not of the individual, but of the subject himself in his being as subject.

There is no doubt an enormous objection to everything I have been saying, an objection to which it will be necessary to return, and which is, of course, the gnosis.[49] However, the gnosis, and the whole Gnostic movement, is precisely a movement that overloads the act of knowledge (*connaissance*), to [which] sovereignty is indeed granted in access to the truth. This act of knowledge is overloaded with all the conditions and structure of a spiritual act. The gnosis is, in short, that which tends to transfer, to transpose, the forms and effects of spiritual experience into the act of knowledge itself. Schematically, let's say that throughout the period we call Antiquity, and in quite different modalities, the philosophical question of "how to have access to the truth" and the practice of spirituality (of the necessary transformations in the very being of the subject which will allow access to the truth), these two questions, these two themes, were never separate. It is clear they were not separate for the Pythagoreans. Neither were they separate for Socrates and Plato: the *epimeleia heautou* (care of the self) designates precisely the set of conditions of spirituality, the set of transformations of the self, that are the necessary conditions for having access to the truth. So, throughout Antiquity (in the Pythagoreans, Plato, the Stoics, Cynics, Epicureans, and Neo-Platonists), the philosophical theme (how to have access to the truth?) and the question of spirituality (what transformations in the being of the subject are necessary for access to the truth?) were never separate. There is, of course, the exception, the major and fundamental exception: that of the one who is called "the" philosopher,[50] because he was no doubt the only philosopher in Antiquity for whom the question of spirituality was least important; the philosopher whom we have recognized as the founder of philosophy in the modern sense of the term: Aristotle. But as everyone knows, Aristotle is not the pinnacle of Antiquity but its exception.

Now, leaping over several centuries, we can say that we enter the modern age (I mean, the history of truth enters its modern period) when it is assumed that what gives access to the truth, the condition for the subject's access to the truth, is knowledge (*connaissance*) and knowledge alone. It seems to me that what I have called the "Cartesian moment" takes on its position and meaning at this point, without in any way my wanting to say that it is a question of Descartes, that he was its inventor or that he was the first to do this. I think the modern age of the history of truth begins when knowledge itself and knowledge alone gives access to the truth. That is to say, it is when the philosopher (or the scientist, or simply someone who seeks the truth) can recognize the truth and have access to it in himself and solely through his activity of knowing, without anything else being demanded of him and without him having to change or alter his being as subject. Of course, this does not mean that the truth is obtained without conditions. But these conditions are of two orders, neither of which fall under the conditions of spirituality. On the one hand, there are the internal conditions of the act of knowledge and of the rules it must obey to have access to the truth: formal conditions, objective conditions, formal rules of method, the structure of the object to be known.[51] However, in any case, the conditions of the subject's access to the truth are defined within knowledge. The other conditions are extrinsic. These are conditions such as: "In order to know the truth one must not be mad" (this is an important moment in Descartes).[52] They are also cultural conditions: to have access to the truth we must have studied, have an education, and operate within a certain scientific consensus. And there are moral conditions: to know the truth we must make an effort, we must not seek to deceive our world, and the interests of financial reward, career, and status must be combined in a way that is fully compatible with the norms of disinterested research, etcetera. As you can see, these are all conditions that are either intrinsic to knowledge or extrinsic to the act of knowledge, but which do not concern the subject in his being; they only concern the individual in his concrete existence, and not the structure of the subject as such. At this point (that is, when we can say: "As such the subject is, anyway, capable of truth"—with the two reservations of conditions intrinsic to knowledge and conditions extrinsic to the individual*), when the subject's being is not put in question by the necessity of having access to the truth, I think we have entered a different age of the history of relations between subjectivity and truth. And the consequence—or, if you like, the other aspect of this—is that access to truth, whose sole condition is henceforth knowledge, will find reward and fulfillment in nothing else but the indefinite development of knowledge. The point of enlightenment and fulfillment, the moment of the subject's transfiguration by the "rebound effect" on himself of the truth he knows, and which passes through, permeates, and transfigures his being, can no longer exist. We can no longer think that access to the

---

*The manuscript (by which we designate the written notes Foucault used to support the delivery of this course at the Collège de France) allows this last point to be understood as extrinsic, that is to say individual, conditions of knowledge.

truth will complete in the subject, like a crowning or a reward, the work or the sacrifice, the price paid to arrive at it. Knowledge will simply open out onto the indefinite dimension of progress, the end of which is unknown and the advantage of which will only ever be realized in the course of history by the institutional accumulation of bodies of knowledge, or the psychological or social benefits to be had from having discovered the truth after having taken such pains to do so. As such, henceforth the truth cannot save the subject. If we define spirituality as being the form of practices which postulate that, such as he is, the subject is not capable of the truth, but that, such as it is, the truth can transfigure and save the subject, then we can say that the modern age of the relations between the subject and truth begin when it is postulated that, such as he is, the subject is capable of truth, but that, such as it is, the truth cannot save the subject. Okay, a short rest if you like. Five minutes and then we will begin again.

1. From 1982, Foucault, who previously had both lectured and held a seminar, decided to give up the seminar and just lecture, but for two hours.
2. See the summary of the 1980-1981 course at the Collège de France in M. Foucault, *Dits et Écrits, 1954-1988*, ed. Daniel Defert and François Ewald (Paris: Gallimard, 1994), vol. 4, pp. 213-18; English translation by Robert Hurley "Subjectivity and Truth" in Michel Foucault, *Essential Works of Foucault 1954-1984, vol. 1: Ethics: Subjectivity and Truth*, ed. Paul Rabinow, translations by Robert Hurley et al (New York: The New Press, 1997), pp. 87-92.
3. For the first elaboration of this theme, see the lecture of 28 January 1981, but more especially M. Foucault, *L'Usage des plaisirs* (Paris: Gallimard, 1984), pp. 47-62; English translation by Robert Hurley, *The Use of Pleasure* (New York: Pantheon Books, 1985), pp. 38-52. By *aphrodisia* Foucault understands an *experience*, which is a *historical* experience: the Greek experience of pleasures as opposed to the Christian experience of the *flesh* and the modern experience of *sexuality*. The *aphrodisia* are identified as the "ethical substance" of ancient morality.
4. In the first lecture of the 1981 course ("Subjectivité et verité," 7 January 1981) Foucault states that what is at stake in his research is whether it was not precisely paganism that developed the strictness and sense of decency of our moral code (which, furthermore, would problematize the break between Christianity and paganism in the field of a history of morality).
5. In the 1981 lectures there are no analyses explicitly concerned with the care of the self, but there are lengthy analyses dealing with the arts of existence and processes of subjectivation (the lectures of 13 January, 25 March, and 1 April). However, generally speaking, the 1981 course continues to focus exclusively on the status of the *aphrodisia* in pagan ethics of the first two centuries A.D. while maintaining that we cannot speak of subjectivity in the Greek world, the ethical element being determined as *bios* (mode of life).
6. All the important texts of Cicero, Lucretius, and Seneca on these problems of translation have been brought together by Carlos Lévy in his article, "Du grec au latin," in *Le Discours philosophique* (Paris: PUF, 1998), pp. 1145-54.
7. "If I do everything in my own interest, it is because the interest I have in myself comes before everything else *(Si omnia propter curam mei facio, ante omnia est mei cura.)*." Seneca, *Letters*, CXXI.17.
8. See P. Courcelle, *Connais-toi même, de Socrate à saint Bernard* (Paris: Études augustiniennes, 1974), 3 volumes.
9. Epictetus, *Discourses*, III.i.18-19.
10. For the Greeks, Delphi was the geographical center of the world (*omphalos*: the world's navel), where the two eagles sent by Zeus from the opposite sides of the Earth's circumference came together. Delphi became an important religious center at the end of the eighth century B.C. (the sanctuary of Apollo from which Python delivered oracles) and continued to be so until the end of the fourth century A.D., extending its audience to the entire Roman world.
11. W. H. Roscher, "Weiteres über die Bedeutung des *E[ggua]* zu Delphi und die übrigen *grammata Delphika*," *Philologus* 60, 1901, pp. 81-101.
12. The second maxim is: *eggua, para d'atē*. See Plutarch's statement in *Dinner of the Seven Wise Men*, 164b: "Until I have learned it from these gentlemen, I won't be able to explain to you the meaning of the precepts *Not too much* and *Know yourself*, and the famous maxim which has stopped so many from getting married, has made so many others mistrustful and others silent: Commitment brings misfortune (*eggua para d'ata*)."
13. J. Defradas, *Les Thèmes de la propaganda delphique* (Paris: Klincksieck, 1954), ch. 3, "La sagesse delphique," pp. 268-83.
14. "Then Socrates demanded: 'Tell me, Euthydemus, have you ever been to Delphi?'
    'Yes, by Zeus,' Euthydemus answered, 'I have even been twice.'
    'Then did you notice somewhere on the temple the inscription: Know yourself?'

'Yes.'
'Did you just idly glance at it, or did you pay attention to it and try to examine who you are?' " Xenophon, *Memorabilia*, IV.II.24.

15. For his lectures Foucault usually uses the Belles Lettres edition (otherwise called the Budé edition) that enables him to have the original Greek or Latin facing the translation. This is why for the important terms and passages he accompanies his reading with references to the text in the original language. Moreover, when Foucault reads French translations in this way, he does not always follow them to the letter, but adapts them to the demands of oral style, multiplying logical connectors ("and," "or," "that is to say," "well," etc.) or giving reminders of the preceding arguments. Usually we restore the original French translation while indicating, in the text, significant additions (followed by "M.F.") in brackets.
16. Plato, *Apology*, 29d.
17. Foucault here cuts a sentence from 30a: "If it seems clear that, despite what he says, he does not possess virtue, I shall reproach him for attaching less value to what has the most value and more value to what has the least." Ibid.
18. Ibid., 30a.
19. "I tell you, being what I am, it is not to me that you do the most wrong if you condemn me to death, but to yourselves." Ibid., 30c.
20. Foucault refers here to a development of the exposition from 31a to 31c.
21. In 35e-37a, on being told of his condemnation to death, Socrates proposes an alternative penalty. Actually, in the kind of trial Socrates undergoes, there is no penalty fixed by law: it is up to the judges to determine the penalty. The penalty demanded by the accusers (and indicated in the charge) was death, and the judges acknowledge that Socrates is guilty of the misdeeds of which he is accused and therefore liable to incur this penalty. However, at this moment of the trial, Socrates, recognized as guilty, must propose an alternative penalty. It is only after this that the judges must fix a punishment for the accused on the basis of the penal proposals of the two parties. For further details see C. Mossé, *Le Procès de Socrate* (Brussels: Éd. Complexe, 1996) as well as the lengthy introduction by L. Brisson to his edition of the *Apologie de Socrate* (Paris: Garnier-Flammarion, 1997).
22. *Apology*, 36b-d.
23. This alludes to the famous passage of 28d: "The true principle, Athenians, is this. Someone who occupies a post (*taxē*), whether chosen by himself as most honorable or placed there by a commander, has to my mind the duty to remain firmly in place whatever the risk, without thought of death or danger, rather than sacrifice honor." Epictetus praises steadfastness in one's post as the philosophical attitude par excellence. See, for example, *Discourses*, I.ix.24, and III.xxiv.36 and 95, in which Epictetus alternates between the terms *taxis* and *khōra*. See also the end of Seneca's *On the Firmness of the Wise Man*, XIX.4: "Defend the post (*locum*) that nature has assigned you. You ask what post? That of a man."
24. Socrates warns the Athenians of what will happen if they condemn him to death: "You will spend the rest of your life asleep." *Apology*, 31a.
25. "If you put me to death you will not easily find another man . . . attached to you by the will of the gods in order to stimulate you like a horsefly stimulates a horse." *Apology*, 30e.
26. "Did Socrates manage to persuade all those who came to him to take care of themselves (*epimeleisthai heautōn*)?" Epictetus, *Discourses*, III.i.19.
27. It is found in the *Letter to Menoeceus*, 122. More exactly the text says: "For no-one is it ever too early or too late for ensuring the soul's health . . . So young and old should practice philosophy." This quotation is taken up by Foucault in Michel Foucault, *Histoire de la sexualité*, vol. 3, *Le Souci de soi* (Paris: Gallimard, 1984), p. 60; English translation by Robert Hurley, *The Care of the Self* (New York: Pantheon, 1985), p. 46.
28. Actually, the Greek text has "*to kata psukhēn hugiainon*." The verb *therapeuein* appears only once in Epicurus, in *Vatican Sayings*, 55: "We should treat (*therapeuteon*) misfortunes with the grateful memory of what we have lost and with the knowledge that what has come about cannot be undone."
29. The center of gravity for the whole of this theme is Epicurus's phrase: "The discourse of the philosopher who does not treat any human affection is empty. Just as a doctor who does

not get rid of bodily illnesses is useless, so also is a philosophy if it does not get rid of the affection of the soul (221 Us.)." Translated by A.-J. Voelke in his *La Philosophie comme thérapie de l'âme* (Paris: Éd. du Cerf, 1993), p. 36. In the same work, see the articles: "Santé de l'âme et bonheur de la raison. La fonction thérapeutique de la philosophie dans épicurisme" and "Opinions vides et troubles de l'âme: la médication épicurienne."

30. Seneca, *On Benefits*, VII.i.3-7. This text is analyzed at length in the lecture of 10 February, second hour.

31. For a conceptualization of the notion of culture of the self, see the lecture of 6 January, first hour.

32. On the concept of the event in Foucault, see "Nietzsche, la généalogie, l'histoire" (1971) in *Dits et Écrits*, vol. 2, p. 136, for the Nietzschean roots of the concept; and "Mon corps, ce papier, ce feu" in *Dits et Écrits*, vol. 2, p. 260 on the polemical value of the event in thought against a Derridean metaphysics of the originary (English translations by Robert Hurley and others, as "Nietzsche, Genealogy, History" and "My Body, This Paper, This Fire," in *Essential Works of Foucault, 1954-1984, vol. 2: Aesthetics, Method and Epistemology*, ed., J.D. Faubion, translations by Robert Hurley et al [New York: New Press, 2000]), "Table ronde du 20 mai 1978" for the program of an "*événementialisation*" of historical knowledge, *Dits et Écrits*, vol. 4, p. 23; and, in particular, "Polémique, politique, et problématisations" in *Dits et Écrits*, vol. 4, concerning the distinctiveness of the history of thought (translated by Lydia Davis as "Polemics, Politics, and Problematizations: An Interview with Michel Foucault" in *Ethics: Subjectivity and Truth*).

33. "Considering the seventh day to be very holy and a great festival, they accord it a special honor: on this day, after caring for the soul (*tēs psukhēs epimeleian*), they anoint their bodies with oil." Philo of Alexandria, *On the Contemplative Life*, 477M, IV.36.

34. "Then we will contemplate the same objects as [the soul of the universe], because we also will be well prepared thanks to our nature and our effort (*epimeleiais*)." Plotinus, *The Enneads*, II.9.18.

35. "The law eliminates fate by teaching that virtue is taught and develops if one applies oneself to it (*ex epimeleias prosginomenēn*)." Methodius of Olympus, *The Banquet*, 172c.

36. "*Hote toinun hē agan hautē tou sōmatos epimeleia autō te alusitelēs to sōmati, kai pros tēn psukhēn empodion esti; to ge hupopeptōkenai toutō kai therapeuein mania saphēs*" ("When excessive care for the body becomes useless for the body and harmful to the soul, submitting to it and attaching oneself to it seems an obvious madness"). Basil of Caesarea, *Sermo de legendis libris gentilium*, 584d, in J.-P. Migne, ed. *Patrologie grecque* (SEU Petit-Montrouge, 1857), vol. 31.

37. "Now that [Moses] had raised himself to the highest level in the virtues of the soul, both by lengthy application (*makras epimeleias*) and by knowledge from on high, it is, rather, a happy and peaceful encounter that he has with his brother... The help given by God to our nature... only appears... when we are sufficiently familiarized with the life from on high through progress and application (*epimeleias*)." Grégoire de Nysse [Gregory of Nyssa], *La Vie de Moïse, ou Traité de la perfection en matière de la vertue*, translations by J. Daniélou (Paris: Éd. du Cerf, 1965), 337c-d, 43-44, pp. 130-131; see also 55 in 341b, setting out the requirement of a "long and serious study (*toiautēs kai tosautēs epimeleias*)," p. 138.

38. "But now I have returned here to this same grace, joined by love to my master; also strengthen in me what is ordered and stable in this grace, you the friends of my fiancé, who, by your cares (*epimeleias*) and attention, preserve the impulse in me towards the divine." Grégoire de Nysse, *Le Cantique des cantiques*, translations by C. Bouchet (Paris: Migne, 1990), p. 106.

39. "*Ei oun apokluseias palin di'epimeleias biou ton epiplasthenta tē kardia sou rupon, analampsei soi to theoeidēs kallos* (If, on the other hand, you purify the dregs spread out in your heart by taking care of your life, the divine beauty will shine within you)." Gregory of Nyssa, *De Beatitudinibus*, Oratio VI, in *Patrologie grecque*, vol. 44, p. 1272a.

40. Gregory of Nyssa, *Treatise on Virginity*. See in the same book the parable of the lost drachma (300c-301c, XII), often cited by Foucault to illustrate the care of the self. See the lecture ("Technologies of the Self" in *Ethics: Subjectivity and Truth*, p. 227); "Les techniques de soi" in *Dits et Écrits*, vol. 4, p. 787: "By filth, we should understand, I think, the taint of the flesh: when one has 'swept it away' and cleared it by the 'care' (*epimeleia*) that one takes of one's life, the object appears in broad daylight." 301c XII, 3.

41. In an interview in January 1984, Foucault notes that in this text by Gregory of Nyssa (303c-305c, XIII) the care of the self is essentially defined as "the renunciation of all earthly attachments. It is the renunciation of all that may be love of self, of attachment to an earthly self" ("L'éthique du souci de soi comme pratique de la liberté," in Dits et Écrits, vol. 4, p. 716; English translation by P. Aranov and D. McGrawth, "The Ethics of the Concern for Self as a Practice of Freedom" in Ethics: Subjectivity and Truth, p. 288).
42. On the meaning of meletē, see the lecture of 3 March, second hour, and 17 March, first hour.
43. On the techniques of meditation, and the meditation on death in particular, see the lectures of 27 February, second hour, 3 March, first hour, and 24 March, second hour.
44. On examination of conscience see the lecture of 24 March, second hour.
45. On the technique of screening representations, in Marcus Aurelius in particular, and in comparison with the examination of ideas in Cassian, see the lecture of 24 February, first hour.
46. In "moral dandyism" we can see a reference to Baudelaire (see Foucault's pages on "the attitude of modernity" and the Baudelairean *ethos* in "What is Enlightenment?" in *Ethics: Subjectivity and Truth*, pp. 310-12 [French version "Qu'est-ce que les Lumières?" in *Dits et Écrits*, vol. 4, pp. 568-71) and in the "aesthetic stage" there is a clear allusion to Kierkegaard's existential triptych (aesthetic, ethical, and religious stages), the aesthetic sphere (embodied by the Wandering Jew, Faust, and Don Juan) being that of the individual who exhausts the moments of an indefinite quest as so many fragile atoms of pleasure (it is irony that allows transition to the ethical). Foucault was a great reader of Kierkegaard, although he hardly ever mentions this author, who nonetheless had for him an importance as secret as it was decisive.
47. This thesis of the Hellenistic and Roman philosopher no longer finding the basis for the free use of his moral and political action in the new sociopolitical conditions (as if the Greek city-state had always been its natural element), and finding in the self a last resort into which to withdraw, became a *topos*, if not unchallenged self-evidence of the history of philosophy (shared by Bréhier, Festugière and others). During the second half of the century, the articles on epigraphy and the teaching of a famous scientist with an international audience, Louis Robert (*"Opera minora selecta"*. Épigraphie et antiquités grecques [Amsterdam: Hakkert, 1989], vol. 6, p. 715) made this vision of the Greek lost in a world which was too big and in which he was deprived of his city-state outmoded (I owe all this information to Paul Veyne). This thesis of the obliteration of the city-state in the Hellenistic period is thus strongly challenged by, among others, Foucault in *Le Souci de soi* (*The Care of the Self*, part three, ch. 2, "The Political Game", pp. 81-95, and see also pp. 41-43). For Foucault it is primarily a question of challenging the thesis of a breakup of the political framework of the city-state in the Hellenistic monarchies (pp. 81-83) and then of showing (and again in this course) that the care of the self is basically defined as a mode of living rather than as an individualistic resort ("The care of the self... appears then as an intensification of social relations," p. 53). P. Hadot, in *Qu'est-ce que la philosophie antique?* (Paris: Gallimard, 1995), pp. 146-47, traces this prejudice of a disappearance of the Greek city-state back to a work by G. Murray, *Four Stages of Greek Religion* (New York: Columbia University Press, 1912).
48. Descartes, *Méditations sur la philosophie première* (1641), in *Œuvres* (Paris: Gallimard/ Bibliothèque de la Pléiade, 1952); English translation by John Cottingham, in Descartes, *Meditations on First Philosophy*, ed. John Cottingham (Cambridge: Cambridge University Press, 1996).
49. Gnosticism represents an esoteric philosophico-religious movement that developed in the first centuries A.D. This extremely widespread movement, which is difficult to delimit and define, was rejected both by the Church Fathers and by philosophy inspired by Platonism. The *"gnosis"* (from the Greek *gnōsis*: knowledge) designates an esoteric knowledge that offers salvation to whomever has access to it, and for the initiated it represents knowledge of his origin and destination as well as the secrets and mysteries of the higher world (bringing the promise of a heavenly voyage), uncovered on the basis of secret exegetical traditions. In this sense of a salvationist, initiatory, and symbolic knowledge, the "gnosis" covers a vast set of Judeo-Christian speculations based on the Bible. The "Gnostic" movement, through the

revelation of a supernatural knowledge, thus promises liberation of the soul and victory over the evil cosmic power. For a literary reference see Michel Foucault, "La prose d'Actéon" in *Dits et Écrits*, vol. 1, p. 326. It is likely, as A. I. Davidson has suggested to me, that Foucault was familiar with the studies of H. C. Puech on this subject (See *Sur le manichéisme et Autres Essais* [Paris: Flammarion, 1979]).

50. "The" philosopher is how Aquinas designates Aristotle in his commentaries.
51. In the classification of the conditions of knowledge that follow we find, like a muffled echo, what Foucault called "procedures of limitation of discourse" in his inaugural lecture at the Collège de France, *L'Ordre du discours* (Paris, Gallimard, 1971). However, in 1970 the fundamental element was discourse, as an anonymous and blank sheet, whereas everything here is structured around the articulation of the "subject" and "truth."
52. We can recognize here an echo of the famous analysis devoted to the *Meditations* in Foucault's *Histoire de la folie* (Paris: Gallimard/Tel, 1972). In the exercise of doubt, Descartes encounters the vertigo of madness as a reason for doubting, and he excludes it *a priori*, refuses to countenance it, preferring the gentle ambiguities of the dream: "madness is excluded by the doubting subject" (p. 7). Derrida immediately challenged this thesis in "Cogito et Histoire de la folie" (in *L'Écriture et la Différence*, Paris: Éd. du Seuil, 1967; English translation by A. Bass, "Cogito and the History of Madness," in *Writing and Difference*, London: Routledge and Kegan Paul, 1978), which takes up a lecture delivered on 4 March 1963 at the Collège philosophique, showing that the peculiarity of the Cartesian Cogito is precisely to take on the risk of a "*total madness*" by resorting to the hypothesis of the evil genius (pp. 81-82; English translation pp. 52-53). We know that Foucault, openly stung by this criticism, some years later published a masterly response, raising a specialist quarrel to the level of an ontological debate through a rigorous textual explanation ("My Body, This Paper, This Fire," and "Réponse à Derrida," in *Dits et Écrits*, vol. 2). Thus was born what is called the "Foucault/Derrida polemic" about Descartes' *Meditations*.

## two

## 6 JANUARY 1982

### Second hour

*Presence of conflicting requirements of spirituality: science and theology before Descartes; classical and modern philosophy; Marxism and psychoanalysis.* ∼ *Analysis of a Lacedaemonian maxim: the care of the self as statutory privilege.* ∼ *First analysis of Plato's* Alcibiades. ∼ *Alcibiades' political expectations and Socrates' intervention.* ∼ *The education of Alcibiades compared with that of young Spartans and Persian Princes.* ∼ *Contextualization of the first appearance of the requirement of care of the self in* Alcibiades: *political expectation and pedagogical deficiency; critical age; absence of political knowledge* (savoir). ∼ *The indeterminate nature of the self and its political implications.*

I WOULD LIKE TO say two or three more words because, despite my good intentions and a well-structured use of time, I have not entirely kept within the hour as I hoped. So I will say a few more words on this general theme of the relations between philosophy and spirituality and the reasons for the gradual elimination of the notion of care of the self from philosophical thought and concern. I was saying that it seemed to me that at a certain moment (and when I say "moment," there is absolutely no question of giving it a date and localizing or individualizing it around just one person) the link was broken, definitively I think, between access to the truth, which becomes the autonomous development of knowledge (*connaissance*), and the requirement of the subject's transformation of himself and of his being.* When I say "I think it was definitively broken," I don't need to tell you that I don't believe any such thing, and that what is interesting is precisely that the links were not broken abruptly as if by the slice of a knife.

Let's consider things upstream first of all. The break does not occur just like that. It does not take place on the day Descartes laid down the rule of self-evidence or discovered the Cogito, etc. The work of disconnecting, on the one hand, the principle of an access to truth accomplished in terms of the knowing subject alone from, on the other, the spiritual necessity of the subject's work on himself, of his self-transformation and expectation of enlightenment and transfiguration from the truth, was underway long before. The dissociation had begun to take place long before and a certain wedge had been inserted between these two components. And of course, we should look for this wedge... in science? Not at all. We should look for it in theology (the theology which, precisely, with Aquinas, the scholastics, etc., was able to be founded on Aristotle—remember what I was just saying—and which will occupy the place we know it to have in Western reflection). This theology, by claiming, on the basis of Christianity of course, to be rational reflection founding a faith with a universal vocation, founded at the same time the principle of a knowing subject in general, of a knowing subject who finds both his point of absolute fulfillment and highest degree of perfection in God, who is also his Creator and so his model. The correspondence between an omniscient God and subjects capable of knowledge, conditional on faith of course, is undoubtedly one of the main elements that led Western thought—or its principal forms of reflection—and philosophical thought in particular, to extricate itself, to free itself, and separate itself from the conditions of spirituality that had previously accompanied it and for which the *epimeleia heautou* was the

---

*More precisely, the manuscript states that the link was broken "when Descartes said: philosophy by itself is sufficient for knowledge, and Kant completed this by saying: if knowledge has limits, these limits exist entirely within the structure of the knowing subject, that is to say in precisely what makes knowledge possible."

most general expression. I think we should be clear in our minds about the major conflict running through Christianity from the end of the fifth century—St. Augustine obviously—up to the seventeenth century. During these twelve centuries the conflict was not between spirituality and science, but between spirituality and theology. The best proof that it was not between spirituality and science is the blossoming of practices of spiritual knowledge, the development of esoteric knowledge, the whole idea—and it would be interesting to reinterpret the theme of Faust along these lines[1]—that there cannot be knowledge without a profound modification in the subject's being. That alchemy, for example, and a whole stratum of knowledge, was at this time thought to be obtainable only at the cost of a modification in the subject's being clearly proves that there was no constitutive or structural opposition between science and spirituality. The opposition was between theological thought and the requirement of spirituality. Thus the disengagement did not take place abruptly with the appearance of modern science. The disengagement, the separation, was a slow process whose origin and development should be located, rather, in theology.

Neither should we think that the break was made, and made definitively, at the moment I have called, completely arbitrarily, the "Cartesian moment." Rather, it is very interesting to see how the question of the relation between the conditions of spirituality and the problem of the development of truth and the method for arriving at it was posed in the seventeenth century. Take, for example, the very interesting notion that is typical of the end of the sixteenth and the beginning of the seventeenth century: the notion of "reform of the understanding." Take, precisely, the first nine paragraphs of Spinoza's *Treatise on the Correction of the Understanding*.[2] You can see quite clearly there—and for well-known reasons that we don't need to emphasize—how in formulating the problem of access to the truth Spinoza linked the problem to a series of requirements concerning the subject's very being: In what aspects and how must I transform my being as subject? What conditions must I impose on my being as subject so as to have access to the truth, and to what extent will this access to the truth give me what I seek, that is to say the highest good, the sovereign good? This is a properly spiritual question, and the theme of the reform of the understanding in the seventeenth century is, I think, entirely typical of the still very strict, close, and tight links between, let's say, a philosophy of knowledge and a spirituality of the subject's transformation of his own being.

If we now consider things downstream, if we cross over to the other side, starting with Kant, then here again we see that the structures of spirituality have not disappeared either from philosophical reflection or even, perhaps, from knowledge (*savoir*). There would be... but then I do not really want to outline it now, I just want to point out a few things. Read again all of nineteenth century philosophy—well, almost all: Hegel anyway, Schelling, Schopenhauer, Nietzsche, the Husserl of the *Krisis*,[3] and Heidegger as well[4]—and you see precisely here also that knowledge (*connaissance*), the activity of knowing, whether [it] is discredited, devalued, considered critically, or rather, as in Hegel, exalted, is nonetheless still linked to the requirements of spirituality. In all these philosophies, a certain structure of spirituality tries to link knowledge, the activity of knowing, and the conditions and effects of this activity, to a transformation in the subject's being. *The Phenomenology of Mind*, after all, has no other meaning.[5] The entire history of nineteenth-century philosophy can, I think, be thought of as a kind of pressure to try to rethink the structures of spirituality within a philosophy that, since Cartesianism, or at any rate since seventeenth-century philosophy, tried to get free from these self-same structures. Hence the hostility, and what's more the profound hostility, of all the "classical" type of philosophers—all those who invoke the tradition of Descartes, Leibniz, etcetera—towards the philosophy of the nineteenth century that poses, at least implicitly, the very old question of spirituality and which, without saying so, rediscovers the care of the self.

However, I would say that this pressure, this resurgence, this reappearance of the structures of spirituality is nonetheless quite noticeable even within the field of knowledge (*savoir*) strictly speaking. If it is true, as all scientists say, that we can recognize a false science by the fact that access to it requires the subject's conversion and that it promises enlightenment for the subject at the end of its development; if we can recognize a false science by its structure of spirituality (which is self-evident; every scientist knows this), we should not forget that in those forms of knowledge (*savoir*) that are not exactly sciences, and which we should not seek to assimilate to the structure of science, there is again the strong and clear presence of at least certain elements, certain requirements of spirituality. Obviously, I don't need to draw you a picture: you will have immediately identified forms of knowledge like Marxism or psychoanalysis. It goes without saying that it would be completely wrong to identify these with religion. This is meaningless and contributes nothing. However, if you take each of them, you know that in both Marxism and psychoanalysis, for completely different reasons but with relatively homologous effects, the problem of what is at stake in the subject's being (of what the subject's being must be for the subject to have access to the truth) and, in return, the question of what aspects of the subject may be transformed by virtue of his access to the truth, well, these two questions, which are once again absolutely typical of spirituality, are found again at the very heart of, or anyway, at the source and outcome of both of these knowledges. I am not at all saying that these are forms of spirituality. What I mean is that, taking a historical view over some, or at least one or two millennia, you find again in these forms of knowledge the questions, interrogations, and requirements which, it seems to me, are the very old and fundamental questions of the *epimeleia heautou*, and so of spirituality as a condition of access to the truth. What has happened, of course, is that neither of these two forms of knowledge has openly considered this point of view clearly and willingly. There has been an attempt to conceal the conditions of spirituality specific to these forms of knowledge within a number of social forms. The idea of the effect of a class position or of the party, of allegiance to a group or membership of a school, of initiation or of the analyst's training, etc., all refer back to these questions of the condition of the subject's preparation for access to the truth, but conceived of in social terms, in terms of organization. They have not been thought of in terms of the historical thrust of the existence of spirituality and its requirements. Moreover, at the same time the price paid for transposing or reducing these questions of "truth and the subject" to problems of membership (of a group, a school, a party, a class, etc.), has been, of course, that the question of the relations between truth and the subject has been forgotten.* The interest and force of Lacan's analyses seems to me to be due precisely to this: It seems to me that Lacan has been the only one since Freud who has sought to refocus the question of psychoanalysis on precisely this question of the relations between the subject and truth.[6] That is to say, in terms which are of course absolutely foreign to the historical tradition of this spirituality, whether of Socrates or Gregory of Nyssa and everyone in between, in terms of psychoanalytic knowledge itself, Lacan tried to pose what historically is the specifically spiritual question: that of the price the subject must pay for saying the truth, and of the effect on the subject of the fact that he has said, that he can and has said the truth about himself. By restoring this question I think Lacan actually reintroduced into psychoanalysis the oldest tradition, the oldest questioning, and the oldest disquiet of the *epimeleia heautou*, which was the most general form of spirituality. Of course, a question arises, which I will not answer, of whether pysychoanalysis itself can, in its own terms, that is to say in terms of the effects of knowledge (*connaissance*), pose the question of the relations of the subject to truth, which by definition—from the point of view of spirituality, and anyway of the *epimeleia heautou*—cannot be posed in terms of knowledge (*connaissance*).

That is what I wanted to say about this. Now let's go on to a more simple exercise. Let's return to the texts. So, there is obviously no question of me rewriting the entire history of the notion, practice, and rules of the care of the self I have been referring to. This year, and once again subject to my sloppy timekeeping and inability to keep to a timetable, I will try to isolate three moments which seem to me to be interesting: the Socratic-Platonic moment, the appearance of the *epimeleia heautou* in philosophical reflection; second, the period of the golden age of the culture of the self, of the cultivation of oneself, of the care of oneself, which we can place in the first two centuries A.D.; and then, roughly, the transition from pagan philosophical ascesis to Christian asceticism in the fourth and fifth centuries.[7]

---

*The manuscript notes that the fact that for psychoanalysis this has "never been thought theoretically" has entailed "a positivism, a psychologism" with regard to this truth-subject relation.

The first moment: Socratic-Platonic. Basically, then, the text I would like to refer to is the analysis, the theory itself of the care of the self; the extended theory developed in the second part, the conclusion, of the dialogue called *Alcibiades*. Before reading some of this text, I would like to recall two things. First, if it is true that the care of the self emerges in philosophical reflection with Socrates, and in the *Alcibiades* in particular, even so we should not forget that from its origin and throughout Greek culture the principle of "taking care of oneself"—as a rule and positive requirement from which a great deal is expected—was not an instruction for philosophers, a philosopher's interpellation of young people passing in the street. It is not an intellectual attitude; it is not advice given by wise old men to overeager young people. No, the assertion, the principle "one ought to take care of oneself," was an old maxim of Greek culture. In particular it was a Lacedaemonian maxim. In a text which, since it is from Plutarch, is fairly late, but which refers to what is clearly an ancestral and centuries-old saying, Plutarch reports a comment supposedly made by Anaxandridas, a Lacedaemonian, a Spartan, who is asked one day: You Spartans really are a bit strange. You have a lot of land and your territory is huge, or anyway substantial. Why don't you cultivate it yourselves, why do you entrust it to helots? And Anaxandridas is supposed to have answered: Well, quite simply, so that we can take care of ourselves.[8] Of course, when the Spartan says here: we have to take care of ourselves and so we do not have to cultivate our lands, it is quite clear that this has nothing to do [with philosophy]. In these people, for whom philosophy, intellectualism, etcetera, had no great positive value, taking care of themselves was the affirmation of a form of existence linked to a privilege, and to a political privilege: If we have helots, if we do not cultivate our lands ourselves, if we delegate all these material cares to others, it is so that we can take care of ourselves. The social, economic and political privilege of this close-knit group of Spartan aristocrats was displayed in the form of: We have to look after ourselves, and to be able to do that we have entrusted our work to others. You can see then that "taking care of oneself" is not at all philosophical but doubtless a fairly common principle linked, however, and we will find this again and again in the history of the *epimeleia heautou*, to a privilege, which in this case is political, economic, and social.

So when Socrates takes up and formulates the question of the *epimeleia heautou*, he does so on the basis of a tradition. Moreover, Sparta is referred to in the first major theory of the care of the self in the *Alcibiades*. So, let's move on now to this text, *Alcibiades*. Today, or next week, I will come back to the problems, not of its authenticity, which are more or less settled, but of its dating, which are very complicated.[9] But it is no doubt better to study the text itself and see the questions as they arise. I pass very quickly over the beginning of the dialogue of *Alcibiades*. I note only that right at the start we see Socrates accosting Alcibiades and remarking to him that until now he, Socrates, in contrast to Alcibiades' other lovers, has never approached Alcibiades, and that he has only decided to do so today. He has made up his mind to do so because he is aware that Alcibiades has something in mind.[10] He has something in mind, and Alcibiades is asked the old, classic question of Greek education, which goes back to Homer, etcetera:[11] Suppose you were offered the following choice, either to die today or to continue leading a life in which you will have no glory; which would you prefer? Well, [Alcibiades replies]: I would rather die today than lead a life that will bring me no more than what I have already. This is why Socrates approaches Alcibiades. What is it that Alcibiades has already and in comparison with which he wants something else? The particulars of Alcibiades' family, his status in the city, and his ancestral privileges place him above others. He has, the text says, "one of the most enterprising families of the city."[12] On his father's side—his father was a Eupatrid—he has connections, friends, and wealthy and powerful relatives. The same is true on the side of his mother, who was an Alcmaeonid.[13] Moreover, although he had lost both of his parents, his tutor was no nonentity, but Pericles. Pericles rules the roost in the city, even in Greece, and even in some barbarian countries.[14] Added to which, Alcibiades has a huge fortune. On the other hand, as everyone knows, Alcibiades is beautiful. He is pursued by numerous lovers and has so many and is so proud of his beauty and so arrogant that he has rejected all of them, Socrates being the only one who continues to pursue him. Why is he the only one? He is the only one precisely because Alcibiades, by dint of having rejected all his lovers, has come of age. This is the famous critical age of boys I spoke about last year,[15] after which one can no longer really love them. However, Socrates continues to take an interest in Alcibiades. He continues to be interested in Alcibiades and even decides to speak to him for the first time. Why? Because, as I said to you a moment ago, he has clearly understood that Alcibiades has in mind something more than just benefiting from his connections, family, and wealth for the rest of his life, and as for his beauty, this is fading. Alcibiades does not want to be satisfied with this. He wants to turn to the people and take the city's destiny in hand: he wants to govern the others. In short, [he] is someone who wants to transform his statutory privilege and preeminence into political action, into his effective government of others. It is inasmuch as this intention is taking shape, at the point when Alcibiades—having taken advantage or refused to take advantage of others with his beauty—is turning to the government of others (after *erōs*, the *polis*, the city-state), that Socrates hears the voice of the god who inspires him to speak to Alcibiades. He has something to do: to transform statutory privilege and preeminence into the government of others. It is clear in the *Alcibiades* that the question of the care of the self arises at this point. The same thing can be found in what Xenophon says about Socrates. For example, in book III of the *Memorabilia*, Xenophon cites a dialogue, a meeting between Socrates and the young Charmides.[16] Charmides is also a young man on the threshold of politics, no doubt a little older than the Alcibiades of Plato's text since he is already mature enough to participate in the Assembly and give his views. Except that the Charmides who is heard in the Assembly, who gives his views and whose views are listened to because they are wise, is shy. He is shy, and although he is listened to and knows that everyone listens to him when considering things in a small group, he shrinks from speaking in public. And it is about this that Socrates says to him: Even so, you should pay heed to yourself; apply your mind to yourself, be aware of your qualities and in this way you will be able to participate in political life. He does not use the expression *epimeleia heautou* or *epimelei sautou*, but the expression "apply your mind." *Noūn prosekhei*:[17] apply your mind to yourself. But the situation is the same. It is the same, but reversed: Charmides, who despite his wisdom dares not enter political activity, must be encouraged, whereas with Alcibiades we are dealing with a young man champing at the bit, who only asks to enter politics and to transform his statutory advantages into real political action.

Now, asks Socrates, and this is where the part of the dialogue I want to study more closely begins, if you govern the city, if you are to be able to govern it, you must confront two sorts of rivals.[18] On the one hand there are the internal rivals you will come up against in the city, because you are not the only one who wants to govern. And then, when you are governing them, you will come up against the city's enemies. You will come up against Sparta and the Persian Empire. Now, says Socrates, you know very well how it is with both the Lacedaemonians and the Persians: they outmatch Athens and you. In wealth first of all: However wealthy you may be, can you compare your wealth to that of the Persian King? As for education, can you really compare your education with that of the Lacedaemonians and Persians? There is a brief description of Spartan education, which is not put forward as a model but as a mark of quality at least; an education that ensures firmness, greatness of soul, courage, endurance, the taste for victory and honor, etcetera. Persian education, and the passage here is interesting, also has great advantages. In the education given to the King, from the earliest age—in short, from when he is old enough to understand—the young prince is surrounded by four teachers: one is the teacher of wisdom (*sophia*), another of justice (*dikaiosunē*), the third a master of temperance (*sōphrosunē*), and the fourth a master of courage (*andreia*). With regard to the date of the text, the first problem to reckon with is the following: on the one hand, as you know, fascination and interest in Sparta is constant in Plato's dialogues, starting with the Socratic dialogues; however, the interest in and fascination with Persia is something which is thought to appear late in Plato and the Platonists [...*]. How then has Alcibiades been trained in comparison with this education, whether Spartan or Persian? Well, says Socrates, consider what has happened. After the death of your parents you were entrusted to Pericles. For sure, Pericles "may lord it over his

---

*Only "... that we hear in late Platonism, in the second half of Platonism at any rate" is audible.

city, Greece and some barbarian States." However, in the event, he could not educate his sons. He had two of them, both good for nothing. Consequently you have come out badly. But one should not count on a serious training from this direction. And then again, your tutor Pericles entrusted you to an old slave (Zopyrus the Thracian) who was a monument to ignorance and so had nothing to teach you. Under these conditions, Socrates says to Alcibiades, you should make a little comparison: you want to enter political life, to take the destiny of the city in hand, and you do not have the wealth of your rivals, and above all you do not have their education. You should take a bit of a look at yourself, you should know yourself. And we see appearing here, in fact, the notion or principle of *gnōthi seauton* (an explicit reference to the Delphic principle).[19] However, it is interesting to see that this *gnōthi seauton*, appearing before any notion of care of the self, is given in a weak form. It is simply a counsel of prudence. It does not appear with the strong meaning it will have later. Socrates asks Alcibiades to reflect on himself a little, to review his life and compare himself with his rivals. A counsel of prudence: Think a bit about who you are in comparison with those you want to confront and you will discover your inferiority.

His inferiority consists in this: You are not only not wealthy and have not received any education, but also you cannot compensate for these defects (of wealth and education) by the only thing which would enable you to confront them without too much inferiority—a know-how (*savoir*), a *tekhnē*.[20] You do not have the *tekhnē* that would enable you to compensate for these initial inferiorities. Here Socrates demonstrates to Alcibiades that he does not have the *tekhnē* to enable him to govern the city-state well and be at least on an equal footing with his rivals. Socrates demonstrates this to him through a process which is absolutely classical in all the Socratic dialogues: What is it to govern the city well; in what does good government of the city consist; how do we recognize it? There is a long series of questions. We end up with this definition advanced by Alcibiades: The city is well governed when harmony reigns amongst its citizens.[21] Alcibiades is asked: What is this harmony; in what does it consist? Alcibiades cannot answer. The poor boy cannot answer and then despairs. He says: "I no longer know what I am saying.

Truly, it may well be that I have lived for a long time in a state of shameful ignorance without even being aware of it."[22] To this Socrates responds: Don't worry; if you were to discover your shameful ignorance and that you do not even know what you are saying when you are fifty, it really would be difficult for you to remedy it, because it would be very difficult to take care of yourself (to take pains with oneself: *epimelēthēnai sautou*). However, "here you are at the time of life when one ought to be aware of it."[23] I would like to stop for a moment on this first appearance in philosophical discourse—subject once again to the dating of the *Alcibiades*—of this formula "taking caring of oneself," "taking pains with oneself."

First, as you can see, the need to be concerned about the self is linked to the exercise of power. We have already come across this in the Lacedaemonian or Spartan maxim of Anaxandridas. Except, however, that in the apparently traditional formula—"We entrust our lands to our helots so that we can take care of ourselves"—"taking care of oneself" was the consequence of a statutory situation of power. Here, rather, you see that the question of the care of oneself, the theme of the care of oneself, does not appear as an aspect of statutory privilege. It appears rather as a condition for Alcibiades to pass from his position of statutory privilege (grand, rich, traditional family, etcetera) to definite political action, to actual government of the city-state. However, you can see that "taking care of oneself" is entailed by and inferred from the individual's will to exercise political power over others. One cannot govern others, one cannot govern others well, one cannot transform one's privileges into political action on others, into rational action, if one is not concerned about oneself. Care of the self: the point at which the notion emerges is here, between privilege and political action.

Second, you can see that this notion of care of the self, this need to be concerned about oneself, is linked to the inadequacy of Alcibiades' education. But the target here is, of course, Athenian education itself, which is wholly inadequate in two respects. It is inadequate in its specifically pedagogical aspect (Alcibiades' master was worthless, a slave, and an ignorant slave, and the education of a young aristocrat destined for a political career is too important to be handed over to a family slave).

There is also criticism of the other aspect, which is less immediately clear but lurks throughout the beginning of the dialogue: the criticism of love, of the *erōs* of boys, which has not had the function for Alcibiades it should have had, since Alcibiades has been pursued by men who really only want his body, who do not want to take care of him—the theme reappears a bit later—and who therefore do not encourage Alcibiades to take care of himself. Furthermore, the best proof of their lack of interest in Alcibiades himself, of their lack of concern that he should be concerned about himself, is that they abandon him to do what he wants as soon as he loses his desirable youth. The need for the care of the self is thus inscribed not only within the political project, but also within the pedagogical lack.

Third, something as important as and immediately connected to the former feature is the idea that it would be too late to rectify matters if Alcibiades were fifty. This was not the age for taking care of oneself. One must learn to take care of oneself at the critical age when one leaves the hands of the pedagogues and enters political activity. To a certain extent, this text contradicts or raises a problem with regard to another text I read to you a short while ago, the *Apology*, in which Socrates, defending himself in front of his judges, says: But the job I have followed in Athens was an important one. It was entrusted to me by the gods and consisted in placing myself in the street and stopping everyone, young and old, citizens and noncitizens, to tell them to take care of themselves.[24] Here, the *epimeleia heautou* appears as a general function of the whole of life, whereas in the *Alcibiades* it appears as a necessary moment of the young man's training. A very important question, a major debate and a turning point in the care of the self, arises when the care of the self in Epicurean and Stoic philosophy becomes a permanent obligation for every individual throughout his life. But in this, if you like, early Socratic-Platonic form, the care of the self is, rather, an activity, a necessity for young people, within a relationship between them and their master, or them and their lover, or them and their master and lover. This is the third point, the third characteristic of the care of the self.

Fourth, and finally, the need to take care of the self does not appear to be urgent when Alcibiades formulates his political projects, but only when he sees that he is unaware of . . . what? Well, that he is unaware of the object itself, of the nature of the object he has to take care of. He knows that he wants to take care of the city-state. His status justifies him doing this. But he does not know how to take care of the city-state; he does not know in what the purpose and end of his political activity will consist (the well-being of the citizens, their mutual harmony). He does not know the object of good government, and that is why he must pay attention to himself.

So, two questions arise at this point, two questions to be resolved that are directly linked to each other. We must take care of the self. But this raises the question: What, then, is this self with which we must be concerned when we are told that we must care about the self? I refer you to the passage that I will comment upon at greater length next time, but which is very important. The dialogue of *Alcibiades* has a subtitle, but one which was added much later, in the Alexandrian period I think, but I am not sure and will have to check for next time. This subtitle is "*of human nature.*" [25] Now when you consider the development of the whole last part of the text—which begins at the passage I pointed out to you—you see that the question Socrates poses and attempts to resolve is not: You must take care of yourself now you are a man, and so I ask, what is a man? Socrates asks a much more precise, interesting, and difficult question, which is: You must take care of yourself; but what is this "oneself" (*auto to auto*),[26] since it is your self you must take care of? Consequently the question does not concern the nature of man but what we—that is us today, since the word is not in the Greek text—will call the question of the subject. What is this subject, what is this point towards which this reflexive activity, this reflected activity, which turns the individual back to himself, must be directed? The first question, then, is what is this self?

The second question to be resolved is: If we develop this care of the self properly, if we take it seriously, how will it be able to lead us, and how will it lead Alcibiades to what he wants, that is to say to knowledge of the *tekhnē* he needs to be able to govern others, the art that will enable him to govern well? In short, what is at stake in the whole of the second part, of the end of the dialogue, is this: "oneself," in the expression "caring about oneself," must be given a definition which entails, opens up, or gives access to a knowledge necessary for good government. What is at stake in the dialogue, then, is this: What is this self I must take care of in order to be able to take care of the others I must govern properly? This circle, [which goes] from the self as an object of care to knowledge of government as the government of others, is, I think, at the heart of the end of this dialogue. Anyway, the question of "caring about oneself" first emerges in ancient philosophy on the back of this question. So, thank you, and next week we will begin again at 9:15. I will try to conclude this reading of the dialogue.

1. Foucault examines the Faust myth at greater length in the lecture of 24 February, second hour.
2. B. Spinoza, *Tractatus de intellectus emendatione*, in *Benedicti de Spinoza Opera quotquot reperta sunt*, ed. J. Van Vloten and J. P. N. Land (The Hague, 1882-1884); English translation by R. H. M. Elwes, "On the Improvement of the Understanding," in *Works of Spinoza*, vol. 2 (New York: Dover, 1955).
3. E. Husserl, *Die Krisis der europäischen Wissenschaften und die transzendentale Phänomenologie* (Belgrade: Philosophia, 1936); English translation by D. Carr, *The Crisis of European Sciences and Transcendental Phenomenology* (Evanston, Ill.: Northwestern University Press, 1970).
4. In this period Foucault identified himself as an heir to this tradition that he recognized as that of "modern" philosophy. See, Michel Foucault "Qu'est-ce que les Lumières?" in *Dits et Écrits*, vol. 4, pp. 687-88; English translation by Colin Gordon, "Kant on Enlightenment and Revolution" in *Economy and Society*, vol. 15, no.1 (London: Routledge and Kegan Paul, 1986), pp. 403-04; and "The political technology of individuals" in *The Essential Works of Foucault, 1954-1984, vol. 3: Power* ed. J.D. Faubion (New York: New Press, 2000) pp. 403-04; French translation by P.-E. Dauzat, "La technologie politique des individus" in *Dits et Écrits*, vol. 4, pp. 813-14.
5. G. W. F. Hegel, *Phänomenologie des Geistes* (Wurtzbourg: Anton Goebhardt, 1807; French translation by J. Hyppolite, *Phénomenologie de l'Esprit* (Paris: Aubier-Montaigne, 1941); English translation by A.V. Miller, *The Phenomenology of Spirit* (Oxford: The Clarendon Press, 1979).
6. On Lacan's reopening of the question of the subject, see *Dits et Écrits*, vol. 3, p. 590; IV, pp. 204-05, and p. 435. For Lacan's texts going in this direction, see: "Fonction et champ de la parole et du langage en psychanalyse" (1953), "Subversion du sujet et dialectique du désir dans l'inconscient freudien" (1960), "La Science et la vérité" (1965), and "Du sujet enfin la question" (1966), all in Jacque Lacan, *Écrits*, Paris: Le Seuil, 1966 (English translations by Alan Sheridan in *Écrits. A Selection*, [London: Tavistock/Routledge, 1989]); *Le Séminaire I: Les Écrits techniques de Freud* (1953-1954) (Paris: Le Seuil, 1975), pp. 287-99; *Le Séminaire II: Le Moi dans la théorie de Freud et dans la technique de la psychanalyse (1954-1955)*, (Paris: Le Seuil, 1978); *Les Quatre concepts fondamentnaux de la psychanalyse* (1964) (Paris: Le Seuil, 1973), pp. 31-41, pp. 125-35; English translation by Alan Sheridan, *The Four Fundamental Concepts of Psychoanalysis* (London: The Hogarth Press, 1977), pp. 29-41 and pp. 136-49; "Réponse à des étudiants en philosophie sur l'objet de la psychanalyse," *Cahiers pour l'analyse* 3, 1966, pp. 5-13; "La Méprise du sujet supposé savoir," *Scilicet* 1 (Paris: Le Seuil, 1968), pp. 31-41; *Le Séminaire XX: Encore* (Paris: Le Seuil, 1975), pp. 83-91; "Le Symptôme," *Scilicet* 6/7 (Paris: Le Seuil, 1976), pp. 42-52. (I am indebted to J. Lagrange and to M. Bertani for this note).
7. This third moment will not be developed in this year's course, or in the following year.
8. "As someone asked why they entrusted work in the fields to the helots, instead of taking care of them themselves (*kai ouk autoi epimelountai*). 'Because,' he answered, 'it was not in order to take care of them that we acquired them, but to take care of ourselves (*ou toutōn epimelomenoi all'hautōn*)'." Plutarch, *Sayings of Spartans*, 217a. See the summary of this example in *Le Souci de soi*, p. 58; *The Care of the Self*, p. 44.
9. They are examined in the second hour of the lecture of 13 January.
10. All of this takes place in the beginning of the text, *Alcibiades I*, from 103a to 105e.
11. Foucault is thinking here of Achilles' double destiny: "For my mother Thetis the goddess of the silver feet tells me/I carry two sorts of destiny toward the day of my death. Either,/if I stay here and fight beside the city of the Trojans,/ my return home is gone, but my glory shall be everlasting;/but if I return home to the beloved land of my fathers,/the excellence of my glory is gone, but there will be a long life/left for me, and my end in death will not come to me quickly." Homer, *The Illiad*, translation by Richmond Lattimore (Chicago:

1961) Book IX, 410-16, p. 209; French translation by P. Mazon, *Iliade* (Paris: Les Belles Lettres, 1937) p. 67.
12. *Alcibiades*, 104a.
13. Through his father Clinias, Alcibiades was a member of the *genos* of the "Eupatrids" (i.e., "those of good fathers"), a family of aristocrats and big landowners who dominated Athens politically from the archaic period. His mother (daughter of Megacles, a victim of ostracism) belongs to the family of Alcmaeonids, who undoubtedly played the most decisive role in the political history of classical Athens.
14. *Alcibiades*, 104b.
15. The problem of the critical age of boys was broached by Foucault in the lecture of 28 January 1981 in particular, which was devoted to the structuring of the ethical perception of *aphrodisia* (principle of socio-sexual isomorphism and principle of activity) and the problem raised within this framework by the love of young boys from good families.
16. Xenophon, *Memorabilia*, III.vii.
17. More precisely, the Greek text has: "*alla diateinou mallon pros to seautō prosekhein.*" Ibid.
18. This passage is found in *Alcibiades*, 119a-124b.
19. "Ah, naïve child, believe me and the words inscribed at Delphi: 'Know yourself'." *Alcibiades*, 124b.
20. Ibid. 125d.
21. Ibid. 126c.
22. Ibid. 127d.
23. Ibid. 127e.
24. Plato, *Apology*, 30a.
25. According to Diogenes Laertius, *Lives of Eminent Philosophers*, III.57-62, the catalogue of Thrasylus (astrologer of Tiberius and philosopher at Nero's court in the first century A.D.) adopts the division of Plato's dialogues into tetralogies and for each dialogue fixes a title, which usually corresponds to the name of Socrates' principal interlocutor—but it may be that this way of designating the dialogues goes back to Plato himself—and a second title indicating the main subject matter.
26. The expression is found in *Alcibiades*, 129b.

three

# 13 JANUARY 1982

## First hour

> *Contexts of appearance of the Socratic requirement of care of the self: the political ability of young men from good families; the (academic and erotic) limits of Athenian pedagogy; the ignorance of which one is unaware. ∼ Practices of transformation of the self in archaic Greece. ∼ Preparation for dreaming and testing techniques in Pythagoreanism. ∼ Techniques of the self in Plato's* Phaedo. *∼ Their importance in Hellenistic philosophy. ∼ The question of the being of the self one must take care of in the* Alcibiades. *∼ Definition of the self as soul. ∼Definition of the soul as subject of action. ∼ The care of the self in relation to dietetics, economics, and erotics. ∼ The need for a master of the care.*

LAST WEEK WE BEGAN reading Plato's dialogue, the *Alcibiades*. I would like to begin this reading without going into the question, to which we will have to return, if not of the authenticity of this dialogue, of which there is hardly any doubt, then at least of its date. We halted at the appearance of the expression that I would like to study this year in its full extension and development: "caring about oneself" (*heautou epimeleisthai*). You no doubt recall the context in which this expression appears. In the dialogues of Plato's youth—those called the Socratic dialogues—there is a very familiar context of a political and social milieu comprising the small world of young aristocrats whose status makes them leading figures in the city-state and who are destined to exercise a certain power over their city-state, over their fellow citizens. They are young men who from an early age are consumed by the ambition to prevail over others, their rivals within as well as outside the city-state—in short, to enter active, authoritarian and triumphant politics. However, the problem is whether the authority initially conferred on them by birth, membership of the aristocratic world, and great wealth—as was the case with Alcibiades—also gives them the ability to govern properly. It is a world, then, in which relations between the status of the "preeminent" and the ability to govern are problematized: the need to take care of oneself insofar as one has to govern others. This is the first circle, the first contextual element.

The second element, linked of course to the first, is the problem of pedagogy. This is the criticism of the two forms of pedagogy familiar to us from the Socratic dialogues. There is criticism, of course, of education, of educational practice in Athens, which is compared extremely unfavorably with Spartan education, with its unremitting severity and strong integration within collective rules. Athenian education is also compared unfavorably—and this is stranger and less frequent in the Socratic dialogues, more typical of the last Platonic texts—with oriental wisdom, with the wisdom of the Persians who can at least give their young princes the four necessary masters who can teach them the four fundamental virtues. This is one aspect of the criticism of pedagogical practices. The other aspect concerns, of course, the way in which love between men and boys takes place and develops. The love of boys in Athens cannot fulfill the task of instruction that would be able to justify it and give it a foundation.[1] Adults, men, pursue young people in the bloom of their youth. However, they abandon them precisely at that critical age when, having left childhood behind and got away from the guidance and lessons of their schoolmasters, they need a guide to train them for this other, new thing for which they have received absolutely no training from their teacher: the practice of politics. As a result of this double failing of pedagogy—academic and amorous—it is necessary to take care of the self. In this case the question of "taking care of oneself" (of the *epimeleia heautou*) is no longer linked to the question of "governing others" but, if you like, to the question of "being governed." Actually, you can see that the two things are connected: taking care of oneself in order to be able to govern, and taking care of the self inasmuch as one has not been governed sufficiently and properly. "Governing," "being governed," and "taking care of the self" form a sequence, a series, whose long and complex history extends up to the establishment of pastoral power in the Christian Church in the third and fourth centuries.[2]

The third element of the context in which the question, imperative, or prescription to "take care of yourself" appears is of course ignorance, and once again we are familiar with this from the Socratic dialogues. It is an ignorance that is both ignorance of things one should know and ignorance of oneself, inasmuch as one does not even know that one is ignorant of these things. Alcibiades, you recall, thought it would be easy to answer Socrates' question and to define the nature of good government of the city-state. He even thought he could define good government by designating it as that which ensures harmony between citizens. And he does not even know what harmony is, demonstrating both that he did not know and was unaware that he did not know. So you can see that these three questions of the exercise of political power, pedagogy, and ignorance that is unaware of itself form a familiar context in the Socratic dialogues.

However, since it is precisely the emergence, the appearance of the requirement "to care about oneself" that we are considering, I would like to point out that there is something strange about the exposition of the text of the *Alcibiades* in which this requirement is introduced at 127e. The exposition is quite simple. It is already outlined in the general context I have been talking about: Socrates shows Alcibiades that he does not know what harmony is and that he is not even aware of his ignorance of what it is to govern well. So Socrates demonstrates this to Alcibiades, and Alcibiades immediately despairs. Socrates then consoles him, saying: But this is not serious, do not panic, after all you are not fifty, you are young and so you have time. But time for what? At this point we could say that the answer that could come, the answer we would expect—the answer Protagoras would no doubt give[3]—would be this: Okay, you are ignorant, but you are young and not fifty, so you have time to learn how to govern the city, to prevail over your adversaries, to convince the people and learn the rhetoric needed to exercise this power, etcetera. But it is precisely this that Socrates does not say. Socrates says: You are ignorant; but you are young and so you have time, not to learn, but to take care of yourself. It is here, I think, in the gap between "learning," which would be the usual result expected from this kind of reasoning, and the necessity to "take care of the self," between pedagogy understood as apprenticeship and this other form of culture, of *paideia* (we will return at length to this later), which revolves around what could be called the culture of the self, the formation of the self, the *Selbstbildung* as the Germans would say,[4] it is in this gap, this interplay, this proximity that a number of problems rush in which concern, it seems to me, the whole interplay between philosophy and spirituality in the ancient world.

But first of all, a comment. I told you that this expression "caring for the self" emerges and appears in Plato with the *Alcibiades*, but once again the question of the dialogue's date will have to be posed. As you will soon see when I come back to it at greater length, the question of the nature of this caring about oneself is posed explicitly and systematically in this dialogue. The question has two parts: what is "one's self" and what is "taking care of"? We truly have the first, and we could even say the only, comprehensive theory of the care of the self in all of Plato's texts. We may regard it as the first major theoretical emergence of the *epimeleia heautou*. Even so, we should not forget and must always keep in mind the fact that this requirement to care for the self, this practice—or rather, the set of practices in which the care of the self will appear—is actually rooted in very old practices, in ways of acting and types and modalities of experience that constituted its historical basis well before Plato and even Socrates. That the truth cannot be attained without a certain practice, or set of fully specified practices, which transform the subject's mode of being, change its given mode of being, and modify it by transfiguring it, is a prephilosophical theme which gave rise to many more or less ritualized procedures. Well before Plato, the *Alcibiades*, and Socrates, there was, if you like, an entire technology of the self related to knowledge (*savoir*), whether this involved particular bodies of knowledge (*connaissances*) or overall access to truth itself.[5] The idea that one must put a technology of the self to work in order to have access to the truth is shown in Ancient Greece, and what's more in many, if not all, civilizations, by a number of practices, which I will just list and recall in a completely schematic way.[6] First, rites of purification: You cannot have access to the gods, you cannot make sacrifices, you cannot hear the oracle and understand what he says, and you cannot benefit from a dream which will enlighten you through ambiguous but decipherable signs, without first being purified. The practice of purification as a necessary preliminary rite, not only before contact with the gods, but also [with] the truth they may vouchsafe us, is an extremely common theme, well-known and attested for a long time in Classical Greece and even in Hellenistic Greece and throughout the Roman world. Without purification there can be no relationship with the truth possessed by the gods. There are other techniques (and I cite them somewhat randomly without in any way undertaking a systematic study). There are techniques for concentrating the soul. The soul is something mobile. The soul, the breath, is something that can be disturbed and over which the outside can exercise a hold. One must avoid dispersal of the soul, the breath, the *pneuma*. One must avoid exposing it to external danger and something or someone having a hold over it. One must avoid its dispersal at the moment of death. One must therefore concentrate the *pneuma*, the soul, gather it up, condense it, and unite it in itself in order to give it a mode of existence, a solidity, which will enable it to last, to endure, and hold out throughout life and not be scattered when death comes. Another technique, another procedure falling under these technologies of the self, is the technique of withdrawal (*retraite*), for which there is a word, which as you know will have a prominent future in all of Western spirituality: *anakhōrēsis* (withdrawal or disengagement from the world). Withdrawal is understood in these archaic techniques of the self as a particular way of detaching yourself and absenting yourself from the world in which you happen to be, but doing so "on the spot": somehow breaking contact with the external world, no longer feeling sensations, no longer being disturbed by everything taking place around the self, acting as if you no longer see, and actually no longer seeing what is there before your eyes. It is, if you like, a technique of visible absence. You are always there, visible to the eyes of others. But you are absent, elsewhere. A fourth example, and these are only examples, is the practice of endurance, which is linked, moreover, to the concentration of the soul and to withdrawal (*anakhōrēsis*) into oneself, and which enables one either to bear painful and hard ordeals or to resist temptations one may be offered.

This whole set of practices then, and still many others, existed in ancient Greek civilization. We find traces of them for a long time afterwards. Moreover, most of them were already integrated within the well-known spiritual, religious, or philosophical movement of Pythagoreanism with its ascetic components. I will consider just two examples of these components of the technology of the self in Pythagoreanism.[7] I take these examples because they too will be popular for a long time, and are still attested in the Roman period of the first and second centuries A.D., having spread in the meanwhile into many other philosophical schools. There is, for example, the purifying preparation for the dream. Since dreaming while you sleep is, for the Pythagoreans, to be in contact with a divine world, which is the world of immortality, beyond death, and also the world of truth, you must prepare yourself for the dream.[8] Before sleep, then, you must engage in a number of ritual practices that will purify the soul and thus enable it to enter into contact with this divine world and understand its meanings, the more or less ambiguous messages and truths it reveals. Among these techniques are those of listening to music, inhaling perfumes, and also, of course, examination of conscience.[9] Reviewing the whole of one's day, recalling the faults you have committed, and thus purging and purifying yourself of them by this act of memory, is a practice whose paternity was always attributed to Pythagoras.[10] Whether or not he really was the first to instigate it is not important. It is anyway an important Pythagorean practice whose diffusion you are familiar with. I will take also another example from the many examples of the technology of the self, of the techniques of the self we can find in the Pythagoreans: the techniques of testing. That is to say you try something, you organize a tempting situation and test your ability to resist it. These were also very ancient practices. They lasted for a long time and are still attested quite late. As an example, consider a text from Plutarch (at the end of the first and the beginning of the second century). In the dialogue on *Socrates' Daemon*, Plutarch recounts, or rather, he gets one of his interlocutors, who is clearly a spokesman for the Pythagoreans, to recount the following little exercise: you start the morning with a series of lengthy, difficult, and tiring physical exercises, which give you an appetite. Having done this you have sumptuous tables served with extraordinarily rich dishes filled with the most attractive food. You place yourself before them, gaze on them, and meditate. Then you call the slaves. You give this food to the slaves and content yourself with their extremely frugal food.[11] We will no doubt have to come back to all this to examine its developments.[12]

I have pointed this out in order to show you that a whole series of techniques coming under something like the care of the self is generally attested, and particularly in the Pythagoreans, even before the emergence of the notion of *epimeleia heautou* in Plato's philosophical thought. Staying within this general context of techniques of the self, we should not forget that there are many traces of these techniques even in Plato, even if it is true—as I will try to show—that Plato brings the whole of the care of the self back to the form of knowledge and self-knowledge. For example, the technique of concentrating the soul, of gathering it and bringing it together, is very clearly attested. In the *Phaedo*, for example, it is said that one must accustom the soul to gather together from all points of the body, to concentrate itself on itself and dwell in itself as much as possible.[13] Also in the *Phaedo* it is said that the philosopher must "take the soul in hand"[14] [...*]. The practice of seclusion, of *anakhōrēsis*, of withdrawing into oneself, which is basically expressed in immobility, is also attested in the *Phaedo*.[15] Immobility of the soul and the body: of the body which resists, and of the soul which does not move, which is fixed, as it were, on itself, on its own axis, and which nothing can turn away from itself. This is the famous image of Socrates evoked in the *Symposium*. As you know, during the war Socrates was able to remain alone, immobile, standing with his feet in

---

*Only "and the [...] philosophy as guide or as therapy for the soul, the integration, within philosophical practice, of this technique of gathering together, concentrating and tightening of the soul on itself" is audible.

the snow, impervious to everything going on around him.[16] Plato refers to all these practices of endurance and resistance to temptation. In the *Symposium* there is also the image of Socrates successfully controlling his desire while lying with Alcibiades.[17]

The dissemination of these techniques of the self within Platonic thought was, I think, only the first stage in a set of shifts, reactivations, organizations, and reorganizations of these techniques in what becomes the great culture of the self in the Hellenistic and Roman period. Of course, it goes without saying that these kinds of techniques are also found in the Neo-Platonists and Neo-Pythagoreans. But you find them in the Epicureans as well. You find them in the Stoics, transposed and rethought differently, as we will see. If you take, for example, immobility of thought, the immobility of thought undisturbed by either external excitation, ensuring *securitas*, or internal excitation, ensuring *tranquillitas* (to take up Roman Stoic terms),[18] then this immobilization of thought is quite clearly the transposition and reelaboration of the practices I have been talking about within a technology of the self whose general expressions are clearly different. The notion of withdrawal, for example. The theory of this kind of withdrawal, already called *anakhōrēsis*, by which the individual withdraws into himself and cuts himself off from the external world, is found again in Roman Stoicism. In Marcus Aurelius in particular, there is a long passage which I will try to explain and the explicit theme of which is the *anakhōrēsis eis heauton* (the withdrawal [*anachorèse*] into oneself, withdrawal into and towards the self).[19] In the Stoics also there is a series of techniques for the purification of representations, for checking *phantasiai* as they appear, enabling one to recognize those that are pure and those that are impure, those to be admitted and those to be dismissed. Behind all of this there is then a great arborescence, if you like, which may be interpreted as a continuous development, but in which there are a number of important moments attesting to transfers and overall reorganizations. It seems to me that Plato, the Platonic moment, and particularly the *Alcibiades* bear witness to one of these moments in the progressive reorganization of this old technology of the self, which goes back well beyond both Plato and Socrates. It seems to me that these old technologies of the self underwent fairly profound reorganization in Plato, in the *Alcibiades*, or somewhere between Socrates and Plato. At any rate, the question of the *epimeleia heautou* (of care of the self) in philosophical thought takes up elements—at a completely different level, for completely different purposes, and with partially different forms—that were previously found in these techniques I have been talking about.

So, having said that about the first appearance of these elements in philosophy and at the same time their technical continuity, I would like to return to the text of *Alcibiades* itself and in particular to the passage (127e) where it is said: One must care about oneself. One must care about oneself, but ... and this is why I emphasize this text: Socrates has scarcely said "One must care about oneself" than he is seized by a doubt. He halts for a moment and says: It's all very well to take care of oneself, but there is a grave danger of going wrong. We risk not really knowing what we should do when we want to take care of ourselves, and instead of blindly obeying the principle "we care about ourselves" we should ask: *ti esti to hautou epimeleisthai* (what is it to take care of oneself?).[20] After all, Socrates says, we know quite well, or more or less, what it means to take care of our shoes. There is an art for this, the cobbler's art. The cobbler knows perfectly well what it means to take care of them. We also know perfectly well what it means to take care of our feet. The doctor (or the gymnastics teacher) advises you about this and is the specialist in this matter. But who knows exactly what "taking care of one's self" is? The text then naturally divides into two parts, on the basis of two questions. First, in the imperative "one must take care of the self," what is this thing, this object, this self to which one must attend? Secondly, there is the care in "care of the self." What form should this care take, in what must it consist, given that what is at stake in the dialogue is that I must be concerned about myself so as to be able to govern others and the city-state? The care of myself must therefore be such that it also provides me with the art (the *tekhnē*, the know-how) which will enable me to govern others well. In short, the succession of the two questions—what is the self and what is the care?—involve responding to one and the same demand: one's self and the care of the self must be given a definition from which we can derive the knowledge required for governing others. This is what is at stake in the second half, the second part of the dialogue beginning at 127e. This is what I should now like to examine. First of all, the question: What is one's self that we must take care of? Secondly: What is this attending to, this care, this *epimeleia*?

First question: What is one's self? We should note straightaway how the question is posed. It is posed in an interesting way because, naturally—with regard to this question "what is one's self?"—there is once again reference to the Delphic oracle, to Pythia, and to what she says, namely, that one must know oneself (*gnōnai heauton*).[21] This is the second reference to the oracle in the text, or rather to the precept given to those who consult the oracle at Delphi. You may recall that the first time was when Socrates was conversing with Alcibiades and said to him: All right, very well, you want to govern Athens; you will have to outmatch your rivals within the city itself and you will also have to fight or compete with the Lacedaemonians and Persians. Do you really think you are strong enough, that you have the capabilities, wealth, and education required? Since Alcibiades was not very sure of being able to give a positive answer—or whether he should give a positive or negative answer to this—Socrates said to him: But at least pay some attention, reflect a bit on what you are, look at the education you have received, you would do well to know yourself a little (a reference, which is explicit, moreover, to the *gnōthi seauton*).[22] However, you can see that this first reference, which is in the part of the text I analyzed last week, is, I would say, weak and fleeting. The *gnōthi seauton* is called upon merely to encourage Alcibiades to reflect a little more seriously on what he is, what he is capable of doing, and the formidable tasks awaiting him when he will have to govern the city. Now we see the *gnōthi seauton* appear in a completely different way and at a completely different level. Actually, we now know that one should take care of oneself and the question now concerns the nature of "oneself." What is the *heautou* in the expression *epimeleisthai heautou*? One should *gnōnai heauton*, the text says. I think we should be clear about this second use of, this second reference to, the Delphic oracle. It is certainly not a question of Socrates saying: Okay, you must know what you are, your abilities, your passions, whether you are mortal or immortal, etcetera. It is certainly not this. In a way it is a methodological and formal question, but one that is, I think, absolutely fundamental in the development of the text: one must know what this *heauton* is, what this "oneself" is. Not, then: "What kind of animal are you, what is your nature, how are you composed?" but: "[What is] this relation, what is designated by this reflexive pronoun *heauton*, what is this element which is the same on both the subject side and the object side?" You have to take care of yourself: It is you who takes care; and then you take care of something which is the same thing as yourself, [the same thing] as the subject who "takes care," this is your self as object. Moreover, the text says it very clearly: we must know what is *auto to auto*.[23] What is this identical element present as it were on both sides of the care: subject of the care and object of the care? What is it? This is then a methodological question concerning the meaning of what is designated by the reflexive form of the verb "taking care of oneself." This second reference to the precept "one must know oneself" is quite different from the simple counsel of prudence given a bit earlier when Alcibiades was told: Pay some attention to your bad education and all your inabilities. What then is this *heauton*, or rather, what is referred to by this *heauton*? I will go immediately to the answer. The answer, as you know, is given a hundred times in Plato's dialogues: "*psukhēs epimelēteon*" (one must take care of one's soul),[24] it is said, at the start of an exposition to which I will return. In this the *Alcibiades* corresponds exactly with a series of other expressions found elsewhere, as in the *Apology* for example, when Socrates says that he encourages his fellow citizens, and everyone he meets, to care for their soul (*psukhē*) in order to perfect it.[25] We also find the expression in the *Cratylus*, where, with regard to the theories of Heraclitus and the universal flux, it is said that we should not entrust the "*therapeuein hauton kai tēn psukhēn*" (the concern of taking care, of attending to oneself, to one's soul) to the power of names: the *heauton/psukhēn* coupling is clear here.[26] In the *Phaedo* there is the famous passage: if the soul is immortal, then "*epimeleias deitai*" (it needs that you attend to it, it needs your zeal and care, etcetera).[27] So, when the *Alcibiades* reaches the expression, "What is this 'oneself' one must care for?—Well, it is the soul," it matches up with many things, many themes which are found in many other Platonic texts. However, even so, I think the way in which we arrive at this definition of the *heauton* as the soul, the way in which this soul is conceived of here, is quite different from what is found elsewhere. Because, in fact, when it is said in the *Alcibiades*, "that which one must take care of is one's soul, one's own soul," it might be thought that this is basically very close to what is said in *The Republic*. The *Alcibiades* could be the reverse form, so to speak, of *The Republic*, in which the interlocutors, wondering what justice is and what it is for an individual to be just, are quickly talked into not being able to give an answer and, passing from justice writ small in the individual, refer to the large letters of the city-state so as better to decipher what justice might be: to know what justice is in the individual's soul, let's see what it is in the city-state.[28] Okay, it might be thought that the approach taken by the *Alcibiades* is in some way the same, but turned around; that is to say, in trying to find out what it is to govern well and the nature of good harmony and just government in the city, the interlocutors of the *Alcibiades* inquire about the nature of the soul and look for the *analogon* and model of the city in the individual soul. After all, the hierarchies and functions of the soul might be able to enlighten us on this question concerning the art of governing.

Now, this is not at all how things take place in the dialogue. We must examine how, through their discussion, Socrates and Alcibiades arrive at this (both obvious but even so possibly paradoxical) definition of one's self as soul. Significantly, the analysis that takes us from the question, "What is myself?" to the answer, "I am my soul," begins with a small group of questions which I will summarize, more or less, in the following way.[29] What does it mean when we say: "Socrates speaks to Alcibiades"? The answer given is: we mean that Socrates makes use of language. This very simple example is at the same time very revealing. The question posed is the question of the subject. "Socrates speaks to Alcibiades," what does that mean, says Socrates; that is to say, what subject do we presuppose when we evoke this activity of speech, which is the speech activity of Socrates towards Alcibiades? Consequently it involves drawing the dividing line within a spoken action that will make it possible to isolate and distinguish the subject of the action from the set of elements (words, sounds etc.) that constitute the action itself and enable it to be carried out. In short, it involves revealing the subject in its irreducibility. This kind of dividing line between the action and the subject, which the Socratic question introduces, is utilized and applied in a number of easy and obvious cases which make it possible to distinguish, within an action, between the subject of the action and all the instruments, tools, and technical means he may put to work. In this way it is easy to establish, for example, that in the cobbler's art there are tools, such as the leather knife, on the one hand, and then the person who uses these tools on the other. However, what appears to be very simple in the case of, if you like, "instrumentally mediated" actions, may also apply when we are investigating an action that takes place within the body itself, rather than an instrumental activity. For example, what do we do when we move our hands to manipulate something? Well, there are the hands and then there is the person who uses the hands; there is the part, the subject, who makes use of the hands. What do we do when we look at someone? We use our eyes, that is to say there is a part that uses the eyes. When the body does something there is generally a part that uses the body. But what is this part that uses the body? Obviously, it is not the body itself: the body cannot make use of itself. Can we say that man, understood as a combination of soul and body, uses the body? Certainly not. Because the body, even as a simple part, even supposing it to be alongside the soul, as auxiliary, cannot be what uses the body. What, then, is the only element that really uses the body, its parts and organs, and which consequently uses tools and finally language? It is and can only be the soul. So, the subject of all these bodily, instrumental, and linguistic actions is the soul: the soul inasmuch as it uses language, tools, and the body. Thus we have arrived at the soul. However, you see that the soul we have arrived at through this bizarre reasoning around "uses" (I will return shortly to this question of the meaning of "uses") has nothing to do with, for example, the soul which, as prisoner of the body, must be set free, as in the *Phaedo*;[30] it has nothing to do with the soul as a pair of winged horses which must be led in the right direction, as in the *Phaedrus*;[31] and it is not the soul structured according to a hierarchy of levels which must be harmonized, as in *The Republic*.[32] It is only the soul as such which is the subject of the action; the soul as such uses the body, its organs and its tools etcetera. The French word I employ here, "*se servir*" ["use" in English—G.B.], is actually the translation of a very important Greek verb with many meanings. This is the verb *khrēsthai*, with the substantive *khrēsis*. These two words are difficult and have had a lengthy and very important historical destiny. *Khrēsthai* (*khraōmai*: "I use") actually designates several kinds of relationships one can have with something or with oneself. Of course, *khraōmai* means: I use, I utilize (an instrument, a tool), etcetera. But equally *khraōmai* may designate my behavior or my attitude. For example, in the expression *ubriskhōs khēsthai*, the meaning is: behaving violently (as when we say, "using violence" when "using" does not at all mean utilizing, but rather behaving violently). So *khraōmai* is also a certain attitude. *Khrēsthai* also designates a certain type of relationship with other people. When one says, for example, *theois khrēsthai* (using the gods), this does not mean that one utilizes the gods for any end whatever. It means having appropriate and legitimate relationships with the gods. It means honoring the gods, worshipping them, and doing what one should with them. The expression *hippō khrēsthai* (using a horse) does not mean doing what one likes with a horse. It means handling it properly and using it in accordance with the rules of the art entailed by the yoked team or the cavalry. *Khraōmai, khrēsthai* also designate a certain attitude towards oneself. In the expression *epithumiais khrēsthai*, the meaning is not "to use one's passions for something" but quite simply "to give way to one's passions." *Orgē khrēsthai*, is not "to use anger" but "to give way to anger," "to behave angrily." So you see that when Plato (or Socrates) employs this notion of *khrēsthai/khrēsis* in order to identify what this *heauton* is (and what is subject to it) in the expression "taking care of oneself," in actual fact he does not want to designate an instrumental relationship of the soul to the rest of the world or to the body, but rather the subject's singular, transcendent position, as it were, with regard to what surrounds him, to the objects available to him, but also to other people with whom he has a relationship, to his body itself, and finally to himself. We can say that when Plato employs this notion of *khrēsis* in order to seek the self one must take care of, it is not at all the soul-substance he discovers, but rather the soul-subject.

This notion of *khrēsis* recurs throughout the history of the care of the self and its forms.* The notion of *khrēsis* will be especially important in the Stoics. It will even be at the center, I think, of the entire theory and practice of the care of the self in Epictetus.[33] Taking care of oneself will be to take care of the self insofar as it is the "subject of" a certain number of things: the subject of instrumental action, of relationships with other people, of behavior and attitudes in general, and the subject also of relationships to oneself. It is insofar as one is this subject who uses, who has certain attitudes, and who has certain relationships etcetera, that one must take care of oneself. It is a question of taking care of oneself as subject of the *khrēsis* (with all the word's polysemy: subject of actions, behavior, relationships, attitudes). It seems to me that the outcome of the argument of the *Alcibiades* on the question "what is oneself and what meaning should be given to oneself when we say that one should take care of the self?" is the soul as subject and not at all the soul as substance.

Having reached this point, as a corollary, or a consequence, we can note three small reflections in the text, which may seem secondary and relatively marginal to the structure of the argument, but which I believe are very important historically. In fact, when care of the self becomes concerned with the soul as subject, it can be distinguished from three other types of activity which, at first glance at least, may seem to be forms of care of the self: the activities of the doctor, the head of the household, and the lover.[34]

First, the doctor. Can we not say that the doctor takes care of himself when, because he is ill, he applies to himself his knowledge of the art of medicine and his ability to make diagnoses, offer medication, and cure illnesses? The answer is, of course, no. What is it in fact he takes care of when he examines himself, diagnoses himself, and sets himself a regimen? He does not take care of himself in the meaning we have just

---

*The manuscript notes here that it "is found in Aristotle."

given to "himself" as soul, as soul-subject. He takes care of his body, that is to say of the very thing he uses. It is to his body that he attends, not to himself. The first distinction then is that the *tekhnē* of the doctor who applies his knowledge to himself and the *tekhnē* that enables the individual to take care of himself, that is to say to take care of his soul as subject, must differ as to their ends, objects, and natures.

Second distinction: Can we say that a good family father, a good head of the household, or a good landowner takes care of himself when he takes care of his goods and wealth, takes care that his property thrives, and takes care of his family, etcetera? The same argument applies and there is no need to take it further: he takes care of his goods and of what belongs to him, but not of himself.

Finally, third, can we say that Alcibiades' suitors take care of Alcibiades himself? Actually, their behavior, their conduct proves that they do not care for Alcibiades but merely for his body and its beauty, since they abandon him as soon as he is no longer absolutely desirable. To take care of Alcibiades himself, in the strict sense, would mean therefore attending to his soul rather than his body, to his soul inasmuch as it is subject of action and makes more or less good use of his body and its aptitudes and capabilities, etcetera. You see, then, that the fact that Socrates waits until Alcibiades has come of age and has lost his most dazzling youth before speaking to him shows that, unlike Alcibiades' other suitors and lovers, Socrates cares for Alcibiades himself, for his soul, for his soul as subject of action. More precisely, Socrates cares about the way in which Alcibiades will be concerned about himself.

This, I think, is what we should hold onto and what defines the master's position in the *epimeleia heautou* (care of the self). For, as we shall see, the care of the self is actually something that always has to go through the relationship to someone else who is the master.[35] One cannot care for the self except by way of the master; there is no care of the self without the presence of a master. However, the master's position is defined by that which he cares about, which is the care the person he guides may have for himself. Unlike the doctor or the family head, he is not concerned about the body or about property. Unlike the teacher, he is not concerned with teaching aptitudes or abilities to the person he guides; he does not seek to teach him how to speak or how to prevail over others, etcetera. The master is the person who cares about the subject's care for himself, and who finds in his love for his disciple the possibility of caring for the disciple's care for himself. By loving the boy disinterestedly, he is then the source and model for the care the boy must have for himself as subject. So, if I have stressed these three short remarks about the doctor, the head of the family, and the lover, if I have emphasized these three little passages whose role in the text is mainly transitional, it is because I think they allude to problems that will be very important in the history of the care of the self and of its techniques.

First, we will see that the question regularly arises of the relation between care of the self and medicine, treatment of the body and regimen—let's say between care of the self and dietetics. And if in this text Plato clearly shows the radical difference of kind distinguishing dietetics from care of the self, in the history of the care of the self we see them increasingly intertwined—for a number of reasons, which I will try to analyze—to such an extent that dietetics is a major form of the care of the self in the Hellenistic and especially the Roman period of the first and second centuries A.D. At any rate, as the general regimen of the existence of the body and the soul, dietetics will become one of the crucial forms of the care of the self.

Second, another regular question will be that of the relation between the care of the self and social activity, between care of the self and the private duties of the family head, of the husband, of the son, of the landowner, of the master of slaves, etcetera, that is to say, between care of the self and all those activities that Greek thought grouped together as "economic." Is the care of the self compatible or incompatible with all these duties? This again will be a fundamental question and the different philosophical schools will answer it in different ways. Roughly speaking, the Epicureans tend to favor separating economic obligations as much as possible from the urgency of care of the self. In the Stoics, rather, there is an intricate connection between care of the self and the economic, which they try to make as strong as possible.

Finally, the question of the relation between care of the self and the love relationship will endure for centuries: Must the care of the self, which takes shape and can only take shape by reference to the Other, also go through the love relationship? Here we will see a lengthy labor, on the scale of the whole history of Greek, Hellenistic, and Roman civilization, which gradually separates care of the self from the erotic, and which lets the erotic fall on the side of a strange, dubious, disturbing, and possibly even blameworthy practice to the same extent as care of the self becomes a major theme of this same culture. So, separation of the erotic and care of the self; problem of the relation [between] care of the self and the economic, with opposed solutions in the Stoics and Epicureans; and intricate connection, rather, between dietetics and care of the self: these will be the three major lines of evolution [...*].[36]

---

*All that is audible is "and you can see that these problems of the relation between the care of the self and medicine, family management, private interests and the erotic."

1. On pederasty as education, see the old clarifications of H. I. Marrou in his *Histoire de l'éducation dans l'Antiquité* (Paris: Seuil, 1948) part one, ch. III; English translation by G. Lamb, *A History of Education in Antiquity* (London and New York: Sheed and Ward, 1956).
2. Foucault describes the establishment of a "pastoral power" by the Christian Church (as renewal-transformation of the Jewish pastoral theme) for the first time in the 1978 Collège de France course (lecture of 22 February). There is a clarification and synthesis in a lecture of 1979, "*Omnes et singulatim*: Towards a Critique of Political Reason" in Foucault, *Power*, pp. 300-303; French translation by P.E. Dauzat, " '*Omnes et singulatim*': vers une critique de la raison politique," in *Dits et Écrits*, vol. 4, pp. 145-47 and Foucault studies the structure of the relationship between the spiritual guide and the person guided more precisely and deeply in the 1980 course, but not so much in terms of "pastoral power" than of the relationship linking the subject to "truth acts" (see the course summary, "Du gouvernement des vivants," in *Dits et Écrits*, vol. 4, pp. 125-29; English trans, Robert Hurley "On the Government of the Living" in Foucault, *Ethics: Subjectivity and Truth*, pp. 87-92).
3. Born at Abdera early in the fifth century B.C., Protagoras was a well-known Sophist in Athens in the middle of the century. Plato puts him in the famous dialogue named after him in which Protagoras claims to be able to teach virtue, for which he demands payment. However, the following account given by Foucault—concerning apprenticeship in the rhetorical techniques of persuasion and domination—suggests rather Gorgias' reply in Plato's dialogue of this name (452e).
4. *Bildung* is education, apprenticeship, formation (*Selbstbildung*: "self-formation"). The notion was especially widespread through the category of the *Bildungsroman* (the novel of apprenticeship, the model for which remains Goethe's *The Apprenticeship of Wilhelm Meister*).
5. On the notion of "technology of the self" (or "technique of the self") as a specific historical domain to be explored, and on processes of subjectivation as irreducible to a symbolic game, see "On the Genealogy of Ethics: An Overview of Work in Progress," in *Ethics: Subjectivity and Truth*, p. 277 (French translation by G. Barbedette and F. Durand-Bogaert, "À propos de la généalogie de l'éthique: une aperçu du travail en cours," in *Dits et Écrits*, vol. 4, pp. 627-28), and for a definition, "Usage des plaisirs et techniques de soi," in *Dits et Écrits*, vol. 4, p. 545; English translation by Robert Hurley, "Introduction" to *The Use of Pleasure* (New York: Pantheon, 1985), p. 10: "reflected and voluntary practices by which men not only fix rules of conduct for themselves but seek to transform themselves, to change themselves in their particular being, and to make their life an oeuvre" (translation slightly modified; G. B.).
6. The history of techniques of the self in Ancient Greece was broadly investigated before Foucault's studies of the eighties. For a long time its focal point was the exegesis of a text by Empedocles on Pythagoras, who was presented as a "man of rare knowledge (*savoirs*), more than anyone else the master of all kinds of wise works, who acquired an immense wealth of knowledge (*connaissances*), for when he flexed the full strength of his mind, he saw everything in detail without effort, for ten and twenty human generations." Porphyry, *Vie de Pythagore*, translation E. des Places (Paris: Les Belles Lettres, 1982) 30, p. 50. First L. Gernet, in *Anthropologie de la Grèce antique* (Paris: Maspero, 1968;) English translation by B. Nagy, *The Anthropology of Ancient Greece* [Baltimore and London: Johns Hopkins University Press, 1981), and then J.-P. Vernant, in *Myth et Pensée chez les Grecs* (Paris: Maspero, 1965); English translation *Myth and Thought Among the Greeks* [London: RKP, 1983]), saw a clear reference in this text to a spiritual technique consisting in the control of breathing to allow the soul's concentration so as to free it from the body for journeys in the beyond. M. Detienne also mentions these techniques in a chapter of *Maîtres de la vérité dans la Grèce ancien* (Paris: Maspero, 1967), pp. 132-33 (English translation Janet Lloyd, *The Masters of Truth in Archaic Greece* [New York: Zone Books, 1999], p. 123). See also Detienne's *La Notion de daïmon dans le pythagorisme ancien* (Paris: Les Belles Lettres, 1963),

pp. 79-85. But E. R. Dodds preceded all of these in 1959, in his book, *The Greeks and the Irrational* (Berkeley and Los Angeles: University of California Press, 1973); see the chapter "The Greek Shamans and the Origin of Puritanism." Later, H. Joly, *Le Renversement platonicien Logos-Epistemē-Polis* (Paris: Vrin, 1974), studied the resurgence of these spiritual practices in Platonic discourse and the Socratic move, and finally we know that P. Hadot considers these techniques of the self to be an essential grid for reading ancient philosophy (see *Exercices spirituals et Philosophie antique* (English translation *Philosophy as a Way of Life: Spiritual Exercises from Socrates to Foucault*).

7. The organization of the first Pythagorean groups and their spiritual practices are known to us almost solely through later writings such as the *Life of Pythagoras* by Porphyry or the *Life of Pythagoras* by Iamblichus, which are from the third and fourth centuries. In *The Republic*, Plato eulogizes the Pythagorean mode of life in 600 B.C., but only formally. See W. Burkert, *Weisheit und Wissenschaft. Studien zu Pythagoras, Philolaus, und Platon* (Nuremberg: H. Karl, 1962); English translation by Edwin L. Milnar, *Lore and Science in Ancient Pythagoreanism* (Cambridge, Mass.: Harvard University Press, 1972, edition revised by Burkert).

8. Foucault refers here to descriptions of the early Pythagorean sect: "Considering that one begins to take care of men through sensation, by getting them to see beautiful forms and figures and hear beautiful rhythms and melodies, [Pythagoras] began education with music, with certain melodies and rhythms, thanks to which he brought about cures in the character and passions of men, restored harmony to the soul's faculties, as they originally were, and invented means of controlling or getting rid of diseases of the body and the soul... In the evening, when his companions were getting ready for sleep, he relieved them of the cares and turmoil of the day and he purified their agitated mind, giving them a peaceful sleep, full of beautiful and sometimes even prophetic dreams." Iamblichus, *Life of Pythagoras*, 64-65. On the importance of the dream in the early Pythagorean sect, see M. Detienne, *La Notion de* daïmon, pp. 44-45. See also the lecture of 24 March, second hour.

9. See the lecture of 27 January, second hour, and of 24 March, second hour.

10. For the examination of the Pythagorean evening, see the lecture of 24 March, second hour.

11. Plutarch, *Socrates' Daemon*, 585a. Foucault takes up this example again in a lecture of October 1982 at the University of Vermont, "Technologies of the Self" in *Ethics: subjectivity and truth*, p. 240; French translation by F. Durant-Bogaert, "Les techniques de soi," in *Dits et Écrits*, vol. 4, p. 801. See also, *Le Souci de soi*, p. 75 (*The Care of the Self*, p. 59).

12. The examination of testing techniques will be taken up in the lecture of 17 March, first hour.

13. One must "separate the soul from the body as much as possible, accustom it to draw back and concentrate itself on itself by withdrawing from all points of the body." Plato, *Phaedo*, 67c. In the manuscript Foucault notes that these techniques may act "against the dispersion that dissipates the soul" and he refers to another passage in the *Phaedo* (70a) concerning the fear expressed by Cebes of the soul's dissipation.

14. "Once philosophy has taken in hand the souls in this condition, it gently persuades it." *Phaedo*, 83a.

15. "[Philosophy] undertakes to release them... by persuading them [the souls] to detach themselves (*anakhōren*) from the objects of the senses except where necessary." Ibid.

16. Foucault here confuses two scenes recounted by Alcibiades in the *Symposium*. The first, 220a-220b, is Socrates insensitive to the cold of winter: "He, rather, on this occasion went out wearing only the same coat he usually wore, and in his bare feet walked more easily on the ice than the others wearing shoes." The second, which immediately follows this, 220c-220d, is of Socrates standing motionless, deep in thought, for a whole day and night.

17. This is the passage 217d-219d.

18. This couple is found in Seneca, who sees the fulfillment of the philosophical life in these two conditions (along with *magnitudo*, greatness of soul). See, for example: "What is happiness? It is a state of peace and constant tranquility (*securitas et perpetua tranquillitas*)." *Letters*, XCII.3. On the importance and definition of these conditions in Seneca, see I. Hadot, *Seneca und die griechisch-römische Tradition der Seelenleitung* (Berlin: De Gruyter, 1969,) pp. 126-37. *Tranquillitas*, as entirely positive internal calm, as opposed to *securitas*, as armor

of protection directed towards the exterior, is Seneca's theoretical innovation, perhaps inspired by Democritus (*euthumia*).
19. Marcus Aurelius, *Meditations*, IV.3.
20. Foucault refers here to the text's argument from 127e to 129a.
21. "Except, is it an easy thing to know oneself (*gnōnai heauton*)? And was the person who put these words on Pytho's temple just anybody?" *Alcibiades*, 129a.
22. "Ah, naïve child, believe me and the words inscribed at Delphi: 'Know yourself'." *Alcibiades*, 124b.
23. Ibid., 129b.
24. Ibid., 132c.
25. Plato, *Apology*, 29e.
26. "Perhaps it is not very sensible to leave oneself and one's soul (*hauton kai tēn hautou psukhēn therapeuein*) to the good offices of names with complete confidence in them and their authors." *Cratylus*, 440c.
27. *Phaedo*, 108c.
28. "If we gave shortsighted people some small letters to read at a distance, and one of them found the same letters written elsewhere in larger characters and on a bigger surface, I presume it would be their good fortune to begin with the big letters and afterwards the small... There may well be justice on a larger scale and in a larger framework, and so easier to decipher. So if you agree, we will examine justice in the State first of all, and then we will study it in the individual, to try to find the resemblance of the bigger in the features of the smaller." *The Republic*, II.368d and 369a.
29. The passage in *Alcibiades* goes from 129b to 130c.
30. *Phaedo*, 64c-65a.
31. *Phaedrus*, 246a-d.
32. *The Republic*, IV.443d-e.
33. Actually, the notion of the use of representations (*khrēsis tōn phantasiōn*) is central in Epictetus for whom this faculty, which testifies to our divine descent, is the supreme good, the final end to be pursued, and the essential foundation of our freedom (the essential texts are *Discourses*, I.iii.4; I.xii.34; I.xx.5, and 15; II.viii.4; III.iii.1; III.xxii.20; III.xxiv.69).
34. These activities are examined in *Alcibiades*, 131a-132b.
35. See the lecture of 27 January, first hour.
36. This tripartite division into medical, economic, and erotic provides the structure of the plan of *The Use of Pleasure* and *The Care of the Self* (See "On the Genealogy of Ethics," p. 258; "À propos de la généalogie de l'éthique," p. 385).

## four

## 13 JANUARY 1982

### Second hour

> *Determination of care of the self as self-knowledge in the* Alcibiades: *conflict between the two requirements in Plato's work.* ~ *The metaphor of the eye: source of vision and divine element.* ~ *End of the dialogue: the concern for justice.* ~ *Problems of the dialogue's authenticity and its general relation to Platonism.* ~ *Care of the self in the* Alcibiades *in its relation to political action, pedagogy, and the erotics of boys.* ~ *Anticipation in the* Alcibiades *of the fate of care of the self in Platonism.* ~ *Neo-Platonist descendants of* Alcibiades. ~ *The paradox of Platonism.*

[IS THERE] ANOTHER ROOM you can use? Yes? And are those people there because they cannot get into the other room or because they prefer to be there? I am sorry that the conditions are so bad, I can do nothing about it and as far as possible I would like to avoid you suffering too much.[1] Okay, earlier, while talking about these techniques of the self and their existence prior to Platonic reflection on the *epimeleia heautou*, it came to mind, and I forgot to mention it to you, that there is a text, one of the rare texts it seems to me, one of the few studies in which these problems are touched on in terms of Platonic philosophy: Henri Joly's *Le Renversement platonicien Logos-Epistemē-Polis*. There are a dozen pages on this prior existence of techniques of the self, which he attributes to the "shamanistic structure." We may argue with the word, but it is not important.[2] He insists on the prior existence of a number of these techniques in archaic Greek culture (techniques of breathing and of the body, etcetera). You can look at this.[3] Anyway, it is a text that has given me some ideas and so I was wrong not to have referred to it earlier. Okay, a third remark, also on method. I am not unhappy with this arrangement of two hours. I don't know what you think about it, but it at least allows us to go more slowly. Obviously, eventually I would very much like to use part at least of the second hour for discussion with you, to answer questions or things like that. At the same time I must confess that I am a bit skeptical, because it is difficult to have a discussion with such a large audience. I don't know. If you really think it is possible and that we can do it seriously, it's fine by me. In a part of the hour I am happy to try to answer any questions you may have. Well, you will tell me shortly. We could do it in the Greek way: draw lots and extract twenty or thirty auditors each time with whom to have a small seminar... Now I would like to finish our reading of the *Alcibiades*. Once again, for me it is a sort of introduction to what I would like to speak to you about this year. Because my project is not to take up the question of every aspect of the care of the self in Plato, which is a very important question since it is referred to not only in the *Alcibiades*, although only the *Alcibiades* gives its complete theory. Neither do I intend to reconstitute the continuous history of the care of the self, from its Socratic-Platonic expressions up to Christianity. This reading of the *Alcibiades* is the introduction as it were, a reference point in classical philosophy, after which I will go on to Hellenistic and Roman philosophy (in the imperial period). It just picks out a landmark, then. I would now like to finish reading this text and then to indicate some of the problems, some of its specific features; some of the features, rather, which will be found again later and which will allow the question of the care of the self to be set out in its historical dimension. So, the first question dealt with in the second part of the *Alcibiades* was: What is the self we must take care of?

The second part, the second detailed exposition of the subject, the second question of the second part—the whole dialogue is structured in a way which is at once simple, clear, and perfectly legible—is: In what must this care consist? What is this caring? The answer comes at once, immediately. We do not even have to adopt the somewhat subtle and curious approach we took with regard to the soul, when, on the basis of this notion of *khrēsis/khrēsthai*, etcetera, we discovered that it was the soul one had to take care of. No. In what does taking care of the self consist? Well, quite simply, it consists in knowing oneself. And here, for the third time in the text, there is again reference to the *gnōthi seauton*, to the Delphic precept. But the significance, the meaning of this third reference, is completely different from the first two. You recall that the first was simply a counsel of prudence: Tell me, Alcibiades, you have many great ambitions, but attend a little to what you are, do you think you are able to fulfill them? This first reference was, if you like, introductory, an encouragement to the *epimeleia heautou*: by taking a bit of a look at himself and by grasping his own inadequacies, Alcibiades was encouraged to take care of himself.[4] The second occurrence of the *gnōthi seauton* came immediately after the injunction to take care of himself, but in the form of a methodological question as it were: What is the self one must take care of, what does this *heauton* mean, to what does it refer? This was the second time the Delphic precept was quoted.[5] Now, finally, the third occurrence of the *gnōthi seauton* is when the question is what "taking care of the self" must consist in.[6] And this time we have, if you like, the *gnōthi seauton* in all its splendor and fullness: Care of the self must consist in knowledge of the self; *gnōthi seauton* in its full meaning. This is, of course, one of the decisive moments of the text, one of the constitutive moments, I think, [of] Platonism, and precisely one of those fundamental episodes in the history of the technologies of the self, in this long history of the care of the self, and it will be very important, or in any case have considerable effects, throughout Greek, Hellenistic, and Roman civilization. [More] precisely, as I reminded you earlier, in texts like the *Phaedo, Symposium*, and so on, there are a number of allusions to practices which do not appear to fall purely and simply under the "know yourself": practices of the concentration of thought on itself, of the consolidation of the soul around its axis, of withdrawal into the self, of endurance, and so on. At first sight at least, these ways of caring about oneself cannot be purely and simply, or directly, assimilated to self-knowledge. In fact, it seems to me that by taking over and reintegrating a number of these prior, archaic, preexisting techniques, the whole movement of Platonic thought with regard to the care of the self is one of organizing them around and subordinating them to the great principle of "know yourself." It is in order to know oneself that one must withdraw into the self; it is in order to know oneself that one must detach oneself from sensations which are the source of illusions; it is in order to know oneself that one must establish one's soul in an immobile fixity which is not open to external events, etcetera. It is both in order to know oneself and inasmuch as one knows oneself that all this must and can be done. It seems to me then that there is a general reorganization of all these techniques around the prescription "know yourself." Anyway, we can say that in this text, in which there is no mention of all these prior techniques of the self, as soon as the space of the care of the self is opened up and the self is defined as the soul, the entire space thus opened up is taken over by the principle of "know yourself." We can say that there is a forced takeover by the *gnōthi seauton* in the space opened up by the care of the self. Obviously, "forced takeover" is a little metaphorical. You recall that last week I referred to—and this is basically what I will try to speak about this year—the difficult and historically long-lasting problematic relations between the *gnōthi seauton* (knowledge of the self) and the care of the self. It seemed to me that modern philosophy—for reasons which I tried to identify in what I called, as a bit of a joke although it is not funny, the "Cartesian moment"—was led to put all the emphasis on the *gnōthi seauton* and so to forget, to leave in the dark, and to marginalize somewhat, this question of the care of the self. So this year I would like again to bring out the care of the self from behind the privileged status accorded for so long to the *gnōthi seauton* (knowledge of the self). To bring out the care of the self in this way is not to say that the *gnōthi seauton* did not exist, had no importance, or had only a subordinate role. Actually, what I would like to say (and we have a superb example of it here) is that the *gnōthi seauton* ("know yourself") and the *epimeleia heautou* (care of the self) are entangled. Throughout the text you can see two things entangled: by reminding him that he would do well to take a look at himself, Alcibiades is led to say: "Yes, it is true, I should care about myself"; then, when Socrates has laid down this principle and Alcibiades has accepted it, [the problem] is posed anew: "We must know this self we must take care of"; and then now, a third time, when we consider what caring consists in, we find again the *gnōthi seauton*. There is a dynamic entanglement, a reciprocal call for the *gnōthi seauton* and for the *epimeleia heautou* (knowledge of the self and care of the self). This tangle, this reciprocal appeal, is, I think, typical of Plato. We find it again throughout the history of Greek, Hellenistic, and Roman thought, obviously with different balances and relations, with different emphases on one or the other, and with a different distribution of the moments of self-knowledge and care of the self in the various systems of thought encountered. But it is this tangle that is important, I believe, and neither of the two elements should be neglected to the advantage of the other.

Let us return then to our text and to the triumphant reappearance of the *gnōthi seauton* for the third time: To care for the self is to know oneself. Here again we find a text with a number of echoes in Plato's other dialogues, especially the later ones: the well-known and often employed metaphor of the eye.[7] If we want to know how the soul can know itself, since we know now that the soul must know itself, then we take the example of the eye. Under what conditions and how can the eye see itself? Well, when it sees the image of itself sent back to it by a mirror. However, the mirror is not the only reflecting surface for an eye that wants to look at itself. After all, when someone's eye looks at itself in the eye of someone else, when an eye looks at itself in another eye absolutely similar to itself, what does it see in the other's eye? It sees itself. So, an identical nature is the condition for an individual to know what he is. The identical nature is, if you like, the reflecting surface in which the individual can recognize himself and know what he is. Second, when the eye perceives itself in this way in the other's eye, does it see itself in the eye in general or is it not, rather, in that particular part of the eye, the pupil, the part in which and by which the act of vision itself is carried out? In actual fact, the eye does not see itself in the eye. The eye sees itself in the source of vision. That is to say, the act of vision, which allows the eye to grasp itself, can only be carried out in another act of vision, the act we find in the other's eye. Okay, what does this well-known comparison say when applied to the soul? It says that the soul will only see itself by focusing its gaze on an element having the same nature as itself, and more precisely, by looking at the element of the same nature as itself, by turning towards and fixing its gaze on that which is the very source of the soul's nature, that is to say, of thought and knowledge (*to phronein, to eidenai*).[8] The soul will be able to see itself by turning round towards the part that ensures thought and knowledge. What is this element? Well, it is the divine element. So it is by turning round towards the divine that the soul will be able to grasp itself. A problem arises here which I am, of course, unable to resolve, but which is interesting, as you will see, for its echoes in the history of thought, and which concerns a passage whose authenticity has been challenged. It begins with Socrates' reply: "Just as true mirrors are clearer, purer and brighter than the mirror of the eye, so God (*ho theos*) is purer and brighter than the best part of our soul." Alcibiades replies: "It really does seem so Socrates." Socrates then says: "It is God, then, that we must look at: for whoever wishes to judge the quality of the soul, he is the best mirror of human things themselves, we can best see and know ourselves in him." "Yes" says Alcibiades.[9] You see that this passage says that the best mirrors are those that are purer and brighter than the eye itself. Similarly, since we see ourselves better when the mirror is brighter than our own eye, we will see our soul better if we look at it, not in a soul similar to our own, with the same brightness, but if we look at it in a brighter and purer element, that is to say in God. In fact, this passage is only cited in a text of Eusebius of Caesarea (*Préparation évangélique*),[10] and because of this it is suspected of having been introduced by a Neo-Platonist, or Christian, or Platonist-Christian tradition. In any case, whether this text really is Plato's or was introduced afterwards and much later, and even if it takes to extremes what is thought to be Plato's own philosophy, it nevertheless seems to me that the general development of the text is quite clear independently of this passage, and even if one omits it. It makes knowledge of the divine the condition of knowledge of the self. If we suppress this passage, leaving the rest of the dialogue so that we are more or less sure of its authenticity, then we have this principle: To care for the self one must know oneself; to know oneself one must look at oneself in an element that is the same as the self; in this element one must look at that which is the very source of thought and knowledge; this source is the divine element. To see oneself one must therefore look at oneself in the divine element: One must know the divine in order to see oneself.

So, on this basis I think we can quickly deduce the end of the text as it unfolds. In opening onto this knowledge of the divine, the movement by which we know ourselves, in our care for ourselves, enables the soul to achieve wisdom. The soul will be endowed with wisdom (*sōphrosunē*) as soon as it is in contact with the divine, when it has grasped it and been able to think and know the divine as the source of thought and knowledge. When the soul is endowed with *sōphrosunē* it will be able to turn back towards the world down here. It will be able to distinguish good from evil, the true from the false. At this point the soul will be able to conduct itself properly, and being able to conduct itself properly it will be able to govern the city. I summarize very briefly a slightly longer text, but I want to arrive quickly at the last, or rather the penultimate reply of the text in an interesting reflection found at 135e.

Having come back down, and supported by knowledge of the self, which is knowledge of the divine, and which is the rule for conducting oneself properly, we now know that we will be able to govern and that whoever has made this movement of ascent and descent will be well qualified to govern his city-state. Then Alcibiades makes a promise. What does he promise at the end of this dialogue in which he has been encouraged so insistently to take care of himself? What does he promise Socrates? He says the following, which is precisely the penultimate reply, the last given by Alcibiades, which is then followed by a reflection of Socrates: Anyway, it's decided, I will begin straightaway to *epimelesthai*—to "apply myself" to, to "be concerned with" ... myself? No: "with justice (*dikaiosunēs*)." This may seem paradoxical given that the whole dialogue, or anyway the second part of the dialogue, is concerned with the care of the self and the need to take care of the self. Then, at the point at which the dialogue comes to an end, Alcibiades, who has been convinced, promises to concern himself with justice. But you see that, precisely, there is no difference. Or rather, this was the point of the dialogue and the effect of its movement: to convince Alcibiades that he must take care of himself; to define for him that which he must take care of; to explain to him how he must care for his soul by looking towards the divine in which the source of wisdom is found, [so that] when he looks towards himself he will discover the divine and, as a result, will discover the very essence of wisdom (*dikaiosunē*), or, conversely, when he looks in the direction of the essence of wisdom (*dikaiosunē*)[11] he will at the same time see the divine element in which he knows himself and sees himself, since the divine reflects what I am in the element of the identical. Consequently, taking care of oneself and being concerned with justice amount to the same thing, and the dialogue's game—starting from the question "how can I become a good governor?"—consists in leading Alcibiades to the precept "take care of yourself" and, by developing what this precept must be, what meaning it must be given, we discover that "taking care of oneself" is to care about justice. And that is what Alcibiades commits himself to at the end of the dialogue. This, then, is how the text unfolds.

On this basis I think we can now make some more general reflections. Let us start by speaking a little about the dialogue and the problem it raises, since at several points I have referred to either the authenticity of a passage or of the dialogue itself, which at one time some considered to be inauthentic. Actually, I do not think there is a single expert who really, seriously questions its authenticity.[12] However, a number of questions about its date remain. There is a very good article on this by Raymond Weil in *L'information littéraire*, which makes, I think, a closely argued assessment, a clarification, of the questions concerning this text and its dating.[13] Because, certainly, many elements of the text suggest it was written early: the Socratic elements of the first dialogues are very clear in the type of problems posed. I indicated them earlier: the question of the young aristocrat who wants to govern, the inadequacy of pedagogy, the role to be played by the love of boys, etcetera, the dialogue's approach with its somewhat plodding questions: all this indicates both the sociopolitical context of the Socratic dialogues and the method of the aporetic dialogues which do not reach a conclusion. Now, on the other side, a number of elements in the dialogue, external elements, which I am not in a position to judge, seem to suggest a much later date. I take them directly from Raymond Weil's article. For example, as you know, at a certain point there is the allusion to the wealth of Lacedaemonia, of Sparta, when Socrates tells Alcibiades: You know you will have to deal with strong opposition; the Lacedaemonians are wealthier than you. It seems that reference to Sparta being wealthier than Athens only makes sense after the Peloponnesian War, and after an economic development of Sparta that certainly did not take place at the time of the first Platonic dialogues. A second, somewhat extreme element, if you like, is the interest in Persia. There are references to Persia in Plato, but in his later work. There is no other example of this in the early dialogues. However, it is above all the internal examination of the dialogue that interests me with regard to its dating. On the one hand, there is the fact that the beginning of the dialogue is completely in the style of the Socratic dialogues: questions concerning what it is to govern, on justice, and then of the nature of happiness in the city. And all these dialogues, as you well know, generally end with questions without a definite outcome, or at least without a positive answer. But here, after this lengthy marking time, there is suddenly a conception of knowledge of the self as recognition of the divine. This analysis, which founds *dikaiosunē* with a kind of unproblematic self-evidence, is not generally the style of the early dialogues. Then there are a number of other components. As you know, the theory of the four virtues, which is attributed to the Persians, is the theory of the four virtues of established Platonism. Similarly, the metaphor of the mirror, of the soul that looks at itself in the mirror of the divine, belongs to late Platonism. The idea of the soul as agent, or rather as subject, the idea of *khrēsis*, much more than as a substance imprisoned in the body, etcetera, is an element which is found again in Aristotle and would seem to indicate a quite astonishing inflection of Platonism if it dates from the earliest period. In short, we have a text which is chronologically odd and seems to straddle, as it were, Plato's entire work: the youthful references and style are clearly and undeniably present, and then, on the other hand, the presence of the themes and forms of established Platonism are also quite apparent. I think the hypothesis of some people—and it seems to me that this is what Weil proposes, with some reservations—is that maybe there was a kind of rewriting of the dialogue at some time in Plato's old age, or even after Plato's death: two elements, two strata in the text, as it were, are joined together; two strata, which interact and are stitched together at a certain point in the dialogue. Anyway, since I have neither the competence nor the intention to discuss this, what interests me and what I find quite fascinating in this dialogue, is that basically we find here in outline an entire account of Plato's philosophy, from Socratic questioning to what appear to be elements quite close to the final Plato or even to Neo-Platonism. This is why the presence and perhaps insertion of the concocted passage, quoted by Eusebius of Caesarea, does not seem out of place within this great movement of the trajectory of Platonism itself, which is not present in all of its components, but whose basic drift is at least indicated. That is the first reason why this text seems to me to be interesting.

Then, on the basis of this overall trajectory, it seems to me that we can isolate a number of components which no longer raise the specifically Platonic question of the *epimeleia heautou*, but that of the pure history of this notion, of its practices and philosophical elaboration in Greek, Hellenistic, and Roman thought. To start with, a number of questions appear quite clearly in this text: its relationship to political action, to pedagogy, and to the erotics of boys. In their formulation and the solutions given to them in the text, these questions are typical of Socratic-Platonic thought, of course, but they are found again more or less continuously in the history of Greco-Roman thought, right up to the Second and Third centuries A.D., with only slightly different solutions or formulations of the problems.

First: the relationship to political action. You remember that in Socrates, in the dialogue of the *Alcibiades*, it is quite clear that the care of the self is an imperative addressed to those who wish to govern others and as an answer to the question, "how can one govern well?" Being concerned about the self is a privilege of governors, or it is also a duty of governors because they have to govern. It will be very interesting to see how this demand for care of the self is, as it were, generalized as a requirement "for everyone," but immediately I put "everyone" in inverted commas. There is a generalization of this imperative—I will try to show this next week—but a generalization that is nevertheless very partial and with regard to which two considerable limitations must be taken into account. The first is, of course, that to take care of the self one must have the ability, time, and culture, etcetera, to do so. It is an activity of the elite. And even if the Stoics and Cynics say to people, to everyone, "take care of yourself," in actual fact it could only become a practice among and for those with a certain cultural, economic, and social capability. Second, we should also remember that there is a second principle of limitation to this generalization. This is that the effect, meaning, and aim of taking care of oneself is to distinguish the individual who takes care of himself from the crowd, from the majority, from the *hoi polloi*[14] who are, precisely, the people absorbed in everyday life. There will be an ethical divide then, which is entailed as a consequence of the principle "take care of yourself," [which in turn—second divide—] can only be carried out by a moral elite and those with the ability to save themselves. The intersection of these two divisions—the de facto division of a cultivated elite and the division imposed or obtained as a result of the practice of the care of the self—thus constitute considerable limitations on this generalization which is nevertheless demanded, expressed, and proclaimed by later philosophers.

Second: You see that Socrates and Plato directly link the care of the self to the question of pedagogy. Concern about the self is needed because education is inadequate. Later we will see a second shift concerned with age rather than generality. One must take care of oneself, not when one is young and because Athenian education is inadequate, but one must take care of the self anyway, because this care cannot be provided by any education. And one must take care of the self throughout one's life with the crucial, decisive age being maturity. The privileged age at which care of the self is necessary will no longer be the end of adolescence, but the development of maturity. As a result, it is not entry into adult and civic life that paves the way for the care of the self, as it was for the adolescent. The young man will not take care of himself in order to become the citizen, or rather the leader who is needed. The adult must take care of himself... to prepare for what? For his old age;

in order to prepare for the fulfillment of life in that age—old age—when life itself will be fulfilled and suspended, as it were. Care of the self as preparation for old age is very clearly distinguished from care of the self as an educational substitute or complement for the preparation for life.

And finally (I indicated this earlier and won't return to it): the relationship to the erotics of boys. Here again, the link was very clear in Plato. Gradually this link is broken and the erotics of boys disappears, or tends to disappear, in the technique and culture of the self in the Hellenistic and Roman epoch, but with notable exceptions and a series of delays and difficulties. When you read the third or fourth satire of Persius, you see that his master Cornutus is definitely referred to as a lover,[15] and the correspondence between Fronto and Marcus Aurelius is the correspondence between lovers and their loved ones.[16] So the problem will be much more long-lasting and difficult.

Let's say then, that these themes (the relationship to the erotic, to pedagogy, and to politics) are always present, but with a series of shifts which constitute the history of the care of the self in post-classical civilization. If we can say that the problems raised by the *Alcibiades* initiate a very long history, the dialogue also clearly reveals what the specifically Platonic or Neo-Platonist solution to these problems will be in this period. To that extent the *Alcibiades* does not attest to or anticipate the general history of the care of the self, but only the strictly Platonic form it takes. Actually, it seems to me that what characterizes the care of the self in the Platonic and Neo-Platonist tradition is, first of all, that the care of the self finds its form and realization in self-knowledge as, if not the only then at least the absolutely highest form of, the care of the self. Secondly, the fact that self-knowledge, as the major and sovereign expression of the care of the self, gives access to truth, and to truth in general, is also typical of the Platonic and Neo-Platonic movement. And finally, that access to the truth enables one to see at the same time what is divine in the self is also typical of the Platonic and Neo-Platonist form of the care of the self. Knowing oneself, knowing the divine, and seeing the divine in oneself are, I think, fundamental in the Platonic and Neo-Platonist form of the care of the self. These elements—or at least this organization and distribution of these elements—are not found in the other Epicurean, Stoic, and even Pythagorean forms [of the care of the self], notwithstanding any later interactions which take place between the Neo-Pythagorean and Neo-Platonist movements.

Anyway, I think this enables us to understand a number of the aspects of the great "paradox of Platonism" in the history of thought, and not just in the history of ancient thought, but also in the history of European thought until at least the seventeenth century. The paradox is this: in a way Platonism has been the leaven, and we can even say the principal leaven, of a variety of spiritual movements, inasmuch as Platonism conceived knowledge and access to the truth only on the basis of a knowledge of the self, which was a recognition of the divine in oneself. From that moment you can see that for Platonism, knowledge and access to the truth could only take place on condition of a spiritual movement of the soul with regard to itself and the divine: with regard to the divine because it was connected to itself, and with regard to itself because it was connected to the divine. For Platonism, this condition of a relationship with the self and the divine, with the self as divine and with the divine as self, was one of the conditions of access to the truth. To that extent we can see how it continued to be the leaven, the soil, the climate, and the environment for a series of spiritual movements at the heart or pinnacle of which were all the Gnostic movements. However, at the same time you can see how Platonism could provide the climate for the development of what could be called a "rationality." And inasmuch as it is meaningless to contrast spirituality and rationality, as if they were two things at the same level, I would say, rather, that Platonism was the constant climate in which a movement of knowledge (*connaissance*) developed, a movement of pure knowledge without any condition of spirituality, precisely because the distinctive feature of Platonism is to show how the work of the self on itself, the care one must have for oneself if one wants access to the truth, consists in knowing oneself, that is to say in knowing the truth. To that extent, knowledge of the self and knowledge of the truth (the activity of knowledge, the movement and method of knowledge in general) absorb, as it were, or reabsorb the requirements of spirituality. So it seems to me that Platonism plays this double game throughout ancient culture and European culture: continuously and repeatedly raising the question of the necessary conditions of spirituality for access to truth and, at the same time, reabsorbing spirituality in the movement of knowledge alone, of knowledge of the self, of the divine, and of essences. Broadly speaking this is what I wanted to say about the *Alcibiades* and the historical perspectives it opens up. So, if you like, next week we will move on to the question of the *epimeleia heautou* in a different historical period, that is to say in Epicurean, Stoic, and other philosophies of the first and second centuries A.D.

1. The Collège de France made a second room available to the public, outside the main lecture theater where Foucault taught, to which Foucault's voice was directly relayed by a system of microphones.
2. It is precisely because of the strict definition of shamanism as a "social phenomenon fundamentally connected to hunting civilizations" that P. Hadot refuses to refer to it in this context." See P. Hadot, *Qu'est-ce que la philosophie antique?*, p. 279.
3. H. Joly, *Le Renversement platonicien Logos-Epistemē-Polis*, ch. III: "L'archaïsme du connaître et le puritanisme," pp. 64-70: "La pureté de la connaissance."
4. *Alcibiades*, 124b; see the lecture 6 January, second hour.
5. *Alcibiades*, 129a; see this lecture, first hour.
6. "But, in the name of the gods, are we sure we have really understood the just precept of Delphi which we have just recalled?" *Alcibiades*, 132c.
7. See one of the last developments of the *Alcibiades*, 132d-133c.
8. *Alcibiades*, 133c.
9. *Alcibiades*, 133c [not included in the English, Loeb, edition—G.B.].
10. Eusebius of Caesarea, *La Préparation évangélique*, translation. G. Favrelle (Paris: Éd. du Cerf, 1982), book XI, ch. 27, pp. 178-91.
11. In both of these references to *dikaiosunē* Foucault no doubt means to say *sōphrosunē*, unless he wishes to say "justice" rather than "wisdom."
12. The debate on the authenticity of the *Alcibiades* was launched at the beginning of the nineteenth century by the German scholar Schleiermacher, who considered it to be a school text drafted by a member of the Academy. The debate has continued without end since then. Undoubtedly the major French commentators with whom Foucault may have been familiar (M. Croiset, L. Robin, V. Goldschmidt, R. Weil) acknowledged its authenticity, but many Anglo-Saxon or German experts continued to raise doubts, still in Foucault's time. Today, eminent French specialists (like L. Brisson, J. Brunschwig, and M. Dixsaut) still question its authenticity, while others (J.-F. Pradeau) resolutely defend it. For a complete picture of the places and an exhaustive picture of the positions taken, see J.-F. Pradeau's introduction and appendix 1 to his edition of *Alcibiades* (Paris: Garnier-Flammarion, 1999), pp. 24-29 and 219-20.
13. R. Weil, "La place du *Premier Alcibiade* dans l'œuvre de Platon," *L'Information littéraire* 16 (1964), pp. 74-84.
14. The literal meaning of this expression is "the several" or "the many," and since Plato it designates the majority as opposed to the competent and scientific elite. (For an exemplary use of this expression in Plato, see *Crito*, 44b-49c, where Socrates shows that the dominant opinion is worthless in questions of ethical choice.)
15. In fact it is the fifth satire. Foucault is thinking especially of verses 36-37 and 40-41: "I placed myself in your hands, Cornutus; you took up my tender years in your Socratic bosom... With you, I remember, did I pass long days, with you pluck for feasting the early hours of night." Persius, Satire V, 36-7 and 40-1, in Juvenal and Persius, *Satires*, translation G. G. Ramsey (London and New York: Loeb Classical Library), 1918, p. 373.
16. On this correspondence, see the lecture of 27 January, second hour.

## five

## 20 JANUARY 1982

### First hour

> *The care of the self from* Alcibiades *to the first two centuries* A.D.: *general evolution.* ~ *Lexical study around the* epimeleia. ~ *A constellation of expressions.* ~ *Generalization of the care of the self: principle that it is coextensive with the whole of life.* ~ *Reading of texts: Epicurus, Musonius Rufus, Seneca, Epictetus, Philo of Alexandria, Lucian.* ~ *Ethical consequences of this generalization: care of the self as axis of training and correction; convergence of medical and philosophical activity (common concepts and therapeutic objective).*

I WOULD LIKE NOW to take some different chronological reference points and move to the period covering more or less the first and second centuries A.D.: let's say, taking some political reference points, the period going from the establishment of the Augustinian, or Julian-Claudian dynasty, up to the end of the Antonines,[1] or again, taking some philosophical reference points—or at any rate reference points in the domain I want to study—let's say that I will go from the period of Roman Stoicism in its prime, with Musonius Rufus, up to Marcus Aurelius, that is to say the period of the renaissance of the classical culture of Hellenism, just before the spread of Christianity and the appearance of the first great Christian thinkers: Tertullian and Clement of Alexandria.[2] This, then, is the period I want to select because it seems to me to be a genuine golden age in the history of care of the self, that is, of care of the self as a notion, practice, and institution. How, briefly, might we describe this golden age?

You recall that in the *Alcibiades* there were, it seems to me, three conditions which determined both the raison d'être and form of care of the self. One of these conditions concerned the field of application of care of the self: Who must take care of themselves? On this the *Alcibiades* was quite clear: Those who must take care of themselves are the young aristocrats destined to exercise power. This is clear in the *Alcibiades*. I am not saying that we find this in other texts of Plato, or even in other Socratic dialogues, but those who must take care of themselves in this text are Alcibiades and those like him, young aristocrats whose status determines that one day they will have to run the city-state. The second determination, obviously linked to the first, is that care of the self has an objective, a precise justification: It is a question of taking care of oneself so that one will be able to exercise properly, reasonably, and virtuously the power to which one is destined. Finally, the third limitation, which appeared quite clearly at the end of the dialogue, is that the major if not exclusive form of the care of the self is self-knowledge: To take care of the self is to know oneself. I think we can say, again as a schematic overview, that when we move to the period I am now talking about, that is to say the first and second centuries A.D., these three conditions appear to have fallen away. When I say that they have fallen away I certainly do not mean, and I would like to stress this once and for all, that this happens at a precise moment and that something brutal and sudden took place at the time of the establishment of the Empire that made the care of the self suddenly and all at once take on new forms. In reality these different conditions laid down for the practice of the care of the self in the *Alcibiades* finally disappeared at the end of a long evolution that is already visible in Plato's work. This evolution, then, can already be seen in Plato and it continues throughout the Hellenistic period largely as the effect of, and driven by, all those Cynical, Epicurean, and Stoic philosophies that are put forward as arts of living. Anyway, in the period I now want to consider these three determinations (or conditions), which characterized the need to be concerned about oneself in the *Alcibiades*, have disappeared. At any rate, at first sight, it does seem as if they have disappeared.

First, being concerned about the self became a general and unconditional principle, a requirement addressed to everyone, all the time, and without any condition of status. Secondly, the specific activity of governing others no longer seems to be the raison d'être for being concerned about the self. It seems that this specific and privileged object, the city-state, is not the ultimate objective of caring about the self. Rather, if one now takes care of the self it is for oneself and with oneself as its end. Let's say again that, schematically, in the analysis of the *Alcibiades* the self is quite clearly defined as the object of the care of the self, and one has to question oneself about the nature of this object (and the text is very clear about this since the question is repeated several times: What is the self one must take care of? What is my self I must take care of?). But the end, as opposed to the object, of this care of the self, was something else. It was the city-state. Of course, inasmuch as the one who governs is part of the city-state, he is, in a way, also the end of his own care of the self, and in the texts of the classical period we often find the idea that the governor must apply himself to governing properly in order to save himself and the city-state—himself inasmuch as he is part of the city-state. However, in the Alcibiades type of care of the self we can say that there is a rather complex structure in which the object of care was indeed the self, but in which the end of the care of the self was the city-state, in which the self reappears, but merely as a part. The city-state mediated the relationship of self to self so that the self could be the object as well as the end, but the self was only the end because it was mediated by the city-state. Now I think we can say—and I will try to show you this—that in the form taken by the care of the self developed by neoclassical culture in the bloom of the imperial golden age, the self appears both as the object one cares for, the thing one should be concerned about, and also, crucially, as the end one has in view when one cares for the self. Why does one care for the self? Not for the city-state, but for oneself. Or again, the reflexive form structures not only the relationship to the object—caring about the self as object—but also the relationship to the objective and end. There is, if you like, a sort of self-finalization of the relationship to the self: this is the second major feature I will try to elucidate in future lectures. Finally, the third feature is that the care of the self is plainly no longer determined solely in the form of self-knowledge. Not that this imperative or form of self-knowledge disappears. Let's just say that it is attenuated or that it is integrated within a much wider whole, which is attested and can be marked out, in a wholly preliminary and approximate way, by indicating elements of vocabulary and picking out certain types of expression.

First of all, we should be clear that this canonical and fundamental expression, "*epimeleisthai heautou*" (to take care of oneself, to be concerned about oneself, to care for the self), which, once again, is found from Plato's *Alcibiades* up to Gregory of Nyssa, has a meaning that must be stressed: *epimeleisthai* does not only designate a mental attitude, a certain form of attention, a way of not forgetting something. Its etymology refers to a series of words such as *meletan, meletē, meletai*, etcetera. *Meletan*, often employed and coupled with the verb *gumnazein*,[3] means to practice and train. The *meletai* are exercises, gymnastic and military exercises, military training. *Epimeleisthai* refers to a form of vigilant, continuous, applied, regular, etcetera, activity much more than to a mental attitude. For example, in the classical language, consider Xenophon's *Œconomicus*. Talking about all the activities of the landowner, of the kind of gentleman farmer* whose life he describes in the *Œconomicus*, Xenophon refers to his *epimeleiai*, to the activities which, he says, are very advantageous both to him as a landowner, since they keep him fit, and to his family as well, since they enrich it.[4] The series of words, *meletan, meletē, epimeleisthai, epimeleia*, etcetera, thus designate a set of practices. And in the Christian vocabulary of the fourth century you will see that *epimeleia* commonly has the meaning of exercise, of ascetic exercise. So we keep in mind that *epimeleia/epimeleisthai* refer to forms of activity. In the philosophical literature, or even in literary texts strictly speaking, it is easy to pick out around this fundamental and central word a nebula of terms and expressions that quite clearly go well beyond the domain demarcated by the

---

*In English in the original—G.B.

activity of knowledge alone. We can, if you like, identify four families of expressions.

Some do, in fact, refer to cognitive activities, to attending to, looking at and the possible perception of oneself: paying attention to the self (*prosekhein ton noūn*);[5] turning round to look at the self (in Plutarch, for example, there is an analysis of the need to close the windows and doors which open onto the court outside, and to turn round to look towards the inside of one's house and of oneself);[6] examining oneself (one must examine oneself: *skepteon sauton*).[7] But with regard to the care of the self there is also a vocabulary referring not merely to this sort of conversion of looking, to this necessary watchfulness over the self, but also to an overall movement of existence, which is encouraged and called upon to pivot on itself, as it were, and to direct itself or turn round towards the self. Turning round towards the self: this is the famous *convertere*, the famous *metanoia* about which we will have to speak again.[8] There are a series of expressions: withdrawing into the self, retiring into the self,[9] or again, descending to the depths of oneself. There are expressions that refer to the activity, to the attitude which consists in gathering oneself around oneself, in collecting oneself in the self, or again in establishing or installing oneself in the self as in a place of refuge, a well-fortified citadel, a fortress protected by walls, etcetera.[10] A third group of expressions contains those which refer to particular activities and conduct concerning the self. Some are quite directly inspired by a medical vocabulary: one must treat oneself, cure oneself, conduct amputations on oneself, lance one's own abscesses, etcetera.[11] There are also expressions which still refer to activities one engages in with regard to oneself, but which are, rather, of a legal kind: you must, "lay claim to yourself," as Seneca says in his first letter to Lucilius.[12] That is to say: One must lay down this legal claim, assert the rights one has over oneself, over the self currently weighed down by debts and obligations from which one must detach oneself, or over the self that is enslaved. Thus one must free oneself; one must emancipate oneself. There are also expressions that designate religious kinds of activity with regard to the self: One must hold one's self sacred, honor oneself, respect oneself, feel shame in front of oneself.[13] Finally, the fourth nebula or group of expressions contains those which designate a certain kind of constant relationship to the self, whether a relationship of mastery and sovereignty (being master of the self), or a relationship of sensations (having pleasure in oneself, experiencing delight with oneself, being happy to be with oneself, being content with oneself, etcetera).[14]

You see then that we have a whole series of expressions which clearly show that the care of the self, as it was developed, as it appears and is expressed in the period I will be considering, goes far beyond the simple activity of knowledge, and that actually an entire practice of the self is involved. Having said this, so as to situate a little what we could call the dramatic rise of the care of the self, or at any rate its transformation (the transmutation of the care of the self into an autonomous, self-finalized practice with a plurality of forms), and to study this more closely, I would like today to analyze the process of the generalization of the care of the self, which develops along two axes, in two dimensions. On the one hand, there is generalization in the individual's life. How does the care of the self become coextensive with the individual life, and must it be coextensive with this life? I will try to explain this in the first hour. In the second hour I will try to analyze the generalization by which the care of the self must be extended to all individuals, whomsoever they may be, with, as you will see, important restrictions, which I will talk about. First, then: extension to the individual life, or coextensiveness of care of the self and the art of living (the famous *tekhnē tou biou*), the art of life or art of existence which we know, from Plato, and especially in the post-Platonic movements, becomes the fundamental definition of philosophy. Care of the self becomes coextensive with life.

Once again taking the *Alcibiades* as a historical landmark and as a key for the intelligibility of all these processes, you remember that care of the self appeared in the *Alcibiades* as necessary at a given moment of life and on a precise occasion. This moment and occasion is not what is called in Greek the *kairos*,[15] which is the particular conjuncture, as it were, of an event. This occasion and moment is what the Greeks call *hōra*: the moment or season of life when one must take care of oneself. This season of life—I won't go into this again since I have already drawn your attention to it—is the critical age for education, as also for the erotic, and for politics: it is the moment at which the young man is no longer in the hands of teachers and ceases to be the object of erotic desire, and at which he must enter life and exercise his power, his active power.[16] Everyone knows that in every society the adolescent's entry into life, his transition to the phase we ourselves call "adult," poses problems, and that most societies strongly ritualize this difficult and dangerous passage from adolescence to adulthood. What seems to me to be interesting, and what no doubt deserves some investigation, is basically that in Greece, or anyway in Athens, because in Sparta it must have been different, it seems that one always suffered from and complained about the lack of a strong, well-regulated, and effective institution of passage for adolescents at the moment of their entry into adult life.[17] The criticism that Athenian education could not ensure the passage from adolescence to adulthood, that it could not ensure and codify this entry into adult life, seems to me to be a constant feature of Greek philosophy. We can even say that it was here—with regard to this problem, in this institutional gap, in this educational deficit, in the politically and erotically disturbed moment of the end of adolescence and entry into adult life—that philosophical discourse, or at least the Socratic-Platonic form of philosophical discourse, took shape. Let's not return to this point that I have mentioned several times.[18]

One thing is certain at any rate, which is that after Plato, and of course up to the period I am talking about, the need to take care of the self is not asserted at this point of life, at this disturbed and critical stage of the end of adolescence. Henceforth, the care of the self is a requirement that is not linked solely to the critical pedagogical moment between adolescence and adulthood. The care of the self is an obligation that should last for the whole of one's life. And we don't have to wait for the first and second centuries for this to be asserted. In Epicurus, at the start of his *Letter to Menoeceus*, you can read: "We must not hesitate to practice philosophy when we are young or grow weary of it when we are old. It is never too early or too late for taking care of one's soul. Who says that it is not yet time or that there is no longer time to practice philosophy, is like someone who says that it is not yet time or that there is no longer time for happiness. We must therefore practice philosophy when we are young and when we are old, the latter [the old, then: M.F.] to grow young again in contact with good things, through the memory of days gone by, and the former [the young: M.F.] in order to be, however young, as steadfast as an old man in facing the future."[19] You can see that this text is actually very dense and includes a series of components that should be looked at closely. I would like to emphasize just some of them here. There is, of course, the identification of "practicing philosophy" with "taking care of the soul"; you can see that the objective of this activity of practicing philosophy, of taking care of our soul, is to arrive at happiness; and you can see that the activity of taking care of our soul should be practiced at every moment of our life, when we are young and when we are old, but with very different functions in each case, however. When young, we have to prepare ourselves for life—this is the famous *paraskheuē* to which I will return later and which is so important for both the Epicureans and the Stoics[20]—we have to arm ourselves, to be equipped for life. On the other hand, to practice philosophy in old age is to grow young again. That is to say, it is to turn time around, or at any rate to tear ourselves free from time thanks to an activity of memorization that, in the case of the Epicureans, is the remembering of past moments. All this, in fact, puts us at the very heart of this activity, of this practice of the care of the self, but I will come back to the components of this text. You see, then, that for Epicurus we must practice philosophy all the time; we must constantly take care of the self.

If we now consider the Stoic texts we find the same thing. From hundreds of them I will just quote Musonius Rufus who says that we can save ourselves by constantly treating ourselves (*aei therapeuontes*).[21] Taking care of the self is therefore a lifetime's occupation, for the whole of life. In fact, when you see how the care of the self, the practice of the self, is practiced in the period I am talking about, you realize that it really is an activity for the whole of life. We can even say that it is an adult activity and that far from adolescence being the focal point and the privileged temporal axis in the care of the self, it is, rather, the middle of adult life. And, as you will see, it is perhaps even the end of adult life rather than the end of adolescence. At any rate, we are no longer in the world of those ambitious and eager young people who sought to exercise power in Athens of the fifth and fourth centuries B.C. We are dealing, rather, with a whole little world, or a large world, of young men, or fully mature men, or men whom we would consider to be old, who teach themselves, spur each other on and train themselves, either alone or collectively, in the practice of the self.

Some examples. In practices of an individual kind, consider the relations between Seneca and Serenus. Serenus consults Seneca at the beginning of *De Tranquillitate Animi* in which he writes—or is supposed [to have written], or probably wrote—a letter to Seneca in which he describes the state of his soul, asks Seneca to give him advice, to make a diagnosis and play, so to speak, the role of doctor of the soul for him.[22] So who was this Serenus then, to whom the *De Constantia* was also dedicated and probably *De Otio*,[23] as far as we know?[24] He was certainly not an adolescent of the Alcibiades type. He was a young provincial (from a family of notables, distant relatives of Seneca) who had come to Rome and begun a career in politics and even as a courtier. He had advanced Nero's relations with I no longer know which one of his mistresses, it doesn't matter.[25] It is more or less in this period that Serenus, already advanced in life and having already made his choices and begun a career, addresses himself to Seneca. Still in this domain of individual relationships, and still with Seneca, consider Lucilius, with whom Seneca engages in a lengthy correspondence from 62 A.D., and to whom Seneca also addresses and dedicates his *Natural Questions*. Who is Lucilius? He is a man twelve years younger than Seneca.[26] If we think about it, Seneca is sixty when he retires and begins this correspondence and writing *Natural Questions*.[27] So Lucilius must have been about forty or fifty. Anyway, he was procurator in Sicily at the time of the correspondence. For Seneca, the purpose of the correspondence is to get Lucilius to develop from, let's say, a somewhat lax and poorly theorized Epicureanism, towards strict Stoicism. Okay, you will tell me that, all the same, Seneca is a very particular case: this is a case of a strictly individual practice on the one hand, and of high political responsibility on the other, and after all he definitely did not have the time, leisure, or desire to address himself to all young people and tell them what to do.

However, if you take Epictetus who, unlike Seneca, is a teacher by profession, then he really does have a school. He opens a school which is called "school" and in which he has students. And, of course, among his students there are a number, no doubt a considerable number, of young people who come to be trained. The training function of Epictetus's school is indicated, it is demonstrated, in many places in the *Discourses* collected by Arrian.[28] For example, he attacks those young people who have led their family to believe that they were training at a good philosophical school but who in fact think only of returning home in order to shine and occupy important positions. There is also criticism of all those students who arrive full of zeal and who then leave the school after a while, put off by a training that does not teach them how to be successful and which demands too much of them from the moral point of view. The rules on how one should conduct oneself when one has been sent on an errand in town also concern these young people. This seems to indicate that it was not just a matter of delicate young people, but that they were kept under a firm hand and in a kind of fairly well-disciplined boarding school. So it is quite true that Epictetus addressed himself to these young people. It should not be thought that the care of the self, as principal axis of the art of life, was reserved for adults. But alongside this, intertwined with this training of young people, we can say that in Epictetus's school there is also what could be called, employing an unjust metaphor no doubt, an open shop: an open shop for adults. And in fact adults come to his school to hear his teaching for one day, for a few days or for some time. Here also, in the social world evoked in the *Discourses*, you see, for example, a town inspector passing through, a sort of tax procurer if you like. He is an Epicurean who comes to consult Epictetus and ask him questions. There is a man sent to Rome by his town who, passing through Asia Minor to Rome, stops to ask Epictetus questions and get advice on how he can best accomplish his mission. Moreover, Epictetus by no means disregards this clientele, or these adult interlocutors, since he advises his own students, young people therefore, to find prominent people in their town and to shake them up a bit by saying: Tell me then, how do you live? Do you really take proper care of yourselves?[29]

We could of course cite the well-known activity of Cynic orators who, in public places, at the corner of the street, or sometimes at solemn festivals, address the public in general, a public obviously made up of both young and old. In the noble, solemn genre of these diatribes or public discourses there were, of course, the great texts of Dio Chrysostom of Prusa,[30] several of which are devoted to these problems of ascesis, withdrawal into oneself, of the *anakhōrēsis eis heauton*, etcetera.[31]

Finally, I will take one last example of this problem of, if you like, the adult's insertion within the practice of the self. This concerns an important but enigmatic and little known group that we know about only through a text of Philo of Alexandria: the famous Therapeutae, about whom I will say more later. For the moment, let us leave aside the problem of who they are and what they do, etcetera. In any case, it is what we can call an ascetic group from around Alexandria, at least one of whose objectives is, as the text says, the *epimeleia tēs psukhēs*. What they want to do is take care of the soul. Now, a passage from Philo's *De Vita contemplativa*, which is where he speaks about them, says this about these Therapeutae: "Their desire for immortality and a blessed life leads them to think that they have already ended their mortal life [I will come back to this important passage later, with regard to old age; M.F.], they leave their possessions to their sons, their daughters, or other close relatives; they willingly give them their inheritance in advance, and those with no family give everything to their companions or friends."[32] You can see that we are dealing here with a world that is completely different from, and even the reverse of, the world of the *Alcibiades*. In the *Alcibiades*, the young man who took care of himself was someone who had not been sufficiently well brought up by his parents or, in the case of Alcibiades, by his tutor, Pericles. It was with regard to this that when he was young he came to question, or at any rate let himself be stopped and questioned by, Socrates. Now, rather, it is people who already have children, sons and daughters, a whole family, and at a given moment, feeling that their mortal life has ended, depart and concern themselves with their soul. One takes care of one's soul not at the beginning, but at the end of one's life. At any rate, let's say that rather than the transition to adulthood, it is much more adult life itself, or perhaps even the passage from adult life to old age, which is now the center of gravity, the sensitive point of the practice of the self.

As a final confirmation I will take an amusing text by Lucian. You know that at the end of the second century Lucian wrote a series of satires, let's say ironic texts, which are very interesting for the subject I want to talk about. There is the text, which was translated into French and published twelve years ago, sadly under very poor conditions, with the title *Philosophes à l'encan*,[33] although actually the title means something quite different, namely the market of lives[34] (that is to say, of modes of life) promoted by different philosophers and put on offer to people, set out at the market as it were, each philosopher seeking to sell his own mode of life by recruiting students. There is this text and another, which is also interesting, called *Hermotimus*, in which there is a discussion between two individuals, which naturally is presented ironically.[35] It is very funny and should be read a bit in the way we see Woody Allen's films set in the New York psychoanalytic milieu: in a rather similar way, Lucian presents the relationship people have with their philosophy master and their relationship to their own search for happiness through the care of the self. Hermotimus is walking in the street. He is, of course, mumbling to himself the lessons he has learned from his master and he is approached by Lycinus, who asks him what he is doing—he has either left his master or is going to him, I no longer remember, but it doesn't matter.[36] How long have you been going to your master? Lycinus asks Hermotimus, who answers:

Twenty years now.
For twenty years, you must have given him a lot of money?
But of course. I have given him a lot of money.
But won't this apprenticeship in philosophy, in the art of living and happiness soon be at an end?
Oh yes, Hermotimus answers, of course, it won't be long! I reckon to have finished in another twenty years.

A bit further on in the text, Hermotimus explains that he began to study philosophy when he was forty. We know that he has been going to his philosophy master for twenty years, and so at sixty he is exactly midway in his journey. I do not know if any references or correlations have been established between this text and other philosophical texts, but you recall that the Pythagoreans divided human life into four periods of twenty years: in the Pythagorean tradition, you are a child for the first twenty years, an adolescent from twenty to forty, young from forty to sixty, and an old man after sixty.[37] You see that Hermotimus is exactly sixty years old, at the cusp. He has had his youth: the twenty years during which he learned philosophy. There are only twenty years left to continue studying philosophy—the twenty years left for him to live, which still separate him from death. When he discovers that Hermotimus began when he was forty, Lycinus—the skeptic, the character around whom and from whom the ironic gaze is focused on Hermotimus and all this practice of the self—says: But this is fine, I am forty, exactly at the age to begin my training. He addresses Hermotimus, saying: Be my guide and lead me by the hand.[38]

Okay, I think this recentering, or decentering, of the care of the self from adolescence to maturity, or the end of maturity, will have a number of important consequences. First, when the care of the self becomes this adult activity, its critical function obviously becomes more pronounced, and increasingly so. The function of the practice of the self will be as much correction as training. Or again: the practice of the self will become increasingly a critical activity with regard to oneself, one's cultural world, and the lives led by others. Of course, this is not at all to say that the practice of the self only has a critical role. The training component remains and is always present, but it is fundamentally linked to the practice of criticism. We can say, if you like, that in the *Alcibiades*, as in other Socratic dialogues, the frame of reference of the need to be concerned about the self is the individual's state of ignorance. We discover that Alcibiades is ignorant about what he wants to do, that is to say, how to act in order to govern the city-state well, and we realize that he is unaware of his ignorance. Inasmuch as this implies a criticism of teaching, it was above all to show Alcibiades that he had learned nothing at all and that what he thought he had learned was only hot air. In the practice of the self that develops during the Hellenistic and Roman period, however, there is a training aspect that is fundamentally linked to the individual's preparation. But this is not a professional kind of preparation or preparation for social activity: it is not a question of training the individual to become a good governor, as in the *Alcibiades*, but rather of training him, independently of any professional specification, to withstand in the right way all the possible accidents, misfortunes, disgrace, and setbacks that may befall him. Consequently it involves constructing an insurance mechanism. It does not involve inculcating a technical and professional knowledge linked to a particular type of activity. This training, this protective armature with regard to the rest of the world and any accidents and events which may occur, is what the Greeks call the *paraskheuē* and which is roughly translated by Seneca as *instructio*.[39] The *instructio* is the individual's armature for dealing with events rather than training for a definite professional goal. So, there is this training aspect of the practice of the self in the first and second centuries.

However, this training aspect cannot be entirely dissociated from a corrective aspect, which becomes, I think, increasingly important. The practice of the self is no longer imposed simply against a background of ignorance, and of ignorance unaware of itself, as in the case of Alcibiades. The practice of the self is established against a background of errors, bad habits, and an established and deeply ingrained deformation and dependence that must be shaken off. What clearly is crucial is that the practice of the self develops more on the axis of correction-liberation than on that of training-knowledge. For an example of this I refer you to letter 50 from Seneca to Lucilius, where he says: We should not think that the evil that afflicts us comes from outside; it is not external to us (*extrinsecus*) but within us (*intra nos est*). Or again, a bit further on: "*in visceribus ipsis sedet*" (the evil is therefore in our vitals).[40] [ . . . *] In this practice of ourselves we must work to expel and expurgate this evil within us, to master it, throw it off and free ourselves from it. He adds: Of course, it is much easier to cure this evil if we get hold of it when it is still young and tender and not yet deeply ingrained. But you can see in any case that the practice of the self has to correct and not train, or

---

* At this point the manuscript has simply: "One must seek a master."

not only train: above all it has to correct an evil that is already there. We must treat ourselves already when we are young. And a doctor obviously has greater chance of success if he is called in at the start of the illness rather than at its end.[41] Anyway, it is always possible to be corrected, even if we were not corrected in our youth. Even if we are hardened, there are means by which we can recover, correct ourselves, and become again what we should have been but never were.[42] To become again what we never were is, I think, one of the most fundamental elements, one of the most fundamental themes of this practice of the self. Seneca refers to what happens to physical elements, to physical bodies. He says: However bent, even thick beams can be straightened; even more so, the human mind, which is pliable, can also be put right.[43] In any case, he says, the *bona mens* (the noble soul) never comes before the *mala mens*, before, as it were, the soul's imperfection.[44] The soul's nobility can only ever come after the soul's imperfection. We are, he says in the same letter, *praeoccupati*: we are already possessed by something at the very moment we undertake to do good.[45] Here he rediscovers an expression that was an important element of the Cynic vocabulary. He says: "*Virtutes discere vitia dediscere est* (learning virtue is unlearning vices)."[46] This notion of unlearning was crucial for the Cynics[47] and reappears in the Stoics. Now this idea of an unlearning which must begin anyway, even if the practice of the self is got under way in youth, this critical reformation, this reform of the self whose criterion is a nature—but a nature that was never given and has never appeared as such in the human individual, whatever his age—all naturally takes on the appearance of a stripping away of previous education, established habits, and the environment. First of all there is a stripping away of everything that may have taken place in early childhood. Here we find the repeatedly voiced, well-known criticism of the first education, of the famous nursery tales that already obliterate and deform the child's mind. There is Cicero's famous text in the *Tusculan Disputations*: "As soon as we are born and admitted into our families we find ourselves in an entirely distorted milieu in which the perversion of judgment is so complete that we can say we took in error with our nursemaid's milk."[48] Then there is criticism of early childhood and the conditions under which it develops. There is also criticism of the family milieu, not only of its educational effects, but also of the set of values it transmits and lays down, a criticism of what we in our terms would call the "family ideology." I am thinking of Seneca's letter to Lucilius in which he says: Find a safe place and try to return to yourself, "I am well aware that your parents wished you things very different from these; my wishes for you are also quite the opposite of those of your parents; I desire for you a general contempt for everything that your parents wished for you in abundance."[49] Consequently, the care of the self must completely reverse the system of values conveyed and laid down by the family. Third and finally, and I will not stress this since it is well known, the entire critique of pedagogical training, the training given by the masters of what we will call primary education, is above all a critique of the teachers of rhetoric. Here we meet again—and again, this is known so I do not stress it—the great polemic between philosophical practice and teaching on the one hand, and the teaching of rhetoric [on the other].* See, for example, the amusing teasing by Epictetus of the young student of rhetoric.[50] The physical portrait of the young student of rhetoric is itself interesting, because it clearly shows you and situates the major point of conflict between the philosophical practice of the self and rhetorical teaching: the young student of rhetoric arrives all made up and adorned with his hair elaborately dressed, showing by this that the teaching of rhetoric is a teaching of embellishment, pretence, and seduction. It is not a matter of taking care of oneself but of pleasing others. It is precisely on this point that Epictetus questions the student, saying to him: Fine, you are all dolled up; you thought to take care of yourself. But reflect a little: What is it to take care of oneself? We can see the analogy, which was probably quite explicit and recognizable for readers or auditors of the time, the resumption, the echo of the question posed by the *Alcibiades*: You must take care of yourself, how can you do this and what is your self? And we come back to: It is to take care of one's soul and not to take

---

* In the manuscript Foucault illustrates this polemic by taking the paradoxical example of Dio of Prusa, who began his life as a rhetor with attacks directed against Musunius and ended his life as a philosopher, praising philosophy.

care of one's body. So, the first consequence of the chronological shift of the care of the self from the end of adolescence to adulthood was this critical function of the care of the self.

The second consequence will be a very clear and pronounced drawing together of the practice of the self and medicine.[51] You can see that when the major function, or one of the major functions of the practice of the self is to correct, restore, and reestablish a condition that may never have actually existed, but whose nature is indicated by the principle, we are close to a medical type of practice. Of course, philosophy was always thought to have a privileged relationship with medicine and we do not have to wait until the first and second centuries A.D. to see its appearance. It is already very clear in Plato.[52] It is even clearer in the post-Platonic tradition: the *ontōs philosophein* of Epicurus is the *kat'alētheian hugiainein* (that is treating, curing according to the truth);[53] and in the Stoics, starting with Posidonius,[54] the relationship between medicine and philosophy—more precisely, the identification of philosophical practice as a sort of medical practice—is very clear. Musonius says: We call on the philosopher as we call on the doctor in cases of illness.[55] The philosopher's action on the soul is in every respect analogous to the doctor's action on the body. We could also quote Plutarch saying that medicine and philosophy have, or more precisely are, *mia khōra* (a single region, a single country).[56] Okay.* This ancient, traditional, well-established, and always repeated bond between medicine and care of the self is shown in different ways.

It is shown first of all, of course, by the identity of the conceptual framework, of the conceptual structure of medicine and philosophy. At the center there is, of course, the notion of *pathos*, which is understood by both the Epicureans and the Stoics as passion and as illness, with the whole series of analogies that follow from this, and about which the Stoics were more prolix and, as usual, more systematic than the others. They describe the development of a passion as the development of an illness. The first stage is what in Greek they called the *euemptōsia* (the *proclivitas*), that is to say the constitution that predisposes to illness.[57] Then

---

\* The manuscript adds here, giving as backing—see *supra*—Seneca's letter 50: "Our cure is all the more difficult, because we do not know that we are sick."

comes the *pathos* strictly speaking, an irrational impulse of the soul, which Cicero translates into Latin as *pertubatio* and Seneca as *affectus*. After the *pathos*, the illness strictly speaking, there is the *nosēma*, which is the transition to the chronic state of the illness: this is the transition to the *hexis*, which Seneca calls the *morbus*. Then comes the *arrōstēma*, which Cicero translates as *aegrotatio*, that is to say, a permanent condition of illness, which may manifest itself in one way or another but which keeps the individual constantly ill. Finally, in the last stage, there is the vice (*kakia*), the *aegrotatio inveterata* says Cicero, or the *vitium malum* (the *pestis*)[58] says Seneca, which is when the individual is completely warped, gripped by, and lost within a passion that completely possesses him. So there is this system of analogies, which I skip over quickly because it is well known.

No doubt more interesting is the fact that the practice of the self as it is defined, set out, and prescribed by philosophy is itself conceived of as a medical operation at the center of which we find the fundamental notion of *therapeuein*. *Therapeuein* means in Greek three things. *Therapeuein* means, of course, to perform a medical action whose purpose is to cure or to treat. However, *therapeuein* is also the activity of the servant who obeys and serves his master. Finally, *therapeuein* is to worship (*rendre un culte*). Now, *therapeuein heauton*[59] means at the same time to give medical care to oneself, to be one's own servant, and to devote oneself to oneself. There are, of course, a number of variations of all of this, and I will try to come back to some of them.

However, let us take for example the fundamental text of Philo of Alexandria concerning the Therapeutae, those people who at a certain point withdrew and established a community near Alexandria, the rule of which I will come back to later, and who Philo says call themselves Therapeutae. Why, Philo says, do they call themselves Therapeutae? Because, he says, they treat the soul as doctors treat the body. Their practice is *therapeutikē*, he says, as the doctors' practice is *iaktrikē*.[60] Like some Greek authors, but not all, Philo distinguishes between therapeutic and iatric activity, the former being precisely a broader, more spiritual, and less directly physical form of caring activity than that of doctors, for which they reserve the adjective *iatrikē* (iatric practice is applied to the body). And, he says, they call themselves the Therapeutae because they wish to treat the soul in the same way as doctors treat the body, and also because they practice the worship of Being (*to on: therapeuousi to on*). They look after Being and they look after their soul. It is by doing these two things at once, in the correlation between care of Being and care of the soul, that they can be called "the Therapeutae."[61] I will, of course, come back to this, because all these themes in Philo of Alexandria are very important. I just want to indicate the close correlation that emerges between practice of the soul and medicine in what is clearly a religious practice. In this increasingly insistent and pronounced correlation between philosophy and medicine, practice of the soul and medicine of the body, I think we can see three elements, to which I draw particular attention because they concern precisely the practice.

First, there is the appearance of the idea of a group of people joining together to practice the care of the self, or of a school of philosophy established in reality as a clinic for the soul: it is a place you go to for yourself or to which you send your friends, etcetera. You come for a period to be treated for the evils and passions from which you suffer. This is exactly what Epictetus says about his philosophy school. He conceives of it as a hospital or clinic of the soul. See discourse 21 in book II in which he strongly reproaches students who have only come, as we would say, to get "some philosophy," to learn to argue and the art of syllogisms, etcetera:[62] You have come for this and not for your cure, not expecting to be treated (*therapeuthēsomenoi*).[63] You haven't come for that. Now this is what you should be doing. You should remember that you are basically here to be cured. Before you throw yourself into learning syllogisms, "cure your wounds, stop the flow of your humors, and calm your mind."[64] Again, in discourse 23 in book III, he says even more clearly: What is a philosophy school? A philosophy school is an *iatreion* (a clinic). You should not walk out of the philosophy school in pleasure, but in pain. Because you do not come to the philosophy school because you are well and in good health. One comes with a dislocated shoulder, another with an abscess, a third with a fistula, and another has a headache.[65]

Okay, I think there are some problems with the tape recorder requiring urgent attention. So I will stop. There are two or three things I still want to say about medicine, I will come back [to them]. And I will talk a bit about the problem of old age and then of the generalization of the imperative of the care of the self.

1. In 27 B.C. *Octavian Caesar* promoted a new division of power (the Principate) and adopted the title Augustus. He died in April 14 A.D., leaving power to his son-in-law Tiberius (from the Claudian family) who initiated the dynasty of the Julian-Claudians, which ruled until the death of Nero in 68. The Antonines succeeded the Flavians, reigning from 96 to 192 (assassination of Commodus), and their rule was marked by the figures of Trajan, Hadrian, and Marcus Aurelius. This period, selected by Foucault, covers what historians identify as the High Empire.
2. Musonius Rufus, whose moral preaching is known to us due to its preservation by Stobaeus in his *Florilegium*, was a Roman knight from Tuscany who lived as a Cynic, and whose teaching dominated Rome at the beginning of the Flavians' rule. Epictetus, who followed his courses, preserves a lively and often-evoked memory of him in his *Discourses*. He is especially known for his sermons on practices of concrete existence (how to eat, dress, sleep, etcetera). Foucault resorts extensively to his imprecations on marriage in *Le Souci de soi*, pp. 177-80, 187-88, 197-98, and 201-202 (*The Care of the Self*, pp. 150-53, 159-60, 168-69 and 172-73). Marcus Aurelius was born in 121 and succeeded Hadrian in 138. It seems that his *Meditations* were written at the end of his life (at least starting from 170). He died in 180. The first major work by Tertullian (155c-225c), his *Apology*, is from 197. Clement of Alexandria (150c-220c) wrote his treatises on spiritual direction (the trilogy, *The Protreptic*, *The Instructor*, and *The Stromata* [or *The Miscellanies*]) at the beginning of the third century.
3. See the lecture of 3 March, second hour, for a stronger conceptual distinction between *meletan*, as an exercise in thought, and *gumnazein*, as an exercise in real life.
4. "... even the wealthiest cannot hold aloof from husbandry. For the pursuit (*epimeleia*) of it is in some sense a luxury as well as a means of increasing one's estate and of training the body in all that a free man should be able to do." Xenophon, *Économique*, translations by P. Chantraine (Paris: Belles Lettres, 1949) vol. 1, p. 51; English translation by E.C. Marchant, *Œconomicus*, in *Xenophon*, vol. 4 (Cambridge, MSS. and London: Loeb Classical Library, 1979), pp. 400-401.
5. See the exemplary use of this expression in Plato: "you must now examine yourself with even more attention (*mallon prosekhōn ton noun kai eis seauton apoblepsas*)," *Charmides*, 160d; "before all else we must attend to ourselves (*prosekteon ton noun hēmin autois*)," *Meno*, 96d.
6. Plutarch, *On Curiosity*, 515e. Foucault analyses this passage in detail in the lecture of 10 February, first hour.
7. On the theme of turning to look towards the self, see the lecture of 10 February, first hour.
8. On conversion and the Greek and Christian meanings of *metanoia*, see the lecture of 10 February, first hour.
9. On withdrawal or disengagement (*anakhōrēsis*), see the lecture of 12 January, first hour, and of 10 February, first hour.
10. "Remember that your inner guide becomes impregnable when it withdraws into itself and is content not to do what it does not wish to ... The intelligence free from passions is a citadel. Man has no stronger place into which to withdraw and henceforth be impregnable." Marcus Aurelius, *Meditations*, VIII.48; "Philosophy raises an impregnable wall around us that Fortune attacks with its thousand engines without gaining entrance. The soul detached from external things holds an unassailable position, defending itself in the fortress it has constructed." Seneca, *Letters*, 82.5. The same image is found in Epictetus, *Discourses*, IV.i.86, but reversed, since it is a question, rather, of capturing the internal fortress.
11. See *Le Souci de soi*, pp. 69-74 (*The Care of the Self*, pp. 54-58) with references especially to Epictetus and Seneca.
12. First sentence of the first of Seneca's letters to Lucilius: "*vindica e tibi.*" *Letters*, I.1.
13. One thinks especially here of Marcus Aurelius, "venerate your faculty of opinion" (*tēn hupolēptikēn dunamin sebe*), *Meditations*, III.9, and "revere (*tima*) what is highest in yourself," V.21.
14. See Seneca's letters to Lucilius, nos. XXIII.3-6 and LXII.4.

15. In classical culture the *kairos*, the primary meaning of which was spatial (it is the right spot for the archer on the target), designates a qualitative sequence of time: a favorable or opportune moment. See M. Trédé, "*Kairos*": *l'à-propos et l'occasion. Le mot et la notion d'Homère à la fin du IV<sup>e</sup>siècle avant J.-C.* (Paris: Klincksieck, 1992).
16. See the lecture of 6 January, second hour.
17. Only at the end of the fourth century did Athens establish an equivalent of military service, or training for young people before they became adult and responsible citizens. Before this, Athens had no strong institution to mark the passage to adulthood. Sparta, however, always had structures of continuous, strongly regulated and militarized training. See H.-I. Marrou, *A History of Education in Antiquity*. On the Athenian ephebe in particular, see P. Vidal-Naquet, "Le Chasseur noir et l'origine de l'éphébie athénienne" (1968), taken up and completed in *Le Chasseur noir* (Paris: La Découverte, 1983), pp. 151-74.
18. The thesis Foucault develops in part 5 of *L'Usage des plaisirs* (*The Use of Pleasure*) can be recognized here. It was the object of a whole lecture at the Collège de France (28 January 1981).
19. Epicurus, Letter to Menoeceus, in Diogenes Laertius, *Lives of Eminent Philosophers*, X.122-123.
20. See the lecture of 24 February, second hour.
21. "Among the fine maxims of Musonius which we remember, there is this one Sulla: 'one must be under constant treatment (*to dein aei therapeuomenous*) if one wants to live a healthy life (*bioun tous sōzesthai mellontas*)'." Plutarch, *On the Control of Anger*, 453d. Fragment 36 of the O. Hense edition of the *Reliquiae* of Musonius (Leipzig: Teubner, 1905) p. 123.
22. This is in the first part of Seneca's *On Tranquility of Mind*, I.1-18.
23. These three works, *On the Firmness of the Wise Man, On Tranquility of Mind*, and *On Leisure*, traditionally represent the trilogy of Serenus's conversion from Epicureanism to Stoicism under Seneca's influence. However, P. Veyne in his "Preface" to Seneca, *Entretiens, Lettres à Lucilius* (Paris: Robert Laffont, 1993) pp. 375-76, places *De Otio* in the years 62-65, when Seneca resigns himself to retirement and begins to consider it an opportunity. This would exclude it being dedicated to Serenus, who died before 62.
24. Beyond what Foucault says about the relationship between Serenus and Seneca in *Le Souci de soi*, p. 64 and p. 69 (*The Care of the Self*, p. 49 and p. 53) we should remember the pages devoted to this relationship in P. Grimal's classic *Sénèque ou la Conscience de l'Empire* (Paris: Les Belles Lettres, 1979), pp. 13-14, 26-28 and especially pp. 287-92 on his career and supposed Epicureanism. We assume that Serenus was Seneca's relative (he had the same family name) and owed his career to him (a knight; in the 50s he held the office of chief of the guards). He died in 62, poisoned by mushrooms, and was mourned by Seneca in his letter to Lucilius LXIII.14.
25. It was Acte, whose relationship with the Prince was covered up by Serenus: "(Nero) stopped being obedient to his mother and put himself in Seneca's hands, one of whose friends, Annaeus Serenus, pretending to love the same freedwoman (Acte), helped to hide Nero's youthful desire and leant his own name to the presents secretly given by the prince to the young woman, so that the generosity appeared to be his." Tacitus, *Annals*, XIII.xiii.
26. For Seneca's relationship with Lucilius (and the latter's age), we refer to P. Grimal, *Sénèque ou la Conscience de l'Empire*, p. 13 and pp. 92-93, as well as to the older article of L. Delatte, "Lucilius, l'ami de Sénèque," *Les Études classiques*, IV, 1935, pp. 367-545. See also *Le Souci de soi*, p. 64 and p. 69 (*The Care of the Self*, p. 49 and p. 53).
27. For the problems of the date of the *Natural Questions*, the basic text remains P. Oltramare's preface to his edition of the work, *Questions naturelles* (Paris: Les Belles Lettres, 1929). In this text Oltramare places the writing of the *Questions* between 61 and 64 (more precisely, between the end of 63 and the very start of 65), which leads him to the conclusion "that they preceded most of the *Letters to Lucilius*" (p. vii). The date of the letters to Lucilius is discussed at length and in detail by P. Grimal in *Sénèque*, pp. 219-24, and see especially Appendix I: "*Les Lettres à Lucilius*. Chronologie. Nature," pp. 441-56.
28. Arrian—Flavius Arrianus—(circa 40-c.120) was born in Bythinia to an aristocratic family. He took Epictetus as his master in Nicopolis. He then devoted himself to transcribing

faithfully the master's words (see the *Discourses*, which are a unique testimony of Epictetus's oral teaching). According to Simplicius, Arrian is the author of the *Encheiridion*, which is an anthology of his master's best talks. Later, the man who wanted to be the Xenophon of his time became a moneylender and consul under Hadrian, before settling in Athens as a notable.

29. Foucault takes up these examples again within the framework of a systematic analysis of texts in the lecture of 27 January, first hour.
30. Dio of Prusa (40-120) called "Chrysostom"—"golden mouth"—came from one of the most important families of Prusa and began a brilliant career as rhetor under Vespasian (a Sophistic period according to Von Arnim, who follows Themistius) before having to go into exile under Domitian. He then adopted the Cynic mode of life, wandering from town to town and exhorting his contemporaries to morality with long sermons, which have survived. See the full note by Paolo Desideri on Dio in R. Goulet, ed., *Dictionnaire des philosophes antiques* (Paris: CNRS Éditions, 1994) vol. II, pp. 841-56.
31. See discourse 30, *Peri anakhōrēseōs* (*On retirement*), in Dio Chrysostom, *Discourses*, translation J. W. Cohoon (Cambridge, Mass. and London: Loeb Classical Library, 1956) vol. II, pp. 246-69. This discourse is studied in detail in Foucault's dossiers. Foucault sees in this discourse the concept of withdrawal from the world organized in terms of the need for a permanent justification (*logon apodidonai*) of what one is doing.
32. Philo of Alexandria, *De Vita Contemplativa* (*On the Contemplative Life*), 473M, §13.
33. Lucien, *Philosophes à l'encan*, translation T. Beaupère (Paris: Les Belles Lettres, 1967); English translation by H.W. Fowler and F.G. Fowler, Lucian, as *Sale of Creeds*, in *The Works of Lucian of Samosata*, (Oxford: The Clarendon Press, 1905), vol. I.
34. "*Bion prasis*": the market of modes of life, of kinds and styles of life.
35. For a recent French version see Lucien, *Hermotime*, translation. J.-P. Dumont (Paris: PUF, 1993). The original Greek (with an English translation by K. Kilburn) is found in Lucian, *Hermotimus*, in *Works* (Cambridge, Mass. and London: Loeb Classical Library, 1959), vol. IV.
36. He is going: "I guess by your book and the pace you are going at that you are on your way to lecture, and a little late." Lucien, *Hermotime*, p.11; English translation by H.W. Fowler and F.G. Fowler, Lucian, *Hermotimus, or the Rival Philosophies*, in *The Works of Lucian of Samosata* (Oxford: The Clarendon Press, 1905), vol. II.
37. "He divides man's life in this way: 'A child for twenty years, a youth for twenty years, a young man for twenty years, and an old man for twenty years.'" Diogenes Laertius, "Pythagoras," in *Lives of Eminent Philosophers*, VIII.10.
38. "H: 'Oh, I was about your age when I started on philosophy; I was forty; and you must be about that.' L: 'Just that; so take and lead me on the same way.'" *Hermotime*, p. 25 (*Hermotimus*, p. 48). On this text, see *Le Souci de soi*, pp. 64-65 (*The Care of the Self*, pp. 49-50).
39. For this term, see the *Letters*, XXIV.5; LXI.4; CIX.8; and CXIII.38 (quoting Posidonius).
40. "Why do we deceive ourselves? Our evil does not come from outside (*non est extrinsecus malum nostrum*), it is inside us (*intra nos est*), its seat is deep within our entrails (*in visceribus ipsis sedet*); and the reason why it is so difficult for us to attain health is that we do not know we are ill." Seneca, *Letters*, L.4.
41. "The doctor...would have less to do if the vice was young. Tender young souls would obediently follow the way of reason that he would show them." Ibid.
42. "There is work to do (*laborandum est*) and, to tell the truth, even the work is not great, if only, as I said, we begin to form and correct our souls before they are hardened by bad tendencies. But I do not despair even of a hardened sinner. There is nothing that persistent hard work, sustained and intelligent zeal, will not overcome." Ibid., L.5-6.
43. "...however much the timber may be bent, you can make it straight again; heat puts right curved beams, and we change their natural structure to fashion them for our needs. How much more easily does the soul permit itself to be shaped, pliable as it is and more yielding than any liquid! For what else is the soul but air in a certain state? Now, you see that air is more adaptable than any other matter, in proportion as it is rarer than any other." Ibid., L.6.

44. "Wisdom never comes to anyone before a sick mind (*ad neminem ante bona mens vinit quam mala*)." Ibid., L.7.
45. "It is the evil mind that gets first hold on all of us (*omnes praeoccupati sumus*)." Ibid., L.7.
46. Ibid.
47. Foucault here refers to a quotation of Antisthenes given by Diogenes Laertius: "Being asked what learning is the most necessary, he replied, 'How to get rid of having anything to unlearn' (*to periairein ton apomanthanein*)." "Antisthenes," in *Lives of Eminent Philosophers*, II, VI.7. By quickly mastering the division between useful and useless knowledge one avoids learning the latter so as to avoid unlearning it later. More generally, however the Cynic theme of a mode of life *kata phusin* implies that one unlearns customs and other contents of the *paideia* (for the opposition of nature and the law, see the statements by Antisthenes and Diogenes in *Lives of Eminent Philosophers*, VI.11 and 70-71). As M. O. Goulet-Caze notes on this subject: "Cyrus, a typically Antisthenian hero, gives a first answer: 'The most necessary knowledge is that which consists in unlearning evil.' " *L'Ascèse cynique. Un commentaire de Diogène Laërce VI 70-71* (Paris: Vrin, 1986) p. 143; quotation of Stobaeus II, 31, 34. Seneca speaks of *dediscere*: "Give your eyes time to unlearn (*sine dediscere oculos tuos*)." *Letters*, LXIX.2.
48. Cicero, *Tusculan Disputations*, III.I.2.
49. Foucault is referring to letter 32. Foucault uses here an old French translation by Pintreal, revised by La Fontaine, reproduced in *Œuvres complètes de Sénèque le philosophe*, éd. M. Nisard (Firmin Didot, 1869), p. 583 (following references are to this edition).
50. Epictetus, *Discourses*, III.i.
51. See *Le Souci de soi*, pp. 69-74 (*The Care of the Self*, pp. 54-58).
52. The founding text for this complementary relationship between medicine and philosophy is undoubtedly the *Ancient Medicine* from the Hippocratic corpus: "There are, however, certain physicians and scientists who say that it would be impossible for anyone to know medicine who does not know what man consists of, this knowledge being essential for him who is to give his patients correct medical treatment. The question that they raise, however, is a matter for philosophy." Hippocrates, *Ancient Medicine* XX, in W.H.S. Jones, *Philosophy and Medicine in Ancient Greece* (Baltimore: Johns Hopkins Press, 1946), p. 84. For the study of this relationship in Plato and in ancient Greek culture generally, Foucault read the chapter "Greek Medicine as Paideia" in W. Jaeger's *Paideia*, vol. III (Oxford: Basil Blackwell, 1945), as well as: R. Joly, "Platon et la médecine," *Bulletin de l'Association Guillaume Budé*, pp. 435-51; P.-M. Schuhl, "Platon et la médecine," *Revue des études grecques* 83 1960, pp. 73-79; J. Jouanna, "La Collection hippocratique et Platon," *Revue des études grecques* 90 (1977), pp. 15-28. For a recent synthesis, see B. Vitrac, *Médecine et Philosophie au temps d'Hippocrate* (Saint-Denis: Presses universitaires de Vincennes, 1989).
53. "It is not the pretended but the real pursuit of philosophy (*ontōs philosophein*) that is needed; for we do not need to seem to enjoy good health but to enjoy it in truth (*kat'alētheian hugiainein*)." Epicurus, *The Vatican Sayings*, LIV.
54. The essential text on this point is Galen's presentation of the functions of the *hēgemonikon* (the ruling part of the soul) in Posidonius in his *De Placitis Hippocratis et Platonis* (see *Posidonius, I. The Fragments*, ed. L. Edelstein and I. G. Kidd [Cambridge: Cambridge University Press., 1972]). Against Chrysippus, Posidonius maintains the relative independence of the soul's irrational (irascible and lustful) functions. Thus, more than just a correct judgment is needed to master the passions pertaining to the body and its equilibria: a whole therapeutics and dietetics is required in order to dissolve the passions, not just a correction of thought. See the pages of A. J. Voelke, *L'Idée de volonté dans le stoïcisme* (Paris: PUF, 1973) pp. 121-30, and E. R. Dodds, *The Greeks and the Irrational*, pp. 239-40, hailing in Posidonius a return to Plato's moral realism. For a more general presentation of Posidonius, see M. Laffranque, *Poseidonois d'Apamée* (Paris: PUF, 1964), especially the chapter on "L'anthropologie," pp. 369-448.
55. This thesis is not found in the work of Musonius, but Foucault was probably thinking of the discourse XXVII of Dio Chrysostom of Prusa on the appeal to the philosopher: "Most people hate philosophers as they hate doctors; just as one does not buy cures except when

seriously ill, so one neglects philosophy so long as one is not too unhappy. Take a rich man with a large income or huge lands ... if he loses his fortune or his wealth he will lend his ear to philosophy more readily; if now his wife, his son or his brother dies, oh then he will make the philosopher come, he will call him in" (translated in Constant Martha, *Les Moralistes sous l'empire romain* [Paris: Hachette, 1881], p. 244).

56. "Also one should not accuse philosophers of trespass when they discuss matters of health, rather one should blame them if, after having abolished all frontiers, they do not think they should seek renown, as in a single territory common to all (*en mia khōra koinōs*), by pursuing at the same time the pleasant and the necessary in their discussions." Plutarch, *Advice about Keeping Well*, 122e.

57. Foucault merely repeats here the table drawn up by I. Hadot in *Seneca und die grieschisch-römische Tradition der Seelenleitung*, Part II, §2: "Die Grade der seelischen Krankheiten," p. 145. He takes up the same distinctions in *Le Souci de soi*, p. 70 (*The Care of the Self*, p. 54). The main Latin texts used by I. Hadot to find translations of Greek nosographies are: Cicero, *Tusculan Disputations*, IV.10, 23, 27, and 29, and Seneca, *Letters*, LXXV and XCIV. However, this paragraph was undoubtedly inspired by the appearance at this time of J. Pigeaud's thesis, *La Maladie de l'âme. Étude sur la relation de l'âme et du corps dans la tradition médico-philosophique antique* (Paris: Les Belles Lettres, 1981).

58. "They [his natural inclinations] are restored, at least so long as corruption (*pestis*) has not reached as far as them and killed them: in such cases not even the use of the full force of philosophy will succeed in restoring them." Seneca, *Letters*, XCIV.31.

59. The striking reference here is to Marcus Aurelius who, with regard to the inner daemon, writes that one must "surround it with sincere service (*gnēsiōs therapeuein*). This service (*therapeuein*) consists in keeping it pure from all passion." *Meditations*, II.13. The expression *heauton therapeuein* is also found in Epictetus, *Discourses*, I.xix.5.

60. "The choice of these philosophers is immediately revealed by their name: therapeutae (*therapeutai*) and therapeutrides (*therapeutrides*) is their true name, first of all because the therapeutics they practice (*paroson iatrikēn*) is superior to that generally found in our cities—the latter only treat bodies, but the other also treats souls," Philo, *On the Contemplative Life*, I.2.

61. "[If they are called Therapeutae] it is also because they have received an education according to nature and the sacred laws in the worship of Being (*therapeousi to on*), which is superior to the good." Ibid., I.2.

62. Epictetus, *Discourses*, II.xxi.12-22.
63. Ibid., II.xv.
64. Ibid., II.xxii.
65. Ibid., III.xxiii.30. Foucault discusses this text in *Le Souci de soi*, p. 71 (*The Care of the Self*, p. 55).

## six

## 20 JANUARY 1982

### Second hour

> *The privileged status of old age (positive goal and ideal point of existence). ~ Generalization of the principle of care of the self (with universal vocation) and connection with sectarian phenomena. ~ Social spectrum involved: from the popular religious milieu to Roman aristocratic networks of friendship. ~ Two other examples: Epicurean circles and the* Therapeutae *group. ~ Rejection of the paradigm of the law. ~ Structural principle of double articulation: universality of appeal and rarity of election. ~ The form of salvation.*

I HAVE TRIED TO identify two consequences of the chronological shift of the practice of the self from the end of adolescence to maturity and adult life. One concerns the critical function of this practice of the self, which will be added to and overlay the function of training. The second concerns its closeness to medicine, with the following closely connected consequence, about which I have not spoken but to which we will return. In Plato, the art of the body was quite clearly distinguished from the art of the soul. You remember that in the *Alcibiades* it was on the basis of this analysis, or distinction rather, that the soul was identified as the object of the care of the self. [Later], on the contrary, the body will be restored. In the Epicureans, for obvious reasons, and in the Stoics, for whom there is a profound connection between problems of the soul's tension and the body's health,[1] the body reemerges very clearly as an object of concern so that caring for the self involves taking care of both one's soul and one's body. This is obvious in Seneca's letters, which are already rather hypochondriac.[2] Then this hypochondria breaks out very clearly in people like Marcus Aurelius, Fronto,[3] and especially Ælius Aristides, etcetera.[4] We will come back to all this. One of the effects of this drawing together of medicine and the care of the self is, I think, that one has to deal with an intertwining of the mental and the physical, which becomes the center of this care.

Finally, the third consequence of this chronological shift is obviously the new importance and value given to old age. Of course, old age had a traditional and recognized value in ancient culture, but it is a value that I would say is, as it were, limited, offset, and partial. Old age means wisdom, but it also means weakness. Old age means acquired experience, but it also means the inability to be active in everyday life and even in political life. Old age enables one to give advice, but it is also a condition of weakness in which one is dependent upon others: one gives the young advice, but they are the ones who defend the town and the old, and it is the young who work to provide the old with the necessities of life, etcetera. So, traditionally, old age has an ambiguous or limited value. Let's say, roughly, that in traditional Greek culture old age is no doubt honorable, but it is certainly not desirable. One cannot want to become old, even if Sophocles' famous statement that he was glad finally to be old, since it freed him from the sexual appetite, is quoted and will continue to be quoted for a long time.[5] However, it is quoted precisely because it is, as it were, exceptional: he is the one person who wanted to become old, or who at any rate was delighted to be old, because of this liberation, and it is precisely Sophocles' statement that will be frequently employed later. But now that the care of the self must be practiced throughout life, but especially in adult life, now that the care of the self assumes its full dimensions and effects when one is fully adult, we see that the moment of the successful outcome and of the highest form of the care of the self, the moment of its reward, is precisely in old age. Of course, with Christianity and the promise of the hereafter, there will be a different system. But here, in this system that comes up against the problem of death, to which we will have to return, old age constitutes the positive moment, the moment of fulfillment, the peak of this lengthy practice that the individual has pursued or had to submit to throughout his life. Freed from all physical desires and free from all the political ambitions he has renounced, with all the experience he has been able to acquire, the old man will be the person who is sovereign over himself and who can be entirely satisfied with himself. The old man has a definition in this history and in this form of the practice of the self: he is the one who can finally take pleasure in himself, be satisfied with himself, put all his joy and satisfaction in himself, without expecting pleasure, joy, or satisfaction from anything else, neither from physical pleasures, of which he is no longer capable, nor the pleasures of ambition, which he has given up. The old man then is someone who delights in himself, and the point at which old age arrives, if well-prepared by a long practice of the self, is the point at which, Seneca says, the self finally arrives at itself, at which one returns to one's self, and at which one has a perfect and complete relationship to the self of both mastery and satisfaction.

As a result of this, if old age really is this desirable point, then it is understandable (first consequence) that old age should not be seen merely as a limit in life, any more than it is to be seen as a phase of diminished life. Old age should be considered, rather, as a goal, and as a positive goal of existence. We should strive towards old age and not resign ourselves to having it come upon us one day. Old age, with its own forms and values, should orientate the whole course of life. I think there is a letter by Seneca on this that is very important and typical. It is typical because it begins with what is apparently a rather incidental, or anyway enigmatic criticism of those, he says, who adopt a particular mode of life for each age of life.[6] Seneca here refers to the traditional and important theme in Greek and Roman ethics that life is divided up into different ages, each having a particular corresponding mode of life. This division was made differently according to the different schools and cosmo-anthropological speculations. I have referred to the Pythagorean division between childhood, adolescence, youth, and old age, etcetera (there were other modes). But what is interesting is the importance accorded to these different phases and their specific forms of life on the one hand, and, [on the other,] the importance, from the ethical point of view, attached to a good correlation between the mode of life chosen by the individual, the way in which he lived his life, and the time of life he had reached. A young man should live as a young man, a mature man as a mature man, and an old man as an old man. Now, Seneca says, quite probably thinking of this kind of division, I cannot agree with those who cut up their lives and who do not have the same way of living at one age and another. In place of this dividing up Seneca proposes a sort of unity—a dynamic unity, as it were: the unity of a continuous movement striving towards old age. He employs a number of typical expressions in which he says: Act as if you were pursued, you should live as fast as you can, throughout your life you should feel as if there were enemies at your back, people pursuing you.[7] These enemies are the accidents and mishaps of life. Above all they are the passions and disorders these accidents may produce in you, precisely insofar as you are young or adult and still hope for something, insofar as you are attached to pleasure and covet power or money. These are the enemies pursuing you. So, you must flee from these pursuing enemies, and you must flee as quickly as possible. Hasten towards the place that offers you a safe shelter. And this place that offers you a safe shelter is old age. That is to say, old age no longer appears as the ambiguous end of life, but rather as a focal point of life, a positive focal point towards which we should strive. Using an expression that is not found in Seneca and which goes a bit beyond what he says, we could say, if you like: we should now "live to be old." We should live to be old, for in old age we will find tranquility, shelter, and enjoyment of the self.

The second consequence is that this old age at which one must aim is in fact, of course, the chronological old age, which most of the ancients recognized as appearing at sixty—and furthermore, it is roughly at this age that Seneca retires and decides to take full possession of himself. But it is not just this chronological old age of the sixtieth year. It is also an ideal old age; an old age we produce, as it were, which we practice. With regard to our life, and this is the central point of this new ethics of old age, we should place ourselves in a condition such that we live it as if it is already over. In fact, even if we are still young, even if we are adult and still active, with regard to all that we do and all that we are we should have the attitude, behavior, detachment, and accomplishment of someone who has already completed his life. We must live expecting nothing more from our life and, just as the old man is someone who expects nothing more from his life, we must expect nothing from it even when we are young. We must complete our life before our death. The expression is found in Seneca's letter 32: "*consummare vitam ante mortem.*" We must complete our life before our death, we must fulfill our life before the moment of death arrives, we must achieve perfect satiety of ourselves. "*Summa tui satietas*": perfect, complete satiety of yourself.[8] This is the point towards which Seneca wants Lucilius to hasten. You can see that this idea that we must organize our life in order to be old, that we must hasten towards our old age, and that even if we are young we should constitute ourselves in relation to our life as if we are old, raises a series of important questions to which we will return. First of all there is, of course, the question of the death exercise (meditation on death as practice of death): living our life as if on its final day.[9] There is the problem of the type of satisfaction and pleasure we can have with ourselves. There is the problem, which is very important of course, of the relationship between old age and immortality: to what extent did old age prefigure, anticipate or was it correlated with the themes of immortality and personal survival in this Greco-Roman ethic? In short, we are at the heart of a series of problems that need to be disentangled.[10] These are some of the features, some of the consequences marking this chronological shift of the care of the self in the imperial period of the first and second centuries A.D., from adolescent urgency in the *Alcibiades* to adulthood, or a certain turning point between adulthood and real or ideal old age.

The second question I would like to broach today is no longer this chronological extension or shift but the, if you like, quantitative extension. Actually, in the period I am talking about, taking care of the self was no longer, and had not been for a long time, a recommendation restricted to certain individuals and subordinated to a definite aim. In short, people were no longer told what Socrates told Alcibiades: If you wish to govern others, take care of yourself. Now it is said: Take care of yourself, and that's the end of it. "Take care of yourself and that's the end of it" means that the care of the self seems to appear as a universal principle addressed to and laid down for everyone. The methodological and historical question I would like to pose is [the following]: Can we say that the care of the self is now a sort of universal ethical law? You know me well enough to assume that I will immediately answer: no. What I would like to show, the methodological stake of all this (or of a part anyway), is this: we should not be led astray by later historical processes of the progressive juridification of Western culture, which took place in the Middle Ages. This juridification has led us to take law, and the form of law, as the general principle of every rule in the realm of human practice. What I would like to show is that as an episode and transitory form, law itself is, rather, part of a much more general history of the techniques and technologies of practices of the subject with regard to himself, of techniques and technologies which are independent of the form of law and which have priority with regard to it. Basically, law is only one of the possible aspects of the technology of the subject concerning himself. Or, if you like, even more precisely: law is only one of the aspects of this long history, in the course of which the Western subject we are faced with today was formed. Let's return then to the question I posed: Is this care of the self perhaps regarded as a sort of general law in Hellenistic and Roman culture?

First of all, we should note of course that, inasmuch as there was universalization, inasmuch as "take care of yourself" was expressed as a general law, it would obviously have been completely fictitious. For in actual fact it is obvious that such a prescription (take care of yourself) can only be put into practice by a very small number of individuals. After all, you recall the Lacedaemonian expression I spoke about last week or the week before: It is so that we can take care of ourselves that we entrust the cultivation of our lands to the helots.[11] It is an elite privilege asserted as such by the Lacedaemonians, but it is also an elite privilege asserted much later, in the period I am dealing with, when taking care of the self appears in correlation with a notion we will have to consider and elucidate further: the notion of free time (*skholē* or *otium*).[12] We cannot take care of the self unless the life before us, the life available to us, is such that we can—forgive the expression—treat ourselves to the luxury of *skholē* or *otium* (which is not, of course, leisure as we understand it; we will come back to this). Anyway, a certain particular form of life, which is distinct from all other forms of life in its particularity, will in fact be regarded as the real condition of the care of the self. So, in reality, the care of the self in ancient Greek and Roman culture was never really seen, laid down, or affirmed as a universal law valid for every individual regardless of his mode of life. The care of the self always entails a choice of one's mode of life, that is to say a division between those who have chosen this mode of life and the rest. However, I think something else also prevents us from assimilating even the unconditional and self-finalized care of the self to a universal law: actually, in Greek, Hellenistic, and Roman culture, care of the self always took shape within quite distinct practices, institutions, and groups which were often closed to each other, and which usually involved exclusion from all the others. Care of the self is linked to practices or organizations of fraternity, brotherhood, school, and sect. Misusing the word "sect" a little—or rather, giving it the meaning it has in Greek: you know that the word *genos*, which means at once family, clan, genus, race, etcetera, was employed to designate the set of individuals who gathered together like, for example, the Epicurean sect or the Stoic sect—taking the French word "*secte*" in a wider sense than usual, I would say that in ancient culture the care of the self was in fact generalized as a principle, but always by being linked with this phenomenon of sectarian groups and practices.

As a simple indication, just to show or pick out its broad scope, I would say that we should not think that care of the self is only found in aristocratic circles. It is not just the wealthiest, the economically, socially, and politically privileged who practice the care of the self. We see it spread quite widely in a population which it must be said was very cultivated in comparison with any in Europe until the nineteenth-century, apart no doubt from the lowest classes and slaves of course, but even here we need to make some corrections. Well, in this population, it must be said that the care of the self appears and is organized in milieus that were not at all privileged. At one extreme, in the most disadvantaged classes, there are practices of the self that generally are strongly linked with clearly institutionalized religious groups organized around definite cults and often with ritualized procedures. Moreover, this ritual and cultic characteristic reduced the need for more sophisticated and learned forms of personal culture and theoretical research. The religious and cultic framework to some extent dispensed with this individual or personal work of research, analysis, and elaboration of the self by the self. But the practice of the self was nevertheless important in these groups. For example, in cults like that of Isis,[13] participants were subject to very precise requirements concerning abstention from food and sex, the confession of sins, penitential practices, and so on.

Of course, at the other end of the spectrum, there are sophisticated, worked out, and cultivated practices of the self which are obviously much more linked to personal choice, to the life of cultivated free time and theoretical research. This does not mean that these practices were at all isolated; they formed part of what we could call a "fashionable" movement. They depended also, if not on definite cult organizations, at least on preexisting social networks of friendship.[14] Friendship, which had a certain form in Greek culture, had much stronger and more hierarchical forms in Roman culture and society. In Roman society friendship was a hierarchy of individuals linked to one another by a set of services and obligations; it was a system in which no individual occupied exactly the same position as others. Friendship was generally focused on a personage to whom some were close and [others] less so. To pass from one degree of closeness to another was subject to a series of implicit and explicit conditions and there were even rituals, gestures, and expressions indicating to someone that he had advanced in the other's friendship, etcetera. In short, there was a partially institutionalized social network in friendship that, outside of the cult communities I was just talking about, was one of the major supports of the practice of the self. In its individual and inter-individual forms, the practice of the self, the care of the soul, depended on these phenomena. I have spoken many times of Seneca, Lucilius, and Serenus, etcetera. This is exactly the type of relationship involved. Serenus (a young provincial relative who arrives in Rome full of ambition and who tries to edge his way into

Nero's court) sees his uncle or distant relative, Seneca, who is in Rome and who has obligations towards Serenus because he is the elder and who already occupies an important position. Serenus enters the sphere of his friendship and within this relationship of semi-institutional friendship Seneca gives him advice, or rather, Serenus asks him for advice. Among all the services Seneca renders to Serenus—he used his influence with Nero, he provided services at court, and he no doubt helped him financially—he also provides him with what could be called "a soul service."[15] Serenus says: I do not really know what philosophy to attach myself to, I feel ill at ease with myself, I do not know if I am sufficiently or insufficiently Stoic, what I should or should not learn, etcetera. And all these questions are of exactly the same type as requests for help: Whom should I approach at court, should I apply for this post or others? Seneca offers advice on all of this. Soul service is integrated within the network of friendships, just as it developed within cult communities.

Let's say then that there are two major poles: on one side a more popular, religious, cultic and theoretically unpolished pole; and, at the other end, care of the soul, care of the self, practices of the self, which are more individual, personal, and cultivated, which are more linked to and frequent within more privileged circles, and which depend in part on friendship networks. But, of course, in indicating these two poles I certainly do not mean that there are two and only two categories, one popular and crude, the other learned, cultivated, and friendly. Actually, things are much more complicated.[16] We can take two examples of this complication. We could take the example of the Epicurean groups, which were philosophical rather than religious, but which in Greece, to start with at least, were for the most part popular communities, filled with artisans, small shopkeepers, and poor farmers, and which represented a democratic political choice, as opposed to the aristocratic choice of the Platonists or Aristotelians, and which of course, completely working class as they were, also involved an important theoretical and philosophical reflection, or anyway a doctrinal apprenticeship. This did not prevent this same Epicureanism from giving rise to extraordinarily sophisticated and learned circles in Italy, especially in Naples,[17] and, of course, around Maecenas and at the court of Augustus.[18]

However, to show you the complexity and variety of all these institutional dimensions of the care of the self there is also another example: this is the famous group of Therapeutae described by Philo of Alexandria in his treatise *On the Contemplative Life*. This group of Therapeutae, whom I have already spoken about, is enigmatic because in fact only Philo of Alexandria refers to it, and in fact—outside of some texts which may be implicit references to the Therapeutae—in the surviving texts of Philo, he only speaks of them in this text. Consequently some have assumed that the Therapeutae did not exist and that it was in fact the ideal and utopian description of how a community ought to be. Contemporary criticism—and I am, of course, absolutely incompetent to judge the matter—seems, rather, to suppose that this group really did exist.[19] For, after all, much cross-referencing makes it likely all the same. Now, as I have said, the Therapeutae were a group of people who had retired to the surroundings of Alexandria, not into the desert, as will be the practice of Christian hermits and anchorites later,[20] but in kinds of small suburban gardens in which each lived in his cell or room, with some communal areas. This community of Therapeutae had three axes and three dimensions. On the one hand, there are very pronounced cultic or religious practices: praying twice a day, weekly gatherings at which people are placed according to age with each having to adopt the appropriate demeanor[21] [...*]. On the other hand, there is an equally marked stress on intellectual, theoretical work, on the work of knowledge (*savoir*). On the side of the care of the self it is said from the start that the Therapeutae have withdrawn to their spot in order to cure illness caused by "pleasures, desires, sorrows, fears, greed, stupidity, injustice and the countless multitude of passions."[22] These then are the Therapeutae who come to cure themselves. Second, another reference: what they seek above all is *egkrateia* (mastery of the self by the self), which they consider to be the basis and foundation of all the other virtues.[23] Finally, and here the text is very important for its vocabulary, on every seventh day, when they have their gathering, so, just once a week, they add care of the body to their everyday activity of

---

*Only "that is to say ... the care of the self" is audible.

the *epimeleia tēs psukhēs*.[24] The *epimeleia tēs psukhēs* then is care of their soul, to which they must devote themselves every day. And, along with this care of the soul, there is a very strong emphasis on knowledge (*savoir*). Their objective is, as they say, as Philo says, to learn to see clearly.[25] Seeing clearly is having one's gaze clear enough to be able to see God. Their love of science, Philo says, is such that for three days, and for some even six days, they completely forget to eat.[26] They read the Holy Scriptures, they devote themselves to allegorical philosophy, that is to say, to the interpretation of texts.[27] They also read authors about whom Philo gives us no information, the authors who would have founded their sect. Their relationship to knowledge, their practice of study is really so strong, their attention to study is so intense—and we find again here a very important theme for all the practice of the self, and to which I think I have already alluded—that even in their sleep, their dreams "proclaim the doctrines of the sacred philosophy."[28] You have here an example of sleep and dreams as criteria of the individual's relationship to the truth, of the relation between the individual's purity and the manifestation of truth (I think I have already given another example with regard to the Pythagoreans).[29]

So, you see, I take this example because it is clearly a case of a religious group. We have no information about the social origins of its members, but there is no reason to assume they were from aristocratic or privileged circles. But you see also that the dimension of knowledge, meditation, apprenticeship, reading, allegorical interpretation, and so on is very prominent. So, we have to say that the care of the self always takes shape within definite and distinct networks or groups, with combinations of the cultic, the therapeutic—in the sense we have said—and knowledge, theory, but [involving] relationships that vary according to the different groups, milieus, and cases. Anyway, the care of the self is expressed and appears in this splitting into, or rather this belonging to a sect or a group. If you like, you cannot take care of the self in the realm and form of the universal. The care of the self cannot appear and, above all, cannot be practiced simply by virtue of being human as such, just by belonging to the human community, although this membership is very important. It can only be practiced within the group, and within the group in its distinctive character.

I think we touch on something important here. Of course, we can say, and it should be remembered, that most of these groups absolutely refuse to endorse and perpetuate on their own account the status differences which existed in the city-state or society, and this is one of their raisons d'être and was one of the grounds for their success in Greek, Hellenistic, and Roman societies. For the *Alcibiades*, for example, care of the self fell within a difference of status that meant that Alcibiades was destined to govern, and it was because of this, and because of his given status as it were, which was never called into question, that he had to take care of himself. In most of the groups I am talking about, the distinctions between rich and poor, between someone high-born and someone from an obscure family, or between someone who exercises political power and someone who lives in obscurity, were in principle not endorsed, recognized, or accepted. Apart from the Pythagoreans, perhaps, about whom there are a number of questions,[30] it seems that most of these groups did not accept even the distinction between a free man and a slave, in theory at least. The Epicurean and Stoic texts on this are many and repetitive: a slave, after all, may be more free than a free man if the latter has not freed himself from the grip of all the vices, passions, and dependences etcetera.[31] Consequently, since there is no difference of status, we can say that all individuals are in general terms "competent": able to practice themselves, able to carry out this practice of the self. There is no *a priori* exclusion of an individual on the grounds of birth or status. However, from another angle, although access to the practice of the self is open to everyone in principle, it is certainly generally the case that very few are actually capable of taking care of the self. Lack of courage, strength, or endurance, an inability to grasp the importance of the task or to see it through; such is the destiny of the majority in reality. Although the principle of taking care of the self (the obligation of *epimeleisthai heautou*) may well be repeated everywhere and to everyone, listening, intelligence, and putting the care into practice will in any case be scarce. And it is just because there is little listening and few are able to listen that the principle must be repeated everywhere. There is a very interesting text of Epictetus on this. He refers again to the *gnōthi seauton* (the Delphic precept) and says: Look at what happens with this

Delphic precept. It is written, inscribed, carved in stone at the center of the civilized world (he uses the word *oikoumenē*). It is at the center of the *oikoumenē*, that is to say, of the Greek-speaking world of reading and writing, of this cultivated world that is the only acceptable human community. It is written then, where everyone can see it, in the center of the *oikoumenē*. But the *gnōthi seauton*, placed by the god at the geographical center of the acceptable human community, is unknown and not understood. Then, passing from this general law, from this general principle, to the example of Socrates, he says: Look at Socrates. How many young people did he have to stop in the street for there to be a few who, in spite of everything, really wanted to listen to him and to take care of themselves? Did Socrates succeed in persuading all those who came to him to take care of themselves, Epictetus asks? Not even one in a thousand.[32] So you see that in this assertion that the principle is given to all but few can hear, we find again the well-known traditional form of division, so important and decisive throughout ancient culture, between a few and the others, between those of the first rank and the mass, between the best and the crowd (between *oi prōtoi* and *oi polloi*: the preeminent and the many). This dividing line in Greek, Hellenistic, and Roman culture made possible a hierarchical division between the preeminent—the privileged whose privilege could not be questioned, although the way in which they exercised it could—and the rest. You see that now there is again opposition between a few and all the rest, but it is no longer hierarchical: it is a practical division by which those who are capable [of the self] are distinguished from those who are not. It is no longer the individual's status that, in advance and by birth, defines the difference that sets him apart from the mass and the others. What will determine the division between the few and the many is the individual's relationship to the self, the modality and type of his relationship to the self, the way in which he will actually be fashioned by himself as the object of his own care. The appeal has to be made to everyone because only a few will really be able to take care of themselves. And you see that we recognize here the great form of the voice addressed to all and heard only by the very few, the great form of the universal appeal that ensures the salvation of only a few. Here again there is that form that will be so important in our culture. It must be said that this form was not exactly invented at this point. In fact, in all the cult groups I have been talking about, or in some at least, we find the principle that the appeal was directed to all, but that very few were true bacchants.[33]

We find this form again within Christianity, rearticulated around the problem of revelation, faith, Scripture, grace, and so on. But what I think is important, and this is what I wanted to stress today, is that it was already in this form of two elements (universality of appeal and rarity of salvation) that the question of the self and of the relationship to the self was problematized in the West. In other words, let's say that the relationship to the self, the work of the self on the self, the discovery of the self by the self, was conceived and deployed in the West as the route, the only possible route, leading from a universal appeal, which in fact can only be heard by a few, to the rare salvation, from which nevertheless no one was originally excluded. As you know, this interplay between a universal principle which can only be heard by a few, and this rare salvation from which no one is excluded *a priori*, will be at the very heart of most of the theological, spiritual, social, and political problems of Christianity. Now this form is very clearly articulated in this technology of the self. Or rather, since we should no longer speak just of technology, Greek, Hellenistic, and Roman civilization gave rise to a veritable culture of the self that, I believe, assumed major dimensions in the first and second centuries A.D. It is within this culture of the self that we can see the full extent and function of this form, once again so fundamental to our culture, between universal appeal and rarity of salvation. Moreover, this notion of salvation (of being saved, of earning one's salvation) is absolutely central to this. I have not yet spoken about this because we have just come to it, but you can see that the chronological shift taking us from the adolescent care of the self to care of the self in order to become old raises the problem of the objective and end of care of the self: what does it mean that we can be saved? You can see also that the relation between medicine and practice of the self directs us to this problem of "being saved and earning one's salvation": What is it to be in good health, to escape from illnesses, both to be lead to death and in a way to be saved from death? So you see that all this leads us to a theme of salvation, the form of which is clearly defined in the text of Epictetus I quoted a while ago. A salvation, once again, which must answer to a universal appeal but which in fact can only be reserved for some.

Okay, listen, next time I will try to speak about another aspect of this culture of the self, which concerns the way in which "cultivating oneself," "caring about oneself" gave rise to forms of relationships and to a fashioning of the self as a possible object of knowledge (*objet de savoir et de connaissance*) completely different from anything to be found in Platonism.

1. See, for example, what Stobaeus says: "Just as the body's strength is a sufficient tension (*tonos*) in the nerves, equally the soul's strength is a sufficient tension of the soul in judgment or action." *Florilegium*, II, 564. On this problematic of tension (*tonos*) in Stoicism and its monist framework ("the *tonos* is the internal tension which unifies a being in its totality," p. 90), the essential source is A.J. Voelke, *L'idée de volonté dans le stoïcisme*, after E. Brehier's classical analysis in his *Chrysippe et l'ancien stoïcisme* (Paris: PUF, 1950, 2nd edition).
2. With regard to letters LV, LVII, and LXXVIII, Foucault writes: "The letters of Seneca offer many examples of this attention focused on health, on regimen, on the malaises and all the troubles that can circulate between the body and the soul." *Le Souci de soi*, p. 73 (*The Care of the Self*, p. 57).
3. Marcus Cornelius Fronto (100-166), native of Numidia, consul in 143, is known above all for having been the teacher of rhetoric to Marcus Aurelius. It seems that he was a good orator, but all that we have to judge this is his correspondence with the future emperor. This correspondence lasts from 139 to 166 (the death of Fronto). See Foucault's analysis of the correspondence in the lecture of 27 January, second hour.
4. Ælius Aristides is the author of six *Sacred Tales* devoted to his illnesses and cures. Aristides, *Discours sacrés*, translation A.-J. Festugière (Paris: Macula, 1986). See on this topic, *Le Souci de soi*, p. 73 (*The Care of the Self*, p. 57).
5. Reference to the beginning of Plato's *The Republic*, at the point when Cephalus, questioned about the inconveniences of old age, answers: "I have met, rather, old men motivated by very different feelings, including the poet Sophocles. I was once with him when someone asked him: 'What is your view, Sophocles, concerning love? Can you still tackle a woman?'—'Be quiet friend' Sophocles replied, 'I am as delighted to be free from love, as if I had escaped the hands of a wild and fierce beast.'" *The Republic*, I.329b-c.
6. In the description that follows, Foucault in fact confuses two of Seneca's texts. One is a passage from *On Tranquility of Mind*, II.6: "Add those who, tossing and turning like people who cannot get to sleep, try every position one after another until finding rest through tiredness: after having changed the basis of their life a hundred times, they end up in the position in which old age, rather than the dislike of change, takes hold of them." The other is from the letter to Lucilius XXXII.2: "This life is so short! And we shorten it by our thoughtlessness, passing from one new start to another. We divide ourselves up and dissipate our life." *Letters*. See also: "You will see how revolting is the frivolousness of men who every day establish their life on a new basis."*Letters*, XIII.16, and XXIII.9.
7. "Hurry then, my very dear Lucilius. Think how you would double your speed if an enemy were at your back, if you suspected the approach of the cavalry pursuing those in flight. This is your situation: the enemy is after you. Come on, quickly!" *Letters*, XXXII.3.
8. Ibid., XXXII.4.
9. See lecture of 24 March, second hour.
10. For a new examination of the soul's immortal or mortal nature in the Stoics, and especially in Seneca, see the lecture of 17 March, second hour.
11. See the analysis of this expression in the lecture of 6 January, second hour.
12. See J. M. André, *L'Otium dans la vie morale et intellectuelle romaine, des origines à l'époque augustéene* (Paris: PUF, 1966).
13. An Egyptian goddess, Isis is especially known for having collected together the dismembered body of Osiris in a famous legend, a complete account of which can be found in Plutarch's *Isis and Osiris*. In the first centuries A.D. her cult (she is at once the sly woman, the devoted wife, and the brooding mother) expanded and was increasingly popular, to the point that it aroused the keen interest of Roman emperors (Caligula ordered the construction of a temple to Isis at Rome), and she even became a philosophico-mystical entity in

the Gnostics. With regard to abstinence and confessions in these rites, see F. Cumont, *Les Religions orientales dans le paganisme romain* (Paris: E. Leroux, 1929) pp. 36-37 and 218, n. 40; and R. Turcan, *Les Cultes orientaux dans le monde romain* (Paris: Les Belles Lettres, 1989), p. 113 (I am grateful to Paul Veyne for these references).
14. See *Le Souci de soi*, p. 68 (*The Care of the Self*, pp. 52-53).
15. See ibid., p. 69 (Ibid., pp. 53-54).
16. On life and social organization in the ancient philosophy schools, see Carlo Natali, "Schools and Sites of Learning" in J. Brunschwig and G. Lloyd, eds., *Greek Thought: A Guide to Classical Knowledge* (Cambridge, Mass. and London: The Belknap Press of Harvard University Press, 2000) pp. 191-217. Some general indications are also found in P. Hadot, *Qu'est-ce que la philosophie antique?* pp. 154-58.
17. With regard to the organization of the Maecenas Circle (bringing together Virgil, Horace, Propertius, etcetera) at the court of Augustus at the end of thirties B.C., see J.M. André, *Mécène. Essai de biographie spirituelle* (Paris: Les Belles Lettres, 1967).
18. On Roman Epicureanism in Campania, notably around Philodemus of Gadara and Lucius Calpurnius Piso Caesoninus, see the fundamental work of the specialist in this subject, M. Gigante, *La Bibliothèque de Philodème et l'épicurisme romain* (Paris: Les Belles Lettres, 1967).
19. Three "periods" of criticism are usually distinguished (see the Introduction by F. Daumas to his translation of Philo's *De Vita contemplativa*, and the very full bibliography of R. Radice, *Philo of Alexandria, an annotated bibliography 1937-1986* [Leiden: Brill, 1988]): First, the old period (from Eusebius of Caesarea in the third century to B. de Montfaucon in the eighteenth century) identifies the Therapeutae as a Christian community; second, the modern period in the nineteenth century (with Renan and P. Lagrange) considers Philo's description as an ideal picture; third, contemporary criticism, through crosschecking, attests the real existence of the group and pronounces itself in favor of linking it with the Essenians (see M. Delcor, etcetera).
20. In the lecture of 19 March 1980, Foucault develops his major thesis of a resumption of philosophical and pagan techniques of spiritual direction and examination in the Christianity of Cassian around the problem of the anchorite's training prior to departure for the desert.
21. "Hands under their clothes, the right hand between their chest and chin, the left hand down by their side." *On the Contemplative Life*, 476M, §30.
22. Ibid., 471M, §2.
23. "On the basis of self-control (*egkrateian*), they construct the other virtues of the soul." Ibid., 477M, §34.
24. "Considering the seventh day to be a very holy day and a great festival, they accord it a special honor: on this day, after caring for the soul (*tēs psukhēs epimeleian*), they rub their bodies with oil." Ibid., 477M, §36.
25. "But the sect of Therapeutae, whose constant effort is to learn to see clearly, is devoted to the contemplation of Being." Ibid., 473M, §10.
26. Ibid., 476M, §35.
27. Ibid., 475M, §28.
28. Ibid., 475M, §26.
29. See the lecture of 12 January, first hour, and of 24 March, second hour.
30. On the political organization of the Pythagorean society and its aristocratic tendencies, see the classic and invaluable presentation by A. Delatte in the chapter "Organisation politique de la société pythagoricienne" in his *Essai sur la politique pythagoricienne* (Geneva: Slatkine Reprints, 1922, repr. 1979) pp. 3-34.
31. See the crucial texts of Epictetus in the *Discourses*, all of IV.i, and especially II.i.22-28, demonstrating that it is not enough to be free before the praetor to cease being a slave, and *Encheiridion* XIV, as well as Epicurus, *Vatican Sayings* 66 and 67, on the freedom of the sage.
32. "And why is he Apollo? And why does he give out oracles? And why has he established himself in a place that makes him the prophet, source of truth and meeting place for all the

inhabitants of the civilized world (*ek tēs oikoumenēs*)? And why is it written on the temple 'Know yourself,' although no one understands these words? Did Socrates succeed in persuading all those who came to him to take care of themselves? Not even one in a thousand." *Discourses*, III.i.18-19.

33. Allusion to a famous Orphic initiatory expression concerning the small number of the elect; "many bear thyrsus, but the bacchants are few." Plato, *Phaedo*, 69c.

# seven

# 27 JANUARY 1982

## First hour

*Reminder of the general characteristics of practices of the self in the first and second centuries. ∼ The question of the Other: three types of mastership in Plato's dialogues. ∼ Hellenistic and Roman period: the mastership of subjectivation. ∼ Analysis of stultitia in Seneca. ∼ The figure of the philosopher as master of subjectivation. ∼ The Hellenic institutional form: the Epicurean school and the Stoic meeting. ∼ The Roman institutional form: the private counselor of life.*

I WILL TRY THEN to describe what seem to me to be some of the most typical features of this practice of the self, for Antiquity at least, and without prejudging what may take place later in our civilization, in the sixteenth century or the twentieth century for example. So, the typical features of this practice of the self in the first and second centuries A.D.

The first characteristic I noted last week was the integration, the intertwining of the practice of the self with the general form of the art of living (*tekhnē tou biou*), an integration such that care of the self was no longer a sort of preliminary condition for an art of living that would come later. The practice of the self was no longer that sort of turning point between the education of the pedagogues and adult life, and this obviously entails a number of consequences for the practice of the self. First, it has a more distinctly critical rather than training function: it involves correcting rather than teaching. Hence its kinship with medicine is much more marked, which to some extent frees the practice of the self from [...*]. Finally, there is a privileged relationship between the practice of the self and old age, and so between the practice of the self and life itself, since the practice of the self is at one with or merges with life itself. The objective of the practice of the self therefore is preparation for old age, which appears as a privileged moment of existence and, in truth, as the ideal point of the subject's fulfillment. You have to be old to be a subject.

The second characteristic of this practice of the self as it is expressed in the Hellenistic and Roman period. Once again, when I take the first and second centuries I am not situating all the phenomena, and the emergence of all the phenomena I am trying to describe, within this period. I have taken this period insofar as it represents a peak in an evolution which no doubt took place over the whole of the Hellenistic period. So, the second feature: The care of the self is expressed as an unqualified principle. "As an unqualified principle" means that it appears as a rule applicable to everyone, which can be practiced by everyone, without any prior condition of status and without any technical, professional, or social aim. The idea that you should care about the self because you are someone whose status destines you for politics, and so that you can govern others properly, no longer appears, or anyway recedes to a large extent (we will have to come back to this in more detail). So, it is an unconditional practice, but one which in fact is always put to work in exclusive forms. In reality only some can have access to this practice of the self, or at any rate only some can pursue this practice to its end. And the end of this practice of the self is the self. Only some are capable of the self, even if the principle of the practice of the self is addressed to everyone. The two forms of exclusion, of rarefaction if you like, with regard to the unqualified nature of the principle, were: either belonging to a closed group—which was generally the case in religious movements—or the ability to practice *otium*, *skholē*, cultivated free time, which represents, rather, an economic and social kind of exclusion.

---

*Only "even if the word *paideia* [...] it is in individual experience [...] the culture finally" is audible.

Roughly speaking, there is either closure around the religious group or cultural segregation. These were the two major forms on the basis of which tools were defined or provided so that certain individuals, and only these, could accede to the full and complete status of subject through the practice of the self. I pointed out, moreover, that these two principles were not represented and did not function in the pure state, but always in a certain combination: in practice the religious groups always implied a certain form of cultural activity—and sometimes of a very high level, as in the group of Therapeutae described by Philo of Alexandria—and conversely, in social selection by culture there were elements of the constitution of a group with a more or less intense religiosity as, for example, with the Pythagoreans. Anyway, we have reached the point that henceforth, relationship to the self appears as the objective of the practice of the self. This objective is the final aim of life, but at the same time a rare form of existence. It is the final aim of life for every man, but a rare form of existence for a few and only a few: we have here, if you like, the empty form of that major transhistorical category of salvation. You see that this empty form of salvation appears within ancient culture, certainly as an echo of, or in correlation and connection with, religious movements, which will of course have to be defined more precisely, but it should also be said that to a certain extent it appears by and for itself and not merely as a phenomenon or aspect of religious thought or experience. We must now see what content ancient culture, philosophy, and thought give to this empty form of salvation.

However, first of all I would like to raise a prior problem, which is the question of the Other, of other people, of the relationship to the Other as mediator between this form of salvation and the content it will have to be given. This is what I would like to focus on today: the problem of the other as indispensable mediator between the form I tried to analyze last week and the content I would like to analyze next time. In the practice of the self, someone else, the other, is an indispensable condition for the form that defines this practice to effectively attain and be filled by its object, that is to say, by the self. The other is indispensable for the practice of the self to arrive at the self at which it aims. This is the general formula. This is what we must now analyze a little. As a reference point, let's take the situation roughly as it appears in the *Alcibiades*, or at any rate, in the Socratic-Platonic dialogues generally. Through the different characters who appear in this kind of dialogue—whether developed positively or negatively doesn't matter—it is easy to recognize three types of mastership, three types of relationship to the other person indispensable for the young man's training. First, mastership through example. The other is a model of behavior that is passed on and offered to the younger person and which is indispensable for his training. The example may be passed on by tradition: there are the heroes and great men whom one comes to know through narratives and epics etcetera. Mastership through example is also provided by the presence of great prestigious souls, of the glorious old men of the city. This mastership through example is also provided from nearer at hand, by lovers pursuing the young boy who offer him—or should offer him—a model of behavior. A second type of mastership is the mastership of competence, that is to say, quite simply, of the person who passes on knowledge, principles, abilities, know-how and so on, to the younger person. Finally, the third type of mastership is, of course, the Socratic mastership of dilemma and discovery practiced through dialogue. I think we should note that each of these three masterships rests on a particular interplay of ignorance and memory. The problem of mastership is how to free the young man from his ignorance. He needs to be presented with examples that he can honor in his life. He needs to acquire the techniques, know-how, principles, and knowledge that will enable him to live properly. He needs to know—and this is what takes place in the case of Socratic mastership—the fact that he does not know and, at the same time, that he knows more than he thinks he does. These masterships function then on the basis of ignorance, and also on the basis of memory, inasmuch as what is involved is either memorizing a model, or memorizing, learning, or familiarizing oneself with a know-how, or discovering that the knowledge we lack is to be found again quite simply in memory itself and, consequently, if it is true that we did not know that we did not know, it is equally true that we did not know that we knew. The differences between these three categories of mastership aren't important. Let us leave to one side the specificity and singularity of the

Socratic type of mastership and its crucial role with regard to the others. I think the Socratic and two other types of mastership have in common at least the fact that it is always a question of ignorance and memory, memory being precisely what enables one to pass from ignorance to non-ignorance, from ignorance to knowledge (*savoir*), it being understood that ignorance cannot escape from itself on its own. Socratic mastership is interesting inasmuch as Socrates' role is to show that ignorance is in fact unaware that it knows, and therefore that to some extent knowledge can arise out of ignorance itself. However, the fact of Socrates' existence, and the necessity of his questioning, proves nonetheless that this movement cannot take place without another person.

Much later, in the practice of the self in the Hellenistic and Roman period I want to analyze, at the beginning of the Empire, the relationship to the other is just as necessary as in the classical epoch I have just referred to, but obviously in a different form. To a certain extent the need for the other is still always based on the fact of ignorance. But it is especially based on those other elements I spoke about last week: basically, on the fact that the subject is not so much ignorant as badly formed, or rather deformed, vicious, in the grip of bad habits. Above all it is based on the fact that right from the start, at the moment of his birth, even in the lap of his mother, as Seneca says, the individual has never had the relationship to nature of rational will that defines the morally sound action and the morally valid subject.[1] Consequently, the subject should not strive for knowledge to replace his ignorance. The individual should strive for a status as subject that he has never known at any moment of his life. He has to replace the non-subject with the status of subject defined by the fullness of the self's relationship to the self. He has to constitute himself as subject, and this is where the other comes in. I think this theme is rather important in the history of this practice of the self and, more generally, in the history of subjectivity in the Western world. Henceforth, the master is no longer the master of memory. He is no longer the person who, knowing what the other does not know, passes it on to him. No more is he the person who, knowing that the other does not know, knows how to demonstrate to him that in reality he knows what he does not know. Mastership will not work in this way. Henceforth the master is an effective agency (*opérateur*) for producing effects within the individual's reform and in his formation as a subject. He is the mediator in the individual's relationship to his constitution as a subject. We can say that, in one way or another, all the declarations of philosophers, spiritual directors, etcetera, in the first and second centuries, testify to this. Take, for example, fragment 23 of Musonius (in the Hense edition of Musonius's *Œuvres*) in which he says this, which is very interesting: You see, when it is a matter of learning something in the realm of knowledge (*connaissance*) or the arts (*tekhnai*), we always need training, we always need a master. And yet in these domains (knowledge, sciences, arts) we are not in the grip of bad habits. We are merely ignorant. Well, even on the basis of this status of ignorance, we need to be trained and we need a master. All right, he says, when it becomes a question of transforming bad habits, of transforming the *hexis*, the individual's way of being, when we have to correct ourselves, then *a fortiori* we will need a master. Passing from ignorance to knowledge involves the master. Passing from a status of "to be corrected" to the status "corrected" *a fortiori* presupposes a master. Ignorance cannot be the element that brings about knowledge; this was the point on which the need for a master was based in classical thought. The subject can no longer be the person who carries out his own transformation, and the need for a master is now inserted here.[2]

I would like to take as an example a short passage at the beginning of Seneca's letter 52 to Lucilius. At the beginning of the letter he refers quickly to the mental restlessness and irresolution with which we are naturally afflicted. He says: This mental restlessness, this irresolution is basically what we call *stultitia*.[3] *Stultitia* here is something that is not settled on anything and not satisfied by anything. Now, he says, no one is in such good health (*satis valet*) that he can get out of (*emergere*) this condition by himself. Someone must lend him a hand and pull him out: *oportet aliquis educat*.[4] So, I would like to focus on two elements from this short passage. First, you see that the need for a master or an aid arises in connection with good and bad health, and so in fact with correction, rectification, and reform. What is this morbid, pathological condition one must rise above? The word then is given: *stultitia*. Now you know that the description of *stultitia* is a kind of commonplace in Stoic philosophy, starting especially with Posidonius.[5] Anyway, Seneca describes it several times. It is mentioned at the beginning of letter 52 and it is described especially at the beginning of *De Tranquillitate*.[6] When Serenus asks Seneca for advice, Seneca says to him: All right, I will give you the diagnosis that fits your case, I will tell you exactly where you are. But in order to get you to really understand the state you are in, first of all I will describe to you the worst state we can be in and, truth to tell, the state we are in when we have not even begun to make progress in philosophy, or in the work of the practice of the self.[7] We are in this condition of *stultitia* when we have not yet taken care of ourselves. *Stultitia* is, then, if you like, the other pole to the practice of the self. The practice of the self has to deal with *stultitia* as its raw material, if you like, and its objective is to escape from it. What is *stultitia*? The *stultus* is someone who has not cared for himself. How is the *stultus* characterized? Basing ourselves on this text from the beginning of *De Tranquillitate* in particular,[8] we can say that the *stultus* is first of all someone blown by the wind and open to the external world, that is to say someone who lets all the representations from the outside world into his mind. He accepts these representations without examining them, without knowing how to analyze what they represent. The *stultus* is open to the external world inasmuch as he allows these representations to get mixed up in his own mind with his passions, desires, ambition, mental habits, illusions, etcetera, so that the *stultus* is someone prey to the winds of external representations and who, once they have entered his mind, cannot make the *discriminatio*, cannot separate the content of these representations from what we will call, if you like, the subjective elements, which are combined in him.[9] This is the first characteristic of the *stultus*. On the other hand, and as a result of this, the *stultus* is someone who is dispersed over time: he is not only open to the plurality of the external world but also broken up in time. The *stultus* is someone who remembers nothing, who lets his life pass by, who does not try to restore unity to his life by recalling what is worth memorizing, and [who does not] direct his attention and will to a precise and well-determined end. The *stultus* lets life pass by and constantly changes his viewpoint. His life, and so his existence, pass by without memory or will. Hence, the *stultus* is constantly changing his way of life. You maybe recall that last week I referred to Seneca's text where he said that, basically, nothing is more harmful than changing one's mode of life according to one's age, having a certain mode of life when adolescent, another when adult, and a third when old.[10] In reality one must direct one's life as quickly as possible towards its objective, which is the fulfillment of the self in old age. "Hasten to be old," he said in short, old age being the point of orientation that enables life to be set in a single unity. The *stultus* is quite the opposite. He is someone who does not think of his old age and who does not think of the temporality of his life as having to be orientated by the completion of the self in old age. He is someone who constantly changes his life. And here, then, even worse than the choice of a different mode of life for each age, Seneca evokes those who change their mode of life every day and who arrive at old age without ever having thought about it. This passage is important and is found at the beginning of *De Tranquillitate*.[11] The consequence then—both the consequence and the principle—of this openness to representations coming from the external world, and of this being dispersed in time, is that the individual *stultus* is unable to will properly. What is it to will properly? There is a passage right at the beginning of letter 52 that tells us what the will of the *stultus* is and so what the will of someone who rises above the condition of *stultitia* should be. The will of the *stultus* is not a free will. It is a will that is not an absolute will. It is a will that does not always will. What does it mean to will freely? It means willing without what it is that one wills being determined by this or that event, this or that representation, this or that inclination. To will freely is to will without any determination, and the *stultus* is determined by what comes from both outside and inside. Secondly, to will properly is to will absolutely (*absolute*).[12] That is to say, the *stultus* wants several things at once, and these are divergent without being contradictory. So he does not want one and only one thing absolutely. The *stultus* wants something and at the same time regrets it. Thus the *stultus* wants glory and, at the same time, regrets not leading a peaceful, voluptuous life, etcetera. Third, the *stultus* is someone who wills, but he also wills with inertia, lazily, and his willing is constantly interrupted and changes its objective. He does not always will. Willing freely, absolutely, and always characterizes the opposite condition to *stultitia*. And *stultitia* is that will that is, as it were, limited, relative, fragmentary, and unsettled.

Now what object can one freely, absolutely, and always want? What is the object towards which the will can be orientated so that it can be exerted without being determined by anything external? What object can the will want absolutely, that is to say, wanting nothing else? What object is the will always able to want in any circumstances, without having to alter itself according to the occasion or time? It goes without saying that the object, the only object that one can freely will, without having to take into consideration external determinations, is the self. What object can one will absolutely, that is to say without relating it to anything else? It is the self. What object can one always want, without having to change it over time or on different occasions? It is the self. What definition of the *stultus* can we extract then from Seneca's descriptions without, I think, too much extrapolation? The *stultus* is essentially someone who does not will, who does not will himself, who does not want the self, whose will is not directed towards the only object one can freely will, absolutely and always, which is oneself. In *stultitia* there is a disconnection between the will and the self, a nonconnection, a nonbelonging characteristic of *stultitia*, which is both its most manifest effect and deepest root. To escape from *stultitia* will be precisely to act so that one can will the self, so that one can will oneself, so that one can strive towards the self as the only object one can will freely, absolutely, and always. Now you see that *stultitia* cannot will this object since what characterizes it is, precisely, that it does not will it.

Inasmuch as *stultitia* is defined by this nonrelationship to the self, the individual cannot escape from it by himself. The constitution of the self as the object capable of orientating the will, of appearing as the will's free, absolute, and permanent object and end, can only be accomplished through the intermediary of someone else. Between the *stultus* individual and the *sapiens* individual, the other is necessary. Or again, intervention by the other is necessary between, on the one hand, the individual who does not will his own self and, on the other, the one who has achieved a relationship of self-control, self-possession, and pleasure in the self, which is in fact the objective of *sapientia*. For structurally, if you like, the will that is typical of *stultitia* is unable to want to care about the self. The care of the self consequently requires, as you can see, the other's presence, insertion, and intervention. This is a first element I wanted to bring out from this short passage at the beginning of letter 52.

Beyond this definition of *stultitia* and its relationship to the will, the second element I wanted to bring out is that someone else is needed. However, although his role may not be very clearly defined in the passage, it is clear that this other person is not an educator in the traditional sense of the term, someone who will teach truths, facts, and principles. It is also clear that he is not a master of memory. The text does not say at all what the other's action will be, but the expressions it employs (to characterize this action, or rather to indicate it from afar) are typical. There is the expression *porrigere manum* and the expression *oportet educat*.[13] Forgive a tiny bit of grammar: *educat*, of course, is an imperative. So it is not *educare* but *educere*: offering a hand, extricating from, leading out of. You see then that this not at all a work of instruction or education in the traditional sense of the term, of the transmission of theoretical knowledge or of know-how. But it is actually a certain action carried out on the individual to whom one offers a hand and whom one extricates from the condition, status, and mode of life and being in which he exists [...]. It is a sort of operation focused on the mode of being of the subject himself, and not just the transmission of knowledge capable of taking the place of or replacing ignorance.

So the question that arises is this: What is this action of the other that is necessary for the constitution of the subject by himself? How will the other's action be inserted as an indispensable element in the care of the self? What is this helping hand, this "eduction," which is not an education but something different or more than education? Well, you can imagine, you are of course familiar with this mediator who immediately comes forward, this effective agent (*opérateur*) who asserts himself in this relationship, in the construction of the subject's relationship to himself. He puts himself forward, loudly asserts himself, and proclaims that he and he alone can perform this mediation and bring about the transition from *stultitia* to *sapientia*. He proclaims that he is the only one who can see to it that the individual is able to will himself—and can finally arrive at himself, exercise his sovereignty over himself and find his entire happiness in this relationship. This effective agent who puts himself forward is, of course, the philosopher. The philosopher, then, is this effective agent. And this idea is found in all the philosophical tendencies, whatever they are. In the Epicureans: Epicurus himself said that only the philosopher is capable of guiding others.[14] Another text, but of course we can find dozens of them, comes from the Stoic Musonius, who says: "The philosopher is the *hēgemōn* (guide) for everyone in what concerns the things appropriate to their nature."[15] And then, of course, we reach the extreme with Dio Chrysostom of Prusa, the one-time rhetor hostile to the philosophers, who then converted to philosophy and led the life of a Cynic, presenting a number of fairly typical features of Cynic philosophy in his thought. [At the] turn of the first and second centuries, Dio of Prusa says: Philosophers provide us with advice on what it is appropriate to do; by consulting the philosopher we can determine whether or not we should marry, take part in politics, establish a monarchy or democracy or some other form of constitution.[16] You see that in Dio of Prusa's definition, the philosopher's jurisdiction extends beyond the relationship to the self; it extends to the individual's whole life. We should turn to philosophers to find out how we ought to conduct ourselves, and philosophers not only tell us how we ought to conduct ourselves, but even how we ought to conduct other men, since they tell us what constitution should be adopted by the city, whether a monarchy is better than a democracy, etcetera. The philosopher, then, loudly promotes himself as the only person capable of governing men, of governing those who govern men, and of in this way constituting a general practice of government at every possible level: government of self and government of others. He is the one who governs those who want to govern themselves and he is the one who governs those who want to govern others. We have here, I think, the fundamental point of divergence between philosophy and rhetoric as it breaks out and emerges in this period.[17] Rhetoric is the inventory and analysis of the means by which one can act on others by means of discourse. Philosophy is the set of principles and practices available to one, or which one makes available to others, for taking proper care of oneself or of others. Now how, concretely and practically, do philosophers, how does philosophy, join together the requirement of its own presence and the formation, development, and organization within the individual of the practice of himself? What does philosophy propose as an instrument? Or rather, through what institutional mediations does it claim that the philosopher's existence, practice, and discourse, the advice he gives, will enable those who listen to him to practice themselves, to take care of themselves, and to arrive finally at that object and end recommended to them, which is themselves?

There are, I think, two major institutional forms that we can look at quickly: the Hellenic type, if you like, and the Roman type. The Hellenic form is, of course, the school, the *skholē*. The school may be closed, involving a communal life for individuals. This was the case, for example, in Pythagorean schools.[18] This was also the case in Epicurean schools. In the Epicurean and also the Pythagorean schools, spiritual guidance had a very big role. A number of commentators—De Witt in particular, in a series of articles devoted to the Epicurean schools[19]—claim that the Epicurean school was organized according to a very complex and rigid hierarchy and that there was a whole series of individuals at the head of which was, of course, the sage, the only sage who never needed a guide: Epicurus himself. Epicurus is the divine man (the *theios anēr*) whose singularity—a singularity without exception—consisted in the fact that only he was able to extricate himself from nonwisdom and attain wisdom on his own. Outside of this *sophos*, then, all the others needed guides and De Witt proposes a hierarchy: the *philosophoi*, the *philologoi*, the *kathēgētai*, the *sunēthis*, the *kataskeuazomenoi*, and so on,[20] who would have occupied particular positions and functions in the school, and a particular role in the practice of guidance, corresponding to these positions and values (some leading only fairly large groups, others having the right to practice individual guidance and, when they are sufficiently trained, directing individuals towards the practice of the self indispensable for achieving the happiness sought). Actually, it seems that the hierarchy proposed by people like De Witt does not entirely correspond to reality. There are a number of criticisms of this thesis. If you want, you can look at the very interesting volume in the proceedings of the Association Guillaume Budé devoted to Greek and Roman Epicureanism.[21]

No doubt we should be much less certain about the closed, strongly institutionalized hierarchical structure advanced by De Witt. We can be sure about some things in the practice of spiritual direction in the [Epicurean] school. The first is attested by an important text written by Philodemus[22] to which we will have to return (Philodemus was an Epicurean who lived in Rome, was counselor to Lucius Piso, and wrote a text entitled *Parrhēsia*—a notion to which we shall return shortly—of which unfortunately only fragments have survived). Philodemus shows that in the Epicurean school it was absolutely necessary for every individual to have a *hēgemōn*, a guide, a director, who ensured his individual guidance. Second, in the same text, Philodemus shows that individual guidance was organized around, or had to obey, two principles. Individual guidance could not take place without an intense affective relationship of friendship between the two partners, the guide and the person being guided. And this guidance implied a certain quality, actually a certain "way of speaking," a certain "ethics of speech" I will say, which I will try to analyze in the next hour and which is called, precisely, *parrhēsia*.[23] *Parrhēsia* is opening the heart, the need for the two partners to conceal nothing of what they think from each other and to speak to each other frankly. Once again, this notion needs to be elaborated, but it is certain that, along with friendship, it was one of the conditions, one of the fundamental ethical principles of guidance for the Epicureans. A letter by Seneca allows us to be equally certain about something else. In the same letter 52, which I commented on earlier, the passage immediately following the one I tried to analyze refers to the Epicureans. He says that for the Epicureans there were basically two categories of individuals: those it is sufficient to guide because they have hardly any internal difficulties with the guidance offered to them; and then those who, because of a certain natural malignancy, must be forced along, whom one must drive out from the condition in which they exist.

And, interestingly, Seneca adds that for the Epicureans there is no difference of value or quality between these two categories of disciples, of guided individuals—basically, one was no better than the other and did not occupy a higher rank—but that there was basically a difference of technique: one could not be guided in the same way as the other, it being understood that once the work of guidance was completed their virtue would be of the same type, or anyway at the same level.[24]

Among the Stoics it seems that the practice of spiritual direction was less bound up with the existence of a somewhat closed group leading a communal life, and the requirement of friendship in particular is much less evident. We can get an idea of what Epictetus' school at Nicopolis may have been like from Arrian's record of his discourses.[25] First of all, it does not seem to have been a place of real communal life, but simply a place for meetings, which were fairly frequent and demanding. In discourse 8 of book II, there is a short note on students sent into town for some kind of shopping and errands, which I would say implies a certain form of boarding, despite the noncommunal life.[26] During the day, students no doubt wanted to remain in a place that was certainly in town, but that was cut off from, or which did not allow easy access to, its daily life. There were several categories of students in this place. First, the regular students. These were divided into two categories. There were those who came to complete their training, as it were, before going into political or civil life [...*]. [Epictetus] also alludes to the time when they will have to exercise responsibilities, present themselves to the Emperor, and choose between flattery or sincerity, as well as deal with condemnations. So, there are these students who come for a kind of period of training prior to entering life. It is probably a student of this kind who appears in discourse 14 of book II, in which a Roman citizen brings his young son to Epictetus. Epictetus straightaway explains his conception of philosophy, how he sees the philosopher's task and what philosophy teaches.[27] He gives, so to speak, an account of the type of training he is prepared to give to the man's son. So, there are more or less temporary students. There are also regular students who are there

---

*Only "... who would probably be young people, let us say [...] you, the rich" is audible.

not just to complete their training and culture, but who want to become philosophers themselves. It is clearly this kind of student who is addressed in discourse 22 of book III, which is the famous discourse portraying the Cynic. We are told that one of the *gnōrimoi* (students or disciples of Epictetus) raises the question, or rather asserts his desire, of taking up the life of a Cynic,[28] that is to say, of dedicating himself wholly to philosophy, and to this extreme, militant form of philosophy that is Cynicism, which involves setting out and going from town to town in the philosopher's garb, stopping people, holding discourses, conducting diatribes, teaching, shaking the philosophical inertia of the public, and so on. It is with regard to this desire of one of his students that Epictetus paints the famous portrait of the Cynical life in which he gives a very positive picture of this life and, at the same time, makes clear all its difficulties and its necessary asceticism.

However, there are other passages that quite clearly refer to this training of the future professional philosopher. To that extent, the school of Epictetus appears as a sort of *École Normale* for philosophers, where it is explained to them how they must act. A passage in discourse 26 in book II is very interesting. It is quite a short chapter divided into two parts in which there is the slightly modified reformulation of the old Socratic thesis, to which Epictetus so often alludes, that when one does wrong it is because one has made a mistake, a mistake of reasoning, an intellectual mistake.[29] He says that when one does wrong, in reality there is a *makhē*: a battle, a conflict in the person who commits the sin.[30] The conflict consists in the fact that, on the one hand, the person who does wrong is seeking something useful like everyone else. But he does not see that what he does is far from being useful and is in fact harmful. For example, the thief is just like everyone else: he pursues his interest. He does not see that stealing is harmful. So, Epictetus says—in an expression that I think is interesting and should be emphasized—when someone makes a mistake like this it is because he believes something that is not true and the *pikra anagkē*, the bitter necessity of renouncing what he believes to be true, must be made clear to him.[31] How can one make this bitter necessity apparent, or rather how can one impose it on the person who makes this mistake and has this illusion? Well, he must be shown that in actual fact he is doing what he does not wish and is not doing what he wishes. He is doing what he does not wish, that is to say he is doing something harmful. And he is not doing what he wishes, that is to say he is not advancing his interest as he thinks he is. According to Epictetus, someone who can show this to the person he is guiding and who can get him to understand the nature of this *makhē*, this struggle between doing what one doesn't wish and failing to do what one does, is *deinos en logō* (really strong and skillful in the art of discourse). He is *protreptikos* and *elegktikos*. These are two strictly technical terms. *Protreptikos*: this is someone who has the ability to give a protreptic education, that is to say, an education that can turn the mind in a good direction. *Elegtikos*, on the other hand, is someone good in the art of discussion, in the intellectual debate that allows truth to be freed from error, error to be refuted and a true proposition put in its place.[32] The individual who can do this and who therefore has the two typical qualities of the teacher—or, more precisely, the two major qualities of the philosopher: to refute the other person and turn his mind—will succeed in transforming the attitude of the person who errs in this way. For, he says, the mind is like a balance and inclines in one direction or the other. Whether one likes it or not, it yields to the truth it is led to recognize. And when one knows how to [intervene] in the struggle (*makhē*) taking place in the other's mind, when, with a sufficient art of discourse, one can perform this action, which consists in refuting the truth in which he believes and turning his mind in the right direction, then one is truly a philosopher: one will succeed in guiding the other person properly. On the other hand, if one does not succeed, one should not blame the person one is guiding; the person at fault is oneself. One must accuse oneself and not the person one has failed to persuade.[33] We have here, if you like, a fine little instructive example of teaching addressed to those who will have to teach in turn, or rather to perform spiritual direction. So, these are the first category of students: those who are training.

Second are those who are there in order to become philosophers. Then, of course, there are those passing through, and whose roles in the different scenes evoked by the *Discourses* are quite interesting to observe.

For example, in discourse 11 of book I, there is a man in Epictetus's audience who has some official responsibility and so seems to be a notable of the town or surrounding area. He has family problems; his daughter is ill. Epictetus explains to him the value and meaning of family relationships. At the same time, he explains that we must not be attached to things we cannot control or master but must attend to our representation of things, for this is what we can really control and master and what we can use (*khrēstai*).[34] The discourse ends with this important note: To be able to examine your representations in this way, you must become *skholastikos* (that is to say, you must go through the school).[35] This clearly shows that Epictetus suggests a period of training and philosophical formation at school, even to a man already established in life with responsibilities and a family. There is also discourse 4 of book II, in which we see a *philologos*—and here all the representations of those on the side of rhetoric are important in these discourses—who is an adulterer who argues that, by nature, women should be common property and so his action was not really that of an adulterer. Unlike the previous man—who felt an attachment to his sick daughter and who wondered about the nature and effects of this and who thus had a right to become *skholastikos*—the adulterous *philologos* is instead rejected and is forbidden to come to the school.[36] There are also characters who come because they have lawsuits that they put before Epictetus. In some cases Epictetus transforms the request for utilitarian consultation by shifting the question and saying: No, I do not have to respond to this, I am not like a cobbler who mends shoes. If you wish to consult me, you must question me about things within my competence, that is to say, things concerning life, things concerning the choices of existence, and things concerning representations. You find this in discourse 9 of book III.[37] There are also criticisms, specifically philosophical ones in this case, as for example when, in discourse 7 of book III, you see a town inspector, a sort of tax attorney, who is an Epicurean whom Epictetus questions on social duties, which Epicureans were supposed to reject but, like this individual, continue to practice.[38] In this contradiction Epictetus sets out a criticism of Epicureanism in general. So you see that in this school form that is very clearly maintained around Epictetus, there is actually a whole series of different forms of guidance, of expressions of the art of guidance, and quite diverse modalities of guidance.

Opposite this more or less Hellenic or school form, of which Epictetus no doubt gives the most developed example, there is what I will call the Roman form. The Roman form is that of the private counselor. I say it is Roman inasmuch as clearly it does not derive in any way from the structure of the school, but fits into fairly typical Roman client relationships, that is to say, a sort of semi-contractual dependence involving a dissymmetrical exchange of services between two individuals whose social status is always unequal. To that extent we can say that the private counselor represents a method that is almost the reverse of the school. In the school there is the philosopher, and one comes to him and appeals to him. In the system of the private counselor, rather, there is the great aristocratic family with the head of the family, the grand political leader, who takes in and houses a philosopher who serves him as counselor. There are dozens of examples of this in Republican and Imperial Rome. I spoke earlier of Philodemus, the Epicurean who played an important role with Lucius Piso.[39] There is Athenodorus, who performed the function of a sort of cultural chaplain for Augustus.[40] There is Demetrius the Cynic[41] who, a bit later, played a politically important role with Thrasea Paetus and then Helvidius Priscus,[42] and to whom we will have to return. Demetrius, for example, accompanied Thrasea Paetus for an entire period of his life, and when Thrasea Paetus had to kill himself, like many people of this epoch he naturally staged his suicide in a very solemn manner. He called his entourage around him, his family, etcetera. Then, bit by bit, he dismissed everyone. The last to remain with him, when he was closest to death, the only one who kept watch beside him, was precisely Demetrius. When the poison took effect and he began to lose consciousness, he turned his eyes towards Demetrius, who was therefore the last person he saw. Of course, the final words exchanged between Thrasea Paetus and Demetrius concerned death, immortality, the survival of the soul, etcetera[43] (a reconstruction, as you can see, of the death of Socrates, but a death in which Thrasea Paetus was not surrounded by a crowd of disciples, but was accompanied solely by his counselor). As you can see, the role of counselor is not that of private tutor any more than it is entirely that of friendly confidante. He is, rather, what could be called a counselor of existence who gives his views on specific occasions. He is the person who guides and initiates someone who is both his patron, almost his employer, and his friend, but his superior friend. He initiates him into a particular form of life, because one is not a philosopher in general. One can only be a Stoic or an Epicurean or a Platonist or a Peripatetic, etcetera. The counselor is also a sort of cultural agent for a circle into which he introduces both theoretical knowledge and practical schemas of life, as well as political choices. In particular, at the start of the Empire, one of the major objects of discussion addressed by philosophers in their role as counselors concerned the big choices to be made between, for example, a monarchical type of despotism, an enlightened and moderate despotism, or the republican demand. They also addressed the problem of monarchical inheritance. So we find them everywhere, involved in political life and in the great debates, conflicts, assassinations, executions, and revolts that mark the middle of the first century, and we find them again, although in a more self-effacing role, when the crisis breaks out again at the beginning of the third century.[44] So, as this figure of the philosopher develops and his importance becomes more pronounced, so also we see that he increasingly loses his singular, irreducible function external to daily life, to everyday life and political life. We see his function, rather, become integrated within advice and opinion. The practice will be intertwined with the essential problems posed to individuals in such a way that as the profession of philosopher becomes more important, so it is deprofessionalized.* The more one needs a counselor for oneself, the more one needs to have recourse to the Other in this practice of the self, then the more philosophy needs to assert itself, the more the philosopher's specifically philosophical function becomes increasingly blurred as well, and the more the philosopher appears as a counselor of existence who—with regard to everything and

---

*In the manuscript, after noting that the forms he describes are never pure, Foucault cites two other examples of relationships: Demonax and Apollonius of Tyana; Musonius Rufus and Rubellius Plautus.

nothing; with regard to a particular life, to family conduct, and to political conduct as well—does not provide general models of the kind that Plato or Aristotle were able to propose, for example, but advice, counsels of prudence and detailed recommendations. They become genuinely integrated in the daily mode of being. And this leads us to something I wanted to talk about earlier: the practice of spiritual direction as a form of social relationship between any individuals whatever outside of the professional field of philosophers. Good, about five minutes to rest, and we will start again in a moment.

1. On the primary nature of vice, see Seneca's letters to Lucilius, *Letters*, L.7, XC.44 and LXXV.16.
2. There is no fragment 23 of Musonius, but everything suggests that Foucault is referring here to fragment II.3. Despite that, Musonius's argument is not exactly as Foucault presents it. Musonius is concerned rather with establishing the universality of natural dispositions to virtue. This is established through comparison with the "other arts" (*allas tekhnas*): in the latter case error is only blameworthy in the case of the specialist, whereas moral perfection is not only a requirement for the philosopher but for everyone: "Now in the care of the sick the only person we demand to be free from error is the doctor, and in playing the lyre we only ask this of the musician, and in handling the rudder we only ask this of the pilot: but in the art of life (*en de tō biō*) it is not just the philosopher we demand to be free from error, although he alone would seem to take care of virtue (*epimeleisthai arestēs*), but we demand it of everyone equally." Fragment II in A.-J. Festugière, *Deux prédicateurs dans l'Antiquité, Télès et Musonius* (Paris: Vrin, 1978), p. 54. To establish the natural disposition to virtue Musonius appeals, then, less to the need for a master of virtue than takes as an example the claim to be able to do without a master: "For why, in the name of the gods, when it is a question of letters, music or the art wrestling, no one, if he has not learned (*mē mathōn*), says or claims he possesses these arts (*ekhein tas tekhnas*) if he cannot name a master (*didaskalon*) at the school where he learned them, but when it is a question of virtue everyone professes that he possesses it?" Ibid., p. 55. Finally, we should note that this theme of the innate character of moral notions, but the acquired nature of technical skills, is found in Epictetus (see, for example, *Discourses*, II.xi.1-6).
3. Seneca, *Letters*, LII.
4. "How, Lucilius, should we designate this impulse which, if we incline in one direction, drags us in another and pushes us in the direction from which we wish to flee? What is this enemy of our soul, which prevents us from ever willing once and for all? We drift between different plans; we do not will with a free, absolute (*absolute*) will, always firm. 'It is madness (*stultitia*),' you answer, 'for which nothing is constant and nothing satisfies for long.' But how, when will we tear ourselves free from its grip? No one is strong enough by himself to rise above the waves (*nemo per se satis valet ut emergat*). He needs someone to give him a hand (*oportet manum aliquis porrigat*), someone to pull him to the bank (*aliquis educat*)." *Letters*, LII.1-2.
5. See the lecture of 20 January, first hour, note 54 on this author (starting with Posidonius, the irrational functions of *hēgemonikon* are presented as being irreducible to the rational functions).
6. Seneca, *On Tranquility of Mind*, I.1-17 (Serenus's description to Seneca of his condition).
7. The description is found in II.6-15.
8. Here, rather than describing the condition of *stultitia* on the basis of *De Tranquillitate* alone, Foucault makes a kind of synthesis of the major analyses of *stultitia* in all of Seneca's work. On this theme, apart from the two texts cited by Foucault, see *Letters*, I.3 (on wasting time); IX.22 (on the erosion of the self); XIII.16 (on the frittering away of a life constantly starting anew); and XXXVII.4 (on permeability to the passions).
9. Foucault analyzes the term *discriminatio* in the lecture of 26 March devoted to Cassian (metaphors of the miller, the centurion and the money changer): it designates the sorting of representations after testing them, within the framework of the examination of conscience (see the lecture of 24 February, first hour, for a presentation of these techniques).
10. See the analysis of letter XXXII, lecture of 20 January, second hour.
11. In Chapter III there is this quotation from Athenodorus: "An old man burdened with years will often have no proof that he has lived other than his age!" Seneca, *On Tranquility of Mind*, III.8. But Foucault also refers here to a passage from chapter II: "Add those who, tossing and turning like people who cannot get to sleep, try every position one after another until finding rest through tiredness: after having changed the basis of their life a hundred

times, they end up in the position in which old age, rather than the dislike of change, takes hold of them." Ibid., II.6.
12. See above, note 4, quotation from Seneca.
13. Seneca, *Letters*, LII.2.
14. No doubt Foucault wishes to evoke here the hierarchical organization of Epicurean schools more than the example of Epicurus himself (see on this point, mentioned below, the debate between De Witt and Gigante on the Philodemus fragments).
15. Fragment XIV: "*hēgemon tois anthrōpois esti tōn kata phusin anthrōpō prosēkontōn.*" C. Musonius Rufus, *Reliquiae* (O. Hense editor) p. 71.
16. On the figure of the philosopher-counselor in Dio Chrysostom of Prusa, see discourse 22: "On peace and war," *Discourses*, vol. II, translations by J. W. Cohoon, pp. 296-98, as well as discourse 67, "On the philosopher," ibid., vol. V, pp.162-73, and discourse 49, ibid., vol. IV, pp. 294-308.
17. See the old but crucial clarifications of H. von Arnim, *Leben und Werke des Dio von Prusa. Mit einer Einleitung. Sophistik Rhetorik, Philosophie in ihrem Kampf um die Jugendbildung* (Berlin: 1898). The rhetoric/philosophy relationship problematized in the Roman epoch is the subject of a thesis by A. Michel, *Rhétorique et Philosophie chez Cicéron* (Paris: PUF, 1960). See also P. Hadot, "Philosophie, dialectique et rhetorique dans l'Antiquité," *Studia philosophica* 39 (1980), pp. 139-66. For an accurate and general presentation of rhetoric, see F. Desbordes, *La Rhétorique antique* (Paris: Hachette Supérieur, 1996).
18. On the communal life of the Pythagoreans, see the descriptions of Iamblichus, *Life of Pythagoras*, §71-110; Diogenes Laertius, *Lives of Eminent Philosophers*, VIII.10; and the lecture of 13 January, first hour (especially note 7, on the Pythagorean sects).
19. The articles are reprinted in M. W. De Witt, *Epicurus and his Philosophy* (Minneapolis: University of Minnesota Press, 1954, 1973,) 2nd ed.
20. N. W. De Witt, "Organisation and procedure in Epicurean groups," *Classical Philology* 31 (1936), p. 205 sq., reprinted in *Epicurus and his Philosophy*.
21. *Association Guillaume Budé, Actes du VIII[e] congrès, Paris, 5-10 avril 1968* (Paris: Les Belles Lettres, 1970). See Gigante's criticism of De Witt's hierarchy, *La Bibliothèque de Philodeme*, pp. 215-17.
22. Philodemus of Gadara was a Greek from the Near East who first went to Athens with the Epicurean Zeno of Sidon, and then to Rome in the seventies B.C., where he became the friend, confidante, and spiritual guide of L. Calpurnius Piso Caesonius, father-in-law of Caesar and consul in 58 B.C. (on this relationship, see Gigante, *La Bibliothèque de Philodème*, ch. V), before finally establishing himself at Herculaneum in what is now called the Villa of the Papyri, the property of Lucius Piso, whose library contained many important Epicurean texts (see ibid., ch. II).
23. On the need for a guide (called, rather, *kathēgētēs*) and the principle of friendship and speaking freely (*franc-parler*) between the guide and the person he guides, see Foucault's analyses of the *Peri parrhēsias* of Philodemus in the lecture of 10 March, first hour.
24. "Some, Epicurus says, have arrived at the truth without the help of any one; they have beaten their own path. He especially honors these because the impulse has come from themselves and they are the product of their own efforts. Others, he says, need help; they will not advance unless someone goes on ahead, but they are able to follow." *Letters*, LII.3.
25. Epictetus was born in Phrygia around 50 A.D. He was the slave of Epaphroditus (a freedman of Nero, a brutal owner who often appears in the *Discourses*) and an old disciple of Musonius Rufus. When freed, Epictetus opened a school of philosophy in Rome before suffering from the emperor Domitian's banishment of philosophers from Italy at the beginning of the eighties. He then settled in the Greek town of Nicopolis, where he established a new school. He remained there until his death (around 120-130 A.D.), in spite of the new favors of Hadrian.
26. "What's more, when we send a young man from the school for some business (*epi tinas praxeis*), why do we fear that he will behave badly?" Epictetus, *Discourses*, II.viii.15.
27. "One day a Roman came with his son and was listening to one of his lessons: 'Such, said Epictetus, is the style of my teaching.' " Ibid., II.xiv.1.

28. "One of his disciples (*gnōrimōn*), who seemed inclined towards the profession of a Cynic, asked him what sort of man should the Cynic be, and how should one conceive of this profession." *Discourses*, III.xxii.1.
29. See, for example, *Discourses*, I.xxviii.4-9 and II.xxii.36: "he will be tolerant, gentle, kindly, forgiving, as towards someone ignorant, someone who is in error."
30. "Every fault entails a contradiction (*makhēn periekhei*)." *Discourses*, II.xxvi.1.
31. "... a bitter necessity (*pikra anagkē*) compels a man to renounce the false when he perceives that it is false; but as long as it is not apparent, he holds onto it as the truth." Ibid., II.xxvi.3.
32. "The person who can show to each man the contradiction which is the cause of his fault is skilled in reasoning (*deinos en logō*) and knows both how to refute (*protreptikos*) and to convince (*elegtikos*)." Ibid., II.xxvi.4.
33. "[Socrates] knew what moves a rational soul: like a balance it will incline whether or not one wishes it to. Show the governing part of the soul the contradiction and it will relinquish. But if you do not point it out, blame yourself rather than the man you fail to convince." Ibid., II.xxvi.7.
34. "When, therefore, he resumed, you will have really understood this, you will then have nothing more at heart and this will be your sole concern, learning the criterion of what is according to nature, then making use of it (*proskhrōmenos*) to judge each particular case." *Discourses*, I.xi.14-15.
35. "You see, then, that you should become a school student (*skholastikon se dei genesthai*) and become that animal at which everyone laughs, if you wish to undertake the examination of your own opinions." Ibid., I.xi.39.
36. "What would you have us do with you? There is no place where we can put you." *Discourses*, II.iv.7.
37. "Someone who was going to Rome for a lawsuit... came to Epictetus... Help me in this affair.—I have no rule to give you in this matter. And if this was your reason for coming to me, then you have not come as to a philosopher, but as to someone who sells vegetables, as to a cobbler.—So with regard to what do philosophers have rules?—For this: whatever may happen, to maintain and direct the governing part of our soul in accordance with nature." *Discourses*, III.ix.1-11.
38. "You live in an imperial State: you must hold office, judging according to justice... Seek principles in accordance with these ways of acting." Ibid., III.vii.20-22.
39. Lecture of 10 March, first hour.
40. Athenodorus of Tarsus (around 85-30 B.C., usually called "son of Sandon" to distinguish him from another Athenodorus of Tarsus who was in charge of the library at Pergamum), was a Peripatetic philosopher (it is thought that he followed the lessons of Posidonius at Rhodes) and private tutor to Octavian (before the latter became Augustus). See P. Grimal, "Auguste et Athénodore," *Revue des études anciennes*, 47, 1945, pp. 261-73; 48, 1946, pp. 62-79 (reprinted in *Rome, la litérature et l'histoire* [Rome: École française de Rome, Palais Farnèse, 1986], pp. 1147-76). See the more developed summary of this same example in the second hour of the lecture.
41. Demetrius of Corinth, friend of Seneca and Thrasea Paetus, was once famous for his discourses against the monarchy (Caligula tried, unsuccessfully, to win him over with money; see Seneca's account in *On Benefits*, VII.11). After Thrasea's death he was exiled in Greece but returned under Vespasian. Along with others he was banished from Rome by the latter around 71 A.D. (see the note by M. Billerbeck in *Dictionnaire des philosophes antiques*, vol. I, pp. 622-23).
42. Thrasea Paetus was from Padua. He was in the Senate from 56 to 63, where he had considerable influence. He brought the republican opposition together around him under the spiritual banner of Stoicism (he even wrote a life of Cato the Younger). In 66, under Nero, he was obliged to kill himself. His son-in-law, Helvidius Priscus, was legate of the legion in 51 and tribune of the plebs in 56. His father-in-law's condemnation in 66 forced him to flee Rome. Recalled from exile under Galba, he again took up a rebellious attitude and praised the merits of the Republic. Then, exiled by Vespasian in 74, he was condemned to death and

executed despite the imperial counterorder, which arrived too late. On these unfortunate oppositionists, see Dion Cassius, *Histoire romaine*, translations by E. Gros (Paris: Didot frères, 1867) book 66, ch. 12 and 13, and Book 67, ch. 13; English translation by E. Cary, Dio Cassius, *Dio's Roman History*, 9 vols. (Cambridge, Mass. and London: Loeb Classical Library, 1969). See also Tacitus, *Annals*, book XVI. It will not be forgotten that Epictetus presents these two great figures as models of virtue and courage (*Discourses*, I.ii.19 and IV.i.123). See also *Le Souci de soi*, p. 68 (*The Care of the Self*, p. 52).

43. See the classic account in Tacitus, *Annals*, book XVI, ch. 34-35.
44. The relationships of philosophers to those holding power in Rome (between persecution and flattery) and their ideological constructions in the area of political philosophy (between justification and reticence) have for a long time been the subject matter of many publications, especially with regard to Stoicism, under whose banner an outright republican and senatorial opposition was constituted. See, for example, I. Hadot, "Tradition stoïciennne et idées politiques au temps des Gracques," *Revue des etudes latines* 48 (1970), pp. 133-79; J. Gagé, "La propaganda sérapiste et la lutte des empereurs flaviens avec avec les philosophes (Stoïciennes et Cyniques)," *Revue philosophique* 149 (1959-1), pp. 73-100; L. Jerphagnon, *Vivre et Philosopher sous les Césars* (Toulouse: Privat, 1980); J.-M. André, *La Philosophie à Rome* (Paris: PUF, 1977); A. Michel, *La Philosophie politique à Rome, d'Auguste à Marc Aurèle* (Paris: Armand Colin, 1969); and especially, R. MacMullen, *Enemies of the Roman Order* (Cambridge, Mass.: Harvard University Press, 1966).

# eight

## 27 JANUARY 1982

### Second hour

[ *The professional philosopher of the first and second centuries and his political choices. ∼ Euphrates in Pliny's* Letters: *an anti-Cynic. ∼ Philosophy as social practice outside the school: the example of Seneca. ∼ The correspondence between Fronto and Marcus Aurelius: systematization of dietetics, economics, and erotics in the guidance of existence. ∼ Examination of conscience.* ]

I OWE YOU AN apology. Somewhat pretentiously and fancifully, I imagined that I would not fall behind if I allowed two hours to say what I wanted to say, since I would have enough time. However, falling behind must be a way of life for me: Whatever I do I fail to keep to the timetable I have set. Never mind. With reference to a number of texts I want to speak a little about [the way in which] the practice of the self was a requirement, a rule, and a way of going about things which had very privileged relationships with philosophy, philosophers, and the philosophical institution itself. Obviously, it was philosophers who disseminated the rule [of this practice of the self], who spread its notions and methods and proposed models. In most cases, they are the source of the texts that were published and circulated and served more or less as manuals for the practice of the self. There is absolutely no question of denying this. But I think there is also something else to be stressed. As this practice of the self is disseminated, so the figure of the professional philosopher—who, as you well know, since Socrates at least, had always been somewhat mistrusted and had provoked quite a few negative reactions—becomes increasingly ambiguous. Naturally, he is criticized by the rhetoricians, and—this becomes clearer with the development of what are called the second Sophists[1] in the second century A.D.—he is also mistrusted for political reasons. In the first place this is, of course, because of his choices in favor of this or that political movement. For example, there was a neorepublican movement at the beginning of the Empire in which the Stoics, and no doubt the Cynics also, played an important part.[2] So, there was resistance due to this. But, more generally, the very existence of professional philosophers—preaching, questioning, and insisting that one care for the self—raised a number of political problems on which very interesting discussions took place. In particular, it seems that in the entourage of Augustus, right at the start of the Empire, the problem [arose] as to whether or not philosophy, putting itself forward as an art of oneself and encouraging people to care for themselves, was useful. Jean-Marie André, who has published two very interesting studies on *otium* and the character of Maecenas,[3] [has advanced a number] of hypotheses. According to him, it seems there were different tendencies around Augustus, with changes of attitude on the part of different people and of Augustus himself. It seems that Athenodorus, for example, represented a fairly distinct tendency of depoliticization: Only concern yourself with politics if you really must, if you want to, if circumstances demand it, but withdraw from politics as quickly as possible. It seems that Augustus was favorable towards this depoliticization, at a particular moment at least. On the other hand, Maecenas and the Epicureans around him represented a tendency that sought a balance between political activity around and for the Prince, and the need for a life of cultivated free time. The idea of a Principate,[4] in which most power would be in the hands of the Prince, in which there would not be the kind of political struggles found in the Republic and everything would be in good order, but in which one would have to concern oneself with the Empire however, would have represented to these people—Maecenas and the Epicureans, who were still mistrustful of political activity—the most adequate formula: One can concern oneself with the things of the state, of the Empire, with political matters and affairs within this framework in which tranquility is ensured by the political order, by the Principate, and then, on the side, one can still have enough free time in one's life to care for oneself. In short, there are a number of interesting discussions around the professional activity of philosophers. I will come back to the problem "activity of oneself/political activity" later and deal with it in greater detail.[5] With regard to the hostility towards or mistrust of philosophers, I would like to refer to just one text. I intended to cite several. I could have cited—but I already referred to them last week—the satirical texts of Lucian, which caricature philosophers as greedy individuals demanding vast sums of money by promising happiness, selling ways of life on the market, and who, claiming to be perfect, having arrived at the pinnacle of philosophy, are at the same time people who practice usury, quarrel with their opponents, lose their temper, etcetera, and have none of the virtues they claim to possess.[6] Okay, I will skip all these texts.

I would like to draw your attention to another text that seems to me to be quite interesting and which is well known, but on whose interpretation I think we should dwell for a moment. It is the famous passage devoted to Euphrates[7] in the tenth letter in the first book of Pliny's *Letters*.[8] Euphrates was an important Stoic philosopher who appears in several texts. In Philostratus's *Life of Apollonius of Tyana* there is a very strange and interesting comparison between Apollonius and Euphrates[9]—and we may come back to the question of the Prince and the philosopher as the Prince's adviser. Anyway, in Pliny's letter about this important character, this important philosopher Euphrates, we read that Euphrates was living in Syria and Pliny got to know him when "*adulescentulus militarem*," that is to say, when as a young man he was not doing his military service exactly, but holding a military office. He is young then, but even so he is not a child or an adolescent of school age. In this text we see that Pliny had seen a lot of him and that their association had been close. "*Penitus et domi inspexi.*" I have seen him, I have been able to observe and examine him *penitus* (in depth) *et domi* (at home). So, if he did not share his life, he had at least a continuous relationship with him, which led them to share a number of moments and periods of life. Third, it is very clear that they had an intense affective relationship, since it is said that: "*Amari ab eo laboravi, etsi non erat laborandum.*"[10] That is to say: I have worked to be loved by him, though that was not difficult. It is interesting that he does not mention the fact that he loved him. I think this emerges from the whole of the text and from his very intense eulogy [of him]. He says that he worked to be loved by him, and this is quite interesting, because this seems to me a typically Roman notion that we can tie up with a number of things. In particular, in Seneca's *De Beneficiis* it is said that one must not only provide services in a friendship, but that it is quite a job, quite a labor to get oneself loved by the person whose friendship one desires. This work proceeds according to a number of phases and by applying a number of rules sanctioned by the relative positions occupied by different individuals in the circle of friends of the person whose friendship one desires.[11] In other words, friendship is not exactly a one-to-one relationship; it is not immediate communication between two individuals, as in the Epicurean formula. We are dealing here with a social structure of friendship revolving around an individual, but in which there are several [others] around him who have a place that changes according to the elaboration, the effort made by both of them. This labor should probably be seen here as Pliny's application to lessons and the zeal with which he accepted the teaching, model, examples, and recommendations of Euphrates. Very probably it also involves a number of services provided by each in a form quite close to Roman friendship. In short, Pliny advanced in this friendship that, as you see, does not at all have the form of a "loving friendship" (to use contemporary terms, which do not entirely coincide with the experience of the period). It has nothing to do with—at any rate, it is something very different from—the love, the *erōs*, that may have existed between Socrates and his disciples, or the *erōs* found in Epicurean friendship. The text is also interesting with regard to the character Euphrates. His description is familiar, and you could even say banal, cloying in its blandness, yet its elements are interesting when we examine it [closely].[12] Euphrates is said to have great physical bearing—he has the beard, the famous philosopher's beard—and his clothes are neat and tidy. He is also said to speak ornately, pleasantly, and convincingly, and what's more he is so convincing that after being convinced by him one regrets it, because one would like to hear him again so as to be convinced anew. He is said to recall Plato in the breadth of his views, to practice the virtues he preaches, and to receive one with great generosity. In particular, he does not chastise those who have done wrong or who are not in the desirable moral condition. He does not chastise these individuals or scold them. Rather, he is extremely indulgent with them, with a great *liberalitas*. Finally, his teaching is characterized by the fact that he constantly tells his disciples that dispensing justice and administering town affairs—in short, roughly speaking, doing one's job as either a local notable or a representative of Roman and imperial authority—is doing the work of the philosopher.[13] So, it seems to me that what we can retain beneath the somewhat cloying blandness of this portrait is, in a way, a very pronounced and emphatic glorification. (We should remember, of course, that Pliny is not a philosopher and has a rather vague, a very vague smattering of Stoic philosophy, which besides he no doubt picked up from Euphrates.) Pliny, who is not a philosopher, glorifies this character Euphrates. He decks him out with every virtue and makes him into a sort of exceptional character with whom one can establish very intense affective bonds; at any rate, without knowing whether or not it was involved, there is no mention of money in this affair. Anyway, through him, through this character, one can have the best possible relationship with philosophy. When [we look at] the character traits and descriptive features of this glorification, we realize that the traditional typical features of the professional philosopher are systematically excluded. Having a well-combed beard and neat and tidy clothes obviously runs counter to, or is opposed to, those professional philosophers wandering the streets with an unkempt beard and rather disgusting clothes, that is to say, to the figure of the Cynic, who is both the extreme point and, in the eyes of the people, the negative model of philosophy. When Pliny explains how Euphrates speaks well, how ornate his language is, how he is so convincing that after being convinced one would like to continue listening to him although one no longer needs convincing, what is he doing but showing that Euphrates is not the philosopher of coarse, rough language, limited to the sole objective of convincing his auditor and changing his soul, but is at the same time something of a rhetor who has managed to integrate the pleasures [...] of rhetorical discourse [...] within philosophical practice? This, then, erases the famous division between rhetor and philosopher, which was one of the most typical features of the philosopher's professionalization. Third, and finally, by not being harsh with those who come to him, by welcoming them generously and liberally without reprimanding them, he does not adopt the rather aggressive role of someone like Epictetus, or *a fortiori* of the Cynics, whose purpose was to throw the individual off-balance, as it were, to disturb him in his mode of life and force him to adopt a different mode of life by pushing and pulling him. Finally, and above all, to say that dispensing justice and administering town affairs is to practice philosophy is again to obliterate anything specific about the philosophical life and thus to dispense with philosophy's withdrawal from political life. Euphrates is precisely someone who does not draw a line between philosophical practice and political life. So, in my view, the praise of philosophy in this famous text of Pliny's about Euphrates is not a sort of homage rendered by Pliny to the old teacher of his youth, displaying the fascination that he, like any young Roman noble, would have had for a prestigious philosopher of the Middle East. That is not what it is. This eulogy has to be grasped in all its elements and with all the notes it strikes. It is a valuation that is produced by repatriating philosophy, so to speak, in a way of being, a mode of conduct, a set of values, and also a set of techniques, which are not those of traditional philosophy but, rather, of a cultural system in which the old values of Roman liberality, the practices of rhetoric and political responsibilities etcetera, are apparent. Basically, Pliny only eulogizes Euphrates by deprofessionalizing him in comparison with the traditional portrait of the philosopher who practices nothing but philosophy. He displays him as a sort of great lord of socialized wisdom.

I think this text opens up a track, which I do not intend to follow in detail, but that seems to me [to involve] one of the most typical features of the period with which we are concerned, the first and second centuries: the practice of the self became a social practice outside the institutions, groups, and individuals who, in the name of philosophy, called for the absolute moral authority of the practice of the self. It began to develop among individuals who were not strictly speaking professionals. There was a tendency to practice, disseminate, and develop the practice of the self outside the philosophical institution, and even outside the philosophical profession, and to turn it into a mode of relationship between individuals by making it a sort of principle of the individual's supervision by others, of the formation, development, and establishment for the individual of a relationship to himself which finds its fulcrum, its mediating element, in another person who is not necessarily a professional philosopher, although having studied some philosophy and having some philosophical notions is, of course, indispensable. In other words, what I think is at stake here is the problem of the figure and function of the master. In the time of the Sophists, of Socrates and Plato, the master's specificity was based either on his competence and Sophistical know-how, or, with Socrates, on his vocation as *theios anēr* (divine and inspired man), or, as in Plato's case, on the fact that he had already achieved wisdom. Well, this kind of master is not exactly in the process of disappearing, but of being outflanked, encircled, and challenged by a practice of the self that is a social practice at the same time. The practice of the self links up with social practice or, if you like, the formation of a relationship of the self to the self quite clearly connects up with the relationships of the self to the Other.

Seneca's series of interlocutors can be taken as an example of this. Seneca is a very interesting character from this point of view: we can say that he is a professional philosopher, at least in the obviously very broad sense of the word "professional" at this time. He began his career by writing philosophical treatises, especially when he was in exile. And it was as a philosopher that he became Nero's private tutor, or anyway counselor, when recalled from exile in Sardinia. Even so, we cannot compare him to a philosophy teacher in the sense that Epictetus and also Euphrates were teachers. He had had a whole political and administrative career. When we see the kind of people to whom he addresses himself, gives advice, and with whom he plays the role of spiritual teacher or director, we see that [they are] always people with whom he had other relationships elsewhere. These may be family relationships, in the case of his mother, Helvia, to whom he writes a consolation when he is sent into exile. When he sends a consolation to Polybius, the latter is for him a sort of ambiguous and distant protector from whom he solicits friendship and protection in order to be repatriated from exile.[14] Serenus,[15] to whom he sends a series of treatises—*De Tranquillitate*, possibly *De Otio*, and a third[16]—was a distant relative who came from Spain to pursue his career at the court and was becoming Nero's confidante. Seneca addresses Serenus, or listens to his questions and gives him advice, on a semi-kinship and semi-clientage basis. Lucilius, who is a bit younger than him but who already has high administrative functions, is a sort of friend, perhaps a client or an old protégé, anyway someone who is quite close to him and with whom his relationships were quite different from the professional relationship of spiritual guidance.[17] The same thing could be shown in the case of Plutarch who, whenever he intervenes to direct and advise someone, basically only modulates a social, statutory, or political relationship.[18] Plutarch plugs this work of spiritual guidance into these relationships, grafts it onto them. So, Seneca and Plutarch do not step in to guide others as more or less professional philosophers. They do so insofar as their social relationships with this or that person (friendship, clientage, protection, etcetera) involve soul service as a dimension—and at the same time as a duty, an obligation—and a possible basis for interventions, for counsel, which will enable the other to make his own way properly. And this is where I come to a final text, which I would like to examine a bit more closely. It seems to me to be interesting and very significant in the history of the practice of the self, because most of the texts we have concerning the practice of the self are solely from those doing the guiding and giving advice. Consequently, inasmuch as they are giving advice and are therefore prescriptive texts, we can always think, and have good grounds for thinking, that they were vain, empty recommendations which were not really taken up in people's behavior and experience; that it was a sort of code without real content and application; and that at bottom it was a way of developing philosophical thought into an everyday moral rule without it much affecting people's everyday life. In Seneca, at the start of *De Tranquillitate*, we do have a confession from Serenus, who asks Seneca for advice and reveals to him the state of his soul.[19] We may think that this is the expression of an experience someone has of himself and of the way in which, as a result, he thinks about himself through the eyes of a possible guide and in terms of possible guidance. Even so this text appears in Seneca's treatise. Even if Serenus really did write it, and even if it was not, as is likely, largely rewritten by Seneca, we can say that it forms part of the same treatise, the *De Tranquillitate*. It is part of Seneca's game, and only with some difficulty, and indirectly, can it be taken as evidence of what takes place on the side of the person being guided.

Even so, we do have some documents that show the other side, Fronto's correspondence with Marcus Aurelius for example[20] [...].* This correspondence is virtually inaccessible in France [...] and it is fairly easy to see why it has not been published. It's rather strange all the same. Fortunately, if you are interested in this text there is an English edition of the Fronto-Marcus Aurelius correspondence, in the Loeb Classical Library, which should be read.[21] And you will see why. Fronto is (and we should keep this in mind) Marcus Aurelius's teacher.[22] But he is not the philosophy teacher. He is a teacher of rhetoric. Fronto was a rhetor, and in the first chapter of the *Meditations* Marcus Aurelius refers to different people to whom he is indebted for this or that, who have been in some way models for his life and who have contributed components from which he has composed his behavior and his principles of conduct. And then there is a passage, quite brief moreover, on Fronto. There is a series of portraits, which are very impressive and fine. There is the famous portrait of Antoninus, which is both superb and also a little theory, not so much of imperial power as of the imperial character.[23] There are, then, some lengthy, detailed expositions on the subject and then a quite short one, a simple reference to Fronto, in which he says: I am indebted to Fronto for understanding the extent to which the exercise of power involves hypocrisy and for having understood how much our aristocracy is "incapable of affection."[24] These two elements show Fronto to be a person of frankness, in contrast

---

*Only "and these documents definitely show [...] French edition of the translation, and which is Fronto's correspondence with Marcus Aurelius" is audible.

to hypocrisy, flattery, etcetera; this is the notion of *parrhēsia*, to which I will return. And then, on the other hand, there is affection, which is the basis on which Marcus Aurelius and Fronto develop their relationship. So I will quote what, in my view, is the most characteristic letter on what spiritual direction may have been from the point of view of the person guided. This is letter 6 in book IV from Marcus Aurelius to Fronto. He writes to him:[25] "We are well. I slept little due to being a bit feverish, which now seems to have subsided. So I spent the time, from eleven at night until five in the morning, reading some of Cato's *Agriculture* and also in writing: happily less than yesterday. After paying my respects to my father, I relieved my throat, I will not say by gargling—though the word *gargarisso* is, I believe, found in Novius and elsewhere—but by swallowing honey water as far as the gullet and ejecting it again. After easing my throat I went off to my father and attended him at a sacrifice. Then we went to luncheon. What do you think I ate? A little bread, though I saw others devouring oysters, beans, onions and fat sardines. We then worked on the grape harvest, building up a good sweat and shouting out loud.[26] ... After six o' clock we came home. I studied little and that to no purpose. Then I had a long chat with my little mother as she sat on the bed ...[27] While we were chatting in this way and disputing which of us two loved the one or other of you two the better [that is to say, I think, whether Marcus Aurelius loved Fronto more than his mother loved Gratia, Fronto's daughter; M.F.], the gong sounded, announcing that my father had gone to his bath. So we had supper after we had bathed in the oil-press room; I do not mean bathed in the oil-press room, but when we had bathed, had supper there, and enjoyed hearing the cheerful banter of the villagers. After coming back, before turning on my side to sleep, I go through my task (*meum pensum expliquo*) and give my dearest of masters an account of the day's doings (*diei rationem meo suavissimo magistro redo*). This master whom I would like, even at the cost of my health and physical well being, to desire and miss even more than I do. Good health, dear Fronto, you who are *meus amor mea voluptas* (my love, my delight). I love you."[28] That's it. So, on the one hand, with regard to this text we should remember, as I said, that Fronto is not a philosophy master. He is not a professional philosopher, but a rhetor, a *philologos*, as the little philological comment on the use of the word "gargled" recalls. This letter should not then be situated in a professional and technical relationship of spiritual direction. Actually it is based upon friendship, affection, and tenderness, which you see plays a major role. This role appears here in all its ambiguity, and it is difficult to decipher in the other letters moreover, in which there is constantly a question of love for Fronto, of their reciprocal love, of the fact that they miss each other when they are separated, that they send each other kisses on the neck, etcetera.[29] Let's remember that Marcus Aurelius must be between eighteen and twenty years old at this time, and Fronto a bit older. It is an "affective" relationship: once again, I think it would be completely out of place—I mean, wholly inappropriate historically—to ask whether or not this is a sexual relationship. It is a relationship of affection, of love, which thus involves a whole range of things. We should just note that these things are never expressed, spelled out, or analyzed within these repeated intense, affective affirmations of love: "my love, my delight." Now, if we look at how the letter is constructed against this background, not of a technical, philosophical relationship, but of a relationship of affection with a master, we see that it is quite simply a very meticulous account of a day, from the moment of waking to the moment of going to sleep. In short, it is an account of the self through an account of the day. What are the components of the day he describes in this way, what elements does Marcus Aurelius consider relevant for producing his account, for giving Fronto an account of his day? Very schematically, but without falsifying things, I think everything in the letter can be grouped according to three categories.

First are details of health, of regimen. This begins with feeling a bit feverish and medication. At several points in Seneca's letters there are these bits of information, where he says: Oh dear! I didn't sleep last night; I had a slight chill. Or: I woke up sick this morning, I had a bit of nausea, I was shivery, etcetera. This, then, is a traditional touch: noting his chills and the medication taken (he gargled, he took some honey water, etcetera). Generally these comments are about sleep. Note, for example, "turning on my side to sleep," which is an important medico-ethical precept of the time. Sleeping on your back exposes you to erotic visions; sleeping on your side promises a chaste sleep. There are notes about food: he only ate some bread while the others were eating... etcetera. There are notes on bathing and exercises. Sleeping, waking, food, bathing, exercises, and then of course medications: since Hippocrates, these are typical components of the regimen, of the medical or dietetic regimen.[30] He gives an account, then, of his medical regimen.

Second, he gives an account of his family and religious duties. He went to his father, he attended a sacrifice with him, and he spoke with his mother, etcetera. To these family duties are added, or we can add, agricultural activities. Marcus Aurelius is describing the farmer's life. It should be understood that the farmer's life is directly related to a number of models. He refers to one of these and the other is implicit. The one cited is Cato's *De Agricultura*.[31] Cato wrote a book on agriculture, that is to say a book on domestic economy identifying how, when the book was written, a Roman agricultural landowner had to behave in order to ensure his prosperity, ethical training and, at the same time, the greatest good of the city. Behind this model we should, of course, remember the model for Cato's text itself, that is to say Xenophon's *Œconomicus*, which described the life a country gentleman ought to lead in fifth and fourth century Attica.[32] These models are very important. Of course, as the adopted son of Antoninus, destined for the Empire, Marcus Aurelius had absolutely no need to lead such a life: the life of a country gentleman was not his normal life. However—and this is very clear from the end of the Republic and even more so under the Empire—agricultural life, the period of training in agricultural life, as it were, was not exactly a holiday, but a moment you had to set aside for yourself so as to have a sort of politico-ethical reference point for the rest of the time in your life. In this country life, in fact, we are closer to the basic, elementary needs of existence and to that archaic, ancient life of centuries past, which ought to be our model. In this life there is also the possibility of practicing a sort of cultivated *otium*. That is to say one [also] exercises physically: you see that he participates in the grape harvest, which enables him to really sweat and shout, exercises forming part of the regimen. He leads, then, this life of *otium*, which has physical elements and also leaves him enough time for reading and writing. So, the country period is, if you like, a sort of reactivation of Xenophon's and Cato's old model: a social, ethical, and political model which is now taken up as an exercise. It is a sort of retreat that you go on with others, but for yourself and to better train yourself, to advance in your work on yourself, to reach yourself. This aspect of economic life, in Xenophon's sense of the term, that is to say, the entire world of family relationships, the work of the head of the household who has to take care of his entourage, his family and friends, his goods and his servants etcetera, is reutilized but, once again, for the purpose of personal exercise.

The third component mentioned in the letter is, of course, those elements concerning love. In the conversation on love the question debated is rather odd, as you can see, since it is no longer the traditional question—"What is true love?"[33]—that, as you know, normally puts to work the usual four elements: Is it love for boys or love for women; is it love including sexual consummation or not? The problem of true love does not appear here. There is a rather strange sort of individual question comparing the intensity, value, and form of this love—whose nature, once again, it would be completely fanciful to want to discuss—between two men (Fronto and Marcus Aurelius) and between two women (Marcus Aurelius's mother and Gratia).

The body; the family circle and household; love. Dietetics, economics, and erotics. These are the three major domains in which the practice of the self is actualized in this period, with, as we see, constant cross-referencing from one to the other. It is out of care for the regimen, for the dietetic, that one practices the agricultural life and participates in the harvests, etcetera, that is to say, enters the economic. And it is within family relationships, that is to say, within the relationships that define the economic, that the question of love arises. The first point is the existence of these three domains, the link, the very strong and clear reference from one to the other, from the dietetic to the economic, from the economic to the erotic. Secondly, we should remember that we have already come across these three elements, if you recall, in a passage of the *Alcibiades*. You remember that at a certain moment Socrates had just arrived at the definition of the self that one had to be concerned about, what this self was. He demonstrated that this self for which one had to be concerned was the soul. Now, starting from this definition, he said: If we must take care of the soul, you can see that care of the self is not care of the body any more than it is care for one's goods or the lover's care, at least not as conceived by the lovers who pursue Alcibiades. That is to say, in Plato's text, in Socrates' contribution, care of the self is definitely distinguished from the care of the body, that is to say dietetics, the care for one's goods, that is to say economics, and the lover's care, that is to say erotics. Well, you see now, rather, that these three domains—dietetics, economics, erotics—are reintegrated, but as a reflecting surface, as the occasion, so to speak, for the self to test itself, train itself, and develop the practice of itself which is its rule of life and its objective. Dietetics, economics, and erotics appear as domains of application for the practice of the self.

This, it seems to me, is what we can extract from the letter's contents, but clearly we cannot end our commentary on this letter here without returning to those lines I quoted in which he says: "After coming back, before turning on my side to sleep, I go through my task (*meum pensum expliquo*) and give my dearest of masters an account of the day's doings (*diei rationem meo suavissimo magistro redo*)." What is this? Back at home, he is going to sleep, and before turning on his side, that is to say taking the position for sleep, he "goes through his task (*déroule sa tâche*)."* This is obviously the examination of conscience as described by Seneca. And these two texts, Seneca's *De Ira* and Marcus Aurelius's letter, are extraordinarily close to each other. Seneca, you remember, said: Every evening I extinguish the lamp, and when my wife has become silent, I withdraw into myself and take stock of my day (he uses exactly the same expression; he "gives an account").[34] In another text—sadly I couldn't find the reference last night, but it's not important—Seneca refers to the need from time to time to unroll the scroll (the *volumen*) of his life and of

---

*This part of Foucault's commentary depends on the French translation of the Latin *expliquo* as *déroule* (to unroll, unwind, uncoil, but also to go over or through something, to review something, etc.)—G.B.

time passed.³⁵ You see that what Marcus Aurelius does in this recalling is this going through (*déroulement*) the task, what one had to do and how one did it. He goes through (*déroule*) his task, he unrolls (*déroule*) the book of the day in which the things he had to do were written, a book that is probably the book of his memory and not a book in which he really wrote, although it could be that too, but anyway it is not of great importance. Whether it involves memory or reading, what is fundamental is the review of the day, a review that is obligatory at the end of the day before going to sleep and which enables one to draw up a balance sheet of the things one had to do and a comparison of how one did them with how one should have done them. One justifies the day. To whom does one justify it? Well, to the person who is "my dearest of masters." You see that this is the exact translation of the fundamental principle of the examination of conscience. In the end, what is this letter? The letter itself, written in the morning of the following day, is nothing other than what Marcus Aurelius had done the previous night when he had gone to bed before sleeping. He had unrolled the *volumen* of his day. He had summarized his day and gone through it (*l'a déroulée*). The previous evening he did this for himself, and the next morning he does it by writing to Fronto. So you see that we have here a quite interesting example of the way in which guidance became, was becoming, or had no doubt already become for some time, a completely normal and natural experience. You make your examination of conscience to a friend, to someone dear to one and with whom you have intense affective relations. You take him as your spiritual director, and it is quite normal to take him as a guide regardless of his qualification as a philosopher—and in this case he is not a philosopher—simply because he is a friend. With regard to the self (to the day you have passed, to the work you have done, and to your sources of entertainment), you have the attitude, the stance, of someone who will have to give an account of it to someone else, and you live your day as a day that may be and anyway should be presented, offered, deciphered to someone else—who will have what kind of relationship to it? Well, we will see later: the judge or inspector, the master, etcetera. Unfortunately it is too late, but I would have liked to say a bit more about how, through this development of the practice of the self, through the fact that the practice of the self becomes a sort of social relationship that, if not universal, is at least always possible between individuals, even when their relationship is not that of philosophy master and pupil, something very new and very important develops, I believe, which is not so much a new ethic of language or discourse in general, but of the verbal relationship with the Other. This new ethic of the verbal relationship with the other is designated by the fundamental notion of *parrhēsia*. *Parrhēsia*, generally translated as "frankness," is a rule of the game, a principle of how one should conduct oneself verbally with the other in the practice of spiritual direction. So, I will begin by explaining this next week, *parrhēsia*, before going on to see how this verbal relationship to the other in spiritual direction is given a technical form.

1. The second Sophists owe their cultural existence to the *Lives of the Sophists* of Philostratus of Lemnos (beginning of the third century). Since Plato's great portraits, the Sophists were always those orators and teachers wandering from town to town giving lessons on wisdom. But the similarity ends there, for the "second" Sophists were dispersed (rather than concentrated in Athens) and paraded in theaters and other auditoriums (rather than in the homes of rich individuals). Furthermore, "more than any other genre, the second Sophists incarnate the historical compromise between Greek culture and Roman power," since one sometimes sees the Sophist who "tries on the spot to calm down the conflicts that could arise with the local governor and preach harmony to the cities in line with the wishes of the Romans" (S. Saïd, ed., *Histoire de la littérature grecque* [Paris: PUF, 1997]). Finally, we note that, relative to philosophy, the complex seems reversed with regard to the Athenian period: in his *Dissertations*, Ælius Aristides strongly criticizes Plato's condemnation of rhetoric (*Gorgias*) and puts formal apprenticeship in rhetoric above everything else. The superiority of rhetoric is assumed and claimed, and it is philosophy that then appears as a pointless and uncertain game. On the second Sophists see: G. Bowerstock, *Greek Sophists in the Roman Empire* (Oxford: Clarendon Press, 1969); G. Anderson, *The Second Sophists: A Cultural Phenomenon in the Roman Empire* (London: Routledge, 1993); B. Cassin, *L'Effet sophistique* (Paris: Gallimard, 1969); see also the link established in this book between the second Sophists and the birth of Roman Greek.
2. "Also it was not the orators that the Caesars especially mistrusted; they were much more suspicious of the philosophers and regarded them as real enemies of the Empire. Starting with Tiberius, a sort of persecution was organized against them and it continued without respite until the Antonines. Sometimes they were struck singly, sometimes en masse: under Nero, Vespasian and Domitian all were exiled from Rome and Italy. What had they done to deserve this fate? They were accused of having taken as models ... the most determined republicans." G. Boissiere, *L'Opposition sous les Césars* (Paris: Hachette, 1885), p. 97. On Stoic-republican opposition to the Caesars see lecture of 27 January, first hour, note 44, p. 148.
3. J.-M. André, *Recherches sur l' Otium romain* (Paris: Les Belles Lettres, 1962), and *Mécène. Essai de biographie spirituelle*.
4. On the Principate as a new organization of power in Rome, starting with Augustus, see J. Béranger, *Recherches sur les aspects idéologiques du Principat* (Bâle: F. Reinhardt, 1953).
5. Foucault won't have time to deal with this problem and only in some preparatory dossiers (for example, the one entitled "Social relations") is there a study of the relations between care of the self and civic duties, which is based on three basic references: Plutarch, Dio Chrysostom of Prusa, and Maximus of Tyre.
6. See the dialogue *Philosophes à l'encan* (Lucian, *Sale of Creeds*) presented in the lecture of 20 January, first hour.
7. Euphrates of Tyre, Stoic philosopher of the first century A.D., was the student of Musonius Rufus. Philostratus presents him as a not very sympathetic character: a dubious republican, great flatterer, and low calculator. We know he must have been exiled at the beginning of the seventies when Vespasian threw the philosophers out of Rome. Finally, Apuleius recounts that he killed himself when he was ninety years old, not without previously requesting authorization from the emperor Hadrian.
8. Plinius Caecilius Secundus, Caius/Pliny the Younger, *Letters*, translations by W. Melmoth (New York and London: Loeb Classical Library, 1915), vol. I, book 1, X, pp. 32-37. See the analysis of this text in *Le Souci de soi*, p. 63 (*The Care of the Self*, p. 48).
9. Philostratus the Elder, *Life and Times of Apollonius of Tyana*, translation C.P. Eells (Stanford: Stanford University Publications, 1923). On the comparison of the two men, see book V, ch. 33-38, pp. 138-14: Euphrates, who claimed adherence to Stoic dogma, only recognized natural immanence as a guide and became the defender of democracy and political liberty, while Apollonius of Tyana—of the Platonist school—appealed to supra-sensible lessons and declared his adherence to the imperial order in which he saw a guarantee of property and security.

10. Pliny the Younger, *Letters*, vol. 1, book 1, X.2, pp. 32-33.
11. Cf. Seneca, *De Beneficiis/On Benefits*, II.XV.1-2 and XVIII.3-5. On the same theme, see also Cicero, *Laelius de Amicitia*, XVII.63. On this delicate point of the Roman mentality, see P. Veyne's introduction to *Des Bienfaits* in Seneca, *Entretiens, Lettres à Lucilius*, pp. 391-403.
12. Throughout the following section Foucault summarizes the description given in paragraphs 5 to 8, *Letters*, pp. 34-35.
13. "to be engaged in the service of the public... is a part, and the noblest part too of Philosophy," 10, Ibid., p. 37.
14. Seneca, *To Helvia on Consolation* and *To Polybius on Consolation*.
15. See the lecture of 20 January, first hour, above p. 102, note 24 on the relationship between Serenus and Seneca.
16. It is Seneca's *De Constantia (On the Firmness of the Wise Man)*.
17. On the relationship between Lucilius and Seneca, see the lecture of 20 January, first hour, above p. 102, note 26.
18. Plutarch, born into a wealthy and cultivated family at Chaeronea (circa 46), began his apprenticeship with cultural journeys to Athens, Ephesus, Smyrna, and Alexandria, from which he acquired an impressive philosophical, rhetorical, and scientific baggage. He went to Rome twice to give lectures (under Vespasian and Domitian), which met with great success and made him a much sought-after spiritual director. In the nineties, he returned to the town where he was born to teach philosophy and write the major part of his work. The prefaces to his treatises show clearly that his interlocutors are either people close to him (his family or neighbors) or Greek and Roman dignitaries.
19. This takes up the first chapter of the Seneca's treatise, *On Tranquility of Mind*. For Foucault's analysis of Seneca's answer, see this lecture, first hour.
20. See *Le Souci de soi*, p. 73 (*The Care of the Self*, p. 57).
21. *The Correspondence of Marcus Cornelius Fronto with Aurelius Antoninus*.
22. See the lecture of 20 January, second hour, above p. 122, note 3, on Fronto.
23. Marcus Aurelius, *Meditations*, I.16.
24. "I owe Fronto for having observed the extent to which envy, hypocrisy and dissimulation are typical of tyrants and those we call patrician are almost always incapable of affection." Marcus Aurelius, *Meditations*, I.11.
25. Foucault follows literally an old translation by A. Cassan, *Lettres inédites de Marc Aurèle et de Fronton* (Paris: A. Levavasseur, 1830), vol. I, book IV, letter VI, pp. 249-51.
26. Foucault omits from the end of the sentence, "and, as an author says, we left hanging from the trellis some gleanings from the harvest." Ibid., p. 251.
27. Foucault does not read out the beginning of the dialogue between Marcus Aurelius and his mother: "This is what I said: What do you think my Fronto is doing now? And she: What do you think my Gratia is doing? Who? I replied. Our sweet warbler, little Gratia?"
28. Actually, the final sentence of the letter is: "What is our relationship? I love someone who is away (*Quid mihi tecum est? amo absentem*)."
29. We can make it clear that kissing between men was usual under the Empire, including kissing on the mouth. Furthermore, it had a hierarchical significance: A plebian only kisses the hand of someone grand, and only between the grand is there kissing on the mouth or the chest. For the passage we are concerned with, this means that hierarchical superiority has been abolished between Marcus Aurelius and his private tutor. See L. Friedländer, *Sittengeschichte Roms* (Leipzig: 1919), vol. I, pp. 93-93, and A. Alfödi, *Die monarchische Rapräsentation im römischen Kaiserreiche* (Darmstadt: Wissenschaftliche Buchgesellschaft, 1980), p. 27, pp. 41-42, and p. 64 (I am indebted to Paul Veyne for these references).
30. See Foucault's analysis of the Hippocratic treatise *Regimen in Health* in *L'Usage des plaisirs*, pp. 124-32 (*The Use of Pleasure*, pp. 109-16).
31. Marcus Porcius Cato, *On Agriculture*, translation W.D. Hooper and H.B. Ash, in Cato and Varro, *De Re Rustica* (Cambridge, Mass. and London: Loeb Classical Library, 1934).
32. Xenophon, *Oeconomicus*, translation E. C. Marchant, in Xenophon, *Memorabilia* (Cambridge, Mass. and London: Loeb Classical Library, 1923).

33. An allusion to Plato's *Symposium* as founding text. See the chapter "True Love" in *L'Usage des plaisirs*, pp. 251-69 (*The Use of Pleasure*, pp. 229-46).
34. Seneca, *On anger*, III.XXXVI. For a more extended study of the same text, see the lecture of 24 March, second hour, and the seminar at the University of Vermont, October 1982, "Techniques de soi," in *Dits et Écrits*, vol. 4, pp. 797-99 ("Technologies of the Self" in *Ethics: Subjectivity and Truth*, p. 237).
35. The reference could not be found. No Seneca text corresponds to this description.

# nine

# 3 FEBRUARY 1982

## First hour

[ *Neo-Platonist commentaries on the* Alcibiades: *Proclus and Olympiodorus.* ∼ *The Neo-Platonist separation of the political and the cathartic.* ∼ *Study of the link between care of the self and care for others in Plato: purpose, reciprocity, and essential implication.* ∼ *Situation in the first and second centuries: self-finalization of the self.* ∼ *Consequences: a philosophical art of living according to the principle of conversion; the development of a culture of the self.* ∼ *Religious meaning of the idea of salvation.* ∼ *Meanings of* sōtēria *and of* salus. ]

LAST WEEK, DUE TO lack of time, I dropped the analysis of the notion that is, I think, very important in the practice of the self, in the technology of the subject: the notion of *parrhēsia*, which roughly speaking means frankness, open-heartedness, openness of thought, etcetera. I wanted to start by taking up this question again a bit, but then, for several reasons, I would prefer to come back to it a bit later when we will talk more precisely about a number of techniques of the subject in the philosophy, practice, and culture of the first and second centuries, and when we will talk in particular about the problem of listening and the master-disciple relationship. So, I will talk about it again then. And anyway, someone has asked me a question. Sadly I don't get many questions, perhaps because we don't have many opportunities to meet each other. Still, I have received a question to which I would like to respond because I think it will serve quite well as an introduction to the lecture I would like to give today.

Quite simply, the question is this: Why focus on this dialogue, the *Alcibiades*, to which commentators do not usually accord such importance in Plato's work? Why take this dialogue as the reference point not only for talking about Plato, but ultimately for a perspective on a whole section of ancient philosophy? As it happens, for some time I have intended to refer to two or three late but, I think, very enlightening texts on this problem of the *Alcibiades* and its place in ancient thought. So, I will make a digression. Instead of speaking to you about *parrhēsia* now and of the Neo-Platonist commentators later, I would like straightaway to say something about the problem of the Neo-Platonist commentaries on the *Alcibiades*. You know that the great return of *Neo-Platonism* in ancient culture, thought, and philosophy—starting from roughly the second century A.D.—raised a number of problems and the question of the systematization of Plato's works in particular. Let's say, very simply, that it is the problem of their publication in a form and order such that the problems of the philosophy arise successively, in the appropriate place, and in a way that constitutes both a closed system and one that can be used in teaching and pedagogy. This problem, then, of the classification of Plato's works, was taken up by a number of commentators and in particular by Proclus and Olympiodorus.[1] Both these commentators agree that the *Alcibiades*, which I have taken as my starting point, should be placed at the head of Plato's works and that the study of Plato and Platonism, and so of philosophy generally, should be approached through this dialogue. In fact, three major principles allow Proclus and Olympiodorus to give the *Alcibiades* this first place, this initial position, and to place it, so to speak, at the propylaeum of philosophy. First, in their eyes the *Alcibiades* is the summary of Plato's philosophy. Second, it is the first and solemn introduction of the *gnōthi seauton* into philosophy as the essential condition of philosophical practice. And finally, they see in it the first appearance of the divergence of the political and the cathartic. Let's go back over these points a little. I'd like to point out anyway that first of all I could not have told you this if Festugière had not written an interesting article on the classification of Plato's works in the Neo-Platonists, and if he had not extracted from them the principle texts on this question. I no longer know where the article appeared, but anyway you can find it in the *Études de philosophie grecque*.[2] Well, a series of texts are quoted.

There is Proclus's text[3] (from the fifth century) concerning the classification of Plato's works: "This dialogue [he says, speaking of the *Alcibiades*; M.F.] is the source of all philosophy [*arkhē hapasēs philosophias*: the beginning, the source of philosophy; M.F.], as is also precisely the knowledge of ourselves [just as the knowledge of ourselves—the *gnōthi seauton*—is the condition for being able to begin philosophy; M.F.]. That is why many logical considerations are scattered within it and passed on by tradition, many moral considerations contributing to our enquiry on eudemonia are clarified in it, many doctrines suited to lead us to the study of nature or even to the truth about the divine beings themselves are briefly set out in it, so that one and the same general and overall sketch of all philosophy may be contained in this dialogue, as in a model, a sketch which is revealed to us thanks precisely to this first review of ourselves."[4] This is an interesting text first of all because it contains a distinction that is certainly not Platonic but one that was introduced later and which fully corresponds with the teaching and arrangement of philosophy during the Hellenistic, imperial period and in late Antiquity. We see the distinction between logical considerations, moral considerations, doctrines of nature, and truths about divine beings. Logic, morality, the study of nature, and theology—or discourse on the divine—are the four basic components into which philosophy is divided up. So, Proclus assumes then that these four components are actually scattered, are both present and somewhat discretely hidden, in the text of the *Alcibiades*, but that these components are presented on the basis of the review of oneself, which should be their foundation. This outline of philosophy is revealed to us thanks precisely to this first review of ourselves. We take stock of ourselves, become aware of what we are, and in this review we see unfolding what philosophical knowledge (*savoir*) should be. "And it seems to me this is also why [Proclus adds; M.F.] the divine Iamblichus gives first place to the *Alcibiades* in the ten dialogues which, according to him, contain the whole of Plato's philosophy [reference to a lost text by Iamblichus[5] which thus seems to indicate that the *Alcibiades* was considered to be Plato's first dialogue, or anyway the one that should be placed at the head of his dialogues, even before Proclus and this problem of the classification of Plato's works; M.F.]."[6]

In another commentary, Olympiodorus says about the *Alcibiades*: "Concerning the rank [of the *Alcibiades*; M.F.], it must be said that we should place it at the head of all the Platonic dialogues. For, as Plato says in the *Phaedrus*, it is absurd not to know oneself if one aspires to know everything else. In the second place, we should approach Socratic doctrine Socratically: now, it is said that Socrates proceeded to philosophy through the precept 'know yourself.' Moreover, this dialogue should be seen as a propylaeum, and just as the propylaeum precedes the temple's adytum, so also the *Alcibiades* should be likened to a propylaeum and the *Parmenides* to the adytum."[7] You see that Olympiodorus makes the *Alcibiades* the propylaeum and the *Parmenides* the very heart of Platonic philosophy. And you see that Olympiodorus quite explicitly makes the "know yourself" of the *Alcibiades* not only the foundation of philosophical knowledge, but the very model for the practice of someone who wants to study philosophy. We should, he says, "approach Socratic doctrine Socratically," that is to say, to initiate ourselves in the philosophy of Socrates and Plato we must reproduce the Socratic approach itself. And this labor exercised on oneself, in the form of self-knowledge, is the price for being able to advance in philosophical knowledge. This leads us to the third part of what I want to talk about and which will serve us directly as introduction: the problem of the distinction between the political and the cathartic. In the same commentary on the *Alcibiades*, Olympiodorus says in fact: "Since the aim of this dialogue [the *Alcibiades*; M.F.] is knowing oneself, not in terms of the body, not in terms of external objects—the title is, in fact, *Alcibiades, or On the nature of man* [which proves that this obviously non-Platonic title had already been added to the *Alcibiades* in Olympiodurus's time; M.F.]—but in terms of the soul; and not the vegetable, not the irrational soul, but the rational soul; and most certainly not knowing oneself in terms of this soul inasmuch we act in a cathartic, theoretical, theological, or theurgic manner, but inasmuch as we act politically."[8] A bit further on (this time in the commentary on the *Gorgias*) he says: "As a result, the sequence of dialogues also appears. Once we have learned, in the *Alcibiades*, that we are soul and that this soul is rational, we must follow this up with both the political and the cathartic virtues. Since therefore we should know first of all that which concerns the political virtues, we necessarily explain this dialogue (the *Gorgias*) after the other (the *Alcibiades*) and then, after this, the *Phaedo* inasmuch as it contains the cathartic virtues."[9] So what we are dealing with here is, I think, a very important point for basically the entire history of the tradition of the *gnōthi seauton*—and so of the *Alcibiades*—in the Platonic tradition, but probably in ancient thought also. This is: in the *Alcibiades*, laying down then the principle "know yourself," we see the germ of the great differentiation which must exist between the political part (that is to say, "know yourself" insofar as it introduces a number of principles and rules that should enable the individual to be either the citizen he ought to be or the good governor), and, on another side, the "know yourself" that calls for a number of operations by which the subject must purify himself and become, in his own nature, able to have contact with and to recognize the divine element within him. The *Alcibiades*, then, is at the source of this bifurcation. And in the classification, or rather, in the sequencing of Plato's dialogues suggested by Olympiodorus, the *Alcibiades* is therefore placed at the start, with one side going in the direction of the political, and thus the *Gorgias* following the *Alcibiades*. And then, on the other side, there is the *Phaedo*, with the dimension of the cathartic and self-purification. Consequently, according to Olympiodorus the series should be: *Alcibiades*; *Gorgias*, for the political filiation; *Phaedo*, for the cathartic filiation.

[Let's go over these elements again.] First, the privilege of the "Know yourself" as the very foundation of philosophy with, in the Neo-Platonist tradition, the absorption of care of the self into the form of self-knowledge. So, first, the privileged status of the "Know yourself" as the form of care of the self par excellence; second, the theme that "Know yourself" leads to the political; third, the theme that this "Know yourself" also leads to a cathartics. Finally, a fourth thing is that a number of problems arise between the political and the cathartic. The relationship between the cathartic and the political creates a certain problem in the Neo-Platonist tradition. Whereas for Plato—and I will show you this in a moment—there is really no structural difference between the cathartic procedure and the political path, in the Neo-Platonist tradition, rather, the two tendencies separate and the political use of "Know yourself" and the cathartic use of "Know yourself"—or again, the political use and the cathartic use of care of the self—no longer coincide and constitute a fork at which one has to make a choice. That's how the *Alcibiades* was given a new place in at least one of the traditions of Greek philosophy, Platonism and Neo-Platonism, and how its importance was supposed to be fundamental and initiatory. Okay, let's come back a bit to this, and precisely to this problem of "care of the self" and "knowledge of the self" (which, once again, are not identical, but are identified in the Platonic tradition), and to the problem of the "cathartic" and the "political," which are identified in Plato but cease to be identified in the Platonist and Neo-Platonist tradition.

I'd like to recall a few things I said about the *Alcibiades* in the first lecture. You remember that this dialogue involved showing Alcibiades that he had to take care of himself. And you know why he had to take care of himself, in both senses of the question "why"? Both because he did not know what exactly was good for the city-state and in what the harmony of citizens consisted and, on the other hand, in order to be able to govern the city-state and take care of his fellow citizens properly. He had to take care of himself, therefore, in order to be able to take care of others. And you remember also, I pointed out that at the end of the dialogue Alcibiades undertakes to "concern myself" (*epimeleisthai*). He takes up the word used by Socrates. He says: Very well, I will concern myself. But concern myself with what? He does not say: I will concern myself with myself. He says rather: I will concern myself with *dikaiosunē* (with justice). I don't need to remind you that in Plato this notion applies both to the soul and to the city.[10] If, after Socrates' lesson, Alcibiades keeps his promise and concerns himself with justice, he will concern himself first with his soul, with the internal hierarchy of his soul and the relations of order and subordination that should govern the parts of his soul, and then, at the same time, and by virtue of doing this, he will make himself capable of watching over the city, safeguarding its laws and constitution (the *politeia*), and maintaining the right balance in relations between citizens. Throughout this text, care of the self is therefore instrumental with regard to the care of others. Proof that this really is the relationship defined in the *Alcibiades* is found in that other, negative, as it were, or anyway late and already sullied image of Alcibiades in the *Symposium*. He bursts into the middle of the debating guests, already getting on a bit, and anyway completely drunk. He sings the praises of Socrates and, still completely under the spell of his lessons, laments and regrets not having listened to them. And he says: In spite of all that I lack, I continue even so not to care for myself (*epimeleisthai emautou*) while concerning myself with the affairs of Athenians.[11] This phrase clearly echoes the theme of the *Alcibiades* itself. In the *Alcibiades* he undertook to take care of himself in order to be able to take care of the citizens by putting *dikaiosunē* at the heart of his care. Well, in the end he concerned himself with the citizens without taking care of himself. So he does not know what *dikaiosunē* is, etcetera. All the dramas and disasters of the real Alcibiades are picked out in this little gap between the promise of the *Alcibiades* and the drunkenness of the *Symposium*.

We could say that Plato generally establishes the link between care of the self and care of others in three ways. Or again, to go back to what I said a short while ago, self-knowledge is one aspect, element, or form in Plato—no doubt crucial, but only one form—of the fundamental and general requirement to "take care of yourself." Neo-Platonism will reverse this relationship. Conversely, however, the cathartic and the political are not differentiated in Plato. Or rather, the same approach is both cathartic and political. It is so in three ways. Because by taking care of oneself—this is what I was just saying—one makes oneself capable of taking care of others. There is, if you like, a functional relation between taking care of the self and taking care of others. I take care of myself so that I can take care of others. I practice on myself what the Neo-Platonists call *katharsis* and I practice this art of the cathartic precisely so that I can become a political subject in the sense of someone who knows what politics is and as a result can govern. The first link then is one of purpose. Second, there is a link of reciprocity. If, as I desire, I act for the good of the city-state I govern by taking care of myself and practicing the cathartic in the Neo-Platonist sense, if I ensure salvation and prosperity for my fellow citizens and the city's victory as a result of taking care of myself, then in return, inasmuch as I am part of the same community of the city-state, I will benefit from the prosperity of all and from the salvation and victory of the city that I have ensured. The care of the self therefore finds its reward and guarantee in the city's salvation. One saves oneself inasmuch as the city-state is saved, and inasmuch as one has enabled it to be saved by taking care of oneself. The circularity is clearly set out in the construction of *The Republic*. Finally, we could call the third link a link of essential implication. For by taking care of itself, by practicing the "cathartic of the self" (not a Platonic but a Neo-Platonist term), the soul discovers both what it is and what it knows, or rather, what it has always known. It discovers both its being and its knowledge at the same time. It discovers what it is, and in the form of memory it discovers what it has contemplated. In this way, in this act of memory, it can get back to the contemplation of the truths that enable the city's order to be founded anew in full justice. So you see that in Plato there are three ways of linking and firmly attaching to each other what the Neo-Platonists call the cathartic and the political: the link of purpose in political *tekhnē* (I must take care of myself in order to know, to have a proper knowledge of the political *tekhnē* that will enable me to take care of others); the link of reciprocity in the form of the city-state, since by knowing myself I save the city and I save myself by saving the city; and finally, the link of implication in the form of recollection. This is, very roughly if you like, the link Plato establishes between care of the self and care of others, and establishes in such a way that it is very difficult to separate them.

If we now place ourselves in the period I have taken as our reference point, that is to say in the first and second centuries A.D., this separation has by now been broadly carried out. One of the most important phenomena in the history of the practice of the self, and perhaps in the history of ancient culture, is quite probably that of seeing the self—and so the techniques of the self and all the practice of oneself that Plato designated as care of the self—gradually emerge as a self-sufficient end, without the care of others being the ultimate aim and indicator by reference to which care of the self is valued. First, the self one takes care of is no longer one element among others, or, if it appears as one element among others, as you will see shortly, it is following a particular argument or form of knowledge (*connaissance*). In itself, the self one takes care of is no longer pivotal. It is no longer a relay. It is no longer a transitional element leading to something else, to the city-state or others. The self is the definitive and sole aim of the care of the self. Consequently, under no circumstances can this activity, this practice of the care of the self, be seen as purely and simply preliminary and introductory to the care of others. It is an activity focused solely on the self and whose outcome, realization and satisfaction, in the strong sense of the word, is found only in the self, that is to say in the activity itself that is exercised on the self. One takes care of the self for oneself, and this care finds its own reward in the care of the self. In the care of the self one is one's own object and end. There is, so to speak, both an absolutization (please forgive the word) of the self as object of care, and a self-finalization of the self by the self in the practice we call the care of the self. In a word, the care of the self, which in Plato quite clearly opened out onto the question of the city-state, of others, of the *politeia*, of *dikaiosunē*, etcetera, appears—at first sight anyway, in the period of the first two centuries I am talking about—as if it is closed on itself. This, more or less, gives the general outline of the phenomenon that must now be analyzed in detail, because what I have said is both true and not true. Let us say that it is what may appear as true at a certain level, from a certain angle, and by practicing a certain type of survey. Anyway, I think this detachment of what, once again, the Neo-Platonists called the cathartic, with regard to what they called the political, is an important phenomenon. It is important for two or three reasons.

The first is this: The phenomenon is important for philosophy itself. We should remember that from at least the Cynics—the post-Socratics: Cynics, Epicureans, Stoics, etcetera—philosophy increasingly sought its definition, its center of gravity, and fixed its objective around something called the *tekhnē tou biou*, that is to say, the art, the reflected method for conducting one's life, the technique of life. Now, insofar as the self is asserted as being and having to be the object of care—you recall that last week I tried to show you that this care had to be practiced throughout life and to lead man to the point of his life's fulfillment—then there is an increasingly pronounced identification of the art of existence (the *tekhnē tou biou*) with the care of the self, or, to put things more tightly, identification of the art of existence with the art of oneself. "What shall we do in order to live properly?" was the question of the *tekhnē tou biou*: what knowledge will enable me to live properly, as I ought to live as an individual, as a citizen, etcetera? This question ("What shall we do in order to live properly?") will become increasingly identified with or increasingly clearly absorbed by the question: "What shall we do so that the self becomes and remains what it ought to be?" Obviously, a number of consequences follow from this. First of all, of course, during the Hellenistic and Roman period there is the increasingly marked absorption of philosophy (as thought concerning truth) into spirituality (as the subject's own transformation of his mode of being). With this there is, of course, an expansion of the cathartic theme. Or again, there is, if you like, the appearance or development of the fundamental problem of conversion (*metanoia*), which I will talk about today and next week. The *tekhnē tou biou* (the art of living) now increasingly turns on the question: How must I transform my own self so as to be able to have access to the truth? You see that from this also arises the fact that when Christian spirituality develops in its strictest ascetic and monastic form, from the third and fourth centuries, it can present itself quite naturally as the fulfillment of an ancient, pagan philosophy which, following this movement I have just indicated, was already entirely dominated by the theme of the cathartic, or by the theme of conversion and *metanoia*. The ascetic life, the monastic life, will be the true philosophy, and the monastery will be the true school of philosophy, this being, once again, in the direct line of a *tekhnē tou biou* that had become an art of oneself.*

---

*The manuscript here notes: "This is why, finally, Western philosophy can be read throughout its history as the slow disengagement of the question: how, on what conditions can one think the truth? from the question: how, at what cost, in accordance with what procedure, must the subject's mode of being be changed for him to have access to the truth?"

However, beyond this long range and general evolution of philosophy, I think it should also be said that the consequences of this self-finalization of the self in the care of the self did not appear in philosophy alone. It seems to me that these consequences can not only be quite easily identified in the literature, but also in a number of practices attested by history and various documents. It seems to me that this self-finalization had broader effects connected to a series of practices, forms of life, and ways in which individuals experienced themselves, through themselves, which were certainly not universal, but were nonetheless very common. While having trouble with the word and putting it in inverted commas, I think we can say that from the Hellenistic and Roman period we see a real development of the "culture" of the self. I don't want to use the word culture in a sense that is too loose and I will say that we can speak of culture on a number of conditions. First, when there is a set of values with a minimum degree of coordination, subordination, and hierarchy. We can speak of culture when a second condition is satisfied, which is that these values are given both as universal but also as only accessible to a few. A third condition for being able to speak of culture is that a number of precise and regular forms of conduct are necessary for individuals to be able to reach these values. Even more than this, effort and sacrifice is required. In short, to have access to these values you must be able to devote your whole life to them. Finally, the fourth condition for being able to talk about culture is that access to these values is conditional upon more or less regular techniques and procedures that have been developed, validated, transmitted, and taught, and that are also associated with a whole set of notions, concepts, and theories etcetera: with a field of knowledge (*savoir*). Okay. So, if we call culture a hierarchical organization of values that is accessible to everyone but which at the same time gives rise to a mechanism of selection and exclusion; if we call culture the fact that this hierarchical organization of values calls on the individual to engage in regular, costly, and sacrificial conduct that orientates his whole life; and, finally, if the organization of the field of values and access to these values can only take place through regular and reflected techniques and a set of elements constituting a systematic knowledge: then, to that extent we can say that in the Hellenistic and

Roman epoch there really was a culture of the self. It seems to me that the self effectively organized or reorganized the field of traditional values of the classical Hellenic world. You remember that the self, as I tried to explain last week, appears as a universal value but one which in actual fact is only accessible to some. Actually, this self can only be attained as a value on condition of a number of regular, demanding, and sacrificial forms of conduct to which we will return. And finally, access to the self is associated with a number of techniques, with relatively well-constituted and relatively well-reflected practices, and anyway with a theoretical domain, with a set of concepts and notions, which really integrate it in a mode of knowledge (*savoir*). Fine, in short, I think all this allows us to say that from the Hellenistic period a culture of the self developed. And it seems to me that it is hardly possible to undertake the history of subjectivity, of the relations between the subject and truth, without setting it in the framework of this culture of the self that afterwards, in Christianity—in early and then Medieval Christianity—and then in the Renaissance and the seventeenth century, undergoes a series of changes and transformations.

All right, now for this culture of the self. Until now I have tried to show how this practice of the self was formed. I would now like to take up the question again more generally by asking what this culture of the self is as an organized field of values with its behavioral requirements and associated technical and theoretical field. The first question I would like to talk about, because I think it is a very important element in this culture of the self, is the notion of salvation: salvation of the self and salvation of others. Salvation is a completely traditional term. You find it in fact in Plato, where it is associated precisely with the problem of care of the self and care of others. One must be saved, one must save oneself, in order to save others. In Plato at least, the notion of salvation does not appear to have a very specific and strict meaning. On the other hand, when you find this notion again in the first and second centuries, you notice that not only is its extension, its field of application, much wider, but that it has taken on a quite specific value and structure. I would like to talk a little about this. If we consider this notion of salvation retrospectively—that is to say, through our grids or schemas more or less formed by Christianity—it is clear that we associate the idea of salvation with a number of elements which seem to us to be constitutive. First, for us salvation normally appears in a binary system. It is situated between life and death, or between mortality and immortality, or between this world and the other. Salvation effectuates a crossing over: It takes one from death to life, mortality to immortality, this world to the other. Or again, it takes one from evil to good, from a world of impurity to a world of purity, etcetera. It is always on the boundary, therefore, and is something that brings about passage. Second, for us salvation is always linked to the dramatic force of an event, which may be situated either in the thread of worldly events or in a different temporality of God, eternity, and so on. Anyway, these—once again, historical or metahistorical—events are brought into play in salvation: transgression, sin, original sin, the Fall, make salvation necessary. And, on the other hand, conversion, repentance, or Christ's incarnation—again, individual, historical events or metahistorical events—organize salvation and make it possible. Salvation, then, is linked to the dramatic force of an event. Finally, it seems to me that when we speak of salvation we always think of a complex operation in which the subject who earns his salvation is, of course, the agent and effective instrument of his salvation, but in which someone else (an other, the Other) is always required, with a role which is precisely very variable and hard to define. Anyway, this interplay between the salvation brought about by oneself and the one who saves you is the precipitation point for a number of familiar theories and analyses. So it seems to me that through these three elements—binarism, the dramatic force of an event, and the double operation—we always think of salvation as a religious idea. Moreover, we habitually distinguish between religions of salvation and religions without salvation. So, when we come across the theme of salvation in Hellenistic and Roman thought, or in the thought of late Antiquity, we always see the influence of religious thought. Besides, it is a fact that the notion of salvation is important in the Pythagoreans, who played such an important and lasting role in Greek philosophical thought.[12] However, and I think this is fundamental for what I want to say, I would like to emphasize that whatever the origin of this notion of salvation, and whatever reinforcement it may have received from the religious theme in the Hellenistic and Roman period, it is not a notion that is heterogeneous to philosophy, and it functions effectively as a philosophical notion within the field of philosophy itself. Salvation developed and appeared as an objective of philosophical practice and of the philosophical life.

We should keep certain things in mind. In Greek, the verb *sōzein* (to save) or the substantive *sōtēria* (salvation) have a number of meanings. *Sōzein* (to save) is first of all to save from a threatening danger. One will say, for example, to save from a shipwreck, from a defeat, or to save from an illness.* *Sōzein* also means (second major field of signification) to guard, protect, or keep a protective shield around something so that it can remain in its existing condition. There is a text of Plato's on this in the *Cratylus*, which besides is rather odd, in which he says that the Pythagoreans considered the body to be an enclosure for the soul. Not the body as prison or grave of the soul it confines, but rather as a *peribolon tēs psukhēs* (an enclosure for the soul) *hina sōzētai* (so that the soul may be kept safe).[13] This is the second major meaning of *sōzein*. Third, in a similar but clearly more moral sense, *sōzein* means to preserve and protect something like decency, honor, or possibly memory. *Sōtēria mnēmēs* (keeping the memory) is an expression found in Plutarch.[14] However, in Epictetus for example, there is the idea of the preservation of the sense of decency.[15] Fourth signification: the juridical meaning. For a lawyer (or someone who speaks on behalf of someone else), for example, to save [someone] is obviously to help him escape an accusation leveled against him. At the same time, it is to exonerate him. It is to prove his innocence. Fifth, *sōzesthai* (the passive form) means to be safe at that moment, that is to say, to remain, kept in the same condition as one was in previously. Wine, for example, is said to be preserved, to be kept fresh, without alteration. Or again, Dio Chrysostom of Prusa examines how a tyrant can be saved in the sense of being able to hold on to his power and maintain it over time . . .[16] [Or again, one will say] a

---

*The manuscript gives an example from Plutarch: "We should not destroy a friendship by causing distress, but should resort to scathing words as to a remedy which saves and preserves that to which it is applied," *How to Distinguish the Flatterer from the Friend*, 55c, §11.

town will only be saved (*sothēnai*), survive, and be preserved if it does not relax its laws.[17] So, if you like, there is the idea of maintenance in the former condition, in the primitive or original state of purity. Finally, and sixthly, *sōzein* has an even more positive sense. *Sōzein* means to do good. It means to ensure the well-being, the good condition of something, someone, or of a collectivity. For example, Plutarch, in *A Letter of Condolence to Apollonius*, says that when we have suffered bereavement, we should not let ourselves go, shut ourselves away in solitude and silence, and neglect our occupations. We should continue, he says, to ensure the *epimeleia tou sōmatos* (the care of the body) and *sōtēria tōn sumbiountōn* (the "salvation" of those who live with us):[18] of course, it is a question of the head of the family here, the person with responsibility who, as such, must continue to support his family and ensure its status, good condition and well being etcetera, and not use bereavement as a pretext for neglect. Dio Chrysostom of Prusa (discourse 64) says that the king is the one *ho ta panta sōzōn*.[19] If we translate *sōzein* literally by "to save," this would mean: the one who saves everything. In fact the king is the person who spreads his benefits over everything and concerning everything. He is the source of well-being in the State or the Empire. Finally, there is the very revealing Latin expression: *salus augusta*. Augustan salvation does not mean that Augustus saved the Empire, [but] that he is the source of the public good, of the Empire's well-being in general. He is therefore the source of the good. This is the batch of meanings that can be found around the verb *sōzein* and the noun *sōtēria*.

Starting from this, we can see that the meaning of "saving oneself" is not at all reducible to something like the drama of an event that allows one's existence to be commuted from death to life, mortality to immortality, evil to good, etcetera. It is not just a matter of being saved from a danger. *Sōtēria, sōzein* have much wider meanings. The meaning of being saved is not just negative: escaping danger, escaping from the prison of the body, escaping the impurity of the world, etcetera. Being saved has positive meanings. Just as a city is saved by building the necessary defenses, fortresses, and fortifications around it—you remember the idea of the body as *peribolon tēs psukhēs hina sōzētai*[20]—so we will say that a soul is saved, that someone is saved, when he is suitably armed and equipped to be able to defend himself effectively if necessary. The person saved is the person in a state of alert, in a state of resistance and of mastery and sovereignty over the self, enabling him to repel every attack and assault. Similarly "saving yourself" means escaping domination or enslavement; escaping a constraint that threatens you and being restored to your rights, finding your freedom and independence again. "Being saved" means maintaining yourself in a continuous state that nothing can change, whatever events occur around the self, like a wine is preserved, is kept. And finally, "being saved" means having access to goods you did not possess at the outset, enjoying a sort of benefit, which you give yourself, of which you are yourself the effective agent. "Being saved" will mean ensuring happiness, tranquility, serenity, etcetera, for yourself. However, you see that if "being saved" has these positive meanings and does not refer to the dramatic force of an event by which we pass from the negative to the positive, in another respect the term salvation refers to nothing else but life itself. There is no reference to anything like death, immortality, or another world in the notion of salvation found in the Hellenistic and Roman texts. It is not with reference to a dramatic event or to the action of a different agency that you are saved; saving yourself is an activity that takes place throughout life and that is executed solely by the subject himself. And if this activity of "saving yourself" ultimately leads to a final effect, which is its aim and end, this consists in the fact that salvation renders you inaccessible to misfortunes, disorders, and all that external accidents and events may produce in the soul. When the end, the object of salvation, has been attained, you need nothing and no one but yourself. The two great themes of ataraxy (the absence of inner turmoil, the self-control that ensures that nothing disturbs one) and autarchy (the self-sufficiency which ensures that one needs nothing but the self) are the two forms in which salvation, the acts of salvation, the activity of salvation carried on throughout one's life, find their reward. Salvation then is an activity, the subject's constant action on himself, which finds its reward in a certain relationship of the subject to himself when he has become inaccessible to external disorders and finds a satisfaction in himself, needing nothing but himself. In a word, let's say that salvation is the vigilant, continuous, and completed form of the relationship to self closed in on itself. One saves oneself for the self, one is saved by the self, one saves oneself in order to arrive at nothing other than oneself. In what I will call this Hellenistic and Roman salvation, this salvation of Hellenistic and Roman philosophy, the self is the agent, object, instrument, and end of salvation. You can see that we are a long way from the salvation in Plato that is mediated by the city-state. We are also a long way from the religious form of salvation linked to a binary system, to a drama of events, to a relationship to the Other, and which in Christianity involves self-renunciation.[21] Rather, salvation ensures an access to the self that is inseparable from the work one carries out on oneself within the time of one's life and in life itself. I will stop there, if you like. We will take a rest for five minutes. Then I will try to show, now, how, despite everything and despite these general theses, salvation of the self in Hellenistic and Roman thought is linked to the question of the salvation of others.

1. Proclus (412-85), was born in Byzantium to a family of magistrates, was converted to Platonist philosophy by Plutarch and became the new master of the Athens School. He taught there, as a strict master, until his death, writing numerous works including the *Platonic Theology*. A Neo-Platonist philosopher of the sixth century, Olympiodorus directed the Alexandria School and wrote numerous commentaries on Plato and Aristotle.
2. A.-J. Festugière, "L'ordre de lecture des dialogues de Platon aux v$^e$/vi$^e$ siècles," in *Études de philosophie grecque* (Paris: Vrin, 1971) pp. 535-50 (first publication: *Museum Helveticum*, 26-4, 1969).
3. Foucault here summarizes the translations given by Festugière.
4. Ibid., p. 540.
5. Iamblichus (around 240-325), who was born at Chalcis in Syria to an influential princely family, taught in Asia Minor (he may have founded a school at Apamea in Syria). He deliberately opened Neo-Platonism to the theurgic dimension; he perfected a spiritual order of reading Plato's dialogues, which became authoritative.
6. A.-J. Festugière, "L'ordre de lecture..."
7. Ibid., pp. 540-41.
8. Ibid., p. 541.
9. Ibid.
10. On the analogy between the soul and the city in the *Alcibiades* and *The Republic*, see the lecture of 13 January, first hour, and supra p. 63, note 28, quotation from *The Republic*.
11. "He forces me to admit to myself that while I am lacking in so much, I persist in not taking care of myself (eti emautou men amelō)." *The Symposium*, 216a.
12. On the notion of salvation in the Pythagoreans, and especially the relationship between salvation and memory exercises, see M. Detienne, *The Masters of Truth in Archaic Greece*, translation Janet Lloyd (Zone Books: New York, 1999) p. 126.
13. "[According to the Orphic poets] the soul is atoning for the sins it has committed... in order to keep it safe (*hina sōzētai*) it has this body as an enclosure (*peribolon*) which represents a prison." Plato, *Cratylus*, 400c.
14. "First and above all, it is really necessary to live in a 'city of renown'... in order... by listening and questioning, to gather everything that has escaped the writers and that, preserved in the memories (*sōtēria mnēmēs*) of men, have more evident authority." Plutarch, *Life of Demosthenes*, 846d.
15. "If we safeguard (*sōzētai*) this distinctive element... if we allow neither his sense of decency, nor his loyalty, nor his intelligence to be corrupted, then it is the man himself who is preserved (*sōzētai*)." Epictetus, *Discourses*, I.xxviii.21.
16. The third of Dio Chrysostom's discourses "On Kingship," "*Ei sōthēsetai tina khronon*," in Dio Chrysostom, *Discourses*, vol. I, p. 130.
17. Discourse 75, "On Law," in Dio Chysostom, *Discourses*, vol. V, p. 48 ("*polin d'ouk eni sōthēnai tou nomou luthentos*").
18. "Let's reject the outward signs of bereavement and think of the care of our bodies (*tēs tou sōmatos epimeleias*) and of securing the well being of those who live with us (*tēs tōn sumbiountōn hēmin sōtērias*)." Plutarch, *A Letter of Condolence to Apollonius*, 118b.
19. The verb *sōzein* is found in discourse 64, but its subject is not the King but Fortune who, Dio tells us, like a good ship, saves all its passengers: "*pantas sōzei tous empleontas.*" *Discourses*, vol. V, p. 48).
20. See above, note 13, reference to Plato's *Cratylus*.
21. See lecture of 24, February, first hour.

## ten

## 3 FEBRUARY 1982

### Second hour

[ *Questions from the public concerning subjectivity and truth.* ∼ *Care of the self and care of others: a reversal of relationships.* ∼ *The Epicurean conception of friendship.* ∼ *The Stoic conception of man as a communal being.* ∼ *The false exception of the Prince.* ]

A SIMPLE TECHNICAL QUESTION about the timetable. I have just been asked whether I will be giving a lecture next week, which will be a university vacation. Does this bother you or not? It's all the same for you? Good, I always have in mind the idea that if maybe you have some questions, maybe it wouldn't be bad if you were to ask them. Since I do two hours in succession, the lectures I am giving are a bit more like a seminar.[1] At any rate, I am trying to introduce a kind of material, or make a number of references, which are usually more difficult to present in a lecture. I would like it to be a bit more like a seminar. Except a seminar implies really that there are some responses or questions or questions-responses. So is there, now for example, anyone who would like to ask any questions, which may be either purely technical questions or general questions on the meaning of what I am doing? Yes?

[*Question from the public:*] Me, if I may. Can we not see some genuinely Lacanian concepts coming up, as operators (opérateurs) *in what you are saying?*

Do you mean in the discourse I am giving, that is to say in the way in which I am talking about what I am talking about, or rather in the things I am talking about?

*They are inseparable.*

Yes, in a sense. Only my answer cannot be the same in both cases. For, in the first case, I would have to give an answer concerning myself. I mean I would have to ask myself what I am doing. In the other case it would involve questioning Lacan and knowing what actually, in a practice, in a conceptual field like psychoanalysis, and Lacanian psychoanalysis, falls in one way or another within the province of this problematic of the subject, of the relationship of the subject to himself, of the relationships of the subject to the truth, etcetera, as it was constituted historically, in this lengthy genealogy I am trying to recount from the *Alcibiades* to Saint Augustine. That's it. So that is why I would like that . . .

*Let's exclude the subject. And let's simply consider the Lacanian concepts. Let's consider the function of the Lacanian concepts . . .*

In my own discourse?

*Yes.*

Well that, I would reply, is for you to say. The ideas, which I cannot even say are at the back of my mind because they are so much out in front in what I say, in the most obvious way, show clearly, in spite of everything, what I want to do. That is to say: to try to situate, in an historical field as precisely articulated as possible, the set of these practices of the subject which developed from the Hellenistic and Roman period until now. And I think that if we do not take up the history of the relations between the subject and truth from the point of view of what I call, roughly, the techniques, technologies, practices, etcetera, which have linked them together and established their norms, we will hardly understand what is involved in the human sciences, if we want to use this term, and in psychoanalysis in particular. So, in a sense I am talking about this. Now, once again, no doubt it is not for me to say what comes from Lacan in the way in which I approach this. I couldn't say.

*For example, when you say "this is true" and "this is not true at the same time." Does not this "it is not true" have a systematic retrospective function* (une fonction économique d'après-coup)?

What do you mean? *[laughter]*

That as a presupposition behind this (that: what has been said, this is not true as it was shortly before) is there not the implicit function of Lacanian concepts that precisely provide this kind of gap between what has been said and what is not yet or maybe never said?

We can say Lacanian, we can also say Nietzschean. In short, let's say that any problematic of the truth as game leads in fact to this kind of discourse. All right, let's take things quite differently. Let's say that there have not been that many people who in the last years—I will say in the twentieth century—have posed the question of truth. Not that many people have posed the question: What is involved in the case of the subject and of the truth? And: What is the relationship of the subject to the truth? What is the subject of truth, what is the subject who speaks the truth, etcetera? As far as I'm concerned, I see only two. I see only Heidegger and Lacan. Personally, myself, you must have heard this, I have tried to reflect on all this from the side of Heidegger and starting from Heidegger. There you are. However, certainly you cannot avoid Lacan when you pose these kinds of questions. Any other questions?

*[A piece of paper is passed to him]*

The question is this: *In the first lecture you set the care of the self and the Cartesian model against each other. It seems to me that this conflict has not been referred to in subsequent lectures. Why?*

It's funny that you ask me this question today, because in fact I thought of taking this up a bit precisely today, with regard to the cathartic, etcetera. It is true that this is the basic question I would like to raise, which is both an historical question and the question of our relationship to the truth. This question, it seems, is that since Plato and, according to the Platonist tradition, since the founding of all philosophy in the *Alcibiades*, the following question is posed: What is the price I have to pay for access to the truth? This price is situated in the subject himself in the form of: What then is the work I must carry out on myself, what fashioning of myself must I undertake, what modification of being must I carry out to be able to have access to the truth? It seems to me that this is a fundamental theme of Platonism, but it is equally so of Pythagoreanism and, I think we can say, of all ancient philosophy, with the enigmatic exception of Aristotle, who anyway is always the exception when you study ancient philosophy. It is a general feature, a fundamental principle, that the subject as such, as he is given to himself, is not capable of truth. And he is not capable of truth unless he carries out or performs a number of operations on himself, a number of transformations and modifications that will make him capable of truth. This is, I think, a fundamental theme in which Christianity very easily finds a place, while adding, of course, a new element which is not found and which obviously you won't find in Antiquity, which is that amongst the conditions is that of the relationship to the Text and faith in a revealed Text. But apart from this, in all ancient philosophy there is the idea of a conversion, for example, which alone can give access to the truth. One cannot have access to the truth if one does not change one's mode of being. So my idea would be that, taking Descartes as a reference point, but obviously influenced by a whole series of complex transformations, there came a point when the subject as such became capable of truth. Obviously the model of scientific practice played a major role in this: To be capable of truth you only have to open your eyes and to reason soundly and honestly, always holding to the line of self-evidence and never letting it go. The subject, then, does not have to transform himself. The subject only has to be what he is for him to have access in knowledge (*connaissance*) to the truth that is open to him through his own structure as subject. It seems to me that this is very clear in Descartes, with, if you like, the supplementary twist in Kant, which consists in saying that what we cannot know is precisely the structure itself of the knowing subject, which means that we cannot know the subject. Consequently, the idea of a certain spiritual transformation of the subject, which finally gives him access to something to which precisely he does not have access at the moment, is chimerical and paradoxical. So the liquidation of what could be called the condition of spirituality for access to the truth is produced with Descartes and Kant; Kant and Descartes seem to me to be the two major moments.

*What surprises me a little is that one has the impression that, before Descartes, Aristotle makes only a fleeting appearance, but that there was no kind of continuity...*

Well, if you like, there was Aristotle. There was, I think I referred to this in the first lecture, the problem of theology.[2] Theology is precisely a type of knowledge with a rational structure that allows the subject—as and only as a rational subject—to have access to the truth of God without the condition of spirituality. Then there were all the empirical sciences (sciences of observation, etcetera). There was mathematics, in short a whole range of processes that did their work. That is to say, generally speaking, scholasticism was already an effort to remove the condition of spirituality laid down in all of ancient philosophy and all Christian thought (Saint Augustine and so forth). You see what I am getting at.

*In these two regimes of truth you are talking about, divided in history by the Cartesian moment (the first requiring a whole transformation of the subject, etcetera, and the second in which the subject can have access to the truth by himself), is the same truth involved in both cases? That is to say a truth that belongs purely to the realm of knowledge* (connaissance), *and a truth that involves the subject's work on himself, is it the same truth...?*

Absolutely not. Yes, you are absolutely right because, amongst all the transformations that have taken place, there was the transformation concerning what I call the condition of spirituality for access to the truth. Second, the transformation of this notion of access to the truth that takes the form of knowledge (*connaissance*), with its own rules and criteria. And finally, third, the transformation of the notion of truth itself. For, here again, very roughly speaking, to have access to the truth is to have access to being itself, access which is such that the being to which one has access will, at the same time, and as an aftereffect, be the agent of transformation of the one who has access to it. And this is the Platonic circle, or anyway the Neo-Platonist circle: by knowing myself I accede to a being that is the truth, and the truth of which transforms the being that I am and places me on the same level as God. The *homoiōsis tō theō* is here.[3] You see what I mean. Whereas it is quite clear that the Cartesian type of knowledge cannot be defined as access to the truth, but is knowledge (*connaissance*) of a domain of objects. So, if you like, the notion of knowledge of the object is substituted for the notion of access to the truth. I am trying to situate here the enormous transformation that is, I think, really essential for understanding what philosophy is, what the truth is, and what the relationships are between the subject and truth, the enormous transformation which this year I am trying to study in terms of the axis "philosophy and spirituality," leaving aside the problem of "knowledge of the object." Shall we go on with the lecture now? Okay.

This then, I believe, is how the notion of salvation is organized in Hellenistic and Roman thought. When salvation is thus defined as the objective of a relationship to self which finds its fulfillment in salvation—the idea of salvation as no more than the realization of the relationship to self—does it at this point become completely incompatible with the problem of the relationship to the Other? Are "salvation of the self" and "salvation of others" definitively disconnected, or, to use the Neo-Platonist vocabulary again, are the political and the cathartic definitively separated? Quite clearly not, at least in the period and forms of thought I am studying here, in the first and second centuries. No doubt it will be different later. Anyway, it seems to me that what is involved is a reversal of the relationship between the cathartic and the political, rather than a separation. You recall that for Plato the salvation of the city-state enveloped the individual's salvation as a consequence. Or, more precisely, albeit still in a general and schematic way, in Plato you cared about the self because you had to take care of others. And when you saved others, you saved yourself at the same stroke. Okay, it seems to me that now the relationship is reversed: You should care about the self because you are the self, and simply for the self. The benefit for others, the salvation of others, or that way of being concerned about others that will make their salvation possible or help them in their own salvation, comes as a supplementary benefit of, or, if you like, follows as what is no doubt a necessary, although only correlative effect of the care you must take of yourself, of your will and application to achieve your own salvation. The care of others is like a supplementary reward for the operation and activity of the salvation you exercise with perseverance on yourself. It seems to me that this reversal of the relationship is illustrated in many ways. Restricting myself to two or three precise examples, I will take the Epicurean conception of friendship, the Stoic conception, or, if you like, the conception specific to Epictetus, of the relationship of self to others (duties towards oneself, duties towards citizens). Then, if I have time, I will also look at the problem of the exercise of Imperial power in Marcus Aurelius.

First, the Epicurean conception of friendship. You know that the Epicurean conception raises a number of problems that oddly enough reveal our own anxious moralizing. Actually, on the one hand we know that Epicurus exalts friendship and, on the other hand, we know, the texts are well known, that Epicurus always derives friendship from utility. This is the famous Vatican Saying 23:[4] "Every friendship is desirable in itself; however it begins with usefulness."[5] Should we say then that Epicurean friendship, as extolled by Epicurus and all his disciples, is no more than usefulness, that is to say, governed entirely by a care of the self that is a concern for utility? I think we should examine this conception of friendship more closely around this notion, this very specific sense of utility. [In fact we must] show that Epicurean friendship is both nothing other than a form of care of the self, and that this care of the self is not thereby a concern for usefulness. Let's consider the Vatican Saying 23 again: "Every friendship is desirable in itself"; *"di'heautēn hairetē"*: it must be chosen for itself, on account of itself; *"arkhēn de eilēphen apo tēs ōpheleias"*: "however, [opposition therefore; M.F.] it begins with usefulness." So, there is a clear opposition between the fact that it is desirable and yet that it began with usefulness. It is as if the more useful it was, the less desirable it would be. Or, it is as if the usefulness of the friendship (which is its beginning, however) and then its intrinsic desirability were mutually exclusive. I don't think it is very difficult to interpret this text and its meaning. Usefulness is *ōpheleia*, that is to say something that designates an external relationship between what one does and why one does it. Friendship is useful. It is useful because it can help me, for example, if I have debts and I want financial assistance. It can be useful in a political career, etcetera. That is how, Epicurus says, friendship begins. That is to say, in fact, it takes place within the regime of social exchanges and services linking men together. But if its origin is here de facto, on the other hand—and the opposition is here—it is *"hairetē di'heautēn,"* that is to say, must be chosen for itself. Why must it be chosen for itself? I think the reason is easily found in Vatican Saying 39: "The friend is neither the one who always seeks what is useful nor the one who never joins usefulness to friendship: for the first makes a trade of the benefit and what is given in return, while the other removes hope for the future."[6] That is to say, friendship will not become *hairetē* (desirable) in itself by suppressing utility, but rather by a certain balance between utility and something other than utility. The person who always seeks what is useful and only seeks what is useful is not a friend, says Vatican Saying 39. But neither should we think that he is a friend who would banish utility entirely from friendship. For if we get rid of utility from friendship, if we exclude it, then at that point we remove any hope for the future. So the problem of Epicurean friendship is this: first, its birth in utility; second, an opposition between the usefulness and the desirability of friendship; third, and finally, the fact that in spite of this opposition, friendship is only desirable if it constantly maintains a certain useful relationship. This combination of usefulness and desirability lies in this fact, and is balanced in the following way: "Of all the things that wisdom prepares for ensuring lifelong happiness, by far the greatest is the possession of friends."[7] And Vatican Saying 34: "We do not welcome the help of our friends, the help that comes to us from them, so much as our trust in the subject of this help."[8] That is to say, friendship is desirable because it is part of happiness. It is part of happiness (*makariotēs*), which consists in what? Happiness consists in knowing that we are as well protected as possible against the evils that may come from the world and that we are completely independent of them. *Makariotēs* is certainty of this independence with regard to evils. And we are assured of this independence by a number of things, among which is that more than providing us with real help, the existence of our friends gives us certainty and confidence that we can get this help. In which case, it is our awareness of friendship, our knowledge that we are surrounded by friends who will reciprocate our attitude of friendship towards them, which constitutes one of the guarantees of our happiness. Insofar as its objective is to establish the soul in a state of *makariotēs*, and so in a state resting on ataraxy, that is to say the absence of inner turmoil, wisdom surrounds itself with friends because we find in these friends, and in the trust we put in their friendship, one of the guarantees of ataraxy and the absence of inner turmoil. You see then that the

Epicurean conception of friendship maintains to the end the principle that in friendship one seeks only oneself or one's own happiness. Friendship is just one of the forms given to the care of the self. Every man who really cares for himself must provide himself with friends. From time to time these friends will enter the network of social exchanges and utility. This usefulness, which is an occasion for friendship, must not be removed. It must be maintained to the end. But what gives this utility its function within happiness is the trust we place in our friends who are, for us, capable of reciprocity. And it is reciprocity of behavior that makes friendship figure as one of the elements of wisdom and happiness. You see then the complex connection between utility and desirability, between the reciprocity of friendship and the singularity of the happiness and tranquility I am assured. And you see that friendship belongs entirely to the domain of care of the self and that it really is for the care of the self that we should have friends. However, the usefulness we get from their friendship, and so the usefulness our friends get from our friendship, is a bonus within this search for friendship for itself. You see this localization of the relationship of reciprocity (usefulness of oneself for others and of others for oneself) within the general objective of our own salvation and of care of the self. It is, if you like, the inverted figure of the Platonic reciprocity I was talking about a short while ago,[9] in which, for Plato, you should take care of the self for others and it was the others who, in the community formed by the city-state, ensured your own salvation. Now Epicurean friendship remains within the care of the self and includes the necessary reciprocity of friends as guarantee of ataraxy and happiness. So, that's Epicurean friendship.

The second indication of this reversal of the relationship between salvation of the self and salvation of others is the Stoic conception of man as a communal being.[10] It is very easy to find this developed in a number of texts. We will take Epictetus as an example. The conception of the link between care of the self and care of others unfolds at two levels in Epictetus. First, at a natural level. This is the conception of the providential bond. Actually, Epictetus says, the order of the world is so organized that all living beings, whatever they are (animals or men, it doesn't matter) seek their own good. Providence, Zeus, God, the rationality of the world, etcetera, have determined that whenever one of these living beings, whatsoever it may be, seeks its own good, at the same time and by the same act, and without wishing to or seeking to, it acts for the good of others. The thesis is set out very clearly in discourse 19 of book I: "he [Zeus] has arranged the nature of the rational animal in such a way that he can attain no particular good without bringing about the common utility. Thus it is not antisocial (*akoinōnēton*) to do everything for oneself (*panta hautou heneka poiein*)."[11] So, doing everything for oneself is not asocial, it is not antisocial. You will say that the text says that Zeus has constituted the nature of the rational animal [...*] [However, more generally, Epictetus establishes the] natural [bond] between usefulness for others and the selfish pursuit of what is useful or indispensable to each. Second, and on the other hand, this bond is transposed when it involves the rational being strictly speaking, the human being. At this point the bond is established at a reflexive level. As you know, according to Epictetus, though animals seek and obtain their own good, they do not obtain this by having taken care of themselves. Another aspect of Providence is precisely that it has determined not only that animals benefit others by pursuing their own good, but also that they do not have to take care of themselves in order to do what is good for them.[12] They have been endowed with a number of advantages like fur, for example, which frees them from having to weave their own clothes—these are old commonplaces on the advantages of animals over men. Men, however, have not been endowed with the advantages that exempt them from taking care of themselves. Zeus has entrusted men to themselves. Zeus has determined that unlike animals, and this is one of the fundamental differences between the rational animal and nonrational animals, men are entrusted to themselves and have to take care of themselves. That is to say, in order to realize his nature as a rational being, in order to conform to his difference from animals, man must in fact take himself as the object of his care. Taking himself as the object of his care, he has to ask himself

---

*Only "... unfortunately I have forgotten the reference; if you like, I will give it to you next time..." is audible.

what he himself is, what he is and what are the things that are not him. He has to ask himself what depends on him and what does not depend on him. And finally he has to ask himself what it is appropriate for him to do or not do, in accordance with the categories of *kathēkonta* or *proēgmena*, etcetera.[13] Consequently, the person who takes care of himself properly—that is to say, the person who has in fact analyzed what things depend on him and what things do not depend on him—when he has taken care of himself so that when something appears in his representations he knows what he should and should not do, he will at the same time know how to fulfill his duties as part of the human community. He will know how to fulfill the duties of father, son, husband, and citizen, precisely because he will attend to himself. Epictetus repeats this thesis many times. Look, for example, at discourse 14 in book II: those who succeed in taking care of themselves "have a life free from pain, fear, and distress, and they observe the order of natural and acquired relationships: those of son, father, brother, citizen, wife, neighbor, fellow-traveller, and subject and ruler."[14] I refer you also to a very interesting discourse in book I. It is the eleventh discourse and involves an example of precisely this problem of care of the self/care of others.[15] It is a very concrete example. It is the story of a father of a family who has problems because his daughter is ill. She has fallen seriously ill, so he has run away and left his daughter's bedside and his household, thus leaving her in the care of others, that is to say of women, servants, etcetera. Why has he done this? Out of selfishness? Not at all. Rather, he did it because he loved his daughter. He loved her so much that her illness upset him, and so it was out of concern for his daughter that he abandoned the sick child to the care of others. Obviously, Epictetus will criticize this attitude. And he will criticize it by emphasizing what? Well, by pointing out that love of the family is natural, in the prescriptive as much as descriptive sense of the word; it is natural to love your family. You should love your family because you love your family and because it is inscribed in nature that you love it. Because it is natural to love your family, it is reasonable to follow the principles governing the bonds between individuals within a family. And, Epictetus says, imagine if your daughter was abandoned by all those who, like you, really love her—she would now be dead. Neither

her mother nor the servants would have remained. In short, Epictetus says, you have made a mistake. You have committed an error and rather than considering your relationship with your daughter as inscribed in and prescribed by nature, instead, then, of conducting yourself in terms of this imperative dictated both by nature and by your reason as a natural individual, as a rational animal, you attended only to your daughter, you thought only of her, and you allowed yourself to be affected by her illness to the extent of being upset by it and, unable to bear the sight of it, you left. You have committed an error by forgetting to care about yourself in order to care about your daughter. If you had attended to yourself, if you had thought of yourself as a rational individual, if you had examined the representations which came to mind concerning your daughter's illness, if you had paid close attention to what you are, what your daughter is, and to the nature and foundation of the bonds established between you, then you would not have let yourself be disturbed by passion and affection for your daughter. You would not have been passive when faced with these representations. Rather, you would have been able to choose the appropriate attitude to adopt. You would have remained cold before your daughter's illness, that is to say you would have stayed to look after her. So, Epictetus concludes, you must become *skholastikos*, that is to say spend some time at the school and learn how to examine your opinions systematically. This is a lengthy undertaking, not the work of an hour or a day.[16] So, as you can see, in this affair Epictetus shows that the father's apparently selfish conduct was rather, in fact, behavior whose raison d'être was only the erratic care or erratic concern, as it were, for the other, and if the father really takes care of himself properly, if he follows the advice Epictetus gives him and learns at school to take care of himself properly, then he would not be upset by his daughter's illness in the first place, and secondly he would stay to look after her. Here, in a very concrete example, we see how care of the self, in itself and as a consequence, must produce or induce behavior through which one will actually be able to take care of others. But all is lost if you begin with the care of others.

Well, you will tell me, there is at least one case in society in which the care of others must, or should, prevail over care of the self, because there is at least one individual whose entire being must be turned towards others, and this is obviously the Prince. For the Prince, the political man par excellence, the only one in the political field of the Roman world who has to be wholly concerned about others, unlike what occurs in the Greek city-state, should not his care for himself be dictated simply by the care he must have for others, as in Plato's *Alcibiades*? Is not the Prince the only one in society, the only one among human beings, who must care about himself only insofar as [he must]—and so that he can in fact—take care of others? Well, we encounter here that character, the Prince, whom we will no doubt meet on a number of occasions in this study of the care of the self. He is a paradoxical character, a central character in a whole series of reflections, an exceptional character who exercises a power over others that constitutes his whole being and who in principle could have a type of relationship to himself and to others completely different from anyone else. No doubt we will have an opportunity to take another look at some of these texts, whether those of Seneca in *De Clementia* or especially those of Dio Chrysostom of Prusa on the monarchy.[17] However, I would like to concentrate on the texts of Marcus Aurelius inasmuch as they give us—*in concreto*, in the case of someone who really was the Prince—the actual way in which he conceived of the relationship between "taking care of others," because he is the emperor, and "taking care of the self."[18] You are well aware that in the *Meditations* of Marcus Aurelius—in the text we call the *Meditations*[19]—there are relatively few direct references to the exercise of imperial power, and that when he does speak about this it is always with regard to, as it were, everyday questions. For example, there is the lengthy and famous exposition on how to greet others, speak to subordinates, and conduct relations with those who seek favors, etcetera. And in this long passage there is absolutely no question of Marcus Aurelius emphasizing the specific tasks of the Prince. Rather, with regard to others—subordinates, those seeking favors, etcetera—he proposes rules of conduct that could be common to the Prince and absolutely anyone else. The general principle of conduct for anyone who would be Prince, like Marcus Aurelius, is precisely to remove everything from his behavior that could be seen as specifically "princely" in a task, and in certain functions, privileges, or even duties. You have to forget that you are Caesar, and you will only perform your work, your task, and fulfill your obligations as Caesar if you conduct yourself like any man: "Be careful not to affect the Caesar too much and impregnate yourself too much with this spirit. Keep yourself simple, honest, pure, serious, natural, the friend of justice, pious, benevolent, affectionate and resolute in the performance of duties."[20]

Now you can see that all these elements of the Prince's good conduct are elements of the daily good conduct of any man whomsoever. The passage in which Marcus Aurelius performs his morning examination of conscience is also very interesting.[21] You know—we will come back to this—that the examination of conscience in Stoic practice, and in Pythagorean practice as well, had two forms and two moments: the evening examination in which you reconstruct the deeds of the day in order to measure them against what you ought to have done,[22] then the morning examination in which you prepare yourself for the tasks you have to perform. You review your use of future time and equip yourself; you reactivate the principles that must be enacted in order to exercise your duty. So, in Marcus Aurelius there is a morning examination that is interesting because he says: Every morning, when I wake up, I recall what I have to do. And he says, I recall that everyone has something to do. In the morning the dancer must remember the exercises he has to perform in order to become a good dancer. The shoemaker or artisan (I no longer know what example he takes[23]) must also remember the different things he has to do during the day. So, I too must do this, and I must be better at it inasmuch as the things I have to do are more important than dancing or an artisan's trade. They are more important, yes, but they are not different in kind, they are not specific. There is simply a responsibility, a heavy responsibility, which is of the same type as any profession or trade, with merely a kind of quantitative supplement. We see here what is no doubt the first clear appearance of the question that will later be of major importance in the European monarchies, and especially in the problematization of the monarchies in the sixteenth century: that of sovereignty as a job, that is to say as a task whose moral structure and fundamental principles are those of any other professional activity. [Marcus Aurelius] clearly expresses the idea that to be emperor—or chief or the one who commands—not only imposes duties, of course, we knew that, but that these duties should be considered, fulfilled, and executed on the basis of a moral attitude like that of any other man with regard to his tasks. The Empire, the principality, becomes an occupation and profession. Why does it become an occupation and profession? Quite simply because for Marcus Aurelius the primary objective, the very end of his existence, the target to which he must always strive, is not to be emperor, but to be himself. And it is in his care for himself, in his concern about himself, that he will encounter all his occupations as emperor. Just as the philosopher who cares about himself must think of his obligations as philosopher—of the teaching he must give, the spiritual guidance he must practice, etcetera, or just as the shoemaker who cares about himself must think, in this care of himself, of what his task is as shoemaker, so the emperor, because he will care about himself, will meet and accomplish tasks that must be accomplished only insofar as they form part of this general objective of: himself for himself. Book VIII: "Keeping your eyes fixed on your task, examine it well and, remembering that you must be an honest man and what nature demands [of man], perform it without a backward glance."[24] This is an important text. You can see its elements. First: keeping your eyes fixed on the task. The Empire, sovereignty, is not a privilege. It is not the consequence of a status. It is a task, a job like any other. Second: you must really examine it, but—and here we encounter what is particular, specific in this task— it is singular, because in all the works, professions, etcetera, all the occupations you may exercise, imperial power can be exercised by one and only one person. So you must examine it, but as you would examine any task with its particular features. Finally, this examination of the task must be measured against or oriented by something [that] you always remember. What do you always remember? That you must be a good emperor? No. That you must save humanity? No. That you must dedicate yourself to the public good? No. You should always remember that you must be an honest man and you should remember what nature demands. Moral candor, which in the case of the emperor is not defined by his specific task and privileges but by nature, by a human nature shared with no matter who, must form the very foundation of his conduct as emperor and, consequently, must define how he must care for others. And he must do this without looking back, that is to say we find again that image, to which we will frequently return, of the morally good man as one who fastens once and for all on a certain objective in his life from which he must not deviate in any way: he must look neither to the right nor the left, at men's behavior, at pointless sciences, or at knowledge of the world with no importance for him; no more must he look back in order to find foundations for his action behind him. His objective is the foundation of his action. What is this objective? It is himself. The emperor will not only produce his own good but also the good of others in this care of the self, in this relationship of the self to the self as a relationship of the self striving towards itself. It is in caring for himself that he will inevitably care [for others]. Okay. There we are. So next time we will talk about the problem: conversion of the self and knowledge of the self.

1. See lecture of 6 January, first hour, above p. 20, note 1.
2. See same lecture, second hour.
3. This expression is found in Plato's *Theaetetus*, 176a-b, and signifies "assimilation to the divine"; see lecture of 17 March, first hour, below, p. 434, note 7.
4. The *Vatican Sayings* derive their name from their discovery in a Vatican manuscript that included a compilation of 81 sayings of an ethical character. The *Principal Doctrines* bring together a set of crucial statements that may have been put together, at least in the beginning, by Epicurus himself.
5. Epicurus, *The Vatican Sayings*, XXIII.
6. Ibid., XXXIX.
7. *Principal Doctrines*, XXVII.
8. *Vatican Sayings*, XXXIV.
9. See the first hour of this lecture, above pp. 175-76.
10. See, for example, the classic texts of Cicero, *De Officiis* (*Treatise on Duties*), III.V, or Marcus Aurelius, *Meditations*, V.16 and VI.54.
11. Epictetus, *Discourses*, I.19.13-15.
12. "Animals do not exist for themselves, but for service, and it would not have been worthwhile to have created them with all these needs. Think a little how tiresome it would be for us not only to have to watch over ourselves, but also our sheep and asses." *Discourses*, I.xvi.3. See the analysis of this text in the lecture of 24 March, first hour.
13. In Stoicism *kathēkonta* (translated by Cicero as *officia*: duties, functions, offices) designates activities that conform to and realize a being's nature; the *proēgmena* refer to those actions that, although not of absolute value from the moral point of view, are liable to be preferred to their contraries. On these notions, see Cicero, *De finibus bonorum et malorum* book III, VI and XVI, translation H. Rackham (London and New York: Loeb Classical Library, 1914) pp. 236-41 and pp. 270-75.
14. Epictetus, *Discourses*, II.xiv.8.
15. Ibid., I.xi. For Foucault's first analysis of this passage, see the lecture of 27 January, first hour.
16. "You see, then, that you must become a school student (*skholastikon*) and become that animal at which everyone laughs, if, that is, you wish to make an examination of your own opinions. And that this is not the work of a single hour or day you know as well as I do." Ibid., I.xi.39-40.
17. In fact, Foucault does not come back to this point. A number of dossiers found with the manuscripts indicate however the extent to which Foucault elaborated the articulation of care of the self and care of others within the framework of a general politics of the Prince. We find traces of these reflections in *Le Souci de soi*, pp. 109-10 (*The Care of the Self*, pp. 88-89).
18. *Le Souci de soi*, pp 110-12 (*The Care of the Self*, pp. 89-91).
19. "It is highly likely that when Marcus was writing what we now call the *Meditations*, he had no idea of giving a title to these notes intended only for himself. In antiquity, moreover, as long as a book remained unpublished—through a public reading, for instance—it was almost always the case that the author did not give it a title ... The Vatican manuscript gives no title to the Emperor's work. Some manuscript collections of extracts from it do bear the notice: *ta kath'heauton*, which could be translated: 'Writing concerning Himself' or 'Private Writing.' The *editio princeps* offers the title: 'Writings for himself' (*ta eis heauton*)." Pierre Hadot, *La Citadelle intérieure* (Paris: Fayard, 1992) p. 38; English translation by Michael Chase, *The Inner Citadel. The* Meditations *of Marcus Aurelius* (Cambridge, Mass. and London: Harvard University Press, 2001) pp. 23-24.
20. Marcus Aurelius, *Meditations*, VI.30.
21. Foucault focuses his analysis on two passages from the first paragraph of book V of the *Meditations*: "In the morning, when it pains you to rise, have this thought present: I am

rising to do the work of man ... Others, who love their occupations, wear themselves out with the labor they bring to them, neither washing nor eating. Do you hold your nature in lower regard than does the engraver his art, the dancer the dance?"
22. See the lecture of 24 March, second hour.
23. It is the engraver.
24. Marcus Aurelius, *Meditations*, VIII.5.

## eleven

## 10 FEBRUARY 1982

### First hour

> *Reminder of the double opening up of care of the self with regard to pedagogy and political activity.* ~ *The metaphors of the self-finalization of the self.* ~ *The invention of a practical schema: conversion to the self.* ~ *Platonic* epistrophē *and its relation to conversion to the self.* ~ *Christian* metanoia *and its relation to conversion to the self.* ~ *The classical Greek meaning of* metanoia. ~ *Defense of a third way, between Platonic* epistrophē *and Christian* metanoia. ~ *Conversion of the gaze: criticism of curiosity.* ~ *Athletic concentration.*

UNTIL NOW I HAVE tried to follow the broadening of the theme of care of the self that we picked out in the *Alcibiades*, to follow it to the point at which it opens out onto a veritable culture of the self, which takes on its full dimensions, I think, at the beginning of the imperial epoch. What I have tried to show in the previous lectures is that this broadening appears, if you like, in two major ways. First: the opening up of the practice of the self with regard to pedagogy. That is to say, the practice of the self no longer appears, as it did in the *Alcibiades*, as a complement, an element indispensable to or a substitute for pedagogy. Henceforth, instead of being a precept laid down for the adolescent at the moment of entry into adult and political life, the practice of the self is an injunction valid for the entire course of life. The practice of the self is identified and united with the art of living itself (the *tekhnē tou biou*).

The art of living and the art of oneself are identical; at least they become, or tend to become, identical. As we have seen, this opening out with regard to pedagogy also has a second consequence: henceforth the practice of the self is no longer just a small matter concerning two people that takes place in the unique and dialectical love relationship between master and disciple. The practice of the self is now integrated within, mixed up, and intertwined with a whole network of different social relations in which mastership in the strict sense still exists, but in which there are also many other possible forms of relationships. So, first: opening out in relation to pedagogy. Second: There is an opening out in relation to political activity. You recall that what was involved in the *Alcibiades* was looking after the self so as to be able to take care of others and the city-state properly. Now one must take care of the self for itself, the relationship to others being deduced from and entailed by the relationship one establishes of self to self. You recall: Marcus Aurelius does not look after himself in order to be more sure of properly looking after the Empire, that is to say, in sum, mankind. But he knows that above all, and in the final account, he will be able to look after mankind, which has been entrusted to him, insofar as he knows how to take care of himself properly. The emperor finds the law and principle of the exercise of his sovereignty in the relationship of self to self. One takes care of the self for the self. What I tried to show last week was that the notion of salvation is, I believe, based on this self-finalization.

Okay, I think that all of this now refers us, as you see, not exactly to a notion, I stress this, but to what I will call, provisionally if you like, a sort of nucleus, a central nucleus. Perhaps even a set of images. You are familiar with these images. We have come across them elsewhere many times. They are these, which I list together: we must, of course, apply ourselves to ourselves, that is to say we must turn away from everything around us. We must turn away from everything that is not part of ourselves but which might grab our attention, our diligence, and arouse our zeal. We must turn away from this in order to turn round to the self. Our attention, eyes, mind, and finally our whole being must be turned towards the self throughout our life. We must turn away from everything that turns us away from our self, so as to turn ourselves around towards our self. This is the great image of turning around towards oneself underlying all the analyses I have been talking about until now. Furthermore, on this problem of the turning around on oneself, there is a series of images, some of which have been analyzed. One of these in particular, analyzed by Festugière some time ago now, is very interesting. You will find its analysis, or rather the schema, in a summary of the lectures at Les Hautes Études. It is the history of the image of the spinning top.[1] The spinning top is indeed something that turns on itself, but the way in which it does so is precisely not how we should turn around towards our self. For what is the top? Well, the top is something that turns on itself at the behest and on the instigation of an external impulse. On the other hand, by turning on itself, the top successively presents different faces in different directions and to the different components of its surroundings. And finally, although the top apparently remains immobile, in reality it is always in movement. Now, in contrast with this movement of the top, wisdom consists, rather, in never allowing ourselves to be induced to make an involuntary movement at the behest of or through the instigation of an external impulse. Rather, we must seek the point at the center of ourselves to which we will be fixed and in relation to which we will remain immobile. It is towards ourselves, towards the center of ourselves, in the center of ourselves, that we must fix our aim. And the movement we must make must be to turn back to this center of ourselves in order to immobilize ourselves there, definitively.

All these images, then, of turning around—of turning around towards the self by turning away from what is external to us—clearly bring us close to what we could call, perhaps anticipating a bit, the notion of conversion. And it is a fact that we regularly find a series of words that can be translated, and translated legitimately, as "conversion." For example, there is the expression, *epistrephein pros heauton* (turning towards the self, converting to the self), which is found in Epictetus,[2] Marcus Aurelius,[3] and also in Plotinus.[4] In Seneca there is an expression like [*se*] *convertere ad se* (converting to the self).[5] To convert to the self is, once again, to turn around towards oneself. It seems to me, however—and this what I will try to show you—that through all these images one is not in fact dealing with a rigorous, "constructed" notion of conversion. It is much more a kind of practical schema, which although it is rigorously constructed, did not produce something like the "concept" or notion of conversion. Anyway, I would like to dwell a little on this today for the obvious reason that this notion of conversion, of the return to the self, of the turning around towards oneself, is certainly one of the most important technologies of the self the West has known. And when I say it is one of the most important, I am thinking, of course, of its importance in Christianity. But it would be quite wrong to view and gauge the importance of the notion of conversion only in connection with religion, and with Christian religion. After all, the notion of conversion is also an important philosophical notion that played a decisive role in philosophy, in practical philosophy. The notion of conversion is also crucially important in connection with morality. And finally, we should not forget that from the nineteenth century the notion of conversion was introduced into thought, practice, experience, and political life in a spectacular and we can even say dramatic way. One day the history of what could be called revolutionary subjectivity should be written. What seems to me interesting in this is that basically, and this is a hypothesis, I do not get the impression that there was ever anything of the nature of conversion either in what has been called the English Revolution or what is called "the Revolution" in France of [17]89. It seems to me that schemas of individual and subjective experience of "conversion to the revolution" begin to be defined in the nineteenth century—and again this will have to be checked—around 1830-1840 no doubt, precisely with reference to the French Revolution as the founding, historico-mythical event [for the] nineteenth century. It seems to me that we cannot understand revolutionary practice throughout the nineteenth century, we cannot understand the revolutionary individual and what revolutionary experience meant for him, unless we take into account the notion or fundamental schema of conversion to the revolution. So the problem is to see how this element, which arises from the most traditional technology of the self—I will say, historically the thickest and most condensed, since it goes back to Antiquity—was introduced, how conversion, this element of technology of the self, was plugged into this new domain and field of political activity, and how this element of conversion was necessarily, or at least exclusively, linked to the revolutionary choice, to revolutionary practice. We would also have to see how this notion of conversion was gradually validated, then absorbed, soaked up, and finally nullified by the existence of a revolutionary party, and how we passed from belonging to the revolution through the schema of conversion, to belonging to the revolution by adherence to a party. And you know that these days, now, in our daily experience—I mean the perhaps somewhat bland experience of our immediate contemporaries—we only convert to renunciation of revolution. The great converts today are those who no longer believe in the revolution. Okay. In short, there is a whole history to be written. Let us return to this notion of conversion and to the way in which it is elaborated and transformed in the period I am talking about, that is to say the first and second centuries of our era. There is, then, the very important and constant presence of this image of the return to the self ([*se*] *convertere ad se*).

The first thing I want to stress is that the theme of conversion is obviously not new in the period I am talking about, since you know it is developed in a very important way in Plato. It is found in Plato in the form of the notion of *epistrophē*. The *epistrophē* is characterized—and obviously I am speaking very schematically here—in the following way: it consists first of all in turning away from appearances.[6] There is this element of conversion as a way of turning away from something (from appearances). Second: taking stock of oneself by acknowledging one's own ignorance and by deciding precisely to care about the self, to take care of the self.[7] And finally, the third stage, on the basis of this reversion to the self, which leads us to recollection, we will be able to return to our homeland, the homeland of essences, truth and Being.[8] "Turning away from," "turning around towards the self," "recollecting," "returning to one's homeland (to one's ontological homeland)"—these, very roughly, are the four elements in the Platonic schema of the *epistrophē*. You see anyway that this Platonic *epistrophē* is governed first of all by a fundamental opposition between the world down here and the other world. Second, it is governed by the theme of a liberation, of the soul's release from the body, the prison-body, the tomb-body, etcetera.[9] And finally, thirdly, the Platonic *epistrophē* is, I think, governed by the privileged role of knowing. To know oneself is to know the true. To know the true is to free oneself. And these different elements are joined together in the act of recollection as the fundamental form of knowledge.

It seems to me that the theme of "conversion" in the Hellenistic and Roman culture of the self—which again I put in inverted commas because I do not think it should be taken as a constructed, finished and well-defined notion closed on itself—is very different from the Platonic *epistrophē*. I put to one side, of course, the specifically Platonic movements of thought, which remain faithful to this notion of *epistrophē*. First of all, the conversion found in the Hellenistic and Roman culture and practice of the self does not function on the axis opposing this world here to the other world, as does the Platonic *epistrophē*. It is, rather, a reversion that takes place in the immanence of the world, so to speak, which does not mean, however, that there is not a basic opposition between what does and does not depend on us. However, whereas the Platonic *epistrophē* consisted in the movement leading us from this world to the other, from the world below to the world above, in the Hellenistic and Roman culture of the self conversion gets us to move from that which does not depend on us to that which does.[10] What is involved, rather, is liberation within this axis of immanence, a liberation from what we do not control so as finally to arrive at what we can control. As a result, this leads us to that other characteristic of Hellenistic and Roman conversion: it does not appear as a liberation from the body, but rather as the establishment of a complete, perfect, and adequate relationship of self to self. Conversion does not take place then in the break with my body, but rather in the adequacy of self to self. This is its second major difference from the Platonic *epistrophē*. Finally, the third major difference is that although knowledge certainly plays an important part, nevertheless it is not so decisive and fundamental as in the Platonic *epistrophē*. In the Platonic *epistrophē*, the essential, fundamental part of conversion is knowledge in the form of recollection. Now, in this process of [*se*] *convertere ad se*, the essential element is much more exercise, practice, and training; *askēsis* rather than knowledge. All of this is very schematic and will be developed in more detail later. However, it is just to situate the theme of conversion, to show that it will have to be analyzed in comparison with the great Platonic *epistrophē*.

Second, I would now like to situate [the Hellenistic conversion] with regard to a theme, a form, a notion of conversion that in this case is very precise and which is not found before but after, later, in Christian culture. That is to say, the notion of conversion (*metanoia*) as developed in Christianity from the third and, especially, fourth centuries. Christian conversion, for which Christians use the word *metanoia*, is obviously very different from the Platonic *epistrophē*. You know that the word itself, *metanoia*, means two things: *metanoia* is penitence and it is also radical change of thought and mind. Now—again speaking as schematically as I was a moment ago about *epistrophē*—Christian *metanoia* seems to have the following characteristics.[11] First, Christian conversion involves a sudden change. When I say sudden, I do not mean that it may not have been, or even did not have to be prepared by a whole development over a long period of time. Nevertheless—whether or not there is preparation, development, effort, ascesis—conversion anyway requires a single, sudden, both historical and metahistorical event which drastically changes and transforms the subject's mode of being at a single stroke. Second, in this conversion, this Christian *metanoia*, this sudden, dramatic, historical-metahistorical upheaval of the subject, there is a transition: a transition from one type of being to another, from death to life, from mortality to immortality, from darkness to light, from the reign of the devil to that of God, etcetera. And finally, third, in this Christian conversion there is an element that is a consequence of the other two or which is found at their point of intersection, and this is that there can only be conversion inasmuch as a break takes place in the subject. A fundamental element of Christian conversion is renunciation of oneself, dying to oneself, and being reborn in a different self and a new form which, as it were, no longer has anything to do with the earlier self in its being, its mode of being, in its habits or its *ēthos*.

If we compare this to how conversion is described in the philosophy, morality, and culture of the self in the Hellenistic and Roman period I am talking about, if we look at how this *conversio ad se*[12] (this *epistrophē pros heauton*[13]) is described, I think we see completely different processes at work from those in Christian conversion. First, there is not exactly a break. At least, here we must be a bit more precise and I will try to develop this a bit more later. There are some expressions that seem to indicate something like a break between self and self, and like a sudden, radical change and transfiguration of the self. In Seneca, but practically only Seneca, there is the expression *fugere a se*: to flee oneself, to escape oneself.[14] There are also some interesting expressions in Seneca, in letter 6 to Lucilius for example. He says: It's incredible, I feel I am now making progress. It is not just an *emendatio* (a correction). I am not content with mending my ways; I have the impression that I am being transfigured (*transfigurari*).[15] A bit further on in the same letter he speaks of a change in himself (*mutatio mei*).[16] However, apart from these few indications, what seems to me essential, or anyway typical in Hellenistic and Roman conversion, is that if there is a break, it is not produced within the self. There is not that caesura within the self by which the self tears itself away from itself and renounces itself in order to be reborn other than itself after a figurative death. If there is a break—and there is—it takes place with regard to what surrounds the self. The break must be carried out with what surrounds the self so that it is no longer enslaved, dependent, and constrained. There are then a series of terms or notions referring to this break between the self and everything else, but which is not a break of the self with the self. There are the terms designating flight (*pheugein*)[17] and withdrawal (*anakhōrēsis*). You know that *anakhōrēsis* has two meanings: the retreat of an army before the enemy (when an army disengages from the enemy: *anakhōrei*, it takes off, withdraws, disengages); or again *anakhōrēsis* is the flight of the slave who takes off into the *khōra*, the countryside, thus escaping subjection and his status as slave. These are the breaks involved. We will see that, in Seneca, there is a range of equivalents for this liberation, a range of expressions all referring to the self breaking with everything else (in the preface to the third part of *Natural Questions*,[18] for example, or the letters 1,[19] 32,[20] 8,[21] etcetera). I draw your attention to Seneca's interesting metaphor, which is well known moreover and refers to the pirouette, but with a different meaning from that of the spinning top we were talking about a moment ago. It appears in letter 8. Seneca says that philosophy spins the subject around on himself, that is to say it performs the action by which, traditionally and legally, a master freed his slave. There was a ritual gesture in which the master turned his slave around on the spot in order to show, to demonstrate and effectuate his freedom from subjection.[22] Seneca takes up this image and says that philosophy turns the subject around on the spot, but in order to free him.[23] So, the break takes place for the self. It is a break with everything around the self, for the benefit of the self, but not a break within the self.

The second important theme distinguishing this conversion from the future Christian *metanoia*, is that in Hellenistic and Roman conversion you must turn to look towards the self. You must have the self under your eyes so to speak, under your gaze or in sight. A series of expressions derive from this, like *blepe se* (consider yourself; you find this in Marcus Aurelius),[24] or *observa te* (observe yourself),[25] *se respicere* (looking at yourself, turning your gaze back on the self),[26] applying your mind to the self (*prosekhein ton noun heautō*),[27] etcetera. So, the self must be kept before your eyes.

And finally, third, you must advance towards the self as you advance towards an end. This is not merely a movement of the eyes, but a movement of the whole being, which must move towards the self as the sole objective. Advancing towards the self is at the same time a return to the self, like a return to port or the return of an army to the town and fortress that protect it. Here again a series of metaphors of the fortress-self[28]—the self as the port where you finally find shelter, etcetera[29]—clearly show that this movement by which you direct yourself towards the self is at the same time a movement of return to the self. We have a problem here, moreover, in these images which are not immediately coherent, a problem which marks, I think, the tension of this notion, this practice, this practical schema of conversion, inasmuch as I do not think it is ever completely clear or resolved in Hellenistic and Roman thought whether the self is something to which you return because it is given in advance or an objective you must set for yourself and to which you might finally gain access if you achieve wisdom. Is the self the point to which you return through the long detour of ascesis and philosophical practice? Or is the self an object you keep always before your eyes and reach through a movement that in the end can only be bestowed by wisdom? I think this is one of the elements of fundamental uncertainty, or fundamental oscillation, in this practice of the self.

Anyway, and this is the last feature I want to stress, this notion of conversion involves finally establishing with the self—to which you either return or towards which you direct yourself—a number of relations which do not characterize the movement of conversion, but at least its point of arrival and point of completion. These relations of self to self may take the form of actions. For example, you protect the self, you defend, arm, and equip it.[30] They may also take the form of attitudes: You respect the self, you honor it.[31] And finally they may take the form of a relationship, so to speak, of a condition: You are master of the self, you possess it, it is your own (a legal relationship).[32] Or again: You experience a pleasure in yourself, an enjoyment or delight.[33] You see that conversion is defined here as a movement directed towards the self, which doesn't take its eyes off it, which fixes it once and for all as an objective, and which finally reaches it or returns to it. If conversion (Christian or post-Christian *metanoia*) takes the form of a break or change within the self, if consequently we can say that it is a sort of trans-subjectivation, then I would propose saying that the conversion of the philosophy of the first centuries of our era is not a trans-subjectivation. It is not a way of introducing or marking an essential caesura in the subject. Conversion is a long and continuous process that I will call a self- subjectivation rather than a trans-subjectivation. How, by fixing your self as the objective, can you establish a full and adequate relationship of self to self? This is what is at stake in this conversion.

You see, then, that we are very far, it seems to me, from the Christian notion of *metanoia*. In any case, the term *metanoia* itself (which you come across in the literature and texts of classical Greece, of course, but also in those of the period I am talking about) never means conversion. It is found in a number of usages referring primarily to the idea of a change of opinion. You *metanoei* (you change opinion) when you have been persuaded by someone.[34] You also find the notion of *metanoia*, the idea of a *metanoein* with the meaning of regret and the experience of remorse (you find this usage in Thucydides, book III).³⁵ In this usage it always has a negative connotation, a negative value. *Metanoia* always has a negative rather than a positive meaning in the Greek literature of that period. Thus, in Epictetus you find the idea that we must get rid of the erroneous judgments we may have in our heads. Why must we get rid of these judgments? Because otherwise we will be forced to reproach ourselves, to struggle against ourselves, and to repent on account of and as a consequence of these judgments (so you have the verbs, *makhestai, basanizein*, etc.). We will be forced to repent: *metanoein*.³⁶ So, having no false judgments so as not *metanoein* (so as not to repent). In *The Encheiridion* of Epictetus there is also the idea that we should not let ourselves be carried away by the kind of pleasures which will give rise to repentance (*metanoia*) afterwards.³⁷ In Marcus Aurelius there is the advice: "Of any action we should ask: what is the likelihood that I shall repent of it? [*mē metanoēsō ep'autē*: shall I repent of having done this action? M.F.]."³⁸ Repentance, then, is something to be avoided, and because it is to be avoided there are a number of things not to do, pleasures to refuse, etcetera. *Metanoia* as repentance therefore is what in fact is to be avoided. This amounts to saying that I do not think that what is involved in the theme of conversion to the self, of return to the self, can be assimilated to *metanoia* understood as a founding conversion taking place through a complete change of the subject himself, renouncing the self, and being reborn from himself. This is not what is involved. *Metanoia* in the positive sense of a break with the self and renewal of the self is found in some texts much later. Of course, I am not speaking of the Christian texts which, from the third century, or at least from the establishment of the great rituals of penance, gave a positive meaning to *metanoia*. *Metanoia* with a positive meaning and with the meaning of a renewal of the subject by himself is not found in philosophical vocabulary until the third and fourth centuries. It is found, for example, in the Pythagorean texts of Hierocles in which he says: *Metanoia* is the *arkhē tēs philosophias* (the beginning of philosophy). It is the flight (*phugē*) from all irrational action and discourse. This is the primordial preparation for a life without regrets. Here then, in fact, you have *metanoia* in, if you like, a new sense of the term, in the sense which was, in part at least, developed by the Christians: It is the idea of a *metanoia* as change, disruption, and modification of the subject's being and access to a life without regrets.³⁹

You see, then, that in this sector that I would now like to study we are between the Platonic *epistrophē* and the Christian *metanoia* (*metanoia* in the new sense of the word). In fact, I think neither the Platonic *epistrophē* nor what can be called, schematically, Christian *metanoia* are entirely suitable for describing this practice and this mode of experience, which appears so frequently and is referred to so frequently in the texts of the first and second centuries. I have done all this preparation and taken all these precautions with regard to the analysis of this conversion, between *epistrophē* and *metanoia*, with reference, of course, to a basic text written by Pierre Hadot twenty years ago now.⁴⁰ At a philosophical conference he produced what I think is an absolutely fundamental and important analysis of *epistrophē* and *metanoia* in which he said that there were two great models of conversion in Western culture, that of *epistrophē* and that of *metanoia*. *Epistrophē*, he says, is a notion, an experience of conversion, which implies the soul's return to its source, the movement by which it reverts to the perfection of being and places itself back once again within the eternal movement of being. The model for *epistrophē* is awakening, so to speak, and *anamnēsis* (recollection) is the fundamental mode of this awakening. One opens one's eyes, one discovers the light and reverts to the very source of the light, which is at the same time the source of being. This is the *epistrophē*. As for *metanoia*, he says, it is a different model and conforms to a different schema. It involves a drastic change of the mind, a radical renewal; it involves a sort of rebirth of the subject by himself, with death and resurrection at the heart of this as an experience of oneself and the renunciation of the self. With this distinction, even opposition, between *epistrophē* and *metanoia*, Hadot identifies a permanent polarity within Western thought, within Western spirituality and philosophy. So this opposition between *epistrophē* and *metanoia* is, I think, quite effective and actually constitutes a very good analytical grid for conversion as it exists, and as it was practiced and experienced, starting from Christianity itself. And I think that these two modes of the subject's transformation, of his transfiguration, do in fact constitute two fundamental forms in the experience to which we can now give a single word: conversion. However, I would like to say even so that if we take things in their diachronic development, and if we follow the theme of conversion as it unfolds throughout Antiquity, it seems to me very difficult to establish these two models, these two schemas, as the explanatory and analytical grid for understanding what takes place in the period extending roughly from Plato to Christianity. Actually, it seems to me that if the notion of *epistrophē*, which is a Platonic or perhaps Pythagorean-Platonic notion, is already clearly worked out in the Platonic texts (and so in the fourth century [B.C.]), these elements were, I think, profoundly modified in later thought, outside specifically Pythagorean and Platonic movements. Epicurean, Cynic, and Stoic thought, etcetera, tried—and I think succeeded—in thinking of conversion in terms other than those of the Platonic model of *epistrophē*. But at the same time, in the period I am talking about, in Hellenistic and Roman thought, we have a schema of conversion that is different from the Christian *metanoia* organized around self-renunciation and the sudden, dramatic change of the subject's being. So what I would now like to study a little more precisely is how, between the Platonic *epistrophē* and the establishment of Christian *metanoia*, the movement that called upon the subject to convert to himself, to direct himself to himself, or to revert to himself, was conceived. I would like to study this conversion that is neither *epistrophē* nor *metanoia*. I will do so in two ways.

First of all, today, I would like to study the problem of the conversion of the gaze. I would like to try to see how the question of "turning your gaze on yourself" and "knowing yourself" was established within the general theme of conversion (of conversion to the self). Given the importance of the theme—you must look at yourself, you must turn your eyes on yourself, you must never be out of your sight, you must always have yourself in sight—there seems to be something here which brings us very close to the requirement to "know yourself." And it does seem that the subject's knowledge of himself is entailed by [...] the requirement to "turn your eyes on yourself." When Plutarch, Epictetus, Seneca, and Marcus Aurelius say that you must examine yourself and look at yourself, what type of knowing (*savoir*) is involved in fact? Is it a call to constitute oneself as an object [...] [of knowledge (*connaissance*)? Is it a "Platonic" appeal? Is it not quite similar to the appeal found later in Christian and monastic literature*] in the form of a requirement of vigilance expressed in precepts and advice like: Pay attention to all the images and representations which enter your mind; always examine every movement in your heart so as to decipher in them the signs or traces of a temptation; try to determine whether what comes to your mind has been sent by God or the devil, or even by yourself; is there not a trace of concupiscence in what seem to be the purest ideas that enter your mind? In short, starting from monastic practice, there is a certain type of self-observation that is very different from the Platonic gaze.[41] The question I think we should ask [is this]: when Epictetus, Seneca, Marcus Aurelius, etcetera, lay down "look at yourself" as a requirement, is this a case of the Platonic gaze—look inside yourself to discover the seeds of the truth within yourself—or does it involve having to look at yourself in order to detect the traces of concupiscence within you and to flush out and explore the secrets of your conscience (the *arcana conscientiae*)? Well, here again, I think it is neither the one nor the other and that the instruction to "turn your gaze on yourself" has a quite specific meaning that is distinct from the Platonic "know yourself" and from the "examine yourself" of monastic spirituality. What does "turning your gaze on yourself" mean in these texts of Plutarch, Seneca, Epictetus, Marcus Aurelius, etcetera? In order to understand what "turning your gaze on yourself" means, I think we must first of all ask the question: From what must the gaze be turned away when one receives the injunction to turn it on oneself? Turning one's gaze on the self means turning it away from others first of all. And then, later, it means turning it away from the things of the world.

First: Turning one's gaze on the self is turning it away from others. Turning it away from others means turning it away from everyday apprehension, from the curiosity that makes us interested in other people, etcetera. There is a very interesting text on this subject, a short text

---

*Restoration according to the manuscript.

which, like all of Plutarch's texts, is rather banal and doesn't get very far, but which is, I think, very revealing of what we should understand by this turning the gaze away from others. It is a treatise called, precisely, *On Curiosity*, in which there are two very interesting metaphors right at the beginning. Right at the start of the text Plutarch refers to what happens in towns.[42] He says: Previously towns were built completely randomly, under the worst conditions and in such a way that there was great discomfort because of bad wind blowing through the town and the wrong kind of sunshine, etcetera. A point was reached when a choice had to be made between moving entire towns or reorganizing them, replanning them, as we would say, "reorienting" them. And he uses for this precisely the expression *strephein*.[43] Houses are turned round on themselves, oriented differently, and doors and windows are opened differently. Or again, he says, mountains can be pulled down or walls built so that the wind no longer lashes the town and its inhabitants in a possibly harmful, dangerous, or disagreeable way etcetera. [So:] reorientation of a town. Second, a bit further on (515e), he says, then taking up the metaphor of the house again: The windows of a house should not open onto the neighbors' houses. Or, at any rate, if you have windows that open onto the neighbor, you should be careful to close them and open rather those that open onto the men's rooms, onto the gynaeceum, and onto the servants' quarters, in order to know what is going on there and be able to keep them under constant surveillance. Well, he says, this is what we should do with ourselves: Don't look at what is going on in the houses of other people, but look rather at what is going on in our own. You get the impression—a first impression anyway—that what is at stake is the substitution of a rather serious examination of oneself for knowledge of others or for unhealthy curiosity about others. The same thing is found in Marcus Aurelius where, at several points, there is the injunction: Don't concern yourself with other people, it is much better to take care of yourself. Thus, in II.8, there is the principle: We are generally never unhappy because we pay no heed to what is going on in another person's soul.[44] In III.4: "Don't use up what is left of your life thinking about what the other person is doing."[45] In IV.18: "What free time is gained by the person who pays no attention to what his neighbor has said, done, or thought, but only to what he himself is doing (*ti autos poiei*)."⁴⁶ Therefore, do not look at what is going on in other people; rather, take an interest in yourself.

However, we must look a little at what exactly this turning round of the gaze consists in, and what you must look at in the self when you are no longer looking at others. First of all we should remember that the word translated as curiosity is *polupragmosunē*, that is to say not so much the desire to know as indiscretion. It is meddling in what does not concern us. Plutarch defines it very precisely at the beginning of his treatise: "*philomatheia allotriōn kakōn*."⁴⁷ It is the desire, the pleasure of hearing about the troubles of other people, about what ills the other person is suffering. It is being interested in what is not going well for others. It is being interested in their faults. It is taking pleasure in knowing about their misdeeds. Hence Plutarch's contrary advice: Don't be curious. That is to say: Rather than concern yourself with the imperfections of others, be concerned about your own flaws and misdeeds, with your *hamartēmata*.⁴⁸ Look at the flaws in yourself. But actually, when we examine Plutarch's text in detail, we see that the way in which this turning away of the gaze from others to oneself must be carried out does not consist at all in substituting oneself for the other as the object of a possible or necessary knowledge (*connaissance*).⁴⁹ Plutarch uses words that designate this turning around: he employs the words, for example, *perispasmos*, or *metholkē*, which is moving or shifting. In what does this shifting consist? We should, he says, *trepein tēn psukhēn* (turn our soul round) towards more pleasing things than the ills and misfortunes of other people.⁵⁰ What are these more pleasing things? He gives three examples or indicates three domains of these things.⁵¹ First, it is more worthwhile to study the secrets of nature (*aporrēta phuseōs*). Second, it is more worthwhile to read the histories written by the historians, in spite of all the baseness we read about in them, and in spite of the misfortunes of other people they contain. However, the pleasure we take in these misfortunes is less unhealthy since they have now receded in time. And finally, third, we should retire to the countryside and take pleasure in the calm and comforting scene around us. Secrets of nature, reading history, and, as the Latins would say, *otium* cultivated in the countryside: this is what we should substitute for curiosity. And in addition to these three domains—secrets of nature, history, and the calm of country life—we should add exercises. Plutarch lists the anti-curiosity exercises he suggests: first of all, memory exercises. This is an old theme which was evidently traditional throughout Antiquity, since the Pythagoreans at least: Always remember what you have in your head, what you have learned.[52] We should—and here he cites a proverbial expression—"open our coffers,"[53] that is to say, recite regularly throughout the day what we have learned by heart and recall the fundamental maxims we have read, etcetera. Second, exercise by going for a walk without looking here and there, and in particular, he says, without amusing ourselves by looking at the inscriptions on tombs which give details about the lives and marriages of individuals, etcetera. We should walk looking straight ahead, a bit like a dog on a leash, he says, whose master has taught it to follow a straight line rather than lose itself running around to right and left. Finally, as another exercise, he says we should refuse to satisfy our curiosity when it happens to be aroused by some event. Just as elsewhere Plutarch said that a good exercise was to have absolutely desirable and pleasing dishes put before us and then to resist them[54]—just as Socrates resisted Alcibiades when the latter stretched out beside him—so, for example, when we receive a letter that we think contains important news, we should abstain from opening it and leave it to one side for as long as possible.[55] These are the exercises of non-curiosity (non-*polupragmosunē*) he mentions: being like a dog on a leash looking straight ahead, thinking only of one objective and one aim. You see then that Plutarch's criticism of curiosity, of the desire to know bad things about others, is not so much that this curiosity leads us to neglect looking at what is taking place in ourselves. What he sets against curiosity is not a movement of the mind or of attention that would lead us to detect everything bad in ourselves. What is involved is not the decipherment of weaknesses, defects, and past wrongdoing. If we should free ourselves from this malign, malicious, and malevolent gaze directed at other people, it is so as to be able to concentrate on keeping to the straight line we must follow in heading to our destination. We must focus on ourselves. It is not a matter of deciphering oneself. It is an exercise of the subject's concentration, an exercise by which all the subject's activity and attention is brought back to this tension that leads him to his aim. In no way does it involve either opening up the subject as a field of knowledge (*connaissances*) or undertaking the subject's exegesis and decipherment. In Marcus Aurelius, the opposite of *polupragmosunē* appears in the same way. When he says that we should not look at or pay attention to what is going on in other people, it is, he says, so as better to focus our thought on our own action, so as to head for the goal without looking from side to side.[56] Or again: It is in order not to let ourselves be carried away by the eddy of futile and vicious thoughts. If we must turn away from others, it is so as better to listen solely to the internal guide.[57]

You see then, and I strongly emphasize this, that this demand for a reversal of the gaze, as opposed to unhealthy curiosity about others, does not lead to the constitution of oneself as an object of analysis, decipherment, and reflection. It involves, rather, calling for a teleological concentration. It involves the subject looking closely at his own aim. It involves keeping before our eyes, in the clearest way, that towards which we are striving and having, as it were, a clear consciousness of this aim, of what we must do to achieve it and of the possibility of our achieving it. We must be aware, permanently aware as it were, of our effort. [It does not involve] taking oneself as an object of knowledge (*connaissance*), as a field of consciousness and unconsciousness, but being always acutely aware of this tension by which we advance towards our aim. What separates us from the aim, the distance between oneself and the aim, should be the object, once again, not of a deciphering knowledge (*savoir*), but of an awareness, vigilance, and attention. Consequently, you see that what we should think about is, of course, an athletic kind of concentration. We should think about preparation for the race. We should think about preparation for the struggle. We should think of the action by which the archer launches his arrow towards his target. We are much closer here to the famous archery exercise, which, as you know, is so important for the Japanese, for example.[58] We should think of this much more than of something like a decipherment of the self of the kind found later in monastic practice. Clear a space around the self and do not let yourself be carried away and distracted by all the sounds, faces, and people around you. Clear a space around the self, to think of the aim, or rather of the relation between yourself and the aim. Think of the trajectory separating you from that towards which you wish to advance, or which you wish to reach. All your attention should be concentrated on this trajectory from self to self. Presence of self to self, precisely on account of the distance still remaining between self and self; presence of self to self in the distance of self from self: this should be the object, the theme, of this turning back of the gaze which was previously directed on others and must now be brought back, not to the self as an object of knowledge, but precisely to this distance from your self insofar as you are the subject of an action who has the means to reach your self, but above all whose requirement is to reach it. And this something you must reach is the self.

This, I think, is what can be said about this aspect of the turning back of the gaze to oneself, [as distinguished from the] gaze directed on others. So, in the second hour I will try to show the meaning or form taken by the transfer of the gaze onto the self when it is counterposed to the gaze directed on the things of the world and the knowledge of nature. Good, a few minutes of rest then, please.

1. "Une expression hellénistique de l'agitation spirituelle," *Annuaire de l'École des Haute Études*, 1951, pp. 3-7, reprinted in A.-J. Festugière, *Hermétisme et Mystique païenne* (Paris: Aubier-Montaigne, 1967), pp. 251-55.
2. "You have no good habit, you do not attend to or review your selves (*out'epistrophē eph'hauton*) and you take no care to observe yourselves." Epictetus, *Discourses*, III.xvi.15; "Turn back to yourselves (*epistrepsate autoi*), understand the preconceived ideas you have." Ibid., III.xxii.39; "Tell me, who, on hearing you lecture or giving a discourse, has been seized by anxiety, has taken stock of himself, or left saying: 'The philosopher has really affected me; I must not act like this any longer'?" Ibid., III.xxiii.37; "After, if you turn back to yourself (*epistrephēs kata sauton*) and seek the domain to which the event belongs, you will immediately recall that it belongs 'to the domain of things independent of us.' " Ibid., III.xxiv-106.
3. "Above all, when you reprove a man for his disloyalty or ingratitude, turn your thoughts on yourself (*eis heauton epistrephou*)." Marcus Aurelius, *Meditations*, IX.42.
4. Plotinus, *Enneads*, IV.4.2.
5. For this commitment to conversion, see Seneca, *Letters*, XI.8, LIII.11, and XCIV.68.
6. "Our present discourse argues that every soul has this faculty of learning and an organ for this purpose, and that, like an eye which cannot be turned (*strephein*) from darkness to light unless the whole body is turned at the same time, so this organ must be turned away with the whole soul from the world of change until it can bear the sight of being, and the brightest part of being, which is what we call the good ... Education is this art (*tekhnē*) of turning around this organ and of finding the method which would effect the conversion as easily and effectively as possible; it does not consist in putting sight in the organ, since it already possesses it; but as it is turned in the wrong direction and looks elsewhere, it brings about its conversion." Plato, *The Republic*, VII.518c-d. It is above all in Neo-Platonism that the term *epistrophē* takes on a direct and central value (cf. Porphyry: "the only salvation is conversion to God (*monē sōtēria hē pros ton theon epistrophē*)" in *Letter to Marcella*, 289N. The notion of conversion assumes ontological and not just anthropological importance in Neo-Platonism. It goes beyond the framework of a soul's adventure in order to designate an ontological process: in Neo-Platonism a being only assumes its specific consistency in the movement by which it "turns around" to its source. See, P. Aubin, *Le Problème de la conversion* (Paris: Beauchesne, 1963) and A. D. Nock, *Conversion: The Old and the New in Religion from Alexander the Great to Augustine of Hippo* (Oxford: Oxford University Press, 1933, 2nd ed., 1961).
7. See the lecture of 6 January, second hour: the passage in the *Alcibiades* (127e) in which Socrates, demonstrating to Alcibiades his ignorance, advises him to care about himself.
8. On recollection, see the essential texts of the *Phaedrus*, 249b-c: "Man's intelligence must be exercised according to what we call the Idea, passing from a multiplicity of sensations to a unity which is gathered together by an act of reflection. Now this act consists in a recollection (*anamnēsis*) of the objects previously seen by our soul when it walked with a god"; the *Meno*, 81d: "All nature being homogeneous and the soul having learned everything, nothing prevents a single recollection (what men call knowledge) from leading the soul to all the others"; the *Phaedo*, 75e: "Would not what we call 'learning' consist in recovering a knowledge belonging to us? And surely in calling this 'recollection' (*anamimnēskesthai*) we would be using the correct name."
9. The tomb-body theme first appears in Plato as a play on words between *sōma* (body) and *sēma* (tomb and sign). It is found in *Cratylus*, 400c; *Gorgias*, 493a: "One day I heard a wise man say that our present life is a death and that our body is a tomb"; *Phaedrus*, 250c: "We were pure and did not bear the taint of that tomb we call the body and which we now carry about with us." On this theme, see P. Courcelle, "Tradition platonicienne et Tradition chrétiennne du corps-prison," *Revue des études latines*, 1965, pp. 406-43, and "Le Corps-tombeau," *Revue des études anciennes* 68, 1966, pp. 101-22.
10. This distinction is crucial in Epictetus and is for him the source of strength, the absolute compass; see the *Encheiridion* and *Discourses*, especially I.1 and III.8.

11. In the 1980 course (lectures of 13, 20, and 27 February), Foucault analyzed the theme of *paenitentia* (Latin translation of *metanoia*) taking as the central reference point *De Paenitentia* of Tertullian (around 155 to 225). This course contrasts Christian with Platonic conversion by showing that whereas in Plato conversion makes possible, in a single movement, knowledge of the Truth and of the soul innately linked to it, for Tertullian, there is a separation in penitence between access to an instituted Truth (the faith) and the quest for a dark truth of the penitent's soul to be relieved (confession).
12. See *Le Souci de soi*, p. 82 (*The Care of the Self*, pp. 64-65).
13. See Epictetus, *Discourses*, III.xxii.39; I.iv.18; III.xvi.15; III.xxiii.37; III.xxiv.106.
14. See in the lecture of 17 February, second hour, the analysis of the preface to Book III of Seneca's *Natural Questions* (which concerns the slavery of the self—*servitus sui*—from which one must free oneself).
15. "Lucilius, I feel that I am not only getting better, but that a metamorphosis is taking place in me (*Intellego, Lucili, non emendari me tantum sed transfigurari*)." Seneca, *Letters*, VI.1.
16. "Ah: I wish to inform you of the effects of such a sudden transformation (*tam, subitam mutationem mei*)." Ibid., VI.2.
17. "If you still do not possess this ability [to say to things which do not depend on me that they are nothing to me], flee your old habits, flee the ignorant if you ever want to be someone." Epictetus, *Discourses*, III.xvi.15.
18. For the analysis of this text, see the lecture of 17 February, second hour.
19. "My dear Lucilius: claim your rights over yourself." Seneca, *Letters*, I.1.
20. "Hurry yourself therefore, dearest Lucilius. Think how you would have to quicken your step if you had an enemy at your back, if you suspected the cavalry were approaching, pursuing those fleeing. You are in that situation; someone is pursuing you. Go faster! Escape (*adcelera et evade*)." Ibid., XXXII.3.
21. "I have withdrawn from the world and from the affairs of the world (*secessi non tantum ad hominibus, sed a rebus*)." Ibid., VIII.2.
22. See the reference to this gesture in Epictetus to show that true liberation is not attached to objective emancipation but to the renunciation of desires: "When a man turns his slave about in the presence of the praetor, has he done nothing? ... Has not the man to whom this has been done become free?—No more than he has acquired tranquility of soul." *Discourses*, II.i.26-27.
23. "Here is a sentence I found in [Epicurus] today: 'Become the slave of philosophy and you will enjoy true freedom.' In fact, philosophy does not put off the man who submits and gives himself up to her: he is emancipated on the spot (*statim circumagitur*). Who says slavery to philosophy says precisely freedom." *Letters*, VIII.7.
24. Marcus Aurelius, *Meditations*, VII.55, VIII.3.
25. "Dissect yourself, dig deep in different ways and look everywhere (*Excute te et varie scrutare et observa*)." Seneca, *Letters*, XVI.2
26. "I shall examine myself instantly and, following a salutary practice, I shall review my day. Why are we so wicked? Because none of us casts a backward glance over his life (*nemo vitam suam respicit*)." Seneca, *Letters*, LXXXIII.2.
27. See lecture of 20 January, first hour.
28. See same lecture, above p. XXX, note 10.
29. "Detach yourself from the common herd, dearest Paulinus, and, too much tossed about for the time you have lived, retire at last into a more peaceful harbor." Seneca, *On the Shortness of Life*, XVIII.1.
30. See lecture 24 February, second hour, on the notion of equipment (*paraskeuē*).
31. See lecture 20 January, first hour, concerning *therapeuein heauton*.
32. See *Le Souci de soi*, pp. 82-83 (*The Care of the Self*, pp. 65-66): reference to Seneca, *Letters*, XXXII and LXXV, and *On the Shortness of Life*, V.3.
33. See *Le Souci de soi*, pp. 83-84 (*The Care of the Self*, pp. 66-67) where, referring to Seneca, Foucault contrasts alienating *voluptas* to authentic *gaudium* (or *laetitia*) of the self: "I do not wish you ever to be deprived of gladness. I would have it abound in your house. It will abound there only if it is within yourself ... it will never cease once you have found where

to get it . . . look toward the true good, be happy with your own assets (*de tuo*). And what are these assets? Your self (*teo ipso*) and the best part of you." Seneca, *Letters*, XXIII.3-6.

34. See for example, in this sense: "When we had considered that someone had existed, the Persian Cyrus, who made himself master of a very great number of men . . . reconsidering our opinion, we were forced to recognize (*ek toutou dē enagkazometha metanoein*) that it is neither an impossible nor difficult task to command men, if one knows how to go about it." Xenophon, *Cyropédie*, translations by M. Bizos and E. Delebecque (Paris: Les Belles Lettres, 1971) t.l, 1-3, p. 22.
35. "Next day, however, there was a sudden change of feeling (*metanoia tis euthus en autois*) and people began to think how cruel and unprecedented such a decision was . . ." Thucydides, *History of the Peloponnesian War*, translation R. Warner (London: Penguin, 1972) book 3, 36, p. 212.
36. "In that way, first of all, he will not have to reproach himself, to struggle with himself (*makhomenos*), to repent (*metanoōn*), to torment himself (*basanizōn heauton*)." Epictetus, *Discourses*, II.xxiii.35.
37. "You will later repent and reproach yourself (*husteron metanoēseis kai autos seautō loidorēsē*." Epictetus, *The Encheiridion*, 34.
38. Marcus Aurelius, *Meditatons*, VIII.2.
39. "*Hē de metanoia hautē philosophies arkhē ginetai kai tōn anoētōn ergōn te kai logōn phugē kai tēs ametameletou zōēs hē prōtē paraskeuē.*" Hierocles, *Aureum Pythagoreorum Carmen Commentarius*, XIV-10, ed. F.G. Koehler (Stuttgart: Teubner, 1974) p. 66 (I owe this reference to R. Goulet). In a 1965 edition (Paris: L'Artisan du livre) M. Meunier translates this as: "Repentance, then, is the beginning of philosophy, and abstaining from foolish words and actions is the first condition that prepares us for a life exempt from repentance" (p. 187).
40. P. Hadot, "*Epistrophē* and *metanoia*" in *Actes du XIᵉ congrès international de Philosophie, Bruxelles, 20-26 août 1953* (Louvain-Amsterdam: Nauwelaerts, 1953), vol. XII, pp. 31-36 (see the summary in the article "Conversion," written for the *Encylopaedia Universalis* and republished in the first edition of *Exercises spirituals et Philosophie antique*, pp. 175-82).
41. For an exposition of the establishment of the techniques for deciphering the secrets of conscience in Christianity, see lecture of 26 March 1980 (last lecture of the year at the Collège de France) in which Foucault bases himself on Cassian's practices of spiritual direction.
42. Plutarch, *On Curiosity*, 515b-d.
43. "Thus my homeland, exposed to the west wind, at mid-day suffered the full force of the Sun coming from Parnassus; it is said that it was reorientated (*trapēnai*) to the east by Chaeron." Ibid., 515b.
44. "It is not easy to find a man who is unhappy due to his regarding what is going on in another man's soul. But those who do not examine the movements of their own soul are inevitably unhappy." Marcus Aurelius, *Meditations*, II.8.
45. Ibid., III.4. The passage ends: "unless you propose some end useful to the community."
46. Ibid., IV.18.
47. Plutarch, *On Curiosity*, 515d.
48. Ibid., 515d-e.
49. "Turn this curiosity away from the outside in order to lead it back within." Ibid.
50. "By what means can we flee? The conversion (*perispasmos*), as has been said, and the transfer (*metholkē*) of curiosity, by turning by preference one's soul (*trepsanti tēn psukhēn*) towards more decent and pleasing subjects." Ibid., 517c.
51. Ibid., 5, 6, and 8, and 517c to 519c.
52. "They thought one must keep and preserve in memory all that was taught and said, and that one must acquire knowledge and learning as long as the faculty of learning and remembering can do so, because it is thanks to this faculty that one must learn and in it that one must keep the memory. They always held memory in great esteem and spent considerable time training it and taking care of it . . . The Pythagoreans strove to train their memory extensively, for there is nothing better for acquiring science, experience and wisdom than being able to remember." Iamblichus, *Life of Pythagoras*, §164.
53. Plutarch, *On Curiosity*, 520a, §10.

54. Plutarch, *Socrates' Daemon*, 585a. For a first analysis of this text, see the lecture of 13 January, first hour.
55. Plutarch, *On Curiosity*, 522d.
56. "Pay no attention to the wicked character, advance straight to the aim without looking from side to side." Marcus Aurelius, *Meditations*, IV.18.
57. "... by trying to imagine what so-and-so is doing and why, what he is saying, what he is thinking, what he is planning and other thoughts of this kind you make yourself giddy and neglect your inner guide. Therefore avoid allowing entry into our chain of ideas that which is foolhardy and vain and, above all, futility and wickedness." Marcus Aurelius, *Meditations*, III.4.
58. Foucault, we should recall, was a great reader of E. Herrigel: see, by this author, *Le Zen dans l'art chevaleresque du tir à l'arc* (Paris: Dervy, 1986) [English translation by R.F.C. Hull, *Zen and the Art of Archery* (London: Routledge and Kegan Paul, 1953)]. I owe this reference to D. Defert.

## twelve

## 10 FEBRUARY 1982

### Second hour

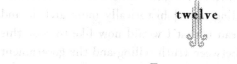

*General theoretical framework: veridiction and subjectivation.* ~ *Knowledge (*savoir*) of the world and practice of the self in the Cynics: the example of Demetrius.* ~ *Description of useful knowledge (*connaissances*) in Demetrius.* ~ *Ethopoetic knowledge (*savoir*).* ~ *Physiological knowledge (*connaissance*) in Epicurus.* ~ *The* parrhēsia *of Epicurean physiologists.*

WE HAVE JUST SEEN what was meant by "turning one's gaze and attention away from others in order to transfer them to the self" in Plutarch and Marcus Aurelius. I would now like to consider what is basically a much more important question, which has given rise to many more discussions, namely the question of what it means to "turn one's gaze away from the world in order to shift it towards the self." Actually, this is a difficult, complex question on which I will dwell at greater length inasmuch as it is right at the heart of the problem I want to pose this year—and what's more have wanted to pose for some time—and which basically is: How is the relationship between truth-telling (veridiction[1]) and the practice of the subject established, fixed, and defined? Or, more generally, how are truth-telling and governing (governing oneself and others) linked and connected to each other? I have tried to look at this problem under a whole range of aspects and forms—whether with regard to madness, mental illness, the prison, delinquency, etcetera—and now, starting from the question I asked myself concerning sexuality, I would like to formulate it differently, in a way that is both more strictly defined and slightly shifted in relation to the domain I chose, and [by calling upon] historically more archaic and ancient [periods]. What I mean is that I would now like to pose this question of the relationship between truth-telling and the government of the subject in ancient thought before Christianity. I would also like to pose it in the form and within the framework of the constitution of a relationship of self to self in order to show how within this relationship of self to self the formation of a certain type of experience of the self became possible which is, it seems to me, typical of Western experience, of the subject's experience of himself in the West, but also of the experience the Western subject may have or create of others. This then, in general terms, is the problem I want to take up.

This question of how the knowledge (*savoir*) of things and the return to the self are linked appears in a number of texts of the Hellenistic and Roman epoch, which I would like to talk to you about, and it appears around that very old, ancient theme which Socrates had already evoked in the *Phaedrus* when, as you know, he said: Should we choose the knowledge (*connaissance*) of trees rather than the knowledge (*connaissance*) of men? And he chose the knowledge of men.[2] We come across this theme again later in the Socratics when, one after the other, they say that what is interesting, important, and decisive is not knowing the world's secrets, but knowing man himself.[3] We find it again in the major Cynic, Epicurean, and Stoic philosophical schools and, inasmuch as they have left us a greater number of texts, which are also more explicit, I would like to try to see how the problem is posed, how it is defined, in these. First, the Cynics, then the Epicureans, and finally the Stoics.

First, the Cynics, at least, the Cynics as we know them for the period in question from a number of elements and indirect indications passed down to us by other authors. Actually, the position of the Cynic movement, or of the Cynics, with regard to this question of the relation between knowledge of nature and self-knowledge (return to the self, conversion to the self) is certainly much more complicated than it seems. We should remember Diogenes Laertius, for example. When he writes the life of Diogenes, he explains that he was appointed tutor for the children... I no longer know whose children.[4] He gave these children an education in which he taught them all the sciences, and in which he saw to it that they knew a fairly precise and accessible summary of these sciences so that they could recall them throughout their life whenever an opportunity arose. So, the Cynic refusal of the knowledge of things must no doubt be considerably qualified. On the other hand, and for the period I am talking about—that is to say, the beginning of the Empire—Seneca, in book VII of *De Beneficiis* quotes, as you know, a relatively long text by Demetrius, a Cynic philosopher who was, let's say, at home in Rome and the aristocratic milieu.[5] This is the famous Demetrius who was the confidante of Thrasea Paetus and who was the witness, the philosophical organizer so to speak, of his suicide: when Thrasea Paetus committed suicide he called Demetrius to him in his last moments. He dismissed everyone else and engaged in a dialogue with Demetrius on the immortality of the soul. He died while engaged in this Socratic kind of dialogue.[6] Demetrius then is a Cynic, but a well-bred Cynic, an adapted Cynic. Seneca often quotes Demetrius, and always with much praise and deference. In the passage quoted by Seneca, Demetrius says that we should always keep the model, the image of the athlete in mind. We will have to come back to this theme—I will try to explain it to you a little—which is absolutely constant but whose role and value in the Cynics seems to have been more important than anywhere else.[7] So, one must be a good athlete. What is a good athlete? The good athlete, he says, is certainly not someone who has learned every possible action that might be needed or which we might be able to perform. Basically, to be a good athlete it is enough to know only those actions that can actually be used and that are used most frequently in the struggle. And these well-mastered actions must have become so familiar that they are always available and can be resorted to whenever the opportunity arises.[8]

Starting with this model there appears what might seem to be a criterion of utility. Let's ignore all those kinds of knowledge we could learn which, being more or less like acrobatic actions, are completely pointless and of no possible use in the real struggles of life. Let's retain then only the knowledge that will be used and which we will be able to resort to, and resort to easily, in the different opportunities of the struggle. Once again, then, we seem to get the impression of a division in the content of knowledge between useless knowledge, which might be knowledge of the external world, etcetera, and useful knowledge, which directly affects human existence. In fact, starting with this reference [and this] model, we should see how Demetrius distinguishes between what is and what is not worth knowing. Is it really a pure and simple difference of content: useful knowledge/useless knowledge, with knowledge of the world, of the things of the world on the side of useless knowledge, and knowledge of man and human existence on the side of useful knowledge? Look at the text; I am quoting an old translation, but it doesn't matter. It says this: "You may not know what causes the ebb and flow of the ocean tides; you may not know why every seventh year imprints a new character on the life of a man [the idea, then, that every seven years one enters a new phase of life, a new character, and that consequently one should take on a new mode of life; M.F.]; why the width of a portico, when you look at it from a distance, does not keep its true proportion, the ends drawing together and getting narrower, and the spaces between the columns finally disappearing; why it is that twins are conceived separately, but are born together; whether in coition one act gives birth to two, or each is born from a separate act; why those who are born together have different destinies; why events put a great distance between them although their births were very close together. You will not lose anything by neglecting things the knowledge of which is denied us and pointless. Obscure truth is hidden in an abyss. Nor can we charge Nature with malevolence. For there is nothing that is difficult to discover except things whose discovery brings no other fruit than the discovery itself. Everything that can make us better or happier, Nature has placed in plain sight and within our reach."⁹ And here are listed the things we should know as opposed to those which are useless: "If man* has fortified himself against the accidents of fortune, if he has risen above fear, if, in the greed of his hopes he does not embrace the

---

*The Latin here is *animus*. The English, Loeb translation has "soul." The translation Foucault uses has "man" (*l'homme*) throughout—G.B.

infinite but learns to seek his riches in himself; if he has cast out the dread of men and gods, convinced that he has little to fear from man and nothing from God; if, despising all frivolities which are the torment as well as the ornament of life, he has come to understand that death produces no evils, and ends many; if he has dedicated himself to Virtue, and finds every path to which she calls him easy; if he sees himself as a social being born to live in a community; if he views the world as the universal home of mankind, if he has opened his conscience to the gods and always lives as if in public—then, respecting himself more than others, free from storms, he is settled in an unalterable calm; then, he has gathered within him all truly useful and necessary science: the rest is only the diversion of leisure."[10]

This, then, is the list, the double list of those things it is pointless to know and those it is useful to know. Among the things it is pointless to know are the cause of tides, the cause of the rhythm of seven year periods which break up human life, the cause of optical illusions, the reason for twins and the paradox of two different lives born under the same sign, etcetera. Now you can see that all these objects of useless knowledge are not distant things of a distant world. Of course, there is, at a pinch, the cause of tides, although, after all, it could be said that this is not so remote from human existence. But in actual fact what is at stake in all these things is, for example, the problem of health, of the mode of life, of the seven-year rhythm, all of which directly affect human life. Optical illusions are a matter of errors, of human errors. What is at stake in the question of twins and the paradoxes arising from the fact that two lives born under the same sign have different destinies is the question of destiny, the question of freedom and of what in the world determines our life and yet leaves us free. All these questions are referred to in the list of things it is unnecessary to know. So you see that we are not dealing with an opposition between the remote and the near, the sky and the earth, the secrets of nature and the things which affect human existence. Actually, what I think characterizes the whole of this list of things it is pointless to know, what constitutes their common character, is not that they are things that will not affect human existence. They affect it and they affect it very closely. As you can see, their common feature and what makes them pointless is that they are knowledge through causes. It is the cause of twins, the cause of the seven-year rhythm, as well as the cause of tides, which do not need to be known. For while making use of their effects, nature has in fact concealed the causes. According to Demetrius, if nature had thought that these causes could be important in any way to human existence and knowledge, she would have shown them, she would have made them visible. She has not hidden the causes because something like a transgression, the infringement of a ban, would be needed to know them. It is quite simply that nature has shown man that knowing the causes of these things is not useful. This does not mean it is pointless to know these things and take them into account. It will be possible for us to know these causes if we wish to. We will be able to know them to a certain extent, and this is what comes in at the end of the text where he says: "A soul already retired to shelter may occasionally lose itself in these speculations which serve to embellish the mind rather than strengthen it." This should be put alongside what is said in the middle of the passage I have just read out, namely that the only fruit of the discovery of these things is the discovery itself. These causes, then, are hidden. They are hidden because it is pointless to know them. Pointless to know does not mean therefore that knowledge is prohibited, but that they are to be known, if we wish to know them, only as an extra, as it were, when the soul, *in tutum retracto*[11] (withdrawn into that region of security which provides it with wisdom), wants additionally to seek out these causes, as diversion and in order to find a pleasure residing precisely solely in discovery itself. Consequently, it is a supplementary, pointless, and ornamental cultural pleasure: this is what nature has pointed out to us by showing us that all these things, which, once again, affect us in our real existence, are not to be investigated, are not to be looked into, at the level of the cause. What Demetrius thus denounces, criticizes, and rejects is knowledge through causes as cultural, ornamental knowledge.

What, by contrast, are the things it is necessary to know (*connaître*)? That there is little to fear from men, that there is nothing at all to fear from the gods, that death is not the source of any evil, that it is easy to find the path [of] virtue, that one should consider oneself a social being born for the community. It is, in short: knowing (*savoir*) that the world is a common dwelling-place in which all men are joined together to constitute precisely this community. You can see that this list of things we should know is not at all part of what could be called, and what Christian spirituality will call, the *arcana conscientiae* (the secrets of conscience).[12] Demetrius does not say: Ignore knowledge of external things and try to know exactly who you are; make an inventory of your desires, passions, and illnesses. He does not even say: Undertake an examination of conscience. He does not put forward a theory of the soul and he does not set out what human nature is. He speaks of the same thing at the level of content, that is to say, of the gods, of the world in general, of other men. This is what he talks about, and here again it is not the individual himself. He does not demand that the gaze be transferred from external things to the inner world. He does not demand that the gaze be directed away from nature to the conscience, or towards oneself, or towards the depths of the soul. He does not wish to substitute the secrets of conscience for the secrets of nature. It is only ever a matter of the world. It is only ever a matter of others. It is only ever a matter of what surrounds us. What is involved is simply knowing them differently. Demetrius speaks of another modality of knowing (*savoir*). He contrasts two modes of knowledge (*savoir*): one through causes, which he tells us is pointless, and another mode of knowledge, which is what? Well, I think we could call it, quite simply, a relational mode of knowledge, because when we now consider the gods, other men, the *kosmos*, the world, etcetera, this involves taking into account the relation between the gods, men, the world and things of the world on the one hand, and ourselves on the other. It is by making us appear to ourselves as the recurrent and constant term of all these relations that our gaze should be directed on the things of the world, the gods, and men. It is in this field of the relation between all these things and oneself that knowledge (*le savoir*) can and must be deployed. It seems to me that this relational knowing (*savoir*) is the primary characteristic of the knowledge (*connaissance*) validated by Demetrius.

It is also a knowledge (*connaissance*) that has the property of being, if you like, immediately translatable—and immediately translatable in

Demetrius's text—into prescriptions. It involves knowing (*savoir*), Demetrius says, that man has very little to fear from men, that he has nothing to fear from the gods, that he should despise the embellishment of life—the torment as well as the embellishment of life—and that he should know that "death produces no evils, and ends many." That is to say, they are kinds of knowledge (*connaissances*) which, while establishing themselves and expressing themselves as principles of truth, are given at the same time, jointly, with no distance or mediation, as prescriptions. They are prescriptive facts. They are principles in both senses of the word: in the sense that they are statements of fundamental truth from which others can be deduced, and in the sense that they are the expression of precepts of conduct to which we should, anyway, submit. What are at stake here are prescriptive truths. So, what we need to know are relations: the subject's relations with everything around him. What we must know, or rather the way in which we must know, is a mode in which what is given as truth is read immediately and directly as precept.

Finally, these are kinds of knowledge such that the subject's mode of being is transformed when he has them, when he possesses them, when he has acquired them, since it is thanks to this, Demetrius says, that he becomes better. It is thanks to this also that, respecting ourselves more than we respect others, free from storms, we are settled in an unalterable calm. *In solido et sereno stare*: We can stand in the firm and serene element.[13] This knowledge makes us *beati* (happy),[14] and it is precisely this that distinguishes it from "cultural embellishment." Cultural embellishment is precisely something that may well be true, but which does not change the subject's mode of being in any way. Once again, the pointless kinds of knowledge rejected by Demetrius are not defined by their content. They are defined by a mode of knowledge, a causal mode of knowledge, which has the double property, or rather the double deficiency, which we can now define with regard to the other knowledge: they are kinds of knowledge which cannot be transformed into prescriptions, which have no prescriptive relevance; and second, when one knows them, they have no effect on the subject's mode of being. On the other hand, a valid mode of knowledge will be knowledge of a kind which, considering all the things of the world (the gods, the *kosmos*, others, etcetera) in their relation to us, we will be able to translate immediately into prescriptions, and these will change what we are. They will change the state of the subject who knows them.

I think this is one of the most clear and distinct descriptions of what seems to me to be a general feature of this ethic of knowledge and truth, which is found again in the other philosophical schools, namely, that what is ruled out, the distinguishing point, the frontier established, does not affect, once again, the distinction between things of the world and things of human nature: it is a distinction in the mode of knowing (*savoir*) and in the way in which what one knows (*connaît*) about the gods, men, and the world can have an effect on the nature, I mean on the subject's way of doing things, on his *ethos*. The Greeks had a very interesting word, which can be found in Plutarch as well as in Denys of Halicarnassus. It exists in the form of a noun, verb, and adjective. It is the expression, or series of expressions, of words: *ēthopoiein*, *ēthopoiia*, *ēthopoios*. *Ēthopoiein* means making *ēthos*, producing *ēthos*, changing, transforming *ēthos*, the individual's way of being, his mode of existence. *Ēthopoios* is something that possesses the quality of transforming an individual's mode of being.[15] [...] We will keep more or less to the meaning found in Plutarch, that is to say: producing *ēthos*, forming *ēthos* (*ēthopoiein*); capable of forming *ēthos* (*ēthopoios*); formation of *ēthos* (*Ēthopoiia*). Okay, it seems to me that the distinction, the caesura introduced into the field of knowledge (*savoir*), is again not that which marks certain contents of knowledge (*connaissance*) as pointless and others useful: it is what distinguishes knowing (*savoir*) as having or not having an "ethopoetic" character. Knowing, knowledge of something, is useful when it has a form and functions in such a way that it can produce *ēthos*. And a knowledge (*connaissance*) of the world is perfectly useful: it (as well as knowledge of others and knowledge of the gods) can produce *ēthos*. And it is this that marks, forms, and characterizes what knowledge useful to man must be. As a result you can see that this criticism of pointless knowledge does not at all direct us to the enhancement of the status of another knowledge with a different content, which would be knowledge of ourselves and what is within us. It directs us to a different functioning of the same knowledge of external things. Knowledge of the self, at this level at least, is not then on the way to becoming the decipherment of the mysteries of conscience and the exegesis of the self which develops later in Christianity. Useful knowledge, knowledge in which human life is at stake, is a relational mode of knowledge that asserts and prescribes at the same time and is capable of producing a change in the subject's mode of being. What seems to me to be quite clear in Demetrius's text can, I think, be found again, with different modalities, in other philosophical schools, and mainly in the Epicureans and Pythagoreans.

Now let's read some Epicurean texts. You have seen that Demetrius's demonstration, or rather analysis, mainly consists in distinguishing or comparing two lists, again not so much of things to be known (*à connaître*) as of the defining characteristics of two ways of knowing (*savoir*): one ornamental, typical of the culture of a cultivated man who has nothing else to do, and the other, the mode of knowledge (*connaissance*) necessary for the person who has to cultivate his own self and takes himself as the objective of his life. It is a more or less empirical list. However, in the Epicureans there is a notion which I think is very important inasmuch as it overlays the knowledge, or rather the mode of functioning of what can be called "ethopoetic" knowledge (*savoir*), that is to say knowledge which provides or forms *ēthos*. This is the notion of *phusiologia*. Actually, in Epicurean texts knowledge (*connaissance*) of nature (knowledge of nature insofar as it is valid) is regularly called *phusiologia* (physiology, more or less). What is *phusiologia*? In the *Vatican Sayings*—paragraph 45—there is a text that gives the precise definition of *phusiologia*. Here again, *phusiologia* is not a distinct branch of knowledge (*savoir*): it is the modality of knowledge (*savoir*) of nature insofar as it is philosophically relevant for the practice of the self. The text says: "The study of nature (*phusiologia*) does not form men who are fond of boasting and who are verbal performers, or those who make a show of the culture which is envied by the masses, but men, rather, who are haughty and independent, and who take pride in what is their own and not what comes from circumstances."[16] Let us go back over this. So, the text says: *phusiologia* does not form (*paraskeuazei*) boasters and verbal performers—I will come back to this—people who make a show of that culture (*paideia*) prized by the masses. It forms men who are haughty and independent (*autarkies*), who take pride in what belongs to them by right and not what comes to them from circumstances, from things (*pragmata*).

You see that this text rests first of all on a classical opposition [the first term of which is] cultural learning, for which Epicurus uses the word *paideia*, a cultural learning whose end is glory, the display that gives men a name, a kind of boastful knowledge. This boastful knowledge (*savoir*) is the knowledge of boasters (*kompous*), of people who want to get a name for themselves, and which actually has no basis. This *paideia* is what we find in those people who are, as the French translation puts it, "*des artistes du verbe*." Very precisely this is: *phōnēs ergastikous*. The *ergastikoi* are artisans, workers, that is to say, those who do not work for themselves, but in order to sell and make a profit. And what is the object on which these *ergastikoi* work? It is the *phōnē*, that is to say speech insofar as it makes sounds, but not insofar as it is *logos* or reason. They are, I would say, "word-spinners" (*faiseurs de mots*). Rather than people who work for themselves at the level of the *logos*, that is to say at the level of the rational structure of discourse, they are people who concoct a number of effects for sale linked to the sound of words. So we have *paideia*, defined as that with which one makes conceited chatter with others, as the very object of the artisans of verbal sounds. And it is the latter, of course, who are appreciated by the masses to whom they display their *paideia*. There are many echoes of this part of *Vatican Sayings* 45 in other texts of Epicurus known to us. When Epicurus says: You must practice philosophy for yourself and not for Greece,[17] he is referring to that activity of the genuine practice of the self whose sole end is oneself. And he contrasts it with those who make a show of having this practice of the self, but who in reality only think about one thing: when they learn something and display it, their only aim is to be admired by Greece. All this comes under the term *paideia*, a term which, as you know anyway, was used with positive connotations in Greece.[18] The *paideia* is, so to speak, the general culture necessary for a free man. Well, Epicurus rejects this *paideia* as a culture of boasters, developed merely by concoctors of words whose only aim is to be admired by the masses.

What does Epicurus set against the *paideia* he criticizes in this way? He sets against it, precisely, *phusiologia*. *Phusiologia* is different from *paideia*. How is it distinguished from *paideia*? First, what does *phusiologia* do instead of producing people who are only pompous and inconsistent boasters? It *paraskeuei*, that is to say it prepares. We find here then that word to which I have already drawn your attention and to which we will have to come back: *paraskeuē*.[19] *Paraskeuē* is the equipping, the preparation of the subject and the soul so that they will be properly, necessarily, and sufficiently armed for whatever circumstance of life may arise. *Paraskeuē* is precisely what will make possible resistance to every impulse and temptation that may come from the external world. *Paraskeuē* is what will enable one both to achieve one's aim and to remain stable, settled on this aim, not letting oneself be swayed by anything. The function of *phusiologia* is, then, *paraskeuein*, to provide the soul with the necessary equipment for its struggle, for its objective and its victory. As such, it is the exact opposite of *paideia*.

In providing this preparation, the effect of *phusiologia* is to give, to produce, and I read the French translation again: "men who are haughty and independent, who take pride in what belongs to them by right and not what comes to them from circumstances, from things." We must take up the words again. The word for haughty is *sobaroi*. It is a rather rare word more readily used with reference to those animals, those horses that are energetic and frisky, but consequently difficult to control and hold back. It is quite clear that this word designates, more or less negatively to start with, the fact that such individuals, thanks to *phusiologia*, will no longer fear. They will no longer suffer from that fear of the gods to which, as you know, Epicurus attaches such importance. But it undoubtedly involves something more than the abolition of fear. *Phusiologia* gives the individual boldness and courage, a kind of intrepidity, which enables him to stand firm not only against the many beliefs that others wish to impose on him, but also against life's dangers and the authority of those who want to lay down the law. Absence of fear, boldness, a sort of recalcitrance and spiritedness if you like: this is what *phusiologia* gives to the individuals who learn it.

Second, these individuals will become *autarkeis*. Here again we find the well-known notion of *autarkeia*. That is to say, they will depend only on themselves. They will be *contenti* (content with themselves, satisfied with themselves). But this is not "pleased with oneself" in the sense we understand it. It is to be satisfied with oneself, again in a negative and positive sense. Negative: that is to say, they will need nothing other than themselves. However, at the same time, they will find a number of resources within themselves, and the possibility in particular of experiencing pleasure and delight in the full relationship they will have with themselves.

Finally, the third effect of *phusiologia* is that of enabling individuals to take pride in what is their own and not what derives from circumstances. That is to say: to make that famous sorting and division that as we know is fundamental in existence for both the Epicureans and the Stoics. At every moment and before every thing, asking oneself and being able to say whether or not it depends on [oneself];[20] putting all one's pride, all one's satisfaction, and all one's self-affirmation with regard to others, in the fact that one can recognize what depends on oneself; and establishing a total, absolute, and limitless mastery over that which depends on oneself. You can see then that *phusiologia*, as it appears in Epicurus, is not a branch of knowledge (*savoir*). It is the knowledge (*connaissance*) of nature, of *phusis*, insofar as this knowledge can serve as the principle of human conduct and as the criterion for setting us free, and also insofar as it can transform the subject (who was filled with fear and terror before nature and by what he had been taught about the gods and things of the world) into a free subject who finds within himself the possibility and means of his permanent and perfectly tranquil delight.

The same definition of *phusiologia* is found in another Vatican Saying, 29, in which Epicurus says: "For my part, speaking freely as one who studies nature, I would rather speak in oracles about the things useful to all men, even if no one should understand me, than gather the praise that comes in abundance from the many by giving my approval to popular opinion."[21] I don't have much time to explain this. I would just like to note two or three things that I think are important. Epicurus says: "for my part, speaking freely." The Greek word is *parrhēsia*—which I said we must come back to—which is essentially not frankness or freedom of speech, but the technique—*parrhēsia* is a technical term—which allows the master to make a proper use, from the true things he knows, of that which is useful or effective for his disciple's work of transformation. *Parrhēsia* is a quality, or rather a technique, used in the relationship between doctor and patient, between master and disciple: it is the free hand, if you like, which ensures one's ability to select from the field of true knowledge that which is relevant for the subject's transformation, change and improvement. And you see that within [the framework of] the *parrhēsia* he lays claim to as a physiologist, that is to say as someone who knows nature but who only employs this knowledge in terms of what is useful to the subject, using this freedom [of speech], he says: I would rather "speak in oracles about the things useful to all men" than give "my approval to popular opinion." "Speaking in oracles about useful things" is, in Greek, *khrēsmōdein*; an important word. You see that when Epicurus refers to the oracle, he refers to a type of discourse that expresses both what is true and what one should do, a discourse that reveals the truth and prescribes. He says: In my freedom as physiologist, in employing then the *parrhēsia* of physiology, I still prefer to be like that oracular expression which speaks the truth, however obscurely, but at the same time prescribes, rather than restrict myself to following current opinion, which is no doubt approved of and understood by everyone, but which in actual fact, precisely because it is accepted by everyone, does not change the subject's being at all. The art and freedom of the physiologist consists in expressing the truths of nature in oracles only to someone who can understand, truths of a kind that can really change his mode of being. It is an art similar to the oracular form of expression. It is also an art similar to medicine, which functions according to an objective and in terms of the subject's transformation.

This is *phusiologia*, and you see, here again, why we could not distinguish useful knowledge and pointless knowledge by their content, but simply by whether or not the form of knowing is physiological. And the introductions to those texts that are combinations of Epicurean fragments (the letters to Herodotus and Pythocles) clearly tell us this. You know that these are texts of physics, of "theoretical" physics if you like, which deal with comets, the composition of the world, atoms and their movements, etcetera. Now these texts are introduced by perfectly clear and distinct statements. The beginning of the letter to Herodotus is as follows: "I recommend continuous activity in *phusiologia*, and through this activity I guarantee life the most perfect serenity."[22] So, Epicurus prescribes continuous activity in *phusiologia*, but he prescribes this knowledge of nature in order to achieve, and inasmuch as it makes it possible to achieve, the most perfect serenity. Similarly, at the beginning of the letter to Pythocles, he says: "You must convince yourself that knowledge of celestial phenomena has no other end than peace of mind and firm confidence ... Our life, in fact, does not need foolishness and empty opinion, it needs untroubled renewal."[23] The knowledge of celestial bodies and of things of the world, of the sky and the earth, the most speculative knowledge of physics, is far from being rejected. However, this knowledge appears and is modalized in *phusiologia* in such a way that knowledge of the world is a relevant part of the subject's practice on himself; an effective and efficient component in the subject's transformation of himself. This, at any rate, is more or less how the opposition between knowledge of things and knowledge of oneself can be interpreted in the Epicureans and the Cynics, as also the opposition between knowledge of nature and knowledge of the human being. This opposition, and the rejection of some kinds of knowledge, bears simply on this mode of knowing. What is required, and of what valid and acceptable knowledge (*savoir*) must consist for both the sage and his disciple, is not a knowledge that would focus on themselves, not a knowledge that would take the soul or the self as the real object of knowledge (*connaissance*). It is, rather, knowledge (*savoir*) concerning things, the world, the gods and men, but whose effect and function are to change the subject's being. This truth must affect the subject. It does not involve the subject becoming the object of a true discourse. This, I think, is the major difference. This is what must be grasped, along with the fact that nothing in these practices of the self and the way in which they are connected to knowledge of nature and things can appear as preliminary to or the sketch of the much later appearance of the decipherment of conscience by itself and the subject's self-exegesis. Okay then, next week I will talk about "knowledge of the self and knowledge of nature" in the [Stoics].

1. On this notion, see "Structuralism and Post-Structuralism" and "Foucault" in Michel Foucault, *Dits et Écrits*, vol. 4, p. 445 and p. 632, English translations (with same titles) by Jeremy Harding and Robert Hurley in *Aesthetics, Method, and Epistemology*, p. 444 and p. 460.
2. Reference to the passage in which Socrates, to whom Phaedrus had remarked that he never ventured beyond the walls of Athens, replies: "The country and the trees teach me nothing, but men in the towns teach me much." *Phaedrus*, 230d.
3. Historians usually designate as the "Socratics" those contemporary philosophers and friends of Socrates who claim to be his direct disciples. Among the best known, we can mention Antisthenes (the teacher of Diogenes the Cynic), who rejected both logic and physics and retained only ethics, and Aristippus of Cyrene, who also rejected the sciences for research solely into the principles of the gentle way of life.
4. The children in question are those of Xeniades. Diogenes Laertius writes: "These children also learned many passages from poets, prose writers and even from the writings of Diogenes himself, who gave them a summary and précis of every science so that they could retain them more easily." Diogenes Laertius, *Lives of Eminent Philosophers*, VI.31. It may be, however, that Foucault allowed himself to be misled by Genaille's somewhat free and often incorrect translation. The new translation (*Vies et Doctrines des philosophes illustres*) by M.-O. Goulet-Cazé gives: "These children learned by heart many passages from the poets, prose writers and the works of Diogenes himself; he made them practice every method for remembering quickly and well" (VI.31, p. 712).
5. See lecture of 27 January, first hour, above p. 147, note 41 on Demetrius.
6. On this scene and its characters, and for the historical references, see the same course, notes 42 and 43.
7. See lecture of 24 February, second hour.
8. "The great wrestler, he says, is not the one who has a thorough knowledge of every postures and grip, which he will rarely use on the ground, but the one who has well and conscientiously trained himself in one or two of them and waits attentively to use them, for the number of things he knows is not important if he knows enough to win; thus in the study which concerns us, there are many diverting notions, but few which are decisive." Seneca, *On Benefits*, VII.i.4.
9. Foucault uses here an old, nineteenth-century edition of Seneca: *Œuvres completes de Sénèque le philosophe, Bienfaits*, VII.i.5-6, p. 234 (the *Bienfaits* are here translated by M. Baillard).
10. Ibid., VII.i.7.
11. The Latin text has, more precisely, "*in tutum retracto animo*" ("a soul already withdrawn to safety"). Ibid.
12. See lecture of 26 March 1980.
13. "free from storms, he is settled in an unalterable calm (*in solido ac sereno stetit*)" *On Benefits*, VII.i.7.
14. "Everything that can make us better or happier (*meliores beatosque*), Nature has placed in plain sight and within our reach." Ibid. VII.i.6.
15. In Denys of Halicarnassus, the word *ēthopoiia* is found in the sense of a painting of mores: "I see then in Lysias this quality that is so distinguished that it is generally called painting of mores (*hētopoiian*)." "Lysias" in *Les Orateurs antiques*, translation G. Aujac, Paris, Les Belles Lettres, 1978, §8, p. 81. In Plutarch, however, the practical meaning is present: "Moral beauty ... does not at all form the mores (*ēthopoioun*) of the person who contemplates it for imitation alone." *Pericles* 153b.
16. Epicurus, "Vatican Sayings," 45 in *Letters, Principal Doctrines and Vatican Sayings*.
17. "As you grow old you are such as I advise myself to be, and you really have been able to distinguish between practicing philosophy for yourself and practicing philosophy for Greece (*Helladi*)." Epicurus, "Vatican Sayings," 76.

18. On the notion of *paideia*, see the classical works of W. Jaeger, *Paideia, the Ideals of Greek Culture*, translation G. Highet (Oxford and New York: Oxford University Press, 1943) vol. 2, and H.-I. Marrou, *Histoire de l'éducation dans l'Antiquité* (*A History of Education in Antiquity*).
19. See lecture of 24 February, second hour.
20. See this lecture, first hour, and above, p. 224, note 10.
21. Epicurus, "Vatican Sayings," 29.
22. Epicurus, "Letter to Herodotus," 37a, in *Letters, Principal Doctrines, and Vatican Sayings*.
23. Epicurus, "Letter to Pythocles," 85-87, in *Letters, Principal Doctrines, and Vatican Sayings*.

## thirteen

## 17 FEBRUARY 1982

### First hour

> *Conversion to self as successfully accomplished form of care of the self.* ~ *The metaphor of navigation.* ~ *The pilot's technique as paradigm of governmentality.* ~ *The idea of an ethic of return to the self: Christian refusal and abortive attempts of the modern epoch.* ~ *Conversion to self without the principle of a knowledge of the self.* ~ *Two eclipsing models: Platonic recollection and Christian exegesis.* ~ *The hidden model: Hellenistic conversion to self.* ~ *Knowledge of the world and self-knowledge in Stoic thought.* ~ *The example of Seneca: criticism of culture in Seneca's* Letters to Lucilius; *the movement of the gaze in* Natural Questions.

[…][I HAVE SHOWN FIRST of all how] the care of the self—the old care of the self whose first theoretical and systematic exposition we saw in the *Alcibiades*—was freed from its privileged connection with pedagogy, how it was freed from its political purpose and consequently how, all in all, it was separated from the conditions under which it appeared in the *Alcibiades* in, let's say, a more or less Socratic-Platonic context. The care of the self thus took the form of a general and unconditional principle. This means that "caring about the self" is no longer a requirement valid at a given moment of life and in the phase of life when the adolescent enters adult life. "Caring about the self" is a rule coextensive with life. Second, care of the self is not bound up with the acquisition of a particular status in society. It involves the entire being of the subject, who must be concerned with the self, and with the self as such, throughout his life. In short, we arrive at this notion that gives a new content to the old requirement to "care about the self," a new notion, which I began to disentangle last week: that of conversion to oneself. The whole subject must turn around towards himself and devote himself to himself: *eph'heauton epistrephein*,[1] *eis heauton anakhōrein*,[2] *ad se recurrere*,[3] *ad se redire*,[4] *in se recedere*,[5] *se reducere in tutum*[6] (return to oneself, revert to oneself, review oneself, etcetera). Okay, you have a set of expressions in Latin and Greek that I think we should hold onto on account of at least two of their essential components. First, in all of these expressions there is the idea of a real movement of the subject with regard to himself. It is not just a matter of attending to yourself, of focusing your gaze on yourself, or remaining alert and vigilant with respect to yourself, as in the, if you like, "naked" idea of the care of the self. It involves a real shift, a certain movement of the subject with regard to himself, whose nature we will have to investigate. The subject must advance towards something that is himself. Shift, trajectory, effort, and movement: all of this must be retained in the idea of a conversion to self. Second, in this idea of a conversion to self there is the important, difficult, not very clear, and ambiguous theme of return. What does it mean to return to the self? What is this circle, this loop, this falling back that we must carry out with regard to something, yet something that is not given to us, since at best we are promised it at the end of our life? The two elements we must try to disentangle are movement and return; the subject's movement towards himself and the self's turning back on itself. And, as a final, slightly marginal note, I think there is a significant and frequently recurring metaphor concerning this conversion to the self and return to the self, one to which we will no doubt have to return.

It is the metaphor of navigation and it includes several components. [First,] there is, of course, the idea of a journey, of a real movement from one point to another. Second, the metaphor of navigation implies that this movement is directed towards a certain aim, that it has an objective. This aim, this objective, is the port, the harbor, as place of safety where we are sheltered from everything. Also in this idea of navigation, there is the theme that the port we are seeking is the homeport, the port in which we will find again our place of origin, our homeland. The path towards the self will always be something of an Odyssey. The fourth idea linked to this metaphor of navigation is that the journey to reach the homeport is dangerous, and it is because the journey is dangerous that we wish so much to reach this place of safety. During the journey you encounter unforeseen risks that may throw you off course or even lead you astray. Consequently, the journey will be in fact the one that leads you to the place of safety through a number of known and little known, known and unfamiliar dangers, etcetera. Finally, from this idea of navigation I think we should keep hold of the idea that this dangerous journey to the port, the port of safety, implies a knowledge (*savoir*), a technique, an art, in order to be undertaken well and to arrive at its objective. It is a complex, both theoretical and practical knowledge, as well as being a conjectural knowledge, which is very close, of course, to the knowledge of piloting.

I think the idea of piloting as an art, as a theoretical and practical technique necessary to existence, is an important idea which might be worth analyzing more closely, inasmuch as at least three types of techniques are usually associated with this model of piloting: first, medicine; second, political government; third, the direction and government of oneself.[7] In Greek, Hellenistic, and Roman literature, these three activities (curing, leading others, and governing oneself) were regularly analyzed by reference to the image of piloting. And I think that this image of piloting picks out quite well a type of knowledge (*savoir*) and practices between which the Greeks and Romans recognized a certain kinship and for which they sought to establish a *tekhnē* (an art, a reflected system of practices referring to general principles, notions, and concepts): The Prince, insofar as he must govern others, govern himself, and cure the ills of the city, of citizens and of himself; the person who governs himself as one governs a city, by curing his own ills; the doctor, who has to give his views not only on bodily ills but on the ills of the souls of individuals. In short, I think there is here a whole batch, a set of notions in the mind of the Greeks and Romans which, I think, fall within the province of a single type of knowledge (*savoir*), a single type of activity, and a single type of conjectural knowledge (*connaissance*).

And I think we could follow the entire history of this metaphor practically up to the sixteenth century, at which point, precisely, the definition of a new art of governing centered around *raison d'État* will make a radical distinction between government of oneself, medicine, and government of others, but not without this image of piloting remaining linked, as you know, to the activity that is called, precisely, the activity of government.[8] In short, in all of this you see that in this practice of the self, as it appeared and was expressed in the last centuries of the so-called pagan era and the first centuries of the Christian era, the self basically appeared as the aim, the end of an uncertain and possibly circular journey—the dangerous journey of life.

I think we should be clear about the possible historical importance of this prescriptive figure of the return to the self, and especially its singularity in Western culture. For although this prescriptive theme of the return to the self is quite clearly and evidently present in the period I am talking about, I think we should keep two things in mind. First of all, in Christianity there is, I believe, as the principal axis of Christian spirituality, a rejection, a refusal, which is obviously not without ambiguities, of this theme of the return to the self. The fundamental principle of Christian asceticism is that renunciation of the self is the essential moment of what enables us to gain access to the other life, to the light, to truth and salvation.[9] You cannot be saved unless you renounce yourself. Of course, there is ambiguity and difficulty in this theme of a search for salvation of the self for which self-renunciation is a fundamental condition, and we will have to come back to this. However, I think this self-renunciation is one of the fundamental axes of Christian asceticism. As for Christian mysticism, you know that it is also at least permeated by, if not entirely governed or exhausted by, the theme of the self being absorbed into God and losing its identity, individuality, and subjectivity, in the form of the self, through a privileged and immediate relationship to God. So, if you like, throughout Christianity the theme of return to the self has been a counter-theme much more than one that was really taken up and integrated within Christian thought. Second, I think we should also note that the theme of return to the self has undoubtedly been a recurrent theme in "modern" culture since the sixteenth century.

However, I also think that we cannot fail to be struck by the fact that this theme of return to the self has basically been reconstituted—but in fragments and scraps—in a series of successive attempts that have never been organized in the overall and continuous way that it was in Hellenistic and Roman antiquity. The theme of return to the self has never been dominant for us as it was possible for it to be in the Hellenistic and Roman epoch. To be sure, there is an ethics and also an aesthetics of the self in the sixteenth century, which refers explicitly, moreover, to what is found in the Greek and Latin authors I am talking about.[10] I think Montaigne should be reread in this perspective, as an attempt to reconstitute an aesthetics and an ethics of the self.[11] We could also take up the history of nineteenth century thought a bit in this perspective. Here, no doubt, things would be much more complicated, ambiguous, and contradictory. However, a whole section of nineteenth-century thought can be reread as a difficult attempt, a series of difficult attempts, to reconstitute an ethics and an aesthetics of the self. If you take, for example, Stirner, Schopenhauer, Nietzsche, dandyism, Baudelaire, anarchy, anarchist thought, etcetera, then you have a series of attempts that are, of course, very different from each other, but which are all more or less obsessed by the question: Is it possible to constitute, or reconstitute, an aesthetics of the self? At what cost and under what conditions? Or should the ethics and aesthetics of the self ultimately be inverted in the systematic refusal of the self (as in Schopenhauer)? In short, there is a question here, a series of problems, which could be raised. At any rate, what I would like to point out is that, after all, when today we see the meaning, or rather the almost total absence of meaning, given to some nonetheless very familiar expressions which continue to permeate our discourse—like getting back to oneself, freeing oneself, being oneself, being authentic, etcetera—when we see the absence of meaning and thought in all of these expressions we employ today, then I do not think we have anything to be proud of in our current efforts to reconstitute an ethic of the self. And in this series of undertakings to reconstitute an ethic of the self, in this series of more or less blocked and ossified efforts, and in the movement we now make to refer ourselves constantly to this ethic of the self without ever giving it any content, I think we may have to suspect that we find it impossible today to constitute an ethic of the self, even though it may be an urgent, fundamental, and politically indispensable task, if it is true after all that there is no first or final point of resistance to political power other than in the relationship one has to oneself.

In other words, what I mean is this: if we take the question of power, of political power, situating it in the more general question of governmentality understood as a strategic field of power relations in the broadest and not merely political sense of the term, if we understand by governmentality a strategic field of power relations in their mobility, transformability, and reversibility,[12] then I do not think that reflection on this notion of governmentality can avoid passing through, theoretically and practically, the element of a subject defined by the relationship of self to self. Although the theory of political power as an institution usually refers to a juridical conception of the subject of right,[13] it seems to me that the analysis of governmentality—that is to say, of power as a set of reversible relationships—must refer to an ethics of the subject defined by the relationship of self to self. Quite simply, this means that in the type of analysis I have been trying to advance for some time you can see that power relations, governmentality, the government of the self and of others, and the relationship of self to self constitute a chain, a thread, and I think it is around these notions that we should be able to connect together the question of politics and the question of ethics.

Having stated the meaning I want to give to this analysis of the care of the self and the relationship of self to self, which may appear to you to be rather plodding and meticulous, I would like now to return to the question I raised last week, which was this: What were the relations between the principle of conversion to the self and the principle of self-knowledge in the period I am talking about? In this simple and crude form this question will be: When the precept "care about the self" takes on the scope, the generality, the radical and absolute character of "one must change one's life to turn around on oneself and seek to get back to oneself," does not the precept "convert to the self" then entail the partial or no doubt total transfer of the gaze, of attention, of the focal point of the mind, away from others and from things of the world and towards oneself? More precisely, does not "convert to the self" basically imply constituting oneself as an object and domain of knowledge (*connaissance*)? Or again, posing the same question in the linear terms of an historical perspective, we could say the following: In this Hellenistic and Roman precept of conversion to the self, do we not find the origin, the first root of all those practices and forms of knowledge developed later in the Christian world and the modern world (practices of the investigation and direction of conscience), [do we not find here the] first form of what later it will be possible to call the sciences of the mind, psychology, the analysis of consciousness, the analysis of the *psukhē*, etcetera? Is not knowledge of the self, in the Christian and then modern sense, not rooted in this Stoic, Epicurean, Cynic episode that I am trying to analyze with you? Well, what I said to you last week concerning the Cynics and Epicureans tends to show, I think, that things are not so simple, and that what is constituted in this period and in these forms of the practice of the self is not knowledge of the self, as we understand it today, and that it is not even decipherment of the self, as Christian spirituality understood this. I would like now to go back to this point we referred to with regard to the Cynics and Epicureans, [but] I would like to return to it with regard to the Stoics, because I think there is a problem here that is important for me inasmuch as it is at the heart of the problems I want to pose, since basically the question I ask myself is this: How was the question of the truth of the subject constituted through the set of phenomena and historical processes we call our "culture"? How, why, and at what cost did we undertake to hold a true discourse on the subject: on the subject we are not, in the cases of the mad or delinquent subject; on the subject we are in general, inasmuch as we speak, work, and live; and on the subject we are directly and individually, in the particular case of sexuality?[14] I have tried to address this question of the constitution of the truth of the subject in these three major forms, perhaps with blameworthy stubbornness.*

---

*In conclusion to this methodological note, the manuscript has the following: "If the critical question is knowing 'the general conditions for the subject to possess truth,' the question I would like to pose is, rather, 'to what specific and historically definable transformations has the subject had to submit for there to be an injunction to speak the truth about the subject?' "

Anyway, I would like then to return to this point, which is no doubt an important historical issue: When, in Hellenistic and Roman culture, the care of the self becomes an autonomous, self-finalized art imparting value to the whole of life, is this not a privileged moment for seeing the development and formulation of the question of the truth of the subject? Forgive me for once again being slow and plodding, but I think confusions are easy here, facilitated, I believe, by the presence and prestige of two great models, two great schemas of the relation between care of the self and knowledge of the self—or again, if you like, [between] conversion to the self and knowledge of the self—which ultimately obscured what was specific in the model I want to analyze through Cynicism, Epicureanism, and especially Stoicism. These two great models hid from view what I will call, to make things easy and merely to give a purely historical name, a simple chronological reference point, the Hellenistic model. This Hellenistic model, which I want to analyze with you through Epicurean, Cynic, and Stoic texts, was concealed historically and for later culture by two other great models: the Platonic and the Christian models. What I would like to do is to free it from these two other models.

What is the Platonic model? I remind you that we saw it schematically through the *Alcibiades*. In this Platonic schema the relation between care of the self and self-knowledge is established around three basic points. First, if one must care about the self it is because one is ignorant. We are ignorant, we don't know we are ignorant, but then we discover (as the result, precisely, of an encounter, an event, a question) that we don't know and are unaware of the fact that we don't know. This is what happens in the *Alcibiades*. Compared with his rivals, Alcibiades was ignorant. Through Socratic questioning he discovers his ignorance. He even discovers that he was unaware of his ignorance and that consequently he must attend to himself in order to respond to this ignorance or, rather, to put an end to it. This is the first point. It is ignorance and the discovery of being unaware of this ignorance that gives rise to the requirement of caring for the self. Second, in the Platonic model, when care of the self is asserted and one actually undertakes to be concerned about the self, this essentially consists in "knowing oneself."

The entire surface of the care of the self is occupied by this requirement of self-knowledge which, as you know, takes the form of the soul's grasp of its own being, which it carries out by looking at itself in the mirror of the intelligible in which, precisely, it has to recognize itself. This leads us to the third point of the Platonic schema of the relation between care of the self and self-knowledge: Recollection is situated exactly at the point where care of the self and self-knowledge meet. The soul discovers what it is by recalling what it has seen. And it is by recalling what it is that it finds again access to what it has seen. In Platonic recollection we can say that knowledge of the self and knowledge of the true, care of the self and return to being are brought together and sealed off in a single movement. This, then, is the Platonic model.

The Christian model was formed, beginning in the third and fourth centuries, opposite, or alongside, or rather, later with regard to this model. We should say "ascetic-monastic" model rather than Christian in the general sense of the word. However, let's call it "Christian" to begin with. How is this Christian model, which I shall talk about in greater detail if I have time, characterized? I think we can say that in this model knowledge of the self is linked in a complex way to knowledge of the truth as given in the original Text and by Revelation: knowledge of the self is entailed and required by the fact that the heart must be purified in order to understand the Word; it can only be purified by self-knowledge; and the Word must be received for one to be able to undertake purification of the heart and realize self-knowledge. There is then a circular relation between self-knowledge, knowledge of the truth, and care of the self. If you want to be saved you must accept the truth given in the Text and manifested in Revelation. However, you cannot know this truth unless you take care of yourself in the form of the purifying knowledge (*connaissance*) of the heart. On the other hand, this purifying knowledge of yourself by yourself is only possible on condition of a prior fundamental relationship to the truth of the Text and Revelation. This circularity is, I think, one of the fundamental points of the relations between care of the self and knowledge of the self in Christianity. Second, in Christianity self-knowledge is arrived at through techniques whose essential function is to dispel internal illusions, to recognize the temptations that arise within the soul and the heart, and also to thwart the seductions to which we may be victim. And this is all accomplished by a method for deciphering the secret processes and movements that unfold within the soul and whose origin, aim, and form must be grasped. An exegesis of the self is thus required. This is the second fundamental point of the Christian model of the relations between self-knowledge and care of the self. Finally, third, the function of self-knowledge in Christianity is not to turn back to the self in an act of recollection in order to rediscover the truth it had once contemplated and the being that it is: rather, as I said a moment ago, if we turn round on the self, it is essentially and fundamentally in order to renounce the self. With Christianity then we have a schema of a relation between knowledge and care of the self that hinges on three points: first, circularity between truth of the Text and self-knowledge; second, an exegetical method for self-knowledge; and finally the objective of self-renunciation.

These two great models—the Platonic and the Christian, or, if you like, the model of recollection and the model of exegesis—have obviously had an immense historical prestige which has hidden the other model, the nature of which I would like to separate out for you. I think it is easy to find the reason for the prestige of these two great models (exegetical model and model of recollection) in the fact that they confronted each other throughout the first centuries of Christianity. It should not be forgotten that the Platonic model—organized around the theme of recollection, that is to say of the identification of care of the self and self-knowledge—was basically taken up, on the frontiers of Christianity, both within and outside Christianity, by those extraordinary movements that we have called the Gnosis, the Gnostic movements.[15] Actually, in all these movements we find again the same schema, which broadly speaking can be called "Platonic," that is to say, the idea that knowledge of being and recognition of the self are one and the same thing. Returning to the self and taking up again the memory of the true is one and the same thing for the Gnosis, and in this respect all the Gnostic movements are more or less Platonic movements. The exegetical model developed in confrontation with the Gnostic model and so on the borders of Christianity, of the Christian church—and this is precisely how monastic spirituality and asceticism was used—and its function (or anyway, effect) was to assure the great caesura and division with regard to the Gnostic movement, and its effect within Christian spirituality was not to give knowledge of the self the memorial function of rediscovering the subject's being, but rather the exegetical function of detecting the nature and origin of internal impulses produced within the soul. I think that these two great models—Platonic and Christian, or, if you like, the model of the subject's recollection of himself and the model of the subject's exegesis of himself—both dominated Christianity and were afterwards transmitted through Christianity to the whole of Western culture.

I would like to show you that there is a third schema between the great Platonic model—which survived throughout Antiquity, became vigorous again from the second and third centuries, appeared and developed in the Gnosis on the borders of Christianity, remained the more or less privileged interlocutor of Christianity, and which to some extent Christianity has always tried both to combat and take back into itself—and the exegetical model of Christian spirituality and asceticism. A third schema: this is the schema that was, precisely, put to work and developed during the last centuries of the old era and the first centuries of our era. The form of this schema is neither recollection nor exegesis. Unlike the Platonic model, it neither identifies care of the self and knowledge of the self, nor absorbs care of the self within knowledge of the self. Rather, it tends to accentuate and privilege care of the self, to maintain its autonomy at least with regard to knowledge of the self whose place is, as I think you will see, limited and restricted even so. Second, the Hellenistic model, unlike the Christian model, far from moving in the direction of self-exegesis or self-renunciation, tends, rather, to make the self the objective to be attained. Throughout the Hellenistic and Roman period, between Platonism and Christianity, an art of oneself was constituted, which for us will no doubt be just an episode permanently bracketed off by these two great models, the earlier and the later, which then dominated it and concealed it. As a result we might consider it to be no more than a sort of archeological curiosity within our culture, were it not for the fact—and this is undoubtedly the paradox to be grasped—that an exacting, rigorous, restrictive, and austere morality was developed within this neither Platonic nor Christian, but Hellenistic model. Christianity certainly did not invent this morality, because Christianity, like all good religions, is not a morality. At any rate, Christianity is a religion without morality. Well, it was this morality that Christianity utilized and repatriated, first of all as a strong support explicitly taken in from outside (see Clement of Alexandria),[16] and then that it adapted, fashioned, and honed precisely through those practices of the exegesis of the subject and self-renunciation. At the level of practices of the self, we have then, if you like, three great models which historically succeeded each other: the model I will call "Platonic," which gravitated around recollection; the "Hellenistic" model, which turns on the self-finalization of the relationship to the self; and the "Christian" model, which turns on self-exegesis and self-renunciation. For historical reasons, which I have tried to sketch out, the first and the third models have hidden the middle model from us moderns. However, this middle model, the Hellenistic model, centered on the self-finalization of the relationship to self and conversion to self, was nevertheless the site for the formation of a morality which Christianity accepted, took into itself, and developed so as to make it what we now mistakenly call "Christian morality,"[17] and which at the same time it linked, precisely, to exegesis of the self. The strict morality of the Hellenistic model was taken up and shaped by techniques of the self that were defined by the specifically Christian model of self-exegesis and self-renunciation. This, if you like, is a bit of the general historical perspective in which I would like to place all this.

Now let's return at last to this Hellenistic model, centered on the theme of "converting to the self," and try to see the role played by self-knowledge in this model. Does "converting to the self" in fact entail or call for a fundamental and continuous task of knowledge of what we will call the human subject, the human soul, human interiority, the interiority of consciousness, etcetera? With reference to Cynic texts—to one text at least, that of Demetrius—and some Epicurean texts, I have tried to show, first of all, that if self-knowledge was indeed a fundamental theme in the demand to "convert to the self," this self-knowledge was definitely not an alternative to the knowledge of nature. It was not a question of either knowing nature or knowing ourselves. Second, [I have tried to show] that within the theme of "converting to the self," self-knowledge found its place, rather, in a certain relationship of reciprocal links between knowledge of nature and knowledge of the self. "Converting to the self" is still a way of knowing nature.

I would now like to pose this question again with regard to the Stoics because, as you know, the question of the knowledge of nature occupies a much bigger place and has much greater importance and value in the Stoics, greater anyway than in the Cynics; I am not talking about the Epicureans. Schematically, we can say there is no doubt that in the Stoics, as in the Cynics as well as the Epicureans, there is a tradition of criticism of useless knowledge and a preference for all knowledge and learning, and all techniques and precepts that may concern human life. The theme that all the knowledge we need must be knowledge prescribed by the *tekhnē tou biou* (art of living) is found equally in the Stoics, Epicureans, and Cynics. This is so much the case that in what we can call, in inverted commas, certain "heretical" currents of Stoicism, there are, if you like, drastic, or anyway thoroughly restrictive assertions on what knowledge of the world or of nature could be. You find this, of course, in the famous Ariston of Khios[18] who, as you know, according to Diogenes Laertius rejected logic and physics from philosophy (physics because is it beyond our reach, and logic because it does not concern us).[19] According to Ariston, only morality mattered, and even then, he said, it is not the precepts (everyday precepts, counsels of prudence, etcetera) that are a part of philosophy, but just a number of general moral principles, a number of *dogmata*,[20] reason by itself, with no need of any other counsel, being capable of knowing what must be done in any circumstance without referring to the realm of nature. Ariston of Khios is a kind of extreme point, if you like, for in actual fact the general tendency of Stoicism is not towards mistrust of the knowledge of nature and its rejection as pointless. You know how morality, logic, and physics are defined within the strongly systematizing character of Stoic thought, and how they are linked to a cosmology and system of speculations about the order of the world. Stoicism in practice, even apart from its theoretical propositions, was actually associated with a set of scientific projects, sometimes indirectly and sometimes much more directly. The great encyclopedias of the naturalists of the first and second centuries, Galen's enormous medical encyclopedia, were in fact imbued with Stoic thought[21] [...*]. However, I think the question arises in the following way: What can the Stoics mean when they insist on the need to organize all knowledge in terms of the *tekhnē tou biou*, to direct the gaze on the self, and when, at the same time, they associate this conversion and inflection of the gaze onto the self with the entire course of the order of the world and with its general and internal organization? I will consider two texts to see how the Stoics deal with this question of directing the gaze on the self and at the same time exploring the order of the world. Well, I will certainly consider a first set of texts in Seneca and, if I have time, I will also talk about a number of texts from Marcus Aurelius.

First of all, Seneca. In Seneca—I will go over this very quickly, just to point it out—there is a series of completely traditional texts. Some refer to the criticism of the vanity of knowledge found in certain individuals who are interested in the luxury of libraries and books, and in the ostentation of books, rather than in what they may contain. There is an interesting critical reference in *De Tranquillitate*: it is a criticism of the library of Alexandria, in which he says that in reality the hundreds of thousands of books collected in this library were only [there] to satisfy the king's vanity.[22] Another series of texts, which I also pass over quickly, are recommendations made to his disciple in the first *Letters* to Lucilius:[23] don't read too much, don't seek to increase your reading, don't dissipate your curiosity. Just take one or two books and try to go into them more deeply; and from these books hold onto certain aphorisms, like those precisely that Seneca himself frequently looks for in Epicurus, which he extracts, as it were, from their context and from the books in which they are found and offers to Lucilius as subjects for meditation. This meditation, this exercise of thought on the truth—to which I will return one of these days[24]—does not proceed by way of a cultural journey

---

*Only "... did Stoicism separate useful and pointless knowledge?" is audible.

undertaken by knowledge in general. It is conducted, rather, according to a very old Greek technique, on the basis of maxims, of propositions, which are both the statement of truth and the pronouncement of a prescription, both assertion and prescription. This is what constitutes the element of philosophical reflection, and not a cultural field to be explored through a system of knowledge. The third series of texts concern the criticism of education, of the pointless and harmful education provided by traditional pedagogy. These texts are equally concerned with the place of different sciences in the education given to children, or in the education given in the name of philosophy. In the long letter 88,[25] there is a consideration and analysis of the liberal arts and of the uncertain and pointless, or at any rate purely instrumental, character of the knowledge provided by the liberal arts. So, there is this series of texts, but these are not what I want to refer to.

I would like to take the text in which Seneca puts to work the encyclopedic knowledge of the world to which Stoicism always accorded value, a positive value, while claiming that we must turn our gaze on ourselves. This is, of course, his *Natural Questions*, the comparatively lengthy and important work written by Seneca when he had gone into retirement and therefore after the sixties.[26] He wrote it in retirement when, on the one hand, he was writing regularly to Lucilius a large number of letters of spiritual and individual guidance. So, he was writing *Natural Questions* while also writing to Lucilius, and he sends him his work, the accompanying letters serving as prefaces to some of the books of *Natural Questions*. In this period he writes at the same time a *Treatise on Morality*.[27] On the other hand, you know that *Natural Questions* amounts to a sort of immense exploration of the world embracing the sky and earth, the path of the planets and the geography of rivers, the explanation of fire and meteors, etcetera. Moreover, everything is presented in an organization which reconstitutes a kind of descending and re-ascending movement: the first book is about the sky; the second, the air; the third and fourth, rivers and the seas; the fifth is on the wind; the sixth is on the earth; and the seventh, beginning the re-ascent, speaks of meteors. Now in this big book, which is therefore an exploration of the world, there are at least two places where Seneca wonders why he is writing in this way about these subjects which are, after all, so distant from us. These two texts are precisely the accompanying letters sent to Lucilius. They are the preface to the first book of *Natural Questions*, which functions as a general preface to the enterprise, and another letter, the preface to the third book, which is placed therefore more or less in the middle of the text. There are other letters-prefaces, to the fourth book for example, concerning flattery, which we can put to one side for the moment. I would like to consider these two letters-prefaces: One introducing the first part and the other introducing the third part. I will start with the letter introducing the third part,[28] because in this letter Seneca is still asking the reader and asking himself and wondering as it were: What after all am I doing here, what does it mean for me, at this point in my life, to be writing a book like this?—a book whose principle and objective he sums up very precisely in two phrases. For him, he says, it is actually a matter of *mundum circuire* (encompassing the entire world); and secondly, of investigating *causas secretaque* (causes and secrets). What he is doing is scouring the world and penetrating its internal causes and secrets.[29] Now, he says, what sense is there in this? Why do it? And here—from this observation: I am in the process of scouring the world, investigating its causes and secrets—begins a series of considerations that, for the sake of convenience, divide into four movements.

First, there is the question of age: I am in the process of exploring the world, I am investigating its causes and secrets, and, Seneca says, I am *senex* (an old man). This introduces, or rather reintroduces some familiar themes and questions: the theme I have spoken about of old age, haste, and the quickest possible path of life. For Seneca—as also for other Stoics, but Seneca gives it a quite specific importance—we must hasten to complete our lives as quickly as possible.[30] We must hasten to its point of completion, not in the sense that it will have reached its most distant chronological term, but complete by the fact of having achieved its fullness. We must pass through our life at the greatest speed, at a stroke, evenly, without even dividing it up into distinct phases with distinct modes of existence. We must pass through our life at the greatest speed, at a stroke, in order to arrive at that ideal point of ideal old age.

Seneca takes up this theme again here, accentuated by the consideration that when he writes *Natural Questions*, he is in fact old. He is old and he has lost time: time, he says, devoted to *vana studia* (to pointless, vain studies); and time lost through having had so many years in his life *male exemptae* (badly occupied, badly used, misspent). Hence, he says (since I am so old and have lost so much time), *labor* (work) is needed,[31] which must be undertaken with all the more *velocitas* (speed).[32] What is the work to which he must hasten due to his advanced age and all the time he has lost? He says he must concern himself not with an estate, a property far from its master: I must take care of the estate close by. This is what must detain me entirely. And what is this estate close by if not myself? It is necessary, he says, that "*sibi totus animus vacet*" (that the whole mind cares for, attends to itself). This expression "*sibi vacare*" (caring entirely for the self, attending to oneself) is found in other texts of Seneca and in letter 17 in particular: "*si vis vacare animo*" (if you want to attend to your *animus*).[33] So, not concerning oneself with distant estates but taking care of the estate closest at hand. This estate is oneself. We must, he says, "*ad contemplationem sui saltem in ipso fugae impetus respiciat*" (turn around to contemplate the self, in the very movement of flight).[34] It is the flight of time that is involved here, rather than the sage's flight or retreat. In the movement of time that carries us to the final point of our life, we must turn our gaze around and take ourselves as the object of contemplation. So everything indicates that at his age, in this flight of time and in this rush or *velocitas* that is now imposed on him, the only object with which Seneca must concern himself and on which he must work, is himself.[35] If he must be concerned with himself, what is it that this means he should not be concerned with? The rest? Yes, if you like. But what is this rest?

At this point we approach the second part of the text's exposition. We might think that having arrived at this point in his reasoning he says: Since I must only care about myself and not with distant estates, with distant property, let's put aside nature, meteors and the stars etcetera. Not at all. He does not say this. He says: What we must turn away from is historical learning. What does this historical learning tell us? It relates the history of foreign kings and their adventures, exploits, and conquests. All of this is basically only the history of kings, the history of suffering, transformed into praise. It matters little whether it is suffering inflicted on the people or inflicted by peoples, in the end this is all that is conveyed by the chronicles under the glorious drapery of the history of kings. And he stresses that it would be much better to overcome and defeat our own passions than to recount the passions of others, as historians do.[36] Instead of researching and investigating what has been done like historians, we should find out *quid [faciendum]* (what we should do).[37] Finally, third, when we read these accounts we are in danger of mistaking what is great for what is not, and of being deluded about true human greatness, only seeing human greatness in what are always fragile victories and uncertain fortunes. This whole argument against history is also completely in line with what is found in many of Seneca's other texts, and especially in his *Letters* to Lucilius, which were written at the same time and in which he regularly expressed his opposition to the verbosity of chronicles and their praise of great men like Alexander, whom he particularly detested. Against the verbosity of the chronicles he set the genuine value of the historical *exemplum*, which does not look for models in the lives of foreign kings. The historical *exemplum* is good inasmuch as it gives us native (Roman) models and reveals the true features of greatness, which are precisely not the visible forms of brilliance and power, but individual forms of self-mastery. Cato's modesty is an example. Scipio too is an example, leaving Rome in order to secure his town's freedom and retiring modestly, without glamour, to a villa.[38] So, in this criticism of history and the chronicle of great events and great men, we have the point, the example, the type of learning from which we should in fact turn away if we want to care for the self. You see, then, that it is not knowledge of nature that is to be avoided, but the form of historical knowledge that is not an exemplary knowledge, the form of historical chronicle, of historical learning.

So, the third development, the third moment of the text is this: Since history cannot teach us true greatness, in what does true greatness consist? This is what he explains, and it is to this, he says, that we must devote ourselves. "What is great down here? Is it crossing the seas in fleets, planting our flags on the shores of the Red Sea and, when we lack land for our devastation, wandering the ocean in search of unknown shores? No: it is seeing the whole of this world with the eyes of the mind and having carried off the most beautiful triumph, triumph over the vices. Those who have made themselves masters of towns and entire nations are countless; but how few have been masters of themselves! What is great down here? It is raising one's soul above the threats and promises of fortune; it is seeing that we can expect nothing from it that is worthy of us. What actually is there to wish for when our eyes return to earth from the sight of celestial bodies, and find only shadows, as when one passes from a clear sun to the dark night of dungeons? What is great is a steadfast soul, serene in adversity, a soul that accepts every event as if it were desired. In fact, should we not desire them if we know that everything happens by God's decree? What is great is to see the features of fate fall at one's feet; it is to remember that one is a man; it is, when one is happy, saying to oneself that one will not be happy for long. What is great is having one's soul at one's lips, ready to depart; then one is free not by the laws of the city but by the law of nature."[39] In this long list—I have skipped a few paragraphs, but it doesn't matter—the well-known principles are easily recognizable. First, it is important to defeat one's vices; this is the principle of self-control. Second, it is important to be steadfast and serene in the face of adversity and misfortune. The third—I skipped this paragraph, but no matter—concerned struggling against pleasure.[40] That is to say, we have here the three traditional forms of struggle: the internal struggle, which enables vices to be corrected, and the external struggle, which involves either standing up to adversity or resisting the temptations of pleasures of the flesh. What is great, [fourth], is not pursuing fleeting goods but rather the *bons mens*.[41] That is to say, we should seek our objective, happiness and ultimate good in ourselves, in our minds, in the quality of our souls. Finally, fifth, what is important is to be free to depart, to have the soul on our lips. So, after the three forms of struggle, the final objective is defined, the *bona mens*, with its criterion of having really acquired the necessary quality and plenitude of the relationship to the self and being ready to die.

Having arrived at this point of the definition of what we should do when we are old men, and that we must hasten to work for and on ourselves, we may wonder how these kinds of consideration are compatible with all the analyses produced in this same work, *Natural Questions*, how they can be inserted in the middle of this work on air, water, and meteors, etcetera, and how Seneca can resolve the paradox which he himself experienced and pointed out at the start of the text when he said: Well, I want to scour the world and extract its causes and secrets even though I am an old man. This is the question I would now like to address. So, if you like, we will take a break for two or three minutes and then, on the basis of this and other texts from Seneca, I will try to show how all the objectives of traditional Stoic morality are in fact not only compatible with, but can only really be attained, can only be met and accomplished at the cost of the knowledge of nature that is, at the same time, knowledge of the totality of the world. We can only arrive at the self by having passed through the great cycle of the world. I think this is what we find in some of Seneca's texts that I will now talk about.

1. "One of you, turning away from external things, focuses his efforts on his own self (*tēn proairesin epestraptai tēn hautou*)" *Discourses*, I.iv.18; "Turn back to yourselves (*epistrepsate autoi eph'heautous*)" *Discourses*, III.xxii.39; "Then, if you go back into yourself (*epistrepsate autoi eph'heautous*) and consider to what domain the event belongs, you will remember at once that it is 'the domain of things independent of us.'" *Discourses*, III.xxiv.106.
2. "We seek retreats (*anakhōrēseis*) in the country, by the sea, in the mountains; and you too are in the habit of wanting these things intensely. But this is very simple-minded since whenever we choose we can withdraw into overselves (*eis heauton anakhōrein*)." Marcus Aurelius, *Meditations*, IV.3.
3. "Vices beset us and surround us on every side, and they do not permit us to rise up anew and raise our eyes to discern truth. They keep us down, sunk in passion; their victims are never allowed to return to themselves (*numquam illis recurrere ad se licet*)." Seneca, *On the Shortness of Life*, II.3.
4. See Seneca, *Letters*, XV.5.
5. "Moreover, we ought to withdraw into ourselves (*in se recedendum est*) very often." Seneca, *On Tranquility of Mind*, XVII.3; "Virtue is no less great, even when, discouraged, it has retreated into itself (*in se recessit*)." Seneca, *Letters*, LXXIV.29.
6. "Nevertheless, let us, insofar as we can, not only avoid dangers but discomforts as well, and withdraw to a safe place (*in tutum nos reducamus*), by thinking continually of ways to avoid all objects of fear." Seneca, *Letters*, XIV.3.
7. We may recall that the *kubernētēs*, the person responsible for the conduct and direction of a ship, is given in Latin as *gubernator*. See the article *gubernator/kubernētēs* in E. Saglio, ed., *Dictionnaire des antiquités grecques et romaines* (Paris: Hachette, 1926) vol. II-2, pp. 1673-74. Moreover, the comparison between medical and navigational arts frequently appears in Plato (see *Alcibiades*, 125e-126a; *Gorgias*, 511d-512d; *The Republic*, 332d-e, 341c-d, 360e, 389c, 489b, etcetera). However, it is in a long passage from *The Statesman* (297-299c) that the arts of medicine, navigation, and political government are connected to each other (this is the passage that Foucault studies, to determine the distinction between government of the city-state and pastoral government, in his lecture at the Collège de France, 15 February 1978). The key text for this analogy between the pilot and the doctor remains, however, Hippocrates' *Ancient Medicine*: "It seems that the same thing happens to doctors as to pilots. Insofar as the latter govern in calm weather, any error they may make is not apparent." A trace of this analogy is found again in Quintilian: "Similarly a pilot will desire to bring his ship safe to harbour; but if he is swept out of his course by a storm, he will not for that reason cease to be a pilot, but will say in the well-known words of the old poet, 'Still let me steer straight on!' So too the doctor seeks to heal the sick; but if the violence of the disease or the refusal of the patient to obey his regimen or any other circumstance prevent his achieving his purpose, he will not have fallen short of the ideals of his art, provided he has done everything according to reason." *The Institutio Oratorie of Quintilian*, in 4 volumes, trans. H.E. Butler (London and New York: Loeb Classical Library, 1920-1922) vol. I, II.xvii.24-25, pp. 335-36; French translation by J. Cousins, *Institution oratoire*, vol. II, I.17.24-25 (Paris: Les Belles Lettres, 1976) p. 95.
8. For the analysis of modern *raison d'État*, see the Collège de France lectures 8 and 15 March, 1978, and the course summary "Sécurité, territoire et population," *Dits et Écrits*, vol. III, pp. 720-21 (English translation by Robert Hurley et al., "Security, Territory, and Population," in *Ethics: Subjectivity and Truth*, pp. 68-69) and "'Omnes et singulatim': vers une critique de la raison politique," *Dits et Écrits*, vol. 4, pp. 150-53 (English translation by Robert Hurley et al, "*Omnes et Singulatim*: Toward a Critique of Political Reason" in, *Power*, pp. 314-19).
9. See Collège de France lecture 26 March 1980, which studies the schema of Christian subjectivity in which the production of the truth of the self is linked to self-renunciation: I only produce the truth of myself in order to renounce myself.

10. On the theme of life as a work of art (aesthetic of existence), see lecture 17 March, first hour and below, pp. 434-35, note 14.
11. See the statements along similar lines in "On the Genealogy of Ethics," In *Ethics: subjectivity and truth*, pp. 255-56; French translation by G. Barbedette and Durand-Bogaert, "À propos de la généalogie de l'éthique," *Dits et Écrits*, vol. 4, p. 410.
12. On an analysis of power in strategic terms (as opposed to the juridical model), see "Questions à Michel Foucault sur la géographie" in *Dits et Écrits*, vol. 3, p. 33, and "Pouvoirs et stratégies," *Dits et Écrits*, vol. 3; English translation of latter by Colin Gordon, "Powers and Strategies," in Michel Foucault, *Power/Knowledge: Selected Interviews and Other Writings 1972-1977*, ed. Colin Gordon (Brighton: Harvester Press, 1980).
13. On the criticism of a juridical conception of power, Foucault's classic text is *La Volonté de savoir* (Paris: Gallimard, 1976), pp. 177-211 (English translation by Robert Hurley, *The History of Sexuality: Volume 1: An Introduction* [London: Allen Lane, 1979] pp. 81-114); *"Il faut défendre la société." Cours au Collège de France, 1975-1976*, M. Bertani and A. Fontana, eds. (Paris: Gallimard/Seuil, 1997), *passim* (English translation by David Macey, *"Society must be defended." Lectures at the Collège de France, 1975-1976* [New York: Picador, 2003]); "Subjectivité et vérité," *Dits et Écrits*, vol. 4, p. 214 (English translation by Robert Hurley, "Subjectivity and Truth," in *Ethics: Subjectivity and Truth*, p. 88) and "The Subject and Power" in *Power*, p. 329 (French translation by F. Durand-Bogaert, "Le sujet et le pouvoir," *Dits et Écrits*, vol. 4, p. 214).
14. For a similar presentation of his work (the figure of the mad in *Madness and Civilization* and of the delinquent in *Discipline and Punish*), rearticulated around the notion of the subject, see "Sexuality and Solitude" in *Ethics: Subjectivity and Truth*, p. 177 (French translation by F. Durand-Bogaert, "Sexualité et solitude," *Dits et Écrits*, vol. 4, p. 170); "Foucault," *Dits et Écrits*, vol. 4, p. 633 (English translation by Robert Hurley, "Foucault," *Aesthetics, Method, and Epistemology*, pp. 459-60); "The Subject and Power" in, *Power*, pp. 326-27 (French translation by F. Durand-Bogaert, "Le sujet et le pouvoir," *Dits et Écrits*, vol. 4, p. 227); and "Interview de Michel Foucault," *Dits et Écrits*, vol. 4, p. 657.
15. On the Gnostics, see lecture 6 January, first hour and above, pp. 23-24, note 49.
16. Concerning the summary of passages from Musonius Rufus in Clement of Alexandria's *The Instructor* (II.10), see, for example, Foucault's analysis in *Le Souci de soi*, p. 198 (*The Care of the Self*, p. 170). Foucault read extensively the classic work of M. Spanneut, *Le Stoïcisme des Pères de l'Église, de Clément de Rome à Clément d'Alexandrie* (Paris: Éd. du Seuil, 1957).
17. On the difficulty of talking of a "Christian morality," see the beginning of the lecture 6 January, first hour.
18. Zeno's dissident disciple, Ariston of Chios, was not satisfied with ignoring logic (pointless) and physics (inaccessible), but also maintained a radical morality that consisted in asserting that, outside of virtue, everything is of equal value (the postulate of indifference, preventing the prescription of standard duties). Some maintain that it was through reading him that Marcus Aurelius was converted to philosophy. See the note by C. Guérard on Ariston in the *Dictionnaire des philosophes antiques*, pp. 400-03.
19. "He wished to discard both Logic and Physics, saying that Physics was beyond our reach and Logic did not concern us: all that did concern us was Ethics," Diogenes Laertius, "Ariston," in *Lives of Eminent Philosophers*, VII.160. Seneca takes up the same presentation in *Letters*, LXXXIX.13 and XCIV.2.
20. See Seneca's presentation: "That part of philosophy which gives precepts (*praecepta*) appropriate to the each individual, which does not train man in general, but which prescribes how a husband should conduct himself toward his wife, or how a father should bring up his children, or how a master should govern his slaves, has been the only part of philosophy accepted by some theoreticians; the rest they reject, seeing in it only digressions having no relation to our needs, as if one could formulate prescriptions on points of detail without first having embraced the whole of human life. But Aristo the Stoic, on the contrary, thinks this part of philosophy has no solidity and fails to penetrate to the heart, being only the proverbs of old women. Nothing is more profitable than pure dogmatic philosophy (*decreta philosophiae*)." *Letters*, XCIV.1-2.

21. The work of the physician Galen of Pergamum (129-200) is impressive: it comprises tens of thousands of pages and covers all the medical sciences of his time. He was quickly translated into Arabic and was established as an unavoidable monument until the Renaissance. We can further note, for the second century, the works of Élien de Préneste (172-235), a compilation of natural and historical knowledge (*Histoire variée, Caractéristique des animaux*). Finally, for the Latin language it will be recalled that Pliny's great *Natural History* is from the first century, as are the books of Celsus.
22. "Forty thousand books were burned at Alexandria. Others may praise this library as the most noble monument to royal munificence, as did Titus Livius, who says that it was the masterpiece of the good taste and solicitude of kings. I see neither good taste nor solicitude, just a literary orgy; and when I say literary, I am wrong, the care for literature has nothing to do with it: these fine collections were created solely for show." Seneca, *On Tranquility of Mind*, IX.5.
23. The recommendations for reading are essentially in the second letter. *Letters*, II.
24. See the lecture 27 February, second hour, and lecture 3 March, first hour.
25. *Letters*, LXXXVIII.
26. On the dating of *Natural Questions*, see lecture 20 January, first hour, and above p. 102, note 27.
27. These are the last letters to Lucilius (CVI.2; CVIII.39; CIX.17), which speak of the drafting of *Moralis philosophiae libri*, presupposing a drafting around 64 AD.
28. Foucault again makes use of the old edition of Seneca's works: *Questions naturelles* in Œuvres complètes de Sénèque le philosophe, Preface to book III.
29. "I am aware, my excellent friend, of the vast project for which I am laying the foundations at my age; an old man (*senex*), I wish to encompass the universe and discover the causes of things and their secrets (*qui mundum circuire constitui, et causas secretaque ejus eruere*) in order to pass them on to the knowledge of men." Ibid.
30. See lecture 20 January, second hour.
31. "When will I be able to put an end to so much research, bring together so many scattered facts, penetrate so many mysteries? Old age presses on me and reproves me for the years sacrificed to idle studies (*objecit annos inter vana studia consumptos*), a further reason for me to hasten and make up with work for a misspent life (*damna aetatis male exemptae labor sarciat*)." *Natural Questions*, Preface to book III.
32. "Let me do what one does on a journey; if one starts late, one makes up for the delay by speed (*velocitate*)." Ibid.
33. "If you wish to take care of your soul (*vacare animo*); be a poor man, or live like a poor man." Seneca, *Letters*, XVII.5.
34. The Belles Lettres edition does not draw this conclusion, but "*ad contemplationem sui saltem in ipso fine respiciat*," which Oltramare translates as: "that, in its last moments [the mind] is no longer interested in anything but what it is." *Questions naturelles*, t.1, p. 113.
35. "Join night to day, cut out pointless concerns; drop concern for property too far from its owner; so that the mind may be entirely for itself and its own study, and at the moment when the flight of age is fastest, we at least cast our mind back on ourselves (*sibi totus animus vacet, et ad contemplationem sui saltem in ipso fugae impetus respiciat*)," *Natural Questions*, Preface to book III.
36. "How much wiser to stifle one's own passions than to recount for posterity those of others?" Ibid.
37. "Ah! Rather investigate what ought to be done (*quid faciendum sit*) than what has been done," Ibid.
38. On the condemnation of the chronicles of Alexander and the praise of the *exemplum* of Cato or Scipio, see the *Letters* to Lucilius, XXIV, XXV, LXXXVI, XCIV, XCV, XCVIII and CIV. Cato is again given as someone who should be taken as the ideal of wisdom in *On the Firmness of the Wise Man*, VII.1, and *On Providence*, II.9.
39. *Natural Questions*.
40. "What is great is that this soul, strong and steadfast against reverses, rejects the pleasures of the flesh and even fights them to excess," Ibid.
41. "What is most great? ... to lay claim to the only treasure that no one will dispute, wisdom (*bonam mentem*)." Ibid.

## fourteen

## 17 FEBRUARY 1982

### Second hour

> End of the analysis of the preface to the third part of Natural Questions. ~ Study of the preface to the first part. ~ The movement of the knowing soul in Seneca: description; general characteristic; after-effect. ~ Conclusions: essential implication of knowledge of the self and knowledge (connaissance) of the world; liberating effect of knowledge (savoir) of the world; irreducibility to the Platonic model. ~ The view from above.

SO, LET'S RETURN TO this preface of the third part of *Natural Questions*. Now that he is old, Seneca explores the world. When you are old you must take care of your own property. Taking care of your own property certainly doesn't mean reading the chronicles of historians who recount the exploits of kings. Rather, it means defeating your passions, being steadfast in the face of adversity, resisting temptation, setting your own mind as your objective, and being ready to die. How is it that at this point Seneca couples with this objective, defined in opposition to the historical chronicles, the possibility and necessity of exploring the world? Well, I think the germ of the return to the knowledge of nature, the usefulness of which he was wondering about, is in the last sentence I read out: "What is great is having one's soul at one's lips, ready to depart; then one is free not by the laws of the city, but by the law of nature (*non e jure Quiritium liberum, sed e jure naturae*)."[1] One is free by the law of nature. One is free, but free for what? What is this freedom given to us when we have practiced these different exercises, waged these struggles, fixed this objective, practiced meditation on death and accepted its arrival? In what does freedom acquired in this way consist? What is it to be free? asks Seneca. And he answers: To be free is *effugere servitutem*.[2] It is to flee servitude, of course, but servitude to what? *Servitutem sui*: servitude to the self. This is clearly a remarkable assertion when we recall everything the Stoics say, everything Seneca says elsewhere about the self, the self we must free from everything that may enslave it, the self we must protect, defend, respect, worship, and honor: *therapeuein heauton* (devoting oneself to oneself).[3] This self must be our objective. He says so himself when, a bit earlier in the text, he speaks of the contemplation of the self: We must have the self before our eyes, not let it out of our sight and order our life around this self which we have set as our objective; this self, in short, with regard to which Seneca frequently tells us that by being in contact with it, close to it, in its presence, we can experience the greatest delight, the only joy, the only *gaudium* which is legitimate, without fragility, neither exposed to danger nor subject to any lapse.[4] How can we say that the self is this thing to honor, pursue, keep in our sight, and in the presence of which we experience this absolute delight, while at the same time saying that we must free ourselves from the self?

Now—Seneca's text is perfectly clear here—self-servitude, servitude with regard to oneself, is defined here as what is to be struggled against. Developing this proposition—that to be free is to flee servitude to oneself—he says the following: To be the slave of oneself (*sibi servire*), is the most serious and grave (*gravissima*) of all servitudes. Second, it is an unremitting servitude, that is to say it weighs upon us constantly. Day and night, Seneca says, without interval or break (*intervallum, commeatus*). Third, it is ineluctable. And by "ineluctable" he does not mean, as you will see, that it is utterly insurmountable. Anyway, he says it is inevitable and no one is exempt from it: we always start from this. However, we can struggle against this grave, unremitting servitude which anyway is forced on us. It is easy to shake it off, he says, on two conditions. These two conditions are the following: first, that we stop demanding too much of ourselves. He explains what he means by this a bit further on. Demanding too much of yourself is giving yourself difficulties, imposing great effort and toil on yourself, for example in managing your affairs, exploiting your land, working the soil, pleading at the forum, pestering the political assemblies, etcetera.[5] In short, it is taking on all the obligations of the traditional active life. Second, we can free ourselves from this self-servitude by not granting ourselves what we usually give ourselves as salary, reward and recompense, as it were, for the work we have done. You must stop *"mercedem sibi referre"* (making a profit for yourself) if you want to free yourself from the self.[6] You can see then, although it is indicated only very briefly in the text, that Seneca describes this self-servitude as a series of commitments, activities, and rewards: it is a sort of obligation-indebtedness of the self to the self. It is this type of relationship to the self from which we must free ourselves. We impose obligations on ourselves and we try to get back some profit (financial profit or the profit of glory and reputation, of pleasures of the body and life, etcetera). We live within this system of obligation-reward, of indebtedness-activity-pleasure. This is the relationship to the self from which we must free ourselves. In what, then, does freeing ourselves from this relationship to the self consist? At this point Seneca lays down the principle that the study of nature enables us to free ourselves from this type of relationship to the self, from this system of obligation-indebtedness, if you like. Seneca ends this part of the preface to the third part of *Natural Questions* by saying: *"proderit nobis inspicere rerum naturam"* (observing, inspecting the nature of things will help us in this liberation). In this text Seneca does not go beyond this assertion that the self from which we must free ourselves is this relationship to self, and that the study of nature assures us of this liberation.

At this point I think we can turn to the preface to the first part that I skipped in order to get to this text which is much closer to Seneca's personal questions: Why is he taking up this study now he is old? Here, in the preface to the first part, there is, rather, what could be called the general and abstract theory of the study of nature as the effective agency that brings about the liberation of self, in the sense I was just talking about. This preface begins with the distinction between two parts of philosophy, which is completely in line with other of Seneca's texts.

There are, he says, two parts of philosophy. There is the part that attends to, is concerned with, and examines men (*ad homines spectat*). This part of philosophy says *quid agendum in terris* (what we must do on earth). Then there is the other part of philosophy. This part does not examine men, but the gods (*ad deos spectat*).[7] And this part of philosophy tells us *quid agatur in caelo* (what happens in the heavens). There is, he says, a great difference between these two parts of philosophy, between that concerning men, telling us what must be done, and that concerning the heavens and telling us what takes place there. The difference between the first and second of these philosophies is as great as that between the ordinary arts (*artes*) and philosophy itself. What different areas of knowledge, the liberal arts he spoke about in letter 88,[8] are to philosophy, so the philosophy that looks towards men is to the philosophy that looks towards the gods. You can see then that there is a difference in importance and dignity between the two forms of philosophy. There is also, and this is another point to stress, an order of succession, which moreover Seneca brings into play in other texts: In the letters to Lucilius, considerations concerning the order of the world and nature in general come, in fact, after a very long series of letters concerning what should be done in everyday life. It is also expressed very simply in letter 65, in which Seneca tells Lucilius that one must "*primum se scrutari, deinde mundum*" (first examine yourself, take yourself into consideration, and then the world).[9] So, this succession of the two forms of philosophy—one concerning men and the other concerning the gods—is called for by the incompleteness of the first with regard to the second, and by the fact that only the second (philosophy concerning the gods) can complete the first. The first—concerning men: "what is to be done?"—allows us, Seneca says, to avoid errors. It casts the light on earth that enables us to discriminate between life's ambiguous paths. The second, however, is not content with using this light to light up life's paths, as it were. It leads us to the source of light by dragging us out of the shadows: "*illo perducit, unde lucet*" (it leads us to the place from which the light comes to us). In this second form of philosophy, therefore, what is involved is something that is, of course, completely different from a knowledge of rules of existence and behavior, but you can see also that it involves something completely different from a knowledge *tout court*. It involves dragging us from the shadows down here and leading us (*peducere*) to the point from where the light comes to us. What is involved then is a real movement of the subject, of the soul, which is thus lifted above the world and dragged from the shadows made by this world here [...] but which really is a movement of the subject himself. Okay, this movement has, I think—forgive me, I schematize—four characteristics.

First, this movement is a flight, a tearing free from one's self that finishes off and completes the detachment from flaws and vices. Seneca says this in this preface to the first part of *Natural Questions*: You have escaped, he says, the vices of the soul—and it is quite clear that Seneca is referring here to his other letters to Lucilius, to the work of spiritual direction he has undertaken, at a point and moment when this internal struggle against vices and flaws is effectively over: it is then that he sends him the *Natural Questions*. You have escaped the vices of the soul, you have stopped composing your features and your speech, you have stopped lying and deceiving (the theory of active and passive flattery), and you have renounced greed, lust, and ambition, etcetera. And yet, he says, it is as if you have done nothing: "*multa effugisti, te nondum*" (you have escaped many things, but you have not escaped yourself). It is then this flight from ourselves, in the sense that I was just talking about, that knowledge of nature can ensure. Second, this movement which leads us to the source of light, leads us to God, but not in the form of losing oneself in God or of a movement which plunges deep into God, but in the form that allows us to find ourselves again, the text says, "*in consortium Dei*": in a sort of co-naturalness or co-functionality with God. That is to say, human reason is of the same nature as divine reason. It has the same properties and the same role and function. What divine reason is to the world, human reason must be to man. Third, in this movement which carries us to the light, which tears us free from ourselves and puts us in the *consortium Dei*, we rise towards the highest point. However, at the same time, at the very moment at which we are thus borne above this world, as it were, above this universe in which we exist—or rather, when we are borne above the things at whose level we exist in this world—we are able, by virtue of this, to penetrate the innermost secret of nature: "*interiorem naturae sinum [venit]*" (the soul reaches the heart, the most internal, innermost bosom of nature).[10]

Let's be clear, I will come back to this shortly, about the nature and effects of this movement. What is involved is not an uprooting from this world into another world. It is not a matter of freeing oneself from one reality in order to arrive at a different reality. It is not a matter of leaving a world of appearances so as finally to reach a sphere of the truth. What is involved is a movement of the subject that is carried out and effectuated within the world—really going towards the point from which the light comes, really gaining a form that is the same form of divine reason—and which places us, inasmuch as we are in the *consortium Dei*, at the very peak, the highest point (*altum*) of this universe. However, we do not leave this universe and this world, and at the very moment we are at the summit of this world, and by virtue of this, the inner recesses, secrets, and very heart of nature are opened to us. You see finally, and for the same reason, that this movement which places us at the highest point of the world, and at the same time opens up to us the secrets of nature, will allow us to look down to earth from above. At the very moment that, participating in divine reason, we grasp the secret of nature, we can grasp how small we are. You know why I am emphasizing all this, and I will come back to it shortly: despite some analogies, you see how far we are from the Platonic movement. Whereas the Platonic movement consisted in turning away from this world in order to look towards another—even if souls, who, through recollection, have rediscovered and savored the reality they have seen, are led more by force than by their own will back to this world in order to govern it—the Stoic movement defined by Seneca is completely different. It involves a sort of stepping back from the point we occupy. This liberation enables us to reach the highest regions of the world without, as it were, ever losing ourselves from sight and without the world to which we belong ever being out of our sight. We reach the point from which God himself sees the world and, without our ever actually turning away from this world, we see the world to which we belong and consequently can see ourselves within this world. What will be permitted us by the view we have obtained by this stepping back from the world and by this ascent to the summit of the world from where nature's secrets are opened up?

Well, it will enable us to grasp the pettiness and the false and artificial character of everything that seemed good to us before we were freed. Wealth, pleasure, glory: all these transitory events will take on their real proportions again when, through this stepping back, we reach the highest point where the secrets of the whole world will be open to us. When, he says, we have encompassed the entire world (*"mundum totum circuire"*: you see that we find again exactly the same expression that I read out from the beginning of the preface to the third book),[11] when we have gone round the world in its general circle, by looking down from above on the circle of the planets (*"terrrarum orbem super ne despiciens"*), we are then able to despise all the false splendors built by men (ivory ceilings, forests transformed into gardens, diverted rivers, etcetera).[12] This point of view—the text does not say this, but you can see how the two prefaces harmonize—also enables us to situate those famous historical glories that, in the text I quoted a moment ago,[13] Seneca said we should shun. They are not what matter because, seen again from the height of the point where the exploration of the whole of nature places us, we see how few things matter and endure. Reaching this point enables us to dismiss and exclude all the false values and all the false dealings in which we are caught up, to gauge what we really are on the earth, and to take the measure of our existence—of this existence that is just a point in space and time—and of our smallness. What are armies for us, Seneca asks, when seen from above, when we see them after having covered the world's great cycle? All armies are no more than ants. Like ants, in fact, they move around a great deal, but over a very small space. "You sail on a point," he says, and no more than a point.[14] You think you have crossed immense spaces: you remained on a point. You wage war on a point, and you share out empires on a point, and only on a point. You can see that the great exploration of nature is not used to tear us from the world, but to enable us to grasp ourselves again here where we are. We are not at all in a world of unrealities, a world of shadows and appearances, and the exploration of nature does not serve to detach us from what is only shadow so that we rediscover ourselves in a world which is only light: Its use is to measure quite precisely our perfectly real existence, but an existence which is only a punctual existence, which is punctual both in space and in time. Being for ourselves, in our own eyes, what we are, namely a point, "punctualizing" ourselves in the general system of the universe, is the liberation really brought about by the gaze we can cast over the entire system of natural things. So, we can now draw some conclusions on the role of the knowledge of nature in the care of the self and in the knowledge of the self.

First consequence. What is involved in this knowledge of the self is not something like an alternative: either we know nature or we know ourselves. In fact, we can only know ourselves properly if we have a point of view on nature, a knowledge (*connaissance*), a broad and detailed knowledge (*savoir*) that allows us to know not only its overall organization, but also its details. Whereas the role and function of Epicurean analysis, of the Epicurean need for a knowledge of physics, was basically to free us from the fears, apprehensions, and myths that have encumbered us from birth, the Stoic need to know nature, the need to know nature in Seneca, is not so much, or anyway is not only, in order to dispel these fears, although this dimension is also present. Above all, this form of knowledge involves grasping ourselves again here where we are, at the point where we exist, that is to say of placing ourselves within a wholly rational and reassuring world, which is the world of a divine Providence; a divine Providence that has placed us here where we are and which has therefore situated us within a sequence of specific, necessary, and rational causes and effects that must be accepted if we really want to free ourselves from this sequence in the form, the only possible form, of acknowledgement of its necessity. Knowledge of the self and knowledge of nature are not alternatives, therefore; they are absolutely linked to each other. And you can see—this is another aspect of this question of the relations between them—that knowledge of the self is in no way knowledge of something like interiority. It has nothing to do with a possible self-analysis, with the analysis of one's secrets (of what Christians will later call *arcana conscientiae*). Later we will see that we must inspect the depth of ourselves, the illusions we create about ourselves, the soul's secret movements, etcetera. But the idea of an exploration, the idea of a particular domain of knowledge that above all else we must know and untangle—because the power of illusion about ourselves is so great, both within ourselves and due to temptation—is absolutely foreign to Seneca's analysis. Rather, if "knowing oneself" is linked to knowledge of nature, if, in this search for the self, knowing nature and knowing oneself are linked to each other, it is inasmuch as knowledge of nature reveals to us that we are no more than a point whose interiority is clearly not a problem. The only problem that is posed to this point is precisely both being there where it is and accepting the system of rationality that has inserted it at this point of the world. This is the first set of conclusions I would like to draw with regard to knowledge of the self and knowledge of nature, their connection and the fact that knowledge of the self is not in any way, and in no way resembles, what will later be the self-exegesis of the subject.

Second, you see that the effect of knowing nature, of this great gaze that scours the world, or which, stepping back from the point we occupy, ends up grasping the whole of nature, is liberating. Why does knowing nature free us? You can see that in this liberation there is nothing like an uprooting from this world, a transfer to a different world, or a break with and abandonment of this world. Rather, it involves two essential effects. First: to obtain a sort of maximum tension between the self as reason—and consequently, as such, as universal reason, having the same nature as divine reason—and the self as individual component, placed here and there in the world, in an absolutely restricted and delimited spot. So the first effect of this knowledge of nature is to establish the maximum tension between the self as reason and the self as point. Second, the knowledge of nature is liberating inasmuch as it allows us, not to turn away from ourselves, not to turn our gaze away from what we are, but rather to focus it better and continuously take a certain view of ourselves, to ensure a *contemplatio sui* in which the object of contemplation is ourselves in the world, ourselves inasmuch as our existence is linked to a set of determinations and necessities whose rationality we understand. You see then that "not losing sight of oneself" and "exploring the whole of the world" are two absolutely inseparable activities, on condition that there has been this stepping back, this spiritual movement of the subject establishing the maximum distance from himself so that the subject becomes, at the summit of the world, *consortium Dei*: closest to God, participating in the activity of divine rationality. It seems to me that all of this is perfectly summarized in Seneca's letter 66 to Lucilius in which he says—it is a lengthy and important description of the virtuous soul—that the virtuous soul is a soul "in contact with the whole universe and careful to explore all its secrets" (*"toti se inserens mundo et in omnis ejus actus contemplationem suam mittens"*). "Every *actus*," we could almost say, every action and process. So, the virtuous soul is a soul which is in contact with the whole universe and which carefully contemplates everything making up its events, activities and processes. Then, "it controls itself in its actions as in its thoughts" (*cogitationibus actionibusque intentus ex aequo*). The soul's virtue consists in penetrating the world and not tearing itself free from it, in exploring the world's secrets rather than turning away towards inner secrets.[15] However, by virtue of this, and by the fact that it is "in contact with the whole universe" and that it "explores all its secrets," the soul can control its actions, "controlling itself in its actions and in its thoughts."

Finally, the third conclusion I would like to draw is that, as you can see, we are very close here to what we might see as a Platonic type of movement. It is clear that the memory of, reference to, and Plato's terms themselves are very close to, are actually present in this text from the preface to the first part of *Natural Questions*. This kind of text can also be found elsewhere in Seneca. I am thinking of letter 65, in which Seneca says: "What is our body? A weight upon the soul for its torment. It oppresses the soul and keeps it in chains, but philosophy has appeared, and at last invites the soul to breathe in the presence of nature; it has made it abandon the earth for divine realities. This is how the soul becomes free, this is how it can take flight. Occasionally it breaks out from its dungeon and is recreated in heaven [by heaven: *caelo reficitur*; M.F.]."[16] This recollection is so clearly Platonic, in Seneca's own eyes, that he gives a kind of little mythology of the cave. He says: Just as artisans (who work in their dark, shadowy, and smoky workshops) love to leave their workshop and walk in the open air, in the free light (*libera luce*), "so the soul, enclosed within its sad and dark abode, rushes out to the open air whenever it can to rest in the contemplation of nature."[17] So we are very close to Platonic themes and a Platonic form. We could also cite the much earlier text *De Brevitate vitae*. As you know, this was addressed to his father-in-law[18] who was the *praefectus annonae* and so concerned with the grain supply to Rome.[19] He says to him: Compare being concerned with wheat (its price, its storage, taking care that it is not spoiled, etcetera) to another activity, that of knowing God, his substance (*materia*), his pleasure (*voluptas*), his condition, and his form. Compare your own occupations to those of knowing the organization of the universe and the revolution of the stars. Having left the ground (*relicto solo*), do you really want to turn the eyes of your mind toward these things (the nature of God, the organization of the universe, the revolution of the stars, etcetera)?[20] There are clear Platonic references here. However, it seems to me—I was saying this a short while ago; I want to come back to it because it is important—that we should not be deceived by the undeniable existence of these references. The movement of the soul that Seneca describes with Platonic images is, I think, very different from the movement found in Plato, and it arises from a quite different spiritual framework or structure. You see first of all that in Seneca's description of this movement of the soul as, in fact, a kind of uprooting from the world, a transition from darkness to light, etcetera, there is no recollection, even if reason recognizes itself in God. What is involved is a journey over the world, an investigation into the things of the world and their causes, rather than a rediscovery of the soul's essence. There is no question of the soul withdrawing into itself and questioning itself in order to discover within itself the memory of the pure forms it had once seen. Rather, what is involved is really seeing the things of the world, of really grasping their details and organization. What is actually involved in this real investigation is understanding the rationality of the world in order to recognize, at that point, that the reason that presided over the organization of the world, and which is God's reason itself, is of the same kind as the reason we possess that enables us to know it. To reiterate, this discovery that human and divine reason share a common nature and function together is not brought about in the form of the recollection of the soul looking at itself, but rather through the movement of the mind's curiosity exploring the order of the world: this is the first difference. The second difference from the Platonic movement is, as you can see, that there is absolutely no passage to another world here. The world to which we gain access through the movement Seneca describes is the world in which we live. The whole game, precisely what is at stake in this movement, is never to lose sight of any of the components that characterize the world in which we exist and, in particular, which characterize our own situation, in the very spot we occupy. We must never lose sight of this. We distance ourselves from it, so to speak, by stepping back. And stepping back we see the context in which we are placed opening out, and we grasp again this world as it is, the world in which we exist. So it is not a passage to another world. It is not a movement by which we turn away from this world to look elsewhere. It is the movement by which we are [enabled to] grasp this world here as a whole, without ever losing sight of this world here, or of ourselves within it, or of what we are within it. You can see, in short, that there is no question here, as in Plato's *Phaedrus*, of raising our sights as high as possible to the super-terrestrial.[21] You can see that the movement outlined here is not that of an effort by which we attempt to see another reality by detaching ourselves from this world and looking away from it. Rather, it is a matter of placing ourselves at a point that is both so central and elevated that we can see below us the overall order of the world of which we ourselves are parts. In other words, rather than a spiritual movement borne upwards by the impulse of *erōs* and memory, what is involved is a completely different kind of effort, that of the real knowledge of the world, of placing ourselves so high that from this point, and below us, we can see the world in its general order, the tiny space we occupy within it, and the short time we remain there. What is involved is a view from above (*une vue plongeante*) looking down on the self, rather than looking up to something other than the world in which we live. It is the self's view of itself from above which encompasses the world of which we are a part and which thus ensures the subject's freedom within this world itself.

This theme of a view of the world from above, of a spiritual movement which is nothing other than the movement by which this view becomes ever deeper—that is to say, ever more encompassing because one rises higher and higher—is, as you can see, quite different from the Platonic kind of movement. It seems to me to define one of the most fundamental forms of spiritual experience found in Western culture. The theme of the view from above is found in certain Stoic texts, and especially in Seneca. I am thinking of one of these texts, which I think is the first he wrote. It is *To Marcia, On Consolation*.[22] Consoling Marcia for the death of one of her children, Seneca deploys traditional Stoic arguments and makes room for this experience, referring to this possibility of a view of the world from above. Here again the reference to Plato is implicit, but quite clear I think. We are quite close to *The Republic* and the choice of souls, you know, when those who have merited it are given the power to choose the type of existence they will have when they enter life.[23] In *To Marcia, On Consolation*, there is a strange passage which echoes this, I think, in which Seneca says: Listen, imagine you could see what is going to happen before you enter life, before your soul is sent into this world. Note that it is not the possibility of choice here, but the right to a view, and to a view that is precisely the view from above I have been talking about. Basically he suggests that Marcia imagine herself before life, in the same position as he wishes and prescribes for the sage at the end of his life, that is to say when one is at the frontier of life and death, on the threshold of life. Here it is the threshold of entrance rather than departure, but Marcia is asked to look in the same way as the sage will have to look at the end of his life. He has the world before him. And what can we see in this world, in this view of the world from above? First of all, he says, if, at the point of entering life you could see in this way, you would see "a city ... shared by gods and men," you would see the stars, their regular course, the moon, and the planets whose movements govern men's fortune. You would admire "the accumulated clouds," "the jagged lightning and the roar of heaven." Then, when you "lower [your eyes] to earth," you will find many different and wonderful things; the plains, mountains, and towns, the ocean, sea monsters, and the ships which cross the seas and ply their trade: "you will see nothing that has not tempted human audacity, both witness to and industrious partner of these great efforts." But at the same time, in this grand view from above (if you could have it at the moment of your birth), you would see that in this world there will also be "a thousand plagues of the body and the soul, wars and robberies, poisonings and shipwrecks, bad weather and illness, and the premature loss of those close to us, and death, maybe gentle or maybe full of pain and torture. Consider and weigh carefully your choice; once you have entered this life of marvels, you must pass through these things to leave it. It is up to you to accept it on these conditions."[24] Now this text seems to me to be very interesting. First of all because there is this theme, which will be so important in Western spirituality as well as in Western art, in painting, of the view of the whole world from above, which seems to me to be both specific to Stoicism and which I think Seneca in particular emphasizes more than any other Stoic. You see also that there is a clear reference to Plato, but that what is evoked here is a completely different kind of experience or, if you like, a different kind of myth. It is not the deserving individual's possibility of choice between the different kinds of life offered to him. Rather, it involves saying to him that there is no choice and that, in his view of the world from above, he really must understand that all the wonders to be found in heaven, in the stars and meteors, in the beauty of the earth, in the plains, in the sea and the mountains, are all inextricably bound up with the thousand plagues of the body and soul, with wars, robbery, death, and suffering. He is shown the world not so that he can, like Plato's souls, choose his destiny. He is shown the world precisely so that he clearly understands that there is no choice, that nothing can be chosen without choosing the rest, that there is only one possible world, and that we are bound to this world. The only thing, and the only point of choice is this: "Consider and weigh carefully your choice; once you have entered this life of marvels, you must pass through these things to leave it." The only point of choice is not: What life will you choose, what character will you give yourself, do you want to be good or bad? The only choice given to the soul on the threshold of life, at the moment of being born into this world, is: Consider whether you want to enter or leave, that is to say, whether or not you want to live. We have here the point symmetrical to, but as it were prior to, what we will find as the form of wisdom, precisely when it is acquired at the end of life and life is completed. When we reach that ideal completion of life, in ideal old age, then we will be able to ponder whether or not we want to live, whether we want to kill ourselves or go on living. The point symmetrical to suicide is given here: You can ponder, Marcia is told in this myth, whether or not you wish to live. But be fully aware that if you choose to live, you will have to choose the whole of this world spread out before your eyes, with all its marvels and sorrows. In the same way, at the end of his life, when he has the whole world before his eyes—its sequence, and its sorrows and its splendors—thanks to this great view from above that ascent to the summit of the world, in the *consortium Dei*, has given him through the study of nature, the sage will then be free to choose whether to live or die. There you are. Thank you.

1. *Natural Questions*, preface to book III.
2. "To be free is to no longer be slave of oneself (*liber autem est,qui servitutem effugit sui*)." Ibid.
3. See lecture of 20 January, first hour.
4. "The wise man's joy is all of a piece (*sapientis vero contexitur gaudium*)." Seneca, *Letters*, LXXII.4; "who has reached the highest point, who knows what he should find joy in (*qui scit, quo gaudeat*)... Your first duty, my dear Lucilius, is: learn joy (*disce gaudere*)." Ibid., XXIII.2-3.
5. "Why such foolishness, effort and sweat? Why plough the soil and besiege the forum? I need so little, and for a short time." *Natural Questions*, preface to book III.
6. "Who is slave to himself suffers the harshest (*gravissima*) yoke; but it is easy to shake it off if you no longer make a thousand demands of yourself and no longer seek to reward yourself for your own merit (*si desieries tibi referre mercedem*)." Ibid.
7. Ibid.
8. See the analysis of this letter in the first hour of this lecture.
9. "When I have finished searching myself, I search for the secrets of this world (*et me prius scrutor, deinde hunc mundum*)." Seneca, *Letters*, LXV.15.
10. "Until now, however, you have done nothing: you have escaped many pitfalls, but you have not escaped yourself (*multa effugisti, te nondum*). If the virtue we seek is worthy of being desired, this is not because it is so good in itself to be free from all vice, but because it enlarges the soul and prepares it for knowledge of heavenly things and makes it worthy to associate with God himself (*dignumque efficit, qui in consortium Dei veniat*). Full and complete happiness is to spurn all evil desire, to launch oneself into the heavens and to penetrate the most hidden folds of nature (*petit altum, et in interiorem naturae sinum venit*)." *Natural Questions*, preface to book I.
11. Actually, the exact expression in the preface to book III is "*mundum circumere.*"
12. "To despise colonnades, brilliant ivory ceilings, forests turned into gardens and rivers diverted through palaces, one must have encompassed the circle of the universe (*quam totum circumeat mundum*) and looked down from on high on this limited globe (*terrarum orbem super ne despiciens, angustum*), most of which is submerged, while where it emerges, parched or frozen, it presents from afar dreadful desolation." Ibid.
13. See the first paragraphs of the preface to the third part of *Natural Questions* analyzed by Foucault at the end of the first hour of this lecture.
14. *Natural Questions*, preface, book I.
15. "A soul turned towards the truth, educated in what it should flee and what it should seek, judging things according to their natural value and not according to opinion, in communication with the entire universe and careful to explore all its secrets (*actus*), controlling itself in its actions and in its thoughts... such a soul identifies itself with virtue." Seneca, *Letters*, LXVI.6-7.
16. *Letters*, LXV.16.
17. *Letters*, LXV.17. The beginning has exactly: "Just as after some delicate work which absorbs their attention and tires their eyes, craftsmen, if their workshop is poorly or uncertainly lit, find some place devoted to public recreation to delight their eyes in the free light, so the soul..."
18. *De Brevitate vitae* (*On the Shortness of Life*) was sent to a certain Paulinus, a close relative of Seneca's wife Pompeia Paulina.
19. The *praefectura annnonae*, instituted by Augustus, supervised income from taxes in kind made up of grain harvests.
20. "Do you think it is the same thing whether you take care that the wheat is poured into the granaries without being damaged by either the fraud or negligence of those who transport it, that it does not get damp, spoil and ferment, that its measure or weight is exact, or that you start upon these sacred and sublime studies in order to know the essence of God, his pleasure (*quae materia sit dei, quae voluptas*), his condition and his form...? Do you really

wish to leave the earth and turn your mind and eyes towards these beauties (*vis tu relicto solo mente ad ista respicere*)?" Seneca, *On The Shortness of Life*, XIX.1-2.
21. Plato, *Phaedrus*, 274d.
22. In *Sénèque ou la Conscience de l'Empire*, pp. 266-69, P. Grimal writes that the first text was written between autumn or winter of 39 A.D. and spring 40 A.D.
23. Foucault alludes here to the myth of Er that closes *The Republic*, X.614a-620c, and especially to the passage (618a-d) on the choice of lives offered.
24. *To Marcia, On Consolation*, XVIII.7-8.

# fifteen

## 24 FEBRUARY 1982

### First hour

*The spiritual modalization of knowledge* (savoir) *in Marcus Aurelius: the work of analyzing representations; defining and describing; seeing and naming; evaluating and testing; gaining access to the grandeur of the soul.* ∼ *Examples of spiritual exercises in Epictetus.* ∼ *Christian exegesis and Stoic analysis of representations.* ∼ *Return to Marcus Aurelius: exercises of the decomposition of the object in time; exercises of the analysis of the object into its material components; exercises of the reductive description of the object.* ∼ *Conceptual structure of spiritual knowledge* (savoir). ∼ *Faust.*

[...] THE PROBLEM POSED LAST week was: What place does knowledge of the world occupy in the theme and general precept of conversion to the self? I tried to show that, within this general theme of conversion to the self, the specific precept of "turn your gaze on yourself" did not exclude knowledge of the world. Neither did it give rise to a knowledge of the self that would have meant the investigation and decipherment of interiority, of the inner world. But this principle ("turn your gaze on yourself"), connected to the double necessity of converting to the self and knowing the world, gave rise instead to what could be called a spiritual modality, a spiritualization of knowledge of the world. I tried to show how this took place in Seneca, you recall, with that very typical figure which, in one sense, is very close to what is found in Plato, yet is very different, I believe, in its structure, dynamic, and purpose: the figure of the subject who steps back, who draws back to the highest point, the summit of the world, from which a view of the world from above opens up for him, a view from above that on the one hand penetrates into the innermost secret of nature (*"in interiorem naturae sinum venit"*),[1] and then at the same time allows him to gauge the infinitesimal size of the point in space he occupies and of the moment in time in which he lives. This then is what I think we find in Seneca. I would now like to study this same spiritual modalization of knowledge in a different, later Stoic text from Marcus Aurelius.

In the *Meditations* of Marcus Aurelius I think there is in fact a figure of spiritual knowledge that corresponds, in a sense, to the figure found in Seneca, but which at the same time is opposite, or symmetrically opposite. It seems to me that in Marcus Aurelius there is a figure of spiritual knowledge that does not consist in the subject stepping back from his place in the world in order to grasp this world as a whole, a world in which he himself is placed. Rather, the figure in Marcus Aurelius defines a movement of the subject who, starting from the point he occupies in the world, plunges into this world, or at any rate studies this world, down to its smallest details, as if to focus the gaze of a nearsighted person onto the finest grain of things. This figure of the subject who looks within things in order to grasp their fine texture is expressed in many texts of Marcus Aurelius. One of the simplest, most schematic, is in book VI: "Look at the inside (*esō blepe*). Neither the quality (*poiotēs*) nor the value (*axia*) of any thing must escape."[2] What is involved, if you like, is the infinitesimal view of the subject who looks into things. This is the figure I would like to analyze in the first hour of today's lecture. I will take what I think is the most detailed text concerning this procedure, this spiritual figure of knowledge. It is found in book III. I will read almost all of it. I use the Budé translation, which is an old translation about which I will try to say a couple of things: "To the aforementioned precepts yet another is added." And this additional precept is: "Always define and describe the object whose image (*phantasia*) appears in the mind." So, define and describe the object whose image appears in the mind "in such a way that you see it distinctly, as it is in essence, naked, whole, and in all its aspects; and say to yourself its name and the names of the parts of which it is composed and into which it will be resolved. Nothing, in fact, is so able to enlarge the soul for us as being able to identify methodically and truthfully each of the objects which appear in life and to see them always in such a way that we consider at the same time in what kind of universe each is useful, what this use is, and what value it possesses with regard to the whole and with regard to man, this citizen of the most eminent city in which other cities are like households. What is this object which causes this image in me, of what elements is it composed, how long is its natural life, and what virtue do I need with regard to it: gentleness, courage, sincerity, good faith, simplicity, abstinence, etcetera."[3] If you like, I will go over this text a little. First phrase: "To the aforementioned precepts yet another is added." In fact the Greek term here is *parastēmata*. The *parastēma* is not exactly a precept. It is not exactly the expression of something to be done. *Parastēma* is something to which we hold fast, which we must have in mind, which we must always keep before our eyes: it is the statement of a fundamental truth as well as the founding principle of behavior. [There is then] this connection, or rather this nonseparation of things that for us are so different: the principle of truth and the rule of conduct. You know that this separation did not exist, or not in a systematic, regular, and constant way, in Greek thought. *Parastēma*, then, is some thing or things that we must have in mind, which we must keep before our eyes. What are these aforementioned *parastēmata* to which Marcus Aurelius refers when he says: "To the aforementioned *parastēmata* yet another is added"? There are three of these aforementioned *parastēmata*. They are found, of course, in the preceding paragraphs. One concerns what we should consider good: What is good for the subject?[4] The second of the *parastēmata* concerns our freedom and the fact that in reality, for us, everything depends upon our own freedom to form an opinion. Nothing can quell or master this power; we are always free to form an opinion as we wish.[5] The third of the *parastēmata* is the fact that there is basically only one level of reality for the subject, and the only level of reality that exists for the subject is the moment itself: the infinitely small moment that constitutes the present, prior to which nothing exists any longer and after which everything is still uncertain.⁶ So, we have the three *parastēmata*: definition of the good for the subject; definition of freedom for the subject; definition of reality for the subject. Paragraph 11, consequently, will add one more to these three principles. Actually, the additional principle is not of the same order or exactly at the same level. Before there were three principles, and what is now set out is much more a prescription, a schema of something like an exercise: a spiritual exercise whose role and function will be precisely, on the one hand, always to keep in mind the things that we must have in mind—namely: the definitions of the good, of freedom, and of reality—and, at the same time as this exercise must always remind us of them and reactualize them for us, it must also enable us to link them together and thus define what, in terms of the subject's freedom, must be recognized by this freedom as good in the only element of reality that belongs to us, namely, the present. So, this is the objective of this other *parastēma*, which is actually a program of exercises rather than a principle to keep in view. I am not inventing this idea that many of the elements in the text of Marcus Aurelius are schemas of exercises. It wouldn't have occurred to me on my own. In Hadot's book on spiritual exercises in Antiquity there is a remarkable chapter on spiritual exercises in Marcus Aurelius.⁷ Anyway, here, in this paragraph, we are certainly dealing with a spiritual exercise that refers to principles to have in mind and link together. How will this exercise unfold and in what does it consist? Let us go over it again item by item.

First moment: always define and describe the object whose image appears in the mind. The Greek expression for "to define" is *poieisthai horon*. *Horos* is the demarcation, the limit, the border. *Poieisthai horon* is, if you like, "to trace the border." Actually, this expression *poieisthai horon* has two meanings. It has a technical meaning in the realms of philosophy, logic, and grammar. This is quite simply to state or give an adequate definition. Second, *poieisthai horon* also has a meaning that is hardly technical, which arises, rather, from everyday vocabulary, but which even so is fairly precise and means to fix the value and price of something. Consequently, the spiritual exercise must consist in giving definitions in logical or semantic terms, and then, at the same time, fixing a thing's value. Defining and "describing." The Greek expression for "to describe" is *hupographēn poieisthai*. And of course, here, as in the philosophical and grammatical vocabulary of the period, the *hupographē* is contrasted with the *horos*.[8] The *horos* then is the definition. The *hupographē* is the description, that is to say, the more or less detailed record of the intuitive content of the form and components of things. The spiritual exercise involved in these paragraphs will thus consist in giving a description and a definition—but of what? Well, the text says, of everything appearing to the mind. The object whose image appears to the mind, everything that comes under the mind (*hupopiptontos*) must be put under surveillance, as it were, and must be the pretext, the occasion, the object for a work of definition and description. The idea that we must [intervene] in the flux of representations as they appear, as they occur, as they file past in the mind, is frequently found in the themes of the spiritual experience of Antiquity. In the Stoics in particular it was a frequently recurring theme: screening the flux of representations, taking hold of the representation as it occurs, as it appears on the occasion of thoughts appearing spontaneously in the mind, or on the occasion of anything falling within the field of perception, or on the occasion of the life we lead, the encounters we have, the objects we see, etcetera; taking, then, the spontaneous and involuntary flux of representation and focusing on it a voluntary attention whose function will be to determine its objective content.[9] This is an interesting formulation which, because it permits a simple, clear but I think nevertheless fundamental opposition, allows us to make a comparison between what we can call intellectual method and spiritual exercise.

The spiritual exercise—and it is found in Antiquity, in the Middle Ages of course, in the Renaissance and the seventeenth century; we will have to see if it is found in the twentieth century—consists precisely in allowing the thread and flux of representations to unfold spontaneously. The spiritual exercise on representations involves the free movement of representation and work on this free movement. Intellectual method will consist, rather, in providing ourselves with a voluntary and systematic definition of the law of succession of representations, and only accepting them in the mind if there is a sufficiently strong, constraining, and necessary link between them for us to be conveyed, logically, without doubt or hesitation, from the first to the second. The Cartesian progression belongs to the realm of intellectual method.[10] Analysis, or rather attention focused on the flux of representation, is typical of the spiritual exercise. The transition from spiritual exercise to intellectual method is obviously very clear in Descartes. I do not think we can understand the meticulousness with which he defines his intellectual method unless we have clearly in mind his negative target, that from which he wants to distinguish and separate himself, which is precisely these methods of spiritual exercise that were frequently practiced within Christianity and which derived from the spiritual exercises of Antiquity, and especially from Stoicism. This then is the general theme of this exercise: a flux of representations on which a work of analysis, definition, and description will be carried out.

Given this theme, the "interception," if you like, of the representation as it appears, in order to grasp its objective content, is now developed in two exercises, which are specified and effectively give this purely intellectual work its spiritual value. These two exercises, which join up on the basis of this general theme, are what we could call eidetic meditation and onomastic meditation. Briefly, this is what I mean by these barbarous terms. Marcus Aurelius has said then that the object whose image appears in the mind must be defined and described in such a way that we see it distinctly—as it is in essence, naked, in its entirety, from every side—and saying to ourselves its name and the name of the elements of which it is composed and into which it will be resolved. So first of all: "in such a way that you see it distinctly, as it is in essence, naked, whole, and in all its aspects." It is a question, then, of contemplating the object as it is in essence (*"hopoion esti kak'ousian"*). And it is necessary to point out that it is in apposition to and as commentary on this general injunction ("contemplate the represented object as it is in essence") that the sentence continues and says that we must grasp the object as it is represented: *gumnon*, that is to say, naked, without anything else, shorn of anything that could conceal and surround it; secondly, *holon*, that is to say in its entirety; and thirdly, *"di'holōn diēremenōs,"* by distinguishing its constituent elements. All of this—this gaze on the represented object that must reveal it in the naked state, in its totality, and in its elements—is what Marcus Aurelius calls *blepein*. That is to say: looking closely, contemplating well, fixing your eyes on, acting so that nothing escapes you, neither the object in its singularity, freed from its surroundings, naked, [nor] in its totality and its particular elements. At the same time as one performs this work, which belongs to the realm of looking, of contemplation of the thing, we must say to ourselves its name and the names of the elements of which it is composed and into which it will be resolved. This is the other branch of the exercise. Saying to ourselves (the text is quite explicit: "*legein par'heautō*"), means not just knowing or recalling the names of the thing and its elements, but saying them to ourselves within ourselves, saying them for ourselves. That is to say, it really does involve an utterance, which is internal certainly, but quite explicit. We must name, we must speak to ourselves, we must say it to ourselves. Even if it is internal, the real expression of the word, of the name, or rather of the name of the thing and the names of the things of which this thing is composed, is absolutely important in this exercise. This exercise of verbalization is obviously very important for fixing the thing and its elements in the mind, and consequently, on the basis of these names, for the reactualization of the whole system of values we will talk about shortly. One of the aims of expressing the names of things is memorization. Second, you see that this exercise of memorizing names must be simultaneous with and directly connected to the exercise of looking. We must see and name. Looking and memory must be linked with each other in a single movement of the mind that, on one side, directs the gaze towards things, and, on the other, reactivates the names of these different things in memory. Third, we should note—still with regard to this double-sided exercise, this partly double exercise—that, due to this double exercise, the essence of the thing will be displayed in its entirety, as it were. In fact, by looking we see the thing itself in the naked state, in its totality and in its parts, but by naming the thing itself and its different components, we see, and the text says it clearly, what components make up the object and into what components it will be resolved. This is in fact the third function of this doubling of looking by naming. Through this exercise we can not only recognize how the object is currently composed, but also what its future will be, into what it will be resolved, when, how, and under what conditions it will come apart and be undone. Through this exercise, therefore, we grasp the complex plenitude of the object's essential reality and the fragility of its existence in time. That then is the nature of the analysis of the object in its reality.

The second phase of the exercise will not consist in considering the object in its reality as it is given—in the reality of its composition, of its actual complexity and temporal fragility—but in trying to assess its value. "Nothing, in fact, is so able to enlarge the soul for us as being able to identify methodically and truthfully each of the objects which appear in life and to see them always in such a way that we consider at the same time in what kind of universe each is useful, and what this use is, what value it possesses with regard to the whole and with regard to man, this citizen of the most eminent city in which other cities are like households." In this passage Marcus Aurelius recalls the aim of this analytical exercise, of this eidetic and onomastic meditation. The aim of this exercise, the end one seeks through its performance, is to "enlarge the soul": "Nothing, in fact, is so able to enlarge the soul for us"; "enlarge the soul for us": actually the text translates here *"megalophrosunē"* (a kind of grandeur of soul). Actually, what this involves for Marcus Aurelius is the condition in which the subject sees himself independent of the bonds and constraints to which he has had to submit his opinions and, following his opinions, his passions. To make the soul great means to free it from this framework, from all this tissue that surrounds, fixes, and delimits it, and thus to enable it to find its true nature and, at the same time, its true destination, that is to say its perfect equivalence to the general reason of the world. Through this exercise the soul finds its true grandeur, which is that of the rational principle organizing the world. The grandeur ensured by this exercise is the freedom entailed both by indifference to things and tranquility with regard to events. This is clearly confirmed by other texts. For example, in book XI it is said that "the soul *adiaphorēsei* (will be indifferent) if it considers each thing *diēremenōs kai holikōs*."[11] This repeats exactly the terms found here: By considering each thing *diēremenōs* (analytically, part by part) *kai holikōs* (and in its totality), the soul acquires at that moment the sovereign indifference of its tranquility and its perfect equivalence to divine reason. This, then, is the aim of the exercise.

Now, this aim is attained when we use the examination of the thing in order to test it, as I will shortly describe to you—and here we must refer to the text of Marcus Aurelius. The word used here is *elegkhein*.[12] This analytical examination (which grasps the thing in its naked state, its totality and its parts) will secure for the soul the grandeur to which it must aspire, permitting what? *Elegkhein*: testing the thing. The word *elegkhein* has several meanings.[13] In philosophical practice, in the terminology of the dialectic, *elegkhein* is to refute. In judicial practice, *elegkhein* is to accuse, to make an accusation against someone. And in everyday language, the language of everyday morality, it means quite simply to make a reproach. This analytical examination will thus have the value of freedom for the soul, it will secure for the soul the real proportions of its grandeur, if it subjects the object—as we picture and grasp it in its objective reality through description and definition—to suspicion, possible accusation, moral reproach, and intellectual refutation which dispels illusions, etcetera. In short, it is a matter of testing the object. In what does this trial, this test of the object consist? In seeing, says Marcus Aurelius, what its utility (*khreia*) is for what universe, for what *kosmos*. What is involved then is placing the object—as we see it, as it has been delineated in its naked reality, grasped in its totality, analyzed into its parts—within the *kosmos* to which it belongs in order to see what use it has, what place it occupies, and what function it performs there. This is what Marcus Aurelius spells out in the rest of the sentence I read out a moment ago. He [asks] "what value (*axia*)" does this object have for the whole, and second, what value does it have for man as the "citizen of the most eminent city in which other cities are like households?"[14] I think this rather enigmatic phrase is easy to explain. It is a matter of grasping the value of the object for the *kosmos*, and also the value of the object for man as citizen of the world, that is to say as a being placed by nature within the natural realm, within this *kosmos*, in accordance with divine Providence. If you like: the utility of this object for man as a citizen of the world in general, but also as a citizen of "those particular cities"—by which we should understand not only towns, but different forms of community, social belonging, etcetera, including the family—which are like households of the great city of the world. This well-known Stoic theme of the interlocking of different forms of social community across the great community of humankind is called upon here to show that the examination of the thing must focus on its relationship to man as citizen, but equally, by virtue of this and within the general framework of citizenship of the world, it must define the object's utility for man as citizen of this particular country, as belonging to this particular town, as member of this particular community, as father of a family, and so on. Thanks to this we will be able to determine what virtue the subject needs with regard to these things. When these things appear to the mind and when the *phantasia* presents them to the subject's perception, should the subject, with regard to these things and in accordance with the content of the representation, employ a virtue like gentleness, or courage, or sincerity, or good faith, or *egkrateia* (self-control)? This is the type of exercise Marcus Aurelius gives here, and many other examples of it elsewhere.

Many more or less systematized, more or less developed exercises of this kind are found in the Stoics. The idea that the flux of representation must be put under continuous and fastidious surveillance is a theme already frequently developed by Epictetus. At several points in Epictetus there are schemas for exercises of this kind,[15] in two forms in particular. In the form of the stroll-exercise:[16] Epictetus recommends, for example, that from time to time we take a walk outside and look at what is going on around us (things, people, events, etcetera). We exercise ourselves with regard to all the different representations offered by the world. We exercise ourselves on them in order to define, with regard to each, in what they consist, to what extent they can act on us, whether or not we depend on them or they on us, etcetera. And we will define the attitude to adopt towards them on the basis of this examination of the content of the representation. He also proposes the exercise that could be called memory-exercise: recalling an event—either an historic event or one that took place more or less recently in our life—and then, with regard to this event, saying to ourselves: But in what did this event consist? What was its nature? What form of action can this event have on me? To what extent do I depend on it? To what extent am I free from it? What judgment must I bring to bear on it and what attitude should I adopt towards it? The exercise I have cited, with the example of Marcus Aurelius, is then a frequent and regular exercise in the practice of ancient spirituality, and of Stoic spirituality in particular.

You know that this type of exercise is found again very insistently and very frequently in Christian spirituality. There are examples of it in the monastic literature of the fourth and fifth centuries, and there are examples of it in Cassian in particular. I think it was last year, or two years ago, I no longer know,[17] that in beginning to study this kind of thing a little I cited Cassian's texts: Cassian's text on the mill and also his text on the money changer's table, I don't know if some of you recall this. Cassian said that the mind is always in movement. At every instant new objects appear to it, new images present themselves to it, and we cannot allow these representations free entry—as in a mill let's say; Cassian doesn't say this—and at every instant we must be sufficiently vigilant so that we can decide what must be done with regard to this flux of representations presented to us, what is to be accepted and what rejected. Thus, he says, when the miller sees the grain passing before him he separates the good grain from the bad and prevents the latter from being ground by the millstone.[18] Or again, the money changer, the banker to whom one goes to change coins of one currency into those of another, does not accept any money whatsoever. He checks and tests each coin, examines what he is given and only accepts those he thinks are good.[19] As you see, what is involved in both cases is a test, something like the *elegkhos* I was talking about a moment ago, which Marcus Aurelius recommended we carry out at every instant. So you see that we have what seems to me a quite similar form of exercise. There is the necessarily mobile, variable, and changing flux of representations: adopting an attitude towards these representations of surveillance and mistrust, and trying to check and test each one. However, I would like to stress the nevertheless profound difference between the Stoic exercise of the examination of representations, which is highly developed in Marcus Aurelius—but which, once again, is found at least in the late Stoic tradition, and especially in Epictetus—and what is found later among Christians, in apparently the same form of an examination of representations. The problem for Christians is not at all one of studying the objective content of the representation. Cassian, as well as all those who inspired him and whom he in turn will inspire, analyzed the representation itself, the representation in its psychical reality. Knowing the nature of the object represented is not a problem for Cassian. His problem is that of knowing the degree of purity of the representation itself as idea, as image. The problem is basically that of knowing whether or not the idea is mixed with concupiscence, if it really is the representation of the external world or if it is a simple illusion. And through this question directed at the nature, the very materiality of the idea, the question raised is that of its origin. Does the idea I have in my mind come from God?—in which case it is necessarily pure. Does it come from Satan?—in which case it is impure. Or possibly even: does it come from myself, in which case, to what extent can we say it is pure or impure? Consequently, it is a question of the actual purity of the representation in its nature as representation and, secondly, of its origin.

Now, you see that there is nothing of all this in Marcus Aurelius, notwithstanding a certain resemblance which you see straightaway. In fact the text I read a short while ago continues in the following way. Marcus Aurelius says: "This is why [so: after having said, with regard to each representation, that we must examine what it represents and, consequently, the virtues to be set against it or put to work concerning it; M.F.]: we must say in connection with each case [each of the objects given in the representation; M.F.]: this comes to me from God; this comes from the chain, the close weave of events and the encounter thus produced by coincidence and chance; and this again from my stock, my kin and fellows, etcetera."[20] You see that Marcus Aurelius also poses the question of origin. But he does not pose the question of the origin of the representation. He does not ask whether the representation in itself came from him, was suggested by God, or was whispered to him by Satan. The question of origin he poses is that of the origin of the thing represented: Does the represented thing belong to the necessary order of the world? Does the represented thing come directly from God, from his Providence and from his benevolence towards me? Or again: Does the represented thing come to me from someone who is part of my society and part of humankind? So you see that what is essential in the Stoic analysis, here represented by Marcus Aurelius, concerns the analysis of the representational content, whereas what is essential in Christian meditation and spiritual exercise concerns the nature and origin of the thought itself. Marcus Aurelius's question is addressed to the external world; the question Cassian will pose is addressed to the nature and interiority of thought itself. In one case what is involved, once and for all, is knowing the external world: it is again and always knowledge of the world which Marcus Aurelius and the Stoics put to work. In the case of Cassian and others it will be a decipherment of interiority, the subject's exegesis of himself. So, in Marcus Aurelius's *Meditations* there is a whole series of exercises of this kind. The same principle is expressed in book XII of the *Meditations*,[21] in VIII.11,[22] in VIII.13,[23] and so on.

I skip all of this. I would now like to see how this general principle of the examination of the representational content is actually put to work by Marcus Aurelius in a series of exercises, all of which have a precise and quite specific moral function [...*]. First, exercises decomposing the object in time; second, exercises decomposing the object into its constituent parts; third, exercises of reductive, disqualifying description. First, the exercises of decomposition in time. There is a striking example in [book XI]. It involves musical notes, or dance movements, or movements of that kind of more or less danced gymnastics, the pancratium.[24] The exercise proposed by Marcus Aurelius is this: When you hear a piece of music, he says, or melodic, enchanting songs, or when you see a graceful dance or pancratic movements, try not to see them as a whole, but try as far as possible to focus a discontinuous and analytical attention on them so that within your perception you will be able to isolate each note from the others and each movement from the others.[25] Why perform this exercise? Why try to put out of one's mind the whole movement presented by dance or music, in order to abstract from it or isolate each specific component so as to grasp the reality of the moment

---

*Only "... the general exercise whose example I have just given" is audible.

in its absolute singularity? The meaning of this exercise is given at the beginning and the end of the paragraph where Marcus Aurelius says: "You will scorn a delightful song, a dance or a pancratium if you etcetera." Then he gives the advice I have just referred to. At the end he takes up the same idea and theme again. After explaining the rule of discontinuous perception, he says: "always remember to go straight for the parts themselves, and by analysis (*diairesis*), come to scorn them."[26] The word used at the beginning and end of the text (translated here as "scorn"), is *kataphronein*. *Kataphronein* is very precisely: to consider from above, to look down on. And why should things be considered in this way, looking down on and scorning them? Because if we look at a dance in the continuity of its movements, or if we hear a melody in its unity, we will be carried away by the beauty of the dance or the charm of the melody. We will be weaker than it. If we want to be stronger than the melody or the dance, if we want to prevail over it—that is to say, to remain master of our self with regard to the enchantment, flattery, and pleasure they arouse—if we want to retain this superiority, if we do not want to be weaker (*hēttōn*) than the whole of the melody and therefore want to resist it and ensure our own freedom, it will be by dissecting it instant by instant, note by note, movement by movement. This is to say that by putting to work this law of the real—which is what was at issue earlier, you know, at the start: the law that there is no reality for the subject except what is given in the present instant—each note or movement will appear in its reality. And its reality will show the subject that it is no more than a note or a movement, without power in themselves because without charm, seduction, or flattery. We realize at once that there is nothing good in these notes and movements. And as soon as there is nothing good in them, we do not have to seek them out, we do not have to let ourselves be dominated by them, we do not have to let ourselves be weaker than them, and we can ensure our own mastery and domination. You see how the principle of the present as level of reality, the principle of the law of determination of the good and of the assurance of the individual's freedom, in short the principle [in terms of which] the individual must assure his own freedom with regard to everything around him, is all assured by this exercise of introducing discontinuity into continuous movements, into connected instants. The law of instantaneous perception is an exercise of freedom that guarantees for the subject that he will always be stronger than each element of reality presented to him. In another text there is a very beautiful image to represent this. He says: Things should be looked at in their multiplicity and discontinuity. "If we take to loving one of those sparrows flying past, it has already vanished from our sight."[27] So, let us see things not in the great unity, but in their dispersion, like a flock of sparrows in the sky. We are not in love with a sparrow passing in the sky. This is, if you like, an example of the exercise of temporal discontinuity.

This text I have just been reading on musical notes and dance ends, however, with something I would like to comment on for a moment and it is this: "In short, save in the case of virtue and what is connected to virtue, always remember to go straight for the parts themselves, and by analysis, come to scorn them. And now, apply the same procedure to life as a whole."[28] He says we should apply this analysis of the perception of continuities, of the analytical perception of continuities, "to life as a whole." By this he means not only apply it to everything around us, but also to our own existence and to ourselves. I think this brief instruction ("apply the same procedure to life as a whole") should be brought together with a series of other texts in the *Meditations*. For example, in II.2, where Marcus Aurelius says: We must never forget that our *pneuma* is no more than a breath. Here then is the reduction to the material element we will talk about in a moment. Our *pneuma* is a breath, a material breath. And again, he says, this breath is replaced with every respiration. Whenever we breathe we give up a little of our *pneuma* and take in a little of another *pneuma*, so that the *pneuma* is never the same. And inasmuch as we have a *pneuma* we are never the same and consequently should not fix our identity in this.[29] Again, in VI.15, he says: "Each man's life is something comparable to evaporation from the blood and inhalation from the air. In fact, at every moment we exhale the air we inhale."[30] So, the exercise of rendering something discontinuous we should apply to things should also be applied to ourselves, to our own life. And in applying it to ourselves we realize that what we think to be our identity, or that in which we think we should place it or seek it, does not itself guarantee our continuity. As body, even as *pneuma*, we are always something discontinuous in comparison with our being. Our identity is not here. Actually, I am commenting here on the phrase that begins the text I was just reading: "Save in the case of virtue and what is connected to virtue, always remember to go straight for the parts themselves... And now, apply this procedure to life as a whole."[31] Ultimately there is only a single element in which we can find, or on the basis of which we can establish our identity, and this is virtue, which, in terms of the Stoic doctrine with which you are familiar, cannot be broken down into parts.[32] It cannot be broken down into parts for the good reason that virtue is nothing other than the unity, the coherence, the cohesive force of the soul itself. It is its nondispersion. And it cannot be broken down into parts for the other good reason that virtue escapes time: An instant of virtue is equivalent to eternity. It is then in this cohesion, and only in this cohesion of the indissociable soul, of the soul that cannot be divided up into elements and which makes an instant equivalent to eternity, that we can find our identity. This is, if you like, a type of exercise of breaking down reality in terms of the instant and the discontinuity of time.

There are other exercises in Marcus Aurelius that are also analytical exercises, but this time bearing on the decomposition of things into their material elements. In a sense this is simpler. For example, in VI.13, there is a meditative text, which says: Basically, what is a cooked dish that we like and eat with so much pleasure? Remember that it is the carcass of an animal. It is a dead beast. What is this *praetexta*\* bearing the famous *laticlave* that is so envied?[33] Well, it is wool and dye. What is wool? It is hair, sheep's hair. What is the dye? It is blood, the blood of a shellfish. What, he says in the same passage, is copulation (*sunousia*)? Copulation is nerves rubbed against each other. It is a spasm followed by a bit of secretion, nothing more.[34] You see that, through these representations, what is involved is uncovering the components of things. However, the text in which Marcus Aurelius comments on this decomposition of things into their components is quite interesting because he

---

\*Robe (*robe-prétexte*)—G.B.

says: What is it we do by applying this method, by recalling that copulation is a friction of nerves with spasms and excretions, and that the robe is sheep's wool tinted with the bloody purple of a shellfish? We get to grips with the things themselves, we get to the heart of them and completely penetrate them so that they can be seen as they are. Thanks to which, he says, we will be able to lay them bare (*apogumnoun*: strip things bare) and get to the bottom of them (*kathoran*), see their *euteleian* (that is to say their scarce value, their cheapness). In this way we will be able to free ourselves from the bombast (*tuphos*), from the bewitchment with which they are in danger of capturing and captivating us.[35] Here again you see the same objective of the exercise: establishing the subject's freedom by looking down on things from above, which enables us to penetrate them thoroughly, to get to the bottom of them, and thereby show us the little value they possess. In this passage, as in the previous one, Marcus Aurelius adds: It is not enough to apply this method to things; we must also apply it to our own life and to ourselves. And here again a series of exercises are referred to. For example, in II.2, when Marcus Aurelius asks himself: Who am I, what am I? I am flesh, I am breath, I am a rational principle.[36] As flesh, what am I? I am earth, blood, bones, nerves, veins, and arteries. As breath, at every instant I expel a part of my breath in order to draw in another. And the rational principle, the guiding principle, is what remains and what must be freed. This exercise combines the different elements, the different exercises I have been talking about. We make a material analysis of the flesh through its constituent elements: earth, blood, water, nerves, etcetera. Of breath we make a temporal analysis of its discontinuity and perpetual renewal. And finally there is only reason, the rational principle, in [which] we can recognize our identity. In IV.4, there is the same kind of analysis: What are we? We are an earthy element, a watery element, of heat, fire, a breath, and then we are an intelligence.[37] These then are exercises of analysis into constituent elements.

Finally, there is the third type of exercise over which I will pass quickly because it is very simple: this is reductive description, or description that aims to discredit. This exercise consists in providing ourselves with the most exact and detailed representation possible whose role is to reduce the thing as it appears; to reduce it with regard to the appearances surrounding it, the embellishments that accompany it, and the seductive or frightening effects it may induce. So, what should we do when we are faced with a powerful, arrogant man who wants to display his power, impress us with his superiority, and frighten us with his anger? Imagine him eating, sleeping, copulating, and excreting. And then, he may always puff himself up again. We have just seen what master this man was a slave to; tell yourself that he will soon fall back under the tutelage of similar masters.[38] These are the exercises of infinitesimal analysis found in Marcus Aurelius. You see that at first glance this figure of spiritual exercise through knowledge of the world seems to be the opposite of what we found in Seneca.

However, a number of remarks are called for. You see that even so there is in Marcus Aurelius, as in Seneca, a certain looking down from above. But whereas in Seneca looking down takes place from the summit of the world, in Marcus Aurelius the point of departure for this downward gaze is not the summit of the world but at the same level as human existence. We look precisely from the point where we happen to be, and the problem is to descend, as it were, beneath this point in order to plunge into the heart of things so as to penetrate them thoroughly. For Seneca it involved seeing the whole of the world set out below us. For Marcus Aurelius, rather, it involves a disqualifying, reductive, and ironic view of each thing in its specificity. Finally, in Seneca there was a perspective on oneself such that the subject, finding himself at the summit of the world and seeing the world set out below him, came to see himself in his own dimensions, which were of course limited, miniscule dimensions, but the function of which was not to dissolve the subject. While the gaze Marcus Aurelius directs towards things of course refers back to himself, it does so in two ways, and here there is something important which undoubtedly introduces a distinction, an important inflection in Stoicism. On the one hand, in penetrating to the heart of things and grasping all their most singular elements we demonstrate our freedom with regard to them. However, at the same time, it also involves showing the extent to which our own identity—that little totality we constitute in our own eyes: continuity in time and space—is in reality only made up of singular, distinct elements, which are separate from each other, and that basically we are dealing with a false unity. The only unity of which we are capable and which can provide us with a foundation in what we are, in this identity as subject that we can and must be in relation to ourselves, is our unity insofar as we are rational subjects, that is to say as no more than part of the reason that presides over the world. Consequently, if we look at ourselves below us, or rather if we look down on ourselves from above, we are nothing but a series of separate, distinct elements: material elements and discontinuous moments. But if we try to grasp ourselves as reasonable and rational principle, we will then realize that we are no more than part of the reason presiding over the entire world. So, the spiritual exercise of Marcus Aurelius tends towards a sort of dissolution of individuality, whereas the function of Seneca's spiritual exercise—with the subject's move to the world's summit from where he can grasp himself in his singularity—was, rather, to found and establish the subject's identity, its singularity and the stable being of the self it constitutes. There is a lot more I would like to say. I would like merely, quickly, to finish this, by saying ... oh dear! ... I'm not sure if I will ... Would you like to go on? No, perhaps we have had enough of Marcus Aurelius.* A few more words to finish with this history of spiritual knowledge (*savoir*).

I have mentioned all this with regard to Seneca and Marcus Aurelius for the following reason. As I reminded you, within this general theme of conversion to the self and within this general prescription, "one must

---

*The manuscript includes here some lengthy arguments (which Foucault deliberately leaves to one side) on the positive function of the infinitesimal order (which he studies with regard to the *Meditations* X.26, II.12, and IX.32). In addition, he finds coincidences between the *Meditations* (XII.24 and IX.30) and Seneca's texts on the contemplation of the world from above. However, here and there, this overhanging vision leads to different ethical consequences: it leads Seneca to the irony of the miniscule; in Marcus Aurelius it leads to effects of repetition of the identical ("from this point of view Marcus Aurelius sees not so much the singular point he occupies as the profound identity between different things and events separated in time"). Analyzing certain *Meditations* (XII.24, XII.27 and II.14), Foucault distinguishes between a "dive (*plongeon*) on the spot" (with effects of singularization) and a "dive (*plongeon*) from the summit" (with the opposite effect of annulment of differences and return to the same).

return to the self," I wanted to define the meaning given to the particular precept "turn your gaze on yourself," "turn your attention on yourself," "apply your mind to yourself." In posing this question and seeing how Seneca or Marcus Aurelius resolves it, it seems perfectly clear to me that it is not in any way a matter of constituting knowledge of the human being, of the soul, or of interiority, alongside, in opposition to, or against knowledge of the world. What, then, is involved is the modalization of the knowledge of things, with the following characteristics. First, it involves the subject changing his position, either rising to the summit of the universe to see it in its totality, or striving to descend into the heart of things. In any case, the subject cannot properly know by remaining where he is. This is the first point, the first characteristic of this spiritual knowledge. Second, on the basis of this shift in the subject's position there is the possibility of grasping both the reality and the value of things. And what is meant by "value" is the place, relations, and specific dimension of things within the world, as well as their relation to, their importance for, and their real power over the human subject insofar as he is free. Third, this spiritual knowledge involves the subject's ability to see himself and grasp himself in his reality. It involves a kind of "self-viewing" ("*héauto-scopie*"). The subject must see himself in the truth of his being. Fourth, and finally, the effect of this knowledge on the subject is assured by the fact that the subject not only finds his freedom in it, but in his freedom he also finds a mode of being, which is one of happiness and of every perfection of which he is capable. In sum, knowledge involving these four conditions (the subject's change of position, the evaluation of things on the basis of their reality within the *kosmos*, the possibility of the subject seeing himself, and finally the subject's transfiguration through the effect of knowledge) constitutes, I believe, what could be called spiritual knowledge. It would no doubt be interesting to write the history of this spiritual knowledge. It would be interesting to see how, however prestigious it was at the end of Antiquity or in the period I am talking about, it was gradually limited, overlaid, and finally effaced by a different mode of knowledge which could be called the knowledge of intellectual knowledge (*le savoir de connaissance*), and no longer the knowledge of spirituality (*le savoir de spiritualité*).\* It is no doubt in the sixteenth and seventeenth centuries that the knowledge of intellectual knowledge finally completely covered over the knowledge of spirituality, but not without having taken up a number of its elements. It is clear that, with regard to what took place in the seventeenth century with Descartes, Pascal, and Spinoza of course, we could find again this conversion of the knowledge of spirituality into the knowledge of intellectual knowledge.

I cannot help thinking that there is a figure whose history it would be interesting to trace, because it would clearly show, I think, how the problem of the relationship between the knowledge of intellectual knowledge and the knowledge of spirituality was posed between the sixteenth and eighteenth centuries. This figure is obviously that of Faust. From the sixteenth century, that is to say from when the knowledge of intellectual knowledge began to advance its absolute rights over the knowledge of spirituality, Faust was the figure who, until the end of the eighteenth century, represented the powers, enchantments, and dangers of the knowledge of spirituality. There is Marlowe's *Doctor Faustus*, of course.[39] In the middle of the eighteenth century there is Lessing's *Faust*: you know that we only know of this Faust from the seventeenth letter on literature, which is nonetheless very interesting,[40] in which Lessing transforms Marlowe's Faust, who was a condemned hero because he was the hero of an accursed and forbidden knowledge. Lessing saves Faust. He saves Faust because, according to Lessing, Faust converts the spiritual knowledge he represents into belief [in the] progress of humanity. The spirituality of knowledge becomes faith and

---

\*It is extremely difficult to render clearly in a simple English phrase the distinction Foucault intends here. Shortly before he introduces this distinction here he gives an account of what he means by spiritual knowledge (*le savoir spirituel*) or the mode of knowing involved in spirituality (*le savoir de spiritualité*). However, *le savoir de connaissance*, involving both the French terms for "knowledge," with all their well-known uncertainties and ambiguities, requires some reconstruction. Earlier and later in the course Foucault contrasts a mode of knowledge, or knowing, that transforms the subject's being, a spiritual knowledge (*le savoir spirituel*), with a knowledge (*une connaissance*) directed towards a particular object or domain of objects (in which the subject could be included *as an object*), and in this lecture he contrasts the knowledge arising from spiritual exercise with knowledge based upon "intellectual method" and also, perhaps, "science." All these distinctions should be borne in mind when reading the translation I have offered—G.B.

belief in a continual progress of humanity. Humanity will be the beneficiary of everything that was demanded of spiritual knowledge, [that is to say] the transfiguration of the subject himself. Consequently, Lessing's Faust is saved. He is saved because, from the angle of faith in progress, he succeeded in converting the figure of the knowledge of spirituality into the knowledge of intellectual knowledge. As for Goethe's Faust, he is precisely the hero again of a world of the spiritual knowledge that is disappearing. However, if you read the beginning of Goethe's *Faust*, the famous monologue at the start of the first part, there you will find again precisely the most basic elements of spiritual knowledge, precisely those figures of knowledge that ascends to the summit of the world, grasps all its elements, penetrates it through and through, seizes hold of its secret, delves into its elements and, at the same time, transfigures the subject and gives him happiness. Recall what Goethe says: "Philosophy, sadly! jurisprudence, medicine, and you also, sad theology! ... I have studied you in depth, with passion and patience; and now here I am, poor fool, no wiser than before." This is knowledge that is precisely not spiritual knowledge. It is the knowledge of intellectual knowledge. The subject cannot expect anything by way of his own transfiguration from this knowledge. What Faust demands from knowledge are spiritual values and effects, which neither philosophy, nor jurisprudence, nor medicine can give him. "I fear nothing from the devil, or from hell; but also all my joy has been taken away [by this knowledge; M.F.]. It only remains for me to throw myself into magic [withdrawal of knowledge of intellectual knowledge into knowledge of spirituality; M.F.]. Oh! if the power of mind and speech revealed to me the secrets I do not know, and if I were no longer forced to say with difficulty what I do not know; if finally I could know everything the world conceals within itself, and, no longer bound by useless words, see the secret energy and eternal seeds which nature contains! Star of silver light, silent moon, deign one last time to look down on my pain! ... So many nights I've kept watch by this desk! It was then you appeared to me, melancholy friend, over piles of books and papers! Ah! If only I might climb high mountains in your soft light, wander in caverns with spirits, dance on the pale prairie turf, forget the miseries of science, and bathe, young again, in the cool of your dew!"⁴¹ I think we have here the last nostalgic expression of a knowledge of spirituality which disappeared with the Enlightenment, and the sad greeting of the birth of a knowledge of intellectual knowledge. That's what I wanted to say about Seneca and Marcus Aurelius. So in a moment, in a few minutes, I will go on to another problem: no longer the problem of knowledge of the world, but of the exercise of the self. After *mathēsis, askēsis*.

1. *Natural Questions*, preface to book I, analyzed in the lecture of 17 February, second hour.
2. Marcus Aurelius, *Meditations*, VI.3 (French translation modified by Foucault).
3. *Meditations*, III.11.
4. "For you then, I say, choose frankly and freely the highest good and do not let it go!—But what is good is what is to our interest.—If it is to your interest as a rational being, follow it." Ibid., III.6.
5. "Revere the faculty of opinion. Everything depends on it!" Ibid., III.9.
6. "Remember that each of us lives only in the present, this infinitely small moment. The rest is either already past or uncertain." Ibid., III.10.
7. "La physique comme exercice spirituel ou pessimisme et optimisme chez Marc Aurèle," in P. Hadot, *Exercices spirituals et Philosophie antique*, pp. 119-33.
8. This conceptual distinction is clearly expressed by Diogenes Laertius in his book on Zeno: "A definition is, as stated by Antipater in his first book *On Definitions*, a statement, deriving from an analysis, formulated in a way adequate (to the object), or, according to Chrysippus in his book *On Definitions*, is an explanation of the distinctive characteristic. A description is a statement introducing realities in a schematic way." Diogenes Laertius, *Lives of Eminent Philosophers*, VII.60.
9. On this screening of representations, in Epictetus in particular, see *Le Souci de soi*, pp. 79-81 (*The Care of the Self*, pp. 62-64), in which the main reference is to *Discourses*, III.xii.15: "We should not accept a representation without examination, but should say to it: 'Wait, let me see who you are and where you are from,' just as night watchmen say: 'Show me your papers,'" and *Discourses*, I.xx.7-11.
10. See Foucault's classical presentation of the Cartesian method (on the basis of the *Regulae*) in *Les Mots et les Choses* (Paris: Gallimard, 1966), pp. 65-71; English translation by Alan Sheridan, *The Order of Things* (London: Tavistock/Routledge, 1970, 1989), pp. 52-56.
11. *Meditations*, XI.16.
12. Foucault refers here to book III.11: "Nothing, in fact, is so able to enlarge the soul for us as being able to identify (*elegkhein*) methodically and truthfully each of the objects which appear in life."
13. In ancient Greek, the *elegkhos* signifies "shame," then "refutation" in classical vocabulary (see P. Chantraine, *Dictionnaire étymologique de la langue grecque* [Paris: Klincksieck, 1968-1980] pp. 334-35). For a study of this notion, especially in its Socratic sense, see L. A. Dorion, "La Subversion de *l'elenchos* juridique dans *l'Apologie de Socrate*," *Revue philosophique de Louvain* 88 (1990), pp. 311-44.
14. *Meditations*, III.11.
15. For an overall view of these exercises in Epictetus, see the work of B. L. Hijmans, often cited by Foucault, *Askēsis: Notes on Epictetus' Educational System* (Utrecht: 1959).
16. *Discourses*, III.iii.14-19.
17. Cassian's texts are analyzed in the lecture of 26 March 1980.
18. J. Cassian, "Première Conférence de l'abbé Moïse," in *Conférences*, vol. 1, §18, translations by Dom E. Pichery (Paris: Éd. du Cerf, 1955), p. 99. With reference to the same text, see "Technologies of the Self" in *Ethics: Subjectivity and Truth*, pp. 240-41; French translation by F. Durant-Bogaert, "Les techniques de soi," *Dits et Écrits*, vol. 4, p. 811.
19. Ibid., §20-22, pp. 101-7; see "Technologies of the Self."
20. *Meditations*, III.11.
21. "The salvation of life is seeing what each object is in its entirety, its matter and its formal cause." Ibid., XII.29.
22. "This object, what is it in itself, in its specific constitution? What is its substance, matter and formal cause?" Ibid., VIII.11.
23. "Continually, and whenever possible, apply the science of nature to every idea (*phantasias phusiologein*)." Ibid., VIII.13.

24. Actually the pancratium was a violent exercise, a combination of boxing and wrestling, in which: "The aim was to knock one's opponent out or to make him raise one of his arms as a sign that he gave in. Anything was allowed—not only the usual boxing punches and wrestling holds but kicks in the stomach, twisting the arms and legs, biting, strangling, etc." H. I. Marrou, *Histoire de l'éducation dans l'Antiquité*, p. 190 (*A History of Education in Antiquity*, p. 190).
25. "You can succeed in disdaining (*kataphronēsis*) a delightful song, the dance or the pancratium. If it is a melodic tune, it suffices to break it down into its notes and ask yourself of each whether you cannot resist it (*ei toutou hēttōn ei*). You would not dare to acknowledge this. For dance use a similar method with each movement or pose, and the same for the pancratium." *Meditations*, XI.2.
26. Ibid., French translation modified by Foucault.
27. Ibid., VI.15.
28. Ibid., XI.2.
29. "All that I am amounts to this: flesh, breath and the internal guide. Give up books, do not be distracted by them any more; it is no longer allowed; but in the thought that you are dying, despise the flesh: it is only mud and blood, bones and a tight network of nerves, veins, and arteries. Look also at your breath: it is just some air, and not even always the same, for at every moment you expel it in order to breathe in different air anew. Then, thirdly, remains the internal guide." Ibid., II.2.
30. Ibid., VI.15.
31. See above, note 28.
32. The Stoic theme of an eternity, understood not as forever but as an instant that short-circuits time, conquered in the perfect and strictly immanent act, is set out in V. Goldschmidt's classic work, *Le Système stoïcien et l'Idée de temps* (Paris: Vrin, 1985), pp. 200-210.
33. This is the purple stripe sewn to the tunic, indicating a status (senator or knight).
34. "It is the same when one thinks of meat and other similar foods if one says to oneself: this is the dead body of a fish, this is the dead body of a bird or a pig; or again that this Falernian wine is only the juice of a bunch of grapes; this purple marked robe only sheep's wool stained with the blood of a shellfish; what happens in copulation (*sunousia*) is friction of the nerves accompanied by a certain spasm and the excretion of mucous." *Meditations*, VI.13.
35. "In the same way as these ideas fully reach their object (*kathiknoumenai autōn*), as they go to the heart of things so that we see their reality; so too should this be so throughout your life (*houtōs dei par'holon ton bion poiein*). When objects seem most worthy of your confidence, strip them (*apogumnon*), see at bottom (*kathoran*) their scant value (*euteleian*), strip them of the appearance of which they are so proud. Pride (*tuphos*) is really a formidable sophist, and it is when you think you are applying yourself more than ever to serious matters that it succeeds most in deceiving you." Ibid.
36. Ibid., II.2.
37. "As, in fact, that which is terrestrial in me has been taken from some earth, the liquid part from a different element, the breath from another source, heat and fire from yet another source ... so therefore must the intellect come from somewhere." Ibid., IV.4.
38. Ibid., X.19.
39. *Doctor Faustus* in *The Works of Christopher Marlowe*, ed. Tucker Brooke (Oxford: 1910).
40. *Letter* of 16 February 1759, in G. E. Lessing, *Briefe die neueste Literatur betreffend* (Stuttgart: P. Reclam, 1972) pp. 48-53.
41. Goethe, *Faust*, translations by Gérard de Nerval (Paris: Garnier, 1969), Part One: "La Nuit," pp. 35-36. [An English translation gives: "I've studied, alas, philosophy,/Law and medicine, recto and verso,/ And how I regret it, theology also,/Oh God, how hard I've slaved away,/With what result? Poor fool that I am,/I'm no whit wiser than when I began!" "I'm not afraid of Hell or the Devil—/But the consequence is, my mirth's all gone; ... Which is why I've turned to magic,/Seeking to know, by ways occult,/From

ghostly mouths, many a secret;/So I no longer need to sweat/Painfully explaining what/I don't know anything about;/So I may penetrate the power/That holds the universe together,/Behold the source from whence all proceeds/And deal no more in words, words, words. O full moon, melancholy-bright,/Friend I've watched for, many a night,/Till your quiet shining face/Appeared above my high-piled desk—/If this were only the last time/You looked down on my pain!/If only I might stray at will/Beneath your light, high on the hill,/Haunt with spirits upland hollows,/Fade with you in dim-lit meadows,/And soul no longer gasping in/The stink of learning's midnight lamp,/Bathe in your dews till well again." Goethe, *Faust*, part One, "Night," translations by Martin Greenberg (New Haven and London: Yale University Press, 1992), pp. 12-13.

## sixteen

## 24 FEBRUARY 1982

### Second hour

> Virtue and its relation to askēsis. ~ The absence of reference to objective knowledge of the subject in mathēsis. ~ The absence of reference to law in askēsis. ~ Objective and means of askēsis. ~ Characterization of the paraskeuē: the sage as athlete of the event. ~ Content of the paraskeuē: discourse-action. ~ Mode of being of these discourses: the prokheiron. ~ Askēsis as practice of the incorporation of truth-telling in the subject.

IN THE LAST TWO lectures I have tried to examine the question of conversion to the self from the angle of knowledge: the relation between return to the self and knowledge of the world. If you like: conversion to the self in comparison with *mathēsis*. Now I would like to take up this question of conversion to the self again, not from the angle of knowledge and *mathēsis*, but from the angle of the type of action, the type of activity, the mode of practice of the self on the self, entailed by conversion to the self. In other words, knowledge apart, what working practice is entailed by conversion to the self? Broadly speaking I think it is what is called *askēsis* (ascesis as exercise of self on self). In a text called, precisely, *Peri askēseōs* (*Of ascesis, Of exercise*),[1] Musonius Rufus, a Roman Stoic, with whom you are no doubt familiar, compared the acquisition of virtue to the acquisition of medicine or music. How is virtue acquired? Do we acquire virtue as we acquire knowledge of medicine or knowledge of music? This was an extremely banal, traditional, and very old kind of question. It is found in Plato, of course, from the first Socratic dialogues. Musonius Rufus said: The acquisition of virtue involves two things. On the one hand there must be theoretical knowledge (*epistēmē theōrētikē*), and then there must also be *epistēmē praktikē* (practical knowledge). This practical knowledge, he says, can only be acquired through zealous, painstaking (*philotimōs, philoponōs*) training; and he uses the verb *gumnazesthai*: "doing exercises, gymnastics," but clearly in a very general sense, as we will see later. So, taking pains, zeal, and practice will enable us to acquire the *epistēmē praktikē*, which is as indispensable as *epistēmē theōrētikē*.[2] That virtue is acquired through an *askēsis* no less indispensable than a *mathēsis* is obviously a very old idea. There is certainly no need to wait for Musonius Rufus to see it expressed, almost in these same terms. The idea is found in the oldest Pythagorean texts.[3] It is found in Plato.[4] It is also found in Isocrates when he speaks of the *askēsis philosophias*.[5] The Cynics, of course, who focused much more on practical exercise than on theoretical knowledge, equally emphasized this idea.[6] In short, it is an entirely traditional idea in the art of oneself, the practice of oneself, whose schema rather than history I am trying to produce for a precise period (the first and second centuries [A.D.]). However, to avoid any ambiguity, I repeat once again that I am certainly not claiming that the practice of the self I am trying to identify in this period was formed at that moment. I am not even claiming that it was a radical novelty in this period. I just want to say that in this period, at the end of, or rather following a very long history (for the end has not yet arrived), in the first and second centuries, we arrive at a culture of the self, a practice of the self of considerable proportions, with extremely rich forms and a scope which, while no doubt not representing any break in continuity, probably allows a more detailed analysis than if we referred to an earlier period. So it is more for reasons of convenience, of the visibility and legibility of the phenomenon, that I speak about this period, without wanting in any way to say that it represents an innovation. Okay, in any case I do not intend to rewrite the long history of the relations between *mathēsis* and *askēsis*, the long history of the notion of ascesis itself, of exercise, as it is found already in the Pythagoreans. I will content myself then with speaking about these first two centuries A.D., but I would like straightaway to emphasize something that is, I think, quite surprising.

When we cease to consider conversion to the self from the angle of *mathēsis*—of knowledge (*connaissance*): knowledge of the world, is there knowledge of the self? etcetera—but consider it instead from the angle of practice, of the exercise of self on self, will we not find ourselves in a realm that is no longer one of truth, of course, but one of law, the rule, and the code? Will we not find at the founding source of this *askēsis*, of this practice of the self by the self, of the self on the self, the founding and primary authority of law? I think it should be clearly understood—and this is one of the most important and, for us at least, most paradoxical features, because it will not be the same for many other cultures—that what distinguishes ascesis (*askēsis*) in the Greek, Hellenistic, and Roman world, whatever the effects of austerity, renunciation, prohibition, and pernickety prescriptiveness this *askēsis* may induce, is that it is not and basically never was the effect of obedience to the law. *Askēsis* is not established and does not deploy its techniques by reference to an authority like the law. In reality *askēsis* is a practice of truth. Ascesis is not a way of subjecting the subject to the law; it is a way of binding him to the truth. I think we should have these things clearly in mind, because, due to our culture and our own categories, there are not a few schemas in our heads that risk confusing us. And, if you like, I am examining the similarities and differences between what I said about knowledge of the world and what I am going to say now about the practice of the self, or again, what I said about *mathēsis* and what I would now like to say about *askēsis*. In our habitual categories of thought, when we talk about the problem of the relations between the subject and knowledge (*connaissance*) it seems obvious to ask ourselves the question: Can there be knowledge of the subject which is of the same type as knowledge of any other component of the world, or is another type of knowledge required which is irreducible to the first? In other words, I think we quite spontaneously pose the question of the relation between subject and knowledge in the following form: Can there be an objectification (*objectivation*) of the subject? In the last two lectures I wanted to show that when the question of the relation between the subject and knowledge is posed in the culture of the self of the Hellenistic and Roman period, the question never arises of whether the subject is objectifiable (*objectivable*), whether the same mode of knowledge can be applied to the subject as is applied to things of the world and whether the subject is really part of these knowable things of the world. The question never arises in Greek, Hellenistic, and Roman thought. But when the question of the relations between the subject and knowledge (*connaissance*) of the world is posed—and this is what I wanted to show—there is the need to inflect knowledge (*savoir*) of the world in such a way that it takes on a certain form and a certain spiritual value for the subject, in the subject's experience, and for the subject's salvation. This spiritual modalization of the subject is the answer to the general question: What is involved in the relationships of the subject to knowledge of the world? That is what I wanted to show.

Now, I think the same disentangling, the same freeing from our own categories and questions, should be applied to the question of *askēsis*. In fact, when we pose the question of the subject in the realm of practice (not just "what to do?" but "what to make of myself?"), quite spontaneously—I do not mean "quite naturally," but I should say rather "quite historically," and through a necessity that weighs heavily on us—we think it obvious that this question "how should we consider the subject and what he should make of himself?" [must be posed] in terms of the law. That is to say: In what respect, to what extent, on what basis and within what limits should the subject submit to the law? Now, in the culture of the self of Greek, Hellenistic, and Roman civilization, the problem of the subject in his relation to practice leads, I believe, to something quite different from the question of the law. It leads to this: How can the subject act as he ought, how can he be as he ought to be, not only inasmuch as he knows the truth, but inasmuch as he says it, practices it, and exercises it? I have expressed the question badly, more precisely we should say: I think the question the Greeks and Romans pose with regard to the relations between the subject and practice is that of knowing the extent to which the fact of knowing the truth, of speaking the truth, and of practicing and exercising the truth enables the subject not only to act as he ought, but also to be as he ought to be and wishes to be. Let's say, schematically, that where we moderns hear the question "is the objectification of the subject in a field of knowledge (*connaissances*) possible or impossible?" the Ancients of the Greek, Hellenistic, and Roman period heard, "constitution of a knowledge (*savoir*) of the world as spiritual experience of the subject." And where we moderns hear "subjection of the subject to the order of the law," the Greeks and Romans heard "constitution of the subject as final end for himself through and by the exercise of the truth." There is, I think, a fundamental heterogeneity here that should warn us against any retrospective projection. And I would say that whoever wishes to study the history of subjectivity—or rather, the history of the relations between the subject and truth—will have to try to uncover the very long and slow transformation of an apparatus (*dispositif*) of subjectivity, defined by the spirituality of knowledge (*savoir*) and the subject's practice of truth, into this other apparatus of subjectivity which is our own and which is, I think, governed by the question of the subject's knowledge (*connaissance*) of himself and of the subject's obedience to the law. In fact, neither of these two problems (of obedience to the law and of the subject's knowledge of himself) was really fundamental or even present in the thought of ancient culture. There was "spirituality of knowledge (*savoir*)," and there was "practice and exercise of the truth." This is how, I think, the question of *askēsis* should be approached and what I would now like to examine in this and the next lecture.

When we speak of ascesis, it is clear that seen through a certain tradition, which is itself extremely distorted moreover [...] [we understand a] certain form of practice whose components, phases, and successive stages of progress should involve increasingly strict renunciations, with self-renunciation as the target and final passage. We understand ascecis as progressive renunciations leading to the essential renunciation, self-renunciation.[7] We hear it with these resonances. I think ascesis (*askēsis*) had a profoundly different meaning for the Ancients. First of all, because obviously it did not involve the aim of arriving at self-renunciation at the end of ascesis. It involved, rather, constituting oneself through *askēsis*. Or, more precisely, let's say it involved arriving at the formation of a full, perfect, complete, and self-sufficient relationship with oneself, capable of producing the self-transfiguration that is the happiness one takes in oneself. Such was the objective of *askēsis*. Consequently there was nothing to make one think of self-renunciation. Even so, because this history is very complex and I do not intend to recount it in all its details, I just remind you of the very strange and interesting inflection found in Marcus Aurelius, in which ascesis, through the disqualifying perception of things below the self, leads to a questioning of the identity of the self by virtue of the discontinuity of the elements of which we are composed, or by virtue of the universality of reason of which we are a part.[8] However, it seems to me that this is much more an inflection than a fully general feature of ancient ascesis. So, the objective of ascesis in Antiquity is in fact the constitution of a full, perfect, and complete relationship of oneself to oneself.

Second, we should not seek the means of ancient ascesis in the renunciation of this or that part of oneself. Of course, there are elements of renunciation. There are elements of austerity. We can even say that the essentials, or anyway a considerable part of Christian renunciation, was already required by ancient ascesis. But the nature itself of the means, of the tactic if you like, put to work to achieve this objective, is not primarily or fundamentally renunciation. It involves, rather, acquiring something through *askēsis* (ascesis). We must acquire something we do not have, rather than renounce this or that element of ourselves that we are or have. We must acquire something that, precisely, instead of leading us gradually to renounce ourselves, will allow us to protect the self and to reach it. In two words, ancient ascesis does not reduce: it equips, it provides. And what it equips and provides us with is what in Greek is called a *paraskeuē*, which Seneca often translates into Latin as *instructio*. The fundamental word is *paraskeuē*, and this is what I would like to study a little today before going on next week to some other, more precise forms of ascetic exercises. When the objective of ascesis is to arrive at the constitution of this full relationship of oneself to oneself, its function, or rather its tactic or instrument, is the constitution of a *paraskeuē*. What is this? Well, the *paraskeuē* could be called both an open and an orientated preparation of the individual for the events of life. What I mean is this: In the ascesis, the *paraskeuē* involves preparing the individual for the future, for a future of unforeseen events whose general nature may be familiar to us, but which we cannot know whether and when they will occur. It involves, then, finding in ascesis a preparation, a *paraskeuē*, which can be adapted to what may occur, and only to this, and at the very moment it occurs, if it does so.

There are many definitions of the *paraskeuē*. I will take one of the simplest and strictest. It is found in Demetrius the Cynic, in the text Seneca quotes in book VII of *De Beneficiis*,[9] in which Demetrius takes up a commonplace of Cynic philosophy, but also of moral philosophy in general, of all practices of life: the comparison of life, and of the person who wishes to achieve wisdom in life, with the athlete. We will often have to return to this comparison of the sage and the athlete, or of the person who heads for or progresses towards wisdom, and the athlete. Anyway, in this text of Demetrius, the good athlete appears as one who practices. But practices what? Not, he says, every possible move. It is definitely not a matter of deploying all the possibilities open to us. It does not even involve achieving some feat in one or other area that will enable us to triumph over others. It involves preparing ourselves only for what we may come up against, for only those events we may encounter, [but] not in such a way as to outdo others, or even to surpass ourselves. The notion of "excelling oneself" is sometimes found in the Stoics, and I will try to come back to it, but this is definitely not the form found in Christian asceticism of a more or less indefinite gradation towards the most difficult. So it does not involve doing better than others, nor even surpassing oneself, but it involves, still according to the category I have been talking about, being stronger than, or not weaker than, whatever may occur. The good athlete's training, then, must be training in some elementary moves which are sufficiently general and effective for them to be adapted to every circumstance and—on condition of their being sufficiently simple and well-learned—for one to be able to make immediate use of them when the need arises. It is this apprenticeship in some elementary moves, necessary and sufficient for every possible circumstance, that constitutes good training, good ascesis. The *paraskeuē* will be nothing other than the set of necessary and sufficient moves, of necessary and sufficient practices, which will enable us to be stronger than anything that may happen in our life. This is the athletic training of the sage. This theme, which is especially well defined by Demetrius, is found everywhere. I will quote you a text from Marcus Aurelius, but you will also find the theme in Seneca and Epictetus, and so on: "The art of living [what he calls the biotic: *hē biōtikē*; M.F.] is more like wrestling than dancing, in that you must stay on guard and steady on your feet against the blows which rain down on you, and without warning."[10] This contrast between athleticism and dance, wrestling and dance, is interesting. The dancer is of course someone who does his best to achieve a certain ideal that will enable him to surpass others or to surpass himself. The dancer's work is indefinite. The art of wrestling consists simply in being ready and on guard, in remaining steady, that is to say, not being thrown, not being weaker than all the blows coming either from circumstances or from others. I think this is very important. It enables us to distinguish between the athlete of ancient spirituality and the Christian athlete. The Christian athlete is on the indefinite path of progress towards holiness in which he must surpass himself even to the point of renouncing himself. Also, the Christian athlete is especially someone who has an enemy, an adversary, who keeps him on guard. With regard to whom and to what? But with regard to himself! To himself, inasmuch as the most malign and dangerous powers he has to confront (sin, fallen nature, seduction by the devil, etcetera) are within himself. The Stoic athlete, the athlete of ancient spirituality also has to struggle. He has to be ready for a struggle in which his adversary is anything coming to him from the external world: the event. The ancient athlete is an athlete of the event. The Christian is an athlete of himself. This is the first point.

Second, of what is this equipment (*paraskeuē*) made up? Well, this equipment with which we must provide ourselves and which enables us to respond properly, at once and with the simplest and most effective means, is made up of *logoi* (discourses). We must pay close attention here. By *logoi* it is not enough to understand merely a supply of true propositions, principles, and axioms, etcetera. Discourses should be understood as statements with a material existence. The good athlete, who has the sufficient *paraskeuē*, is not merely someone who knows this or that about the general order of nature or particular precepts corresponding to this or that circumstance. He is someone who has—for the moment I will say "in his head," but we will have to come back to this subject and examine it more closely—driven into him, embedded in him (these are Seneca's expressions in letter 50)[11] ... what? Well, who has some actually uttered phrases, phrases that he has really heard or read, phrases that he has embedded in his mind by repeating them, by repeating them in his memory through daily exercises, by writing them, in notes for himself for example, like those made by Marcus Aurelius: you know that in the texts of Marcus Aurelius it is very difficult to know what is his and what is a quotation. It's not important. The problem is that the athlete is someone who provides himself with phrases he has really heard or read, really remembered, repeated, written and rewritten. They are the master's lessons, phrases he has heard, phrases he has spoken or which he has said to himself. It is from this material equipment of *logos*, to be understood in this sense, that the necessary framework is constituted for whoever would be the good athlete of the event, the good athlete of fortune. Second, these discourses—discourses existing, acquired, and preserved in their materiality—are of course not any discourses whatsoever. As the word *logos* indicates, they are propositions justified by reason. Justified by reason means that they are rational, that they are true and constitute acceptable principles of behavior. In Stoic philosophy they are the *dogmata* and the *praecepta*[12]— I will skip this (we will return to it if we can, but it is not absolutely necessary). What I would like you to note is that these really existing phrases, these materially existing *logoi* are then phrases, elements of discourse, of rationality: of a rationality that states the truth and prescribes what we must do at the same time. Finally, third, these discourses are persuasive. That is to say, these *logoi* not only say what is true or say what we must do, but when they constitute a good *paraskeuē* they are not confined to being kinds of orders given to the subject. They are persuasive in the sense that they bring about not only conviction, but also the actions themselves. They are inductive schemas of action which, in their inductive value and effectiveness, are such that when present in the head, thoughts, heart, and even body of someone who possesses them, that person will then act as if spontaneously. It is as if it were these *logoi* themselves, gradually becoming as one with his own reason, freedom, and will, were speaking for him: not only telling him what he should do, but also actually doing what he should do, as dictated by necessary rationality. So, these material elements of rational *logos* are effectively inscribed in the subject as matrices of action. This is the *paraskeuē*. And the aim of the *askēsis* necessary to the athlete of life is to obtain this.

The third characteristic of this *paraskeuē* is the question of its mode of being. Because for this discourse—or rather, these discourses, these material elements of discourse—really to be able to constitute the preparation we need, they must not only be acquired but also endowed with a sort of permanent virtual and effective presence, which enables immediate recourse to them when necessary. The *logos* that makes up the *paraskeuē* must at the same time be an aid. Here we come to an important notion that frequently appears in all of these texts. The *logos* must be *boēthos* (aid).[13] This word *boēthos* is interesting. Originally, in archaic vocabulary, *boēthos* is aid. That is to say, it is the fact that someone responds to the appeal (*boē*) launched by a warrior in danger. The person who comes to his aid responds with a cry that announces that help is on its way and that he is running to his assistance. This is what it is, and the *logos* must be like that. When a circumstance arises, when an event takes place that puts the subject, the subject's mastery, in danger, the *logos* must be able to respond when someone calls on it, and it must be able to make its voice heard announcing to the subject, as it were, that it is there and that it is bringing him help. The aid itself [resides] precisely in the statement, in the reactualization of the *logos*, in the voice making itself heard and promising help. If the *logos* speaks, as soon as the event occurs, if the *logos*, which constitutes the *paraskeuē*, is formulated in order to announce its aid, then the aid telling us what we must do, or rather, actually making us do what we must do, is already there. This, then, is how the *logos* is that which comes to our assistance. There are a thousand metaphors for the *logos boēthos* in the literature, whether in the form of the idea of a *logos*-remedy (*logos-pharmakōn*) for example,[14] or in the idea, also very frequent and to which I have referred already several times,[15] of the piloting metaphor—the *logos* must be like a good pilot on a boat,[16] who keeps the crew in place, who tells it what it must do, and who maintains the direction and orders manoeuvres, etcetera—or again, of course, in the military and warrior form, either of armor or, more often, of the wall and fortress behind which warriors can withdraw when in danger, and from where, well-supported by their walls, from the height of their walls, they can repel the enemy's attacks. In the same way, when the subject feels threatened by events in the open country of daily life, the *logos* must be there: a fortress or citadel perched on high to which he retreats. One withdraws into oneself insofar as one is *logos*. And it is there that we find the possibility of repelling the event, of ceasing to be *hēttōn* (the weaker) than it, and of finally being able to prevail. You see that to play this role in this way, to really have the nature of an aid, and of a permanent aid, this equipment of rational *logoi* should always be ready to hand. It should be what the Greeks called *khrēstikos* (utilizable). And they had a series, or rather a metaphor, which constantly recurs and is very important for trying to define the *paraskeuē* and consequently for what the nature and development of the exercises that form and maintain it should be. To play the role of aid, to really be the good pilot or fortress or remedy, the *logos* must be "ready to hand": *prokheiron*, which the Latins translated as *ad manum*. We must have it here, ready to hand.[17] I think this is a very important notion falling within the category of memory, no doubt fundamental in all Greek thought, but also introducing a particular inflection. In fact, we can say that the basic function of *mnēmē* (memory in its archaic form) was not only to maintain the poet's thought or saying in its being, value, and luster, but also, of course, by thus maintaining the luster of the truth, its function was to be able to enlighten all those who uttered the saying anew, who uttered it because they themselves partook of the *mnēmē*, or who heard it from the mouth of the bard or sage who directly participate in this *mnēmē*.[18] You can see that the idea that the *logoi* (the *logoi boēthikoi*, the *logos* of aid) must be ready to hand, is somewhat different from the idea of the preservation of truth's luster in the memory of those who participate in the *mnēmē*. In reality each must have this equipment ready to hand, and he must have it ready to hand not exactly in the form of a memory that will sing the saying anew and make it shine forth in its light, always new and always the same. We must have it ready to hand, that is to say we must have it, so to speak, almost in our sinews. We must have it in such a way that we can reactualize it immediately and without delay, automatically. In reality it must be a memory of activity, a memory of action, much more than a memory of song. When the day of sorrow comes, of mourning or mishap, when death threatens, when we are sick and suffer, the equipment must come into play to protect the soul, to prevent it being affected, to enable it to preserve its calm. Of course, this does not mean that the formulation, the reformulation of the saying is unnecessary. However, whereas in the great archaic *mnemē* the truth shone forth precisely when the song was raised up anew, here all the verbal repetitions must be part of the preparation so that the saying can be integrated into the individual and control his action, becoming part, as it were, of his muscles and nerves: for this reason, as preparation in the *askēsis*, one will first have to perform all those exercises of remembering by which one will actually recall the sayings and propositions, will reactualize the *logoi*, and reactualize them by actually uttering them. But when the event occurs, the *logos* at that point must have become itself the subject of action, the subject of action must himself have become at that point *logos* and, without having to sing the phrase anew, without even having to utter it, acts as he ought to act. In this general notion of *askēsis*, what I think emerges and is implemented in this way is, if you like, a different form of *mnemē*, a completely different ritual of verbal reactualization and implementation, a completely different relation between the discourse repeated and the action's splendor.

To summarize all this, and by way of introduction [to the] next lecture, I will say this: It seems to me that for the Greeks, and for the Romans also, the essential function, the first, immediate objective of the *askēsis*, on account of its final objective being the constitution of a full and independent relationship of oneself to oneself, is the constitution of a *paraskeuē* (a preparation, an equipment). And what is this *paraskeuē*? It is, I believe, the form that must be taken by true discourse in order for it to be able to be the matrix of rational behavior. The *paraskeuē* is the structure of the permanent transformation of true discourse, firmly fixed in the subject, into principles of morally acceptable behavior.

The *paraskeuē* is, again, the element of transformation of *logos* into *ethos*. And the *askēsis* may then be defined as the set, the regular, calculated succession of procedures that are able to form, definitively fix, periodically reactivate and, if necessary, reinforce this *paraskeuē* for an individual. The *askēsis* is what enables truth-telling—truth-telling addressed to the subject and also truth-telling that the subject addresses to himself—to be constituted as the subject's way of being. The *askēsis* makes truth-telling a mode of being of the subject. I think that this is the definition we can get, well, that we can at least posit, of this general theme of *askēsis*. And you see that when, in this epoch, this period and form of culture, ascesis really is what enables truth-telling to become the subject's mode of being, we are necessarily very far from an *askēsis* of the kind that will be seen in Christianity, when truth-telling will be defined essentially on the basis of a Revelation, of a Text and of a relationship of faith, and ascesis, for its part, will be a sacrifice: the sacrifice of successive parts of oneself and the final renunciation of oneself. Constituting oneself through an exercise in which truth-telling becomes the subject's mode of being: what could be further from what we, in our historical tradition, now understand by an "ascesis," an ascesis which renounces the self according to a true Word spoken by an Other? That's it. Okay, thank you.

1. *Peri askēseōs*, in Musonius Rufus, *Reliquiae*, pp. 22-27; *Musonius Rufus*, 27.
2. "Virtue, he said, is not only a theoretical science (*epistēmē theōrētikē*) but also a practical knowledge (*alla kai praktikē*) like medicine and music. Just as both the doctor and musician must not only accept the principles of their respective art, but also be trained according to these principles (*mē monon aneilēphenai ta theōrēmata tēs hautou tekhnēs hekateron, alla kai gegumnasthai prattein kata ta theōrēmata*), so too the person who wants to be a virtuous man must not only have learned in depth (*ekmanthanein*) all the knowledge which contributes to virtue, but also be trained according to this knowledge with zeal and laboriously (*gumnazesthai kata tauta philotimōs kai philoponōs*)." *Musonius Rufus*.
3. On the idea of an *askēsis tēs aretēs* in the Pythagoreans, see J.-P. Vernant, "Le fleuve 'amelēs' et la 'meletē thanatou,' " in *Myth et Pensée chez le Grecs*, vol. 1, pp. 109-12; English translation, "The River of Amélès and the Méléte Thanatou," in *Myth and Thought among the Greeks*, pp. 106-10.
4. See the conclusion of the myth of Protagoras on virtue as the object of exercise: "In the case of qualities which are thought to be acquired by application (*epimeleias*), exercise (*askēseōs*) and teaching, it is when someone lacks these and they are replaced by the corresponding faults that there is anger, punishment and exhortation," Plato, *Protagoras*, 323d. See also, just after the famous passage of *The Republic*, VII.518d, on education as conversion of the soul: "The other faculties which are called faculties of the soul are analogous to the faculties of the body; for it is true that when they are completely absent to begin with, we can acquire them afterwards through habit and exercise."
5. "For the souls, they [the Egyptian priests] reveal the practice of philosophy (*philosophias askēsin*)." Isocrates, *Busiris*, Oration XI.22.
6. On *askēsis* in Diogenes, see §23 ("he made use of everything to train himself") and especially §70-71 of book VI of Diogenes Laertius, *Lives of Eminent Philosophers*. See also M.-O. Goulet-Cazé, *L'Ascèse cynique. Un commentaire de Diogène Laërce* vol. VI, 70-71.
7. On self-renunciation in Christianity, see lecture of 17 February, first hour.
8. See Foucault's study of the exercises of reductive perception in Marcus Aurelius in the first hour of this lecture.
9. See the analysis of this same text in the lecture of 10 February, second hour.
10. Marcus Aurelius, *Meditations*, VII.61.
11. Reference to the plant metaphor in Seneca, *Letters*, L.8.
12. Foucault no doubt means here *decreta* (Seneca's Latin rendering of the Greek *dogmata*; see Marcus Aurelius, *Meditations* VII.2), which refer to general principles organized in a system and opposed precisely to the *praecepta* (selective practical precepts). See letter 95 in which Seneca preaches a morality of *decreta*: "Only axioms (*decreta*) strengthen us, preserve our security and calm, and embrace at the same time the whole of life and nature. There is the same difference between the axioms of philosophy and its precepts (*decreta philosophiae et praecepta*) as there is between the elements and parts of an organism . . . We do not arrive at the truth without the help of general principles (*sine decretis*): they embrace the whole of life." *Letters*, XCV.12 and 58. See also XCV.60, as well as the lecture of 17 February, first hour, for the presentation of Ariston of Chios, whom Seneca makes the father of this distinction in letter XCIV. For an overall view of this problem, see P. Boyancé, "Les Stoïcisme à Rome," in *Association Guillaume Budé, VII<sup>e</sup> congrès, Aix-en-Provence, 1963* (Paris: Les Belles Lettres, 1964), pp. 218-54.
13. "It is the same for the arguments (*logōn*) which cure the passions (*pros ta pathē boēthousi*). They must be applied before experiencing the passions, if one has good sense, so that, prepared well in advance (*paraskeuasmenoi*), they are more effective." Plutarch, *On Tranquility of Mind*, 465b.
14. This metaphor appears in Plutarch in *A Letter of Condolence to Apollonius*, 101f.
15. See lecture of 17 February, first hour.

16. See this image in Plutarch, *On the Control of Anger*, 453a.
17. "Just as doctors always have their instruments and medical case ready at hand (*prokheira*) for emergencies, so always keep ready the principles (*dogmata*) for understanding things human and divine." Marcus Aurellis, *Meditations*, III.13. See also XI.4, VII.64, VII.1, and V.1, for similar uses of *prokheiron*.
18. See J.-P. Vernant, "Aspects mythiques de la mémoire," in *Mythe et Pensée chez les Grecs*, vol. 1, pp. 80-107; English translation "Mythical Aspects of Memory" in *Myth and Thought among the Greeks*, pp. 75-105; and M. Detienne, "La mémoire du poète," in *Les Maîtres de vérité dans la Grèce achaïque* (Paris: Pocket, 1994), pp. 49-70; English translation by Janet Lloyd, "The Memory of the Poet," in *The Masters of Truth in Archaic Greece* (New York: Zone Books, 1999), pp. 39-52.

## seventeen

## 3 MARCH 1982

### First hour

> *Conceptual separation of Christian from philosophical ascesis. ~ Practices of subjectivation: the importance of listening exercises. ~ The ambiguous nature of listening, between passivity and activity: Plutarch's* Peri tou akouein; *Seneca's letter CVIII; Epictetus' discourse II.23. ~ Listening in the absence of* tekhnē. *~ The ascetic rules of listening: silence; precise non-verbal communication and general demeanor of the good listener; attention (attachment to the referent of the discourse and subjectivation of the discourse through immediate memorization).*

WITH REGARD TO THE general theme of conversion of the self, you remember that I tried first of all to analyze the effects of the principle of "converting to the self" within the realm of knowledge (*connaissance*). I tried to show that these effects should not be sought in the constitution of oneself as an object and domain of knowledge (*connaissance*), but rather in the establishment of certain forms of spiritual knowledge (*savoir*), two examples of which I tried to identify, one in Seneca and the other in Marcus Aurelius. This was, if you like, the side of *mathēsis*. Then I considered the other side of the conversion of the self: the effects introduced into what we can call the practice of the self by the principle of "converting to oneself." And this, I think, is what broadly speaking the Greeks called *askēsis*. As a first approach—and this is what I tried to show briefly at the end of the last lecture—it seems to me that *askēsis*, as it was understood by the Greeks in the Hellenistic and Roman epoch, is very far from being what we traditionally understand by "ascesis," precisely to the extent that our notion of ascesis is more or less modeled on and impregnated by the Christian conception. It seems to me—and once again, I am just giving an outline here, a first sketch—that the ascesis of the pagan philosophers or, if you like, of the practice of the self in the Hellenistic and Roman epoch, is very clearly and precisely distinguished from Christian ascesis on a number of points. First, the final, ultimate objective in the ascesis of the practice of the self is evidently not self-renunciation. Rather, the objective is to fix yourself as the end of your own existence, and to do this in the most explicit, intense, continuous, and persistent way possible. Second, this philosophical ascesis does not involve determining the order of sacrifices or renunciations you must make of this or that part or aspect of your being. Rather, it involves providing yourself with something you have not got, something you do not possess by nature. It involves putting together a defensive equipment against possible events in your life. This is what the Greeks called the *paraskeuē*. The function of ascesis is to form a *paraskeuē* [so that] the subject constitutes himself. Third, it seems to me that the principle of this philosophical ascesis of the practice of the self is not the individual's submission to the law. Its principle is to bind the individual to the truth. Bond with the truth rather than submission to the law seems to me one of the most fundamental aspects of this philosophical ascesis.

In sum, we could say—and I think this is where I stopped last week—that on the one hand ascesis is what makes possible the acquisition of the true discourses we need in every circumstance, event, and episode of life in order to establish an adequate, full, and perfect relationship to ourselves. On the other hand, and at the same time, ascesis is what enables us to become the subject of these true discourses, to become the subject who tells the truth and who is transfigured by this enunciation of the truth, by this enunciation itself, precisely by the fact of telling the truth. In sum, I think we can suggest the following: the meaning and function of philosophical ascesis, of the ascesis of the practice of the self in the Hellenistic and Roman epoch, is essentially to ensure what I will call the subjectivation of true discourse. It ensures that I myself can hold this true discourse, it ensures that I myself become the subject of enunciation of true discourse, whereas it seems to me that Christian ascesis will have a completely different function, which is, of course, self-renunciation. However, on the route to self-renunciation, Christian ascesis will give rise to a particularly important moment which I think I spoke about last year, or two years ago, I no longer remember,[1] and which is the moment of avowal, of confession, that is to say when the subject objectifies himself in a true discourse. It seems to me that in this Christian ascesis there is, therefore, a movement of self-renunciation which proceeds by way of, and whose essential moment is, the objectification of the self in a true discourse. It seems to me that pagan ascesis, the philosophical ascesis of the practice of the self in the period I am talking about, involves rejoining oneself as the end and object of a technique of life, an art of living. It involves coming together with oneself, the essential moment of which is not the objectification of the self in a true discourse, but the subjectivation of a true discourse in a practice and exercise of oneself on oneself. This, basically, is the kind of fundamental difference that I have been trying to bring out since the start of this course. What Seneca is constantly indicating is a method of the subjectivation of true discourse when he says, with regard to learning, the language of philosophers, reading, writing, and the notes you make, etcetera, that what is involved is making the things you know your own (*"facere suum"*),[2] making the discourse you hear, the discourse you recognize as being true or which the philosophical tradition has passed on to you as true, your own. Making the truth your own, becoming the subject of enunciation of true discourse: this, I think, is the very core of this philosophical ascesis.

So you see what the first, initial, indispensable form of ascesis will be when it is conceived of as the subjectivation of true discourse. The first moment, the first stage, but at the same time the permanent support of this ascesis as subjectivation of true discourse, comprises all those techniques and practices concerning listening, reading, writing, and the activity of speaking. As techniques of true discourse, listening, knowing how to listen properly, reading and writing properly, as well as speaking, will be the permanent support and continuous accompaniment of ascetic practice. You see also, we will return to this, the extent to which there is something here which comes close to, but is profoundly different from, hearing the Word or the relationship to the Text in Christian spirituality. These, then, are the three things I will try to explain today, that is to say: first of all, listening as ascetic practice, understood as subjectivation of the true, then reading and writing, and finally, third, speech.

First of all, then, listening. We can say that listening really is the first step, the first move in ascesis and the subjectivation of true discourse, since listening, in a culture which you know was fundamentally oral, is what enables us to take in the *logos*, to take in what is said that is true. However, if conducted properly, listening also makes it possible for the individual to be convinced of the truth spoken to him, of the truth he encounters in the *logos*. And, finally, listening is the first moment of the process by which the truth which has been heard, listened to, and properly taken in, sinks into the subject so to speak, becomes embedded in him and begins to become *suus* (to become his own) and thus forms the matrix for *ēthos*. The transition from *alētheia* to *ēthos* (from true discourse to what will be the fundamental rule of conduct) begins of course with listening. The point of departure and necessity for this ascesis of listening are found in what the Greeks recognized as the profoundly ambiguous nature of audition. This ambiguous nature of audition is expressed in a number of texts. One of the clearest and most explicit on the subject is Plutarch's text called, precisely, *Peri tou akouein* (which is translated *De Audiendo*: *On Listening*).[3] In this treatise *On Listening*, Plutarch takes up a theme which he explicitly says he has borrowed from Theophrastus and which in fact arises, once again, from a wholly traditional Greek problematic. He says that audition, the sense of hearing, is basically both the most *pathētikos* and the most *logikos* of the senses. It is the most *pathētikos*, that is to say—we translate roughly and schematically—the most "passive" sense.[4] That is to say, in audition, more than with any other sense, the soul is passive with regard to the external world and exposed to all the events that come from the outside world and may take it by surprise. Plutarch explains this by saying that we cannot avoid hearing what takes place around us. After all, we can refuse to look; we close our eyes. We can refuse to touch something. We can refuse to taste something. Furthermore, he says, the passivity of audition is proven by the fact that the body itself, the physical individual, risks being surprised and shaken by what he hears, much more than by any other object appearing [to him] through sight or touch. We cannot help jumping at a violent noise that takes us by surprise. The body is passive, then, with regard to the sense of hearing, more than with regard to any other sense. And then, finally, whether through its reception of or sensitivity to verbal flattery, to rhetorical effects, or, of course, its sensitivity to the sometimes positive, but sometimes harmful effects of music, the sense of hearing is more than any other sense capable of bewitching the soul. You will recognize here a very old Greek theme that had many expressions. In all these texts concerning the passivity of audition, there is, of course, the usual reference to Ulysses, who succeeded in conquering all his senses, completely controlling himself, and refusing any pleasures he might be offered. However, when Ulysses approached the area where he encounters the Sirens, nothing, neither his courage nor his self-control, neither his *sōphrosunē* nor his *phronēsis*, could prevent him falling victim to the Sirens, from being bewitched by their songs and their music. He had to block up the ears of his sailors and have himself tied to his own mast, knowing that his sense of hearing is his most *pathētikos* sense.[5] You recall also what Plato says about poets and music, etcetera.[6] The sense of hearing, then, is the most *pathētikos* of the senses. But, Plutarch says, it is also the most *logikos*.[7] By *logikos* he means that it can receive the *logos* better than any other sense. He says the other senses basically give access to the pleasures (the pleasures of sight, taste, and touch). The other senses also give rise to error: there are all the optical errors, the errors of sight. And it is basically through all these other senses of taste, smell, touching, and looking, or through the parts of the body or organs which perform these functions, that vices are learned. On the other hand, the sense of hearing is the only sense through which we can learn virtue. We do not learn virtue by looking. It is and can only be learned through the ear: because virtue cannot be separated from the *logos*, that is to say from rational language, from language really present, expressed, and articulated verbally in sounds and rationally by reason. The *logos* can only penetrate through the ear and thanks to the sense of hearing. The only access to the soul for the *logos*, therefore, is through the ear. Hence the fundamental ambiguity of the sense of hearing: *pathētikos* and *logikos*.

This theme of the ambiguity of audition is found in other texts of the period I am studying (the first and second centuries A.D.), and always with reference to this question of the practice of the self, of the conducting of the soul, etcetera. I would like to refer mainly to two texts: the first is from Seneca's letter 108, and the other from Epictetus. Actually, both of them take up this general theme of the ambiguity of the sense of hearing (*pathētikos* and *logikos*). However, they do so from slightly different points of view. In letter 108, Seneca takes up the question of the passivity of hearing. He considers hearing from this angle and tries to show the ambiguity of this passivity itself. Let's say that Plutarch shows that the sense of hearing is ambiguous because it is at once *pathētikos* and *logikos*. Seneca takes up the theme of the passivity of the sense of hearing (*pathētikos* sense), but he makes this pathos itself a principle of ambiguity, with consequent advantages and drawbacks. This is clearly explained in letter 108. To show the advantages of the passivity of the sense of hearing, he says: After all, it is actually very advantageous that the ear allows itself to be penetrated in this way, without the will intervening, and that it takes in all the *logos* that falls within its range. Thus, he says, it is very good even for philosophy lectures, because even if one does not understand, even if one does not pay close attention and is only passively present, there will always be something to show for it. There will always be something to show because the *logos* enters the ear and then the *logos* carries out some work on the soul, whether the subject likes it or not. "He who studies with a philosopher must anyway reap some benefit every day. At any rate, he returns home on the way to being cured or anyway more easily curable."[8] [We find again] the idea we have already come across that the study of philosophy is actually a therapeutic enterprise; you recall Epictetus saying that the philosophy school is an *iatreion*, a clinic.[9] So, one goes to philosophy lectures as one goes to the clinic. And one leaves always either on the way to being cured or anyway more easily curable.* Such is the virtue of philosophy that everyone benefits from it: the proselytes (this is the [French] translation given for *studentes*: the students) and also the usual entourage (*conversantes*);[10] that is to say, those who study zealously, because they wish either to complete their training or become philosophers themselves, as well as those who merely gather round the philosopher. The latter also profit from philosophy. Just as we get sunburned, he says, when we walk in the sun, although this was not our intention. Or again, when we linger in a perfumer's shop, we are involuntarily impregnated with its scent. So, in the same way, "one doesn't come away from a philosophy lecture without necessarily taking something away which is powerful enough to benefit even the inattentive (*neglegentibus*)."[11]

This anecdotal and amusing passage actually refers to an important part of the doctrine of the seeds of the soul. In every rational soul coming into the world there are seeds of virtue, and these seeds of virtue are awakened and activated by those words of truth uttered around the subject and which he takes in through the ear. Just as he is not responsible for these seeds of virtue, which have been implanted in him by the very nature of his reason, in the same way the awakening may take place through a *logos* which gets through despite his inattention. There is something here like an automatism of the work of the *logos* on virtue, on the soul; [an automatism] which is due both to the existence of the seeds of virtue and to the nature, the very property of the true *logos*. So, this is the advantage from the angle of the pathos or passivity of audition. However, in the same letter Seneca notes that on the other hand there are some drawbacks. And he says that if it is true that we can be impregnated by philosophy when we go to a lecture, a bit like getting sunburned if we stay in the sun, nevertheless, he says, it's still true that some of those who frequent the philosophy school derive no benefit from it. This is because, he says, they were not at the philosophy school

---

*The French here has "plus facilement raisonnable," which seems either to be a slip, since the passage from Seneca quoted before has "plus facilement guérissable," or Foucault's meaning is unclear—G.B.

as *discipuli* (as disciples, pupils). They were there as *inquilini*, that is to say as tenants.[12] They were the tenants of their place at the philosophy lecture, and in the end they stayed without benefiting from it. But since the theory of the seeds of virtue and of the effects, even passive effects, of the *logos* should have enabled them to learn, then if they have remained merely tenants it is because they paid no attention to what was said. They attended only to ornament, to the fine voice and the search for words and style. So, you see that we have here—and I will come back to this shortly—the matrix of the following question: Given that the *logos* can produce effects on the soul spontaneously and automatically, so to speak, because it speaks the truth, how is it that, even in the passivity of attention, it does not always produce positive effects? Well, it is because attention is badly directed. It is because it is not directed towards the right object or target. Hence a certain art is required, or at any rate a certain technique, a correct way of listening.

Now for the Epictetus text. It is from his discourse II.xxiii, where he takes up this theme again, but in this case from the angle of the sense of hearing as *logikos* sense. While Seneca said that the sense of hearing is passive, which has some drawbacks and some advantages, Epictetus starts from hearing as a sense that can receive the *logos*, and he will show that even this is ambiguous, that is to say that there is something necessarily passive even in this logical activity of audition, that there is something that necessarily belongs to the realm of pathos and which, due to this, makes all hearing a bit dangerous, even hearing the word of truth. Epictetus says: "It is by means of the spoken word and instruction (*dia logou kai paradoseōs*) that we should advance to perfection."[13] It is necessary to listen then, to listen to the *logos* and receive this *paradosis*, which is the teaching, the transmitted spoken word. Now, he says, this *logos*, this *paradosis* cannot appear in the naked state, as it were. Truths cannot be conveyed as such. For truths to reach the listener's soul they must be uttered. And we cannot utter them without certain elements linked to speech itself and its organization in discourse. Two things in particular are necessary, he says. First, a *lexis*. The *lexis* is the way of speaking: We cannot express things without a certain way of speaking. And, on the other hand, neither can we express things without using what he calls "a certain variety and subtlety in the wording." By this he means that we cannot convey things without choosing the terms that designate [them] and consequently without certain stylistic or semantic options which prevent the idea itself, or rather the truth of the discourse, being conveyed directly. So, since the truth can only be expressed through *logos* and *paradosis* (through discourse and oral transmission), and as soon as this oral transmission calls upon a *lexis* and semantic choices, you see that the listener risks not focusing his attention on what is expressed but rather on these elements that enable it to be expressed. The listener risks being captivated and getting no further (*katamenoi*).[14] Every individual who speaks and addresses himself to his listeners is exposed to the danger of getting no further than these elements of the *lexis* or these elements of vocabulary. This is what every listener is exposed to if he does not focus his attention properly. So, you can see that we are in any case in an ambiguous world, an ambiguous system, with listening, with audition. Whether we take the aspect of pathos or the *logikos*, audition is in any case always subject to error. It is always subject to misinterpretation or errors of attention.

At this point Epictetus introduces an important notion, I think, which will lead us precisely to the theme of the ascesis of listening. He says: Basically, since we are dealing with a *logos* when we listen, and this logos is inseparable from a *lexis* (a way of speaking) and a certain number of words, we can see that listening is almost as difficult as speaking. For when we speak, it has to be said that sometimes we speak usefully, sometimes we speak pointlessly, and sometimes we even speak harmfully. In the same way, we can listen to our advantage, we can listen in a completely pointless way and without getting any benefit, and we can even listen in a way that is to our disadvantage. Okay, Epictetus says, to be able to speak properly and usefully, and to avoid speaking in a vain or harmful way, we need a *tekhnē*, an art. We also need a *tekhnē* to be able to sculpt properly. Well, he says, to listen we need *empeiria*, that is to say, competence, experience, or, let us say, acquired skill. We also need *tribē* (application, diligent practice). To listen properly, then, we need *empeiria* (acquired skill) and *tribē* (diligent practice), just as we need *tekhnē* to speak properly. You see at once the connection and the difference. You see that Epictetus emphasizes that to speak properly we need *tekhnē*, an art, whereas to listen we need experience, competence, diligent practice, attention, application, and so forth. Now, in technical philosophical vocabulary (in philosophical vocabulary *tout court*), an opposition (a distinction at any rate) is usually recognized or admitted between *tekhnē* on the one hand and *tribē* and *empeiria* on the other. There is a perfectly clear passage about this in the *Phaedrus*. At 270b, Plato speaks about medicine and the art of oratory. He says that it is obvious that much routine and experience, etcetera, are necessary in medicine and oratorical art. However, he says, *empeiria* and *tribē* (the two words are used together, as in the Epictetus text) are not enough. Over and above this we need *tekhnē*. *Tekhnē* rests [on] and implies knowledge—knowledge of what the body is in its very reality. Thus medicine is a *tekhnē*, or at any rate presupposes one, resting on knowledge of the body. And the art of speaking is a *tekhnē* inasmuch as it rests on a knowledge of the soul. Whereas there is no need of knowledge in the case of *empeiria* and *tribē*.[15] You can see why naturally, under these conditions, in Epictetus—but in fact throughout these reflections on listening in connection with the practice of the self—listening cannot be defined as a *tekhnē*, since we are at the first stage of the ascesis. By listening we begin to establish contact with the truth. How then could listening be a *tekhnē* when *tekhnē* presupposes a knowledge that can only be acquired by listening? Consequently, what could be called, but weakening the word, an "art of listening," cannot be an "art" in the strict sense. It is experience, competence, skill, and a certain way of familiarizing ourselves with the demands of listening. *Empeiria* and *tribē*, not yet *tekhnē*. There is a *tekhnē* for speaking, but there is no *tekhnē* for listening.

How then does this assiduous, well-ordered practice, which is not yet a *tekhnē*, arise? Under what rule does it stand and what are its requirements? The problem is this: Since we are dealing with an ambiguous listening, with its part that is *pathētikos* and its *logikos* role, how can we preserve this *logikos* role while eliminating as much as possible the potentially harmful effects of involuntary passivity? In short, this reflected, applied practice of listening involves the purification of logical listening. How can we purify logical listening in the practice of the self?

Basically, by three means. The first, of course, is silence. This is an ancestral, age-old, even millennial rule in practices of the self, which was, as you know, emphasized and laid down by the Pythagoreans. The texts, and Porphyry's *Life of Pythagoras* in particular, repeat this.[16] Five years of silence was required of those who joined and were to be initiated into Pythagorean communities. Obviously, five years of silence does not mean that they had to remain totally silent for five years, but that someone who was still only a novice did not have the right to speak in all the exercises and practices of instruction and discussion, etcetera, in short, whenever dealing with the *logos* as true discourse and whenever participating in these practices and exercises of true discourse. He had to listen, only to listen and entirely without intervening, objecting, giving his opinion and, of course, without teaching. This, I think, is the meaning we should give to the famous rule of silence for five years. This theme, especially pronounced and developed in the Stoics, is found again in milder forms more adapted to everyday life in the texts I am talking about, mainly those of Plutarch and Seneca.[17] In Plutarch in particular there is a whole series of comments about the need for silence. They are found in the treatise *Peri tou akouein* I was talking about a short while ago, and then in another treatise devoted to talkativeness or chattering, this being of course, obviously, the immediate contrary of silence, the first vice we must cure ourselves of when we begin to learn and initiate ourselves into philosophy. Plutarch makes apprenticeship in silence an essential component of good education. Silence, he says—in *Concerning Talkativeness*—possesses something profound, mysterious, and sober.[18] It was the gods who taught men silence, and it was men who taught us to speak. And children who receive a truly noble and royal education learn first of all to keep silent and only learn to speak afterwards. As you know, this history of the system of silence with regard to language has played a role in spirituality, to which we will of course have to return. It has also played a very important role in systems of education. The principle that children must keep quiet before speaking is one that surprises us today, but it should not be forgotten that even some dozens of years ago, before the 1940 war at least, the child's education basically began with an apprenticeship of silence.[19] The idea that a child may speak freely was, from Greek and Roman Antiquity until modern Europe, banished from the system of education. So: education [in] silence. However, this is not what I want to emphasize, but the fact that, for Plutarch, not only should silence, the education of the gods, be the fundamental principle of the education of human beings, but we should impose a sort of strict economy of speech on ourselves. We should keep as quiet as we can. What does it mean to keep quiet as much as we can? It means, of course, that we should not speak when someone else is talking. But equally—and I think this is the important point of Plutarch's text on talkativeness—when we have heard something, when we hear a lesson, a sage speaking, or a poem recited, or a sentence quoted, at that moment we should surround our listening with an aura and crown of silence, as it were. We should not immediately convert what we have heard into speech. We should keep hold of it, in the strict sense, that is to say, preserve it and refrain from immediately converting it into words. Plutarch has fun with the idea that the chatterbox has a very curious physiological anomaly. The ear of the chatterbox, he jokes, is not connected directly with his soul, but rather with his tongue.[20] Consequently, scarcely has something been said than it immediately passes into speech and, of course, is lost. Everything the chatterbox receives through the ear immediately pours out, spills into what he says and, in spilling into what he says, what has been heard cannot have any effect on the soul itself. The chatterbox is always an empty vessel. And the chatterbox is incurable, since the passion for chatter, like the other passions, can only be cured by the *logos*. Now the chatterbox is someone who does not retain the *logos* and immediately lets it spill out into his own speech. Consequently the chatterbox cannot be cured unless he really wishes to keep quiet.[21] You'll say that none of this is either very serious or important. Once again, and I will try to show you this shortly, I think it is interesting to compare all these obligations concerning the language of the person being initiated, to the obligations of listening and speech found in Christian spirituality, where there is a completely different system of silence and speech.[22] So, the first rule, if you like, in the ascesis of listening, and for separating the *pathētikos* and dangerous aspect of listening from its *logikos* and positive aspect, is silence.

But of course this silence is not enough. More than silence, a certain active demeanor is called for. This demeanor is analyzed in different ways which are also quite interesting, despite their apparent banality. In the first place, listening requires a quite precise physical posture on the part of the listener, a posture clearly described in the texts of the period. This precise physical posture has a double function. First of all its function is to allow for maximum listening without any interference or fidgeting. The soul must take in the speech addressed to it without turmoil. Consequently, if the soul must be completely pure and undisturbed to listen to the speech addressed to it, then the body must stay absolutely calm. The body must express and as it were guarantee and seal the tranquility of the soul. Hence a very precise physical posture is required, as immobile as possible. However, and at the same time, in order to stress the soul's attention, in order to express it and make it follow exactly what is being said, the body must demonstrate through a number of signs that the soul really does understand and take in the *logos* as put forward and conveyed to it. There is then both a fundamental rule of the body's immobility, guaranteeing the quality of attention and the soul's transparency to what is going to be said, and at the same time a semiotic system which imposes tokens of attention by which the listener both communicates with the speaker and also assures himself that his attention is following the speaker's discourse.

There is a very interesting and explicit text about this. It is by Philo of Alexandria, from his *De Vita contemplative*, which I have already spoken about.[23] As you know this involves the description of a spiritual group called the *Therapeutae*, whose objective is to treat and save their souls. These *Therapeutae*, then, who live in a closed community, have a number of practices which include banquets during which someone takes the floor and teaches [...] the listener or those seated and participating in the banquet, and then the youngest, least integrated listeners who remain standing around the edges. Now, he says, everyone must maintain the same posture. First, they must turn towards the speaker (*eis auton*). They must turn towards him while keeping "*epi mias kai tēs autēs skheseōs epimenontes*" (while holding themselves in the same *skhesis*, in the same, single and identical posture).[24] This refers then to the obligation of a fixed attention, guaranteed and expressed by immobility. As you know it also refers to something that is very interesting from the point of view of, let's say, the bodily culture of Antiquity: this is the always unfavorable judgment of fidgeting and all involuntary and spontaneous movements of the body, etcetera. The body's immobility, its modeling, the statuesque form of the immobile body, as immobile as possible, is very important. It is very important as a guarantee of morality. It is also very important for imparting maximum semantic value to the speaker's gestures, to the gestures of the person who wants to convince, to gestures that constitute a very precise language. For this language to be very precise, effective, and meaningful, the body itself must again be completely immobile, smooth, and statuelike when in its usual state and one is not speaking. A number of texts refer to the bad moral and intellectual quality of the person who is always fidgeting and making unseemly gestures. This unseemliness of gestures and perpetual mobility of the body is nothing other than the physical version of *stultitia*,[25] which, as you know, is that perpetual restlessness of the soul, mind, and attention, which wanders from one subject to another, from one point of attention to another, which is constantly flitting about and which also has its moral version in the bearing of the *effeminatus*,[26] of the man who is effeminate in the sense of being passive in relation to himself, unable to exercise *egkrateia*, mastery or sovereignty, over the self. All of this is interconnected. On this need for physical immobility, which Philo is talking about, I would like to read you a more or less contemporary text, which comes from Seneca's letter 52, in which he says: You know, you should not behave at school as you do at the theatre.[27] "If you examine them carefully, everything in the world reveals itself through all kinds of external signs, and the smallest details may be enough to give an indication of morality. The man of loose morals [*impudicus*: it is interesting that he uses this word, which has more or less the same meaning as *effeminatus*, indicating bad sexual habits but [also], generally, a bad morality and, again, the expression of the conduct, the typical restlessness of *stultitia* in the realm of *ēthos*; M.F.] is betrayed by his gait, by a movement of the hand, sometimes by a single answer, by his touching his head with a finger [and scratching the top of his head: all of this is a sign of bad mores and bad morality; M.F.]²⁸ ... The cheat is betrayed by his laugh; the madman by his face and general appearance. These defects are revealed by certain perceptible marks. But do you want to plumb the character of an individual? Observe how he gives and receives praise. [Thus in the philosophy class, it happens that—M.F.] everywhere admiring hands are raised and applaud in praise of the philosopher; his head disappears beneath the crowd of enthusiastic listeners. He is covered with praise, or rather, with yells. Let us leave these noisy demonstrations to the professions whose aim is to entertain the people. Let philosophy receive our silent admiration."²⁹ I come back then to Philo's text on the need to maintain one and the same posture for the right listening to the word of truth, without external agitation and gesture. However, he says, while maintaining this posture, first of all the disciples—those listening at the banquet—must indicate that they are following and have understood (that they are following: *sunienai*; that they have understood: *kateilēphenai*). They must show that they follow and have understood. Second, if they approve, and to show they approve, they must express this by a smile and a slight movement of the head. And finally, if they wish to indicate that they are confused, that they do not follow, well, they must gently shake their head and raise the forefinger of the right hand, the gesture we too have all learned at school.³⁰ So, you see that there is this double register of statuesque immobility, which guarantees the quality of attention and thus allows the *logos* to penetrate the soul, but also this semiotic game of the body by which the listener both signals his attention, and indicates to himself and assures himself, as it were, that he really does follow and really has understood, and which also, at the same time, guides the speaker's rhythm, guides the rhythm of the discourse and the speaker's explanations. So a sort of active and meaningful silence is required of the good listener of philosophy. This is the first aspect of the, as it were, physical regulation of attention, of correct attention and correct listening.

There is also a regulation, or rather a more general principle, concerning demeanor in general. This is that being good at listening to the true discourse does not in fact entail only this precise physical posture. Listening, being good at listening to philosophy, should be a kind of commitment, a kind of demonstration of the listener's will, which arouses and supports the master's discourse. I think this is a quite important element, especially of course if we refer it back to Plato, or rather, to Plato's first Socratic dialogues. There are two passages in Epictetus about the correct demeanor to be adopted in general towards the person who tells the truth. These two passages are found in the second book of the *Discourses* and in the first discourse of book III. Both involve a little scene in which we see two young people, very pleasant, nice, perfumed and curly-haired, etcetera, who listen to Epictetus and seek the master's guidance. Now Epictetus greets these young people with his refusal. Or, anyway, he shows his great reluctance to accept their listening. The way in which Epictetus explains his refusal is interesting. In one case in particular it involves a young man, one of those perfumed young men then. He has followed his teaching and then, after a time, gets cross and says to Epictetus: Okay then, I have learned nothing from your teaching. What's more, you haven't paid any attention to me. It's as if I wasn't here: "I often came to you, and you never gave me an answer."[31] The young man continues his complaint. He says: You have not answered me although "I am wealthy," although "I am handsome," although "I am powerful," and although I am a good orator. He has then, and this is an important element, been taught rhetoric and knows how to speak. Epictetus answers him: Oh, you know, there are people wealthier than you; there are people more handsome than you; I know many other powerful people, and better orators as well. This is an old argument constantly found in the Cynic or Stoic diatribe: However wealthy a man may be, there is someone wealthier than him; however powerful a king may be, God is even more powerful, etcetera. Epictetus answers in this way. And after giving this answer he adds: "This is all that I have to say to you [that there is someone wealthier, more handsome, stronger, and a better orator than you; M.F.], and furthermore even this I don't really have the heart to tell you."[32] And why don't you have the heart to tell me, the young man asks. Well, because you have not stimulated me, you have not aroused me. And this "you have not stimulated me" (*erethizein*)[33] refers to a passage coming a bit before this in which Epictetus says to his listener: "Show me, then, what I can get from discussion with you. Arouse my desire [*kinēson moi prothumian*: encourage my desire to discuss with you; M.F.]."³⁴ In this passage Epictetus makes two comparisons. He says: You really must arouse my desire, because one can't do anything without a certain desire. For example, the sheep is only moved to graze if it is shown a green meadow. Or, a knight's interest in a horse is only stimulated when the horse has a fine appearance. So, he says, in the same way: "When you wish to listen to a philosopher, do not ask him, 'What have you got to say to me?' Be content to show you can listen competently [*deiknue sauton empeiron tou akouein*: show yourself skilled, experienced in listening; M.F.]."³⁵ We have the same notion of *empeiria* that I spoke about a moment ago: you must show you can listen competently, therefore, and you will see how then you will stimulate him to speak. This little scene, like the one in the first discourse of book III,³⁶ is interesting in the first place because of the minor character, the arrival of the young man. And clearly there is a definite reference here to Alcibiades, who also came to seduce Socrates and whom Socrates resisted. The *egkrateia* (self-control) of the philosophy teacher is sealed by his reluctance to succumb either to the real and intrinsic beauty of Alcibiades or, with all the more reason of course, to the vain coquetry of these youths. But on the other hand, by appearing so got up, the young man clearly shows that he is not able to give genuine and effective attention to true discourse. He cannot really listen to philosophy properly when he turns up perfumed and with his hair curled, etcetera, for he thereby attests to being interested only in ornament, illusion, and, in short, all the arts of flattery. This is the suitable student for the teacher of rhetoric. An obvious reference to the Socratic theme is also found on the master's side inasmuch as he (Epictetus), like Socrates, resists being bewitched by the beauty of boys. However, you recall that whatever resistance Socrates put up to physical seduction, his interest in his student was based all the same on his love for Alcibiades, or if not for Alcibiades, at any rate for the beauty of the soul displayed by those who pursued Socrates and requested discussion or direction from him. The physical and spiritual beauty of the student was indispensable, as well as the master's *erōs*. In Epictetus [rather], it will be very different. The rejection of the perfumed boy and the absence, apart from these perfumed boys, of any other reference in Epictetus to a possible amorous bond between master and student, shows that by this time the need for *erōs* (for love and desire) in order to listen to the truth has been eliminated. The rejection of all the perfumed young men shows that Epictetus demands solely one thing from those in whom he will be interested. What the rejection of all adornment shows, what the elimination of everything that could belong to the arts of seduction shows is that through an assiduous, strict will, shorn of all adornment, affectation, flattery, and illusion, Epictetus [is only interested], and the master should only be interested, in the truth. Attention to the truth and solely attention to the truth entitles the master to be stimulated and encouraged to care for his student. Consequently we see that these youths do not stimulate the master and do not encourage him to speak. What I think appears clearly in this text by Epictetus is the de-eroticization of listening to the truth in the master's discourse.

So, I have talked about silence first of all, then about the rules of physical demeanor, of precise posture while listening, and of the body's general demeanor and the individual's relationship to his own body—this is what I was showing you with Epictetus. Now, a third set of listening rules: those concerning attention strictly speaking. I would like to return for a moment therefore to the passage in which Epictetus said that philosophical teaching had to pass through the *logos*, which implied a *lexis* and a number of choices of terms. Or again, I would like to return to the letter 108 in which Seneca talks about the benefits we may receive from philosophical instruction, even if we are passive. These two texts show clearly that philosophical discourse is not in fact wholly and entirely opposed to rhetorical discourse. Of course, philosophical discourse is meant to express the truth. But it cannot express it without ornament. Philosophical discourse should be listened to with all the active attention of someone who seeks the truth. But it also has effects that are due to its own materiality, as it were, to its own modeling, its own rhetoric. So there is no actual separation to be made, but in listening to this necessarily ambiguous discourse the listener's work must be precisely to direct his attention properly. What does directing his attention properly mean? Well, it means two things.

First, the listener must direct his attention to what was traditionally called *to pragma*. I'd like to point out that *to pragma* is not just "the thing." It is a very precise philosophical and grammatical term that designates the word's reference[37] (*Bedeutung*, if you like).[38] We must direct ourselves towards the expression's referent. Consequently, we must work at eliminating irrelevant points of view from what is said. Attention should not be directed towards the beauty of the form; it should not be directed towards the grammar and vocabulary; and it should not be directed even to the refutation of philosophical or sophistical quibbles. We must grasp what is said. We must grasp what is said by this *logos* of truth in the sole aspect which is of interest for philosophical listening. For the *pragma* (the referent) of philosophical listening is the true proposition insofar as it can be transformed into a precept of action. And here, if you will allow me a few more minutes, I would like to take up again letter 108, about which I have spoken and which is quite fundamental for this technique of listening. In this passage Seneca gives, I think, a good example of what this active, well-directed listening should be, which could be called the paraenetic listening to a text.[39] He takes as his example a quotation from Virgil's *Georgics*.[40] The text is simply this: "Time flies, time beyond repair."[41] Different forms of attention can be given to this single expression, this simple verse. What will the grammarian think about when he studies this verse: "Time flies, time beyond repair"? Well, it occurs to him that Virgil "always puts disease and old age together." He will make a number of references and cite other texts from Virgil in which there is this association between the flight of time, old age, and illness: "and indeed rightly, for old age is a disease which we cannot cure." Furthermore, what epithet does Virgil usually apply to old age? Well, says the grammarian, generally he employs the epithet "sad": " 'Here comes illness, sad old age.' " Or else he will quote this other text by Virgil: " 'It is the abode of pale disease and sad old age.' We shouldn't be surprised that everyone exploits the same subject according to their inclinations."[42] And the grammarian, the philologist, in short the person interested in the text, will enjoy finding more or less analogous references in Virgil's text. But "the person whose eyes are turned towards philosophy"[43] will see that Virgil never says only that the days "go by." He says that the days "fly." Time "flies," which is the quickest kind of movement. What Virgil says, or anyway what the philosopher must hear, is: "our finest days are also the first to be snatched away; why, then, do we delay to increase our speed to keep up with the thing which is the quickest to flee us? The best of the batch flies past and the bad takes its place. The purest wine flows from the top of the amphora; the thickest, the dregs always fall to the bottom. Thus in our life, the best is at the start. Shall we leave it to others to use it up, keeping only the dregs for ourselves? Let us engrave this on our soul, take it in like a heavenly oracle": time flies, time beyond repair.[44] Okay, you can see two types of commentary: the philological and grammatical commentary, which Seneca dismisses and which consists in finding similar quotations, detecting word associations, etcetera. And then there is philosophical, paraenetic listening, which involves starting from a proposition, an affirmation, an assertion—"time flies"—and gradually, by meditating on it, by transforming it piece by piece into a precept of action, arriving at a rule not only for one's conduct, but for living generally, and making this affirmation something engraved in our soul like an oracle. Philosophical attention then is attention directed towards a *pragma*, which is a referent, a *Bedeutung*, comprising both the idea itself and that in the idea which can and must become a precept.

Finally, another way of focusing our attention in correct philosophical listening is immediately to set about memorizing what we have heard in terms of both the truth expressed and the prescription given. As soon as one has heard something from the mouth of the person uttering it, it must be taken in, understood, firmly grasped by the mind, so that it does not immediately escape. From this follows a series of traditional counsels of this ethic of listening: When you have heard someone say something important, do not start quibbling straightaway but try to collect yourself and spend some moments in silence, the better to imprint what you have heard, and undertake a quick self-examination when leaving the lesson you have listened to, or the conversation you have had, take a quick look at yourself in order to see where you are, whether you have heard and learned something new with regard to the equipment (the *paraskeuē*) you already have at hand, and thus see to what extent and how far you have been able to improve yourself. On this theme Plutarch makes a comparison with what happens at the hairdressing salon. We don't leave the hairdressing salon without casting a discreet glance in the mirror to see how we look. So, in the same way, after a philosophical discourse, after a philosophical lesson, listening must be concluded with this quick inspection of ourselves in order to establish our position with regard to the truth—whether the lesson heard has really brought us closer to the truth, whether it has enabled us to appropriate it—so as to see if we are really in the process of *facere suum* (making it our own). In sum, good philosophical listening involves a necessary work of attention, of a double and forked attention. On the one hand looking towards the *pragma*, towards a specifically philosophical signification in which assertion is equivalent to prescription. And then, on the other, a looking at ourselves in which, memorizing what we have heard, we see it embedding itself and gradually becoming subject in the soul that listens. The soul that listens must keep watch on itself. In paying proper attention to what it hears it pays attention to what it hears as signification, as *pragma*. It also pays attention to itself so that, through this listening and memory, the true thing gradually becomes the discourse that it clutches to itself. This is the first point of this subjectivation of true discourse, which is the final and constant objective of philosophical ascesis. Okay, that is what I had to tell you about listening. Forgive me, it was somewhat anecdotal. In a moment I will talk about the problem of "reading/writing," and then "speech."

1. See lectures at the Collège de France, 5 and 12 March, 1980.
2. *Facere suum* is found in Seneca, but in the sense of appropriating something; see letter CXIX, concerning Alexander and his thirst for possession: "*quaerit quod suum faciat*," Seneca, *Letters*, CXIX.7. On the other hand we find other expressions like *se facere*: "*facio me et formo*" in *On the Happy Life*, XIV.4, or *fieri suum*: "it is a priceless good to belong to oneself (*Inaestimabile bonum est suum fieri*)." *Letters*, LXXV.18.
3. Plutarch, *On Listening*.
4. "I think you would not experience any displeasure in reading as preamble these remarks on the sense of hearing, which Theophrastus claims is of all the senses most connected to the passions (*pathētikōtatēn*). Nothing we may see, taste or touch produces so much panic, disorder and turmoil as those which grip the soul when certain ringing, crashing and screeching noises strike our hearing." Ibid., 37f-38a.
5. See Homer, *The Odyssey*, book XII, 160-200.
6. See the lengthy exposition on the rejection of the poet-imitator and the condemnation of sensual melodies in book III of *The Republic*, 397a-399e.
7. "But this sense has more links with reason (*logikōtera*) than with the passions." Plutarch, *On Listening*, 38a.
8. Seneca, *Letters*, CVIII.4.
9. "What is a philosophy school? It is an *iatreion* (a clinic). When you leave the philosophy school you should not have taken pleasure but have suffered. For you do not enter the philosophy school because you are in good health. One arrives with a dislocated shoulder, another with an abscess, the third with a fistula, and another with a headache." Epictetus, *Discourses*, III.xxiii.30.
10. "Such is the virtue of philosophy that all benefit from it, proselytes and just those who gather round (*ea philosophiae vis est ut non studentis, sed etiam conversantis iuvet*)." Seneca, *Letters*, CVIII.4.
11. Ibid.
12. "What! Do we not know some who have camped in front of a philosopher for years without taking from him just the slightest tinge? Certainly I know them: they are models of perseverance and assiduity who, in my view, are not so much disciples (*non discipulos philosophorum*) as tenants of the school (*inquilinos*)." Ibid., CVIII.5.
13. Epictetus, *Discourses*, II.xxiii.40.
14. "Since teaching the principles must necessarily use a certain diction (*lexis*) and a certain subtlety in the wording, there are people who let themselves be captivated and stay where they are (*katamenousin autou*); one is captivated by style (*lexis*), another by syllogisms." Ibid., xxiii.40-41.
15. "In the one [medicine] as in the other [rhetoric], we must proceed to the analysis of a nature: in the first that of the body, in the other that of the soul, if rather than contenting ourselves with routine (*tribē*) and experience (*empeiria*) we wish to have recourse to art (*tekhnē*)." Plato, *Phaedrus*, 270b.
16. "An exceptional silence prevailed amongst them." Porphyry, *Vie de Pythagore*, §19, p. 44. See also what Isocrates says in his *Busiris* concerning the disciples of Pythagoras: they "are more admired in their silence than the people who accorded speech the greatest reputation" (*Busiris*, §29), as well as the crucial pages of Iamblichus in his *Life of Pythagoras*, §72: "After these three years [of previous examination], he imposed a silence of five years on those who were attached to him, in order to check how far they had mastered themselves, for the most difficult mastery is the mastery one imposes on one's tongue"; but see again in the same sense: "First, then, to examine thoroughly those who came to him, he observed if they could 'hold their tongue' (*ekhemuthein*), this was the actual term he used, he examined if they could keep silent and keep to themselves what they had heard during the instruction they had received. Then he observed if they were modest and concerned themselves more with silence than with speech." Iamblichus, id., §90.

17. "let philosophy have our silent admiration." Seneca, *Letters*, LII.13.
18. "Silence has something profound, religious and sober." Plutarch, *On Talkativeness*, 504a §4.
19. For a personal testimony of education in silence see "Michel Foucault: An Interview by Stephen Riggins," in *Ethics: Subjectivity and Truth*, pp. 121-22; French translation by F. Durand-Bogaert, "Un interview de Michel Foucault par Stephen Riggins," in *Dits et Écrits*, vol. 4, p. 525.
20. "Assuredly the auditory behavior of these people is not at all opened in the direction of the soul, but of the tongue." Plutarch, *On Talkativeness*, 502d §1.
21. "It is a difficult and arduous cure that philosophy undertakes with regard to chatter; the remedy it actually employs, speech, requires listeners, and the chatterers do not listen to anyone because they are constantly talking." Ibid., 502b, §1.
22. For a comparison of the rules of silence in Pythagorean and Christian communities, see A.-J. Festugière, "Sur le *De Vita Pythagorica* de Jamblique," *in Études de philosophie grecque*, pp. 447-51 in particular.
23. See the lecture of 20 January, second hour.
24. "The audience, with attentive ear, eyes fixed on him (*eis auton*), listen to him, remaining immobile in the same position (*epi mias kai tēs autēs skheseōs epimenontes*)." Philo, *On the Contemplative Life*, 483M, IX.77.
25. On *stultitia*, see lecture of 27 January, first hour.
26. With regard to this character, the *effeminatus*, see Foucault's comments in *L'usage des plaisirs*, p. 25 (*The Use of Pleasure*, p. 19).
27. "Do not confuse the cheers of the theater and those of the school: even in praise there is a certain propriety to be observed." Seneca, *Letters*, LII.12.
28. In his edition of Seneca, Paul Veyne notes: "scratching the head with one finger, an 'autistic' action, lacked virile dignity; it was a feminine gesture" (p. 720).
29. Seneca, *Letters*, LII.12-13.
30. "With a nod of the head, a look, they indicate that they have understood (*sunienai kai kateilēphenai*); with a smile, a slight movement of the forehead, they show that they approve of the speaker; with a slow movement of the head and with the forefinger of the right hand, they show that they are confused." Philo, *On the Contemplative Life*, 483M, IX.77.
31. Epictetos, *Discourses*, II.xxiv.1.
32. Ibid., xxiv.27.
33. "Because you have not stimulated me (*ouk ērethisas*)." Ibid., xxiv.28.
34. Ibid., xxiv.15-16.
35. Ibid., xxiv.29.
36. It involves the criticism of a "budding young rhetor" whose "hair was groomed far too much." Ibid., III.i.1. See the analysis of this text in the lecture of 20 January, first hour.
37. See P. Hadot's study in P. Aubenque, ed., *Concepts et Catégories dans la pensée antiqu* (Paris: Vrin, 1980), pp. 309-20.
38. On *Sinn* and *Bedeutung*, see Frege's famous "On Sense and Reference," in P. Geach and M. Black, eds., *Translations from the Philosophical Writings of Gottlob Frege* (Oxford: Basil Blackwell, 1970), pp. 56-78.
39. *Parénétique*: "related to *parénèse*, to moral exhortation" (*Littré*; see the verb *parainein*, which means to advise, to prescribe) [English: *Paraenetic*: hortatory, advisory; from *parainesis* (Greek), exhort]).
40. Sereca, *Letters*, CVIII.25.
41. "But time flies, flies without return (*sed fugit interea, fugit inreparabile tempus*)." Vergil, *Georgics*, book III, v. 284; French translation by H. Goelzer, *Les Géorgiques* (Paris: Les Belles Lettres, 1926); English translation by G.P. Goold in, *Eclogues, Georgics, Aenid I-VII* (Cambridge, Mass. and London: Loeb Classical Library, 1999).
42. Sereca *Letters*, CVIII.29.
43. Ibid., CVIII.25.
44. Actually, the phrase Seneca says should be engraved in the soul is: "The best of our days, for us poor mortals, are always the first to flee," and the verse cited is from the *Georgics*, book III, verse 66. Seneca also quotes this line in *On the Shortness of Life*, IX.2.

## eighteen

## 3 MARCH 1982

### Second hour

[ *The practical rules of correct listening and its assigned end: meditation.* ∼ *The ancient meaning of* meletē/meditatio *as exercise performed by thought on the subject.* ∼ *Writing as physical exercise of the incorporation of discourse.* ∼ *Correspondence as circle of subjectivation/veridiction.* ∼ *The art of speaking in Christian spirituality: the forms of the spiritual director's true discourse; the confession* (l'aveu) *of the person being directed; telling the truth about oneself as condition of salvation.* ∼ *The Greco-Roman practice of guidance: constitution of a subject of truth through the attentive silence of the person being guided; the obligation of* parrhēsia *in the master's discourse.* ]

[...] I WILL BE VERY brief on the questions of reading/writing because these are easier and better-known subjects, and also [because] I already went into too much detail in the previous lecture. Then I will move on quickly to the question of the ethics of speech. Quickly then, reading/writing first of all. Actually, the advice given, with regard to reading at least, arises from a common practice in Antiquity and which the principles of philosophical reading take up, but without fundamentally changing them. That is to say, first, read few books; read few authors; read few works; within these works, read a few passages; chose passages considered to be important and sufficient.[1] What's more, from this come all those well-known practices, like the summaries of works.

This practice was so widespread that it is often the reason that, fortunately, works have been preserved for us. We hardly know the details of the philosophy of Epicurus apart from some summaries, made by his students after his death, of certain propositions considered to be important and sufficient for those undergoing initiation and for those already initiated who need to reactualize or [rememorize] the fundamental principles of a doctrine which must not only be known, but must also be assimilated, and of which one must become the speaking subject, as it were. So, there is the practice of summaries. There is also the practice of anthologies, which bring together the propositions and reflections of different authors, either on a given subject or on a series of subjects. Or again, as was the case for Seneca with Lucilius, for example, there is the practice of noting down quotations from this or that author and then sending them to a correspondent, saying to him: Here is an important or an interesting phrase; I am sending it to you; reflect, meditate on it, etcetera. Obviously this practice rests on certain principles. I would like especially to emphasize that the object or end of philosophical reading is not to learn an author's work, and its function is not even to go more deeply into the work's doctrine. Reading basically involves—at any rate, its principal objective is—providing an opportunity for meditation.

So, we encounter here a notion that we will talk about again later, but on which all the same I would like to dwell for a moment today. This is this notion of "meditation." The Latin word *meditatio* (or the verb *meditari*) translates the Greek substantive *meletē*, the Greek verb *meletan*. This *meletē*, this *meletan*, has a very different meaning from what we today, that is to say in the nineteenth and twentieth centuries, call "meditation." The *meletē* is exercise. *Meletan* is very close to *gumnazein*, for example, which [signifies] "to practice," "to train oneself," but with a somewhat different connotation, however, a different center of gravity of the field of meaning if you like, inasmuch as *gumnazein* generally designates more a sort of test "in real life," a way of confronting the thing, as you confront an adversary, in order to find out if you can resist him or be the stronger, whereas the *meletan* is a sort of mental exercise, rather, an exercise "in thought," but which again is quite different from what we understand by meditation. We think of meditation as an attempt to think of something with a particular intensity without deepening its meaning, or letting our thought develop in a more or less regular order starting from the thing we are thinking about. For us meditation is a bit like that. For the Greeks and Latins the *meletē* or *meditatio* is something else. I think it should really be grasped in its two aspects. First, *meletan* is to perform an exercise of appropriation, the appropriation of a thought. With regard to a given text, it certainly does not involve trying to [think about] what it meant. It does not develop in the direction of exegesis at all. The *meditatio* involves, rather, appropriating [a thought] and being so profoundly convinced of it that we both believe it to be true and can also repeat it constantly and immediately whenever the need or opportunity to do so arises. It involves then ensuring that this truth is engraved in the mind in such a way that it is recalled immediately the need arises, and in such a way that we have it, you remember, *prokheiron* (ready to hand),[2] consequently making it a principle of action. It is an appropriation that consists in ensuring that, from this true thing, we become the subject who thinks the truth, and, from this subject who thinks the truth, we become a subject who acts properly. This is the direction taken by this exercise of *meditatio*. Second, the *meditatio*, and this is its other aspect, consists in making a sort of experiment, an experiment of identification. What I mean is that the *meditatio* involves not so much thinking about the thing itself as practicing the thing we are thinking about. Obviously the most famous example is the meditation of death.[3] Meditating death (*meditari, meletan*), in the sense that the Greeks and Latins understand this, does not mean thinking that your are going to die. It does not even mean convincing yourself that you really are going to die. It is not associating this idea with certain others that follow from it, etcetera. Meditating death is placing yourself, in thought, in the situation of someone who is in the process of dying, or who is about to die, or who is living his last days. The meditation is not therefore a game the subject plays with his own thought, with the object or possible objects of his thought. It is not something like eidetic variation, as we would say in phenomenology.[4] A completely different kind of game is involved: not a game the subject plays with his own thought or thoughts, but a game that thought performs on the subject himself. It is becoming, through thought, the person who is dying or whose death is imminent. Moreover, you see that this idea of meditation, not as the game the subject plays with his thought but as the game thought plays on the subject, is basically exactly what Descartes was still doing in the *Meditations*, and is indeed precisely the meaning he gave to "meditation."[5] So, a history of this practice of meditation should be undertaken: meditation in Antiquity; meditation in early Christianity; its resurgence, and anyway its new importance and dramatic rise in the sixteenth and seventeenth centuries. But in any case, when Descartes performs "meditations" and writes his *Meditations* in the seventeenth century, he does so in this sense. It does not involve a game the subject plays with his thoughts. Descartes is not thinking about everything in the world that could be doubtful. Neither is he thinking about what could not be doubted. Let's say that this is the usual skeptical exercise. Descartes puts himself in the position of the subject who doubts everything, without even wondering about everything that could be doubtful or what could be doubted. And he puts himself in the situation of someone setting out in search of the indubitable. This, then, is not at all an exercise carried out on thought and its content. It is an exercise by which, through thought, the subject puts himself in a certain situation. The subject is shifted with regard to what he is through the effect of thought, and this is basically the meditative function that philosophical reading, as it is understood in the period I am talking about, should have. This meditative function, as an exercise of the subject in which, through thought, he puts himself in a fictional situation in which he tests himself, explains why philosophical reading is, if not totally, at least to a considerable extent, indifferent to the author and context of the phrase or saying.

This explains the effect expected from the reading, which is not to have understood what an author meant, but the creation of an equipment of true propositions for yourself, which really is your own. There is, then, no eclecticism here. It is not a matter of putting together a hodgepodge of propositions from different places, but of building a solid framework of propositions that are valid as prescriptions, of true discourses that are at the same time principles of behavior. What's more, it is easy to see that if reading is conceived of in this way as an exercise, as an experiment, if reading is only for meditating, then it must be immediately linked to writing. We see in this what is undoubtedly an important cultural and social phenomenon of the period I am talking about; the considerable place occupied by, so to speak, personal and individual writing.[6] It is no doubt difficult to date the origin of the process exactly, but when we examine the period I am talking about, the first and second centuries A.D., we notice that writing has already become and is increasingly affirmed as part of the exercise of the self. Reading is extended, reinforced, and reactivated by writing, which is also an exercise, a component of meditation. Seneca said we should alternate between writing and reading. This is in letter 84: We should neither always write nor always read; the former of these activities (writing) will end up exhausting our energy if we keep at it constantly. The second, rather, lessens and dilutes our energy. We should temper reading by writing, and reciprocally, so that the written composition gives body (*corpus*) to what has been obtained by reading. Reading collects *orationes*, *logoi* (discourses, elements of discourse); we must make a *corpus* of them. This *corpus* is put together and assured by writing.[7] This obligation to write, the advice to write, is found continually in the precepts of existence and the rules of the practice of the self. For example, Epictetus offers this advice: We should meditate (*meletan*), write (*graphein*), and train (*gumnazein*).[8] You see then: *meletan*, the exercise of thought often supported by a text which one reads; then *graphein*, writing; and then *gumnazein*, that is to say, training in real life, trying to endure the trial, the test of reality. Or again, after writing a meditation on death, Epictetus concludes by saying: "May death take me while I am thinking, writing and reading these phrases."[9] Writing, then, is a part of exercise with the advantage of two possible and simultaneous uses. The use for oneself, as it were. For simply by writing we absorb the thing itself we are thinking about. We help it to be established in the soul and we help it to be established in the body, to become a kind of habit for the body, or at any rate a physical virtuality. It was a recommended custom to write after having read something, and after having written it, to read it again and, necessarily, read it again out loud since, as you know, words were not separated from each other in Greek and Latin script. That is to say, there was great difficulty in reading. The exercise of reading was not something easy: it was not a matter of just reading, like that, at sight. You had to stress the words properly, you had to utter them in a low voice. So the exercise of reading, writing, and rereading what you had written and the notes you had taken was an almost physical exercise of the assimilation of the truth and the *logos* you were holding on to. Epictetus says: "Keep these thoughts ready at hand (*prokheira*) night and day; put them into writing and read them."[10] The word for reading is the traditional one, *anagignōskein*, which is to say, precisely, to recognize, to recognize in this kind of jumble of signs which are difficult to separate and arrange properly, and so difficult to understand. So, one keeps one's thoughts. To keep our thoughts available, we must put them in writing and read them for ourselves. Let these thoughts "be the object of your conversation with yourself or with another: 'Can you help me in this matter?' And again, find another man and then another. Then, if something undesirable happens to you, you will find immediate relief in the thought that it was not unexpected."[11] Reading, writing, and rereading are part of that *praemeditatio malorum*, which I will talk about next week, or the week after,[12] and which is so important in Stoic asceticism. So, you write after reading so as to be able to reread, rereading to yourself and thus incorporating the true discourse you have heard from the mouth of another or have read under another's name. Writing is of use for yourself; but of course it also has a use, is useful to others. Ah, yes, I forgot to say that these notes which you should take on your reading, or on the conversations you have had, or on the lectures you have heard, are called in Greek, precisely, *hupomnēmata*.[13] That is to say, they are aids to memory. They are notes of memories thanks to which, through reading or memory exercises, you will be able to rememorize things said.[14]

These *hupomnēnata* are of use to oneself, but you can see also that they may be of use to others. And you can see that writing is an important activity in this flexible exchange of favors and benefits, in this flexible exchange of soul services in which we try to be of service to the other in his journey towards the good and towards himself. Here too is a very interesting cultural and social phenomenon of the period. We can see the extent to which what may be called, if you like, a spiritual correspondence—a correspondence of the soul from subject to subject whose end is not so much giving news about the political world (as was still the case, for example, in Cicero's correspondence with Atticus),[15] as giving each other news about ourselves, inquiring about what is happening in the other's soul, or asking the other to give news of what is taking place in him—became an extremely important activity at this time and which you can see has two sides. The correspondence involves allowing the one more advanced in virtue and the good to give advice to the other: he keeps himself informed about the other's condition and gives him advice in return. But, at the same time, you can see that this exercise allows the one who gives advice to rememorize the truths he passes on to the other but which he also needs for his own life. So by corresponding with the other and by serving him as guide, he continues, as it were, to perform personal exercises: he performs an exercise which is addressed to the other as well as to himself, and which enables him, through this correspondence, to maintain himself in a constant state of self-guidance. The advice you give to the other is equally given to yourself. All this is very easily made out in Seneca's letters to Lucilius. Clearly, Seneca gives lessons to Lucilius, but he does so using his *hupomnēmata*. We feel that he always has with him something like a notebook that he uses to recall his important readings, the ideas he has found and which he himself has read. He makes use of them, and in using them for the other, in making them available to the other, he reactivates them himself. For example, there is a letter to Lucilius, I no longer recall which one, but it copies out a letter to [Marullus] who had lost his son.[16] So it is very clear that one and the same letter has three uses. It is of use to Marullus who has lost his son, and Seneca advises him not to give way to excessive grief and to keep it within appropriate limits. Second, when copied out for Lucilius the same letter will serve the latter as an exercise for the day he suffers a misfortune, so he will have *prokheiron* (*ad manum*: ready to hand), the apparatus of truth which will allow him to struggle against this or a similar misfortune, when it arrives. And third, it is of use to Seneca himself as an exercise reactivating what he knows regarding the necessity of death, the probability of misfortune, etcetera. So there is a triple use of the same text. In a similar sense there is the beginning of Plutarch's treatise *Peri euthumias* (*On Tranquility of Mind*) in which Plutarch replies to one of his correspondents, Paccius, who must have said to him: Listen, I really need some advice, some urgent advice. Plutarch replies: I am terribly busy and really don't have the time to draft a complete treatise for you. So I am sending you a whole batch of my *hupomnēmata*. That is to say: I am sending you the notes I have managed to take on this subject of *euthumia*, tranquility of the soul.[17] And this is the treatise. Actually, it is likely even so that the treatise was somewhat rewritten and re-elaborated, but you see here a practice in which reading, writing, taking notes for oneself, correspondence, sending treatises, etcetera, together make up a very important activity in the care of oneself and the care of others.

It would be interesting—okay, these are tracks for those who would like to work on this—to compare these activities, the form and content of these activities of reading, taking notes, writing a sort of ship's log, and correspondence, with what takes place in sixteenth century Europe when, in the context both of the Reformation and of the return, precisely, to ethical forms or concerns quite similar to those of the first and second centuries, we also see the recurrence of this genre of notes, of the personal diary, the diary of life, the log book of existence, and then of correspondence. What is interesting is precisely that in the former texts—in correspondence like that to Lucilius or in treatises like Plutarch's—autobiography, the description of oneself in the unfolding course of one's life, actually plays a very small part, whereas autobiography is absolutely central when this genre reappears in the sixteenth century. Only, meanwhile, there will have been Christianity. And meanwhile there will have been Saint Augustine. And we will have moved on to a regime in which the subject's relationship to truth will not be governed simply by the purpose: "how to become a subject of veridiction," but will have become: "how to be able to say the truth about oneself." That's all on this subject: just an outline.

So then: listening, reading, and writing. Is there a regulation or requirements or precepts concerning speech in the practice of the self and in this art of the practice of the self? I am well aware that the question I am asking has no meaning, or could only exist and be expressed on the basis of an anachronism or, anyway, of a retrospective view. Obviously I only ask it from the moment that, and due to the fact that, there is an extraordinarily complex, complicated, and extremely important development of the art of speaking in Christian spirituality and the Christian pastoral. Actually, we will see this art of speaking developing at two levels in the Christian pastoral and Christian spirituality. On the one hand there will be, of course, the art of speaking on the part of the master. The master's art of speaking is both founded but also, at the same time, made much more complicated and relativized, so to speak, by the fact that there is, of course, a fundamental speech: Revelation. There is a fundamental writing: the Text. The whole of the master's speech must be ordered with regard to [these]. Nevertheless, even if the master's speech refers back to this fundamental speech, it remains the case that it exists in different forms and with multiple strands in Christian spirituality and the Christian pastoral. There will be the function of instruction strictly speaking: teaching the truth. There will be an activity of paraenesis, that is to say of prescription. There will also be the function of the spiritual director, the function [again] of the master of penance and of the confessor, which is not the same function as spiritual director.[18] All these distinct roles of teaching, preaching, confession, and spiritual guidance are undertaken in the ecclesiastical institution either by one and the same person, or, much more often, by different people, with all the doctrinal, practical, and institutional conflicts [to which] this may give rise. Okay, let us leave this. However, what I would like to emphasize today is that in Christian spirituality the master's discourse with its different forms, rules, tactics, and institutional supports [undoubtedly exists], but for the analysis I want to make, what seems to me to be important, what is remarkable, is the fact that even so the person being guided—the person who must be led to the truth and to salvation, the person who consequently is still in the realm of ignorance and perdition—has something to say. He has something to say and he has to say a truth. Only what is this truth that the person led to the truth has to say, what is this truth that the person directed, the person lead by another to the truth, has to say? It is the truth about himself. It is, I think, an absolutely crucial moment in the history of subjectivity in the West, or in the relations between subjectivity and truth, when the task and obligation of truth-telling about oneself is inserted within the procedure indispensable for salvation, within techniques of the development and transformation of the subject by himself, and within pastoral institutions. Of course, this is not a precise and definite moment and is in fact a whole complex process with breaks, conflicts, slow evolutions, sudden surges, etcetera. But still, if we take a historical overview on all this, I think we should consider it a highly significant event in the relations between the subject and truth when truth-telling about oneself became a condition of salvation, a fundamental principle in the subject's relationship to himself, and a necessary element in the individual's membership of a community. The day, if you like, when refusal to confess at least once a year was grounds for excommunication.[19]

Now the subject's obligation to tell the truth about himself, or this fundamental principle that we must be able to say the truth about ourselves in order to be able to establish a relationship to truth in general in which we will be able to find our salvation, did not exist at all in Greek, Hellenistic, or Roman Antiquity. The person who is led to the truth through the master's discourse does not have to say the truth about himself. He does not even have to say the truth. And since he does not have to say the truth, he does not have to speak. It is necessary and sufficient that he keep quiet. In the history of the West, the person who is directed and led only gets the right to speak within the obligation of telling the truth about himself, that is to say in the obligation of confession. Of course, you will say that in the Greek, Hellenistic, and Roman art of oneself, we find (there are examples of) elements along these lines which are comparable to, or that a retrospective look could define as an anticipation of, the future "confession." There are procedures of confession, of the acknowledgement of fault, which are required, or recommended at least, in judicial institutions or in religious practices.[20] There are also, and I will return to this in more detail,[21] a number of practices which are in fact exercises in the examination of conscience; practices of consultation in which the individual seeking advice is obliged to speak about himself. We also find the obligation to be frank with one's friends and to say everything one has on one's mind. However, all these elements seem to me to be profoundly different from what we should call "confession" in the strict, or anyway, spiritual sense of the word.[22] All these obligations for the person being guided to tell the truth, speak frankly to his friend, to confide in his guide, to tell him at any rate where he has got to, are instrumental obligations, as it were. To confess is to appeal to the indulgence of the gods or judges. It is to assist the soul's doctor by providing him with a number of diagnostic elements. It is to demonstrate one's progress by having the courage to confess a fault. All of this, then, is found in Antiquity with this instrumental meaning. But these elements of confession are instrumental, they are not effective modifiers that bring about a change by themselves. As such they do not have a spiritual value. And I think that one of the most remarkable features of the practice of the self in this period is that the subject must become a subject of truth. He must be concerned with true discourse. He must therefore carry out a subjectivation that begins with listening to the true discourses proposed to him. He must therefore become the subject of truth: he himself must be able to say the truth and he must be able to say it to himself. In no way is it necessary or indispensable that he tell the truth about himself. You will tell me that there are all the same many fundamental texts proving that the person being guided, the student or the disciple, has the right to speak. After all, the long history or tradition of the dialogue, from Socrates to the Stoic-Cynic diatribe, clearly shows that the other, if you like, or the person being guided, must and can speak. But we should note that in this tradition, from the Socratic dialogue to the Stoic-Cynic diatribe, the dialogue, diatribe, or discussion does not involve getting the subject to tell the truth about himself. It simply involves testing him, trying him out as a subject capable of telling the truth. Through Socratic questioning, through those kinds of insolent and offhand questionings of the Stoic-Cynic diatribe, it is a matter either of demonstrating to the subject that he knows what he didn't think he knew—which Socrates does—or of showing him that he doesn't know what he thought he knew—which Socrates also does, as well as the Stoics and Cynics. It involves as it were testing him as a subject speaking the truth in order to force him to be aware of the stage he has reached in this subjectivation of true discourse, in his ability to speak the truth. So I do not think that there is really any problem on the side of the discourse of the person being guided, since he does not have to speak, or else what he is made to say is merely a certain way for the master's discourse to get a hold and develop. The discourse of the person being guided has no autonomy; it has no function of its own. Basically, its role is silence. And the kinds of speech dragged, extorted, or extracted from him, or provoked in him through the dialogue or the diatribe, are basically ways of showing that the truth exists wholly and solely in the master's discourse.

There is a problem then: What is involved in the case of the master's discourse? In this ascetic game, that is to say, what part is played by the master's discourse and how he deploys it in this game of the progressive subjectivation of true discourse? This is where I think we encounter the notion we have referred to several times and the examination of which I would like to begin today: the notion of *parrhēsia*. *Parrhēsia* is basically what on the master's side corresponds to the disciple's obligation of silence. Just as the disciple must keep quiet in order to bring about the subjectivation of his discourse, so the master's discourse must obey the principle of *parrhēsia* if, at the end of his action and guidance, he wants the truth of what he says to become the subjectivized true discourse of his disciple. Etymologically, *parrhēsia* is the act of telling all (frankness, open-heartedness, plain speaking, speaking openly, speaking freely). The Latins generally translate *parrhēsia* as *libertas*. It is the openness which makes us speak, which makes us say what has to be said, what we want to say, what we think ought to be said because it is necessary, useful, and true. *Libertas* or *parrhēsia* seems to be primarily a moral quality that basically is demanded of every speaking subject. When speaking entails telling the truth, how could there not be a kind of fundamental pact imposed on everyone who speaks that they speak the truth because they believe it to be true? However, and I would like to stress this, in philosophy, in the art of the self, in the practice of the self I am talking about, this general moral sense of the word *parrhēsia* takes on a very precise technical meaning, which I think is very interesting with regard to the role of language and speech in the spiritual ascesis of philosophers. There are a thousand proofs and indications of this technical meaning. I will just take a fairly short text written by Arrian as a preface to the *Discourses* of Epictetus, since, as you know, the texts by Epictetus which have come down to us represent only a part of his discourses, those preserved by one of his listeners, Arrian, precisely in the form of these *hupomnēmata* I have just been talking about.[23] So, Arrian listens, takes notes, makes *hupomnēmata*, and decides to publish them. He decides to publish them because many texts were circulating under the name of Epictetus at this time, and he wanted to provide a version which was, of course, his own, but which seemed to him to be the most reliable and so the only authentic version. But authentic to what in the discourses of Epictetus? In the short page introducing the *Discourses*, Arrian says: "everything I heard from this man I endeavored to write down (*grapsamenos*) while he was speaking."[24] So, then, there is listening to the speech. He listens, and then he writes. Having written as much as possible word for word—he uses the term *onoma*—"word for word, I endeavored to preserve it *emautō* (for myself), *eis husteron* (for the future) in the form of *hupomnēmata*."

Here again is everything I have just been telling you. One listens, writes, and transcribes what has been said. Arrian draws attention to having truly summarized "word for word." And he makes *hupomnēmata*, kinds of notes of what has been said. He makes them *emautō* (for himself), *eis husteron* (for future use), that is to say with a view to constituting a *paraskeuē* (an equipment), which will permit him to use it all when the occasion arises of various events, dangers, misfortunes, etcetera. Now he is going to publish these *hupomnēmata*, which represent what? "*Dianoia kai parrhēsia*": Epictetus's own thought and free speech. The existence and juxtaposition, then, of these two notions appears to be, I believe, utterly important. By publishing the *hupomnēmata* made for himself, Arrian takes on the task then of reconstructing what other publications were unable to give: *dianoia*, the thought, the content of Epictetus's thought in his discourses; and then *parrhēsia*, his free speech. And we could say, and I will stop here, to continue next week the study of this *parrhēsia*, that basically what is involved in *parrhēsia* is that particular kind of rhetoric, or nonrhetorical rhetoric, which philosophical discourse must employ. Then of course, you are well aware of the enormous division, the enormous conflict that constantly set philosophy and rhetoric against each other from Classical Greece to the end of the Roman Empire.[25] You are aware of the intensity of this conflict in the period I am talking about (first and second centuries) and the acute crisis that developed in the second century. In actual fact, *parrhēsia* should be defined within the space of this conflict. *Parrhēsia* is the necessary form of philosophical discourse, since—as Epictetus himself said, you recall, in a discourse I spoke about a short while ago[26]—when we employ the *logos*, there is necessarily a *lexis* (a way of saying things) and the choice of particular words rather than others. Therefore, there can be no philosophical *logos* without this kind of body of language with its own qualities, its own figures, and its own necessary effects at the level of pathos. But if you are a philosopher, it is not the art or *tekhnē* of rhetoric that is needed to control these elements (verbal elements, elements whose function is to act directly on the soul). It must be this other thing, which is both a technique and an ethics, an art and a morality, and which is called *parrhēsia*. If the disciple's silence is to be fruitful, if the master's truthful words are to settle properly in the depths of this silence, and if the disciple is to make of these words something of his own which will one day entitle him to become a subject of veridiction himself, then the master's discourse must not be an artificial, sham discourse subservient to the rules of rhetoric, seeking only to produce effects of pathos in the disciple's soul. It must not be a discourse of seduction. It must be a discourse that the disciple's subjectivity can appropriate and by which, by appropriating it, the disciple can reach his own objective, namely himself. For this a certain number of rules are necessary on the master's side, rules that once again do not focus on the truth of the discourse, but on the way in which this discourse of truth is formulated. And this is *parrhēsia*, *libertas*, the rules for the expression of the discourse of truth. Okay, next week I will try to explain these rules of the discourse of truth, seen from the angle of the master.

1. "Expenditure on literature, the most elevated one can make, is only reasonable if measured. What is the good of countless books and libraries whose titles the owner can scarcely read through in his lifetime? Abundant reading burdens the mind, but does not furnish it, and it is much better to attach yourself to a few authors than wander about everywhere." Seneca, *On Tranquility of Mind*, IX.4.
2. See lecture of 24 February, second hour.
3. This death meditation is analyzed in the lecture of 24 March, second hour.
4. Eidetic variation refers to the method by which, for a given existent, one disengages the invariant kernel of meaning constitutive of its being, otherwise called its *eidos*. The variation proposes a series of deformations imposed by the imagination on an existent, these deformations revealing limits beyond which the existent is no longer itself and thus making possible the definition of an invariable of meaning (its essence). "Eidetic" thus designates less the variation itself than its result.
5. It should be noted that, in his reply to Derrida (1972), Foucault had already determined the meaning of Cartesian meditation outside of the establishment of pure rules of method, but in irreducible processes of subjectivation: "a 'meditation' produces, as so many discursive events, new utterances that carry with them a series of modifications of the enunciating subject... In meditation, the subject is ceaselessly altered by his own movement; his discourse provokes effects within which he is caught; it exposes him to risks, makes him pass through trials or temptations, produces states in him, and confers on him a status or qualification he did not hold at the initial moment. In short, meditation implies a mobile subject modifiable through the effects of the discursive events that take place." Michel Foucault, "Mon corps, ce papier, ce feu" in *Dits et Écrits*, vol.2, p. 257; English translation by Robert Hurley et al., "My Body, This Paper, This Fire," in *Aesthetics, Method, and Epistemology*, pp. 405-06.
6. Foucault planned to publish a collection of articles devoted to practices of the self. One of these articles was entitled precisely "self writing (*l'écriture de soi*)" in the first century A.D. See, "L'écriture de soi," in *Dits et Écrits*, vol.4, pp. 415-30; English translation by Robert Hurley et al., "Self Writing," in *Ethics: Subjectivity and Truth*, pp. 207-22.
7. "We should no more confine ourselves to writing than we should to reading. The first will depress and exhaust the spiritual energy. The second will overexcite and dilute it. We should have recourse to each of them in turn and temper one by means of the other in such a way that the written composition embodies (*stilus redigat in corpus*) what we have gathered from reading (*quicquid lectione collectum est*)." Seneca, *Letters*, LXXXIV.2.
8. "These are the thoughts that philosophers should meditate, these they write down every day, these that should be the material of their exercise (*tauta edei meletan tous philosophountas, tauta kath'hēmeran graphein, en toutois gumnazesthai*)." Epictetus, *Discourses*, I.i.25.
9. Ibid., III.v.11.
10. Ibid., III.xxiv.103.
11. Ibid., III.xxiv.103-04.
12. See lecture of 24 March, first hour.
13. On the *hupomnēmata*, see Foucault's clarifications in "L'écriture de soi," pp. 418-23 ("Self Writing," pp. 209-14).
14. In Greek, *hupomnēmata* actually has a broader meaning than that of a simple collection of quotations or things said in the form of notes. In the broader sense it designates any commentary or form of written memory. See the article *commentarium, commentaries*—Latin translation of *hupomnēmata*—of the *Dictionnaire des antiquités grecques et romaines*, ed. E. Saglio, vol. I-2, pp. 1404-08. However, it may also designate daily personal notes and reflections without necessarily involving quotations. See P. Hadot, *La Citadelle intérieure*, p. 38 and pp. 45-49 (*The Inner Citadel*, p. 24 and pp. 30-34).

15. Cicero, *Letters to Atticus*, edited and translation D. R. Shackleton Bailey, Cambridge, Mass.: Harvard University Press, Loeb Classical Library, 1999, 4 volumes.
16. It is letter XCIX, in which Seneca copies for Lucilius a letter to Marullus.
17. "I received your letter too late in which you asked me to write to you on the tranquility of the soul... I have not had the time I would have liked to do as you ask, but nor could I bear the idea that this man, coming from me, would arrive at your home empty handed. I have therefore put together some notes (*hupomnētmatōn*) which I made for my own use." Plutarch, *On Tranquility of Mind*, 464e-f, 1.
18. On all these points, see the lectures at the Collège de France from 6 February to 26 March 1980 during which, within the general theoretical framework defined as the study of truth obligations, Foucault examines the connection between the manifestation of the truth and the remission of sins on the basis of the problems of baptism, canonic penitence, and spiritual direction. Reference should also be made to the lectures of 19 and 26 February 1975, in which Foucault examines the development of the pastoral: Michel Foucault, *Les Anormaux. Cours au Collège de France, 1974-1975*, ed. V. Marchetti and A. Salomoni (Paris: Gallimard/Seuil, 1999); English translation by Graham Burchell, *Abnormal: Course at the Collège de France, 1974-1975* (New York: Picador, 2003).
19. On the transition from a technique of confession (*aveu*), restricted to monastic settings, to a practice of generalized confession (*confession*), see *La Volonté de savoir*, pp. 28-29 and pp. 84-86 (*The History of Sexuality. Volume 1: An Introduction*, pp. 18-21 and pp. 63-64).
20. Foucault began the analysis of confessional procedures in the judicial system right from the first courses at the Collège de France, 1970-1971 ("La Volonté de savoir," course summary in *Dits et Écrits*, pp. 240-44 [English translation, "The Will to Knowledge," in *Ethics: Subjectivity and Truth*, pp. 11-16]), starting with the study of the evolution of Greek law from the seventh to the fifth century B.C. Sophocle's *Oedipus Rex* was taken as the example.
21. On the examination of conscience in Stoicism, and especially in Seneca, see the course of 24 March, second hour.
22. For the strict definition of the word confession (*aveu*) in Foucault's unpublished lecture, see, "Mal faire, dire vrai. Fonctions de l'aveu" (Louvain, 1981): "Confession (*l'aveu*) is a verbal act by which the subject, in an affirmation about what he is, binds himself to this truth, places himself in a relationship of dependence with regard to the other person and at the same time modifies the relationship he has with himself."
23. Arrian's transcriptions do not include the first, properly technical and logical part of Epictetus's lectures devoted to the reading and explanation of the fundamental doctrinal principles, but evoke only their testing through free discussion with disciples.
24. "Arrian to Lucius Gellius," in Epictetus, *Discourses*, vol. I.
25. See the course of 27 January, first hour.
26. See this lecture, first hour.

# nineteen

## 10 MARCH 1982

### First hour

> Parrhēsia *as ethical attitude and technical procedure in the master's discourse.* ~ *The adversaries of* parrhēsia: *flattery and rhetoric.* ~ *The importance of the themes of flattery and anger in the new system of power.* ~ *An example: the preface to the fourth book of Seneca's* Natural Questions *(exercise of power, relationship to oneself, dangers of flattery).* ~ *The Prince's fragile wisdom.* ~ *The points of opposition between* parrhēsia *and rhetoric: the division between truth and lie; the status of technique; the effects of subjectivation.* ~ *Positive conceptualization of* parrhēsia: *the* Peri parrhēsias *of Philodemus.*

I HAVE TRIED TO show you that the role and function of ascesis—in the sense that Greek and Roman philosophers gave to the word *askēsis*— was to establish the strongest possible link between the subject and truth that would enable the subject, when he had attained his finished form, to have at his disposal the true discourse that he should have and keep ready to hand and which he could say to himself as an aid when needed. The ascesis constitutes, therefore, and its role is to constitute, the subject as subject of veridiction. This is what I have tried to explain and this has of course led us to the technical and ethical problems of the rules of communication of these true discourses, of communication between the person who delivers them and the person who receives them and constructs from them an equipment for life. In view of the way the question of "the technique and ethics of the communication of true discourse" was posed, obviously it did not focus on the problem of speech as far as the disciple was concerned. The question of what the disciple has to say, of what he must and can say, basically did not arise, at any rate not as a primordial, essential, and fundamental question. What was imposed on the disciple as duty and conduct—as moral duty and as technical conduct—was silence, a particular organized silence obeying a number of rules of posture, and the requirement of giving a number of signs of attention. So, a technique and an ethics of silence, a technique and an ethics of listening, and a technique and ethics also of reading and writing, which are so many exercises for the subjectivation of true discourse. And so it is only when we turn to the master, that is to say to the person who must deliver true speech, that quite naturally the problem arises: what to say and how to say it, according to what rules, technical procedures, and ethical principles? It is around this question, in fact at the very heart of this question, that we encounter the notion I began to speak to you about last week: *parrhēsia*.

It seems to me that the term *parrhēsia* refers both to the moral quality, the moral attitude or the *ēthos*, if you like, and to the technical procedure or *tekhnē*, which are necessary, which are indispensable, for conveying true discourse to the person who needs it to constitute himself as a subject of sovereignty over himself and as a subject of veridiction on his own account. So, for the disciple really to be able to receive true discourse in the correct way, at the right time, and under the right conditions, the master must utter this discourse in the general form of *parrhēsia*. I reminded you last week that, etymologically, *parrhēsia* is "telling all." The *parrhēsia* tells all. In actual fact, it is not so much a question of "telling all" in *parrhēsia*. What is basically at stake in *parrhēsia* is what could be called, somewhat impressionistically, the frankness, freedom, and openness that leads one to say what one has to say, as one wishes to say it, when one wishes to say it, and in the form one thinks is necessary for saying it. The term *parrhēsia* is so bound up with the choice, decision, and attitude of the person speaking that the Latins translated it by, precisely, *libertas*. The telling all of *parrhēsia* was rendered by *libertas*: the freedom of the person speaking. And to translate *parrhēsia*—or to translate *libertas* in this sense—many French translators use the expression *"franc-parler"* (speaking freely), and this seems to me the most exact translation, you will see why.

I would now like to study this notion of *parrhēsia* (*libertas*, speaking freely) a little. It seems to me that if we want to understand what this *parrhēsia*, this *ēthos*, and this *tekhnē*, this moral attitude and technical procedure, require on the part of the person who speaks, the master or the person who dictates, then the best way may be—to begin with a rather negative analysis—to compare this *parrhēsia* with two figures to which it is opposed. Schematically, we can say that the master's *parrhēsia* (his speaking freely) has two adversaries. The first is a moral adversary to which it is directly opposed and against which it must struggle. The moral adversary of speaking freely is flattery. Second, speaking freely has a technical adversary. This technical adversary is rhetoric, with which speaking freely actually has a much more complex relationship than it does with flattery. Flattery is the enemy. Speaking freely must dismiss flattery and get rid of it. Speaking freely must free itself from rhetoric, but not only or solely so as to expel or exclude it, but rather, by being free from its rules, to be able to use it within strict, always tactically defined limits, where it is really necessary. So, there is opposition to and a battle and struggle against flattery. And, with regard to rhetoric there is freedom, a setting free. You notice, moreover, that flattery is the moral adversary of speaking freely, while rhetoric is, if you like, its adversary or ambiguous partner, but its technical partner. What's more, these two adversaries, flattery and rhetoric, are profoundly connected to each other since the moral basis of rhetoric is always flattery in fact, and the privileged instrument of flattery is of course the technique, and possibly the tricks of rhetoric.

First of all, what is flattery, and in what respect and why must speaking freely oppose it? It is striking that there is an abundant literature on the problem of flattery in the texts of this period. For example, it is worth noting that there were immensely more treatises on and examinations of flattery than there were concerning, for example, sexual conduct or problems like the relationship between parents and children. Philodemus (about whom we will have to speak again several times), an Epicurean,[1] wrote a treatise on flattery.[2] Plutarch wrote a treatise on how to distinguish the true friend from the flatterer.[3] And Seneca's letters are full of considerations of flattery. Curiously—I will come back to this text in more detail—the preface to the fourth part of *Natural Questions*, in which one might expect something very different from a consideration of flattery, is entirely devoted to this problem. Why the importance of flattery? What is it that makes flattery such an important stake in this practice of the self, in this technology of the self? Well, it is easy to understand this if we compare flattery with another defect, another vice which also played a crucial role in this period and was, as it were, paired with it: anger. In the matter of vices, anger and flattery go together. In what respect and how? There is also an enormous literature on anger. Moreover, a long time, over sixty years ago I believe, a study was published in Germany written by someone called Paul Rabbow, on the treatises on anger in the Hellenistic period and under the High Empire.[4] What is at stake in these treatises on anger? Obviously, I am going over this very quickly. Here again, there is a mass of texts. There is Seneca's *De Ira* of course, Plutarch's treatise on the control or mastery of anger,[5] and many more. What is anger? Anger is, of course, the uncontrolled, violent rage of someone towards someone else over whom the former, the angry person, is entitled to exercise his power, is in a position to do so, and who is therefore in a position to abuse his power. When you look at these treatises on anger you see that the question of anger is always a question of the anger of the head of the family towards his wife, his children, his household, or his slaves. Or it is the anger of the patron towards his clients or those dependent on him, or of the general towards his troops, and, of course, of the Prince towards his subjects. That is to say, the question of anger, of being carried away by anger or of the impossibility of controlling oneself—let's say more precisely: the impossibility of exercising one's power and sovereignty over oneself insofar as and when one exercises one's sovereignty or power over others—is situated precisely at the point of connection of self-control and command over others, of government of oneself and government of others. Actually, if anger is so important in this period, it is of course because in this period—and even for centuries, let's say from the beginning of the Hellenistic period until the end of the Roman Empire—there is the attempt to pose in new terms the question of the system of power relations in a society in which the structure of the city-state no longer prevails and in which the appearance of the great Hellenistic monarchies, and *a fortiori* of the imperial regime, raises the problem of the individual's adequacy with regard to the sphere of power, the problem of his position in the sphere of the power he may exercise. How can power be something other than a privilege of status to be exercised how one likes, when one likes, and in terms of this inherent status? How can the exercise of power become a precise and circumscribed function whose rules do not derive from the individual's statutory superiority, but from the precise and concrete tasks he has to perform? How can the exercise of power become a function and a job? The question of anger is raised in the general context of this problem. Again, if you like, the difference between power and property is this: Property is, of course, the *jus utendi et abutendi*.[6] A *jus utendi* must be defined with regard to power that will allow the use of power without its abuse. And the ethics of anger is a way of distinguishing between a legitimate use of power and a claim to abuse it. This, then, is the question of anger.

The question of flattery and the moral problem of flattery is the exact opposite and complementary problem. What actually is flattery? If anger, then, is the superior's abuse of power with regard to the inferior, it's perfectly understandable that flattery will be a way for the inferior to win over the greater power he comes up against in the superior, a way for him to gain the superior's favors and benevolence, etcetera. And with what and how can the inferior gain the superior's favors and benevolence? How can he divert the superior's power and utilize it to his own advantage? By the only element, the only instrument, the only technique available to him: the *logos*. He speaks, and it is by speaking that the inferior, boosting the superior's extra power as it were, can get what he wants from him. But in making use of the superior's superiority in this way, he reinforces it. He reinforces it since the flatterer is the person who gets what he wants from the superior by making him think that he is the most handsome, the wealthiest, the most powerful, etcetera, or at any rate, wealthier, more handsome, and more powerful than he is. Consequently, the flatterer may succeed in diverting the superior's power by addressing himself to the superior in a mendacious discourse in which the superior will see himself with more qualities, strength, and power than he possesses. The flatterer is the person who prevents you knowing yourself as you are. The flatterer is the person who prevents the superior from taking care of himself properly. There is, if you like, a whole dialectic of the flatterer and the flattered by which the flatterer, who by definition occupies an inferior position, will be in a position vis-à-vis the superior such that it is as if the superior is impotent with regard to the flatterer, since the superior finds in the flatterer's flattery an incorrect, a false image of himself, which deceives him and so puts him in a weak position with regard to the flatterer, with regard to others, and finally with regard to himself. Flattery renders the person to whom it is directed impotent and blind. This, more or less, is the general schema of flattery.

We have a very precise text on this problem of flattery. Well, we have a series of texts. The one on which I would like to concentrate is in Seneca, in the preface to the fourth book of his *Natural Questions*.[7] This seems to me to provide us with a very clear social and political landscape that enables us to define a little what is at stake in this question of flattery. Seneca wrote these *Natural Questions*, then, when he was in retirement as it were, when he had withdrawn from the exercise of political power and was writing to Lucilius—at that time procurator in Sicily—the famous correspondence that took up the last years of his life. He writes to Lucilius. He writes the letters, and he also composed for him the *Natural Questions*, which has survived, and the famous *Moral Treatise*, which however has not. So, he writes to Lucilius and sends him the different books of the *Natural Questions* as they are written. And, for reasons which are unclear, at least which are not directly clear to me, he begins the fourth book of *Natural Questions*, devoted, I think, to rivers and seas, with some considerations on flattery.[8] The text begins in this way: I have complete confidence in you, I know you conduct yourself well and as you should in your job as procurator. What is it to conduct himself well in his job as procurator? The text says it clearly.

On the one hand, he exercises his functions. He exercises them, but without abandoning what is indispensable for exercising them well, that is to say *otium* and *litterae* (free time and literature). A studious free time, applied to study, to reading and writing, etcetera, as complement, accompaniment, and regulative principle, is the guarantee that Lucilius properly discharges his office as procurator. It is thanks to this, to this correct combination of the exercise of functions and studious *otium*, that Lucilius will be able to keep a firm hold on his functions (*continere intra fines*: contain them within [their] limits). And what is it to contain the function he exercises within its limits? It is to remember—and you Lucilius, he says, never forget this—that you do not exercise the *imperium* (political sovereignty in its totality), but a mere *procuratio*.[9] I think the existence of these two technical terms here is quite significant. The power exercised by Lucilius is exercised well thanks to his studious reflection which accompanies the performance of his functions. And he exercises it well by not taking himself to be another Prince, the Prince's substitute, or even the overall representative of the Prince's total power. He exercises his power as a job defined by the office he has been given. This is a mere *procuratio*, and, he says, thanks to *otium* and study, the reason you thus succeed in performing your functions as *procuratio* within their limits, and not with the presumption of imperial sovereignty, is basically because in all of this you are content with yourself, you know how to be satisfied with yourself (*"tibi tecum optime convenit"*).[10]

We see here then in what respect and how studious *otium* can play the role of delimiting the function he performs. As an art of oneself, which has the aim of ensuring that the individual establish an appropriate and sufficient relationship to himself, studious *otium* ensures that the individual does not invest his own self, his own subjectivity, in the presumptuous delirium of a power that exceeds its real functions. He puts all the sovereignty he exercises in himself, within himself, or, more precisely, in a relationship of himself to himself. And on that basis, on the basis of this lucid and total sovereignty that he exercises over himself, he will be able to define and delimit the performance of his office to only those functions it has been assigned. This, then, is the good Roman functionary. I think we can use this term. He can exercise his power as a good functionary precisely on the basis of this relationship of self to self that he obtains through the culture that is his own. So, he says, this is what you do, Lucilius. However, there are, of course, very few men who can do this. Most of the others, he says, are tormented by either self-love or disgust with themselves. And this disgust with oneself, or this excessive love of oneself, leads, in the former case, to being concerned about things that are really not worth caring about; they are tormented, he says, by *sollicitudo*, by concern, by caring about things external to the self; and, in the latter case, through self-love, it leads to being attracted by sensual pleasures, by all the pleasures through which one tries to please oneself. In both cases, whether disgust with oneself, and as a result constant concern about events that may occur, or self-love, and as a result attachment to sensual pleasure, he says, these people are anyway never alone with themselves.[11] They are never alone with themselves in the sense that they never have that full, adequate, and sufficient relationship to themselves that ensures that we do not feel dependent on anything, neither on the misfortunes that threaten nor on the pleasures we may encounter or obtain from around us. The figure of the flatterer and the dangers of flattery rush in here, in this insufficiency that ensures that we are never alone with ourselves, in this inability to be alone, when we are either disgusted with or too attached to ourselves. In this non-solitude, in this inability to establish that full, adequate, and sufficient relationship to ourselves, the Other intervenes who, as it were, meets the lack and substitutes or rather makes up for this inadequacy through a discourse, and precisely through a discourse that is not the discourse of truth through which we can establish, fasten, and close up on itself the sovereignty we exercise over ourselves. The flatterer will introduce a foreign discourse, one that precisely depends on the other, on him, the flatterer. And this discourse will be a lying discourse. Thus, through the insufficiency of his relationship to himself, the flattered person finds himself dependent on the flatterer, on someone who is an other and who may therefore disappear or transform his flattery into wickedness, into a trap, etcetera. He is therefore dependent on this other, and what's more he is dependent on the duplicity of the flatterer's discourse. The subjectivity, as we would say, the typical relationship of self to self of the flattered person, is therefore a relationship of insufficiency mediated by the other, and a relationship of duplicity mediated by the other's lying. From this it is easy to draw a conclusion, and maybe make some remarks.

The conclusion is that *parrhēsia* (speaking freely, *libertas*) is precisely anti-flattery. It is anti-flattery in the sense that in *parrhēsia*, there is indeed someone who speaks and who speaks to the other but, unlike what happens in flattery, he speaks to the other in such a way that this other will be able to form an autonomous, independent, full and satisfying relationship to himself. The final aim of *parrhēsia* is not to keep the person to whom one speaks dependent upon the person who speaks—which is the case in flattery. The objective of *parrhēsia* is to act so that at a given moment the person to whom one is speaking finds himself in a situation in which he no longer needs the other's discourse. How and why does he no longer need the other's discourse? Precisely because the other's discourse was true. It is insofar as the other has given, has conveyed a true discourse to the person to whom he speaks, that this person, internalizing and subjectivizing this true discourse, can then leave the relationship with the other person. The truth, passing from one to the other in *parrhēsia*, seals, ensures, and guarantees the other's autonomy, the autonomy of the person who received the speech from the person who uttered it. This is what I think can be said about the flattery/*parrhēsia* (speaking freely) opposition. I would like to add two or three remarks to this.

You will tell me that we did not have to wait for the texts I have been discussing, those of the Hellenistic and imperial period, to encounter this problem of flattery, this fear and criticism of flattery as the opposite of the true and healthy guidance of souls. After all, there is powerful criticism of flattery in a number of Plato's texts.[12] I would just like to note that the flattery Plato is talking about, and to which he contrasts the true relationship between philosopher and disciple, is essentially the lover's flattery of the boy. Here, rather, in the Hellenistic and especially Roman texts I am talking about, the flattery in question is not at all the old philosopher's amorous flattery of the boy, but what could be called socio-political flattery. The basis of this flattery is not sexual desire but one's position of inferiority in relation to the other. And this refers to a practice of guidance which I have already spoken about and which is quite different from what we come across or that was exemplified in the first Socratic dialogues: In the Greco-Roman circles of this period, the guide is not so much the old sage, the old possessor of truth who stops young people on the street or at the gymnasium and suggests they take care of themselves. The guide is someone in a socially inferior position to those he addresses; he is someone on the payroll, someone to whom money is given, and someone who comes to your home as a permanent counselor to tell you, should the need arise, what you ought to do in this or that political or private situation; he is someone you ask for advice about your conduct. But he is a kind of friend whose relationship to the person he guides is for the most part that of client to his patron. This social reversal of the guide's relationship to the person he is guiding is quite striking. I think it is one of the reasons why the problem of flattery was so important. The position of the guide as private counselor within a big family or aristocratic circle actually poses the problem of flattery in a completely different way from the way it was posed in classical Greece. Moreover, there is a comment by Galen on this subject or theme that seems a bit strange, but which I think can be explained in this context—we will come back to Galen's text shortly. At a certain point Galen says: The person being guided must not be rich and powerful.[13] Actually, I think the meaning of this comment is only comparative. What I think he is saying is that it would be better if the person being guided were not much richer and more powerful than the person guiding him.

There is also a more general political problem attached to this problem of flattery. When, with imperial government, the political form is one in which the Prince's wisdom, virtue, and moral qualities are much more important than the city-state, and more important even than the legal organization of the State—you remember we spoke about this with regard to Marcus Aurelius[14]—then it is certain that the question of the moral guidance of the Prince will arise. Who will advise the Prince? Who will train the Prince and who will govern the soul of this Prince who has to govern the whole world? And here, of course, the question of frankness with regard to the Prince arises. The problem is connected to the existence of personal power, to the phenomenon of the court surrounding the Prince, which was new to the Roman world. The problem is also connected to the equally new phenomenon, for Rome, of the Emperor's deification. The basic problem in the Roman Empire at this time was evidently not the question of freedom of opinion. It was the question of truth for the Prince:[15] Who will tell the Prince the truth? Who will speak frankly to the Prince? How can one speak truthfully to the Prince? Who will tell the Prince what he is, not as Emperor but as a man, which is indispensable when it is indeed as a rational subject, as purely and simply a human being (as Marcus Aurelius said), that the Prince will be a good Prince? The rules of his government must depend fundamentally on his ethical attitude towards things, men, the world, and God. Inasmuch as it is the law of laws, or the internal law to which all absolute power must be subject, this ethic of the Prince, the problem of his *ēthos*, will obviously give a fundamental place to the *parrhēsia* of the person who advises the Prince (to this "telling the truth" to the Prince).

Let us now leave this question of *parrhēsia* (speaking freely) and flattery and look at the other adversary, the other partner if you like, which is rhetoric. Here I will go a bit quicker because things are more familiar. Rhetoric is better known than flattery. Let's say, schematically, that rhetoric is first of all defined as a technique whose methods obviously do not aim to establish a truth; rhetoric is defined as an art of persuading those to whom one is speaking, whether one wishes to convince them of a truth or a lie, a nontruth. Aristotle's definition in the *Rhetoric* is clear: it is the ability to find that which is capable of persuading.[16] The question of the content and the question of the truth of the discourse delivered do not arise. It is, said Athanaeus, "the conjectural art of persuading listeners."[17] Quintillian, who you know strove to bring as close together as possible the problems of rhetoric, or at least of the art of oratory, and the major themes of the philosophy of the time, raises the question of truth and rhetoric. He says: Of course, rhetoric is not a technique, an art which conveys, and should only convey and persuade someone of things that are true. It is an art and a technique that can persuade the listener of something true and of something that is not true. However, he says, can we at this point really speak of *tekhnē* (technique)?[18] As an orator well-trained in philosophy, Quintillian is fully aware that there can be no effective *tekhnē* that is not directly linked to the truth. A *tekhnē* resting on lies would not be a true technique and would not be effective. Quintillian therefore makes the following distinction: Rhetoric is indeed a *tekhnē* and consequently it really does refer to the truth, but the truth as known by the person speaking and not the truth contained in what he says.[19] Thus, he says, a good general must be able to persuade his troops that the enemy they are about to confront is neither serious nor formidable when in actual fact he is. The good general must therefore persuade them with a lie. How will he do this? He will do this if, on the one hand, he knows the truth of the situation and if, on the other, he truly knows the means by which one can persuade someone by a lie as well as by a truth. Consequently, Quintillian shows how rhetoric as *tekhnē* is directly linked to a truth—the truth known, possessed, and controlled by the person speaking—but not to the truth of what is said and so not from the point of view of the person being spoken to. So, it really is an art capable of lying. This is what is fundamental for rhetoric, its opposition precisely to philosophical discourse and to the technique peculiar to philosophical discourse, namely *parrhēsia*. There can only be truth in *parrhēsia*. Where there is no truth, there can be no speaking freely. *Parrhēsia* is the naked transmission, as it were, of truth itself. *Parrhēsia* ensures in the most direct way this *paradosis*, this transfer of true discourse from the person who already possesses it to the person who must receive it, must be impregnated by it, and who must be able to use it and subjectivize it. It is the instrument of this transfer that does nothing other than put to work the truth of true discourse in all its naked force, without adornment.

Second, as you know, rhetoric is an art organized according to regular procedures. It is also an art that is taught. Quintillian recalls that no one has ever been bold enough to doubt that rhetoric is an art, and an art that is taught.[20] Even the philosophers, he says, the Peripatetics and the Stoics say so and acknowledge this (obviously he does not mention the Epicureans, who say exactly the opposite):[21] Rhetoric is an art and an art that is taught. And he adds: "Is there anyone who on this point is so far removed not only from all culture but also from common sense, who thinks that there could be an art of forging, an art of weaving, an art of making vases, while rhetoric, so important and beautiful, will have reached a level we know it to have without the help of an art, without having become itself an art?"[22] So, rhetoric is indeed an art. And what controls this art? Here again the texts are very clear, especially those of Quintillian, but the same is true of Cicero. This art and its rules are not defined by a personal or individual relationship, let's say by the "tactical situation" of the person speaking face to face with the person he is addressing. So the rules of rhetoric, as it is understood in this period, are not defined by the interaction between persons. And despite what is sometimes said nowadays, we should remember that neither is ancient rhetoric a play on the intrinsic properties of language. The possibilities and rules of rhetoric, what defines it as an art, are not these characteristics of language itself. What defines rhetoric for Cicero and Quintillian is basically, as you know, the subject matter one is dealing with.[23] What we are talking about is what matters for saying how we should talk about it. Does it involve defending a cause, discussing war and peace before an assembly, dismissing a criminal accusation, etcetera? For rhetoric it is this game of the subject matter we are dealing with that defines how the discourse must be organized, how the preamble must be constructed, how the *narratio* (the account of events) must be presented, and how arguments for and against must be discussed. The rhetorical rules of the discourse must be constituted by and derived from the subject matter, from the referent of the discourse in its entirety.

Something completely different is at stake in *parrhēsia*. First of all, *parrhēsia* is not an art. I am a bit hesitant in saying this since, as you will see shortly, there is someone, Philodemus in his *Peri parrhēsias*, who defined *parrhēsia* as an art, but I will come back to this. Anyway, generally speaking—and this is very clear in Seneca—*parrhēsia* (speaking freely, *libertas*) is not an art. I will return shortly to Seneca's texts in which there is, in letter 75 in particular, a veritable theory of speaking freely, which is clearly not organized as an art, or anyway is not presented as an art. What characterizes *parrhēsia* is above all that basically it is not so much defined by the content itself—which, it goes without saying is given, is the truth—but that it is a specific, particular practice of true discourse defined by rules of prudence, skill, and the conditions that require one to say the truth at this moment, in this form, under these conditions, and to this individual inasmuch, and only inasmuch as he is capable of receiving it, and receiving it best, at this moment in time. That is to say, what essentially defines the rules of *parrhēsia* is the *kairos*, the occasion, this being precisely the situation of individuals with regard to each other and to the moment chosen for saying this truth. It is precisely according to the person to whom one speaks and the moment one speaks to him that *parrhēsia* must inflect, not the content of the true discourse, but the form in which this discourse is delivered [...*]. I will take just one example, from Quintillian himself. With regard to the moral teaching, or rather the moral part or aspect of the teaching that the professor of rhetoric must give, Quintillian explains that we should entrust the student to the master of rhetoric as quickly as possible and not delay too long, but that the master of rhetoric has two roles to perform. Obviously, he must teach rhetoric. But he also has a moral role.[24] And how will he perform this moral role, [namely], aiding the individual in his training of himself, in the formation of an appropriate relationship of self to self? Quintillian gives a number of rules[25] for which he does not use the word *libertas*, but which once again take the form of the empirical advice one gives and which correspond roughly to *parrhēsia*. He says: We should not arouse our student's antipathy by being too severe. Neither, by being too lax, should we give the student an excessively arrogant attitude that will lead him to despise the master and what he says. Quintillian continues, saying: Anyway, it is much better to give advice before than have to punish after an act has been committed. We should, he says also, answer questions willingly. Those who remain too quiet and do not ask questions should be questioned. We should correct any errors the student

---

*All that is audible is "... deployed as practice, as reflection, as tactical prudence let us say, between the person who possesses the truth and the person who must receive it."

may make, but we should do so without acrimony. Finally, he says, once a day, and possibly several times a day, the master himself should take the floor and speak so that his listeners "take away with them" what he has said. "No doubt reading provides examples to be imitated, but the living word is more nutritional food, especially when it is the word of the master, for whom his students, if they are properly trained, have affection and respect."[26]

And here I think we come to a third difference between rhetoric and *parrhēsia*. The essential function of rhetoric is to act on others in the sense that it enables one to steer or influence deliberations in assembly, lead the people, direct an army, etcetera. It acts on others, but always to the greater advantage of the person speaking. The rhetor, when he really is a good rhetor, does not give the impression of being just an advocate pleading a cause. He launches lightning and thunder,[27] says Quintillian, and it brings him glory, a present glory that may survive his death. *Parrhēsia*, rather, has a completely different objective and purpose. The positions of the person speaking and person spoken to are completely different. Of course, *parrhēsia* also involves acting on others, but not so much to order, direct, or incline them to do something or other. Fundamentally it involves acting on them so that they come to build up a relationship of sovereignty to themselves, with regard to themselves, typical of the wise and virtuous subject, of the subject who has attained all the happiness it is possible to attain in this world. Consequently, if this is the real object of *parrhēsia*, it is clear that the person who practices *parrhēsia*—the master—has no direct and personal interest in its exercise. The exercise of *parrhēsia* must be dictated by generosity. Generosity towards the other is at the very heart of the moral obligation of *parrhēsia*. In a word, let's say then that speaking freely, *parrhēsia*, is in its very structure completely different from and opposed to rhetoric. Of course, as I was saying at the start, this opposition is not of exactly the same type as that between speaking freely and flattery. Flattery really is the adversary, the enemy. *Parrhēsia* must get rid of it entirely. With regard to rhetoric, rather, the position is a little different. Of course, in its structure, in its game, the discourse of *parrhēsia* is completely different from rhetoric. This does not mean that, in the tactic of *parrhēsia* itself, in order to obtain one's intended outcome it may not be necessary from time to time to call upon some elements and procedures belonging to rhetoric. Let's say that *parrhēsia* is fundamentally freed from the rules of rhetoric, that it takes rhetoric up obliquely and only uses it if it needs to. We touch here on a whole series of problems, which I merely indicate and which concern of course the great fundamental conflict in ancient culture between rhetoric and philosophy.[28] This conflict, which, as you know, was already breaking out in the fifth and fourth centuries B.C., will permeate the whole of ancient culture. It assumes new dimensions and intensity precisely in this period of the High Empire I am talking about, with the reappearance of Greek culture and the appearance of what can be called the second Sophists, that is to say a new literary culture, a new rhetorical culture, and a new oracular and judicial culture which will be very strongly opposed—at the end of the first century and throughout the second century—to this philosophical practice called for by the care of the self.[29] So these differences, if you like, distinguish *parrhēsia* a little from the two figures linked to it and opposed to it (flattery and rhetoric), and enable us to approach at least a negative definition of the nature of *parrhēsia*.

Now, if we want to know what *parrhēsia* is positively, I think we can go to three texts that pose the question very directly and put forward a very direct analysis of what this speaking freely is. These are: first, the text by Philodemus I have spoken about, the *Peri parrhēsias*; second, letter 75 from Seneca to Lucilius; and third, the text by Galen in *On the Passions and Errors of the Soul*, which begins with an analysis of how frankness should be employed in relationships of spiritual guidance. I will not take these texts entirely in their chronological order. Inasmuch as the incomplete literature available prevents us from establishing or clearly identifying an evolution, there would in any case be no point at all in following the chronological order, and it seems to me that in view of the complexity of the texts and the different levels of analysis it would be more worthwhile to begin with the text by Philodemus, which will give us a kind of institutional image of the game of *parrhēsia*;[30] then we will study Galen's text—although it is from much later, the end of the second century A.D.[31]—which gives an image of what *parrhēsia* is within the individual relationship of spiritual guidance; and then [we will return] to Seneca's text from the middle of the first century A.D.,[32] which is, I think, the deepest and most analytical text concerning *parrhēsia*.

First, the text by Philodemus. So, as you know, Philodemus is this Epicurean philosopher, settled in Rome right at the end of the Republic, who was the philosophical counselor, the private counselor of Lucius Piso.[33] Philodemus was very important, first of all because he wrote a number of quite remarkable things, and then because he was one of the founders, one of the inspirers of the Epicurean movement at the end of the first century B.C. and the beginning of the first century A.D. He was the constant reference point for those different Epicurean circles that we come across in Naples, Campania, and also at Rome. And, from Philodemus to Maecenas, the life of Roman Epicureanism, which was so intense, was dominated by the texts of Philodemus. Philodemus wrote a series of treatises on specific points of morality involving the question of the relations between the power relationship and government of oneself, system of truth, etcetera. There is a treatise on anger, one on flattery, and one on vanity (conceit: *huperēphania*). Then there is a *Peri parrhēsias*: "Treatise on speaking freely." We have some relatively important fragments of this "Treatise on speaking freely," with many gaps. It has been published in Germany,[34] not in France, but I think that Monsieur Hadot intends to publish it with a commentary. Given the difficulty of the text, moreover, I must confess that I have been especially guided by an interesting commentary produced by an Italian—Gigante. This commentary is found in the proceedings of the congress of the Budé association devoted to Epicureanism. The congress took place in 1968 and Gigante made a very precise analysis of this *Peri parrhēsias*. So, hobbling badly on the text and following Gigante's text, this is roughly what I think we can say about it.

Gigante's thesis is the following. He says: *Parrhēsia* is put forward by Philodemus as a *tekhnē*. Gigante immediately adds: Note that the text we have by Philodemus does not mention the word *tekhnē*. Nonetheless, he says, there is an element that seems to indicate that Philodemus does indeed have an art (a *tekhnē*) in mind. In an incomplete fragment there is the expression *stokhazomenos*. Philodemus says very precisely: "The wise man and philosopher applies speaking freely (*parrhēsia*) in that he reasons by conjecturing through plausible arguments and without inflexibility."[35] Now you know that, since Aristotle at least, there is an old, traditional contrast [between] two kinds of art: the arts of conjecture and the arts of method. Conjectural art proceeds precisely by merely likely and plausible arguments, and consequently whoever uses these arguments need not follow a rule, and just one rule, but can try to arrive at this likely truth by a series of juxtaposed arguments with no need for a single necessary order. Everything belonging to methodical art (*methodikos*), rather, entails first of all that one arrives at the result of a certain and well-established truth, but after following a single possible line of reasoning which is the only one possible. We may assume then that the use of this word *stokhazomenos* (of the verb to conjecture)[36] seems to be related to the existence of an art, or to the opposition between conjectural and methodical art.[37] Anyway, according to the Philodemus text, on what consideration is this conjectural art based? Well, precisely on the *kairos*, the occasion.[38] Here again, there is fidelity to the Aristotelian lesson. For Aristotle too, a conjectural art is based on taking the *kairos* into account. And, Philodemus says, actually you should take great care when speaking to the disciple; you must delay the occasions of intervention as much as is necessary. But you must not hold back too long. You must choose exactly the right moment. You must also take account of the state of mind of the person you are speaking to, for you can make young people suffer if you admonish them too severely in public. You can also do it in such a way that everything takes place with pleasure and gaiety (*hilarōs*), and this is the path that should be adopted.[39] In this respect, in this seizing of the opportunity, Philodemus says, *parrhēsia* calls to mind the art or practice of the navigator and the practice of medicine. What's more, he develops this parallel between philosophical *parrhēsia* and medical practice. *Parrhēsia*, he says, is an aid (*boētheia*: you recall that we have already come across this notion),[40] a *therapeia* (a therapeutics). And *parrhēsia* must make it possible to treat properly. *Sophos* is a good medicine.[41] Finally, in these fragments of Philodemus there is a new element with regard to everything I have been saying and which we could have identified already through the negative definition of *parrhēsia* as opposed to both flattery and rhetoric. This new, positive, and important element is this. It is found in fragment 25 of Philodemus. The translation of the text says this: By speaking freely (*parrhēsia*) we encourage, intensify, and enliven, as it were, the students' benevolence (*eunoia*) towards each other thanks to having spoken freely.[42] It seems to me that there is something important in this text. This will be the overturning, if you like, of *parrhēsia* (of speaking freely). You can see that it is a question of speaking freely, of the master's *parrhēsia*, having to act on the disciples to encourage them in something: "to intensify" something. But to intensify and enliven what? The students' benevolence towards each other thanks to having spoken freely. That is to say: it is thanks to the fact that the students will have spoken freely that their reciprocal benevolence will thereby be assured and increased. In this text then, there is the sign of a transition from the master's *parrhēsia* to the *parrhēsia* of the students themselves. The practice of free speech on the part of the master must be such that it serves as encouragement, support, and opportunity for the students who will themselves also have the possibility, right, and obligation to speak freely. The students' free speech will increase *eunoia* (benevolence) or friendship between them. We have then, I think, two important elements in this text: the transfer of *parrhēsia* from master to student, and, of course, the traditional importance in Epicurean circles of reciprocal friendship between the disciples, since this is a principle in Epicurean circles—moreover Philodemus explicitly recalls this in his text: the disciples must save each other and be saved through each other (*to di'allēlōn sōzesthai*).[43]

Being very schematic, I think the game of *parrhēsia* can be represented in the following way. What stands out in the Epicurean group is the place of the guide, of the one called the *kathēgetēs*, or the *kathēgoumenos*, it doesn't matter: the guide is an important, central character in the Epicurean group.[44] He is central for a fundamental reason, which is that he is based on a succession; a direct succession from man to man, presence to presence, which goes back to Epicurus. In the dynasty of the Epicurean leaders, the direct line back to Epicurus through the transmission of a living example, a personal contact, is indispensable, and the particular place of the *kathēgētēs* (the one who guides) is founded on this. On the other hand, the position of this *kathēgoumenos* (this master) is characterized by the fact that he can speak on the authority given to him by the living example passed down since Epicurus. He can and will speak the truth, which is precisely the truth of the master from whom he derives indirectly (he is linked indirectly, but through a series of direct contacts). Therefore his discourse will fundamentally be a discourse of truth, and he will have to present it as such and as nothing more. It is the *parrhēsia* of his own discourse that puts the student in the presence of the discourse of the first master, namely Epicurus. But in another respect, apart from the vertical line, as it were, which marks the master's singular place in the historical series going back to Epicurus and on which his authority over all the students is founded, there will be a series of intense, compact, and strong horizontal relationships within the group, which are relationships of friendship that will be of use in reciprocal salvation. *Parrhēsia* circulates in this double, vertical, and horizontal organization. Of course, it comes from the master who has the right to speak and who can only speak, moreover, when he is in contact with the words of Epicurus. However, in another respect, this *parrhēsia* is turned around, reversed, and becomes the practice and mode of relationship between the students themselves. And, according to some texts, which are besides extremely allusive and schematic, this is actually what is found in the Epicurean groups, that is to say, the obligation for the students to assemble in a group before the *kathēgoumenos* and then to speak: to say what they are thinking, what is in their hearts, to tell of the faults they have committed and the weaknesses for which they still feel responsible or to which they still feel exposed. And this is how we find—for the first time, it appears, quite explicitly within this practice of the self of Greco-Roman Antiquity—the practice of confession. This practice of confession is completely different from the ritual, religious practices that actually consisted in going to the temple to deposit a stele or to make an offering when you had committed a petty theft, an offense or a crime, and [by which] you acknowledged your guilt. No, here it is something completely different: it is an explicit, developed, and regular verbal practice by which the disciple must respond to this *parrhēsia* of the master's truth with a certain *parrhēsia*, with a certain open-heartedness, which is the opening of his own soul that he puts in contact with the others' souls, thus doing what is necessary for his own salvation, but also encouraging the others not to have an attitude of refusal, rejection, and blame towards themselves, but one of *eunoia* (benevolence) and, thereby, encouraging all the group's members, all the characters of the group, to undertake their salvation. We have here an utterly unique structure whose mechanism or logic is very readily and clearly found, I think, in this practice, this technique of *parrhēsia*. However, I think you will see that this will be a unique phenomenon. At any rate, it seems to me that we find in these Epicurean circles the first foundation of what will be transformed [with] Christianity. It is a first form that may bring the Christian form to mind, without prejudging any of the historical links of transformation from one to the other. It seems to me that it is the first time that we find this obligation that we will meet again in Christianity, namely: I must respond—I am encouraged, called upon, and obliged to respond—to the words of truth that teach me the truth and consequently help me in my salvation, with a discourse of truth by which I open the truth of my own soul to the other, to others. That's Epicurean *parrhēsia*. So, in a moment I will talk about *parrhēsia* in Galen and *parrhēsia* (*libertas*) in Seneca.

1. Concerning Philodemus, see the lecture of 27 January, first hour. We recall here that this conflict was first orchestrated by Plato in the *Gorgias* (Plato refused the status of *tekhnē* to rhetoric, seeing it as only a vulgar know-how) and the *Phaedrus* (in which rhetoric, in order to achieve authenticity, must become philosophy), and that this conflict takes on a new vigor with the new Sophists, proudly assuming its identity and claiming its divorce from a philosophy reduced to formal amusement (see the same lecture, second hour).
2. "We must place the other great work of the systematization of moral concepts, to which Philodemus gives the title *On contrary vices and virtues (Des vices et des vertus opposes)*, after 50 B.C.... This work is made up of at least six books: in several the theme is sycophancy: *Peri kolakeias*... The different books *On Flattery (De l'adulation)* indicate in an equally polemical way the characteristics of this vice and, above all, their aim could be to determine the correct comportment of the Epicurean sage towards it." M. Gigante, *La Bibliothèque de Philodème et l'épicurisme romain*, p. 59.
3. Plutarch, *How to Distinguish a Flatterer from a Friend*.
4. P. Rabbow, *Antike Schriften über Seelenheilung und Seelenleitung auf ihre Quellen untersucht, I. Die Therapie des Zorns* (Leipzig: Teubner, 1914).
5. Plutarch, *On the Control of Anger*.
6. "According to the compilers of Justinian, property has a *plena potestas* over the thing (I.2, 4, 4). An assertion of the principle of an absolute power that will have a remarkable fortune. In the Middle Ages, scholarly law will rediscover and develop it. The glossators extrapolate a harmless text from the *Digest* in order to extract the successful formula: property is the *jus utendi* and *abutendi* (D., 5, 3, 25, 11: *re sua abuti putant*)." P. Ourliac and J. de Malafosse, *Droit romain et Ancien Droit* (Paris: PUF, 1961), p. 58.
7. Seneca, *Natural Questions*, preface to book IV. On this text, see *Le Souci de soi*, pp. 108-09 (*The Care of the Self*, p. 88).
8. The fourth book is entitled: "On the Nile."
9. "To judge from your letters, wise Lucilius, you like both Sicily and the free time your office of governor leaves you (*officium procurationis otiosae*). You will continue to like them if you are willing to stay within the limits of your office, if you think of yourself as the Prince's minister and not the Prince himself (*si continere id intra fines suos volueris, nec efficere imperium, quod est procuratio*)." *Natural Questions*, IV, Preface, 1.
10. "You, rather, are happy with yourself." Ibid.
11. "I am not surprised that so few people enjoy this happiness: we are our own tyrants and persecutors; sometimes unhappy due to loving ourselves excessively, sometimes from disgust with our existence; in turns the mind is swollen by a deplorable pride or strained by greed; giving ourselves up to pleasures or burning up with anxiety; and, to complete the misery, never alone with ourselves." Ibid., 2.
12. See the famous passage in the *Gorgias*, 463a, on rhetoric: "Well, Gorgias, rhetoric seems to me to be a practice foreign to art, but which requires a soul with imagination, boldness and naturally skilled in dealing with men. For me, the generic name for this kind of practice is flattery (*kolakeian*)." There is a very dark definition of the flatterer also in the *Phaedrus*, 240b.
13. "The man who seeks advice should be neither rich nor endowed with any civic honor." Galen, *On the Passions and Errors of the Soul*, ch. III.
14. See the lecture of 3 February, second hour.
15. See Paul Veyne's judgement: "Towards an unsteady sovereignty, it remains only to go one better in demonstrations of loyalty; the cult of the personality or 'flattery' was this: both a simple stipulation of monarchical style and a strict obligation, on pain of being suspected of high treason." "Préface" to Seneca, *Entretiens, Lettres à Lucilius*, p. xi.
16. "Rhetoric may be defined as the faculty of observing in any given case the available means of persuasion." Aristotle, *Rhetoric*, I.2.1335b, in *The Complete Works of Aristotle* (the revised

Oxford translation), ed. Jonathan Barnes (Princeton: Princeton University Press, 1985) vol. 2, p. 2155.
17. "*Athēnaios de logōn dunamin prosagoreuei tēn rhētorkikēn stokhazomenēn tēs tōn akouontōn peithous*," quoted by Sextus Empiricus, *Against the Professors*, in *Sextus Empiricus*, translation. R.G. Bury (London and Cambridge, Mass.: Loeb Classical Library, 1949) vol. IV, II.62, pp. 218-19 ("And Athanaeus calls rhetoric a power of speech which aims at the persuasion of the audience").
18. Foucault refers here to II.xvii, of book II of the *Institutio Oratoria*.
19. "There is a big difference between having an opinion oneself and trying to get someone else to adopt it." Ibid., II.xvii.9.19.
20. See ibid., book II, *passim*.
21. In his *Peri rhētorikēs*, Philodemus "while professing a hostility towards rhetoric which was indeed part of the Epicurean tradition, granted only to the 'sophistic rhetoric,' that is to say the rhetoric which teaches how to write discourses other than political or juridical discourses, the status of *tekhnē*, of structured knowledge (savoir)." C. Levy, *Les Philosophies hellénistiques* (Paris: Le Livre de Poche, 1997), p. 38. See again on this point the comments of M. Gigante, *La Bibliothèque de Philodème*, pp. 49-51.
22. *Institutio oratoria*, vol. II, bk. II.xvii.3
23. "For my part—and this is not unwarranted—I think that the material of rhetoric is every subject on which it may be called upon to speak." Ibid.
24. Ibid., II.
25. Ibid., II.ii.3-8.
26. Ibid., II.ii.8.
27. This metaphor is first used by Aristophanes when evoking Pericles as an orator in *Acharnians*, verse 530; Aristophanes, *Acharnians and Knights*, translation Jeffrey Henderson (Cambridge, Mass. and London: Loeb Classical Library, 1998), p. 120. Quintillian employs it on several occasions (see, for example, *Institutio oratoria*, VII.xii.10, 24 and 65).
28. See lecture of 27 January, first hour.
29. See the same course, second hour.
30. Following Gigante, we can date this treatise, from the bigger collection devoted to *Modes of Life* (*Peri ēthōn kai biōn*), from the 40s B.C. For a historical presentation of *Peri parrhēsias*, see M. Gigante, *La Bibliothèque de Philodème*, pp. 41-47.
31. We assume, on the basis of an indication in the text of *On the Passions and Errors of the Soul*, that Galen wrote this work when he was 50 years old, which, if we accept 131 A.D. as his date of birth, implies that it was written around 180 A.D.
32. According to P. Grimal's chronological table in his *Sénèque*, p. 45, letter 75 should be placed in the spring of 64 A.D.
33. See the lecture of 27 January, first hour. Cicero caricatured this relationship in which Greek subtlety encounters Roman coarseness; see *Contre Pison*, in Cicero, *Discours*, translation P. Grimal (Paris: Les Belles Lettres, 1966) vol. XVI-1, XXVIII-XIX, pp. 135-37.
34. Philodemus, *Peri parrhēsias*, ed. A. Olivieri (Leipzig: Teubner, 1914).
35. Fragment 1 of *Peri parrhēsias*, p. 3. Gigante's translation of this fragment is found in *Association Guillaume Budé, Actes du VIII<sup>e</sup> congrès* (1968), p. 202.
36. Actually, *stokhazesthai* originally refers to the action of aiming accurately (in the case of a target), and then later shares the meaning of conjecture with the verb *tekmairesthai*. See the argument in Marcel Detienne and Jean-Pierre Vernant, *Les Ruses de l'intelligence. La mètis des Grecs* (Paris: Flammarion, 1974), pp. 292-305; English translation by Janet Lloyd, *Cunning Intelligence in Greek Culture and Society* (Hassocks, U.K.: Harvester Press, 1978), pp. 288-90.
37. The opposition between exact sciences and conjectural arts, the latter bringing together the piloting of ships and medical care, appears for the first time perfectly expressed in *Ancient Medicine*, from the Hippocratic corpus: "It is necessary to aim at some kind of measure (*dei gar metrou tinos stokhazesthai*). Now since there is no measure, neither number nor weight, by reference to which we could know the exact truth, except the body's sensibility, and as it is also a hard task to acquire a science so exact as to make only slight errors here

and there, I myself would highly praise the doctor who only commits slight errors; but absolutely certain judgment is a rare sight. In fact, it seems to me that usually the same thing happens to doctors as happens to bad pilots. When the latter steer in calm weather, any mistake they make is not obvious; but if they are struck by a heavy storm and a violent, opposing wind, then everyone can see that they have lost their ship through their inexperience and stupidity." *Ancient Medicine*, IX. On the notion of stochastic art, in Plato in particular, see Festigière's detailed note (*L'Ancienne Médecine*, pp. 41-42, n. 41). We note however that the opposition between certain knowledge (*savoir certain*) and uncertain knowledge (*connaissance hasardeuse*) is treated in Plato from the perspective of a condemnation of stochastic intelligence. In Aristotle (who privileges then the idea of the "glance"— cf. *eustokhia*), this form of practical intelligence is recognized, rather, as an integral part of prudence (*phronēsis*): what stochastic art loses in demonstrative necessity (in the timelessness of science) it gains in appropriateness of intervention in the *kairos* grasped on the wing.

38. See Gigante translation in *Actes du VIII<sup>e</sup> congrès*, pp. 206-07.
39. See Gigante translation, pp. 211-14 (fragment 61 of *Peri parrhēsias*, p. 29).
40. See the analysis of discourse-aid (*logos boēthos*) in the lecture of 24 February, second hour.
41. See Gigante translation, in *Actes du VIII<sup>e</sup> congrès*, pp. 209-11 (fragment 44 of *Peri Parrhēsias*, p. 21).
42. See Gigante translation, p. 206 (fragment 25 of *Peri Parrhēsias*, p. 13).
43. See Gigante translation, p. 212 (fragment 36 of *Peri parrhesias*, p. 17). This passage is summarized in *Le Souci de soi*, p. 67 (*The Care of the Self*, pp. 51-52).
44. See Gigante translation, pp. 214-17.

# twenty

# 10 MARCH 1982

### Second hour

> *Continuation of the analysis of* parrhēsia: *Galen's* On the
> Passions and Errors of the Soul. ∼ *Characteristics of* libertas
> *according to Seneca: refusal of popular and bombastic eloquence;
> transparency and rigor; incorporation of useful discourses; an art of
> conjecture.* ∼ *Structure of* libertas: *perfect transmission of thought
> and the subject's commitment in his discourse.* ∼ *Pedagogy and
> psychagogy: relationship and evolution in Greco-Roman
> philosophy and in Christianity.*

— ARE THERE STILL TWO lecturers to come?[1]
— That's right.
— *You are governed by the religious festivals...*
— Oh yes, that's right, absolutely. From the Nativity to the Resurrection.[2]

First of all I would like, not exactly to make an appeal for help, but to ask you a question. I understand there are some people recording the lectures. Very well, you are absolutely within your rights. The lectures here are public. It's just that maybe you have the impression that all my lectures are written. But they are less so than they seem to be, and I do not have any transcripts or even recordings. Now it happens that I need them. So, if by chance there is anyone who has (or who knows someone who has) either recordings—I believe there is a Monsieur Lagrange[3]—or obviously transcripts, would you be kind enough to tell me, it could help me. It is especially for the last four or five years. I will try to finish early, and maybe you could ask some questions.

Now, then, Galen's text: skipping a bit, and moving to the end of the second century A.D., Galen writes this famous text, *On the Passions* or more precisely, *On the Treatment of the Passions*.[4] In the first pages of this text, unlike what we find in Philodemus, there is absolutely no "theory" of *parrhēsia*, but I think there are certain interesting elements indicative of what speaking freely should be in this field of connections and relations. He starts from the principle that one can never cure without knowing what is to be cured. Medical science, or rather medical *tekhnē*, obviously needs to know the disease it has to treat. This goes without saying. Now, in *On the Passions and Errors of the Soul*, Galen explains that this text does not speak of the cure (the treatment, the therapy) of diseases, but of the treatment of passions and errors. Now, he says, if it is true that the sick suffer from their disease without really knowing what it is, or feel quite explicit discomforts because of it, [so that they] spontaneously go to the doctor, when it is a matter of the passions and errors, rather, we find ourselves even more blind. For, he says, we always love ourselves too much not to deceive ourselves (this is the *amor sui* we were talking about a short while ago with regard to a passage in Seneca's *Natural Questions*).[5] The fact that we deceive ourselves thus disqualifies the subject from the role he might have or claim to exercise of being his own doctor. This thesis does not authorize us to judge ourselves, but it does authorize others to do so. Consequently, due to this self-love, which deceives us about everything, we need to resort to someone else in order to cure our passions and errors, on condition that this person does not feel indulgent or hostile towards we who are consulting him: I will come back to this shortly, at present I am just following the text.[6] How will we choose and recruit this Other who must be neither indulgent nor hostile and of whom, due to our love of ourselves, we really do need to cure us? Well, Galen says, we must be careful. We must be on the lookout, and when we hear of someone famous, renowned and well known for not being a flatterer, then we go to him.[7] We speak to him, or rather, even before speaking to him directly, we try to confirm and test, as it were, this individual's non-flattery. We observe how he acts in life, whether he associates with the powerful, his attitude towards the powerful people with whom he associates or on whom he is dependent. And depending on his attitude, when we have thoroughly demonstrated and tested that he is not a flatterer, we can then speak to him. We are dealing then with someone unknown, or rather with someone known only to ourselves, and who is known only for his non-flattery. So we had to check that he was not a flatterer. We then speak to him. What will we do, how will things unfold? First of all we will initiate a conversation, a private conversation, in which we will ask him the first question as it were, but which is also the question of confidence: Has he noticed in our comportment, in how we speak, etcetera, the traces, the signs, or the proofs of a passion, a passion that we may have? A number of things may happen at this point. Of course, he may say that he has noticed it. Then the treatment begins, that is to say we ask him for advice in order to treat our passion. Suppose, rather, he says that he failed to detect any passion whatever during this first conversation? Well then, Galen says, we must refrain from rejoicing and from thinking that we have no passions and so no need of a spiritual guide to help us cure them. For, [Galen] says, maybe [the guide] has not yet had time to see these passions; perhaps also he does not want to concern himself with the person who appeals to him; or perhaps he fears that we will bear a grudge against him if he tells us we have this or that passion. So we must therefore persist, insist, and press him with questions to get a different answer than: "no, you have no passions." If need be we must call on the mediation of someone else to find out if this character, whose qualities as a non-flatterer we know, is simply just not interested in advising someone like us. Now let us suppose that instead of saying we have no passions, the person to whom we speak reproaches us, but we feel that these reproaches are not really justified. Well, in this case we must not turn away [from the guide] and say: I asked him for advice and he thought he detected passions in me that I know full well I don't have. We must remember first of all that he may always be right, and that anyway his reproach—to me, to the person who does not feel however that he has this passion—may be an opportunity for me to keep a better eye on myself and to exercise a more attentive vigilance over myself.

Finally, after this first test, after these first, apparently unjustified reproaches which have encouraged the person being advised to keep a better watch on himself, let us suppose that we have reached the conclusion, that we are certain that the guide's reproach is unjust. Let us suppose even that during the treatment the guide continues to make reproaches that we know perfectly well to be unjust. Well, in a rather odd text, Galen says we must be grateful to him for this. We must be grateful to him because this is a test which will exercise us in bearing injustice, and training ourselves, arming ourselves, and equipping ourselves against injustice is indispensable inasmuch as we do in fact continually encounter injustice in life. The guide's injustice is a positive test for the person being guided. This is an odd, astonishing element that, as far as I know, is hardly ever found in other texts of the same kind in this period, but a transposition and full development of which will be found again in Christian spirituality.[8]

I have pointed out this passage from Galen, the first pages of *On the Passions*, for the following reason. First of all, you will have seen that the need for a spiritual guide is, as it were, structural. We cannot dispense with the other. And Galen says this quite explicitly: "I have rarely seen deceived any who have submitted the declaration of their own worth to others, and I have seen all those who have judged themselves excellent, without trusting in the judgment of others, make frequent and serious errors."[9] So the need for spiritual guidance is not just occasional or restricted to the most serious cases. Everyone who wishes to conduct themselves properly in life needs a guide. This is the same theme you find again later in Christianity, which is frequently commented on and based on a Biblical text: Those who are not guided "fall like dead leaves."[10]

Second, you can see that it is quite remarkable that in this text, Galen—who is a doctor and quite evidently transposes certain notions and concepts from medicine to the guidance of souls, who obviously makes use of the basic notion of *pathos* and all the analogies from the body to the soul and from the medicine of the body to the medicine of the soul—at no point considers the person in whom one confides to be a kind of technician of the soul. He is not a technician of the soul: what we require of the guide are certain moral qualities. And there are two things at the heart of these moral qualities. First, frankness (*parrhēsia*), the exercise of speaking freely. This is the principal element. We should test our guide's free speech. This figure [will be] completely reversed later, in Christianity, when the spiritual director will have to try to test the frankness and truthfulness of the person who speaks about himself;[11] in this case it is the person being guided who must test his master's free speech. Second, he should possess a moral quality, which is indicated in a short section of the text where it says that it would be best to choose someone who is already elderly and who has shown by his life that he is a decent man.[12] Finally, third—and this is interesting because it seems quite remarkable to me with regard to a series of other things found in the same period—we choose someone unknown to us as our guide. Whereas in Plato, of course, spiritual guidance rested on the love relationship, whereas in most authors of the imperial period, in Seneca especially, the relationship of guidance is inserted within friendship, esteem, and already established social relationships—in Seneca, the relationship to Lucilius of guide to guided is inserted precisely within this given relationship—[in Galen], although there is clearly no theoretical or explicit consideration of this (but it's enough to follow the text), it is clear that we should not know the person who is to guide us. We should not have had any previous relationship with him, or the least possible relationship, so that there is neither indulgence nor severity. The condition of friendship, which is so explicit in most of the other texts, is dispensed with in this case. Consequently, we have an individual, the guide, who is neither a technician of the soul nor a friend. He is someone neutral, someone outside, in relation to whom we must situate ourselves as the object of his gaze, or rather the target of his discourse. He looks at you, he observes you, and he determines whether or not you have this or that passion. Very well. At this point he will speak, speaking freely, he will speak to you on the basis of his *parrhēsia*. The transaction of spiritual guidance will be practiced in this way, on the basis of this external and neutral point both of the gaze and of the subject of discourse. This is what I wanted to say about Galen's text.

Now, third, Seneca's text. Actually, there are several letters in Seneca's correspondence with Lucilius that, explicitly or implicitly [...] [provide incidental information on this *libertas*].* Unlike what is no doubt found in Philodemus, it is clear that for Seneca *libertas* is not a technique or an art. There is no theory or systematic exposition [on this subject], but there are some perfectly coherent elements. These can be found in letters 40, 38, 29, and 75. First of all we will speak quickly about the first three before studying the text of letter 75. In letter 40, Seneca very clearly, and in a way that recurs in many other texts, compares what the true relationship, the true bond should be between the guide and the person being guided, with the discourse held in the form of popular eloquence, when someone holds forth to a crowd with a violent and bombastic discourse. It is absolutely obvious, clear, and goes without saying, that Seneca is thinking here of those mainly Cynic or Cynic-Stoic popular orators who had such an important role in the forms of preaching, collective guidance, etcetera, which were frequent in Antiquity at this time.[13] Against this collective guidance and popular moralizing, Seneca puts forward the specific rights and richness of what an individual relationship of man to man, between one cultured man and another, can and should be. What basically is the function of popular eloquence? In the first place it is to try to surprise the listeners through strong emotions, without appealing to their judgment. To obtain these strong emotions, popular eloquence does not follow the logical order of things and of truth. It is content with dramatic elements and sets up a kind of theater. Consequently, putting it in our own terms, popular eloquence does not function in terms of truth. It produces emotional, affective effects that consequently do not affect individuals deeply.[14] Seneca contrasts this with what ought to be the controlled and effective discursive relationship between two individuals alone together. This discourse, he says, is a discourse (*oratio*) "*quae veritati dat operam*": that deals with the truth.[15] And for this discourse to make way for the truth, it should, he says, be *simplex*, that is to say,

---

*Reconstruction according to the manuscript.

transparent: that is, it says what it has to say and does not try to dress it up or package it and so disguise it by adorning it or dramatizing it in any way. Simple: it must be simple like pure water; the truth must pass through it. But at the same time it must be *composita*, that is to say it must follow a certain order. Not the dramatic order followed by popular eloquence that is adapted to the emotions of the crowd, but [an order] composed according to the truth one wishes to express. In this way, by employing discourse that is both transparent to the truth and well-ordered in terms of this truth, the discourse will be able to sink into the person to whom it is addressed: *descendere in nos debet*.[16] It must thoroughly penetrate us through its simplicity and reflected composition. This, then, is what there is in letter 40. In letter 38 he also comes back to the contrast between a public eloquence, which seeks to shock with grand gestures, and the true guidance and advice that each must give to the other, which does not involve shocking with grand gestures but plants small seeds in the soul, which are scarcely visible but which will be able to germinate or help germinate the seeds of wisdom planted in us by nature (the seeds, the germs of reason).[17] This implies, of course, that this discourse is particularly attentive to individuals and their present condition. These seeds must not be lost, they must not be crushed.[18] Consequently we need to adjust ourselves to the person we are speaking to, to wait for the good moment when germination will be able to occur. The same theme is found in letter 29.[19]

And now letter 75, which seems to me to be without doubt a complete exposition of the nature of *libertas*, of what the Greeks called *parrhēsia*, again without this actually being said. Here is the text: "You complain that my letters are not to your taste or worked up as they ought to be. Now who thinks of polishing his style except lovers of the pretentious? If we were sitting alone with each other or taking a walk together, my conversation would be unaffected and easygoing (*inlaboratus et facilis*). I should like my letters to be like that; they have nothing studied or artificial about them. If it were possible, I should prefer to show you my thoughts rather than translate them into language [I will come back to this important phrase; M.F.]. Even in an official lecture, I should not stamp my foot, or toss my arms about, or raise my voice, leaving that to the orators and judging my purpose attained if I have conveyed my thought without studied embellishment or platitude. Most of all, my heartfelt wish is to get you to understand that I think whatever I may say, and that I not only think it, but love it. The kisses one gives to one's children are not like those a mistress receives; yet this chaste and restrained embrace displays tenderness. Certainly, I do not condemn discussions concerning such an important matter to a dry and arid tone. Philosophy does not renounce the charms of the mind. But one should not take such great pains over words. This is the essential point of our rhetoric [this is an addition by the translator; *haec sit propositi nostri summa* should rather be translated as, 'this is the essential point of what I assert, of what I am saying, of what I mean'; M.F.]: let us say what we think and think what we say; let speech harmonize with conduct. That man who is the same both when you see him and when you hear him has fulfilled his commitments. We will see the originality of his nature, its greatness. Our discourse should strive not to please, but to be useful. If, however, you can attain eloquence without painstaking, if it comes naturally and at slight cost, accept it, so that it may serve the finest things and so that it shows things rather than displays itself. Other arts are concerned solely with cleverness, but we are concerned only with the soul. A sick man does not go in search of an eloquent doctor. However, if he finds that the man who can cure also discourses elegantly about the treatment to be followed, the patient will reconcile himself to this. But this will be no reason for him to congratulate himself [the patient; M.F.] on having discovered a doctor who, in addition to his skill, is eloquent. The case is similar to that of a skilled pilot who is also a handsome lad. Why do you want to tickle and charm my ear? Something else is at stake: the flame, the iron, the diet I must follow. That is why I called you."[20]

I imagine that you will already have been able to identify a number of familiar elements in this rather long text. First, you will have identified what is said against popular eloquence, along with the privilege accorded to letters sent from one individual to another and which, due to this, as an individual relationship, should have a freedom of style and a flexibility that takes each partner into account. In other texts he says: Instead of sending each other letters, it would be much better if we could converse in a particular way, either sitting idly or taking a walk together.[21] This particular discussion, this tête-à-tête, which is at the same time a living and physical contact, is evidently the best, the ideal form for a relationship of guidance. Second, you will also have been able to identify something in the text about which I have already spoken. This is the attitude towards rhetoric. He does not say as the [French] translator has it: "This is the essential point of our rhetoric."* He never uses this word to designate what he is doing. Nonetheless, he says: Yes, the embellishment of speech may well be useful. There is no reason to disdain the pleasures and charms of listening to fine language. There may even be something quite useful in this, inasmuch as, if eloquence is attained without painstaking, it may make it possible to show things. So: a tactical use of rhetoric, but no fundamental, overall, or total obedience to the rules of rhetoric. Third, you will also have been able to see that thing I have spoken about, which is that the essential function of this "free speaking" discourse is to be turned towards the other, towards the person to whom one speaks, to whom it must be useful. Certain elements of this usefulness are worth recalling here. On the one hand, he characterizes this usefulness by saying it is not addressed so much to the *ingenium* (to the mind, to intelligence, etcetera), but is something which is a matter for the *animi negotium* (for the business, activity, practice of the soul). So *parrhēsia* (speaking freely) is useful in this *animi negotium*, this "management," if you like, of the soul. How will this usefulness manifest itself? Well, this appears at the end of the passage. I have not read out the whole passage, but at the end of this paragraph he shows the useful effect of speaking freely when it is employed properly. He says: You make fine speeches. You attend merely to the words, to their beauty and charm. Fine, this delights you, but: "When will you have finished acquiring all this knowledge? When will it be so indelibly engraved in you that it cannot escape your memory?

---

*Gummere, the English translator, has: "Let this be the kernel of my idea," which is closer to Foucault (and Seneca) than the French version. See, *The Epistles of Seneca*, vol. II, LXXV.4, pp. 138-39—G.B.

When will you put it to the test of experience? For it is not like other things, enough merely to commit these things to memory; you must try to put them to work."[22] Consequently, the final objective of the usefulness of speaking freely in this *animi negotium* is that we should not be satisfied with having some part of what we have heard in our memory, recalling how fine it is. What we hear must be engraved in such a way that we will be able to act as we ought to when we find ourselves in a situation requiring it. The effectiveness and usefulness of the speech heard, the speech conveyed by *parrhēsia*, will have to be measured when it is put to the test. Finally, another element we have already come across in other texts concerning *parrhēsia* is the inevitable but quite fundamental comparison between medicine, navigation, and government, the government of oneself or of others.[23] This comparison is, I believe, really fundamental in the thought and theory of government in the Hellenistic and Greco-Roman period. Governing is, precisely, a stochastic art, an art of conjecture, like medicine and also navigation: Steering a ship, treating a sick person, governing men, and governing oneself all fall under the same typology of rational and uncertain activity.[24]

We have here a wholly familiar landscape. Except, my reason for dwelling on this text is this: at the heart of the text there are certain expressions, whose face, as it were, we have seen breaking through in other texts, in those of Philodemus and Galen; but here, I think, the theme is set out fully. [Seneca] says: What is essential in *parrhēsia* is that the words I use may, if necessary, be somewhat embellished, but in any case what is their role, their function? Here then I would like to quote the phrase. He says: It is a matter of showing (*ostendere*) what I feel (*quid sentiam*) rather than speaking (*loqui*).[25] What does it mean "to show one's thought rather than speaking"? In this showing (*ostention*) of thought, which must be as undramatic as possible, even if it is sometimes embellished, I think there are two important elements, which, moreover, are explicit in the text. First there is the pure and simple transmission of the thought: I shall have achieved my purpose "if I have conveyed my thought without studied embellishment or platitude (*contentus sensus meos ad te pertulisse, quos nec exornasem nec abiecissem*)." Purely and simply to convey, *perferre* [is the verb], as in the expression "convey news by a letter." This is the *paradosis*. It involves then conveying the thought purely and simply, with the minimum embellishment compatible with this transparency (we also find in letter 40 the theme involved here of *oratio simplex*).

Pure and simple transmission of the thought, but—and this is the second element which characterizes this showing (*ostention*) of the thought, this *quid sentiam ostendere* that is the objective of this *parrhēsia*, this *libertas*—the thoughts conveyed must also be shown to be precisely the thoughts of the person conveying them. These are thoughts of the person who expresses them, and what must be shown is not just that this is right, the truth, but also that I who am speaking am the person who judges these thoughts to be really true and I am also the person for whom they are true. The text says this explicitly, one must be convinced that "*omnia me illa sentire, quae dicerem*,"[26] that I myself really experience (*sentire*) the things I say as true. And he adds further "*nec tantum sentire, sed amare*": and not only do I feel and consider the things I say to be true, but I even love them, am attached to them and my whole life is governed by them. The comparison with the kiss given to a child is interesting. The kiss given to one's mistress is an exaggerated and rhetorical kiss, which always lays it on a bit thick. The kiss given to a child is chaste, it is *simplex*: pure in the sense that it is, if you like, transparent, and expresses nothing more than tenderness, but a tenderness felt no less for the child than for the mistress. One is present as it were in the kiss: I make *my* tenderness present in this kiss so simple and pure. I think this directs us to a fundamental element in this notion of *libertas* (of *parrhēsia*). We caught sight of this fundamental element when Galen, for example, said: We must take for a master someone who has shown that he has conducted himself well in his life. We also found it in Philodemus when, concerning the *kathēgētēs* or *kathēgoumenos*, he said that he was formed by the example of the masters.[27] What seems to me the crucial element in this conception of *libertas* and *parrhēsia*, and which Seneca develops in this text, is that in order to guarantee the *parrhēsia* (the frankness) of the discourse delivered, the presence of the person speaking must be really perceptible in what he actually says.[28] Or again: the *parrhēsia*, the truth of what he says, must be sealed by the way he conducts himself and the way in which he actually lives. This is what Seneca says in the following phrase: "This is the essential point [not of our rhetoric but of what I mean; M.F.]: let us say what we think and think what we say; let speech harmonize with conduct. *Ille promissum suum implevit, qui, et cum videas illum et cum audias, idem est.*" [That is to say:] this person has fulfilled the kind of pact (*promissum suum*), the kind of commitment fundamental to the activity of guidance, its basis and condition; he keeps to his commitments and is the same whether you hear him in his discourse or see him in life. The basis of *parrhēsia* is, I think, this *adæquatio* between the subject who speaks, and who speaks the truth, and the subject who conducts himself as this truth requires. Much more even than the need to adjust oneself tactically to the other, it seems to me what characterizes *parrhēsia, libertas*, is this perfect fit between the subject who speaks, or the subject of enunciation, and the subject of conduct. This perfect fit is what gives one the right and possibility to speak outside required and traditional forms, to speak independently of the resources of rhetoric, which one may use, if need be, in order to facilitate the reception of what one is saying.

*Parrhēsia* (*libertas*, speaking freely), then, is this form that is essential to the guide's speech, and it is as such that I will sum up what I wanted to say on *parrhēsia*: *parrhēsia* is free speech, released from the rules, freed from rhetorical procedures, in that it must, in one respect of course, adapt itself to the situation, to the occasion and to the particularities of the auditor. But above all and fundamentally, on the side of the person who utters it, it is speech that is equivalent to commitment, to a bond, and which establishes a certain pact between the subject of enunciation and the subject of conduct. The subject who speaks commits himself. At the very moment he says "I speak the truth," he commits himself to do what he says and to be the subject of conduct who conforms in every respect to the truth he expresses. It is in virtue of this that there can be no teaching of the truth without an *exemplum*. There can be no teaching of the truth without the person who speaks the truth being the example of this truth, and this is also why the individual relationship is necessary—more, of course, than [for] the theatrical teaching given in popular gatherings, where any individual whomsoever exhorts any crowd whatsoever to virtue. Individual relationships in [correspondence]; better still, individual relationships in conversations; even better than conversation, relationships of shared lives, a long chain of living examples, as if passed on from hand to hand.[29] This is not just because the example makes it easier, as it were, to perceive the truth expressed, but because the pact is constantly reproduced in the chain of examples and discourse. I tell the truth, I tell you the truth. What authenticates the fact that I tell you the truth is that as subject of my conduct I really am, absolutely, integrally, and totally identical to the subject of enunciation I am when I tell you what I tell you. Here, I think, we are at the heart of *parrhēsia*. If I have insisted on this, and if I have constructed this analysis of *parrhēsia* so as to bring it to this point, it is because it seems to me that we have here an element, an utterly remarkable distribution of things, especially if we compare it to what we find later in Christianity.[30] All these things are complex and obviously should not be simplified: you have seen how, in the Epicureans for example, there is an expression of *parrhēsia* quite different from what we find in Galen, and what we find in Seneca is equally different. In short, there is a whole range of modalities.

However, if we want to take a bit of an overview, it seems to me that we can say the following. Let us call "pedagogical," if you like, the transmission of a truth whose function is to endow any subject whatever with aptitudes, capabilities, knowledges, and so on, that he did not possess before and that he should possess at the end of the pedagogical relationship. If, then, we call "pedagogical" this relationship consisting in endowing any subject whomsoever with a series of abilities defined in advance, we can, I think, call "psychagogical" the transmission of a truth whose function is not to endow any subject whomsoever with abilities, etcetera, but whose function is to modify the mode of being of the subject to whom we address ourselves. Okay, it seems to me that in the history of these psychagogical procedures, a considerable switch, a considerable mutation took place roughly between Greco-Roman philosophy and Christianity. Let's say that within the psychagogical relationship, the essential burden of truth in Greco-Roman Antiquity, that is, the necessity for telling the truth, the rules to which one must submit oneself in telling the truth, in order to tell the truth and so that the truth can produce its effect—namely, transformation of the subject's mode of being—falls essentially on the master, the guide, or the friend, or anyway on the person who gives advice. These obligations, tasks, and commitments essentially weigh on him, the speaker or transmitter of true discourse. Insofar as the obligations of truth are essentially borne by the master, counselor, or guide, I think we can say that in Antiquity the psychagogical relationship is very close, or relatively close, to the pedagogical relationship. For in pedagogy, the master [is such] inasmuch as he holds the truth, expresses the truth, expresses it properly and within rules intrinsic to the true discourse he conveys. Truth and the obligations of truth fall on the master's side. This is true in all pedagogy. It is, of course, true in ancient pedagogy, but it is true in what we could call ancient psychagogy. And it is in this sense, and for this reason, that ancient psychagogy is so close to pedagogy. It is still experienced as a *paideia*.[31] In Christianity, on the other hand, it seems to me that things will be changed considerably on the basis of a number of quite remarkable mutations, one of which being, of course, that the truth does not come from the person who guides the soul but is given in another mode (Revelation, Text, Book, etcetera). In the Christian type of psychagogy we will see that although it is true that the person who provides spiritual direction must obey a number of rules, and that he has a number of responsibilities and obligations, the most fundamental and essential cost of the truth and of "truth-telling" will be borne by the person whose soul has to be guided. And this person's soul will be able to be guided simply at the cost of his enunciation of a true discourse about himself. It seems to me that from that moment the Christian type of psychagogy will be distinguished from and quite profoundly opposed to the Greco-Roman philosophical type of psychagogy. Greco-Roman psychagogy was still very close to pedagogy. It conformed to the same general structure of the master who delivers the discourse of truth. Christianity will unhook psychagogy and pedagogy by requiring the psychagogized soul, the guided soul, to express a truth; a truth that only it can tell, that it alone holds, and that is not the only element but one of the fundamental elements of the operation by which its mode of being will be changed. Christian confession will consist in this.[32] Let's say, and I will stop there, that in Christian spirituality it is the guided subject who must be present within the true discourse as the object of his own true discourse. In the discourse of the one who is guided, the subject of enunciation must be the referent of the utterance: this is the definition of confession. In Greco-Roman philosophy, rather, the person who must be present within the true discourse is the person who guides. And he does not have to be present in the form of the utterance's reference (he does not have to speak about himself), and he is not present as the person who says: "This is what I am." He is present in a coincidence between the subject of enunciation and the subject of his own actions. "This truth I tell you, you see it in me." That's it.

1. Question from the public.
2. Foucault delivered his lectures from January to April.
3. Jacques Lagrange, historian of psychiatry and philosopher of medicine, remained the most faithful auditor of Foucault's lectures, which he followed from the lectures at Rue d'Ulm at the beginning of the fifties. His recordings (as well as those of G. Burlet for the seventies) are today the basis for the transcripts.
4. The editors hesitate between two titles: *Traité des passions de l'âme et de ses erreurs* (following Marquardt [and the Harkins English edition, *On the Passions and Errors of the Soul*—G.B.]) and *Du diagnostic et du traitement des passions de l'âme* (following Kühn). On these problems, see the "preliminary note" by V. Barras, T. Birchler, and A.-F. Morand to the latest edition of Galen, *L'Âme et ses passions* (Paris: Les Belles Lettres, 1995).
5. See the "unhappy due to loving ourselves excessively (*amore nostri*)" in the preface to book IV of *Natural Questions*, studied in the first hour of this lecture.
6. Actually Foucault gives a summary of chapter 2 of *On the Passions and Errors of the Soul*.
7. Foucault here moves to the recapitulation of chapter III.
8. See the lecture of 19 March 1980 at the Collège de France (with reference to John Cassian's *Cenobite Institutions* and *Conferences*) and, in a different theoretical framework, but resting on the same texts, the lecture of 22 February 1978 at the Collège de France on the Christian pastoral (technique of individualization irreducible to the principles of the governmentality of the Greek city-state).
9. Beginning of chapter II.
10. *Isaiah*, 64: 6. The theme is taken up in the second stanza of the "Rorate, caeli, desuper . . ." sung during Advent.
11. See the description of Christian—as opposed to Hellenistic—spiritual direction, in the lecture at the Collège de France, 19 March 1980.
12. "[Prefer] old men who have lived excellent lives." *On the Passions and Errors of the Soul*.
13. For a general presentation of this movement of popular preaching, see the chapter "La prédication populaire," in J.-M. André, *La Philosophie à Rome*. It will be noted that one of its oldest representatives, Sextius the elder, was the master of Sotion, who gave the young Seneca his first lessons in philosophy. But for Greek literature we should mention in particular the names of Musonius Rufus and Dio Chrysostom.
14. "Popular eloquence has nothing to do with the truth. What is its aim? To stir up the crowd by surprising listeners who lack judgment." Seneca, *Letters*, XL.4.
15. "Besides, speech that deals with the truth should be unadorned and plain (*adice nunc, quod quae veritati operam dat oratio, et composita esse debet et simplex*)." Ibid.
16. "Don't you see that discourse whose aim is to cure us must sink deep within us (*descendere in nos debet*)." Ibid.
17. On the theory of logical seeds, see Cicero: "Undoubtedly we carry the seeds of virtue at birth (*semina innata virtutum*)." *Tusculan Disputations*, vol. II, III.i.2, and Seneca, "It is easy to encourage one's listener in the love of good: nature has placed in every heart the foundation and first seed of the virtues (*semenque virtutum*),"*Letters*, CVIII.8. The theme is the object of a note by Diogenes Laertius in his general presentation of Stoicism in *Lives of Eminent Philosophers*, vol. II, book VII, 157.
18. "The greatest profit comes from free discussion, because it creeps gradually into the soul . . . advice is not given at the top of one's voice . . . we must speak in a lower tone. In this way the words penetrate and are engraved more easily; we do not ask for many words but for effective ones. Scatter them like seed which, quite tiny, fallen on good ground, displays its vigor." Seneca, *Letters*, XXXVIII.1-2.
19. "Truth must only be spoken to the person who wishes to hear it. That is why, regarding Diogenes and the Cynics generally, who used their freedom in speaking indiscriminately and gave lessons to anyone, it is often wondered whether they should have followed such

a course. What a fine effect if you were to chide the deaf or those who are speechless from birth or by accident?" Ibid., XXIX.1-2.
20. Ibid., LXXV.1-7.
21. See for example: "direct speech and daily contact will benefit you more than written discourse." Ibid., VI.5.
22. Ibid., LXXV.7.
23. See the lecture of 17 February, first hour.
24. See the analyses in the first hour of this lecture. On navigation and government as matters of a stochastic intelligence, see M. Détienne and J.-P. Vernant, *Les Ruses de l'intelligence. La mètis des Grecs*, especially pp. 201-41, concerning maritime Athena, and pp. 295-302 (*Cunning Intelligence in Greek Culture and Society*, pp. 215-48 and pp. 288-96).
25. Seneca, *Letters*, LXXV.2.
26. Ibid., LXXV.3.
27. See this lecture, first hour.
28. In the lecture of 12 January 1983 (devoted to the study of *parrhēsia* in classical Greece— Pericles' speech, Euripides' *Ion*, Plato's dialogues, etcetera), Foucault retains the subject's commitment in his words to define *parrhēsia*, but with the supplementary idea of a risk incurred by the subject, whose frankness may cost him his freedom or his life.
29. Allusion to the memory of Epicurus, passed on by disciples who had a living contact with the master and, by virtue of this, enjoyed an unequalled prestige, Foucault discusses this in the first hour of the lecture.
30. The analysis of *parrhēsia* in Christianity will undergo an initial elaboration in the final course Foucault delivered at the Collège de France in 1984. He mentions there its usage in Philo of Alexandria (*parrhēsia* as full and positive modality of the relationship to God) and in New Testament literature (*parrhēsia* as the Christian's assurance making prayer possible).
31. On this notion (based on a text from Epicurus), see the lecture of 10 February, second hour.
32. During 1980 Foucault traced the history of the confession (see the course summary, "Du gouvernement des vivants," in *Dits et Écrits*, vol. 4, pp. 125-29; English translation by Robert Hurley et al, "On the Government of the Living," in *Ethics: Subjectivity and Truth*, pp. 81-85). It should be noted that Foucault's argument then consisted in showing that the coupling of the remission of sins and the verbalization of a truth about oneself does not belong to the original forms of Christianity, but gets its meaning from an apparatus of subjection established by monastic institutions around the fifth and sixth centuries (see the lengthy analyses of Cassian's *Cenobite Institutions* in the lecture of 26 March 1980).

# twenty-one

# 17 MARCH 1982

### First hour

> *Supplementary remarks on the meaning of the Pythagorean rules of silence.* ~ *Definition of "ascetics."* ~ *Appraisal of the historical ethnology of Greek ascetics.* ~ *Reminder of the* Alcibiades: *withdrawal of ascetics into self-knowledge as mirror of the divine.* ~ *Ascetics of the first and second centuries: a double decoupling (with regard to the principle of self-knowledge and with regard to the principle of recognition in the divine).* ~ *Explanation of the Christian fate of Hellenistic and Roman ascetics: rejection of the gnosis.* ~ *Life's work.* ~ *Techniques of existence, exposition of two levels: mental exercise; training in real life.* ~ *Exercises of abstinence: the athletic body in Plato and the hardy body in Musonius Rufus.* ~ *The practice of tests and its characteristics.*

AS AN APPENDIX TO last week's lecture I would like to read you a text I came across during the week, which I really should have known about, concerning listening, the sense of hearing (relations between listening and silence) in the Pythagorean schools. This text delighted me for a number of reasons. In the first place, of course, because it confirms what I said to you about the meaning of the famous Pythagorean instruction of silence, which is a pedagogical silence, silence with regard to the master's speech, silence within the school and as opposed to the speech permitted to more advanced students. Then certain other elements in the text seemed to me to be interesting. It is a text by Aulus Gellius from book I of *Attic Nights*. Here it is: "According to tradition, this was the progressive method of Pythagoras, and then of his school and successors, for admitting and training disciples. First of all Pythagoras studied the 'physiognomy' of the young people who came to him in order to follow his teaching. This word indicates that one inquired about the nature and character of the person by drawing inferences from the look of their face and expression and the whole structure of their body as well as its appearance. Then the person who had been examined and judged suitable [in terms of these positive physiognomic features; M.F.], was immediately admitted into the sect and Pythagoras imposed silence on him for a definite time, not the same for all, but for each according to the judgment of his capacity to progress [so: silence according to what one had been able to recognize, identify, or divine according to the student's physiognomy; M.F.]. The person listened in silence [this points to what I was saying, that is to say, the function of silence in relation to listening: pedagogical silence; M.F.] to what the others said and was not allowed to ask questions [you see that this really was involved; M.F.] if he had not understood well, or to note down what he had heard." So this is something I was unaware of, but which confirms the idea that this silence is essentially an exercise of memory: Not only does the student not have the right to speak, to ask questions, to interrupt the master, and to participate in this game of questions and answers which is nevertheless so important in all ancient pedagogy—he does not have the right to participate in this game, he is not qualified to take the floor—but at the same time he does not have the right to take notes, that is to say, he must record everything in the form of memory; the exercise of pure memory is involved here, which is, if you like, the positive side of the prohibition on speaking. "No-one [so not even among those who had the best physiognomic features; M.F.] maintained silence for less than two years. In the period during which they kept quiet and listened they were called *akoustikoi*, auditors. But when they had learned the two most difficult things of all, keeping quiet and listening [you remember what I was saying to you last week on silence and listening as the first basis for all the exercises of apprenticeship, of all the spiritual exercises, as first moment of the training: keeping quiet and listening so that what is said, the true word spoken by the master, is inscribed in pure memory; M.F.], and had begun their instruction with silence, which was called *ekhemuthia* [that is to say: keeping silence, the safekeeping of silence; M.F.], they then had the right to speak and ask questions, and they had the right to write down what they had heard and to expound on what they themselves thought [so the right to speech and the right to take notes appear, simultaneously, at the end of the necessary and initial stage of silence; M.F.]. During this period [in which they had the right to speak and write; M.F.] they were called *mathēmatikoi*, mathematicians, from the name of the sciences which they had begun to learn and study: for the ancient Greeks called geometry, gnomonics, music, and the other somewhat abstract disciplines, *mathēmata*."[1] Then "our dear Taurus [a philosopher before Aulus Gellius of Pythagorean inspiration, I think; M.F.][2] after giving us this information about Pythagoras" said: Now, sadly, things are not done in the same way. This gradation going from silence and listening to participation in speech and apprenticeship in the *mathēmata*, this fine order, is no longer respected. This is how Taurus describes the schools of philosophy in his period: " 'Now people are admitted straightaway at the philosopher's establishment, their feet badly washed, and it is not enough that they are ignorant, incapable of learning the arts and geometry, they themselves decree the order in which they will learn philosophy. One of them says: "Teach me this first of all." Another says: "I want to learn this, not that." One is keen to start with Plato's *Symposium*, because of the debauchery of Alcibiades. The other wants to begin with *Phaedrus* because of the beauty of the speech made by Lysias. There are even those, by Jupiter, who ask to read Plato, not in order to make their conduct more beautiful but in order to embellish their language and style, not in order to govern themselves more strictly [*nec ut modestior fiat*: not in order to behave better; M.F.] but in order to acquire more charm.' These were the usual remarks of Taurus when he compared the new mode of philosophy students with the old Pythagoreans."[3] This, then, is what I should have read to you when I spoke about this problem of the silence of the Pythagoreans. And so you see that for the good students—those who wash their feet and do not ask to begin with the *Symposium*—it actually constitutes, I believe, the first basis of apprenticeship. So, in short, through the rules of silence and the principles of *parrhēsia*, of speaking freely, I am trying to study the rules of the expression, transmission, and acquisition of true discourse. You know that this true discourse should make up the soul's necessary equipment, the *paraskeuē*, which enables individuals to confront, or anyway to be ready to confront, all the events of life as they occur. This then is the first basis of ascesis.

I would like now to move on to a completely different stratum of ascesis, in which the principal axis is no longer this listening to and reception of true discourse. The principal axis of this new stratum, of this new domain of ascesis, will be precisely putting these true discourses to work, activating them, not merely in the memory or thought, which grasps them again by returning to them regularly, but in the subject's activity, that is to say: how to become the active subject of true discourse. This other phase, this other stage of ascesis must transform true discourse, the truth, into *ēthos*. This is what is usually called *askēsis* in the strict sense. In order to designate this other stratum, this other level of ascesis (of exercise), I will employ the term "ascetics," but with some misgivings because I am not very fond of these kinds of plays on words, but in the end it is a bit more convenient. I would like to avoid, on the one hand, using the word "asceticism" which has, as you know, quite specific connotations and refers to an attitude of renunciation, mortification, etcetera, which is not what is involved; it is not an asceticism. I would also like to avoid the word "ascesis" which is related either to this or that particular exercise or to the individual's undertaking of a series of exercises from which he will ask—what? Well, it may be his pardon, it may be his purification, it may be his salvation, it may be some kind of spiritual experience, and so on. So, since to designate this set of exercises we use neither the term "asceticism" nor the term "ascesis," I will call it, if you like, "ascetics." Ascetics, that is to say the more or less coordinated set of exercises that are available, recommended, and even obligatory, and anyway utilizable by individuals in a moral, philosophical, and religious system in order to achieve a definite spiritual objective. By "spiritual objective" I understand a certain transformation, a certain transfiguration of themselves as subjects, as subjects of action and as subjects of true knowledge. This objective of spiritual transmutation is what ascetics, that is to say the set of given exercises, must make it possible to achieve.

What then are these exercises? What is the nature of this ascetics introduced and defined, generally speaking, in the philosophy of the High Empire, in the practice and culture of the self that I am trying to define and describe in this period? In a sense, the question of ascetics, of the whole system of ascesis-exercises, is essentially a question of technique. It can be analyzed as a technical question. That is to say, in this period it involves defining the different exercises prescribed or recommended, what they consist in, how they differ from each other, and what the internal rules are to which each must conform. We could draw up a table including abstinence, meditation, meditation on death, meditation on future evils, the examination of conscience, etcetera (there is a whole set of exercises of this kind). I will try to bring out this technical side; at any rate I will concentrate on the framework of a certain technicality of these exercises of ascesis, of this ascetics.

We could besides, and I think it would be quite interesting, try to make a bit of a systematic examination of all this and, if you like, again using a rather solemn word which I put in inverted commas, do a kind of "ethnology of ascetics," comparing the different exercises and following their evolution and diffusion. For example, I think there is a very interesting problem raised by Dodds, which was taken up by Vernant and Joly, and which provoked a discussion, or anyway aroused the skepticism of Hadot: the problem of the continuity between exercises of probably shamanist origin, which appeared in Greece towards the seventh and sixth centuries B.C., and the spiritual exercises we see emerging in Greek philosophy strictly speaking.[4] Dodds' hypothesis, taken up by Vernant and Joly, is that when the Greeks came into contact with northeastern European civilizations in the seventh century (thanks to navigation in the Black Sea), they encountered shamanistic practices and techniques of the self peculiar to this form of culture, among which there were things like: regimens of feats of abstinence (up to what point can one bear hunger or the cold, etcetera?); also, the system of tests of abstinence (the contest to see who will go furthest in this kind of exercise); techniques for concentrating thought and breathing (holding the breath or breathing as little as possible so as to try to concentrate oneself, dispersing oneself as little as possible in the external world, as it were); meditation on death, in the form of a kind of exercise by which one separates the soul from the body and anticipates one's death, so to speak. The Greeks then would have known all these exercises through and on the basis of shamanistic cultures. According to Dodds, Vernant, and Joly, there are traces of these exercises in the first Socratic dialogues in which Socrates arouses the admiration of his contemporaries and his circle: thus at the battle of Matinee, when he remains alone throughout the night, in the cold, immobile, and really feeling and experiencing nothing around him.[5] So these are the forms of the practice of the self, of the technique of the self, which would be attested in the character of Socrates. These are the exercises that would be transposed and transfigured in spiritual practices in which there are in fact the same rules of abstinence as well as relatively analogous practices of concentration on the self, examination of oneself, and the withdrawal of thought into itself, etcetera. So should continuity be admitted or not? Should we take it that in fact a kind of transfer, implanting, and decanting took place at the same time as these basically magical and somatic practices became philosophical and spiritual practices? Or are there actually two sets of different practices that cannot be brought together? I think Hadot would be on the side of discontinuity. Dodds and Vernant, rather, would support continuity. However, I leave it there, because it is not really my problem.

I will try nevertheless to stick to the technical framework suggested by the table of these exercises, but the problem I would like to pose, what I would like to propose as the stake of the analysis, is both historical and philosophical. Let's return for a moment to the text that was our point of departure, the *Alcibiades*, Plato's dialogue about whose dating there are many uncertainties. You recall that the whole of the *Alcibiades*—or at any rate all of the second half of the dialogue—was devoted to the question of the *epimeleia heautou* (the care of the self).

Socrates had convinced Alcibiades that if he really wanted to fulfill his political ambition—namely, to govern his fellow citizens and hold his own against both Sparta and the King of Persia—then first of all he had to pay a bit of attention to himself, to attend to himself, to be concerned about himself. And then the whole of the second part of the *Alcibiades* was therefore devoted to the question: What is it to take care of oneself? What, first of all, is one's self which one should take care of? Answer: it is the soul. And in what does this care applied to the soul consist? Well, in the *Alcibiades*, this care applied to the soul was described as being essentially the soul's knowledge of itself, self-knowledge. The soul, in looking at itself in the element that constitutes its essential part, namely the *noūs*,[6] must recognize itself, that is to say, recognize both its divine nature and the divinity of thought. In this sense the dialogue of the *Alcibiades* shows, or rather brings about in its development, what could be called the specifically Platonic "covering up" of the *epimeleia heautou* by the *gnōthi seauton* (of care of the self by knowledge of the self). Self-knowledge, the requirement "know yourself," completely covers over and occupies the entire space opened up by the requirement "take care of yourself." Ultimately "take care of yourself" will mean: "know yourself." Know yourself, know the nature of your soul, ensure your soul contemplates itself in this *noūs* and recognizes itself in its essential divinity. This is what we found in the *Alcibiades*.

Now, if we move on to the analysis of these exercises, of this ascetics that I would now like to begin to analyze—this ascetics developed mainly by the Stoics and Stoico-Cynics in the period of the High Empire—what I think appears quite clearly is that, contrary to what can be found in the *Alcibiades* and in classical Platonism, and especially in the long continuation of Neo-Platonism, this Stoico-Cynic ascetics is not organized around the principle of self-knowledge. It is not organized around the principle of recognition of the self as a divine element. In saying this I do not mean at all that the absorption of the care of the self into knowledge of the self absolutely excludes any exercise or ascetics in Platonism or Neo-Platonism. On the contrary, the Platonists and Neo-Platonists lay great stress on this. Moreover, in the texts of Plato himself, in classical Platonism if you like, it is a fundamental principle that *philosophia* is an *askēsis*. But what is involved is precisely a different type of exercise. Neither do I want to say that self-knowledge is not involved, and is excluded in Stoico-Cynic exercises, in this ascetics. A different type of knowledge is involved, however. I would say that in its precise historical form, and when compared with what is said and formulated in the *Alcibiades*, the ascetics of the Stoics and Cynics in the Hellenistic and Roman period is characterized by a double decoupling. [First:] decoupling of the whole of this body of ascetics (of all these exercises) from the requirement of self-knowledge; a shift, if you like, in which self-knowledge will have a certain role, of course, as something indispensable that cannot be eliminated, but it will no longer be the central axis of the *askēsis*; a shift, then, of the whole of the *askēsis* with regard to the axis of self-knowledge. And second, a shift, a decoupling of the self-knowledge that can be obtained—and as it must be practiced, moreover, in these exercises—from recognition of the self as divine element. This component is still found here. It is not eliminated and is by no means to be neglected. You know how the principle of *homoiōsis tō theō*, of assimilation to God, how the necessity of recognizing oneself as participating in divine reason, or even as being a substantial part of the divine reason that organizes the whole world, is very present in the Stoics. However, I do not think this recognition of oneself as divine element occupies the central place it has in Platonism and Neo-Platonism.[7] So, there is decoupling of the set of these exercises from the principle of self-knowledge, and decoupling of self-knowledge from the Platonists' central axis of recognition of the self as divine element. Okay, I think it was this double decoupling that was at the source of the historical success of these exercises, of their historical success, paradoxically, in Christianity itself.

What I would now like to say is that if these exercises have been so important historically—not just in the imperial period, but for a long time after, and in Christianity, being found again in sixteenth- and seventeenth-century spirituality—if they were indeed incorporated into Christianity where they survived and lived for so long, it is precisely inasmuch as they were non-Platonist, inasmuch as there was this displacement of ascetics with regard to self-knowledge and of self-knowledge with regard to recognition of the self as divine element. Non-Platonism assured this survival for a very simple reason, which is that, as you know, the mainspring, the major principle—I was going to say, the strategic principle—of the development of Christian spirituality in monastic institutions, from the end of the third century and throughout the fourth and fifth centuries, was in fact the construction of a Christian spirituality freed from the gnosis.[8] That is to say, Christian spirituality, as developed in the monastic environment, was engaged in a sharp polemic. It had a strategic line which was the line dividing it from the gnosis, which was fundamentally Neo-Platonist[9] inasmuch as the stake of all Gnostic spirituality, of all Gnostic practices and exercises of life, consisted precisely in focusing all ascesis around knowledge (of the "gnosis") and all knowledge on the act by which the soul recognizes itself, and is recognized, as divine element. This was the center of the gnosis, and the, as it were, Neo-Platonist heart of the gnosis. Inasmuch as Christian spirituality, that is to say the spirituality that develops in the East from the fourth century, was fundamentally anti-Gnostic and strove to detach itself from this gnosis, it was natural that monastic institutions—and more generally, the spiritual practices of the Christian East—resorted to this ascetic equipment, to this ascetics I have just been talking about, which was originally Stoic and Cynic and which distinguished itself from Neo-Platonism through the two features I have mentioned: not focusing on the practice of knowledge, and not focusing the question of knowledge on the principle of "recognizing oneself as divine element." Let's say that, up to a certain point and taking things very broadly, this Stoico-Cynic ascetics had no special vocation to become Christian. It would not have had to become Christian were it not precisely for this question posed within Christianity when it had to free itself from the Gnostic temptation. For Christianity, this philosophical, or originally philosophical ascetics, was the technical guarantee, as it were, against falling into Gnostic spirituality. It put to work exercises that, to a large extent, did not belong to the domain of knowledge. And, precisely, the significance of these exercises, of abstinence for example, of tests, etcetera, about which I will speak again, [was entirely due to the absence of direct connections] with knowledge, and with self-knowledge. This set of abstinences was therefore important. Then, second, there were certainly knowledge exercises, but their primary meaning and final aim was not recognition of oneself as divine element, but rather exercises of knowledge and self-knowledge whose function and aim were directed at oneself. Not the great movement of recognition of the divine, but the constant anxiety of suspicion. It is not the divine element that I must first of all recognize within me and in myself. First of all I must try to decipher in myself anything that may be the traces... the traces of what? Well, in the Stoics; [the traces] of my faults, of my weakness the traces of my fall in the Christians, as well as the traces, not of God, but of the Other, of the Devil. The exercises of self-knowledge, which Christian spirituality will develop in terms of, on the basis of, and following the model of the old Stoic suspicion towards oneself, basically consisted in this decipherment of the self as a tissue of impulses of thought and of the heart, which carry the mark of evil and which may be instilled in us by the close or even internal presence of the Devil.[10] These are exercises, then, that are far from being focused on knowledge and which, when they do focus on knowledge, focus on suspicion of the self more than on recognition of the divine: this, more or less, explains the transfer of these originally philosophical exercises to the very heart of Christianity. They are visibly and royally implanted in the spirituality of the fourth and fifth centuries. Cassian's texts are very interesting on this. And, broadly speaking, from Seneca to Cassian you see the same type of exercises transposed and taken up again.[11] And then, these are the exercises that will live throughout Christianity and reappear with new, greater dimensions and a new, stronger intensity from the fifteenth and sixteenth centuries and, of course, in the Reformation and Counter-Reformation.

This provides, if you like, some explanation for the fact that these exercises, this philosophical ascetics, strangely found in Christianity a particularly favorable milieu for reception, survival, and development. Now then, what are these exercises? To tell the truth, it is not very easy to find a way to pinpoint this ascetics and try to analyze it. Even so, for whoever wants to analyze these things, Christianity has in this respect a considerable advantage over the philosophical ascetics of the imperial period I am talking about. You know—and this is striking in the sixteenth and seventeenth centuries—how important it was for Christianity to define each exercise in its specificity, to prescribe the ordering of these exercises in relation to each other and their temporal succession according to the day, week, month, year, and also of the individual's progress. At the end of the sixteenth and the beginning of the seventeenth century, a truly pious person's life—and I am not even talking about members of seminaries or monks in the Counter-Reformation; I am talking about the Catholic world, since it is somewhat different in the Protestant world—was literally carpeted and lined with exercises which had to be kept up and practiced daily and hourly, according to times of the day, circumstances, moments of life, and degrees of advancement in spiritual exercise. There were entire manuals explaining all the exercises you had to do at each of these moments. There was no moment of life that did not have to be doubled, prompted, and underpinned by a certain type of exercise. Each of these exercises was meticulously defined in its object, purpose, and procedures. Without going as far as this kind of lining of life, and each moment of life, with these exercises, if you take the texts of the fourth and fifth centuries—the first great Cenobite rules, I am thinking of Basil of Caesarea, for example[12]—you see here also that, without being so dense and well-defined as in the sixteenth and seventeenth centuries in the Counter-Reformation, the exercises are nonetheless very clearly defined and divided up in relation to each other. Now there is none of this in the ascetics I am talking about. There are some indications of regularity. Certain forms of examination are recommended for the morning: the examination you should make in the morning concerning the tasks you will have to perform during the day. There is the well-known recommendation of the evening exercise (examination of conscience).[13] However, beyond these few reference points, it is much more a matter of the subject's free choice of exercises when he finds he needs them. One just gives some rules of prudence or advice on the way in which an exercise should be followed. If there is this liberty and such a slight definition of these exercises and their sequence, we should not forget that all this is not taking place within the framework of a rule of life but of a *tekhnē tou biou* (an art of living). I think we should remember this. Making one's life the object of a *tekhnē*, making one's life a work—a beautiful and good work (as everything produced by a good and reasonable *tekhnē* should be)—necessarily entails the freedom and choice of the person employing this *tekhnē*.[14] If a *tekhnē* was a body of rules to which one had to submit from start to finish, minute by minute, at every moment, if there were not precisely this freedom of the subject making use of his *tekhnē* according to his objective, desire, and will to make a beautiful work, then there would be no perfection of life. I think this is an important element that should be firmly grasped because it is precisely one of the dividing lines between these philosophical exercises and the Christian exercise. We should not forget that one of the major elements of Christian spirituality will be precisely that life must be "well-ordered." The *regula vitae* (the rule of life) is essential. Why then? We need to come back to this. Certainly, many elements have played a part. To take the most external, but not the most indifferent, the model of the army and of the Roman legion was an organizing model for at least some cenobites in the Christian East and West. The model of the army certainly played its part, but this was not the only reason why the Christian life must be a regular life. It is a problem anyway. The philosophical life, rather, or the life as defined and prescribed by philosophers as the life obtained thanks to a *tekhnē*, does not obey a *regula* (a rule): it submits to a *forma* (a form). It is a style of life, a sort of form one gives to one's life. For example, to build a beautiful temple according to the *tekhnē* of architects, one must of course follow some rules, some indispensable technical rules. But the good architect is one who uses enough of his liberty to give the temple a *forma*, a beautiful form. In the same way, the person who wants to make his life a work, the person who wants to employ the *tekhnē tou biou* in the proper way, must have in his mind not so much the framework, fabric, and thick covering regulations which he follows constantly and to which he has to submit. In the mind of a Roman or a Greek, neither obedience to the rule nor obedience *tout court* can constitute [a] beautiful work. A beautiful work is one that conforms to the idea of a certain *forma* (a certain style, a certain form of life). This is no doubt the reason why in the ascetics of the philosophers there is absolutely nothing of this exact catalog of all the exercises to be performed, at every moment of life and each time of the day, that there is in the Christians. So we are dealing with a much more tangled set which we can begin to untangle a little in the following way: by focusing on two words, two terms, both of which refer to this domain of exercises, of ascetics, but which refer, I think, to two of its aspects or, if you like, to two families. On the one hand there is the term *meletan*, and on the other the term *gumnazein*.

The Latins translate *meletan* by *meditari*, and *meletē* by *meditatio*. We must keep in mind also—I think I have already pointed this out[15]—that (the Greek) *meletan-meletē* and (the Latin) *meditari-meditatio* designate something active, a real activity. It is not just a sort of withdrawal of thought freely playing on itself. It is a real exercise. In certain texts the word *meletan* may well designate the activity of agricultural work, for example.[16] *Meletē* performs real work, the work of *meletan*. *Meletan* is also a term employed in the technique of teachers of rhetoric to designate the kind of preparatory work the individual must undergo when he has to speak, and when he has to speak freely by improvising, that is to say when he does not have a text to read or declaim after learning it by heart. It is a sort of preparation that is both very constraining, very concentrated on itself, but which also prepares the individual to speak freely. This is the *meletē* of the rhetoricians.[17] When the philosophers speak of exercises of the self on the self, the expression *meletan* designates, I think, something like the *meletē* of the rhetoricians: a work thought exercises on itself, a work of thought, but whose basic function is to prepare the individual for what he will soon have to do.

Then there is the *gumnazein*, or *gumnazesthai*, the usual form, which indicates the fact that one does exercises for oneself, which means "to practice," "to train," and which seems to me to be related much more to a practice in real life. *Gumnazein* actually involves being present in a real situation, either that one has artificially called for and organized, or that one encounters in life, and in which one tries out what one is doing. This distinction between *meletan* and *gumnazein* is both quite clear and quite uncertain. I say it is uncertain because there are many texts in which there is clearly no difference between them, and Plutarch, for example, employs *meletan/gumnazein* roughly as equivalents, with no difference between them. However, it is very clear that there is a difference in other texts. In Epictetus the series *meletan/graphein/gumnazein* appears at least twice.[18] *Meletan* then is to meditate, if you like, to practice in thought. One thinks about things, about principles, one reflects on them, and one prepares oneself through thought. *Graphein* is writing these things; so one thinks and one writes. And then *gumnazein*: one practices in real life. The series is clear. So here, if you like, I will base myself a bit on this series, or rather on the distinction *meletan/gumnazein*, and although in one sense and logically we [should begin with *meletan*, for a] number of reasons, which I hope will become apparent, [I would like] to present things in the reverse order and begin with *gumnazein*, that is to say, work on the self in real life. Then I will move on to the problem of *meletan*, of meditation and the work of thought on itself.

I think we can [make a distinction] within this vein of *gumnazein*, of training in real life. However, you will see that this distinction, which I try to introduce for ease of exposition, is somewhat arbitrary. There is a huge amount of overlap. On the one hand, in actual fact this is a domain of prescribed practice with its rules and game: There is a real technicality; but once again we are also in a space of freedom in which to some extent each improvises according to his needs, requirements, and situation. I will therefore introduce two things somewhat abstractly: the regimen of abstinence, and secondly the practice of tests.

The regimen of abstinence. To begin with I will look at some fairly, even completely simple things. Stobaeus, in his *Florilegium*, has preserved a text, part of a treatise by Musonius Rufus, which is precisely on exercises and is called the *Peri askēseōs*.[19] In this treatise, or rather in this fragment of his treatise, Musonius Rufus—you know he was a Stoic philosopher at the beginning of the Empire who had a number of problems with Nero and his successors[20]—says that the body must not be neglected in the exercises, even when it is a matter of practicing philosophy. For, he says, if it is true that the body is no great thing, or anyway no more than an instrument, it is an instrument that the virtues really have to make use of for the actions of life. Virtue must go through the body in order to become active. Therefore one must take care of one's body, and *askēsis* (ascetics) must include the body. So, Musonius says, what sorts of exercise may one engage in? Well, he says, there are exercises of the body itself, of the soul itself, and of the body and the soul. Now what is typical of this passage preserved from his *Treatise* is that Musonius says absolutely nothing about exercises of the body in the strict sense, and the only things that interest him, precisely from the point of view of philosophy and the *tekhnē tou biou*, are exercises of the soul and exercises of the soul and the body together. He says these exercises of the soul and the body must have two objectives. On the one hand, training and strengthening courage (*andreia*), which we should understand as resistance to external events, the ability to bear them without suffering, collapsing, and letting oneself be overcome by them; resistance to external events, misfortunes, and all the rigors of the world. Then, second, training and strengthening that other virtue, *sōphrosunē*, that is to say, the ability to control oneself. Let's say that *andreia* enables us to bear what comes from the external world, and *sōphrosunē* enables us to limit, regulate, and master all the internal impulses, the impulses of one's self.[21] In saying this—that the exercises of the soul and the body are for training *andreia* and *sōphrosunē*, courage and self-control—Musonius Rufus seems very close to what can be found in Plato, in *The Laws* for example, when Plato explains how, in order to train a good citizen or a good guardian, we need to train both his courage and then his moderation, his *egkrateia* (self-control).[22] But if the objective in Plato and Musonius is the same, the nature of the exercise is completely different. In Plato these two virtues—courage with regard to the external world; control of oneself—are secured by physical exercises, literally by gymnastic exercise. For Plato, athleticism, the exercise of fighting with another person, all the preparations necessary for competing not only in fighting, but also in racing and jumping, etcetera, all this specifically athletic training is one of the guarantees that one will not be afraid of external adversity, that one will not be afraid of the adversaries with whom one learns to fight, the struggle with another person having to serve as the model for the struggle with events and misfortunes. And then, athletic preparation involves of course many renunciations, many abstentions, if not abstinences, and sexual abstinence in particular: It is well known that one cannot win a contest at Olympia unless one has led a particularly chaste life.²³ In Plato, then, gymnastics provides the training of these two virtues, courage and self-control. Now what is interesting in Musonius is precisely that gymnastics has completely vanished. By what means will the same objective— training *andreia* and *sōphrosunē* through exercises of the body and the soul—be achieved? Not by gymnastics but by abstinence or, if you like, by a regime of endurance with regard to hunger, cold, heat, and sleep. One must accustom oneself to bear hunger and thirst, and to bear extreme cold and heat. One must get used to sleeping rough. One must get used to coarse and inadequate clothing, etcetera. So these exercises in Musonius do not involve—and I think the difference here is very important—the athletic body, the stake or point of application of the physical or physico-moral ascesis, but a body of patience, endurance, and abstinence. Now this is in actual fact what is involved in Musonius. And the same thing is found in most Stoic and Cynic texts.

It is found in Seneca in particular, where there is a quite explicit and clear criticism of gymnastics in the strict sense. In letter 15 to Lucilius, he has fun at the expense of those people who spend their time exercising their arms, developing their muscles, thickening their neck, and broadening their shoulders. This, he says, is an occupation that is vain in itself, which exhausts the mind and burdens it with all the weight of the body. So, in these exercises in which the body is activated, the objective must be that the body does not burden the soul; gymnastics burdens the soul with all the weight of the body. Seneca, therefore, prefers light exercises suitable for supporting a body, a valetudinary body like his own, asthmatic, coughing, breathing with difficulty, and so on, a valetudinary body which must be prepared so that it is free for intellectual activity, for reading and writing, etcetera. So he gives advice which consists in saying: You should jump from time to time in the morning, go for a ride in a litter, shake yourself up a little.²⁴ In short, all this is both very interesting in itself, but also, again, for the difference between the Platonic gymnastics for training virtue and the abstinence or very light work on one's own body suggested by the Stoics. But, in addition to this kind of light work of support for the valetudinary body in bad health—bad health is central in this reflection and ascesis of the body: Stoic ethics is concerned with the bodies of old men, of quadragenarians, not with the young man's athletic body—Seneca adds exercises of abstinence, which I have spoken about and will briefly recall. For example, letter 18,[25] which dates from the winter of 62, a short time before Seneca's suicide. In December 62 he writes a letter to Lucilius in which he says: Life's not much fun at the moment! All around me everyone is preparing for the Saturnalia, the period of the year when licentiousness is officially authorized. He asks Lucilius: Should we participate in this kind of festival, of should we abstain from it? Abstain from it? We are in danger of wanting to distinguish ourselves, of displaying a rather arrogant kind of philosophical snobbery. Well then, it would be more prudent to participate a little, at arm's length. But, he says, there is one thing to do anyway, which is that when people are getting ready for the Saturnalia, already beginning to eat and drink, we will have to prepare in a different way. We must prepare for them with a number of exercises of both real and sham poverty.[26] Sham, since in actual fact Seneca, who had stolen millions of sesterces in his colonial exploitations, was not really poor;[27] but real in the sense that he recommends that one live the life of the poor for three, four, or five days, sleeping on a pallet, wearing coarse clothes, eating little, and drinking water. This kind of (real) exercise, he says, should enable us to train, just as a soldier continues to practice the javelin in peacetime in order to be stronger in war. In other words, what Seneca is aiming for in this kind of exercise is not the great conversion to the general life of abstinence, which was the rule for some Cynics and will of course be the rule in Christian monasticism. Rather than converting oneself to abstinence, what is involved is the integration of abstinence as a sort of recurrent, regular exercise to which one returns from time to time and which enables a *forma* (a form) to be given to life, that is to say, which enables the individual to have the appropriate attitude [towards] himself and the events of his life: sufficiently detached to be able to bear misfortune when it arises; but already sufficiently detached to be able to treat the wealth and goods around us with the necessary indifference and with correct and wise nonchalance. In letter 8 he says: "Hold to this rule of life" (in fact this is *forma vitae*: this principle of life, this form or style of life) "of granting your body only precisely what is necessary for looking after it. Treat it severely so that it obeys the soul. Eat to relieve hunger, drink to quench thirst, clothe yourself to keep out the cold and let your house be a shelter from [bad weather]."[28] You can see what is involved then. Once again, Seneca has never really lived by eating only to relieve his hunger or drinking only to quench his thirst. However, in the use of wealth and thanks to these recurrent exercises of abstinence, the philosopher must always keep in mind that the principle and measure of what he eats must be what is actually necessary to relieve his [hunger]. He must only drink knowing that the final purpose and real measure of what he drinks should be what enables him to quench his thirst, etcetera. Thus, a whole way of relating to food, clothes, and housing is formed through these exercises of abstinence: exercises of abstinence for forming a style of life, and not exercises of abstinence for regulating one's life in accordance with precise interdictions and prohibitions. This is what we can say about Stoic abstinence.* Second, I would now like to talk about the other set of ascetic practices: the practice of tests.

Actually there are numerous overlaps between tests and abstinence. However, there are, I think, a number of particular features that characterize the test and distinguish it from abstinence. First, the test always includes a certain questioning of the self by the self. Unlike abstinence, a test basically involves knowing what you are capable of, whether you can do a particular kind of thing and see it through. You may succeed or fail, win or lose in a test, and through this kind of open game of the test it is a matter of locating yourself, of measuring how far you have advanced, and of knowing where you are and basically what you are. There is an aspect of self-knowledge in the test, which does not exist in the simple application of abstinence. Second, the test should always be accompanied by a certain work of thought on itself. Unlike abstinence,

---

* The manuscript here makes the distinction between these tests and the Epicurean exercises of abstinence which would give rise rather to an "aesthetic of pleasure" ("avoid all pleasures which may turn into pains and arrive at a technical intensification of simple pleasures").

which is a voluntary deprivation, the test is only really a test if the subject adopts a certain enlightened and conscious attitude towards what he is doing and towards himself doing it. Finally [the third difference], and this is the essential point which I will try to develop at greater length. As you have seen, for the Stoics abstinence is, as it were, a localized exercise in life on which you must fall back from time to time so as better to develop the *forma vitae* you are aiming for. Here, rather, and once again this is something important, the test must become a general attitude towards reality. Ultimately, and this is the meaning of the test for the Stoics, the whole of life must become a test. I believe a decisive historical step is taken here in the history of these techniques.

If you like, I will quickly refer to the first two points of the test and then we will stop and I will talk about life as a test afterwards, in the following lectures. First: the test as self-questioning. I mean that in test exercises you try to gauge where you are in relation to what you were, the progress you have already made, and the point you must reach. In the test there is always, if you like, a certain question of progression and an effort of location, and therefore of self-knowledge. As an example of these tests, Epictetus says the following: What should you do to struggle against anger? Well, you must commit yourself not to get angry for one day. Then you make a pact with yourself for two days, and then for four days, and finally, when you have made a pact with yourself not to get angry for thirty days, then it is time to offer a sacrifice to the gods.[29] The type of test-contract by which one ensures, and at the same time measures, one's progress, is also found in Plutarch, in the text on the control of anger, in which he says: I try not to get angry for several days, and even for a month. It seems that in Stoic ascetics a month without anger really was the maximum. So: not getting angry for several days and even for a month, "testing myself (*peirōmenos hemautou*), bit by bit, to see if I have progressed in patience, forcing myself to pay attention."[30] A somewhat more sophisticated kind of test is also found in Plutarch. This concerns justice and injustice. In *Socrates' Daemon* he says that you should, of course, practice not committing an injustice according to the same progressive commitment as for anger.[31] Avoiding [being unjust] for a day, a month. However, he says, you should even practice something more subtle, which is foregoing even your honest and legitimate advantage for a time. This is for the purpose of rooting out from yourself the desire for gain which is the source of all injustice. So, more or less, practicing a sort of super-justice which makes one forego gain, however just, so as to be more certain of avoiding injustice. Okay: the system of test as test-location of oneself.

Second, the test as a partly double exercise, by which I mean as an exercise in real life and on thought. This kind of test does not just involve imposing a rule of action or abstention on yourself, but of developing an internal attitude at the same time. You must both confront reality and then check your thought at the same time as you are faced with this reality. This may seem somewhat abstract, but it is very simple. It is very simple, but it will have important historical consequences. When you meet a beautiful young girl in the street, says Epictetus, it is not enough to restrain yourself, not to follow her or try to tempt her away or profit from her services. This is not enough. It is not enough to refrain in a way that would be accompanied by thinking to yourself: My God! I give up this young girl, but even so I really would like to go to bed with her. Or: How happy this young girl's husband must be! When in reality you meet this young girl, from whom you refrain, you must try not to imagine yourself with her, not to picture in thought (*zōgraphein*) being with her, benefiting from her charms and consent. Even if she is willing, even if she displays her consent, even if she approaches you, you must succeed in no longer feeling anything at all, no longer thinking anything at all, having your mind completely empty and neutral.[32] There is an important point here. It will be precisely one of the major points of distinction between Christian purity and pagan abstinence. In all the Christian texts on chastity you will see what a dim view is taken of Socrates, who abstained from Alcibiades to be sure, when Alcibiades lay down beside him, but who nonetheless continued to desire him. Here we are halfway between the two. A work of neutralizing thought, desire, and imagination is involved. And this is the work of the test. One must accompany abstention with this work of thought on itself, of self on self. In the same way, in book III there is another example of this mental work of self on self when you are in a real life situation, where Epictetus says: When you are in a situation in which there is a danger of being carried away by your passion, you must face up to the situation, refrain of course from anything that could carry you away and, through a work of thought on itself, control yourself and check yourself.[33] Thus, he says, when we kiss our own child, or when we embrace a friend, natural feelings, social duty, and our whole system of obligations require us to show them our affection and to really experience the joy and contentment of having our children or our friends with us. But then a danger appears in this situation. The danger comes from the famous *diakhusis*,[34] that kind of exuberance of the soul which, authorized as it were by obligations or by the natural impulse which draws us to others, is in danger of pouring out our feelings, that is to say of getting out of control, not as the result of an emotion and a *pathos*, but as a result of a natural and legitimate impulse. This is *diakhusis*, and we must avoid *diakhusis*. We must avoid *diakhusis*, then what? It is very simple, he says. When your child, your little boy or girl, is on your knees, and you quite naturally express your affection for him or her, at the very moment you are kissing your child in a legitimate impulse and expression of natural affection, say to yourself constantly, repeat in a whisper, for yourself, or say anyway in your soul: "tomorrow you will die."[35] Tomorrow, you, the child I love, will die. Tomorrow you will disappear. This exercise, in which one both displays legitimate attachment and in which one detaches oneself through this work of the soul that clearly sees the real fragility of this bond, will be a test. Similarly, when kissing a friend, we must constantly say to ourselves in a sort of internal repetition of thought focused on itself: "tomorrow you will go into exile," or: "tomorrow it is I who will go into exile and we will be parted." These are the test exercises as presented by the Stoics.

Finally, all of this is a bit anecdotal and secondary with regard to something that is much more important and which is the transformation of the test—or the relationship or practice of the test—or rather its transmutation at a level which is such that life in its entirety will take the form of the test. This is what I will now try to explain.

1. Aulus Gellius, *Les Nuits attiques*, translation R. Marache (Paris: Les Belles Lettres, 1967) vol. 1, book I, IX, 1-6, pp. 38-39.
2. Aulus Gellius' master, Calvisius Taurus, philosopher of the second century A.D., a Platonist.
3. *Les Nuits attiques*, livre I, IX, 9-11, p. 40.
4. E. R. Dodds, *The Greeks and the Irrational*, pp. 135-78; J.-P. Vernant, *Mythe et Pensée chez les Grecs*, vol. 1, p. 96 and vol. 2, p. 111 (*Myth and Thought Among the Greeks*, p. 87 and pp. 354-56); H. Joly, *Le Renversement platonicien Logos-Epistemē-Polis*, pp. 67-69. For a final critical summary of this theme, see P. Hadot, *Qu'est-ce que la philosophie antique?* pp. 276-89.
5. See the analysis of this point in the lecture of 13 January, first hour.
6. In Plato, the *noūs* is the highest part of the soul, the intellect inasmuch as it accomplishes specifically divine spiritual acts; see the pessimistic declaration of *Timaeus*, 51e: "the gods have a share in intellection (*noū*), but very few men." In the Neo-Platonists, the *noūs* will become a fully fledged ontological level situated between the One and the Soul. See J. Pépin, "Éléments pour une histoire de la relation entre l'intelligence et l'intelligible chez Platon et dans le Néo-Platonisme," *Revue philosophique de la France et de l'étranger* 146 (1956), pp. 39-55.
7. One of the first times the concept of *homoiōsis theō* is expressed is in Plato's *Theaetetus*, 176a-b: "the escape consists in assimilating oneself to God (*homoiōsis tō theō*) as far as possible." This passage is widely quoted by middle Platonism (Apuleius, Alcinous, Arius Didyme, Numenius), which will make it the expression of the *telos*, the expression of the sovereign good, and then it is widely taken up by Neo-Platonism (see the essential text of Plotinus, *Enneads*, I, 2, 2). It is found again in the Peripatetic schools to describe the contemplative life (echoing chapter VII of the tenth book of the *Nichomachean Ethics*; see Cicero, *De Finibus*, V.11). The mystical resonances of this passage from the *Theaetetus* will be exploited by Jewish and Christian mysticism (see Philo of Alexandria, *De Fuga et Inventione* [*On Flight and Finding*]), 63 (English translation by C. D. Youge, *The Works of Philo* [Headnickson Publishers: 1993]), and Clement of Alexandria, *Stromata (The Miscellanies)*, II.22 (English translation in *Aute-Nicene Christian Library*, vol. 4, *Clement of Alexandria* [Edinburgh: T. and T. Clark, 1867]) and by the Neo-Pythagoreans. It will only be used again by Stoicism (see Cicero, *De Natura deorum* II.147 and 153) at the cost of important reorganizations, since the first *telos* remains, in the school of the Porch, the *oikeiōsis* as exercise of immediate articulation on a nature good in itself (principle of ethical immanence), whereas *homoiōsis* (principle of ethical transcendence) always includes an effort of tearing away from the world (see the article by Carlos Lévy, which has been a major source for this note, "Cicéron et le Moyen Platonisme: le problème du Souverain Bien pour Platon," *Revue des études latines* 68 (1990), pp. 50-65.
8. On this movement, see the lecture of 6 January, first hour.
9. We should nonetheless bear in mind that Plotinus constantly combated the Gnostics. See *Enneads*, II.9, entitled by Porphyry, precisely, *Against the Gnostics*.
10. For a description of the procedures of decipherment of the self in Christian spirituality (that is to say of the way in which the verbalization of sins is carried out belatedly from a self-exploration, in the establishment of the monastic institution from the fifth to eighth centuries), see the lecture of 12 and especially 26 March 1980 at the Collège de France.
11. On this transplantation of spiritual exercises (particularly of the techniques of self-examination), see the seminar of October 1982 at the University of Vermont: "Technologies of the Self."
12. Born in Caesarea of Cappadocia (330), Basil studied at Constantinople and Athens. He composed *Rules* for monastic communities he founded in Asia Minor.
13. See the lecture of 24 March, second hour.
14. We find here the theme of what will soon be called "the aesthetics of existence." See the interview with A. Fontana in May 1984, "Une esthétique de l'existence," *Dits et Écrits*,

vol. 4, pp. 731-32; English translation by Alan Sheridan, "An Aesthetics of Existence," in M. Foucault, *Politics, Philosophy, Culture. Interviews and Other Writings 1977-1984*, ed. L. D. Kritzman (London and New York: Routledge, 1988), pp. 49-50; the interview with P. Rabinow and H. Dreyfus, "On the Genealogy of Ethics: An Overview of Work in Progress," in *Ethics: Subjectivity and Truth*, p. 271 and p. 278; French translation by G. Barbedette, "A propos de la généalogie de l'éthique: un aperçu du travail en cours," in *Dits et Écrits*, vol. 4, pp. 610-11 and p. 615; and "Usage des plaisirs et techniques de soi," in *Dits et Écrits*, vol. 4, p. 545; English translation by Robert Hurley, "Introduction" to *The Use of Pleasure*, p. 12.
15. See the lecture of 20 January, first hour, and especially of 3 March, second hour.
16. See Hesiod: "who neglects his need (*meletē de toi ergon ophellei*) will not fill his barn." *Works and Days*, 412.
17. H. Marrou, *Histoire de l'éducation dans l'Antiquité*, pp. 302-03 (*A History of Education in Antiquity*, pp. 202-03), distinguishes two types of exercises (*meletai*) perfected by the teachers of rhetoric in the Hellenistic period: imaginary pleadings, on ridiculous subjects, and improvisations in the deliberative genre, in which the subjects were also fanciful. In Latin the *meletē* will become the *declamatio*.
18. See, for example, Epictetus, *Discourses*, I.i.25, III.v.11, IV.iv.8-18, and IV.vi.11-17.
19. Musonius Rufus, *Reliquiae*, pp. 22-27. Cf. Stobaeus, *Florilegium*, III.29.78, the section entitled: "*peri philoponias kai meletēs kai hoti asumphoron to oknein.*" On this text, see the lecture of 24 February, second hour.
20. In 65, Nero, thwarting Piso's conspiracy, made some heads fall: Seneca was invited to open his veins, as well as Lucian. While he was at it, Nero decided to exile prominent Stoic or Cynic personalities: Musonius Rufus left for the island of Gyara, Demetrius was banished. Musonius was recalled by Galba and, no doubt protected by Titus, was left alone at the time of decrees of exile pronounced against many philosophers (Demetrius, Euphrates, etcetera), this time by Vespasian at the start of the seventies.
21. "For how will someone become temperate if he knows only that one must not be vanquished by pleasures and has not practiced resistance to the pleasures? How will he become just if he has learned only that one must love equality and has not applied himself to fleeing greed? How will we acquire courage if we have seen only that those things which appear terrible to the masses are not to be feared and we have not applied ourselves to remain without fear in their presence? How will we be prudent if we have recognized only what are the true goods and the true evils but we have not trained ourselves to despise what only appears to be a good?" *Musonius Rufus*.
22. This problematic is the object of a chapter of *L'Usage des plaisirs*, "Enkrateia" [egkrateia], pp. 74-90 (*The Use of Pleasure*, pp. 63-75).
23. "Have we not heard what Iccus of Tarentum did in view of the Olympic competition and other competitions? We are told that in order to win, he, who in his soul combined technique and strength with temperance, never touched either a woman or young boy so long as he was in the heat of training." Plato, *The Laws*, VIII.840.a.
24. Seneca, *Letters*, XV.1-4 and LV.1.
25. Ibid., letter XVIII. On this letter, see *Le souci de soi*, pp. 76-77 (*The Care of the Self*, pp. 59-60).
26. Ibid., letter XVIII.5-8.
27. On Seneca as a rich thief, see the declarations of P. Suillius reproduced by Tacitus: "By what knowledge, by what precepts of the philosophers, did he amass three hundred million sesterces in four years of royal friendships [those of Nero]? In Rome, his [Seneca's] prey was the testaments of those without children, Italy and the provinces were exhausted by his limitless usury." *Annals*, XIII.xlii. We cannot help thinking that Tacitus had Seneca in his sights again when he wrote about Nero: "He enriched his closest friends with his generosity. There was no shortage of those who reproached men who professed austerity for taking advantage of this and sharing out houses and villas like bounty." Ibid. XIII.xviii. It will be recalled that Nero had made a gift to Seneca of domains that had belonged to Britannicus, who died in suspicious circumstances. On Seneca's revenues, see the declarations

of Dion Cassius, *Dio's Roman History*, translation E. Cary (London and New York: Loeb Classical Library, 1914-1927), LXI.10.3, and for a modern presentation, P. Veyne, who speaks of "one of the biggest fortunes of his century" in "Préface" to *Sénèque, Entretiens, Lettres à Lucilius*, pp. xv-xvi. The whole of Seneca's *De Vita Beata* (*On the Happy Life*) is a clever and violent attempt to defend himself against reproaches leveled at affluent philosophers who sing the praises of the simple life.

28. Seneca, *Letters*, VIII.5.
29. "Do you wish to no longer be quick-tempered? Don't feed your habit; give it nothing which will make it grow. Calm down the first manifestation and then count the days on which you have not been angry. 'I used to get angry every day, then on every other day, then every third, and then every fourth day.' If you control yourself for thirty days, offer a sacrifice to God." Epictetus, *Discourses*, II.xviii.12-13.
30. Plutarch, *On the Control of Anger*, 464c.15.
31. Plutarch, *Socrates' Daemon*, 585a-c.
32. "To-day I saw a handsome boy or a beautiful girl and I did not say to myself: 'Would to God I had lain with her,' and, 'Her husband is a happy man,' for whoever says this also says 'The adulterer is a happy man.' I did not even represent to myself (*anazōgraphō*) the following scene: the woman is with me, she is undressing and lying next to me." Epictetus, *Discourses*, II.xviii.12-13.
33. Ibid., III.xxiv.84-85.
34. "If you kiss your child, your brother, your friend, never give free rein to your imagination and do not let your effusions (*diakhusin*) run away with themselves." Ibid., 85.
35. Ibid., 88.

## twenty-two

## 17 MARCH 1982

### Second hour

> *Life itself as a test.* ~ *Seneca's* De Providentia: *the test of existing and its discriminating function.* ~ *Epictetus and the philosopher-scout.* ~ *The transfiguration of evils: from old Stoicism to Epictetus.* ~ *The test in Greek tragedy.* ~ *Comments on the indifference of the Hellenistic preparation of existence to Christian dogmas on immortality and salvation.* ~ *The art of living and care of the self: a reversal of relationship.* ~ *Sign of this reversal: the theme of virginity in the Greek novel.*

ONE OF THE IMPORTANT things in this philosophers' ascetics in the imperial period is the appearance and development of the idea that the test (the *probatio*), unlike abstinence, can and must become a general attitude in life, and not just a sort of training exercise whose limits one fixes at a certain moment of life. That is to say, I think we see the appearance of the crucial idea that life must be recognized, thought, lived, and practiced as a constant test. Of course, this is mostly an idea lurking in the background in the sense that I do not think that there is any systematic reflection on or general theorization of the principle that life is a test, at any rate I have not come across one. Anyway, there is no theorization on a scale resembling what will be found in Christianity. However, it seems to me to be an idea that is nevertheless quite clearly expressed in a number of texts, particularly in Seneca and Epictetus.

For Seneca then, the basic text on this theme of "life as test" is, of course, the *De Providentia*, in which one of the guiding threads is the old, very classical Stoic theme of God the father (father in relation to the world and father in relation to men) who must be recognized and honored on the model of the family relationship. Except that from this old, well-known theme of God as father, Seneca draws a number of interesting consequences. Seneca says: God is a father, that is to say he is not a mother. What I mean is this: typically a mother is indulgent towards her children. The mother—and here he clearly refers to what the maternal relationship to a boy reaching school age or adolescence would be—is made to be indulgent. She is made to be permissive. She is made to console, etcetera.[1] As for the father, he is responsible for education. And Seneca has an interesting expression. He says: The father, and consequently God as father, *amat fortiter*[2] (there will be a certain *pecca fortiter* which will become important later[3]). *Amat fortiter*: He loves with courage, unrelenting vigor, thoroughgoing severity, roughly if necessary. He loves his children with this courage and unrelenting vigor. What does loving them with unrelenting vigor mean? Mainly it means overseeing their proper training, that is to say, through the strains, difficulties, and even suffering by which these children can be prepared for the real strains and the actual sorrows, misfortunes, and hardships they may experience in life. In loving *fortiter* (strongly and vigorously), he will ensure the strong and vigorous education of men who will also be strong and vigorous. So, the paternal love of God for man should not be conceived on the maternal model of providential indulgence, but in the form of a pedagogical vigilance towards men. A pedagogical vigilance, but which even so contains a paradox the reasons for which *De Providentia* sets out to explain and tries to resolve. The paradox is this: In this pedagogical strictness, the Father-God nevertheless makes a distinction. He distinguishes between good and wicked men. But the distinction is very paradoxical, since we constantly see the good men, whom the divinity favors, working, striving, and sweating to climb the steep paths of life. They constantly come up against difficulty, misfortune, hardship, and suffering, whereas we see the wicked at rest, passing their life in undisturbed delights. Okay, Seneca says, this paradox is very easily explained.

In reality it is entirely logical and rational that the wicked are favored in this education, while the good men are persecuted and constantly tested. It is because these men are wicked, he says, that God abandons them to sensual pleasures, neglecting their education as a result, whereas the good men, rather, precisely those whom he loves, he submits to tests in order to harden them, to make them courageous and strong and thus to prepare them. "*Sibi* [*parare*]."[4] God prepares men for himself, and he prepares the men he loves for himself because they are good men. And he prepares them for himself through a series of tests that make up life. Okay, I think we should focus on this text for a while because it includes at least two important ideas.

First there is this. You see that we have this idea that life with its system of tests and hardships, life in its entirety, is an education. Here then, we come across again, you see, the things I referred to when we started with the *Alcibiades*. You recall that the *epimeleia heautou* (the practice of the self, the culture of the self) was essentially the substitute for an inadequate education; and the *epimeleia heautou*—I do not say in all of Platonism, but at least in the *Alcibiades*[5]—was something that the young man on the threshold of his political career had to practice so as to be able to fulfill this career properly. We saw the generalization of this idea of the *epimeleia heautou* and I tried to show how "taking care of the self" in this culture of the self of the Hellenistic and imperial epoch was not just an obligation for the young man, due to an inadequate education: one had to take care of the self throughout one's life.[6] And now we find again the idea of education, but of education that is also generalized: the whole of life must be the individual's education. The practice of the self, which must develop and be put to work from the beginning of adolescence or youth until the end of life, is inserted within a providential schema whereby God responds in advance, as it were, and organizes for this training of oneself, for this practice of oneself, a world which has a formative value for man. In other words, the whole of life is an education. And the *epimeleia heautou*, now that its scale encompasses the whole of life, consists in educating oneself through all of life's misfortunes. There is now something like a sort of spiral between education and form of life. We must educate ourselves constantly through the tests, which are sent to us, and thanks to this care of ourselves, which makes us take these tests seriously. We educate ourselves throughout our life, and at the same time we live in order to be able to educate ourselves. That life and training are coextensive is the first characteristic of the life-test.

Second, you can see that this generalization of the test as life, or the idea that the care of the self should permeate the whole of life inasmuch as life should be devoted entirely to our training, is connected to a fundamental but enigmatic discriminating function, since the whole of this analysis of life as test rests on the dichotomy, given in advance, between those who are good and those who are wicked. The life as test is reserved, is made for the good people. It is constructed so that good people are distinguished from others, while precisely those who are not good (the wicked) not only do not pass the test, or do not recognize a test in life, but their life is not even organized as a test. And if they are abandoned to pleasure, it is to the extent they are not even worthy of being confronted with the test. In other words, we can say that what appears in *De Providentia* is the principle that the test (the *probatio*) constitutes at the same time the general, educative, and discriminating form of life.

Seneca's text (in *De Providentia*) echoes many texts by Epictetus in the *Discourses*, in which there are quite similar ideas. For example, in book I of the *Discourses*, God is not at all compared to a strict father as opposed to an indulgent mother, but to a gymnasium instructor who, in order to give a good training to the students he has accepted or gathered around him and to whom he wants to teach endurance and strength, surrounds them with the toughest adversaries possible. Why has he chosen tough adversaries for the students to whom he has granted his favors and interest? So that they become champions at the Olympic games. You don't become a champion at the Olympic games without sweat: God, then, appears as a gymnasium instructor who reserves the toughest adversaries for the students he prefers so that his students take the palm on the day of the games. In the same discourse you see, in outline at least, the distinction between those who are good and those who are not, the discriminating function of the *probatio*, in the very interesting form of the scout, which again will have many echoes later.[7]

Epictetus says: There are men who are naturally so virtuous, who have already amply demonstrated their strength, that God, rather than letting them live amongst other men, with the advantages and drawbacks of ordinary life, sends them as scouts into the greatest dangers and difficulties. It is these scouts of hardship, misfortune, and suffering who, on the one hand, will set especially tough and difficult tests for themselves but, as good scouts, will then return to their city in order to tell their fellow citizens that, after all, they should not worry themselves so much about those dangers they so greatly fear, since they themselves have experienced them. Sent as scouts, they faced up to these dangers and were able to vanquish them, and since they were able to vanquish them, so will the others be able to as well. They return thus as scouts who have fulfilled their contract, who have carried off their victory, and who are able to teach others that one can triumph over these tests and evils, and that there is a path for this that they can teach them. Such is the philosopher, such is the Cynic—what's more, in Epictetus's great portrait of the Cynic, this metaphor of the scout is employed again[8]— the philosopher-scout in the game of tests, sent ahead to confront the toughest enemies, and who returns to say that the enemies are not dangerous, or not very dangerous, not as dangerous as one thinks, and to say how one can defeat them [...].

Okay, we should no longer consider these tests, these misfortunes, as evils. We are really forced to consider them as goods that we should benefit from and put to use in the individual's formation. We do not encounter a single difficulty that, precisely as difficulty, suffering, and misfortune, is not as such a good. Epictetus says: We can benefit from every difficulty and trouble.—From every difficulty?—Yes, all of them. Epictetus takes up, sketches out a diatribe-kind of dialogue between master and student: From every difficulty? the student asks.—Yes, from every difficulty.—Is it a benefit, is it useful if a man insults you? The master's answer: What advantages does the athlete get from his training? He gets the greatest advantages. Well, he also, the person who insults me, "becomes my trainer: he exercises my patience, my calmness, my mildness; [if someone exercises my calmness, does he not provide me with a service? M.F.] ... Is my neighbour wicked?—Yes, for himself; but for me [and because he is bad; M.F.], he is good; he exercises my mildness and tolerance. Bring disease, bring death, bring [poverty], insult and condemnation to the final torture, under Hermes' wand all of this will acquire usefulness."[9] Hermes' wand turns every object into gold. Okay, I think we have here an important idea actually, because in one sense it is quite close to a wholly traditional Stoic theme. It is close to it, and yet it is very different. It is close to the theme according to which what initially appears to us to be an evil, coming to us from the external world, from the domain of things, is not really an evil. This is a fundamental thesis of Stoicism, from its earliest forms.[10] But how is this elimination of evil as evil brought about in the traditional Stoic thesis? That is to say: how do we discover that what we experience as, or believe to be an evil, is not really an evil? Well, you know that we discover it through an essentially intellectual and demonstrative kind of operation. Confronted by something that happens to us, for example the death of someone close to us, an illness, loss of wealth, or an earthquake, we should say to ourselves that each of these events, whatever it may be and however accidental it may seem, is really part of the order of the world and its necessary sequence. The God or rational principle that organized the world, and organized it well, has organized this necessary sequence. Consequently we must recognize that from the only point of view that we should take, namely [that of a] rational being, we should consider that what we believe to be an evil is not really an evil. It is only our opinion that separates us and distances us from the rational point of view and from rational being. Only this opinion makes us think that it is an evil. In actual fact it is not an evil. Let us take the attitude and stance of the rational subject: all these events are part of the order of the world, and consequently not an evil, with, as you know, the frequently repeated question, which Cicero for example came back to many times,[11] which is: it may well not be an evil, but when I am ill and I am really suffering, is this or is this not an evil? But anyway the Stoic thesis, the schema, if you like, of the nullification of evil in classical Stoicism, arises through the analysis or reflection by the rational subject as such on the order of the world, and it enables him to place all these events in an order that is ontologically good. Consequently, ontologically at least, the evil is not an evil.

Now you see that it is completely different in the text of Epictetus, in this little story of the insulter who does me good and whose insult is a good. For it involves something quite different from the sort of analysis I have just been talking about. It involves the transfiguration of evil into good, but of evil into good precisely inasmuch as it harms me. Cicero objected to a kind of surplus in the classical Stoic analysis: if in the end I recognize that it is not an evil, inasmuch as it is part of the world's rational order, it nevertheless remains the case that it still harms me. Now what shifts Epictetus's analysis so that it escapes Cicero's kind of objection is the fact that this non-evil (for Epictetus, of course, according to the classical doctrine, it is not an evil ontologically) at the same time harms me and is pain and suffering, and this affects me if and so long as I do not have absolute control of myself, well then, this itself is a good in its relation [to] me. The transfiguration or nullification of evil does not take place then merely and solely in the form of the adoption of a rational position for looking at the world. The transfiguration into good takes place at the very heart of the suffering caused, insofar as this suffering is actually a test that is recognized, lived, and practiced as such by the subject. We can say that in classical Stoicism it is the thought of the whole that is supposed to nullify the personal experience of suffering. In the case of Epictetus, and within this same theoretical postulate that Epictetus upholds, there is, if you like, another type of mutation due to the test attitude, which doubles and adds a value to every personal experience of suffering, pain, and misfortune, a value that is directly positive for us. This added value does not nullify the suffering; it attaches itself to it, rather, and makes use of it. It is insofar as it harms us that the evil is not an evil. This is something quite fundamental and, I think, very new with regard to what may be considered the general theoretical framework of Stoicism.

I would like to make several remarks concerning this idea of life as formative test and the idea that misfortune is a good precisely insofar as it is misfortune and is recognized as such by the test attitude. Of course, in a sense you will tell me: but this is not as new as all that, and even if it seems to represent, and actually does represent, a certain mutation or change of accent with regard to Stoic dogma, in actual fact the idea that life is a long fabric of misfortunes by which men are tested is an old Greek idea. After all, does it not underpin all classical Greek tragedy and all the great classical myths? Prometheus and his test, Heracles and his tests,[12] Oedipus and the test both of the truth and of the crime, etcetera. Except I think that what characterizes the test in classical Greek tragedy, what underpins it anyway, is the theme of the confrontation, the joust, of the game between the jealousy of the gods and the excess of men. In other words, it is when the gods and men confront each other that the test really appears as the sum of misfortunes sent by the gods to men in order to know whether men will be able to resist, how they will resist, and whether men or the gods will prevail. The story of Prometheus is obviously the clearest example of this.[13] There is an agonistic relationship between gods and men at the end of which, struck down by misfortune, man emerges grown in stature, but with a grandeur of reconciliation with the gods, which is the grandeur of rediscovered peace. For this nothing is clearer than *Oedipus at Colonus* or, if you like, the contrast between *Oedipus the King* and *Oedipus at Colonus*.[14] Oedipus at Colonus, definitively struck down by misfortune, having really suffered all the ordeals with which the gods have pursued him arising from an ancient vengeance which weighs less on him than on his family, finally arrives at the place where he will die, exhausted by his ordeals. And, at the end of the battle in which he has been vanquished, but from which he nevertheless emerges grown in stature, he arrives at Colonus able to say: Of all this I was innocent. No one can reproach me. Who then would not have killed an insolent old man as I did, since I did not know he was my father? Who then would not have married a woman, not knowing it was my mother? Of all this I was innocent and the gods have pursued me with a vengeance that was not and could not be a punishment. But now we are here, exhausted by ordeals, I come to give a power to the earth where I will die, a new, protective power given to me precisely by the gods. And if I really have been ruined, [due to] a crime of which I was unaware and for which the gods pursued me, in a struggle in which I was the weaker, if I brought the plague to my country, well now I will give serenity, tranquility, and omnipotence to the earth where I will now rest.[15] It is a wrestling match in which there was a loser (Oedipus), but in which finally, the defeat having been consummated, man regains his power and is reconciled with the gods who now protect him. Now this wrestling match, this great joust between the power of the gods and the power of men, is not at all what underpins the Stoic test as defined by Seneca and Epictetus. Rather, it is out of I must say a rather pernickety paternalism of suffering that the gods surround good men with the series of tests, misfortunes, etcetera, necessary to form them. It is not the joust but a protective benevolence which is there in order to arrange misfortunes.

The second remark is that this theme of considering life itself, the whole of life in its generality and continuity, as a formative and discriminating test, obviously raises many theoretical difficulties. After all, Seneca says, for example, by surrounding good men with a series of tests, God prepares them (*sibi* [*parat*]): the men he tests he prepares for himself.[16] But what is this preparation; preparation for what? Is it a preparation for the relationship of the soul's identification with or its assimilation to universal and divine reason? Does it involve preparing man for the fulfillment of his own life up to the decisive and revealing point of death? Is it a matter of preparing man for immortality and salvation, and immortality founded on universal reason or personal immortality? Actually, it would be difficult to find a precise theory for all this in Seneca.[17] There are no doubt many elements of an answer, and the fact that we can adduce several is precisely what shows that for Seneca [this] is not really the important problem. God prepares men, but even so, although "life is a preparation" is a fundamental theme for Seneca, it does not raise for him, at least not urgently, what will be the crucial question for Christianity: preparation for what? It is as if this theme of the technique of the self, of the culture of the self, had an autonomy with regard to the theoretical problems that we feel hover around this practice. But it was serious and important enough to hold itself up as a principle of conduct without the theoretical problems it raised having to be confronted directly and systematically. The same could be said about the question of discrimination: but in the end what does this mean? Should we assume that there are good and bad men from the start? And that God directs the good to misfortunes and the bad to sensual pleasures? Or should we accept that there seems to be a reversal: God submitting men to tests, seeing those who withstand them, who do well at them, and so multiplying the tests around them, whereas the others, those who have demonstrated their incapacity in the first tests, he abandons to pleasures of the flesh? None of this is clear, and here again what strikes me is that neither Seneca nor Epictetus gives the impression of taking the problem seriously. Again, there are elements of an answer, and we should not think that it is just thrown out without being inserted within a theoretical field. But there is no precise problematization of these two themes. The question "For what is this life a preparation?" is not theorized. The question, "What is this discrimination, which is both a condition and an effect of life as test?" is not theorized. This is the second remark I wanted to make.

There is a third remark, which is this: these two major themes of life being a test throughout its course, and of the test as discrimination, were, of course, transferred from the philosophical ascetics I am talking about to Christian spirituality, as you know, but obviously with a very different appearance. On the one hand this is because in Christianity the idea of life as test will become not just a kind of high idea, but rather an absolutely basic idea. It is not just some particularly refined philosophers who lay down the principle or ideal that we should consider and live our life as a constant test. Rather, every Christian will be called upon to regard life as nothing but a test. Except, at the same time as the principle is generalized and becomes prescriptive for every Christian, then the two questions I have just been talking about, and which are strangely untheorized in the Stoics, become one of the most active focal points of Christian reflection and thought. This is, of course, the problem of what it is that life as preparation prepares us for. It is obviously the question of immortality, of salvation, etcetera. As for the question of discrimination, this is the fundamental question around which what is essential to Christian thought has no doubt revolved: What is predestination; what is human freedom in the face of divine omnipotence; what is grace; how can it be that God loved Jacob and hated Esau even before they were born?[18] So, there is both a transposition of these questions and, at the same time, a completely different system in both theory and practice.

I have referred to all this because I wanted to show what seems to me to be an important phenomenon in the history of this vast culture of the self which developed in the Hellenistic and Roman epoch and which I have tried to describe this year. Roughly speaking I would say that from the classical period, the problem seems to me to have been one of defining a certain *tekhnē tou biou* (an art of living, a technique of existence). And you recall that the principle of "taking care of oneself" was formulated within this general question of the *tekhnē tou biou*. The human being is such, his *bios*, his life, his existence is such, that he cannot live his life without referring to a certain rational and prescriptive articulation which is that of *tekhnē*. We touch here on what is doubtless one of the major nuclei of Greek culture, thought, and morality. However pressing the city-state may be, however important the idea of *nomos* may be, and however widespread religion may be in Greek thought, it is never the political structure, the form of law or religious imperatives that can say what a Greek or Roman, but especially a Greek, must do concretely throughout his life. In Greek classical culture, the *tekhnē tou biou* is, I believe, inserted in the gaps left equally by the city-state, the law, and religion regarding this organization of life. For a Greek, human freedom has to be invested not so much, or not only in the city-state, the law, and religion, as in this *tekhnē* (the art of oneself) which is practiced by oneself. It is, then, within this general form of the *tekhnē tou biou* that the principle or precept "take care of yourself" is formulated. And we have seen precisely how someone like Alcibiades, wanting to make a political career and direct the life of government, is reminded by Socrates of the principle of which he was ignorant: You cannot develop the *tekhnē* you need, you cannot make a rational object of your life as you wish, if you do not attend to yourself. The *epimeleia heautou* is inserted therefore within the necessity of the *tekhnē* of existence.

Now what I think happened, and what I have tried to show you in the course of this year, is this: in the period I am talking about—let's say in the Hellenistic period, and certainly in the period of the High

Empire which I have especially studied—we see a sort of reversal, a twisting on the spot between technique of life and care of the self. It seems to me that what actually happens is that the care of the self is no longer a necessary and indispensable element of the *tekhnē tou biou* (the technique of life). The care of the self is not something with which one must begin if one wishes to define properly a good technique of life. It seems to me that henceforth the care of the self not only completely penetrates, commands, and supports the art of living—not only must one know how to care for the self in order to know how to live—but the *tekhnē tou biou* (the technique of life) falls entirely within the now autonomized framework of the care of the self. [What] emerges from the idea that life must be grasped as a test? What is the meaning and objective of life with its formative and discriminating value, of life in its entirety seen as a test? Well, it is precisely to form the self. One must live one's life in such a way that one cares for the self at every moment and that at the enigmatic end of life—old age, moment of death, immortality (immortality as diffusion in the rational being or personal immortality, it doesn't matter)—what one finds, what anyway must be obtained through the *tekhnē* one installs in one's life, is precisely a certain relationship of self to self which is the crown, realization, and reward of a life lived as test. The *tekhnē tou biou*, the way of dealing with the events of life, must be inserted within a care of the self that has now become general and absolute. One does not take care of the self in order to live better or more rationally, and one does not take care of the self in order to govern others properly, which was Alcibiades' question. One must live so as to establish the best possible relationship to oneself. Ultimately I would say, in a word: one lives "for oneself," but obviously giving to this "for" a completely different meaning than is given in the traditional expression "living for oneself." One lives with the relationship to one's self as the fundamental project of existence, the ontological support which must justify, found, and command all the techniques of existence. Between the rational God, who, in the order of the world, has set around me all the elements, the long chain of dangers and misfortunes, and myself, who will decipher these misfortunes as so many tests and exercises for me to perfect myself, between this God and myself, henceforth the issue is only myself. It seems to me that we have here a relatively important event in the history of Western subjectivity. What can we say about this?

First, of course, I have tried to pinpoint this movement—this turning around which is so important, I think, and which shifted the relationship between care of the self and technique of life—through the texts of philosophers, but it seems to me that we could find many other signs of it. I do not have the time this year, but I would have liked, for example, to talk about novels. The appearance of the Greek novel in precisely this period I am talking about (the first and second centuries A.D.) is very interesting. Greek novels are long adventure stories which are also stories of voyages, misfortunes, and trials and tribulations, etcetera, across the Mediterranean world and which in one sense slip easily into and lodge within the major form defined by the *Odyssey*.[19] However, whereas the *Odyssey* (the epic story of the trials and tribulations of Odysseus) already involved that great wrestling match I was talking about a short while ago—it involved knowing who would finally prevail, man or gods, or rather some gods in relation to others: it is a universe of struggle and joust—with the Greek novel, rather, the theme that life must be a formative test of the self appears very clearly. Whether it is *An Ethiopian History* by Heliodorus, better known as *Theagenes and Chariclea*, or the *The Ephesian Story* by Xenophon of Ephesus,[20] or the adventures of *Cleitophon and Leucippe* by Achilles Tatius,[21] all are dominated by the theme that everything that may happen to man, all the misfortunes that may befall him (shipwrecks, earthquakes, fires, encounters with bandits, death threats, imprisonment, enslavement), everything that happens to these characters with an accelerated rhythm which, as in the *Odyssey*, actually leads back home, all of this displays life as a test. A test whose outcome should be what? Reconciliation with the gods? Not at all. The outcome must be purity; it must be purity of the self in the sense of that over which one exercises vigilance, surveillance, protection, and mastery. That is why the guiding thread of all these novels is not the problem of knowing whether the gods will prevail over man, or if this god will prevail over another god, as in the *Odyssey*. The question permeating these novels is quite simply that of virginity.[22] Will the girl keep her virginity, will the boy keep his virginity, will those who, either with regard to the god or with regard to each other, are committed to preserving this personal purity, keep their virginity? All the tests these two characters are set, swept up in the series of trials and tribulations, all these episodes are constructed in order to know the extent to which they will be able to preserve this virginity which, in this literature, seems to me to be like the visible form of the relationship to the self in its transparency and mastery. The theme of virginity, which is so fundamental and which will be found again with so many consequences in Christian spirituality, can be seen emerging here as a metaphorical figure of the relationship to self. Preserving virginity so that it is still intact, integral, for both the boy and the girl when, having finally returned home, they find each other again and are legally married. It seems to me that the preservation of this virginity is nothing other than the figurative expression of what, throughout the trials and tribulations of life, must be preserved and maintained to the end: the relationship to one's self. Once again, one lives for one's self.

Okay, that is what I had to say on life as test. So there is still one lecture in which I will try to talk a little about the other set of exercises: no longer the *gumnazein* (that is to say, exercise, training in real life), but the exercise of thought (*meletan*, meditation). Clearly then I won't have time to finish. I don't know if I will still lecture after Easter. Do you all leave at Easter? In short, I don't know, we'll see. Thank you.

1. "Do you not see the difference between a father's tenderness and that of a mother? The father wakes his children early to send them to work, he does not even allow them rest on holidays, he makes them sweat when they are not in tears. The mother, rather, smothers them in her breast, keeps them in the shade, protects them from sorrow, tears and weariness. Towards good men God has the soul of a father and loves them vigorously (*illos fortiter amat*)." Seneca, *On Providence*, II.5-6.
2. Ibid., 6.
3. An allusion to Luther: "*esto peccator, et peca fortiter, sed fortius fide et gaude in Christo qui victor est peccati, mortis et mundi... ora fortiter; es enim fortissimos peccator.*" Letter to Melanchton of 1 August 1521, quoted in L. Febvre, *Un Destin. Martin Luther* (Paris: PUF, 1968), p. 100. It could be translated as: "Be sinner and sin strongly, but keep still more strongly your faith and joy in Christ, conqueror of sin, death and the world! Pray strongly! for you are an even greater sinner."
4. "God...does not spoil the good man; he tests him, hardens him, and makes him worthy of him (*sibi illum parat*)." *On Providence*, I.6. E. Bréhier translates: "he sets him aside for himself" in *Les Stoïciens*, p. 758.
5. See the development of this theme in the lecture of 6 January, second hour.
6. See the lecture of 20 January, first hour.
7. "It is difficulties that show what men are. Also, when a difficulty occurs, remember that God, like a gymnasium master, has put you in the hands of a tough young partner.—To what end? you ask.—So that you win at the Olympic games... Now we are sending you to Rome as a scout. But no one sends a coward as a scout." Epictetus, *Discourses*, I.xxiv.1-2.
8. "In fact the Cynic really is a scout for men, finding out what is favorable to them and what is hostile. First he must scout accurately, then return to tell the truth, without being paralyzed by fear so that he designates as enemies those who are not." Epictetus, *Discourses*, III.xxii.24-25.
9. *Discourses*, III.xx.10-12.
10. See Cicero's statement: "Some people reduce these duties to just one: to show that what is thought to be evil is not evil—this is the view of Cleanthes," *Tusculan Disputations*, III.XXXI.76. Cleanthes, with Chrysippus, was the first scholar after the foundation of the school of the Porch by Zeno at the beginning of the third century B.C.
11. See the whole of book III of *Tusculan Disputations*, as well as Foucault's analysis of chapter XV of this book in the lecture of 24 March, first hour.
12. On Heracles, an essential reference for Cynicism with regard to athletic ascesis, is R. Höistad, *Cynic Hero and Cynic King. Studies in the Cynic Conception of Man* (Uppsala: 1948).
13. See the tragedy by Aeschylus, *Prometheus Bound*. Prometheus, bound to the summit of a mountain for having stolen fire, continues to defy Zeus, claiming to possess a secret that will dethrone him. Prometheus remains inflexible in the face of threats from Hermes who presses him to reveal his secret, and Zeus sends a bolt of lightning to the rock to which Prometheus is bound, plunging him into the depths of the earth.
14. This is the first time that Foucault examines *Oedipus at Colonus* in his Collège de France lectures. *Oedipus the King*, however, was a regular object of analysis: with regard to "The Will to Knowledge" (the first year's course at the Collège de France), Foucault shows how Sophocles' tragedy should be understood as a chapter in the great narrative of historical forms of constraints on true discourse, and above all, in 1980 (the course "On the Government of the Living") he develops (in the lectures of 16 and 23 January, and 1 February) an "alethurgic (*aléthurgique*) reading" of *Oedipus the King* (the relationship between manifestation of truth and the art of governing).
15. "August goddesses, goddesses of the terrible eyes, since you were the first of the land on whose soil I must settle, do not be pitiless towards me or Phoebus. When this god told me of all the misfortunes I would suffer, he told me they will come to an end after a long time,

when I would finally arrive in a land where the venerable gods would grant me a place to settle, there to be welcomed. It is there, he said, that I will end my miserable life, a source of prosperity for those who have welcomed me." Sophocles, *Oedipus at Colonus*, 84-93.
16. See *supra*, p. 451, n. 4.
17. See R. Hoven, *Stoïcisme et Stoïciens face au problème de l'au-delà* (Paris: Les Belles Lettres, 1971), and P. Veyne, "Préface" to Seneca, *Entretiens, Lettres à Lucilius*, pp. cxxi-xxiii.
18. "And not only this; but when Rebecca also had conceived by one, even by our father Isaac; (For the children not being yet born, neither having done any good or evil, that the purpose of God according to election might stand, not of works, but of him that calleth;) It was said unto her, *The elder shall serve the younger*. As it is written, *Jacob have I loved, but Esau have I hated*." St. Paul, *Epistle to the Romans*, IX.10-13. Paul's *Epistle to the Romans* is of course Luther's principal source for establishing the primacy of grace over works. For a general and historically decisive presentation, see also, Pascal, *Écrits sur la Grâce*.
19. Homer, *The Odyssey*, translation R. Lattimore (New York: Harper and Row, 1965).
20. Xenophon of Ephesus, *The Ephesian Story*, translation Paul Turner (London: The Golden Cockerel Press, 1957).
21. P. Grimal's translations of the novels of Heliodorus and Achilles Tatius appear in a volume of the "Bibliothèque de la Pléiade," *Romans grecs et latins*.
22. For a more developed analysis of this theme, see the final chapter, "Une nouvelle érotique," of *Le Souci de soi*, pp. 262-63 (English translation by Robert Hurley, "A New Erotics," *The Care of the Self*, p. 228): "But one can nonetheless call attention to the presence, in these long narratives with their countless episodes, of some of the themes that will subsequently characterize erotics, both religious and profane: the existence of a 'heterosexual' relation marked by a male-female polarity, the insistence on an abstention that is modeled much more on virginal integrity than on the political and virile domination of desires; and finally, the fulfillment and reward of this purity in a union that has the form and value of a spiritual marriage."

# twenty three

## 24 MARCH 1982

### First hour

> *Reminder of results of previous lecture.* ~ *The grasp of self by the self in Plato's* Alcibiades *and in the philosophical texts of the first and second centuries* A.D.: *comparative study.* ~ *The three major forms of Western reflexivity: recollection, meditation, and method.* ~ *The illusion of contemporary Western philosophical historiography.* ~ *The two meditative series: the test of the content of truth and the test of the subject of truth.* ~ *The Greek disqualification of projection into the future: the primacy of memory; the ontologico-ethical void of the future.* ~ *The Stoic exercise of presuming evils as preparation.* ~ *Gradation of the test of presumption of evils: the possible, the certain, and the imminent.* ~ *Presumption of evils as sealing off the future and reduction of reality.*

SO, IT SEEMED TO me that we could distinguish two principal groups in the large family of typical exercises of the philosophers' ascetics. There were those we could group under the rubric *gumnazein* (training in real life, if you like). And it seemed to me that in this group we could distinguish, somewhat schematically of course, and for the sake of convenience, practices of abstinence on the one hand, and the regime of tests on the other. I tried to show how, on the basis of this idea, of this principle of the regime of tests, we arrive at what I think is a quite fundamental theme in this form of thought, namely, that the whole of life must be exercised and practiced as a test. That is to say, life, which since classical Greek thought was the point of departure and object of a *tekhnē*, now became a sort of great ritual, the constant occasion for the test. I think this shift or, if you like, re-elaboration of the *tekhnē* as test, or the fact that now the *tekhnē* must be a sort of permanent preparation for a test that lasts as long as life, was something quite important.

This week then, which is the last for this year, I would like to talk about the other group of ascetic exercises, which can be grouped around the terms *meletē*, *meletan*, *meditatio*, and *meditari*: meditation then, understood in the very general sense of the exercise of thought on thought. The term has a much wider meaning than the word meditation has for us. We can clarify it a little by recalling the use of the word *meletē* in rhetoric. In rhetoric, *meletē* is the internal preparation—preparation of thought on thought, of thought by thought—which prepares the individual to speak in public, to improvise.[1] Since we must go quickly, to understand the significance and general meaning of these exercises of "meditation"—once again we must use inverted commas—I would like to return for a moment to the text which was the point of departure for the whole of this year's course, Plato's *Alcibiades*. You recall that the approach consisted first in stopping Alcibiades and showing him that he really should take care of himself, and then in wondering what this care of the self was that Alcibiades was exhorted to undertake. The question was subdivided into two. First, what is this self about which one must be concerned? Second, how must one care for oneself? And here again you recall that Socrates defined the fundamental modality of the care of the self. Essentially he described the practice of the care of the self as the exercise of looking, of a looking that focuses precisely on the self, on oneself. "One must be concerned about the self," [this was the translation] of *blepteon heauton*: [one must] look at oneself.[2] Now what I think we should note is that what made this looking important—what gives it its value, what precisely will enable it to lead to the dialogue's real objective, namely: how must one learn to govern?—was precisely the fact that it established a relation of same to same. It was precisely this relation, in the general form of identity, which gave looking its fecundity. The soul saw itself, and it was precisely in this grasp of itself that it also grasped the divine element, the divine element that constituted its own virtue. By looking at itself in this mirror of itself that was absolutely pure—since the mirror is the mirror of the divine luminosity itself—and in seeing itself in this divine luminosity, it recognized the divine element that was its own.[3] There is then both a relation of identity, which is fundamental, the motor of development as it were, and, as point of arrival, the recognition of a divine element that will have two effects. First, that of provoking the soul's ascent [to] essential realities, and, on the other hand, of opening to him the knowledge of the essential realities that will enable him to give a rational foundation to his political action. Very schematically, let's say that if we ask ourselves what the nature of this *gnōthi seauton* is in this movement described in *Alcibiades*, the principle of which, moreover, is recalled at the beginning and at several points during the dialogue,[4] then we see that it involves the soul knowing its own nature and, on this basis, of having access to what is connatural to the soul. The soul knows itself, and in this movement by which it knows itself, it recognizes in the depths of its memory what it knows already. You see then, and I would like to emphasize this, that in this modality of the *gnōthi seauton* we are not dealing with a knowledge of the self in which the relation of self to self, the looking at ourselves would open onto a sort of domain of internal objectivity on the basis of which we could eventually infer the soul's nature. It is a matter of a knowledge that is neither more nor less than the knowledge of what the soul is in its own essence, in its own reality; and it is the grasp of the soul's own essence that will open up a truth: not the truth with regard to which the soul would be an object to be known, but a truth which is the truth the soul knew. That is to say, the soul grasps itself both in its essential reality, and it grasps itself at the same time as subject of a knowledge of which it was the subject when it contemplated the essences in heaven, at the summit of heaven where it had been placed. Consequently, we can say that self-knowledge turns out to be the key of an essential memory. Or again, the relation between the reflexivity of the self on the self and knowledge of the truth is established in the form of memory. One knows oneself so as to recognize what one knew. Okay, it seems to me that the relation is established quite differently in the philosophical ascetics

I would now like to talk about. In fact, again schematically and in a quick overview, how can we say what happens in the *meletē* (in this meditation which precisely is not a memory)? I will try to show this later with some concrete examples.

First of all, and this is, of course, the fundamental difference from the *gnōthi seauton* and the *epimeleia heautou* of the *Alcibiades*, self-knowledge is not arrived at in the element of identity. It is not the element of identity which is relevant in the self's grasp of itself, but rather a sort of internal reduplication which entails a shifting of levels. There is a very explicit text by Epictetus on this. It is in discourse 16 of book I, in which Epictetus explains how what distinguishes the fact of man having to be concerned about himself, the fact that he can and must be concerned about himself, is his having at his disposal a certain faculty which is different in its nature, or rather in its functioning, from the other faculties.[5] The other faculties—those, for example, which enable me to speak or play a musical instrument—know, in fact, how to make use of an instrument, but they never tell me if I ought to use these instruments, if I should use the flute or use language. They can tell me how to do so, but if I want to know if I ought to do so and whether it is good or bad to do so, I must turn to another faculty, which is the faculty of the use of the other faculties. This faculty is reason, and it is [through reason], occupying the position of the control of and free decision regarding the use of other faculties, that the care of the self must be realized. Caring for oneself means not just using the faculties one has, but using them only after determining the use to which they are put through recourse to this other faculty that determines whether the use is good or evil. So care of the self and self-knowledge is carried out in this shifting of levels, and not in the soul's recognition by itself, as in Plato. There is, then, a shifting of the level of the faculties in order to situate, fix, and establish the relationship of self to self.

Second, what is grasped in this movement described by the Stoics, and which defines or describes the gaze one focuses on oneself, is not, as in Plato, as in the *Alcibiades*, the soul's substantial and essential reality. What will be grasped and become the object of the gaze and attention one focuses on the self are the impulses taking place in thought, the representations that appear in thought, the opinions and judgments which accompany representations, and the passions which act on the body and the soul. So you can see that, in this respect, grasping the substantial reality of the soul is not involved. It is a gaze looking down, as it were, and a gaze that enables reason in its free employment to observe, check, judge, and evaluate what is taking place in the flow of representations and the flow of the passions.

The third difference concerns the recognition of kinship with the divine. It is true that in the Stoic texts I am talking about there is a certain acknowledgement of the soul's kinship with the divine, even through the exercise of looking at oneself, contemplating oneself, examining oneself, and taking care of oneself. But I think this kinship with the divine is established in a quite different way. If you like, in Plato the divine is discovered in the self, in the soul, but on the side of the object as it were. What I mean is that it was by seeing itself that the soul discovered, in this other than itself that is itself, the divine element thanks to which it could see itself. In the Stoic meditation, it seems to me that the divine is discovered, rather, on the side of the subject, that is to say in the exercise of the faculty that freely employs the other faculties. This is what shows my kinship with God. Maybe all this is not very clear, but there is a text by Epictetus that I think explains what is involved and how the soul's kinship with the divine is established in the exercise of the *epimeleia heautou* and through self-examination. Epictetus says: "Just as Zeus lives for himself, reposes in himself, reflects on the nature of his government, occupies himself with thoughts which are worthy of him, so also should we be able to converse with ourselves, be able to do without others, and not be at a loss as to how we spend our time; we must reflect on the divine government, on our relations with the rest of the world, to consider what our attitude hitherto has been towards events, what it is now, what things affect us, how we might remedy them also, and how we might eradicate them."[6] To understand this text I think we should recall another passage in which Epictetus says that the great difference between animals and humans is that animals do not have to look after themselves. They are provided with everything, and they are provided with everything so that they can be of use to us. Imagine our difficulty if we had to look after animals as well as ourselves.[7] So, in order that they can be of use to us, animals find everything they need around them. As for humans, they are—and this is what distinguishes them—living beings who must take care of themselves. Why? Precisely because Zeus, God, has entrusted them to themselves, by giving them the reason I was just talking about which enables them to determine the use to which all the other faculties may be put. So God has entrusted us to ourselves, so that we have to look after ourselves.

If now, instead of passing from animals to humans, we go from humans to Zeus, what then is Zeus? He is simply the being who does nothing else but attend to himself. What distinguishes the divine element is the *epimeleia heautou* in the pure state as it were, in its total circularity and absence of dependence with regard to anything whatsoever. What is Zeus? Zeus is the being who lives for himself. "*Autos heautō sunestin*" the Greek text says. This is not completely "living for himself" as the [French] translation says, it is rather: the one who is forever himself with himself.* Divine being consists in this being with oneself. "Zeus lives for himself, reposes in himself (*ēsukhazei eph'heautou*), reflects on the nature of his government, occupies himself with thoughts that are worthy of him (*ennoei tēn dioikēsin tēn heautou oia esti*)." He reflects, he thinks of the government of himself, of his own government, that is to say the government he exercises, and he reflects on it in order to know *oia esti*—what it is—and he occupies himself with thoughts that are worthy of him. Living with himself, reposing in himself, being therefore in a condition of ataraxy; reflecting on the nature of his own government, that is to say knowing how his reason, the reason of God, will be exercised on things; and finally occupying himself with thoughts that are worthy of him, conversing with himself: these are the four [distinctive features], as you know, which characterize the position of the sage when he has achieved wisdom. Living in complete independence; reflecting on the nature of the government one exercises on oneself and on others; conversing with one's own thoughts; speaking with oneself: this is the

---

*Oldfather translates, "Zeus communes with himself,"—G.B.

portrait of the sage; it is the portrait of Zeus. But precisely, whereas the sage has arrived at this progressively, by stages, Zeus is put in this position by his very being. Zeus is the one who has only to take care of himself. Now, taking this position of Zeus as the model of all care of oneself, what should we do? Well, he says, we should be able to converse with ourselves, know how to do without others, not be at a loss as to how we spend our time. You see how the great divine model of the care of the self now falls back on men, element by element, as duty and prescription. We must reflect. And whereas Zeus reflects on his own government, now we must reflect on the divine government, that is to say on the same government, but seen from outside so to speak, and as being a government imposed on the whole world and on us. We must reflect on our relations with the rest of the world (how we should conduct ourselves and govern ourselves with regard to others); we must consider what our attitude has been hitherto vis-à-vis events (what affects us, how might we remedy them, and how might we eradicate them). These are precisely the objects of the *meletē*, of the *meletan*. We must meditate, we must exercise our thought on these different things: attitude towards events; what things affect us; how might we remedy them; how might we eradicate them? These are the four great domains of the exercise of thought in Epictetus. So, you can see that in this exercise of thought on itself there is something that brings us closer to the divine. But whereas in Plato, by looking at itself the soul recognized itself as being, substantially and in essence, of divine nature, in Epictetus there is the definition of a looking at oneself analogous to what constitutes the divine being entirely and solely concerned with himself.

Finally, the fourth major difference between the Platonic looking spoken about in the *Alcibiades* and the looking spoken about in Stoic meditation is that, in Plato's case, the truth grasped is ultimately that essential truth that will enable us to lead other men. Towards what will the gaze be turned in the case of the Stoics? It won't be a gaze directed towards the reality of essences, but one directed towards the truth of what we think. It is a matter of testing the truth of representations and of the opinions that accompany them. It also involves knowing if we will be able to act according to this tested truth of opinions, and if we can be the ethical subject, so to speak, of the truth that we think. Let's say, schematically and abstractly, looking at oneself in Platonism makes possible a memory-type of recognition, a mnemonic recognition if you like, which founds access to the truth (the essential truth) on the reflexive discovery of what the soul is in its reality. In Stoicism, a quite different apparatus is at work. In Stoicism, looking at oneself must be the constitutive test of the self as subject of truth, and it is this through the reflexive exercise of meditation.

As "background"* to all this, I would like to outline the following hypothesis: basically, in the West, we have known and practiced three major forms of the exercise of thought, of thought's reflection on itself; three major forms of reflexivity. [First,] reflexivity in the form of memory. This form of reflexivity gives access to the truth, to truth known in the form of recognition. In this form, which consequently leads to a truth which one recollects, the subject is modified since in the act of memory he brings about his liberation; his return to his homeland and to his own being. Second, there is, I think, the major form of meditation, which is of course set out above all by the Stoics. This form of reflexivity carries out the test of what one thinks, the test of oneself as the subject who actually thinks what he thinks and acts as he thinks, with the objective of the subject's transformation and constitution as, let's say, an ethical subject of the truth. Finally, the third major form of reflexivity of thought on itself is, I think, what is called method. Method is a form of reflexivity that makes it possible to fix the certainty that will serve as criterion for all possible truth and which, starting from this fixed point, will advance from truth to truth up to the organization and systematization of an objective knowledge.[8] It seems to me that these are the three major forms (memory, meditation, and method) which in the West have successively dominated the practice and exercise of philosophy, or, if you like, the practice of life as philosophy. Roughly speaking we could say that the whole of ancient thought was a long movement from memory to meditation with, obviously, Saint Augustine as its

---

*In English in the original—G.B.

point of arrival. From Plato to Saint Augustine there was this movement from memory to meditation. Of course, the form of memory is not entirely [absent] in Augustinian meditation, but I think that the traditional exercise of memory in Augustine is founded and given meaning by meditation. And, of course, let's say there was a different trajectory from the Middle Ages to the start of the modern age, to the sixteenth and seventeenth centuries: this was the movement from meditation to method in which the fundamental text is obviously that of Descartes, who, in the *Meditations*, produced the foundation of what constitutes a method. Anyway, let us leave this, if you like, and this general hypothesis.

What I have wanted to show in this year's course is, among other things, the following: that the historical tradition, and so the philosophical tradition—in France at least and, it seems to me, in the West generally—has always privileged the *gnōthi seauton*, self-knowledge, as the guiding thread for all analyses of these problems of the subject, reflexivity, knowledge of the self, etcetera. Now it seems to me that by only considering the *gnōthi seauton* in and for itself alone we are in danger of establishing a false continuity and of installing a factitious history that would display a sort of continuous development of knowledge of the self. This would be reconstructed either as a process of radicalization that would extend, more or less, from Plato to Husserl[9] through Descartes, or as a continuous history which would develop in the direction of an empirical extension going... from Plato to Freud through Augustine. And in both cases—that is to say, in taking the *gnōthi seauton* as a guiding thread which can be followed continuously in the direction of either radicalization or extension—we allow an explicit or implicit, but anyway undeveloped theory of the subject to run behind it all. Now what I have tried to show, what I have tried to do, is precisely resituate the *gnōthi seauton* alongside, or even within the context and on the basis of what the Greeks called the care of the self (*epimeleia heautou*). The principle of *gnōthi seauton* is not autonomous in Greek thought. And I do not think we can understand either its specific meaning or history if we do not take into account this permanent relation between knowledge of the self and care of the self in ancient thought. Care of the self, precisely, is not just a knowledge (*connaissance*). So if, as I would like to show today, the care of the self is always strongly linked to the problem of knowledge, even in its most ascetic forms, those closest to exercise, it is not fundamentally, exclusively, and from end to end a movement and practice of knowledge. It is a complex practice, which gives rise to completely different forms of reflexivity. So that, if we accept in fact this junction between *gnōthi seauton* and *epimeleia heautou*, if we accept a connection, an interaction between them; even if we accept, as I have tried to show, that the *epimeleia heautou* is the real support of the imperative "know yourself," if one must know oneself because one must take care of the self, then in that case I think we should seek the intelligibility and principle for the analysis of the different forms of knowledge of the self in the different forms of the *epimeleia heautou*. The *gnōthi seauton* does not have the same form or function within this history of the care of the self. The consequence of this is that the *gnōthi seauton* will not always open up or deliver the same contents of knowledge in every case. Which means that the actual forms of knowledge put to work are not the same. Which also means that the subject himself, as constituted by the form of reflexivity specific to this or that type of care of the self, will be modified. Consequently, we should not constitute a continuous history of the *gnōthi seauton* whose explicit or implicit postulate would be a general and universal theory of the subject, but should, I think, begin with an analytics of the forms of reflexivity, inasmuch as it is the forms of reflexivity that constitute the subject as such. We will therefore begin with an analytics of the forms of reflexivity, a history of the practices on which they are based, so as to be able to give the old traditional principle of "know yourself" its meaning—its variable, historical, and never universal meaning. This, then, in short, was what was at stake in this year's course.

Having made this introduction, I would like to move on to the examination of the forms of *meletai* (of meditations, of exercises of thought on itself) in this ascetics I am talking about. I think we can divide them into two categories. Here again this is schematic, so as to clarify things a little. On the one hand, we could say that the meditations, the different forms of *meletai* are [first of all] those that focus on the examination of the truth of what we think: keeping a watch on representations as they appear, seeing in what they consist, to what they are related, whether the judgments we pass on them, and consequently the impulses, passions, emotions, and affects they may arouse, are true or not. This is one of the major forms of *meletē*, of meditation. I will not talk about this form, because in fact (without remembering clearly why exactly) I know I have already spoken about it once or twice in the course.[10] Still, it could very well find its place here if the course had been more systematically structured.

Today I would like to talk about the other series of tests, not those concerning the examination of the truth of what we think (examination of the truth of opinions which accompany representations), but those that test oneself as the subject of truth. Am I really the person who thinks these true things? This is the question to which these exercises must respond. Being the person who thinks these true things, am I the person who acts as someone knowing these true things? What I mean by this expression is: Am I really the ethical subject of the truth I know? Okay, the Stoics have several exercises for responding to this question, the most important of which are, of course, the *praemeditatio malorum*, the exercise of death, and the examination of conscience.

First, *praemeditatio malorum*: the premeditation or presumption of evils. This exercise gave rise, in fact, to many discussions and debates throughout Antiquity, from the Hellenistic period up to and including the imperial period. The discussion and debate are, I think, very interesting. First of all we should consider the horizon within which this debate takes place. Throughout Greek thought—anyway from classical thought up to the period I am talking about—this horizon was that there was always a very considerable mistrust of the future, of thinking about the future, and of the orientation of life, reflection, and imagination towards the future. To get some understanding of this mistrust of the future on the part of all Greek moral and ethical thought, or of its mistrust of an attitude orientated towards the future, we would of course have to consider a range of cultural reasons—you are familiar with those things which are no doubt important and have to be taken into consideration. For example, the fact that for the Greeks what we have before our eyes is not our future but our past, that is to say that we advance into the future with our back turned, etcetera. We could refer to all this. Okay, I have neither the time nor the competence to do so. What I would like to emphasize now is that a fundamental theme in the practice of the self is that we should not let ourselves be worried about the future. The future preoccupies. We are *praeoccupatus* by the future.[11] The expression is interesting. We are, as it were, occupied in advance. The mind is pre-absorbed by the future, and this is something negative. The fact that the future preoccupies you, that it absorbs you in advance and consequently does not leave you free, is linked, I think, to three things, to three fundamental themes in Greek thought and more especially in the practice of the self.

First, of course, is the primacy of memory. It is very interesting to see that thinking about the future preoccupies, and so is negative, whereas in general, except for a certain number of particular cases, among which is, of course, remorse, which is negative, memory, that is to say thinking about the past, has a positive value. This opposition between the negative value of thinking about the future and the positive value of thinking about the past is crystallized in the definition of an antinomic relation between memory and thinking about the future. There are people who are turned towards the side of the future, and they are reprimanded. And there are those who are turned towards memory, and these win approval. Thinking about the future cannot be a memory at the same time. Memory cannot be thinking about the future at the same time. When it became possible for us to think that reflection on memory coincides with an attitude towards the future was no doubt one of the great mutations of Western thought. And all the themes like progress, for example, or, let's say, the whole form of reflection on history, this new dimension of historical consciousness in the West, is acquired very late, I think, only when it became possible to think that looking at memory is at the same time looking at the future.[12] I think the establishment of an historical consciousness, in the modern sense, will oscillate, will revolve around this. The other reason why thinking about the future is discredited is, if you like, theoretical, philosophical, and ontological. The future is nothingness: it does not exist, or at any rate not for man. Consequently we can only project on to it an imagination based on nothing. Or else the future pre-exists and, if it pre-exists, it is predetermined, and so we cannot control it. Now what is at stake in the practice of the self is precisely being able to master what one is, in the face of what exists or is taking place. That the future is either nothing or predetermined condemns us either to imagination or to impotence. Now the whole art of oneself, the whole art of the care of the self is constructed against these two things.

To illustrate this I would like to remind you of a text from Plutarch in *Peri euthumias* which seems to me to describe these two attitudes and show in what respect and why thinking about the future, or the attitude, if you like, of turning towards the future, is negative: "The foolish [*oi anoētoi*: this is the term the Latins translate as *stulti*,[13] that is to say, those whose position is exactly the opposite of the philosophical position; M.F.] carelessly neglect good things, even when these are present goods, because they are constantly in the grip of preoccupations about the future [being *anoētos*, being *stultus*, is then to be preoccupied about the future; M.F.], whereas sensible (*phronimoi*) people are clearly in possession of the goods they no longer have, thanks to memory." The [French] translation is not very pretty. Sensible people, then, are clearly in possession of the goods they no longer have thanks to memory—"for the present only allows us to touch it for a very short period of time. Then it escapes perception and the foolish think that it no longer concerns them and no longer belongs to us."[14] So, there are a number of important elements in this first part of the text. You can see the very clear opposition between the *anoētoi* and the *phronimoi*: *anoētoi*, men who are turned towards the future; *phronimoi*, men who are turned towards the past and who make use [of memory]. With regard to the past and the future, there is then a very clear distinction between two categories of people. And this distinction between the two categories of people is made by reference to the distinction between *anoētoi* and *phronimoi*, the philosophical attitude as opposed to the attitude of *stultitia*, of the dispersion and non-reflexivity of thought with regard to itself. The *stultus*, the *anoētos*, is the person who is not concerned about himself: not attending to himself, he worries about the future. You can also see in this text that the reason why the character of the man of the future is negative is because being turned towards the future, he cannot grasp the present. He cannot grasp the present, the actual, that is to say the only thing that is actually real. Why? Because, turned towards the future, he does not pay attention to what is taking place in the present, and he thinks that as soon as the present is swallowed up by the past it is not really important. As a result, the man of the future is the person who, not thinking about the past, cannot think about the present and who is therefore turned towards a future that is only nothingness and nonexistence. This is the first phrase I wanted to read. The second is this: "But just as the rope-maker in the painting of Hades lets the donkey feed on the rushes he is plaiting, so for most insensitive and unpleasant people, oblivion seizes their past, devours it, and makes all action, success, pleasant leisure, social life and enjoyment disappear, without allowing life to form a whole in which the past intertwines with the present; as if the man of yesterday were different from the man of today and equally the man of tomorrow not the same as the man of today, forgetting separates them and, in the absence of memory, turns all that happens into nothingness."[15] I think this phrase is important then for the following reason. It begins by evoking the image of the rope-maker who is letting a donkey feed on the strands of rushes he is in the process of plaiting. It refers to an image here: this is an old saying, an old fable,[16] which traditionally was recounted to show, to illustrate the distracted existence of someone who neither pays attention to what he is doing nor to himself. He is plaiting rushes, but he does not see a donkey eating what he is plaiting (another, somewhat different form of the frequently analyzed water pots of the Danaides).[17] He is engaged in work which is immediately undone. Okay, the man of the future is the person who is like this, who allows what he is doing to be consumed by something else as he does it. Now what is interesting about this illustration are the two details where it is said that the man who allows all that happens to be consumed by forgetting is incapable of action, incapable of success and incapable of pleasant leisure, of *skholē* (that form of studious activity which is so important in the care of the self).[18] He is not even capable of social life or of pleasure. In other words, when you do not practice memory and when you allow it to pass into forgetting, it is no longer possible to totalize social life, active life, the life of pleasure and of leisure. But there is more. Not only cannot these totalizations be carried out, but also you cannot constitute yourself as an identity. For the man who allows himself to be consumed by forgetting in this way (wholly preoccupied as he is with the future), is someone who considers [...*]. He is given over to discontinuity in his own being therefore. The text ends in this way: "Those in the schools who deny growth on the ground that matter is in a continual flux make each of us, in theory, a being always different from itself."[19] This is, of course, a reference to the Cyrenaic school:[20] the perpetual flow of time and matter, discontinuity.[21] Those who dedicate themselves to forgetting are, as it were, the Cyrenaics of life. But the text continues, and he says: But there is worse still. The attitude of those who turn towards the future, and who thus neglect memory and allow themselves to be consumed by forgetting, is worse. They are even worse than the Cyrenaics or those who live in a Cyrenaic way: "They do not preserve the memory of the past, nor recall it, but allow it to disappear gradually, rendering each day in reality destitute and empty, they hang on to the next day and then the next year, and two days before and the day before do not concern them and have absolutely nothing to do with them."[22] That is to say, not only are they doomed to discontinuity and the flux, they are also doomed to dispossession and emptiness. They are really no longer anything. They exist in nothingness.

There are many other echoes of these quite interesting analyses of the attitude of memory and the attitude of the future as two opposed forms, one justified and the other discredited. There are many in Seneca, in *De Brevitate vitae*, for example.[23] In letter 99 also, Seneca says, for example: "We are ungrateful for benefits already obtained, because we count on the future, as if the future, supposing it falls to us in turn, must not swiftly join the past. He who limits the object of his pleasures to the present extremely contracts the field of his satisfactions." Here then, is an interesting note, which shows that the inflection in Seneca is somewhat different from that in Plutarch. He says: "Both the future and past have their charms." It seems, then, that in this text the present is criticized, and he recommends a more open attitude and perception towards the future and the past. However, he adds straightaway: "The future

---

*Only "... the same as today" is audible.

attracts us through hope, the past through memory. But one [the future; M.F.] is still to come and may very well not be [so we must turn away from it; M.F.] while the other [the past; M.F.] cannot not have been. What madness to allow the most assured possession to escape."[24] So you can see, everything turns on the privilege of the exercise of memory, on an exercise of memory which enables us to grasp that form of reality of which we cannot be dispossessed, inasmuch as it has been. Reality that has been is still available to us through memory. Or again, let's say that memory is the mode of being of that which no longer is. To that extent it therefore makes possible a real sovereignty over ourselves, and we can always wander in our memory, says Seneca. Second, the exercise of memory enables us to sing the hymn of gratitude and recognition to the gods. You see, for example, how Marcus Aurelius, at the beginning of his *Meditations*, pays homage to the gods in a sort of biography, which at the same time is not so much his story as a hymn to the gods for the benefits that they have arranged for him. Marcus Aurelius recounts his past, his childhood, his adolescence, how he was raised, the people he met, and so on.

So, everything should direct us to the privileged status, the absolute and almost exclusive privileged status of the exercise of memory over exercises directed towards the future. Nevertheless, within this general context that accords value entirely to memory and the relation to the past, the Stoics developed the famous exercise of *praemeditatio malorum* (premeditation of misfortunes and evils). The Epicureans were savagely opposed to this exercise of the premeditation of evils, saying that we have enough problems in the present without additionally having to worry about evils that, after all, could very well not happen.[25] Against this *praemeditatio malorum*, the Epicureans set two other exercises: the *avocatio*, the function of which is to ward off representations or thoughts of misfortune by turning instead to the thought of pleasures, and to the thought of all the pleasures that could come to us some day in life; and then the exercise of *revocatio*, which protects us, rather, and defends us from the misfortunes or so-called evils that may happen to us, by recalling past pleasures.[26] The Stoics, then, practice *praemeditatio malorum*. The value of the *praemeditatio malorum* is based on the principle I have already referred to: The function of the ascesis in general, let's say of the exercise, is to provide man with the equipment of true discourse on which he will be able to call for aid, for assistance (the *logos boēthos*), should the need arise and an event occur that might, if he is insufficiently attentive, be thought an evil, but which is just an episode in the natural and necessary order of things.[27] One should then equip oneself with true discourse, and this is precisely the meaning of the premeditation of evils. Actually, the Stoics say, a man who is suddenly surprised by an event is really at risk of finding himself in a weak position if he is not prepared for it and the surprise is great. This man does not have the discourse-aid available to him, the discourse-recourse that would enable him to react properly, not letting himself be disturbed and remaining master of himself. In the absence of this equipment he will be permeable to the event, so to speak. The event will enter his soul and disturb and affect it, etcetera. Thus he will be in a passive state with regard to the event. We must therefore be prepared for the events that occur, we must be prepared for evils. In letter 91, Seneca says: "The unexpected overwhelms most, and strangeness adds to the weight of misfortune: there is no mortal to whom surprise does not increase the distress."[28] There are similar texts in Plutarch as well: When misfortune arrives, we should never be able to say: "I didn't expect it." Precisely: "you should have expected it," then "you would not have been taken unawares." Men "who have not trained (*anasketōs diakeimenoi*)," those, so to speak, whose apparatus is untrained, "are unable to resort to reflection in order to play a suitable and useful part."[29] We should therefore be prepared for evils. And how does one prepare for evils? Well, by the *praemeditatio malorum*, which can be described in the following way.

First, the *praemeditatio malorum* is a test of the worst. In what sense is it a test of the worst? First of all, we must assume that not just the most frequent evils may happen to us, those that normally happen to individuals, but that anything that can happen to us will happen to us. The *praemeditatio malorum* consists in training oneself in thought to assume that all possible evils, whatever they may be, are bound to occur. It is an exhaustive review of evils, or, inasmuch as the exhaustive review of possible evils cannot really be practiced, it consists in considering the worst of all evils and assuming that it is bound to occur. Second, the *praemeditatio malorum* is also a test of the worst inasmuch as we must not only assume that the worst evils will occur, but that they will happen in any event and are not just possibilities with a certain margin of uncertainty. So we should not think in terms of probabilities. We must practice misfortune in a sort of certainty that we acquire through the exercise of this *praemeditatio*: it will happen to you anyway. Thus, in his letter to Marullus, which I have already spoken about, Seneca consoles Marullus on the loss of his daughter.[30] The letter of consolation to Marullus is, like all this literature of consolation, a long list of all the misfortunes that have already occurred, will occur, and may occur. And, at the end of this letter of consolation, in which it is only a matter of even worse things that may still happen or which have happened to others, Seneca concludes by saying: I am not writing this to you because I think you expect a remedy from me. For it is too late, my letter will reach you long after the death of your daughter. But I write "to exhort you for the future to lift your soul aloft against fortune, to foresee her offensives not as possible events, but as bound to occur."[31] Finally, the third way for the *praemeditatio malorum* to be a test of the worst is that not only should we think of the most serious misfortunes as occurring, not only should we think of them as happening anyway, regardless of probability, but we should think of them as happening immediately, very shortly, without delay. Seneca's letter 91: The person who said it only needs a day, an hour, or a moment to overturn the greatest Empire of the world has still granted too much time.[32]

Despite the general climate of mistrust with regard to thinking about the future, we might think that even so the *praemeditatio malorum* is an exception to this general rule, and that it is indeed a case of thinking about the future. But looked at in detail you can see that it is not really thinking about the future. It is much more a case of sealing off the future in this *praemeditatio malorum*. It involves thought systematically nullifying the specific dimensions of the future. For what is at stake is not a future with its different open possibilities. All possibilities are given, or the worst at any rate. It is not a matter of a future and its uncertainty. It involves assuming that everything that can happen is necessarily bound to happen. Finally, it does not involve a future with the unfolding of time and its uncertainties, or anyway its successive moments. It is not a successive time but a sort of immediate time, gathered up into a point, which must make one consider that all the worst misfortunes of the world, which will happen to you anyway, are already present. They are imminent with regard to the present you are living. You see then that it is not at all a case of thinking about the future that is an exception to the general mistrust of thinking about the future. In reality, within this mistrust, it is a nullification of the future by making everything possible present, if you like, in a sort of present test of thought. We do not start from the present in order to simulate the future: we give ourselves the entire future in order to simulate it as present. It is therefore a nullification of the future.

This nullifying making present of the future—and I think this is the other aspect of the *praemeditatio malorum*—is at the same time a reduction of reality. We do not make the whole of the future present in this way so as to make it more real. Rather it is to make it as least real as possible, or at least to nullify that which could be envisaged as or considered to be an evil in the future. Seneca's letter 24 is quite interesting on this. He says: "Get it clear in your mind that whatever event you fear will happen without fail." This is right at the beginning of the letter. Lucilius had a problem, a lawsuit that he feared losing. So Seneca consoles him by telling him: "get it clear in your mind that whatever event you fear will happen without fail," and that is, that you will lose your lawsuit. You should get it into your head: this is the rule of the worst I was just talking about. "Whatever the evil may be, take its measure in your thought and weigh up your fears: you will certainly see that what frightens you is unimportant and short-lived."[33] Lucilius is thus urged to assume that he will lose his lawsuit, that he will lose it, that it is lost already, and that it is lost in the worst conditions. This is not at all so as to actualize the misfortune and make it more real, but rather in order to encourage Lucilius to take the measure of the event and discover that in the end it is unimportant and short-lived. And at the end of the same letter there is an interesting passage precisely on this thinking about the future and its relation to imagination. Concerning this mistrust of the future, I was saying a moment ago that one of the reasons why it should be mistrusted is because the future appeals, so to speak, to the imagination. And our uncertainty concerning the future gives us, if not the right, at least the possibility of imagining it in the worst forms. So then, we must both think of the future in the worst forms, but at the same time not imagine it in the worst forms, or rather we must carry out some work so that thinking about the future is shorn as it were of the imagination in which it usually appears and restored to its reality which, as misfortune at least, is nothing. Here is the passage: "What you see happening to boys, we too experience, big children that we are. Those they love, with whom they are familiar, and with whom they play, make them tremble with fear when they appear in a mask. We should remove the mask not only from men but also from things, forcing them to take on their true appearance again. What is the point of showing me these swords, fires and that band of executioners growling angrily around you? Cast off that paraphernalia which hides you and only scares fools. You are death who a short while ago my slave or servant girl defied. What! Why spread your whips and racks before me again in grand display, these tools, one for every joint, each adjusted to dislocate them all, and these thousands of instruments for tearing a man into shreds? Put away all these bogeymen; silence the groans, the broken pleas and sharp cries of the tortured victim broken into pieces. So, you are pain that this gouty person despises, that this dyspeptic suffers in the midst of his delicacies, that the young woman endures in childbirth; pain that is slight if I can bear it, short if I cannot."[34] You have here then a speech to death, to death which, when we think about it, appears with all this imaginary paraphernalia of torture, swords, suffering, and so on. The exercise of *praemeditatio malorum* must start from this, but not in order to form an imaginary world, but rather to quell it and ask oneself: What is there behind a sword, what is this torment we suffer in torture? What do we find when we unmask all these bogeymen? Only a small pain, a small pain which is really no different than the pain of a woman giving birth, of someone with gout suffering pain in his joints, etcetera. It is no more than this, and this pain—which maybe, in fact, we will suffer in death—is "slight if I can bear it, short if I cannot." You know this is the old Stoic aphorism: Either a pain is so violent that you cannot bear it (you die straightaway, and so it is short), or a pain is bearable.[35] And if it is bearable, if it does not kill us, it is because it is slight. Consequently, it is reduced anyway, if not to nothing, at any rate to the least possible being.

You see then that the *praemeditatio malorum* is not imaginary thought about the future. It is a nullification of the future and a reduction of the imagination to the simple and stripped down reality of the evil towards which one is turned. I think the objective of the *praemeditatio malorum* is to seal off the future through the simulation of actuality, to reduce its reality, by stripping it down in imagination. And by this means we can equip ourselves with a truth which, when the event occurs, will be of use to us for reducing to the element of strict truth all representations that could move and disturb our soul if we were not thus prepared. You can see that the *praemeditatio malorum* is a *paraskeuē*. It is a form of *paraskeuē*, of preparation realized through the test of the non-reality of what we actualize in this exercise of thought. So, if you like, I will move on in a moment to another exercise of death, and then, quickly, to the examination of conscience.

1. See the lecture of 17 March, first hour.
2. "If the eye wishes to see itself (*ei mellei idein hauton*), it must look at (*blepteon*) an eye." Plato, *Alcibiades*, 133b.
3. For this analysis of looking, see the lecture of 12 January, second hour.
4. *Alcibiades*, 124b, 129a, and 132c (cf. the lecture of 6 January, second hour, and of 12 January, first hour).
5. "This is what you ought to sing on every occasion, and also the most solemn and divine hymn for the faculty God has given us to comprehend these things and to use it with method (*hodō khrēstikēn*)." Epictetus, *Discourses*, I.xvi.18.
6. Epictetus, *Discourses*, III.xiii.7.
7. "Animals do not exist for themselves, but to serve, and it was not at all beneficial to create them with all these needs. Think a little, how tiresome it would be for us if we had to look out not only for ourselves but for sheep and asses." *Discourses*, I.xvi.3; see the summary of this text in *Le Souci de soi*, pp. 61-62 (*The Care of the Self*, p. 47).
8. On method, and more precisely the Cartesian method, see the lecture of 24 February, first hour.
9. Husserl himself, in the *Krisis*, gives this view of a Greek rationality, which, after the Cartesian refoundation of the *Meditations*, finds its teleological realization (in the sense of an always more radical resumption of the meaning of Reason) in transcendental phenomenology. See *The Crisis of European Sciences and Transcendental Phenomenology: An Introduction to Phenomenological Philosophy*, chapter 73.
10. See the lecture of 24 February, first hour.
11. See the lecture of 20 January, first hour, on Seneca's "*omnes praeoccupati sumus*" (letter to Lucilius, L).
12. The temporal structure of modern consciousness was the object of a lengthy chapter, "Le recul et le retour de l'origine," in *Les Mots et les Choses* ("The retreat and the return of the origin," in *The Order of Things*).
13. On *stultitia*, especially in Seneca, see the lecture of 27 January, first hour.
14. Plutarch, *On Tranquility of Mind*, 473c.
15. Ibid., 473c, p. 118.
16. "Plaiting the rushes of Ocnus" is a proverbial expression that refers to the needy Ocnus, whose spendthrift wife ate everything he earned.
17. Daughters of Danaus, the Danaides (there were fifty of them) were forced to marry their cousins, and all, with the single exception of Clytemnestra, took advantage of their wedding night to slit the throats of their new husbands. As punishment they were condemned to draw water eternally with leaking water-pots that let the water escape as they filled them.
18. See J.-M André, *L'Otium dans la vie morale et intellectuelle romaine, des origines à l'époque augustéenne*.
19. Plutarch, *On Tranquility of Mind*, 473d.
20. A philosophical school of the fifth and fourth centuries B.C., founded by Aristippus of Cyrene. The Cyrenaics professed a morality of pleasure as an irreducible subjective experience, exhausting its virtue in the punctuality of a moment. In Aristippus, however, the ethics of the actuality of pleasure that cannot be surpassed does not lead to the frantic and anxious search for pleasures, but to an ideal of self-control. See the note by F. Caujolle-Zaslawsky on this philosopher in the *Dictionnaire des philosophes antiques*, vol. I, pp. 370-75.
21. "Both pain and pleasure consist in movement, so that neither the absence of suffering nor the absence of pleasure derive from movement ... But they deny that pleasure, if it derives from memory or the expectation of good things, is fulfilled—as Epicurus thought—since the movement of the soul is exhausted with time." Diogenes Laertius, "Aristippus," in *Lives of Eminent Philosophers*, II.8.89.
22. Plutarch, *On the Tranquility of Mind*, 473d-e.

23. "Life is divided into three periods: what has been, what is, and what will be. Of these three, the present is short, the future is doubtful, and the past is certain ... [the past] is the only part of our life which is sacred and inviolable, which has avoided all human mishaps, which is withdrawn from the empire of Fortune, which is upset by neither poverty, fear nor the onset of illness; it cannot be disturbed or stolen from us; its possession is perpetual and serene ... It is the mark of an assured and tranquil mind to wander through all the periods of its life; the mind of those preoccupied, as if under a yoke, can neither turn around nor look behind. Their life therefore advances into an abyss." *On the Shortness of Life*, x.2-5.
24. Seneca, *Letters*, XCIX.5.
25. "[Epicurus] supposes that distress is inevitable whenever we feel struck by an evil, even if this evil was foreseen and expected or is already well established. For time does not lessen it nor foresight lighten it, and it is foolish to think about an evil which may occur but which equally may not: any evil is painful enough when it arrives, and always to be thinking that we may suffer misfortune is itself a perpetual evil; even more so if this evil does not come, for then one has plunged pointlessly into voluntary misery." Cicero, *Tusculan Disputations*, III.XV.32.
26. "As for the alleviation of distress, Epicurus makes it dependent upon two things: detaching oneself from painful thoughts (*avocatione a cogitanda molestia*) and attaching oneself to the thought of pleasures (*revocatione ad contemplandas voluptates*)." Ibid., 33.
27. On the *logos boēthos*, see the lecture of 24 February, second hour.
28. Seneca, *Letters*, XCI.3.
29. Plutarch, *A Letter of Condolence to Appollonius*, 112c-d.
30. For an earlier analysis of this letter, see the lecture of 3 March, second hour.
31. Seneca, *Letters*, XCIX.32.
32. "When the catastrophe arrives quickly, to speak of a day is to give it too much time: an hour, an instant is enough for the overthrow of empires." *Letters*, XCI.6.
33. Seneca, *Letters*, XXIV.2.
34. Ibid., 13-14.
35. A similar idea is found in Seneca himself. See, for example, letter LXXVIII.17: "Which would you prefer? That the illness is long or violent and short? If long it has its respites, allows you to get your breath back, spares you plenty of time; its development is unfailing—after a period of ascent there is the period of decline. If it is a brief and speedy illness there is the alternative: either it will disappear or I will. What difference is there if it ceases or I do? In either case suffering comes to an end." However it should be pointed out that this theme is largely inspired by Epicurean propositions contrasting the length of light suffering to the shortness of extreme suffering: "Pain does not endure uninterruptedly in the body, but intense pain lasts only for the shortest time." Epicurus, "Principal Doctrines," IV. "Every pain is easily despised; intense suffering is of brief duration, and lasting pain is slight." "Vatican Sayings," IV.

## twenty-four

## 24 MARCH 1982

### Second hour

[ *The meditation on death: a sagittal and retrospective gaze.* ~ *Examination of conscience in Seneca and Epictetus.* ~ *Philosophical ascesis.* ~ *Bio-technique, test of the self, objectification of the world: the challenges of Western philosophy.* ]

SO, THE ULTIMATE FORM of this premeditation of evils is, of course, the meditation on death, which I will talk about only briefly, insofar as it is still a philosophical *topos*. I would like to point out that, of course, the *meletē thanatou* did not emerge within this practice of the self as it was defined and organized at the beginning of the Empire or in the Hellenistic period: the meditation on death is found in Plato, in the Pythagoreans, and so on.[1] Consequently, in talking briefly about this death meditation, rather than give the general and complete history of this ancient practice, I will touch on the inflection of the tonality, meaning, and forms it was given within the Hellenistic and Roman practice of the self. In its general form, the death meditation is fully isomorphous with the presumption, the premeditation of evils I have just been talking about, for the simple [primary reason] that death is, of course, not just a possible event; it is a necessary event. It is not just an event of some gravity: for man it has absolute gravity. And finally, as we well know, death may occur at any time, at any moment. So it is for this event, as the supreme misfortune if you like, that we must prepare ourselves by the *meletē thanatou*, which will be a privileged exercise, the one in which or through which this premeditation of evils will be brought to its highest point. There is, however, something specific in the death meditation, and this is what I would like to bring out. Actually, in this meditation on death, in this death exercise, which occupies a very specific place and is accorded great importance, something appears that is not found in the other forms of the meditation or premeditation of evils. This is the possibility of a certain form of self-awareness, or a certain form of gaze focused on oneself from this point of view of death, or of the actualization of death in our life. In fact, the privileged form of the death meditation in the Stoics is, as you know, the exercise that consists in thinking of death as present, according to the schema of the *praemeditatio malorum*, and that one is living one's last day. There is an interesting letter by Seneca, letter 12, on this. In this letter Seneca refers to a sort of speculation on the theme, which was for a long time fairly general in ancient thought, that the whole of life is only one long day with, of course: morning, which is childhood, midday, which is maturity, and evening, which is old age; that a year is also like a day, with the morning of spring and the night of winter; that each month is also like a sort of day; and that all in all a day, the passing of a single day, is the model for the organization of the time of a life, or of different organized times and durations in a human life.[2] Well, the exercise to which Seneca urges Lucilius in this letter consists precisely in living his day as if not just a month or a year, but the whole of his life passes by in that day. We should think of each hour of the day we are living as a sort of age of life, so that when we arrive at the evening of the day we will also arrive at the evening of life as it were, that is to say at the moment of death itself. This is the exercise of the last day. It does not consist merely in saying to oneself: "Ah! I could die today"; "Ah! Something fatal could well happen to me that I have not foreseen." No, it involves organizing and experiencing our day as if each moment of the day was the moment of the great day of life, and the last moment of the day was the last moment of our existence. Okay, if we succeed in living our day according to this model, then when the day is completed, when we get ready to go to sleep, we can say with joy and a cheerful countenance: "I have lived." Marcus Aurelius writes: "Moral perfection (*teleiotēs tou ēthous*) involves living each day as if it were the last."[3]

Now what gives particular importance and meaning to the death meditation and to this kind of exercise is precisely that it enables the individual to see himself, and to see himself in two ways. First, this exercise enables us to take a sort of instantaneous view of the present from above; it enables thought to make a cross section of the duration of life, the flow of activities, and the stream of representations. By imagining that the moment or day we are living is the last, we immobilize the present in a snapshot, so to speak. And from this moment, frozen in this interruption by death, the present, the moment or the day will appear in their reality, or rather, in the reality of their value. The value of what I am doing, of what I am thinking, of my activity, will be revealed if I am thinking of it as the last.[4] Epictetus says: "Don't you know that illness and death must take us in the middle of some activity? They take the laborer at his work, the sailor navigating. And what activity would you like to be engaged in when you are taken? For you will be doing something when death takes you. If you can be taken [by death; M.F.] while engaged in something better than your present activity, practice that."[5] You see, then, that the exercise consists in thinking that death will take you when you are engaged in some activity. Through this kind of gaze of death which you focus on your activity, you will be able to evaluate it, and if you happen to think that there is a finer and morally more worthy activity which you could be engaged in when you die, then this is the activity you should choose, and consequently [you should] place yourself in the best situation for dying at every moment. Marcus Aurelius writes: In performing each action as though it were the last, it will be "stripped of all casualness," of all "repugnance for the empire of reason," of "falsity." It will be free "from egoism and resentment at destiny."[6] So: present gaze, cross-section of the flux of time, grasp of the representation of the action one is performing. Second, the second possibility, the second form of the view of oneself which death makes possible, is no longer this instantaneous gaze and cross-section, it is the retrospective view over the whole of life. When we test ourselves as being at the point of dying, then we can look back over the whole of what our life has been. And the truth, or rather the value of this life will be able to appear. Seneca: "On the moral progress I have been able to make in the course of my life, I trust only in death. I await the day when I will pass judgment on myself and know whether virtue was only in my words or really in my heart... Whether or not you have wasted your time will be revealed when you lose your life."[7] The thought of death, then, makes this looking back and evaluative memorization of life possible. Here again you see that thinking of death is not thinking about the future. The exercise, thinking about death, is only a means for taking this cross-section view of life which enables one to grasp the value of the present, or again to carry out the great loop of memorization, by which one totalizes one's life and reveals it as it is. Judgment on the present and evaluation of the past are carried out in this thought of death, which precisely must not be a thought of the future but rather a thought of myself in the process of dying. This is what I wanted to say quickly about the *meletē thanatou*, which is fairly well known.

I would now like to move on to the other form of exercise about which I want to speak, the examination of conscience.[8] I think I talked about this some years ago,[9] so here again I will be somewhat schematic. You know that the examination of conscience is an old Pythagorean rule, and almost none of the ancient authors who speak about examination of conscience do so without referring to those verses of Pythagoras, which are probably quoted with some additions but whose authentic and primary meaning seems simply to be the following: Prepare a pleasant sleep by examining everything you have done during the day. Unfortunately I have forgotten to bring the text.[10] We should appreciate that this text from Pythagoras signifies that the principal function of the examination of conscience is to enable a purification of thought before sleep. Examination of conscience is not undertaken so as to judge what one has done. It is not, of course, intended to reactualize something like remorse. By thinking about what we have done, and thereby expelling the evil there may be within ourselves, we purify ourselves and make possible a peaceful sleep. This idea that the examination of conscience must purify the soul for the purity of sleep is linked to the idea that dreams always reveal the truth of the soul:[11] in the dream we can see whether a soul is pure or impure, if it is troubled or calm. This is a Pythagorean idea,[12] and it is also found in *The Republic*.[13] It is an idea found throughout Greek thought and is still present in monastic practice and exercises of the fourth or fifth centuries.[14] The dream is the test of the soul's purity. What is interesting here also (as in the *meletē thanatou*), is that the old schema of examination of conscience recommended by Pythagoras takes on a different meaning in the Stoics. In the Stoics two forms of examination of conscience are attested, morning examination and evening examination: what's more, according to Porphyry, the Pythagoreans also had a morning examination and an evening examination.[15] Anyway, in the Stoics, Marcus Aurelius, for example, refers to the morning examination right at the beginning of book V of the *Meditations*.[16] This examination does not at all involve going back over what you could have done in the night or the day before; it is an examination of what you will do. I think this morning examination is the only time in this practice of the self that there is an exercise really turned towards the future as such. However, it is an examination turned towards a near and immediate future. It involves reviewing in advance the actions you will perform in the day, your commitments, the appointments you have made, the tasks you will have to face: remembering the general aim you set yourself by these actions and the general aims you should always have in mind throughout life, and so the precautions to be taken so as to act according to these precise objectives and general aims in the situations that arise. Okay, this is the morning examination. The evening examination is completely different in both its functions and its forms. Epictetus frequently refers to it and there is a well-known example in Seneca's *De Ira*.

I am sure I spoke about this text some years ago and I will recall it quickly.[17] For Seneca it involves, every evening, when he has retired for the night and there is silence and calm around him, going over what he has done during the day. He must consider his different actions. Nothing should be neglected. He must show no indulgence towards himself. And then, in this examination, he will adopt the attitude of a judge; he says, moreover, that he summons himself to his own court in which he is both the judge and the accused. In this program of the examination of conscience, in which you review all the day's actions, and in which you must judge them at your own court, we get the impression of a type of inquest, a type of practice very close to what is found in Christianity, that is to say when penance has taken the juridical form with which we are familiar, and when this penance is accompanied by confessional practices which do in fact involve the retrospective expression of everything you have done and the submission of this to the court of penance.[18] We seem to be dealing with the original form of all this. But in fact, I'd like you to note that there are some quite notable differences between the examination Seneca defines and that which is found later in the court of penance and the medieval Christian examination of conscience. Actually, we should note first of all the nature of the actions and faults that Seneca records in his day. He gives some examples. He says: During a discussion and conversation with a friend, I remember wanting to try to give him a moral lesson to help him progress and correct himself, well then [...] I hurt him. Another example: I spent a long time arguing with some people, wanting to convince them of a number of things I consider to be true. But in fact these people were incapable of understanding so I wasted my time.[19] Now what is interesting is that these examples are of two faults which are, after all, quite relative. First of all, you can see that the faults he commits, anyway which he records, mainly concern the activity of spiritual advice. It is as a spiritual adviser that he committed certain "faults"—in inverted commas. And you can see that these faults should be understood as basically technical errors. He was unable to deploy or handle well the instruments he was using. He was too intense at one moment and wasted time at another. He could not achieve his objectives—correcting someone, convincing a group of people—because he did not use the right means. Basically, then, what he records in his examination is a mismatch between means and ends. The morning examination consists in defining and reminding ourselves of the tasks we will have to do, the objectives and ends we are aiming for and the means to be employed. The evening examination corresponds [to the first] as a balance sheet, a real balance sheet of the action programmed or envisaged in the morning. Second, we should note that although there are a number of metaphors of a juridical and even judicial kind in Seneca's text, in actual fact the principal notions employed are much more of an administrative kind. Of course, he says he is the judge and sits at his own court; he sits as the judge and is present as the accused. But when he refers to the different operations making up the examination he practices, the terms he uses are above all administrative rather than judicial. He uses the verb *excutire*,[20] which means "to shake out," but which in administrative terms would mean: to reexamine an account, an accounting, in order to bring out all its errors. He uses the verb *scrutari*,[21] which is the technical verb meaning to make an inspection of an army, a military camp, or a ship, etcetera. He employs the term *speculator*,[22] which roughly corresponds to the same type of activity (the *speculator* is an inspector). And he employs the verb *remetiri*,[23] which means precisely going back over the measures of a finished piece of work, as an inspector checks the measures again, sees if the thing has been made properly and if the cost really does correspond to the work expended, etcetera. So he performs an administrative labor of self-inspection. Finally, the third thing to be noted is that he does not reproach himself.[24] He says only: I leave nothing out, I recall everything I have done, I show no indulgence, but I do not punish myself. I say to myself simply: from now on you must not do again what you have done. Why? Well, he says, when we speak to friends in order to reproach them, our intention obviously should not be to hurt them, but to get them to progress. When we argue with someone it is in order to convey a truth to him. So if I find myself again in similar situations, I must recall these different ends so that from then on my actions will be adapted to them. You see, then, that it is primarily a test of the reactivation of the fundamental rules of action, of the ends we should have in mind, and of the means we should employ to achieve these ends and the immediate objectives we may set ourselves. To that extent, examination of conscience is a memory exercise, not just with regard to what happened during the day, but with regard to the rules we should always have in our mind. And, on the other hand, this examination of conscience is a sort of test inasmuch as, thanks to the reactivation of these rules and to the memory of what we have done, we can measure our progress [by evaluating the mismatch] between the rules we remember and the actions we have performed: whether we still have to make a big effort, whether we are far from the aim, whether or not we have been able to translate our principles of truth in the realm of knowledge (*connaissance*) into action. How far have I developed as an ethical subject of truth? To what extent, how far, up to what point am I really someone who is able to be the same as subject of action and as subject of truth? Or again: How far are the truths I know—and which through my examination of conscience I verify that I know since I remember them as rules—really the forms, rules, and principles of action in my conduct throughout the day and throughout my life? Where have I got to in this development, which I told you I think is the basic point of the ascetic operations in this form of thought? Where have I got to in this fashioning of myself as ethical subject of truth? Where have I got to in this operation that enables me to superimpose the subject of knowledge of the truth and the subject of right action, to make them exactly coincide in myself?

There are, of course, other examples of the fact that examination of conscience really does have this meaning and that it is the constant barometer, if you like, the measure to be taken up again every evening in the constitution of this ethical subject of truth. I am thinking of the text by Epictetus where it is precisely the verses from Pythagoras that he quotes. He quotes the verses by Pythagoras on the examination of conscience: to prepare yourself for peaceful sleep, etcetera. However, the context in which he presents this text from Pythagoras is quite strange. He presents it right at the beginning of the discourse, which begins in this way: "We should always have ready at hand the judgment of which we feel the need; at table, we should have ready at hand the judgment concerning everything to do with eating; at the bath, we should have ready at hand (*prokheiron*) all the judgments concerning how to behave at the bath. When we are in bed, we should always have ready at hand (*prokheiron*) all the judgments concerning how to behave in bed."[25] It is at this point that he quotes the verses from Pythagoras, within, or on the basis of, this general principle: have *prokheiron* principles of conduct, rules of conduct. It is with this objective, to this end, that we practice examination of conscience: providing ourselves with the availability of these true discourses that enable us to conduct ourselves. He quotes the verses from Pythagoras, and immediately after he says: "We should keep these verses ready at hand for us to employ usefully, and not just to declaim. Similarly, in a fever let us have ready at hand the judgments suitable for that circumstance." A few lines later, in conclusion to the whole paragraph on the need to construct for ourselves an apparatus of true discourse for conduct, he adds: To practice philosophy is to make preparation.[26] "To practice philosophy is to make preparation," to practice philosophy, then, is to put oneself in a frame of mind such that one will regard the whole of life as a test. And the meaning of ascetics, the set of exercises available to us, is that of enabling us to be permanently prepared for this life which will only ever be, until its end, a life test in the sense that it will be a life that is a test.

I think it is at this point that the famous *epimeleia heautou*, the care of the self, which appeared within the general principle or theme that one should have a *tekhnē* (an art of living), occupied as it were the whole of the place defined by the *tekhnē tou biou*. What the Greeks sought in these techniques of life, in this *tekhnē tou biou*, in very different forms over many centuries from the beginning of the classical age, is now entirely taken up in this kind of thought by the principle that we should be concerned about our selves, and that caring about the self means equipping ourselves for a series of unforeseen events by practicing a number of exercises which actualize these events with an unavoidable necessity and in which we strip them of any imaginary reality they may have, in order to reduce their existence to the strict minimum. It is in these exercises, in the interplay of these exercises, that we will be able to live existence as a test throughout our life. To summarize all this I would say briefly that this philosophical ascesis—the ascetic system, the meanings of which and some of its principal elements I have tried to give you—is not at all of the same type as Christian ascesis, the essential function of which is to determine and order the necessary renunciations leading up to the ultimate point of self-renunciation. This is, then, very different, but it would be wholly inadequate to remain at this simple distinction and say that philosophical ascesis is only an exercise for the formation of oneself. I think that philosophical ascesis should be understood as a certain way of constituting the subject of true knowledge as the subject of right action. And, in constituting oneself both as a subject of true knowledge and as a subject of right action, one situates oneself within or takes as the correlate of oneself, a world that is perceived, recognized, and practiced as a test.

I have presented [all this] to you in a rather systematic, condensed way, whereas in actual fact it is a series of fairly complex processes spread out over time, over centuries and centuries. In this somewhat condensed and, due to this, abstract form, with regard to the multiplicity of events and sequences, I have tried to present the movement in ancient thought, from the Hellenistic and imperial period, by which reality was thought of as the site of the experience of the self and as the opportunity for the test of the self. Now if we accept, if not as a hypothesis at least as a reference point—at any rate, a bit more than a hypothesis, a bit less than a thesis—the idea that if we want to understand the form of objectivity peculiar to Western thought since the Greeks we should maybe take into consideration that at a certain moment, in certain circumstances typical of classical Greek thought, the world became the correlate of a *tekhnē*[27]—I mean that at a certain moment it ceased being thought and became known, measured, and mastered thanks to a number of instruments and objectives which characterized the *tekhnē*, or different techniques—well, if the form of objectivity peculiar to Western thought was therefore constituted when, at the dusk of thought, the world was considered and manipulated by a *tekhnē*, then I think we can say this: that the form of subjectivity peculiar to Western thought, if we ask what this form is in its very foundation, was constituted by a movement that was the reverse of this. It was constituted when the *bios* ceased being what it had been for so long in Greek thought, namely the correlate of a *tekhnē*; when the *bios* (life) ceased being the correlate of a *tekhnē* to become instead the form of a test of the self.

That *bios*,[28] that life—by which I mean the way in which the world immediately appears to us in the course of our existence—is a test should be understood in two senses. Test in the sense of experience, that is to say the world is recognized as being that through which we experience ourselves, through which we know ourselves, discover ourselves, and reveal ourselves to ourselves. And then, test in the sense that this world, this *bios*, is also an exercise, that is to say that on the basis of which, through which, in spite of or thanks to which we form ourselves, transform ourselves, advance towards an aim or salvation, or head towards our own perfection. I think the fact that through the *bios* the world became this experience through which we know ourselves, and this exercise through which we transform ourselves or save ourselves, is a transformation, a very important mutation with regard to classical Greek thought, in which the *bios* should be the object of a *tekhnē*, that is to say of a reasonable and rational art. You see then that two processes will thus intersect at different periods, from different directions and according to different movements: one by which the world ceased being thought so as to be known through a *tekhnē*; and the other by which the *bios* ceased being the object of a *tekhnē* and became the correlate of a test, an experience, and an exercise. It seems to me that we have here the root of the question that has been posed to philosophy in the West, or, if you like, the root of the challenge of Western thought to philosophy as discourse and tradition. The challenge is this: How can what is given as the object of knowledge (*savoir*) connected to the mastery of *tekhnē*, at the same time be the site where the truth of the subject we are appears, or is experienced and fulfilled with difficulty? How can the world, which is given as the object of knowledge (*connaissance*) on the basis of the mastery of *tekhnē*, at the same time be the site where the "self" as ethical subject of truth appears and is experienced? If this really is the problem of Western philosophy—how can the world be the object of knowledge (*connaissance*) and at the same time the place of the subject's test; how can there by a subject of knowledge (*connaissance*) which takes the world as object through a *tekhnē*, and a subject of self-experience which takes this same world, but in the radically different form of the place of its test?—if this really is the challenge of Western philosophy, you will see why *The Phenomenology of Mind* is the summit of this philosophy.* That's all for this year. Thank you.

---

*The manuscript has here a concluding sentence that Foucault decided not to utter: "And if the task left by the Aufklärung (which the *Phenomenology* takes to the absolute) is to ask on what our system of objective knowledge rests, it is also to ask on what the modality of the experience of the self rests."

1. On this point, the Platonic *meletē thanatou* (*Phaedo*, 67e and 81a) and its ancient roots, see the old but fundamental article by J.-P. Vernant, "Le Fleuve 'amelēs' et la 'meletēthanatou'" in *Mythe et Pensée chez les Grecs*, vol. 1, pp. 108-23 ("The River of Amélès and the Mélétè Thanatou" in *Myth and Thought among the Greeks*, pp. 106-23).
2. "One day is a stage of life. The whole of life is divided into periods; it is made up of unequal and concentric circles. The function of one of them is to embrace and circumscribe all the others; it extends from birth to our last day. The second encloses the years of youth. The third confines all of childhood in turn. Then there is the year, an ideal entity, the sum of all the moments which when multiplied make up the whole of life. A smaller circumference contains the month. The smallest describes the day, but like all the others, the day goes from its beginning to its end, from sunrise to sundown... Therefore let us regulate each day as if it had to close the progression, as if it were the end our life and its ultimate conclusion... When we go to sleep let us say with joy and cheerful countenance: 'I have lived; I have completed the course that Fortune assigned to me.'" Seneca, *Letters*, XII.6-9.
3. Marcus Aurelius, *Meditations*, VII.69.
4. One cannot help hearing here, like an echo, the *credo* of the Nietzschean eternal return aiming to evaluate every action, not in its capacity to be the last, but to be repeated to infinity: "If this thought [of the eternal return] took hold of you, perhaps it would transform you, and perhaps it would destroy you: you would ask of every thing: 'do you desire this? do you desire its return? once? always? to infinity?' and this question would weigh on you with a decisive and terrible weight!" Friedrich Nietzsche, *The Gay Science*, book IV, 341 (translated from the French [G.B.]: *Le Gai Savoir*, translations by A. Vialatte [Paris: Gallimard, n.d.] p. 17; see English translation by W. Kaufmann, *The Gay Science* [New York: Random House, 1974] p. 274).
5. Epictetus, *Discourses*, III.v.5.
6. "You will free yourself from them [= all other concerns] if you perform each action as if it were the last, stripped of all mental casualness, of impassioned repugnance for the empire of reason, of deceit, egoism, and resentment at destiny." Marcus Aurelius, *Meditations*, II.5.
7. Seneca, *Letters*, XXVI.5-6.
8. See on this theme, *Le Souci de soi*, pp. 77-79 (*The Care of the Self*, pp. 60-62).
9. See the lecture at the Collège de France of 12 March 1980. Foucault attempted an archeology of the Christian coupling of the verbalization of faults and the exploration of oneself, taking great care to indicate an irreducible discontinuity between the Pythagorean-Stoic examination and the Christian examination at the three levels of their field of exercise, instruments, and objectives.
10. "Do not allow gentle sleep to creep into your eyes,/before having examined every action of your day./In what have I sinned? What have I done? What have I failed to do?/Start with the first and go through them all. And then,/if you find you have sinned, rebuke yourself; but if you have acted well, rejoice./Strive to put these precepts into practice, meditate on them; you should love them,/and they will put you on the path of divine virtue." Pythagoras, *Les Vers d'or*, translation M. Meunier, p. 28.
11. See *Le Souci de soi*, pp. 25-26 (*The Care of the Self*, pp. 12-13).
12. See the lecture of 12 January, first hour.
13. "When he has calmed these two parts of the soul [that of the appetite and that of anger], stimulated the third where wisdom resides, and at last abandoned himself to rest, it is under these conditions, as you know, that the soul best arrives at the truth." Plato, *The Republic*, IX.572a-b.
14. Foucault worked especially on this problem of the dream in the Greek culture, taking as his privileged reference *The Interpretation of Dreams* by Artemidorus. See *Le Souci de soi*, pp. 16-50 (*The Care of the Self*, pp. 4-36). For a general presentation of this problem, see S. Byl, "Quelques idées grecque sur le rêve, d'Homère à Artémidore," in *Les Études classiques*, 47 (1979), pp. 107-122.
15. "There were two moments in particular that he [Pythagoras] urged should be considered well: before going to sleep and the moment of rising after sleep. For both of them one had

to examine actions already performed or future actions, in order to give an account to oneself of past action and to foresee the future." Porphyre, *Vie de Pythagore*, translation E. des Places, §40, p. 54. See also the long description of the morning examination by Iamblichus, *Life of Pythagoras*, §165. We may recall that for Pythagoras: "getting up has greater value than going to bed." Diogenes Laertius, *Lives of Eminent Philosophers*, VIII.22.

16. "In the morning, when it pains you to rise, have this thought present: I am rising to do the work of man. Do I go then still in bad humor to do that for which I was made and for which I was cast into the world? Am I made for this, to remain in bed keeping myself warm under the covers?" Marcus Aurelius, *Meditations*, V.1. See the lecture of 3 February, second hour.

17. Foucault analyzed this text by Seneca (*On Anger*, III.XXXVI) in his course at the Collège de France of 12 March 1980. However, the analytical framework was somewhat different, although in 1982 Foucault takes up a large number of the elements developed in 1980 (notably, the theme of an administrative more than judicial vocabulary, and the absence of any attribution of culpability). In 1980 he stressed the anti-Freudian aspect of Seneca's apparatus (the censor serves only to keep the good elements for a good sleep) and on the future horizon projected by this examination (one does not examine oneself in order to release buried secrets of consciousness, but in order to open out embryonic rational schemas of action). In 1980 the essential opposition between Hellenistic and Christian examination of conscience turns on the alternative of either autonomy or obedience. See *Le Souci de soi*, pp. 77-78 (*The Care of the Self*, pp. 61-62) on this text.

18. See the lecture of 19 February 1975 in *Les Anormaux* (*Abnormal*).

19. "You spoke too sharply in that discussion; in the future do not get into arguments with ignorant people; those who have never learned do not wish to learn. You reprimanded that man more severely than you ought and so you have not corrected him but offended him; in the future see not only that what you say is true, but also that the person to whom you are speaking can hear the truth. Virtuous men love admonishments, the vicious find a guide difficult to bear." Seneca, *On Anger*, III.XXXVI.4.

20. "Is there anything more fine than this custom of scrutinizing (*excutiendi*) the whole day?" Ibid., III.XXXVI.2.

21. "When the light has been removed and my wife, accustomed to my ways, is silent, I examine (*scrutor*) the whole of my day." Ibid., III.XXXVI.3.

22. "What sleep follows this examination of oneself... when [the mind] has acted the spy (*speculator*), the secret censor of its own mores?" See *supra*, note 20.

23. "I measure (*remetior*) all my deeds and words." See *supra*, note 21.

24. "Take care not to do that again. I pardon you this once." Ibid., III.XXXVI.4.

25. Epictetus, *Discourses*, III.x.1.

26. "But what is it to practice philosophy? Is it not being prepared for every event?" Ibid., III.x.6.

27. Foucault's implicit references here are no doubt to two famous texts that he read very early and studied in depth: Husserl's *Krisis* (1936) (*The Crisis of European Sciences and Transcendental Phenomenology*), and Heidegger's lecture, "The Question Concerning Technology" (1953), in *The Question Concerning Technology and Other Essays*, translation W. Lovitt (New York: Harper and Row, 1977).

28. It is in the second lecture of the 1981 Collège de France course that Foucault distinguishes between *zōē* (life as the property of organisms) and *bios* (existence as the object of techniques).

# Course Summary*

THE COURSE THIS YEAR was devoted to the formation of the theme of the hermeneutics of the self. It involved studying it not only in its theoretical formulations, but analyzing it in relation to a set of practices which were very important in classical and late Antiquity. These practices were concerned with what was often called in Greek *epimeleia heautou*, and in Latin *cura sui*. To our eyes, the principle that one should "take care of the self," "be concerned about oneself" is no doubt overshadowed by the glory of the *gnōthi seauton*. But we should remember that the rule that one should know oneself was regularly combined with the theme of care of the self. Throughout ancient culture, it is easy to find evidence of the importance given to the "care of the self" and its connection with the theme of self-knowledge.

In the first place, it is found in Socrates himself. In the *Apology*, Socrates appears before his judges as the master of care of the self. He is the person who stops passersby and says to them: You worry about your wealth, reputation, and honor, but you are not concerned about your virtue and your soul. Socrates is the person who sees to it that his fellow citizens "are concerned about themselves." A bit later in the same *Apology*, Socrates says three important things about this role: It is a mission entrusted to him by the god, and he will not relinquish it before

---

*First published in *Annuaire du Collège de France*, 82ᵉ année, *Histoire des systèmes de pensée*, année 1981-1982 (1982), pp. 395-406; reprinted in *Dits et Écrits, 1954-1988*, Paris, 1994, vol. 4, no. 323, pp. 353-65. An alternative translation appears in M. Foucault, *Ethics: Subjectivity and Truth* (*The Essential Works of Foucault, 1954-1984*, vol. 1), ed. Paul Rabinow, translation Robert Hurley and others (New York: The New Press, 1997) pp. 93-106.

his final breath; it is a disinterested task for which he demands no payment, performing it out of pure benevolence; and finally it is a useful function for the city-state, even more useful than an athlete's victory at Olympia,* for by teaching citizens to take care of themselves (rather than their goods) one also teaches them to take care of the city-state itself (rather than its material affairs). Instead of condemning him, his judges would do better to reward Socrates for teaching others to be concerned about themselves.

Eight centuries later the same notion of *epimeleia heautou* appears with an equally important role in Gregory of Nyssa. He uses this term for the impulse that leads one to renounce marriage, detach oneself from the flesh, and, thanks to the virginity of heart and body, rediscover the immortality from which one has fallen. In another passage of the *Treatise on Virginity*, he models the care of the self on the parable of the lost drachma: to find the lost drachma one must light the lamp, turn the house upside down, search in every corner, until one sees the coin's metal shining in the dark. In the same way, to rediscover the effigy imprinted by God on our soul, and covered with filth by the body, it is necessary to "take care of oneself," to shine the light of reason and explore every recess of the soul. We can see, then, that Christian asceticism, like ancient philosophy, places itself under the sign of the care of the self and makes the obligation to know oneself one of the components of this basic concern.

Between these two extreme reference points—Socrates and Gregory of Nyssa—we can see that the care of the self was not just a principle, but also an abiding practice. We can take two other examples, distant from each other in their modes of thought and types of morality. An Epicurean text, the *Letter to Menoeceus*, begins: "It is never too early or too late to take care of one's soul. We should therefore practice philosophy when we are young and when we are old": philosophy is identified

---

*See "Technologies of the Self" in *Ethics: subjectivity and truth*, p. 227, where there is a very similar passage to this, except that in this lecture Foucault says "more useful than the Athenians' military victory at Olympia." The French translation of this lecture, by F. Durant-Bogaert, "Les techniques de soi" in *Dits et Écrits*, vol. 4, also has, "plus utile que la victoire militaire des Athéniens à Olympie."—G.B.

with care of the soul (the term is very precisely medical: *hugiainein*), and this care is a task to be pursued throughout life. In his *On the Contemplative Life*, Philo refers to a practice of the Therapeutae in the same way, as an *epimeleia* of the soul.

We cannot stop there, however. It would be wrong to think that the care of the self was an invention of philosophical thought and that it was a precept peculiar to the philosophical life. In actual fact it was a precept of life that, in a general way, was very highly valued in Greece. Plutarch quotes a Lacedaemonian aphorism that is very revealing with regard to this. Anaxandridas was asked one day why his compatriots, the Spartans, entrusted the cultivation of their lands to slaves instead of keeping this activity for themselves. His answer was: "Because we prefer to take care of ourselves." Taking care of oneself is a privilege; it is the symbol of social superiority, setting one apart from those who have to concern themselves with others so as to serve them, or to concern themselves with a trade in order to live. The advantage conferred by wealth, status, and birth is expressed in the fact that one can take care of oneself. We may note that the Roman conception of *otium* is not unrelated to this theme: the "free time" that it points to is, par excellence, the time one spends taking care of oneself. In this sense, philosophy, in Greece as in Rome, only transposed a much more widespread social ideal into its own requirements.

Anyway, even as a philosophical principle, the care of the self remained a form of activity. The term *epimeleia* itself refers not just to an attitude of awareness or a form of attention focused on oneself; it designates a regular occupation, a work with its methods and objectives. Xenophon, for example, uses the word *epimeleia* to designate the work of the master of the household who manages its farm. The word is also used to designate ritual respects paid to the gods and the dead. The sovereign's occupation of keeping watch over and guiding the city-state is called *epimeleia* by Dio Chrysostom of Prusa. So, when philosophers and moralists recommend taking care of the self (*epimeleisthai heautō*), it should be understood that they are not just advising one to pay attention to oneself, avoid errors, and protect oneself. They are referring to a whole domain of complex and regular activities. We can say that for all of ancient philosophy care of the self was a duty and a technique, a fundamental obligation and a set of carefully fashioned ways of behaving.

❦

The starting point for a study devoted to the care of the self is quite naturally the *Alcibiades*. Three questions appear in this dialogue concerning the connection of the care of the self with politics, pedagogy, and self-knowledge. Comparison of the *Alcibiades* with the texts of the first and second centuries A.D. reveals several important transformations.

1. Socrates advised Alcibiades to take advantage of his youth to take care of himself: "At fifty it will be too late." But Epicurus said: "One should not hesitate to practice philosophy when one is young, and one should not hesitate to practice philosophy when one is old. It is never too early or too late to take care of one's soul." Quite clearly the principle of constant care throughout life prevails. For example, Musonius Rufus says: "If you wish to live healthily, you must take care of yourself all the time." Or Galen: "To become an accomplished man, everyone needs to practice, so to speak, for his whole life," although it is true that it would be better "to have looked after his soul from when he was young."

It is a fact that the friends to whom Seneca or Plutarch give advice are no longer those ambitious adolescents to whom Socrates spoke: they are men, some of whom are young (like Serenus), and some fully mature (like Lucilius, who held the office of procurator of Sicily when he and Seneca engaged in their lengthy spiritual correspondence). Epictetus, who ran a school, had students who were still quite young, but sometimes he too stopped adults—and even "consular figures"—to remind them to take care of themselves.

Attending to the self is not therefore just a brief preparation for life; it is a form of life. Alcibiades understood that he had to take care of himself if he wished to take care of others later. Now it is a matter of taking care of oneself, for oneself. One should be one's own object for oneself throughout one's life.

Hence the idea of conversion to the self (*ad se convertere*), the idea of a whole life activity by which one turns round to examine oneself (*eis *heauton epistrephein*). No doubt the theme of the *epistrophē* is typically Platonic. However, as could be seen in the *Alcibiades*, the movement by which the soul turns to itself is a movement in which one's gaze is drawn "aloft"—towards the divine element, towards essences and the supracelestial world in which they are visible. The turning round urged by Seneca, Plutarch, and Epictetus is a turning round on the spot as it were: its sole end and outcome is to live with oneself, to "dwell in oneself" and to remain there. The final objective of conversion to the self is to establish certain relations with oneself. These are sometimes conceived in terms of the juridico-political model: being sovereign over oneself, exercising perfect control over oneself, being fully independent, being completely "self-possessed" (*fieri suum*, Seneca often says). They are also often represented in terms of the model of possessive enjoyment: self-enjoyment, taking one's pleasure with oneself, finding all one's delight in the self.

2. A second major difference concerns pedagogy. Care of the self in the *Alcibiades* was essential because of the deficiencies of pedagogy; it was a matter of either completing it or replacing it; in any case, it was a question of providing a "training."

When applying oneself to oneself became an adult practice that must be undertaken throughout one's life, its pedagogical role tends to give way to other functions.

*a.* First of all, a critical function. The practice of the self must enable one to rid oneself of all one's bad habits and all the false opinions one may get from the crowd or from bad teachers, as well as from parents and associates. To "unlearn" (*de-discere*) is an important task of the culture of the self.

*b.* But it also has a function of struggle. The practice of the self is conceived as an ongoing battle. It is not just a matter of training a man of courage for the future. The individual must be given the weapons and the courage that will enable him to fight all his life. We know how frequently two metaphors were employed: that of the athletic contest (in life one is like a wrestler who has to overcome successive opponents and who must train even when he is not fighting) and that of war (the soul must be deployed like an army that is always liable to be attacked by an enemy).

c. But most of all this culture of the self has a curative and therapeutic function. It is much closer to the medical model than to the pedagogical model. Of course, we should remember certain very ancient facts of Greek culture: the existence of a notion like *pathos*, which signifies the soul's passion as well as the body's illness; the extent of a metaphorical field that allows expressions like nursing, curing, amputating, scarifying, and purging to be applied to both the body and the soul. We should also remember the principle, familiar to Epicureans, Cynics, and Stoics, that the role of philosophy is to cure the diseases of the soul. Plutarch could say that philosophy and medicine are *mia khōra*, a single region, a single domain. Epictetus did not want his school to be seen as just a place for training, but rather as a "clinic," an *iatreion*; he wanted it to be a "dispensary for the soul," he wanted his students to be aware of being patients: "One" he said "with a dislocated shoulder, another with an abscess, a third with a fistula, and that one with a headache."

3. In the first and second centuries, the relation to the self is always seen as having to rely on the relationship with a master, a guide, or anyway someone else. But the need for this relationship was increasingly independent of the love relationship.

Not being able to take care of oneself without the help of someone else was a generally accepted principle. Seneca said that no one is ever strong enough to extricate himself by his own efforts from the state of *stultitia*: "He needs someone to give him a hand and pull him out." In the same way, Galen said that man loves himself too much to be able by himself to cure himself of his passions: He had often seen men "stumble" who had not agreed to put themselves in someone else's hands. The principle is true for beginners, but it is also true afterwards and until the end of life. Seneca's attitude in his correspondence with Lucilius is typical: albeit he is aged, having given up all his activities, he gives Lucilius advice but also asks him for advice and is glad of the help he gets from this exchange of letters.

What is striking in this practice of the soul is the multiplicity of social relations that can serve as its support.

- There are strictly scholastic organizations: Epictetus's school can serve as an example: temporary auditors were accepted alongside students who remained for a longer period of training; but teaching was also given to those who wanted to become philosophers and the guides of souls themselves; some of the *Discourses* collected by Arrian are technical lessons for these future practitioners of the culture of the self.
- We also come across private counselors, especially in Rome. Set up in the entourage of a great figure, forming part of his group or of his clientele, they would offer political opinions, direct the education of young people, and provide assistance in the important occasions of life. Thus, Demetrius in the entourage of Thrasea Paetus: when the latter was induced to take his own life, Demetrius served as his suicide counselor, so to speak, and gave support in his final moments with a discourse on immortality.
- But there are many other forms in which guidance of the soul is practiced. The latter joins up with and drives a whole set of other relationships: family relationships (Seneca writes a consolation to his mother when he is exiled); relationships of protection (Seneca takes charge of both the career and the soul of the young Serenus, a provincial cousin just arrived in Rome); friendship relations between two persons fairly close in age, culture, and situation (Seneca and Lucilius); relationships with a highly placed figure to whom one pays one's respects by offering useful advice (as Plutarch with Fundanus, to whom he urgently dispatches his own notes on the tranquility of the soul).

In this way what could be called a "soul service" is formed, which is performed through multiple social relations. The traditional *erōs* plays at the most an occasional role in this. This does not mean that affective relationships were not intense, which often they were. Our modern categories of friendship and love are no doubt wholly inadequate for understanding them. The correspondence between Marcus Aurelius and his teacher Fronto can serve as an example of this intensity and complexity.

⁕

The culture of the self comprised a set of practices generally designated by the term *askesis*. It would be best to analyze its objectives first of all. In a passage quoted by Seneca, Demetrius resorts to the very common metaphor of the athlete: We must train like an athlete; the latter does not learn every possible move, he does not try to perform pointless feats; he practices a few movements that are necessary for him to triumph over his opponents in the fight. In the same way, we do not have to perform feats on ourselves (philosophical ascesis is very mistrustful of those characters who draw attention to their feats of abstinence, their fasts, and their knowledge of the future). Like a good wrestler, we should learn only what will enable us to resist possible events; we must learn not to let ourselves be disconcerted by them, not to let ourselves be carried away by the emotions they may arouse in us.

Now what do we need in order to keep our control in the face of the events that may occur? We need "discourses": *logoi* understood as true and rational discourses. Lucretius speaks of *veridica dicta* that enable us to ward off our fears and not let ourselves be crushed by what we believe to be misfortunes. The equipment we need to face up to the future is an equipment of true discourses. These are what will enable us to face reality.

Three questions are raised concerning these discourses.

1. The question of their nature. There were numerous discussions on this point between the philosophical schools and within the same movements. The main point of debate concerned the need for theoretical knowledge. The Epicureans all agreed on this: From their point of view, knowing the principles that govern the world, the nature of the gods, the causes of marvels, and the laws of life and death, is indispensable for preparing oneself for the possible events of life. The Stoics were divided depending on how close they were to cynical doctrines: some accorded the greatest importance to *dogmata*, to the theoretical principles that

complement the practical prescriptions; others gave the main place to these concrete rules of conduct. Seneca's letters 90 and 91 set out these opposing theses very clearly. What we should point out here is that the true discourses we need only concern what we are in our relation to the world, in the place we occupy in the natural order, in our dependence or independence with regard to events that occur. They are not in any way a decipherment of our thoughts, representations, and desires.

2. The second question raised concerns the way in which these true discourses exist within us. To say that they are necessary for our future means that we must be able to resort to them when the need makes itself felt. To protect ourselves from an unexpected event or misfortune we must be able to call upon the appropriate true discourses. They must be available to us, within us. The Greeks had a common expression for this: *prokheiron ekhein*, that the Latins translate as: *habere in manu, in promptu habere*—to have ready to hand.

It should be understood that this involves something very different from a simple memory that one would recall should something occur. Plutarch, for example, resorts to several metaphors to describe the presence within us of these true discourses. He compares them to a medicine (*pharmakon*) with which we supply ourselves to deal with all the vicissitudes of life (Marcus Aurelius compares them to the surgeon's kit, which must always be ready to hand); Plutarch also speaks of them as like those friends "the surest and best of which are those whose useful presence in adversity gives us aid"; elsewhere he refers to them as an internal voice that makes itself heard when the passions begin to grow restless; they must be in us like "a master whose voice is enough to silence the growls of dogs." In a passage of *De Beneficiis* there is a gradation of this kind, going from the instrument one makes use of to the automatism of a discourse that would speak to us by itself. With reference to advice given by Demetrius, Seneca says we should "clasp them with two hands" (*utraque manu*) without ever letting go; but we must also fasten them, attach them (*adfigere*) to our mind, to the point of making them a part of oneself (*partem sui facere*), and finally, through daily meditation, arrive at the point where "healthy thoughts arise by themselves."

The movement here is very different from the movement Plato prescribes when he asks the soul to turn round on itself in order to rediscover its true nature. What Plutarch or Seneca suggest, rather, is the absorption of a truth given by a teaching, reading, or piece of advice; and one assimilates it to the point of making it a part of oneself, an internal, permanent, and always active principle of action. In such a practice we do not find, through recollection, a hidden truth deep within us; we internalize accepted truths through an increasingly thorough appropriation.

3. So a series of questions are raised about the methods of this appropriation. Memory obviously plays a major role here; not in the Platonic form of the soul that discovers its original nature and homeland however, but in the form of progressive exercises of memorization. I would just like to pick out some prominent features in this "ascesis" of truth:

- The importance of listening. Whereas Socrates questioned people and sought to get them to say what they knew (without knowing that they knew it), for the Stoics or Epicureans (as in the Pythagorean sects), the disciple must first of all keep quiet and listen. In Plutarch, or in Philo of Alexandria, there is a set of rules for correct listening (the correct posture to adopt, the way to direct one's attention, how to retain what has been said).
- The importance also of writing. In this period there was a culture of what could be called personal writing: taking notes on the reading, conversations, and reflections that one hears or engages in oneself; keeping kinds of notebooks on important subjects (what the Greeks called *hupomnēmata*), which must be reread from time to time so as to reactualize their contents.
- Finally, the importance of taking stock of oneself, but in the sense of exercises for memorizing what one has learned. This is the precise and technical meaning of the expression *anachorēsis eis heauton*, as Marcus Aurelius employs it: going back into oneself and examining the "wealth" one has deposited there; one must have within oneself a sort of book that one rereads from time to time. This tallies with the practice of the arts of memory studied by Frances Yates.

There is then a whole set of techniques whose purpose is to link together the truth and the subject. But it should be clearly understood that it is not a matter of discovering a truth in the subject or of making the soul the place where truth dwells through an essential kinship or original law; nor is it a matter of making the soul the object of a true discourse. We are still very far from what would be a hermeneutics of the subject. On the contrary, it is a question of arming the subject with a truth that he did not know and that did not dwell within him; it involves turning this learned and memorized truth that is progressively put into practice into a quasi-subject that reigns supreme within us.

We can distinguish between exercises that are carried out in real life situations and which basically form a training in endurance and abstinence, and those which are a training in thought and by thought.

1. The most famous of these thought exercises was the *praemeditatio malorum*, the meditation on future evils. It was also one of the most disputed. The Epicureans rejected it, saying it was pointless to suffer in advance evils that had not yet come about, and that it was more worthwhile to practice calling to mind the memory of past pleasures so as to protect oneself against present evils. The strict Stoics, like Seneca and Epictetus, but also men like Plutarch whose attitude towards Stoicism is very ambivalent, diligently apply themselves to the practice of the *praemeditatio malorum*. It should be clearly understood what this consists in: it seems to be a somber and pessimistic anticipation of the future. In actual fact it is something completely different.

- First of all, it is not picturing the future as it is likely to come about. Rather, it involves imagining very systematically the worst that might occur, even if there is very little likelihood of it happening. Concerning the fire that destroyed the whole town of Lyons, Seneca said: This example should teach us to consider the worst as always certain.
- Next, we should not envisage these things as possible events in a more or less distant future, but imagine them as already present

and already taking place. For example, let us imagine that we are already exiled, already being tortured.

- Finally, we do not imagine these things in their actuality so as to live through in advance the suffering or pain they cause us, but rather in order to convince ourselves that in no way are they real evils and that only our opinion of them makes us take them for true misfortunes.

We can see then that this exercise does not consist in envisaging a possible future of real evils in order to get accustomed to it, but in nullifying both the future and the evil. The future: since we bring it to mind as already given in an extreme actuality. The evil: since we practice no longer considering it as such.

2. At the other end of the exercises are those that are carried out in reality. These exercises had a long tradition behind them: They were exercise of abstinence, privation, or physical resistance. They could have the value of purification or attest the "daemonic" strength of the person who practiced them. However, these exercises have a different meaning in the culture of the self: they involve establishing and testing the individual's independence in relation to the external world.

Two examples. The first from Plutarch's *Socrates' Daemon*. One of the interlocutors refers to a practice, whose origin, moreover, he attributes to the Pythagoreans. First of all one engages in sporting activities that whet the appetite; then one stands before tables loaded with the most delicious dishes; and then, after having gazed on them, one gives them to the servants and takes for oneself the simple and frugal food of a poor man.

In letter 18, Seneca says that the whole town is getting ready for the Saturnalia. For reasons of expediency he considers participating in the festivities, in a way at least. But his own preparation will be that for several days he will dress in a simple, rough cloak, sleep on a pallet, and eat only rustic bread. This is not in order to build up an appetite for the feasts but, rather to establish both that poverty is not an evil and that he is fully capable of bearing it. Other passages, in Seneca or Epicurus, refer to the usefulness of short periods of voluntary trials. Musonius Rufus also recommends periods of training in the country: one lives like the peasants and, like them, one devotes oneself to farm work.

3. Between the pole of the *meditatio*, in which one practices in thought, and that of the *exercitatio*, in which one trains in reality, there is a series of other possible practices designed for testing oneself.

Epictetus in particular gives examples of these in the *Discourses*. They are interesting because there will be practices very similar to these in Christian spirituality. In particular they involve what could be called the "control of representations."

Epictetus requires that one adopt an attitude of constant supervision of representations that may come to mind. He expresses this attitude in two metaphors: that of the night watchman who does not allow just anyone to enter the town or house; and that of the money changer or inspector—the *arguronomos*—who, when given a coin, looks at it, feels its weight, and checks the metal and the effigy. The principle that one should be like a vigilant money changer with regard to one's own thoughts is found again in roughly the same terms in Evagrius Ponticus and in Cassian. However, in the latter it is a matter of prescribing a hermeneutic attitude towards oneself: deciphering possible concupiscence in apparently innocent thoughts, recognizing thoughts coming from God and those coming from the Tempter. In Epictetus it is something different: We must know whether or not we are affected or moved by the thing represented and what reason we have for being or not being so affected.

To this end Epictetus recommends to his students an exercise of control inspired by the Sophistic challenges that were so highly valued in the schools. However, instead of throwing difficult questions at each other, different types of situation will be set out to which one will have to react: "Someone's son has died.—Answer: that does not depend on us, it is not an evil.—Someone's father has disinherited him. What do you think about it?—That does not depend on us, it is not an evil . . . — It distressed him.—That depends on us, it is an evil.—He bore it bravely.—That depends on us, it is a good."

It can be seen that the aim of this control of representations is not to decipher a hidden truth beneath appearances, which would be the truth of the subject himself. Rather, he finds in these representations, as they appear, the opportunity for recalling a number of true principles concerning death, illness, suffering, political life, etcetera. By means of this reminder we can see if we are capable of reacting in accordance with such principles—if they have really become, according to Plutarch's metaphor, that master's voice which is raised immediately the passions growl and which knows how to silence them.

4. At the pinnacle of all these exercises there is the famous *meletē thanatou*—meditation on, or rather, training for death. In fact it does not consist in a simple, albeit insistent, reminder that one will die. It is a way of making death actual in life. Among all the other Stoics, Seneca was very experienced in this practice. It aims to ensure that one lives each day as if it were the last.

To really understand the exercise proposed by Seneca we need to recall the correspondences traditionally established between the different cycles of time: the times of the day are symbolically related to the seasons of the year, from spring to winter; these seasons are in turn related to the ages of life, from childhood to old age. The death exercise as it is evoked in some of Seneca's letters consists in living the length of life as if it were as short as a day and each day as if it contained one's whole life; every morning one should be in the morning of one's life, but living the whole day as if the evening would be the moment of death. In letter 12 he says: "When we get ready to go to sleep, let us say, with joy and a cheerful countenance: I have lived." Marcus Aurelius was thinking of the same type of exercise when he wrote that "moral perfection involves living each day as if it were the last" (VII.69). He even requires each action to be performed "as if it were the last" (II.5).

What gives the meditation on death its particular value is not just that it anticipates what opinion generally represents as the greatest misfortune; it is not just that it enables one to convince oneself that death is not an evil; rather, it offers the possibility of looking back, in advance so to speak, on one's life. By considering oneself as at the point of death, one can judge the proper value of every action one is performing. Death, said Epictetus, takes the laborer while he is working, the sailor while sailing: "And what activity would you like to be engaged in when you are taken?" And Seneca envisages the moment of death as the moment when one will be able to become one's own judge, as it were, and able to measure the moral progress one will have made up to one's final day. In letter 26 he wrote: "On the moral progress I have been able to make in the course of my life, I trust only in death . . . I await the day when I will pass judgment on myself and know whether virtue was only in my words or really in my heart."

# COURSE CONTEXT

## Frédéric Gros*

## THE 1982 COURSE IN FOUCAULT'S WORK

THE EXCEPTIONAL CHARACTER OF the course delivered by Michel Foucault in 1982 at the Collège de France derives from its ambiguous, almost paradoxical status. The previous year (the course of 1980-1981 on "Subjectivity and Truth"), Foucault presented to his public the main results of a study of the experience of pleasures in Greco-Latin Antiquity and, more precisely, on the medical regimens which set limits to sexual acts, on the restriction of legitimate pleasure to the married couple, and on the constitution of heterosexual love as the only possible site of reciprocal consent and the calm truth of pleasure. All of this is developed within the privileged chronological framework of the first two centuries A.D., and it receives its definitive written form in *Le Souci de soi* (*The Care of the Self*), the third volume of the *Histoire de la sexualité*

---

*Frédéric Gros, editor of this year's course, is maître de conferences in the Philosophy department at the university of Paris-XII. He is the author of *Michel Foucault* (Paris: PUF, 1996), *Foucault et la Folie* (Paris: PUF, 1997), and *Création et Folie. Une histoire du jugement psychiatrique* (Parsi: PUF, 1997).

(*History of Sexuality*), published in 1984. Now the 1982 course is anchored in exactly the same historical period as the previous year's course, but with the new theoretical framework of practices of the self. It even appears as a considerably expanded and developed version of one small chapter in *The Care of the Self* entitled "The culture of the self."* This strange situation is clarified if we follow Foucault's intellectual itinerary from 1980 and the editorial hesitations that marked it.

We could start with an enigma: in 1976 Foucault published *La Volonté de savoir* (in English, *The History of Sexuality: An Introduction*, 1978), the first volume of his *History of Sexuality*, which is not so much a work of history as the announcement of a new problematic of sexuality and the presentation of the methodological framework to be followed by the subsequent volumes, which were given as follows: 2. The body and the flesh; 3. The children's crusade; 4. The wife, the mother, and the hysteric; 5. The perverts; and, 6. Populations and races. None of these books ever appeared, although the courses at the Collège de France from 1973 to 1976 were full of material that could have filled out these studies.[1] Foucault does not write these books, although they are ready, planned. An eight-year silence follows, which is broken with the simultaneous publication of *L'Usage des plaisirs* (*The Use of Pleasures*) and *The Care of the Self*, the proofs of which he was still correcting some weeks before his death. Everything had now changed, the historical-cultural framework and the reading grid of his history of sexuality: It is no longer Western modernity (from the sixteenth to the nineteenth century), but Greco-Roman Antiquity; it is no longer a political reading in terms of power apparatuses, but an ethical reading in terms of practices of the self. It is no longer a genealogy of systems, it is a problematization of the subject. There is even a complete change in the style of writing: "I completely abandoned this style [the flamboyant writing of *The Order of Things* and *Raymond Roussel*; F.G.] insofar as I intended to write a history of the subject."[2]

---

*In the English language edition of *Le Souci de soi* (translated by Robert Hurley, *The Care of the Self*) "La Culture de soi" is translated as "The Cultivation of the Self," but see the lecture of 3 February, first hour, for Foucault's comments on the notion of a culture of the self.—G.B.

Foucault will talk at length about this change of mind and the delay forced on writing (but otherwise, he multiplies interviews, lectures, and courses; if he does not immediately pursue his *History of Sexuality*, he does not stop working or abandon his commitments), referring to the weariness and boredom of those books conceived before being written:[3] if it is only the realization of a theoretical program, writing fails its authentic vocation, which is to be the site of an experience, of an attempt: "What is philosophy today—philosophical activity, I mean—if it is not the critical work that thought brings to bear on itself? In what does it consist, if not in the endeavor to know how and to what extent it might be possible to think differently?"[4] We should understand, then, precisely what it was that changed from 1976 to 1984. And for this the 1982 course turns out to be critical, located at the living heart of a change of problematic, of a conceptual revolution. But to speak of a "revolution" is no doubt too hasty, since what is involved, rather, is a slow maturation, of a development with neither break nor commotion, which brought Foucault to the shores of the care of the self.

In 1980 Foucault delivered a course ("On the Government of the Living") devoted to Christian practices of confession (*aveu*), which was introduced by a lengthy analysis of Sophocles' *Oedipus The King*. This course constitutes a first reorientation in the general plan of his work, since we find in it, clearly expressed and conceptualized for the first time, the project of writing a history of "truth activities" understood as regulated procedures which tie a subject to a truth, ritualized activities through which a certain subject establishes his relationship to a certain truth. This study is based on the texts of the first Christian Fathers in which problems of baptism, declarations of faith, catechesis, penance, and spiritual direction etcetera, are linked together. And in this course, neither the condemnation of pleasures, nor the painful freedom of bodies, nor the emergence of the flesh, is involved.[5] Something else is at stake: the emergence in monastic institutions (see Foucault's analyses of Cassian's texts) of new techniques, unknown to early Christianity, demanding several things from the subject for the remission of his sins: a continuous analysis of his representations in order to flush out the Evil One's presence; the verbalization of sins to a superior, of course;

but especially an exhaustive confession (*aveu*) of evil thoughts. In the 1980 course Foucault was concerned to show how, in certain monastic communities in the first centuries of our era, an obligation to tell the truth about oneself was established, structured by the theme of an other (the Other is the superior to whom one confesses everything, but also the Devil who must be flushed out from the inner folds of one's thoughts) and death (since these exercises involved a definitive self-renunciation). Foucault thinks that the subject's production by himself of a discourse in which his own truth could be read is one of the major forms of our obedience. In these monastic institutions the procedures of confession and self-examination are in fact framed by very strict rules of obedience to one's spiritual director. But it is no longer just signs of obedience and marks of respect that are expected of the person being guided; he will have to put the truth of his desire into discourse before an other (his superior): "The government of men demands not only acts of obedience and submission from those who are led, but also 'truth activities,' which have the peculiar feature that the subject is not only required to tell the truth but must tell the truth about himself."[6] This is what confession is for Foucault: a way of subjecting the individual, by demanding from him an indefinite introspection and the exhaustive statement of a truth about himself ("unconditional obedience, uninterrupted examination and exhaustive confession form an ensemble"[7]). Henceforth, and for a long time, the fate of the true subject in the West will be settled, and to seek his innermost truth will always be to continue to obey. More generally, the objectification of the subject in a true discourse only takes on meaning historically from this general, overall, and permanent injunction to obey: in the modern West, I am only a subject of the truth from start to finish of my subjection to the Other. But perhaps there are other ways of being true for a subject, and Foucault hints at this. At the Collège de France (lectures of 12, 19, and 26 March), when studying, through Cassian's texts, these practices of spiritual direction in monastic institutions, practices that determine the relationships between a tyrannical spiritual director and the person being directed, who is subjected to him as he would be to God, Foucault offers a counterpoint in the techniques of existence of late Antiquity that punctuate the temporary relations between the experienced and eloquent sage and the listening applicant, and which are oriented above all by an autonomy to be gained. And Foucault makes some vague, passing references, here and there, to texts which, precisely, will be the object of lengthy and penetrating analysis in 1982: a passage from the *Golden Verses* of Pythagoras, Seneca's *On Anger* concerning the examination of conscience... These texts from Antiquity encourage a practice of the self and of truth in which it is the subject's liberation that is at stake rather than his confinement in a straitjacket of truth which was no less total for being very spiritual.[8] In Seneca, Marcus, Aurelius, and Epictetus, a completely different regime of the subject's relations to the truth, a completely different regime of speech and silence, and a completely different regime of reading and writing are at work. The subject and the truth are not bound together here externally, as in Christianity, as if in the grip of a higher power, but as the result of an irreducible choice of existence. A true subject was possible, therefore, no longer in the sense of subjection, but of subjectivation.

Judging by its effects, the shock must have been as important as it was exciting: it gives Foucault the enthusiasm to revive the *History of Sexuality*, which is now intended to reveal this new dimension, or this dimension of the relationship to the self that until then had remained too implicit. Also, what differentiates paganism from Christianity is above all not the introduction of prohibitions, but the very forms of the sexual experience and the relationship to the self. Everything had to be gone back over again, but from the beginning, from the Greeks especially, and from the Romans. The chronological framework, therefore, the theoretical framework especially, is completely changed. In 1976, sexuality interested Foucault as a privileged marker of what he otherwise described as the great enterprise of normalization of the modern West, in which medicine plays an essential role. We know that for Foucault, in the seventies, disciplinary power cuts individuals to its measure, pinning predefined identities on them. Moreover, it was expected that Foucault's *History of Sexuality* would confirm us in the denunciation of submissive sexualities strictly aligned with established social norms. Volume 1 of *The History of Sexuality* allowed us to be confident that we would learn from him that it is as though our sexual identities are formatted by a dominant power. Informing us, as he did, that this power was not repressive but productive, that rather than the prohibition and censorship of sexuality it involved procedures of incitement, was not an insignificant nuance, but the essential was still that what is involved when we are talking about sex is power. But none of this came about. The books published by Foucault in 1984 are different. The historical study of the relationship to pleasures in classical and late Antiquity is no longer constructed as the demonstration-denunciation of a vast enterprise of normalization undertaken by the State and its laicized henchmen, and Foucault suddenly declares: "Thus, it is not power, but the subject, that is the general theme of my research,"[9] and again: "Thus I am far from being a theoretician of power."[10]

The tone is set, although these declarations should not be taken too literally; Foucault does not abandon politics to dedicate himself to ethics, but *complicates* the study of governmentalities through the exploration of the care of the self. In any case, ethics, or the subject, is not thought of as the other of politics or power. Therefore, Foucault begins his 1981 course and again the 1982 course, recalling that his general axis of research is now the subject's relationship to truth, sexuality being one domain amongst others of the crystallization of this relationship (there is also writing, the medical relationship to the self, etcetera). Sex is no longer then just the indicator of (normalizing, identifying, classifying, reducing, etcetera) power, but also of the subject in his relationship to truth. Soon he maintains that this problem of the subject, and not that of power, is his main concern, and has been for more than twenty years of writing: the emergence of the subject from social practices of division (*Madness and Civilization* and *Discipline and Punish*—on the construction of the mad and criminal subject); emergence of the subject in theoretical projections (*The Order of Things*—on the objectification of the speaking, living, and working subject in the sciences of language, life, and wealth); and finally, with the "new formula" of *History of Sexuality*, the emergence of the subject in practices of the self. This time the subject itself by means of techniques of the self, rather than being constituted by techniques of domination (Power) or discursive techniques (Knowledge). These techniques of the self are defined as: "the procedures, which no doubt exist in every civilization, offered or prescribed to individuals in order to determine their identity, maintain it, or transform it in terms of a certain number of ends, through relations of self-mastery or self-knowledge."[11] These procedures, perhaps hidden by or subordinated to techniques of domination or discursive techniques, did not appear clearly to Foucault so long as he was studying the problematization of the subject in the modern West. So long as Foucault was studying the eighteenth and nineteenth centuries, the subject, as if by a natural tendency, was reflected as the objective product of systems of knowledge and power, the alienated correlate of these apparatuses of power-knowledge from which the individual drew and exhausted an imposed, external identity beyond which the only salvation was madness, crime, or literature. From the eighties, studying the techniques of existence encouraged in Greek and Roman Antiquity, Foucault let a different figure of the subject appear, no longer constituted, but constituting itself through well-ordered practices. For a long time the study of the modern West had hidden the existence of these practices from him, overshadowed as they were in the archive by systems of knowledge and apparatuses of power: "The very important role played at the end eighteenth and in the nineteenth centuries by the formation of *domains of knowledge* about sexuality from the points of view of biology, medicine, psychopathology, sociology and ethnology; the determining role also played by the *normative systems* imposed on sexual behavior through the intermediary of education, medicine, and justice made it hard to distinguish the form and effects of the *relation to the self* as particular elements in the constitution of this experience... In pursuing my analysis of the forms of the relation to the self, in and of themselves, I found myself spanning eras in a way that took me farther and farther from the chronological outline I had first decided on."[12] Thus sexuality, which to start with was to reveal the authoritarian fixing of identities through domains of knowledge and tactics of power, in the eighties reveals techniques of existence and practices of the self.

In the final years there will be an ever-increasing tension that we should put in the balance inasmuch as it involves the status of the 1982 course. Foucault is in fact soon torn between, on the one hand, writing a reorganized history of ancient sexuality in terms of the problematic of techniques of the self, and, on the other, the growing temptation to study these techniques for themselves, in their historico-ethical dimensions, and in domains of effectuation other than sexuality: problems of writing and reading, of physical and spiritual exercises, of the spiritual direction of existence, of the relation to politics. But this was to write two different books: a first on the history of sexuality, and a second on the techniques of the self in Antiquity. For a time at least, this was his intention. We can see this by reading the first version of an interview given at Berkeley in April 1983,[13] in which Foucault gives details of his publishing projects, referring to two very different books. The title of the first is, he says, *The Use of Pleasure*, and deals with the problem of sexuality as an art of living throughout Antiquity. He intends to show "that you have nearly the same restrictive, the same prohibitive code in the fourth century B.C. and in the moralists and doctors at the beginning of the empire. But I think that the way they integrate those prohibitions in relation to oneself is completely different."[14] In this first book, then, what is involved is a description of the evolution of Ancient sexual ethics by showing that starting from the same points of anxiety (pleasures of the body, adultery, and boys),[15] one can identify two distinct styles of austerity between classical Greece and imperial Rome. So we find here, concentrated into a single book, the content of what in 1984 will appear in the form of two distinct volumes (one on classical Greece and another on imperial Rome). However, in the first organization, these two works were just one, to be followed by "The Confessions of the Flesh" (which in 1984 will be announced as the fourth volume of the *History of Sexuality*). In 1983 Foucault, after having announced this first book on ancient sexuality, refers to a different, parallel work "composed of a set of separate studies, papers about such and such aspects of ancient, pagan technologies of the self ... composed of different papers about the self—for instance, a commentary on Plato's *Alcibiades* in which you find the first elaboration of the notion of *epimeleia heautou*."[16] What's more, Foucault calls this work: *The Care of the Self* (the title he will keep in 1984, but for the study of sexual ethics in the first two centuries A.D.: volume three of the present *History of Sexuality*). The fact remains that in this interview he refers to a work devoted entirely to the problem of techniques of the self in Antiquity, and without any particular reference to sexuality.

The subject matter of this book is precisely what forms the content of "The Hermeneutics of the Subject": a commentary on the *Alcibiades*; studies on self-writing and the regular practice of reading, on the emergence of a medical experience of the self, etcetera. This indicates the importance of the 1982 course; it is like the substitute of a projected and thought-out book which never appeared, a book devoted entirely to these techniques of the self in which Foucault found, at the end of his life, the conceptual crowning achievement of his work, something like the principle of its completion. For we should again remember that, as earlier with the apparatuses of power, Foucault does not present the practices of the self as a conceptual novelty, but as the organizing principle of his entire work and the common theme of his first writings. Foucault, and this is the secret of his approach, never proceeds by the juxtaposition of themes, but according to a hermeneutic spiral: what he brings out as new thought he finds again as the unthought of the work preceding it. The fact remains that in 1983 he was still keen to write the book that he had delivered at the Collège de France from January to March 1982, and above all not reduce these practices of the self, these techniques of existence, to the status of a simple methodological and introductory framework for the history of sexuality. No doubt they find a congruent place in the existing second and third volumes of the *History of Sexuality*: a chapter in the second volume ("Modifications") and two chapters in the third volume ("The Culture of the Self" and "Self and Others"). They deserved better and Foucault knew it. And yet, in 1984, his last year, when correcting the French version of this same interview of April 1983, he eliminates and crosses out all reference to this work, on which he set such store, and soberly announces: *The Use of Pleasures* and *The Care of the Self*, volumes 2 and 3 of the *History of Sexuality*, to be published by Gallimard. Had he given up this work; did he want to refer only to completed work; did he think that illness would not leave him time to write it? Or should we refer to that mysterious disappointment that he referred to in his last interview and to which it will be necessary to return: "All of antiquity seems to me to have been a 'profound error.' "[17] We will never know, but this course remains like a double or, since Foucault liked the image so much, like a scout of this lost book.

Not totally lost, however. For the preparation of the course for publication, Daniel Defert loaned us a number of thick, bound dossiers that belonged to Foucault, five in all, some of which held surprises. These dossiers contain folders of colored paper containing, somewhat yellowed, pages and pages covered by fine, lively writing in pale blue or black ink. The first dossier, entitled "Course," is the most important. It contains the actual text of the course delivered in 1982, the present transcription of which we have established on the basis of recordings provided by Jacques Lagrange. Here and there this manuscript of the course has helped us to restore inaudible words or fill in gaps in the recording. It has helped us to enrich the transcript by taking account of content well established in the text of the lectures, but which Foucault did not have time to present. This is the dossier we refer to in footnotes at the bottom of the page when we refer to the "manuscript." This text was actually used by Foucault as an aid to his lectures. Entire passages are written up, notably those of conceptual and theoretical clarification, and it is usually only in commentaries on the ancient texts that Foucault departs a little from his text. There is very little improvisation therefore: everything, or almost everything, was written.

The four following dossiers are entitled: "Alcibiades, Epictetus," "Government of the self and others," "Culture of the self—Rough draft," "The Others." These are thematic classifications; each dossier contains a number of folders, some containing a few pages, others a hundred, dealing with particular points that find their way from one dossier to another. From reading these hundreds of pages we can accept a principal division, details aside. The dossiers entitled "Alcibiades, Epictetus" and "Government of the self and others" comprise a series of thematic studies ("listening, reading, writing," "critique," "government of the self and others," "age, pedagogy, medicine," "retirement," "social relations," "direction," "battle," etcetera). The studies are developed to varying degrees. They are often completely rewritten. Foucault did not stop to go back to them, and every overall reorganization led to the rewriting of these studies, which took up a new place in a new architecture.

The two dossiers we have just referred to undoubtedly constitute the main stages of writing for the promised work on practices of the self. For example, it is in these dossiers that we find the development of the text "Writing the self," which will appear in *Corps écrit* in February 1983, referred to by Foucault as precisely "part of a series of studies on 'the arts of oneself.'"[18] The dossiers entitled "Culture of the self—Rough draft" and "The Others" contain successive versions of two chapters of *The Care of the Self*, published in 1984, entitled respectively: "Culture of the self," "Self and others." But we quickly see that Foucault proceeds here by increasing rarefaction, since the published work finally corresponds to a synthesis of texts which are much more thorough, detailed, and enriched with references.

These dossiers include then entire pages of finished writing dealing with points of which there is still no definitive record: neither in the *History of Sexuality*, nor in *Dits et Écrits*, nor even in the 1982 course published here (for example, on the notion of retirement, on the concept of *paideia*, on the idea of old age, on the self's mode of participation in public life, etcetera). Certainly, Foucault did not have time to give an account of all of his research on ancient techniques of the self in the three months of the course (from January to March 1982). This is all the more unfortunate since many passages throw a crucial light on the whole of this final work, notably concerning the connections between the ethics and politics of the self. What Foucault presents in these dossiers makes possible a better understanding of the 1982 course, as well as the relevance of the problematization, from 1983 at the Collège de France, of *parrhēsia* as "courage of the truth"; so a problematic that is wholly in line with a set of unpublished studies of the politics of the self can only be recaptured on the basis of this set of studies. We will try nonetheless, in an overall perspective on the 1982 course, to take into account, however partially, this precious unpublished work. Foucault's last years, from 1980 to 1984, really were in any case a period of amazing conceptual acceleration, of a sudden proliferation of problematics. Never has what Deleuze called the speed of thought been so palpable as in these hundreds of pages, versions, and rewritings, almost without deletion.

## The Distinctiveness of the 1982 Course

The 1982 course at the Collège de France has, if only formally, some specific features. Having abandoned his research seminar parallel to the main course, Foucault extends the length of his lectures, which, for the first time, extend over two hours divided by a break. The old difference between a lecture course and more empirical and precise research is thereby erased. A new style of teaching is born; Foucault does not expound the results of his work so much as put forward, step by step, and almost hesitantly, the development of a work of research. A major part of the course now consists in a patient reading of selected texts and in a word-by-word commentary on them. Hence we see Foucault "at work," so to speak, immediately extracting some terms, on the spot, from a simple sustained reading, and trying to give them a provisional systematization, sometimes quickly abandoned. What's more, we quickly see that for Foucault it is never a matter of explaining texts, but of inserting them within an ever-changing overall vision. Some general frameworks guide the selection and reading of texts, therefore, but without these texts being instrumentalized thereby, since the reading may lead to a reconfiguration of the initial hypothesis. He follows a constant movement back and forth between vague, general propositions detached from any precise reference (on Platonism, Hellenistic and Roman philosophy, ancient thought) and detailed examinations of fragments from Musonius Rufus or maxims from Epictetus. The course then takes on more the appearance of a living laboratory than of a final balance sheet. It gains analytical clarity from this and there is extreme luminosity in the detail. But it becomes very difficult to keep hold of the course in its generality insofar as in almost every lecture the stakes are shifted, reformulated, or set out in other directions.

In this movement back and forth between original texts and general reading principles, Foucault seems to cut out the secondary literature. Of course, some references emerge: A.-J. Festugière, H. Joly, J.-P. Vernant, E.R. Dodds, P. and I. Hadot, M. Gigante, P. Rabbow, J.-M. André... Certainly, the requirement of sticking to the texts themselves may lead the less prudent to multiply truisms or to ignore obvious criticism. However, the weak role given to criticism must be put in its context. Actually, the gray literature on this Hellenistic and Roman period, which really constitutes the chronological framework for Foucault's course, is today (in France, Germany, Italy, and especially the Anglo-Saxon world) so massive that it would appear pretentious and naïve to speak about Epictetus, Marcus Aurelius, Seneca, Epicurus, or Posidonius without indicating, albeit in passing, the main critical findings. But in 1982 this literature was still slight. There was just one overall approach by A.A. Long (*Hellenistic Philosophy*, London, 1974). Concerning Epicureanism as a whole, we can cite just the eighth congress organized by the Association Guillaume Budé in 1968, the studies of N.W. De Witt (both of these references being mentioned by Foucault), and the *Études sur l'épicurisme antique* (edited by J. Bollack and A. Lacks, Lille, 1976). Stoicism was already better known and studied, especially following the fundamental texts of E. Bréhier on *Chrysippe et l'Ancien Stoïcisme* (Paris, 1910, republished in 1950) and *La Théorie des incorporels dans l'ancien stoïcisme* (Paris, 1908, republished in 1970), of P. and I. Hadot, as well as V. Goldschmidt's book on *Le Système stoïcien et l'Idée de temps* (Paris, first edition 1953). We mention also the general survey by Max Pohlenz, *Die Stoa* (Göttingen, 1959), closer, however, to a book of edification than to one of science.[19] Otherwise, the publication of the proceedings of the recent conference on *Les Stoïciens et leur logique* (edited by J. Brunschwig, Paris, 1978) helped to revive interest in this period. The middle stoicism of Posidonius and Panetius began to be studied more thoroughly thanks to the texts collected by M. Van Straaten (*Panetii Rhodii fragmenta*, Leyde, 1952) and by L. Edelstein and I.G. Kidd (*Posidonius. The Fragments*, Cambridge, 1972).[20] However, it is precisely in the eighties, not to speak of the following decade, that studies of Hellenistic and Roman philosophy truly multiply and expand, with the major references of A.A. Long and D.N. Sedley (*The Hellenistic Philosophers*, Cambridge, 1987, in two volumes), H. Flashar (publication of the fourth volume of *Die Philosophie der Antike: Die hellenistische Philosophie*, Bâle, 1994), R.W. Sharples (*Stoics, Epicureans and Sceptics. An Introduction to Hellenistic Philosophy*, London, 1996), J. Annas (*Hellenistic*

*Philosophy of Mind*, Berkeley, 1992, and *The Morality of Happiness*, Oxford, 1993), M. Nussbaum (*The Therapy of Desire: Theory and Practice in Hellenistic Ethics*, Princeton, 1994), J. Brunschwig (*Études sur les philosophies hellénistiques*, Paris, 1995), and C. Lévy (*Les Philosophies hellénistiques*, Paris, 1997). And we can also mention all the volumes of the *Symposium hellenisticum*, which has met regularly since the eighties. So it cannot be held against Foucault that he did not refer to a critical literature that did not yet exist: he was, rather, a pioneer in these studies.

We have already pointed out that the composition of the course is empirical rather than systematic. Foucault advances step by step. For these reasons we will not give a summary of the course here, and especially since Foucault himself worked on it and has given us a stroke of luck: his "Course summary" for 1982 exactly corresponds (and this is not often the case) to the course delivered that year. To appreciate the success of this synthesis we should again remember that Foucault wanted to turn these lectures on the self into a book, with a precise structure in mind. Instead, we will try here to pick out a certain number of theoretical "effects" induced by the systematic use of the notions of "practices of the self," "techniques of existence," and "care of the self." We would like to understand the stakes of these analyses, their relevance, and why, gathered in the cramped lecture rooms of the Collège, the auditors were sure they were witnessing something other than a presentation of ancient philosophy: how, in talking about Epictetus, Seneca, Marcus Aurelius, and Epicurus, Foucault continued to indicate reference points for thinking a political, moral, and philosophical actuality; why this course is indeed something other than a history of Hellenistic and Roman philosophy, just as *Madness and Civilization* was something other than a history of psychiatry, *The Order of Things* something other than a history of the human sciences, and *Discipline and Punish* something other than a history of the penal institution. Besides, the specialist of Hellenistic and Roman philosophies can only be surprised here, if not irritated: concerning Stoicism, there is no historico-doctrinal presentation of the three periods of the school of the Porch; nothing on the system of logic, physics, and ethics; almost nothing on the problem of duties, preferable things, and indifferent things, nor even on the paradoxes of the sage; concerning Epicureanism, Foucault speaks neither of pleasure nor the physics of atoms; as for skepticism, it is not even mentioned.[21] Explaining in detail the structures of subjectivation (the medical tenor of the care given to the self, the examination of conscience, the appropriation of discourses, the speech of the guide, retirement, etcetera), Foucault carries out transversal sections in these philosophies, finding historical realizations of these structures in the different schools. But his presentation is never doctrinal. As far as Hellenistic and Roman philosophy is concerned, Foucault does not intend to work as an historian. He produces a genealogy: "Genealogy means that I begin my analysis from a question posed in the present."[22]

We should then clarify now the extent of the stakes of this course. For the sake of convenience of exposition we will distinguish between the philosophical, ethical, and political stakes.

## THE PHILOSOPHICAL STAKES OF THE COURSE

We will not go back over the general project of writing a history of sexuality, a history on to which will be grafted a "genealogy of the modern subject."[23] Let it suffice to recall that, with regard to sexuality, the point of view of techniques of the self entailed, on the one hand, not writing a history of actual sexual behavior or of moral codes, but of forms of experience,[24] and, on the other hand, not setting an ancient age of permissiveness against an oppressive Christian epoch from which we could free ourselves by piously invoking the Greeks, but retracing, rather, an evolution in styles of austerity: "the opposition is not between tolerance and austerity but between a form of austerity linked to an aesthetics of existence and other forms of austerity linked to the necessity of renouncing the self and deciphering its truth."[25] Nevertheless, in this course Foucault forsakes the theme of sexuality as the privileged foundation stone and is more interested in the processes of subjectivation in and for themselves. The opposition between Antiquity and the modern age is thus cashed out differently, through two conceptual alternatives, between philosophy and spirituality, care of the self and knowledge of the self.

According to Foucault, philosophy since Descartes develops a figure of the subject who is intrinsically capable of truth: the subject will be capable of truth *a priori*, and only secondarily an ethical subject of right action: "I can be immoral and know the truth."[26] This means that for the modern subject access to a truth does not hang on the effect of an ethical kind of internal work (ascesis, purification, etcetera). Antiquity, rather, would have made a subject's access to the truth depend on a movement of conversion requiring a drastic ethical change in his being. In ancient spirituality, the subject can lay claim to the truth on the basis of a transformation of his being, whereas for modern philosophy it is insofar as he is always enlightened by the truth that the subject can claim to change the way he conducts himself. With regard to this we can quote an entire (unpublished) passage from the manuscript that Foucault used for his course:

> Three questions which, in a way, will run through Western thought:
> 
> — access to the truth;
> — activation of the subject by himself in the care that he takes of himself;
> — knowledge of the self
> 
> With two sensitive spots:
> 
> 1. Can you have access to the truth without bringing into play the very being of the subject who gains access to it? Can you have access to the truth without paying for it with a sacrifice, an ascesis, a transformation, a purification which affects the subject's very being? Can the subject have access to the truth just as he is? To this question Descartes will answer yes; Kant's answer also will be all the more affirmative as it is restrictive: what determines that the subject, just as he is, can know, is what also determines that he cannot know himself.[27]
> 
> 2. The second sensitive spot of this questioning concerns the relation between care of the self and knowledge of the self. In putting itself under the laws of knowledge (*connaissance*) in general,

can self-knowledge take the place of care of the self—thus setting aside the question of whether the subject's being must be brought into play; or should we expect virtues and experiences from self-knowledge which would put the subject's being into play; should this knowledge of the self be given the form and force of such an experience?

The end of this text directs us to a new idea: What structures the opposition between the ancient subject and the modern subject is an opposite relation of subordination between care of the self and knowledge of the self. Care, in the Ancients, is organized by the ideal of establishing a certain relation of rectitude in the self between actions and thoughts: One must act correctly, according to true principles, and a just action must correspond to the words of justice; the sage is someone who makes the uprightness of his philosophy legible in his actions; if a part of knowledge enters into this care, it is inasmuch as I have to gauge my progress in this constitution of a self of ethically correct action. According to the modern mode of subjectivation, the constitution of the self as subject depends on an indefinite endeavor of self-knowledge, which strives only to reduce the gap between what I am truly and what I think myself to be; what I do, the actions I perform, only have value insofar as they help me to know myself better. Foucault's thesis can thus be put in the following way: For the subject of right action in Antiquity is substituted the subject of true knowledge in the modern West.

The 1982 course therefore involves a history of the subject itself in the historicity of its philosophical constitutions. The ambition is considerable and to gauge this we need only read the preparatory version of a lecture that Foucault will give in New York in 1981[28] (found in the dossier "Government of the self and others"):

> For Heidegger, it was on the basis of Western *tekhnē* that knowledge of the object sealed the forgetting of Being. Let's turn the question around and ask ourselves on the basis of what tekhnai was the Western subject formed and were the games of truth and error, freedom and constraint, which characterize this subject, opened up.

Foucault writes this text in September 1980, and we have shown above how decisive this year was in his intellectual itinerary: it is the year of the problematization of techniques of the self as irreducible to techniques of production, techniques of domination, and symbolic techniques. There is an extension of this text in the last words uttered at the end of the 1982 course, but with some crucial inflections. For now it is no longer a matter of circumventing Heidegger, but of recontextualizing Hegel, and it would need several pages to comment on these few words that Foucault throws out at the end of the year's course as a final challenge, or as if to show the conceptual range of the patiently pursued analyses on practices of the self. We confine ourselves here to this schematization: if Heidegger shows how mastery of *tekhnē* gives the world its form of objectivity, Foucault demonstrates how the care of the self, and particularly Stoic test practices, make the world, as occasion of knowledge and transformation of the self, the site where a subjectivity emerges. And Hegel, in the *Phenomenology of Mind*, tries precisely to join together thought about the world and reality as the form of objectivity for knowledge (Heidegger rereading the Greeks) and as the matrix of practical subjectivity (Foucault rereading the Latins). In Plutarch's innocuous texts, the maxims of Musonius Rufus, and Seneca's letters, Foucault finds the outline of the fate of Western philosophy.

This first approach is still held within the history of philosophy. By "philosophical stake" should be understood also the problematic of the care of the self and of techniques of existence as involving a new thinking of truth and the subject. Certainly a new thinking of the subject, and Foucault makes himself clear about this on several occasions. In this respect the clearest text remains the first unpublished version of the 1981 lecture. After noting the adventures of a phenomenology of the founding subject unable to constitute signifying systems, and the meanderings of a Marxism bogged down in a vague humanism, Foucault, taking account of the postwar philosophical horizon, writes:

> There have been three directions in which to find a way out:
> — either a theory of objective knowledge; and we should no doubt look to analytical philosophy and positivism for this;

— or a new analysis of signifying systems; and here linguistics, sociology, psychoanalysis, etcetera, have given rise to what is called structuralism;
— or to try to put the subject back into the historical domain of practices and processes in which he has been constantly transformed.

I have set out in this last direction. I say therefore, with the necessary clarity, that I am not a structuralist and, with the appropriate shame, nor am I an analytical philosopher. Nobody is perfect. I have therefore tried to explore the possibilities of a genealogy of the subject while knowing that historians prefer the history of objects and philosophers prefer the subject who has no history. This does not stop me from feeling an empirical kinship with those who are called historians of "mentalities" and a theoretical debt towards a philosopher like Nietzsche who raised the question of the subject's historicity. It was a matter then for me of getting free from the ambiguities of a humanism that was so easy in theory and so fearsome in reality; it was also a matter of replacing the principle of the transcendence of the ego with research into the subject's forms of immanence.

Foucault rarely expressed his theoretical project so concisely and clearly. But this retrospective view is no doubt too good, and Foucault himself had to trudge for a long time before being able to give this final form to his work. We should remember: for a long time Foucault conceived of the subject as only the passive product of techniques of domination. It is only in 1980 that he conceives of the relative autonomy, the irreducibility, anyway, of techniques of the self. We say relative autonomy because we should be wary of any exaggeration. In 1980 Foucault does not "discover" the native freedom of a subject that he had previously been unaware of. It cannot be maintained that Foucault suddenly forsook the social processes of normalization and alienating systems of identification so as to reveal, in its virginal splendor, a free subject creating itself in the ahistorical ether of a pure self-constitution. He criticizes Sartre for precisely having thought this selfcreation of the authentic subject not rooted in history.[29] Now, precisely what constitute the subject in a determinate relation to himself are historically identifiable techniques of the self, which combine with historically datable techniques of domination. Besides, the individual-subject only ever emerges at the intersection of a technique of domination and a technique of the self.[30] It is the fold of processes of subjectivation over procedures of subjection, according to more or less overlapping linings subject to history. What Foucault discovers in Roman Stoicism is the moment when the excess, the concentration of imperial power, the assumption of powers of domination by a single person, enable the techniques of the self to be isolated as it were, and to burst forth in their urgency. Patiently tracing the long, difficult history of these fluid, historically constituted, and constantly transformed relations to the self, Foucault intends to signify that the subject is not tied to his truth according to a transcendental necessity or inevitable destiny. Discovering his project of a genealogy of the subject in 1980, he writes, again in the first unpublished version of his American lecture:

> I think there is here the possibility of writing a history of what we have done which can be at the same time an analysis of what we are; a theoretical analysis that has a political meaning—I mean an analysis that has meaning for what we want to accept, refuse and change of ourselves, in our actuality. In short, it is a matter of starting out in search of a different critical philosophy: a philosophy that does not determine the conditions and limits of a knowledge of the object, but the conditions and undefined possibilities of the subject's transformation.

Identities are formed in the immanence of history. It is there also that they are unmade. For there is only liberation in and through history. But this is already to speak of resistance, and we will have to come back to this in the section on politics.

Foucault describes the subject in its historical determination but also in its ethical dimension. With regard to the subject he takes up again what he had said concerning power: Power should not be thought as law but as strategy, law being only one strategic possibility among others. In the same way, morality as obedience to the Law is only one ethical possibility among others; the moral subject is only one historical realization of the ethical subject. What Foucault describes as the ideal of active domination of others and of the self in classical Greek philosophy, and as the care of the self in Hellenistic and Roman philosophy, are ethical possibilities of the subject, as is later, in Christianity, the internalization of the Law and of norms. It is a matter of relinquishing the prestige of the juridico-moral subject structured by obedience to the Law, in order to reveal its historical precariousness. Foucault is far from considering these practices of the self as a philosophical fashion; they are rather the spearhead of a new idea of the subject, far from transcendental constitutions and moral foundations.[31]

Furthermore, the 1982 course expresses a new thinking of truth. More precisely, we should say, of true discourse, of *logos*, since this is the term that recurs most frequently. What Foucault finds in Seneca and Epictetus, and what he sets out and develops abundantly in the 1982 course, is the idea that a statement is never of value here for its own theoretical content, even when what is at stake is the theory of the world or the theory of the subject. In these practices of the appropriation of true discourse it is not a matter of learning the truth either about the world or about oneself, but of assimilating, in the almost physiological sense of the term, true discourses which are aids for confronting external events and internal passions. This is the recurring theme, in the course and in the dossiers, of the *logos* as armor and salvation. Two examples illustrate this point. First of all, the analysis of the *paraskeuē* (equipment). One does not acquire discourses for the purpose of improving one's mind but in order to prepare oneself for events. The knowledge required is not what enables us to really know ourselves, but that which helps us to act correctly with regard to circumstances. Let us reread what Foucault writes in the dossier "Culture of the self" concerning this knowledge (*savoir*) understood as preparation for life:

> This equipment should not be understood therefore as the simple theoretical framework from which, if necessary, we could draw the practical consequences we need (even if in its foundations it

includes very general theoretical principles, *dogmata* as the Stoics say); no more should it be understood as a simple code telling us what we should do in this or that case. The *paraskeuē* is a whole in which are expressed, at once and in their inseparable relationship, the truth of knowledge (*connaissances*) and the rationality of conduct, or more precisely, that which in the truth of knowledge founds the rationality of conduct, and that which, of this rationality, is justified in terms of true propositions.

The subject of the care of the self is fundamentally a subject of sound action rather than a subject of true knowledge. The *logos* must actualize the soundness of action rather than the perfection of knowledge. The second example is that of the examination of conscience. When Seneca refers to it in his treatise on anger, we see, Foucault says in the same dossier, that *"the point is not to discover the truth of oneself, but of knowing with what true principles one is equipped, to what extent one is in a position to have them available when necessary."* If you practice examination of conscience, it is not to track down latent truths and other buried secrets, but in order to *"gauge how far you have got in your appropriation of truth as principle of conduct"* (same dossier). It is not difficult to find here the implicit opposition between two types of examination of conscience: that practiced in Antiquity and that inculcated by Christianity, each putting to work irreducible modes of subjectivation: the subject of the care of the self *"must become the subject of truth,"* but *"it is not indispensable that he say the truth about himself"* (same dossier). Think again of the *hupomnēmata*, those collections of quotations from diverse works that are brought together in one's possession: these writings were not recorded in this way with the aim of tracking down what is not-said in them, but of assembling what possesses sense from the already-said so that the subject of action draws from it the necessary constituents of his internal cohesion: "to make one's recollection of the fragmentary *logos*, transmitted through teaching, listening, or reading, a means of establishing a relationship of oneself with oneself, a relationship as adequate and accomplished as possible."[32]

Foucault finally devotes himself to the description of a truth that he qualifies in the course as ethopoetic: a truth such as is read in the weft of accomplished actions and physical postures, rather than as deciphered in the secrets of conscience or worked out in the chambers of professional philosophers. As he writes, this time in the dossier "Government of the self and others," it is a matter of *"transforming true discourse into a permanent and active principle."* Further on he speaks of the *"long process which turns the taught, learned, repeated and assimilated* logos *into the spontaneous form of the acting subject."* Elsewhere he defines ascesis in the Greek sense as "the fashioning of accepted discourses, recognized as true, into rational principles of action."[33]

These declarations all point in the same direction, and Foucault will continue to push forward this quest for true speech finding its immediate translation into sound action and in a structured relationship to the self. In 1983, at the Collège de France, he will turn to the study of political *parrhēsia*, defined as true speech, but true speech in which the speaker risks his life (this is the "courage of the truth" of the final years of the course at the Collège de France). And in 1984 he will put the finishing touches to this movement with the study of the radicalism of the Cynics and the examination of the scandalous lives and provocations of Diogenes and Antisthenes—all these lives flaunted like a grimace or sardonic challenge to the discourses of truth. For Foucault then, truth is not displayed in the calm element of discourse, like a distant and correct echo of the real. It is, in the most accurate and literal sense of the expression, a *reason for living*: a *logos* actualized in existence, which sustains, intensifies, and tests it: which *verifies* it.

## THE ETHICAL STAKES OF THE COURSE

Exploring the philosophical stakes of the subject engaged in practices of the self and techniques of existence, we have already spoken a good deal about ethics, and we would like here to bring out the extent to which this course tries to respond to what today is conventionally called "the crisis of values." Foucault was as aware as anyone else of the litany concerning the loss of the "aura" of moral values and the collapse of traditional landmarks. It would be excessive to say that he unreservedly subscribed to it and had merely, for his part, shown how the moralization of individuals extended the normalization of the masses. But overcoming bourgeois morality does not get rid of ethical questioning: "For a long time many people imagined that the strictness of sexual codes, in the form that we know them, was indispensable to so-called 'capitalist' societies. Yet the lifting of the codes and the dislocation of prohibitions have probably been carried out more easily than people thought they would (which certainly seems to indicate that their purpose was not what it was believed to be); and the problem of an ethics as a form to be given to one's behavior and life has arisen once more."[34] The problem then could be posed in these terms: Can we introduce a new ethic outside of the established morality of the eternal values of Good and Evil? Foucault's answer is positive, but indirect. We must be careful here. Because Foucault has too quickly been made the apologist of that contemporary individualism whose excesses and limits are denounced. It has been said, here and there, that in the face of the collapse of values, Foucault, in appealing to the Greeks, gave in to the narcissistic temptation. That he proposed an "aesthetics of existence" as an alternative ethic, indicating to each the path to personal fulfillment through a stylization of life, as if halting thought, fixed at the "aesthetic stage" with all its narcissistic avatars, could disguise the loss of meaning. Or else it is said that Foucault's morality consists in a call to systematic transgression, or in the cult of a cherished marginality. These generalizations are facile, excessive, but above all wrong, and in a way the whole of the 1982 course is constructed in opposition to these unfounded criticisms. Foucault is neither Baudelaire nor Bataille. There is neither a dandyism of singularity nor a lyricism of transgression in these final texts. What he will think of as the Hellenistic and Roman ethic of the care of the self is actually more difficult and also more interesting. It is an ethic of immanence, vigilance, and distance.

An ethic of immanence first of all, and here we find again that "aesthetics of existence" which is the source of so many misunderstandings. What Foucault finds in ancient thought is the idea of inserting an order into one's life, but an immanent order neither sustained by transcendent values nor externally conditioned by social norms: "Greek ethics is centered on a problem of personal choice, of the aesthetics of existence.

The idea of the *bios* as a material for an aesthetic piece of art is something that fascinates me. The idea that ethics can be a very strong structure of existence, without any relation with the juridical per se, with an authoritarian system, with a disciplinary structure."[35] The ethical fashioning of the self is first of all this: to make of one's existence, of this essentially mortal material, the site for the construction of an order held together by its internal coherence. But we should hold on to the artisanal rather than "artistic" dimension of this word "work." This ethics demands exercises, regularities, and work: but without the effect of anonymous constraint. Training, here, arises neither from civil law, nor from religious prescription: "This government of the self, with the techniques that are peculiar to it, takes its place 'between' pedagogical institutions and the religions of salvation."[36] It is not an obligation for everyone, but a personal choice of existence.[37]

Now this personal choice is not a solitary choice but involves the continuous presence of the Other, and in multiple forms as we will soon see. At this point of the exposition, we refer to a major, cruel disappointment: "All of antiquity seems to me to have been a 'profound error'."[38] To understand the strangeness of these words we must rediscover the crux, in this Greco-Roman ethics, of an aporia, or at least the outline of a dead end. Schematizing a great deal, we will say that in classical Greece there was indeed the search for an ethics as style of existence, and not as moral normativity, but in terms of the assertion of a statutory superiority permitted to a social elite. So, for the educated classes and powerful aristocracy, sexual austerity was only a "trend"[39] allowing them to display their snobbery and pretensions. Now, in Roman Stoicism, there really is a liberation of ethics from social conditions (even a slave can be virtuous), since it is as a rational being that man can lay claim to the good. But in being generalized in this way, ethics gradually tends to be laid down as a universal norm: "In late Stoicism, when they start saying, 'Well, you are obliged to do that because you are a human being,' something changes. It's not a problem of choice; you have to do it because you are a rational being."[40] Thus, when not restricted to a social caste for which it is only the external and disdainful luster, in its universalizing application it is translated into a morality obligatory for all: this is "the misfortune of the philosophy of antiquity."[41] But, it will be said, these words are belated. The fact remains that Foucault's position with regard to Stoicism is not at all one of fascination. Here and there he detects in Stoicism the preparation, the anticipation of a codification of morality as tyrannical and normalizing obligation: a law with universal aspirations. As for the Greek ethic of the active domination of oneself and others, Foucault is far from admiring it. It rests on criteria of social superiority, contempt for the other, non-reciprocity and dissymmetry: "All that is quite disgusting!"[42] We can, at least, find an indication here that helps us understand why Foucault quickly got involved in studying Cynic thought. It is as if, on the one hand, turning away from the elitist and disdainful morality of classical Greece, he feared, on the other, that a Stoic ethic of immanent rigor would inevitably deteriorate into an equally restricting lay-republican morality: "The search for a form of morality acceptable to everybody in the sense that everyone should submit to it, strikes me as catastrophic."[43] It's a long way from a "secular" morality to an authentic (you could say, Nietzschean) ethics of immanence. The final resort to the Cynics? It is as if, confronted with the aporias of an ethics of excellence or of a morality obligatory for everyone, Foucault ended up thinking that basically there could be no legitimate ethics other than one of provocation and political scandal: with the sardonic assistance of the Cynics, ethics becomes then the principle of morality's anxiety, that which unsettles it (return to the Socratic lesson).

However, let us return to a more glorious version of the ethics of the care for the self:

> This long work of the self on the self, this labor that all the authors describe as long and arduous, does not aim to split the subject, but to bind him to himself, to nothing else, to no one but to himself, in a form in which the unconditional character and self-finality of the relationship of the self to the self is affirmed (dossier "Culture of the self").

The immanence of the self to the self is established. All the exercises tend to establish a stable and full relationship of the self to the self that can be thought, for example, in the juridico-political form of the full and entire ownership of the self. Foucault emphasizes that the problem of the soul's survival has no pertinence in Roman stoicism. What is aimed at as salvation is accomplished without any transcendence: "*The self with which one has the relationship is nothing other than the relationship itself . . . it is in short the immanence, or better, the ontological adequacy of the self to the relationship*" (same dossier). Authentic transcendence dwells in the immanent and concentrated fulfillment of the self. This immanence is again distinguished by the notion of a conversion to the self (*epistrophē eis heauton, conversio ad se*) preached by Hellenistic and Roman philosophy, and opposed both to the Platonic *epistrophē*, which proposes the passage to a higher reality through recollection, and to Christian *metanoia*, which installs a sacrificial style of break within the self. In a movement of retroversion, conversion to the self offers a different aim to which old age permits access: the fullness of a perfect relationship to oneself. What is here aimed at, expected, and hoped for is called old age: "*This old age is not just a chronological stage of life: it is an ethical form which is characterized both by independence from everything that does not depend on us, and by the fullness of a relationship to the self in which sovereignty is not exercised as a struggle, but as an enjoyment* (jouissance)" (dossier "Government of the self and others"). In this dossier "Government of the self and others," we find long and beautiful pages on old age inspired by Cicero, Seneca, and Democritus. It appears there as a stage of ethical fulfillment to be striven for: at the twilight of life, the relationship to the self must rise to its zenith.

When describing the ethic of the care of the self, Foucault refers at a number of points to the intense delight gained from the relationship to the self. But care of the self never refers to a satisfied and pleasurable self-contemplation. Thus, with regard to the development of certain forms of introspection that he saw on the West Coast of the United States (the search for a personal way, the pursuit and fulfillment of an authentic self, etcetera), Foucault states: "Not only do I not identify this ancient culture of the self with what you might call the Californian cult of the self, I think they are diametrically opposed."[44] In fact, rather than a narcissistic, fascinated, and delighted quest in pursuit of a lost truth of the self, the care of the self denotes the vigilant tension of the self taking care, above all, not to lose control of its representations and be overcome by either pains or pleasures. In the dossier "Culture of the self," Foucault speaks of a *"pure possession and enjoyment of oneself, which tends to eliminate every other form of pleasure."* In fact, the extreme care not to be affected by pleasure is accompanied by vigilant introspection. It is not narcissistic delight that lies in wait for the care of the self; it is pathological hypochondria. Actually, we should understand that in the Hellenistic and Roman epoch, the domain of application of this new vigilance is not the body on one side, whose naturally restive vigor must be tamed by gymnastics, and the soul on the other, whose courage must be awakened through music (as in Platonic education), but the conjunctions of the body and the soul exchanging their weaknesses and vices:

> In these practices of the self, attention is focused on the point where the evils of the body and soul may communicate with each other and exchange their weaknesses; where the soul's bad habits may bring about physical ills, while the body's excesses display and foster the soul's defects; the concern focuses above all on the point of passage of agitations and disorders, taking into account the fact that it is advisable to correct the soul if one does not want the body to prevail over it, and to rectify the body if one wants the soul to maintain full control over itself. The attention one pays to evils, weaknesses and physical suffering is directed towards this point of contact, as the individual's weak point. The body the adult has to look after, when he takes care of himself, is no longer the young body to be trained by gymnastics; it is a fragile, threatened body, undermined by minor ills, and a body which, in return, threatens the soul not so much by its excessively vigorous demands as by its own weaknesses.[45]

Using certain of Seneca's letters and the *Sacred Tales* of Ælius Aristides, Foucault has no difficulty in showing that a new style of inspection, modeled on and conforming to the dynamics of the binary medical relation, corresponds to this new object (the fragile seam of the soul and the body): "*This medico-philosophical theme which is so amply developed brings with it the schema of a relationship to the self in which one has to constitute oneself permanently as the doctor and patient of oneself*" (dossier "Self and others"). What especially interests Foucault here is establishing continuities, showing how an experience is formed in which to master himself the subject no longer has to extend social schemas of domination into the relationship to the self (controlling oneself as one controls one's wife or slaves), but must put to work a vigilance in which he is suspicious of his own affects:

> The strict agonism that is characteristic of ancient ethics does not disappear, but the form of struggle, the instruments of victory and the forms of domination are modified. To be stronger than the self entails that one is and remains on the lookout, that one is constantly mistrustful of oneself, and that one is so not only in daily life, but in the very flux of representations which may trigger inspection and control.[46]

And this enables us to understand the title of the 1982 course: "The Hermeneutics of the Subject." For it is indeed a matter of showing how the practices of the self of the Hellenistic and Roman period form the experience of a subject who "*scans the subtle episodes of existence with a detailed reading*" (dossier "Self and others"). The suspicious self, tracking down its own agitations, reinforces the theme of the struggle against the self, puts the subject's radical weakness in the foreground, and establishes increasingly strongly links between pleasure and evil. One could say that Stoicism slowly paves the way for Christianity: "If I undertook such a long study, it was precisely to try to uncover how what we call the morality of Christianity was encrusted in European morality, not since the beginning of the Christian world but since the morality of antiquity."[47] So, in the final Foucault, and particularly with regard to Stoicism, we are always oscillating between the clear line of breaks and the insistence on continuities. But after all, Foucault recalls Nietzsche: historical truth is always a question of perspective.

The final and most decisive component of this ethics is distance. There is the danger of more misunderstandings here and the preparatory dossiers are more precious to us, backing up the course and revealing its general direction. The Hellenistic and Roman care of the self is not an exercise of solitude. Foucault thinks of it as an inherently social practice, taking place within more or less tightly organized institutional frameworks (the school of Epictetus or the Epicurean groups described by Philodemus), constructed on the basis of clan or family (Seneca's relationships with Serenus and Lucilius), woven into preexisting social relations (Plutarch's interlocutors), developing on a political basis, at the emperor's court, etcetera. The care of the self goes as far as to entail the Other in principle, since one can only be led to oneself by unlearning what has been inculcated by a misleading education. *"Rescue, even from one's own infancy, is a task of the practice of the self"* Foucault writes (dossier "Government of the self and others"). Here the folders "age, pedagogy, medicine" of the "Government of the self and others" dossier, and "critique" of the "Alcibiades, Epictetus" dossier, are explicit: Taking care of the self does not presuppose the return to a lost origin, but the emergence of a distinct "nature," though one that is not originally given to us. Hence the need for a master:

> Education is imposed against a background of errors, distortions, bad habits and dependencies which have been reified since the start of life. So that it is not even a matter of returning to a state of youth or infancy where there would still have been the human being; but rather of referring to a "nature" ... which has never had the opportunity to emerge in a life immediately seized by a defective system of education and belief. The objective of the practice of the self is to free the self, by making it coincide with a nature which has never had the opportunity to manifest itself in it.[48]

The care of the self is therefore shot through with the presence of the Other: the other as the guide of one's life, the other as the correspondent to whom one writes and before whom one takes stock of oneself, the other as helpful friend, benevolent relative ... It is not, Foucault writes, "*a requirement of solitude, but a real social practice,*" an "*intensifier of social relations*" (dossier "Government of the self and others"). Which is as much to say that the care of the self does not separate us from the world and neither is it a stopping point of our activities. For the sage, for example, what is called "withdrawal or retirement" (*anakhōrēsis*) does not mean withdrawal from human society in order to establish oneself in sovereign solitude. Foucault makes a series of distinctions between the retirement of fulfillment (conversion to the self at the peak of one's life), the strategic withdrawal (one frees oneself from the obligations of civic life in order to concern oneself solely with one's own affairs), the critical break (consisting in the considered rejection of certain conventions), and the temporary and healthy training period (enabling one to review oneself).[49] Above all, withdrawal is not synonymous with an outright and sensational cessation of activities. The Stoics say so: There is a lot of arrogance in those glorious feats by which alleged sages publicly flaunt their solitude and make a display of their withdrawal from society. The authentic withdrawal, required by the care of the self, consists in standing back from the activities in which one is engaged while still pursuing them, so as to maintain the distance between oneself and one's actions that constitutes the necessary state of vigilance. The aim of the care of the self is not removal of oneself from the world, but preparing oneself as a rational subject of action for the events of the world:

> Whatever the exercises may be, one thing is worth noting, which is that they are all practiced by reference to situations that the subject may also have to confront: it is therefore a matter of constituting the individual as rational subject of action, of rationally and morally acceptable action. The fact that all of this art of life is focused on the question of the relationship to the self should not mislead us: the theme of the conversion to the self should not be interpreted as a desertion of the domain of activity, but rather as

> the pursuit of what makes it possible to maintain the relationship of self to self as the principle, as the rule of the relationship to things, events and the world.[50]

The care of the self is therefore quite the opposite of an invitation to inaction: it is what encourages us to really act, it is what constitutes us as the true subject of our actions. Rather than isolating us from the world, it is what enables us to situate ourselves within it correctly.

> We have seen that directing attention on the self did not involve abstaining from the world and constituting oneself as an absolute. Rather it involves the most accurate measure of the place one occupies in the world and the system of necessities in which one is inserted.[51]

The care of the self therefore appears as the constitutive principle of our actions, and by the same token as a restrictive principle since *"in its dominant and most widespread forms, the function of the practice of the self was above all the most accurate definition of the degrees, modalities, duration and circumstances of the activity one was induced to devote to others"* (dossier "Government of the self and others"). Far from generating inactivity, the care of the self makes us act as, where, and when we ought. Far from isolating us from the human community, it appears rather as that which connects us to it most exactly since *"the privileged relationship, fundamental to himself, must enable him [the subject] to discover himself as a member of a human community, which extends from the close bonds of blood to the entire species"* (same dossier). The subject discovered in the care of the self is quite the opposite of an isolated individual: he is a citizen of the world. The care of the self is therefore a regulative principle of activity, of our relationship to the world and to others. It constitutes activity, giving it its worth and form, and it even intensifies it. Withdrawal, to take this example again, was *"a practice, an exercise which was integrated in the interplay of other activities, enabling precisely one's proper application to them"* (same dossier). In conclusion, *"we should then conceive of the culture of the self less as a choice opposed to political, civic, economic and familial activity, than* as a way of keeping this activity within what are thought to be the appropriate limits and forms" (dossier "The Others").

## The Political Stakes of the Course

The care of the self creates then a distance from action, which far from nullifying it, regulates it. However, for Foucault it is a matter at the same time of emphasizing that this culture of the self lays down the primacy of the relationship to the self over any other relationship. There is more than regulation here; there is the assertion of an irreducible independence. With regard to the exercises of abstinence in the Stoics or Epicureans, for example, Foucault shows in fact that it is not a matter of systematically depriving oneself of wealth—it is not Christian renunciation—but rather of ensuring that we will not be seriously disturbed if one day this wealth is lacking. So it is not a matter of shedding all material goods, but of enjoying them with sufficient detachment for us not to feel deprived by their loss. For the only genuine possession is the self's ownership of itself, and ownership of things is only a feeble copy of this. We must make ourselves able to accept privations as necessarily and essentially secondary. We must learn again to bear wealth as one bears poverty. Now the government of others must be thought in the same way, and Foucault sets out then the principle of a new governmentality; governmentality of ethical distance:

> In the first place it involves a "quantitative" limit in the work: not letting yourself be entirely occupied by your activities, not identifying your life with your function, not taking yourself for Caesar, but really knowing that you are the holder of a precise and temporary assignment... It involves above all—and this is a radical reversal of the process of statutory identification—not trying to establish what you are on the basis of the system of rights and obligations which differentiate and situate you with regard to others, but rather questioning yourself about what you are in order to infer from this what it is fitting to do, either in general or in this or that circumstance, but ultimately according to the functions that

you have to exercise. "Consider who you are" is the advice Epictetus gives, not so as to turn away from active life, but so as to give a rule of conduct to someone who is an inhabitant of the world and a citizen of his town. It is the definition of his role that will fix the measure of what he has to do: "If you are a councilor in some city, remember that you are old; if you are a father, remember that you are a father." The relationship to self does not detach the individual from any form of activity in the realm of the city-state, the family or friendship; it opens up, rather, as Seneca said, an intervallum between those activities he exercises and what constitutes him as the subject of these activities; this "ethical distance" is what enables him not to feel deprived of what will be taken from him by circumstances; it is what enables him to do no more than what is contained in the definition of the function.

In laying down the principle of conversion to oneself, the culture of the self fashions an ethic that is and always remains an ethic of domination, of the mastery and superiority of the self over the self. Nonetheless, with regard to this general structure it introduces a number of important modulations.

First of all it defines the relation of power exercised over the self independently of any statutory correlation and any exercise of power over others. It isolates it from the field of other power relations; it gives it no other support and no other purpose than the sovereignty to be exercised over the self.

We have also seen that this ethics of victory over oneself is coupled with the principle that makes the relationship to the self much more complex; the honor, veneration and devotion that one must dedicate to oneself are the other face of the domination one exercises. The objective to be reached is therefore a relationship to self which is at the same time a relationship of sovereignty and respect, of mastery of the self and modesty towards the self, of victory asserted over the self and by the self, and of fears experienced by the self and before the self.

In this reversible figure of the relationships to the self, we can see the source of an austerity that is not only more intense but even more internalized because it concerns, on this side of actions, the permanent presence of self to self in thought. However, in this ethics of conversion to the self this source of austerity is offset by the acknowledged legitimacy of actions entailed by the definition of a social, political or familial role, actions which are performed in the distance ensured by the fundamental character (at once first, permanent and last) of the relationship to self.[52]

This text summarizes the political ethics of the self, at least as Foucault finds it problematized in Roman philosophy. The problem really is one of participation in public and political life. It is not a matter, through the asserted primacy of the care of the self, of refusing public office, but actually of accepting them while giving a definite form to this acceptance. What one takes on in a public office or employment is not a social identity. I temporarily fulfill a role, a function of command, while knowing that the only thing I must and can truly command is myself. And if I am deprived of the command of others, I will not be deprived of this command over myself. This detachment thus enables one to fulfill a function, without ever making it one's own affair, performing only what is part of its definition (objective duties of the leader, the citizen, the father, etcetera), and by dispensing these social roles and their content from a constituent relationship to the self.[53] Whereas the Athenian aristocrat, in accepting to take a position of power over others, was identified with a status that was rightfully his and defined him completely, the Stoic sage accepts the functions bestowed on him by the emperor as a role that he fills as best he can, but starting from the irreducible reserve of an inalienable relationship to himself: *"personal status and public function, without being detached from each other, no longer coincide in principle"* (same dossier). The care of the self thus limits the self's ambition and its absorption in external tasks:

1. the culture of the self offers the active man a rule of quantitative limitation (not allowing political tasks, financial concerns, and diverse obligations to invade life to the extent that he risks forgetting himself);

2. the primacy of the relationship to self also enables the subject to establish his independence in all these other relations whose extension it has helped to limit.[54]

The ethical subject, therefore, never perfectly coincides with his role. This distance is made possible first of all because the sovereignty to be exercised over the self is the only sovereignty that one can and must preserve. It defines in fact the only tangible reality of power. This is an inversion of the *ēthos* of classical Greece. It is not a matter of governing oneself as one governs others, seeking models in military command or the domination of slaves, but, when I have to govern others, I can only do so on the model of the first, only decisive, essential, and effective government: the government of myself. It should not be thought that Foucault was looking in the care of the self for the dazzling and vivid formula of a political disengagement. Rather, through the study of imperial Stoicism in particular, he was looking for principles for a connection between ethics and politics.[55]

The final component to keep hold of from this lengthy quotation is what Foucault says about the worship we should offer to ourselves. The austerity of the care of the self is in fact broadly fed by the fear and trembling that should seize the self before himself. In the dossier "Government of the self and others" there is a folder entitled "religion" in which Foucault examines the notion, present in Marcus Aurelius especially, of the *daimōn*, understood as that internal divinity that guides us and which we must venerate and respect, that fragment of divinity in us that constitutes a self before which we must justify ourselves: "*The daimōn, though it is substantially divine, is a subject in the subject, it is in us like an other to whom we owe worship.*" It would not be possible to take these lengthy expositions into account in a couple of sentences. We note here that the interest of this internal division, at least as Foucault conceives of it, is due to the fact that it can hardly be translated in terms of an internalization of the other's gaze, as a cultural reflex (the lessons of psychoanalysis) might encourage us to think spontaneously. The ethical dimension is not then the effect of an internalization of the other's gaze. We should say, rather, that the *daimōn* is like the mythical figure of a first, irreducible caesura: that of self to self. And the Other takes up its place within this relationship, because there is first of all this relationship. It is the Other who is a projection of the Self, and if we must really tremble, it is before the Self rather than before this Other who is only its emblem.

In clarifying this "governmentality of ethical distance," as we have called it, it really was politics that was involved. In general, Foucault states, "*in the common Stoic attitude, the care of the self, far from being experienced as the great alternative to political activity, was rather a regulating component of it*" (same dossier). However, in conclusion we would like to pose a different problem: How did Foucault think that developing the idea of care of the self, practices of the self, and techniques of existence could influence and foster actual struggles?

The situation of Foucault's research at the end of the seventies can be presented in this way: the State, whose genealogy for modern societies he traced from 1976 to 1979, appears as simultaneously totalizing and individualizing. The modern State, which combines the structures of a pastoral government with those of *raison d'État*, emerged as that which at the same time manages populations and identifies individuals. "Police" appears at the junction of this double control. The Welfare State is seen as the final extension of this century-old double logic, concerning the prosperity and size of populations, the health and longevity of individuals. This double vocation of the State leads to fruitless and initially deflected struggles. To oppose to the State "the individual and his interests ... is just as hazardous as opposing it with the community and its requirements,"[56] since in both cases we are dealing with something produced, regulated, and dominated by the State. Resistance seems nowhere to be found and holds out only in the production of historical micro-knowledges, instruments of fragile struggle and openly reserved to an intellectual elite.

We could distinguish, again following Foucault, three forms of struggle: struggles against (political) domination; struggles against (economic) exploitation; struggles against (ethical) subjection.[57] The twentieth century was marked by these latter struggles, which can be described in the following way: "The main object of these struggles is to attack not so much this or that institution of power, or group, or elite, or class but, rather, a particular technique, a form of power. This form of power is exercised on immediate everyday life, it categorizes individuals and distinguishes them through their own individuality, it attaches them to their identity, and it imposes on them a law of truth that must be recognized in them. It is a form of power that makes individuals subjects."[58]

We will have recognized here pastoral power in its individualizing aspect.[59] The new struggles cannot therefore offer to free the individual from an oppressive State, since the State is precisely the matrix of individualization. The "political, ethical, social, philosophical problem of our days is not to try to liberate the individual from the State and its institutions, but to liberate us both from the State and from the type of individualization linked to the state. We have to promote new forms of subjectivity..."[60] It is only in the eighties that Foucault defines, with conceptual clarity, what we should oppose to the State's managerial, normalizing, individualizing, and identificatory ambitions. It is a matter precisely of these practices of the self, taken up in this relational dimension that he described so well with regard to Roman Stoicism. For at bottom, the individual and the community, their interests and their rights, are complementary opposites: a complicity of contraries. Foucault opposes what he calls "modes of life," "choices of existence," "styles of life," and "cultural forms" to both the demands of community and individual rights together. The case of the struggle for the recognition of homosexuality is exemplary here, and we should not forget that these final years were marked by Foucault's always stronger attraction to the United States, his stays in Berkeley, and his discovery there of original relational forms. The texts on the "social triumph"[61] or on "friendship as a way of life,"[62] devoted to the gay question, contain moreover decisive statements of Foucault's new politics. In these texts this politics does not stop at the demand for legal equality for homosexuals. Even less does it involve defining the truth of a homosexual nature. To normalize homosexuality, to struggle for the recognition of a true identity of the homosexual subject, to confine oneself to the demand for equal rights, all seemed to him a way of falling into the great trap of the institution. Real resistance takes place elsewhere for him: in the invention of a new ascesis, a new ethics, a new mode of homosexual life. For practices of the self are neither individual nor communal: they are relational and transversal.

## Preparation of the Course

The exercise of transcribing a course, of putting together a text on the basis of the spoken word, comes up against a number of difficulties of principle, perhaps happily somewhat attenuated in Foucault's case, since, as we pointed out earlier, he scrupulously read a drafted text more than he improvised freely. Nevertheless one is often caught between the dual requirements of fidelity and legibility. We have attempted a compromise by restoring the text as exactly as possible, while trimming it, occasionally cutting out repetitions or clumsiness that ended up hindering the understanding of a sentence. For example, we have omitted from the text precise references concerning fragments quoted (page or paragraph numbers) when the latter are found in the notes. They remained important, however, when suppressing them upset the balance of the sentence. Otherwise, when Foucault commits unimportant slips (errors on page numbers or letter numbers in a correspondence), we have directly restored the correct version in the text. Terms in square brackets, a few, indicate that the sentence has been slightly reorganized to help its comprehension. We have made use of only a single set of cassettes for the course (the recording made by Jacques Lagrange), which means that the few gaps in this recording have not been corrected, except when the manuscript made it possible to restore the missing sentences. Finally, the notes have a double function. On the one hand they indicate the sources of quotations, they establish links between this Collège de France course and the whole of Foucault's work—other courses, the books, the texts of *Dits et Écrits*—they explain allusions, and they refer to the secondary literature that was available to Foucault at this time. On the other hand, their function is more pedagogical, explaining certain historical points, providing biographical references for little known figures, and referring to works of synthesis on particular points.

✣

My gratitude and all my thanks go to Daniel Defert for letting me enrich and complete the transcript of the course through access to Foucault's work dossiers; to the research team in Hellenistic and Roman philosophy at the University of Paris-XII in general, and to Carlos Lèvy in particular; for their scientific skill and assistance, to Jean-François Pradeau for his Platonic insights, to Paul Veyne for his critical rereadings and such constructive comments, to Cécile Piégay for technical help, and finally to Paul Mengal for friendly and loyal support.

1. "*Il faut défendre la société.*" *Cours au Collège de France, 1976*, ed. M. Bertani and A. Fontana (Paris: Gallimard/Seuil, 1997); English translation by David Macey, ed. Arnold I. Davidson, "*Society must be defended.*" *Course at the Collège de France, 1976* (New York: Picador, 2002); *Les Anormaux. Cours au Collège de France, 1974-75*, ed. V. Marchetti and A. Salomoni (Paris: Gallimard/Seuil, 1999); English translation by Graham Burchell, ed. Arnold I. Davidson, *Abnormal. Course at the Collège de France, 1974-75* (New York: Picador, 2003).
2. "Le Retour de la morale" in *Dits et Écrits*, vol. 4, p. 697; English translation by Thomas Leven and Isabelle Lorenz, "The Return of Morality," in M. Foucault, *Politics, philosophy, culture: interviews and other writings of Michel Foucault, 1977-84*, ed. Lawrence D. Kritzman (New York and London: Routledge, 1988), p. 243.
3. "Le Souci de la vérité," *Dits et Écrits*, vol. 4, p. 668 (English translation by Alan Sheridan, "The Concern for Truth," in Foucault, *Politics, philosophy, culture*, pp. 255-56) and "Une esthétique de l'existence," in *Dits et Écrits*, vol. 4, p. 730 (English translation by Alan Sheridan, "An Aesthetics of Existence," in Foucault, *Politics, philosophy, culture*, pp. 47-48).
4. M. Foucault, "Usage des plaisirs et Techniques de soi," *Dits et Écrits*, vol. 4, p. 543; English translation by Robert Hurley, *The Use of Pleasure* (New York: Viking, 1986), pp. 8-9.
5. We have to go back to the 1975 Collège de France course to find Christian confession analyzed in terms of the theme of the production of a guilty body of pleasure, the twelfth and thirteenth centuries being the frame of reference. See the lectures of 19 and 26 February 1975, in *Les Anormaux (Abnormal)*.
6. "Du gouvernement des vivants," in *Dits et Écrits*, vol. 4, p. 125; English translation by Robert Hurley, "On the Government of the Living," in M. Foucault, *The Essential Works of Michel Foucault, 1954-1984, vol. 1: Ethics: Subjectivity and Truth*, ed. Paul Rabinow, translations by Robert Hurley et al (New York: The New Press, 1997), p. 81 (translation modified).
7. Ibid., p. 129, English translation, ibid., p. 84.
8. It should be remembered, however, that this comparison between ancient and Christian techniques of the direction of existence and examination of conscience were outlined first of all in the lecture of 22 February 1978, within the framework of an analysis of pastoral governmentality.
9. "The Subject and Power" in M. Foucault, *Essential Works of Foucault, 1954-1984, vol. 3: Power*, ed. J. D. Faubion, translations by Robert Hurley et al (New York: The New Press, 2002), p. 327; French translation by F. Durand-Bogaert, "Le sujet et le pouvoir," in *Dits et Écrits*, vol. 4, p. 223.
10. "Structuralisme e poststructuralisme," in *Dits et Écrits*, vol. 4, p. 451; English translation by Jeremy Harding (amended), "Structuralism and Post-Structuralism," in Michel Foucault, *Essential Works of Foucault, 1954-1984, vol. 2: Aesthetics, Method, and Epistemology*, ed. J. D. Faubion, translations by Robert Hurley et al. (New York: The New Press, 2000), p. 452.
11. "Subjectivité et Verité," in *Dits et Écrits*, vol. 4, p. 213; English translation by Robert Hurley, "Subjectivity and Truth," in *Ethics: Subjectivity and Truth*, p. 87.
12. "Préface à *l'Histoire de la sexualité*," in *Dits et Écrits*, vol. 4, p. 583; English translation by William Smock, "Preface to *The History of Sexuality*, Volume II," in Paul Rabinow, ed. *The Foucault Reader* (New York: Pantheon, 1984), pp. 338-39, emphasis added.
13. "On the Genealogy of Ethics: An Overview of Work in Progress" (1983) in *Ethics: Subjectivity and Truth*, pp. 254-55; French translation by G. Barbedette and F. Durand-Bogaert, "À propos de la généalogie de l'éthique: un aperçu du travail en cours," in *Dits et Écrits*, vol. 4, pp. 384-85.
14. Ibid., p. 254 (French, p. 384).
15. These are the "three main prohibitions" (ibid., p. 265 [French, p. 396]), the three points of anxiety (will the sexual act exhaust the body; does adultery represent a risk for the household economy; is the physical love of boys compatible with a good education?) which will remain constant throughout Antiquity, if not throughout the history of the West

(see also, "Usage des plaisirs et Techniques de soi," pp. 549-53 ["Introduction" to *The Use of Pleasure*, pp. 14-24]). According to Foucault, it is not the domains of sexual fears that are transformed in the history of sexuality, but the way in which they are reflected in a relationship to the self. What changes historically are the "good" reasons for not performing the sexual act too much, not deceiving one's wife too much, and not abusing young boys too much (it's not done, it is a sign of weakness, it is prohibited by the Law, etc.).

16. "On the Genealogy of Ethics," p. 255; "À propos de la généalogie de l'éthique," p. 385.
17. "Le Retour de la morale"; "The Return of Morality," p. 244.
18. "L'Écriture de soi," in *Dits et Écrits*, vol. 4, p. 415; English translation by Robert Hurley, "Self Writing," in *Ethics: Subjectivity and Truth*, p. 207.
19. See what Foucault says about it in the interview "Politique et Éthique," in *Dits et Écrits*, vol. 4, p. 585; English translation by Catherine Porter, "Politics and Ethics: An interview," in *The Foucault Reader*, pp. 373-74.
20. For this period we can also cite M. Laffranque, *Poseidonios d'Apamée* (Paris: PUF, 1964).
21. At the fifth international congress of philosophy at Caracas (November 1999, proceedings forthcoming), Carlos Lévy emphasized the extent of this absence. Foucault, in fact, takes the Hellenistic and Roman period as the central framework for his historico-philosophical demonstration, describing it as the golden age of the culture of the self, the moment of maximum intensity of practices of subjectivation, completely ordered by reference to the requirement of a positive constitution of a sovereign and inalienable self, a constitution nourished by the appropriation of *logoi* as so many guarantees against external threats and means of intensification of the relation to the self. And Foucault successfully brings together for his thesis the texts of Epicurus, Seneca, Marcus Aurelius, Musonius Rufus, Philo of Alexandria, Plutarch ... The Skeptics are not mentioned; there is nothing on Pyrrhon and nothing on Sextus Empiricus. Now the Skeptical school is actually as important for ancient culture as the Stoic or Epicurean schools, not to mention the Cynics. Study of the Skeptics would certainly have introduced some corrections to Foucault's thesis in its generality. It is not, however, the exercises that are lacking in the Skeptics, nor reflection on the *logoi*, but these are entirely devoted to an undertaking of precisely de-subjectivation, of the dissolution of the subject. They go in a direction that is exactly the opposite of Foucault's demonstration (concerning this culpable omission, Carlos Lévy does not hesitate to speak of "exclusion"). This silence is, it is true, rather striking. Without engaging in a too lengthy debate, we can merely recall that Foucault took himself for ... a skeptical thinker; see "Le Retour de la morale," pp. 706-7; "The Return of Morality," p. 254.
22. "Le Souci de la vérité," p. 674; "The Concern for Truth," p. 262.
23. "Sexuality and Solitude," in *Ethics: Subjectivity and Truth*, p. 177; French translation by F. Durand-Bogaert, "Sexualité et solitude," in *Dits et Écrits*, vol. 4, p. 170.
24. "On the Genealogy of Ethics," p. 263; "À propos de la généalogie de l'éthique," p. 393.
25. Ibid., p. 274; French, p. 406.
26. Ibid., p. 279; French, p. 411.
27. This assertion is only correct if we only consider the *Critique of Pure Reason*. Foucault will say later that by writing the *Critique of Practical Reason* Kant restored the primacy of an ethical constitution of the self (See "On the Genealogy of Ethics.").
28. "Sexuality and Solitude," pp. 175-85; "Sexualité et solitude," pp. 168-78.
29. See, for example, "On the Genealogy of Ethics," p. 262; "À propos de la généalogie de l'éthique," p. 392.
30. In the first, unpublished version of the 1981 lecture, Foucault defined "governmentality" as precisely the "*surface of contact on which the way of conducting individuals and the way they conduct themselves are intertwined.*"
31. Again, in this sense the ethical self of Antiquity is opposed to the moral subject of modernity. See the statements in this sense: "Le Retour de la morale," p. 706; "The Return of Morality," pp. 253-54.
32. "L'Écriture de soi," p. 420; "Self Writing," p. 211. See also: "In this case—that of the *hupomnēmata*—it was a matter of constituting oneself as a subject of rational action through the appropriation, the unification and the subjectivation of a fragmentary and selected

already-said; in the case of the monastic notation of spiritual experiences, it will be a matter of dislodging the most hidden impulses from the inner recesses of the soul, thus enabling oneself to break free of them." Ibid., p. 430 (English translation, p. 221).
33. Ibid., p. 418 (English translation, p. 209).
34. "Le Souci de la verité," p. 674; "The Concern for Truth," pp. 262-63.
35. "On the Genealogy of Ethics," p. 260; "À propos de la généalogie de l'éthique," p. 390.
36. "Subjectivité et Verité," p. 215; "Subjectivity and Truth," p. 89.
37. "This work on the self with its attendant austerity is not imposed on the individual by means of civil law or religious obligation, but is a choice about existence made by the individual." "On the Genealogy of Ethics," p. 271; "À propos de la généalogie de l'éthique," p. 402.
38. "Le Retour de la morale," p. 698; "The Return of Morality," p. 244.
39. "On the Genealogy of Ethics," p. 261; "À propos de la généalogie de l'éthique," p. 391.
40. Ibid., p. 266; French, p. 397.
41. "Le Retour de la morale," p. 700; "The Return of Morality," p. 246.
42. "On the Genealogy of Ethics," p. 258; "À propos de la généalogie de l'éthique," p. 388.
43. "Le Retour de la morale," p. 706; "The Return of Morality," pp. 253-54.
44. "On the Genealogy of Ethics," p. 271; "À propos de la généalogie de l'éthique," p. 403.
45. Dossier: "The Others."
46. Dossier: "Culture of the self."
47. "Le Retour de la morale," p. 706; "The Return of Morality," p. 254.
48. Dossier: "Government of the self and others."
49. Folders: "withdrawal" and "conversion/withdrawal" in the "Government of the self and others" dossier.
50. Dossier: "Government of the self and others."
51. Dossier: "The Others."
52. Dossier: "Government of the self and others."
53. See from the same dossier: "*In this context, the practice of the self has certainly played a part: not that of offering, in private life and subjective experience, a substitute for political activity which has now become impossible; but that of fashioning an 'art of living,' a practice of existence, starting from the only relationship of which one is master and which is the relationship to the self. This becomes the foundation of an ethos, which is not the alternative choice to political and civic activity; it offers rather the possibility of defining oneself outside of one's function, role and prerogatives, and thereby of being able to exercise these in an adequate and rational way.*"
54. Dossier: "Government of the self and others."
55. We should, however, certainly recall that in *The Use of Pleasure*, with regard to classical Greece, the ethical dimension came up against politics in a different way. With regard to the love of boys, it involved showing how domination is limited and restrains itself, how strength sets duties on itself and recognizes rights in the other: ethics was a kind of fold of politics. With regard to this fold of forces, Deleuze (*Foucault*, translation by S. Hand [Minneapolis: University of Minnesota Press, 1988]), will talk of the emergence of the subject. What we should keep hold of in this is that Foucault always thinks of ethics within politics.
56. " '*Omnes et singulatim*': Toward a Critique of Political Reason," in M. Foucault, *Power*, p. 325; French translation by P. E. Dauzat, " '*Omnes et singulatim*': vers une critique de la raison politique," in *Dits et Écrits*, p. 161.
57. "The Subject and Power," p. 331; "Le Sujet et le pouvoir," in *Dits et Écrits*, p. 228.
58. Ibid., p. 331; French translation, p. 227.
59. For a definition: "This form of power is directed towards salvation (as opposed to political power). It is oblative (as opposed to the principle of sovereignty) and individualizing (as opposed to legal power); it is coextensive and continuous with life; it is linked with a production of truth—the truth of the individual himself." Ibid., p. 333 (French translation, p. 229). From the eighteenth century, this power "spread out into the whole social body. It found support in a multitude of institutions." Ibid., p. 335 (French translation, p. 232).

60. Ibid., p. 336; French translation, p. 232.
61. "The Social Triumph of the Sexual Will," in *Ethics: Subjectivity and Truth*, pp. 157-62; French version "Le triomphe social du plaisir sexuel: une conversation avec Michel Foucault," in *Dits et Écrits*, vol. 4, pp. 308-14.
62. "De l'amitié comme mode de vie," in *Dits et Écrits*, vol. 4, pp. 163-67; English translation by John Johnston (translation amended), "Friendship as a Way of Life," in *Ethics: Subjectivity and Truth*, pp. 135-40.

# INDEX OF NAMES

Achilles Tatius, 449, 452n
Ælius Aristides, 108, 122n, 165n, 534
Alcibiades:
   and care of the self, 51, 57-58, 66-67,
     68-74, 76, 78, 82-86, 91, 161-62,
     224n, 418-20, 454, 455-56,
     494-95, 514
   education of, 31-38
   governing and, 44-46, 50-54, 93-94,
     111, 118
   ignorance of, 36, 45-46, 93, 94, 128,
     254, 447
   Neo-Platonist commentaries on,
     170-75
   Socrates' resistance of, 50, 221, 347, 432
Alföldi, A., 166n
Allen, W., 92
Anaxandridas, 31, 36, 493
Andersen, G., 165n
André, J.-M., 122n, 123n, 148n, 150,
   165n, 410n, 474n, 518
Annas, J., 519
Apollonius of Tyana, 143, 151, 165n
Ariston of Khios, 259
Aristotle, xv, 17, 24n, 26, 144, 189, 190,
   388, 392n, 394n
Arnim, H. von, 103n, 146n
Arrian, 90, 102n, 103n, 367, 370n, 497
Athenodorus, 142, 145n, 147n, 150
Atticus, 361
Aubin, M., 224n
Augustine, Saint, 27, 188, 191, 224n, 362,
   460-61

Augustus, 115, 123n, 142, 147n, 150, 165n,
   183, 286n
Aulus Gellius, 414, 415, 434n

Basil of Caesarea, 10, 22n, 423
Baudelaire, Ch., 23n, 251, 530
Béranger, J., 165n
Bertani, M., 40n, 268n, 547n
Boissier, G., 165n
Bowerstock, G., 165n
Boyancé, P., 328n
Bréhier, E., 23n, 451n, 519
Brisson, L., 21n, 79n
Brunschwig, J., 79n, 123n, 519, 520
Burkert, W., 62n
Burlet, G., xviii, 410n
Byl, S., 488n

Caesar, 101n, 146n, 199-200, 539
Cassian, 23n, 123n, 145n, 299-301, 312n,
   422, 503
Cassin, B., 165n
Cato, 147n, 160, 166n, 269n
Caujolle-Zaslawsky, 474n
Cavell, S., xxvi
Chantraine, P., 101n, 312n
Charmides, 33, 101n
Cicero, 20n, 98, 104n, 105n, 166n,
   203n, 370n, 383, 393n, 410n, 442,
   443, 475n, 533
Clement of Alexandria, 81, 101n,
   258, 434n
Cornutus, 76, 79n

Courcelle, P., 20n, 224n
Croiset, M., 79n
Cumont, F., 123n

Davidson, A.I., 24n, 547n
Defert, D., xvi, xviiin, 20n, 227n, 516, 546
Defradas, J., 4, 20n
Delatte, L., 102n
Deleuze, G., 517, 549n
Demetrius, 9, 142, 147n, 229n, 231-32, 234-36, 245n, 258, 321-22, 435n, 497-99
Democritus, 63n, 533
Demonax, 143
Denys of Halicarnassus, 237, 245n
Derrida, J., xxvii, 24n
Desbordes, F., 146n
Descartes, R., 17, 18, 23n, 24n, 25, 26, 28, 190, 294, 309, 358, 461, 522
Desideri, P., 103n
Détienne, M., 411n
De Witt, N.W., 136-37, 146n, 519
Dio Chrysostom (Dio of Prusa), 91, 96, 103n, 104n, 135, 146n, 165n, 182, 183, 186n, 199, 410n, 493
Dio of Prusa. See Dio Chrysostom
Diogenes Laertius, 41n, 102n, 103n, 104n, 146n, 230, 245n, 259, 268n, 312n, 328n, 410n, 474n, 489n
Dixsaut, M., 79n
Dodds, E.R., 62n, 104n, 417-18, 434n, 518
Dorion, L.-A., 312n
Dreyfus, H., 435n

Epictetus:
  aggressiveness of, 154
  care of the self/others in, 9, 57, 118-19, 195-98, 217, 456, 457, 459
  clinic of the soul, 99
  cynicism and, 440-41, 443, 445, 446
  on decency, 182
  on erroneous judgements, 215
  examination of conscience in, 477, 479, 481, 484

  hearing/listening in, 118, 119, 338-40, 346-48, 359, 360, 367-68
  on knowledge of oneself, 3
  and the philosopher-scout, 441
  on philosophy, 138-42, 336
  use of representations in, 63n, 503-504
  on restraint, 431-33
  school of, 90, 99, 138, 146n, 494-96, 536
  spiritual exercises, 298-99
  teasing by, 96
Epicurus:
  and care of the soul, 8
  on evil, 475n
  on friendship, 193
  and the guide, 389-90
  on knowledge, 239-43
  memory of, 411n
  on philosophy/philosophers, 87-88, 135, 136, 225n, 492
  on truth, 97
  on youth, 146n
Esau, 446, 452n
Euphrates, 149, 151-55, 165n, 435n
Eusebius of Cesarea, 70, 74, 79n, 123n
Evagrius Ponticus, 503
Ewald, F., xviiin, 20n

Faust, xxv, 23n, 27, 40n, 289, 309-10, 313n, 314n
Febvre, L., 451n
Festugière, A.-J., 23n, 122n, 145n, 170, 186n, 207, 224n, 353, 518
Flashar, H., 519
Fontana, A., 268n, 434n, 457n
Freud, S., xxv, 30, 40n, 461
Friedländer, L., 166n
Fronto, 76, 108, 122n, 149, 157-59, 161, 163, 166n, 498

Galen, 269n, 380, 386, 391, 392n, 393n, 396-99, 404, 405, 407, 410n, 494, 496
Gernet, L., 61n

Gigante, M., 123n, 146n, 387, 392n, 393n, 394n, 518
Goethe, J.W. von, xxv, 310, 313n, 314n
Goldschmidt, V., 79n
Goulet, R., 103n, 226n
Goulet-Cazé, M.-O., 104n, 245n, 328n
Gratia, 158, 161, 166n
Gregory of Nyssa, xxvi, 10, 13, 22n, 23n, 30, 84, 492
Grimal, P., 102n, 147n, 287n, 393n
Gros, F., xvi, 148n, 507n

Hadot, I., 62n, 105n, 518, 519
Hadot, P., 23n, 62n, 79n, 123n, 146n, 203n, 216, 226n, 312n, 369n, 387, 417, 418, 434n
Hegel, G.W.F., 28, 40n, 524
Heidegger, M., 28, 189, 523-24
Heliodorus, 449, 452n
Helvia, 156, 166n
Helvidius Priscus, 142, 147n
Heracles, 444, 451n
Heraclitus, 53
Hermotimus, 92-93, 103n
Herodotus, 243, 246n
Hierocles, 215, 226n
Hijmans, B.L., 312n
Hippocrates, 104n, 160, 267n
Höistad, R., 451n
Homer, 32, 40n, 352n, 452n
Hoven, R., 452n
Husserl, E., 28, 40n, 474n
Hyppolite, J., xiii, 40n

Iamblichus, 62n, 146n, 171, 186n, 226n, 352n, 489n
Isis, 114, 122n
Isocrates, 316, 328n, 352n

Jacob, 446, 452n
Jaeger, W., 246
Jerphagnon, L., 148n
Joly, H., 62n, 79n, 417, 418, 434n, 518
Joly, R., 104n
Jouanna, J., 104n

Kant, I., 26, 28, 40n, 190, 548n
Kierkegaard, S., 23n

Lacan, J., xxv, xxvi, 30, 40n, 188-89
Laffranque, M., 104n, 548n
Lagrange, J., xviii, 40n, 410n, 516, 545
Leibniz, G.W., xxv, 28
Lessing, G.E., 309, 313n
Lévy, C., 20n, 434n, 520n, 548n
Long, A.A., 519
Lucian, 92, 103n, 151, 165n, 435n
Lucilius, 85, 89, 94, 96, 101n, 102n, 111, 114, 122n, 130, 145n, 156, 166n, 212, 225n, 260-62, 264, 269n, 274, 275, 280, 286n, 356, 361-62, 370, 376-78, 386, 392n, 399-400, 428-29, 436, 452, 471, 474n, 478, 494, 496, 497, 536
Lucius Piso, 137, 142, 146n, 387
Luther, M., 451n
Lycinus, 92-93

MacMullen, R., 148n
Maecenas, 115, 123n, 150, 387
Malafosse, J. de, 392n
Marcus Aurelius:
  and the art of living, 322
  and the athlete, 323
  and the daimōn, 542
  and the exercise of Imperial power, 193, 199-201, 206, 380-81
  exercises, 294-95, 296-308, 311
  Fronto correspondence, 157-63, 498
  history of, 101n
  and memory, 468
  on moral perfection, 478-79, 504
  on repentance and self-examination, 215-19, 222, 481, 489n, 500
  on sincere service, 105n
  on spiritual modalization of knowledge, 290-92
  technique of screening representations, 23n
  and withdrawal, 50
Marcia, 283, 285, 287n

Marlowe, C., 313n
Marrou, H.-I., 61n, 102n, 246n, 313n, 435n
Martha, C., 105n
Marullus, 361, 370n, 470
Methodius of Olympus, 22n
Michel, A., 146, 148
Montaigne, M. Eyquem de, 251
Mossé, C., 21n
Murray, G., 23n
Musonius Rufus, 81, 88, 101n, 143, 146n, 165n, 268, 315, 316, 328n, 410n, 426, 427, 435n, 494, 502, 518, 524, 548n

Natali, C., 123n
Nero, 101n, 102n, 115, 146n, 147n, 165n, 426, 435n
Nietzsche, F., xv, xviii, 22n, 28, 251, 488, 535
Nock, A.D., 224n
Nussbaum, M., 520

Oedipus, 370n, 444, 445, 451n, 452n, 509
Oltramare, P., 102n, 269n
Olympiodorus, 170, 172-73, 186n
Ourliac, P., 392n

Pascal, B., 309, 452n
Pépin, J., 434n
Pericles, 32, 34-35, 91, 245n, 393n, 411n
Persius, 76, 79n
Petitjean, G., xiv, xviiin
Philo of Alexandria, 22n, 91, 98, 99, 103n, 116, 123n, 127, 343, 411n, 434n, 500, 548n
Philodemus, 123n, 137, 142, 146, 373, 383, 385, 387-89, 392n, 393n, 396, 400, 404, 405, 536
Philostratus, 165n
Pigeaud, J., 105n
Plato:
    and access to the truth, 189, 225n
    and art of the body, 107
    on athletes, 427-28, 435n
    and care for the self, 46, 59-51, 75, 86, 175-77, 195
    on flattery, 379
    on medicine, 97, 340
    meditation on death, 477
    on passions, 56-57
    politics in, 174-77, 185
    Persia in, 34, 73, 419
    and the precept "know yourself," 8, 59, 66, 101n, 172
    on salvation, 192
    and self-control, 427-28
    on the soul, 283, 434n, 456-57, 459, 500
    and spiritual guidance, 399
    on turning away from appearances, 209
    and virtue, 316
    *See also* Alcibiades; Socrates
Pliny, 151-54, 165n, 166n
Plotinus, 10, 22n, 207, 224n, 434n
Plutarch:
    on audition, 334-46, 500
    and care of oneself, 31
    on control of anger, 431
    and ethos, 237
    on examination of self, 85, 217-21
    history of, 166n
    on memory, 182-83, 467, 499
    on preparation, 469
    on silence, 341, 342
    and spiritual guidance, 156
    on temptation, 48-49
    on tranquility of mind, 362
    on true friends, 374
Pohlenz, 519
Polybius, 156, 166n
Porphyry, 61n, 62n, 224n, 352n, 434n, 481
Posidonius, 97, 103n, 104n, 131, 145n, 147n, 519
Pradeau, J.-F., 79n, 546
Proclus, 170-72, 186n
Prometheus, 444, 451n
Protagoras, 45, 61n, 328n

# Index of Names

Puech, H.-Ch., 24n
Pythagoras, 48, 61n, 62n, 103n, 146n, 226n, 341, 352n, 414-15, 480-81, 484, 488n, 489n, 511
Pythocles, 243, 246n

Quintilian, 267n

Rabbow, P., 374, 392n, 518
Radice, R., 123n
Robert, L., 23n
Robin, L., 79n
Roscher, W.H. von, 3-4, 20n
Rubellius Plautus, 143

Saïd, S., 165n
Sartre, J.-P., 525
Schelling, F.W.J. von, 28
Schopenhauer, A., 25, 251
Schuhl, P.-M., 104n
Scipio, 264, 269n
Sedley, D.N., 519
Seneca:
  on athletes, 231, 428-30
  on audition, 336-38
  and care of the self, 9
  consultation by Serenus, 89-90, 114-15
  and ethical distance, 540
  on examination of conscience, 478-79, 481-82
  on flattery, 376
  and grief, 361
  and *instructio*, 94-98, 320-23
  on knowledge, 260-64, 306-307, 311
  on *libertas*, 396, 399-400, 403-407
  on "life as test," 437-38, 440, 444-45
  as philosopher, 155-57, 159, 162
  on philosophy, 348-50
  on the present and past, 467-71
  on relationship to oneself, 85, 109-11, 207, 212, 213, 271-90, 494-505
  and *stultitia*, 129-33, 137, 138
  on writing and reading, 359
Serenus, 89, 102n, 114-15, 131, 145n, 156-57, 166n, 494, 497, 536

Sharples, R.W., 519
Socrates, xxvi
  on care of the self, xx, 4-8, 10, 13, 17, 20n, 21n, 73-75, 111, 119, 161-62, 491-92
  death of, 142
  on ignorance, 129, 365
  and knowledge of oneself, 230
  and listening, 500
  practice of the self, 418-19, 431-32
  questioning of Alcibiades, 32-38, 41-46, 59-54, 58, 62n, 69-71
  resistance of Alcibiades, 50, 221, 347, 432
  and the Socratic approach, 172-75
  and youth, 494
Sophocles, 108, 122n, 451n, 452n, 509
Spanneut, M., 268
Spinoza, B., xxv, 27, 40n, 309
Stirner, M., 251
Stobaeus, 101n, 104n, 122n, 426, 435n

Taurus, 415, 434n
Tertullian, 81, 101n, 225n
Theophrastus, 334, 352n
Thomas Aquinas, Saint, 24n, 26
Thrasea Paetus, 142, 147n, 231, 497
Thucydides, 215, 226n
Trédé, M., 102n
Turcan, R., 123n

Ulysses, 335

Vernant, J.-P., 61n, 328n, 329n, 393n, 411n, 417-18, 434n, 488n, 518
Veyne, P., 23n, 102n, 123n, 166n, 353n, 392n, 436n, 452n, 546
Vidal-Naquet, P., 102n
Virgil, 123n, 349-50
Vitrac, B., 104n
Voelke, A.-J., 22n, 104n, 122n
Vuillemin, J., xiii

# INDEX OF NAMES

Weil, R., 72-74, 79n
Wittgenstein, L., xxvi

Xenophon, 4, 21n, 33, 41n, 84,
    101n, 103n, 160, 161, 166n,
    226n, 493

Xenophon of Ephesus,
    449, 452n

Yates, F., 500

Zopyrus the Thracian, 35

# INDEX OF NOTIONS AND CONCEPTS

Abstinence, 123n, 191, 313, 326, 417-18, 421-22, 426-32, 437, 453, 498, 501, 502, 539
Act, 43, 110, 133, 139, 172, 232, 368, 384, 389, 404, 421, 481, 523, 527, 538
  of consultation, 3
  of knowledge, 15-16, 18
  of memory, 48, 176, 460
  political, 173
  of recollection, 210, 256
  of reflection, 224n
  sexual, 547n, 548n
  of telling, 366
  verbal, 370
  of vision, 69
Activity, 88, 91, 98, 116-17, 239, 538
  of agricultural work, 425
  of audition, 338
  of divine rationality, 280
  of the elite, 75
  of encouraging, 7
  of government, 83, 250
  of guidance, 406
  of knowing, 17, 28
  of knowledge, 77, 85-86
  of memorization, 88
  of paraenesis, 363
  of salvation, 184, 192
  of speech, 54, 333
  of spiritual advice, 482
Adult, 75, 87-88, 90-93, 102n, 107-108, 110, 125, 132, 205, 247, 495, 534

Aesthetics, 251, 434n, 521, 530
Aid (*Boēthos*), 324-25, 388, 394n
*Anakhōrēsis*, 47-50, 91, 101n, 212, 537. See also Retirement; Withdrawal
Analysis, 2, 31, 54, 73, 83, 114, 135, 169, 207, 216, 222, 238, 252, 278-79, 294, 296, 301-306, 312n, 386-87, 418, 419, 440, 442-43, 462, 511, 513, 526-27
  Foucault's, 122n, 166n, 268n, 451n
  of Parrhēsia, 407, 411n
  Stoic, 301, 443
  textual, 1, 65, 203n, 225n, 227n, 353n
Anger, 56, 306, 328n, 374-75, 387, 431, 488n, 511, 528
Apparatus, 319, 361, 411n, 460, 469, 485, 489n
Apprenticeship, 46, 61n, 92, 115, 117, 165n, 166n, 321, 341, 414-16
*Arcana conscientiae*, 218, 235, 278
Art, 38, 51, 54-57, 90, 99, 107, 142, 175, 177-78, 224n, 242, 249-50, 254, 328n, 333, 338-40, 347-48, 352, 366, 368, 381-84, 387, 400, 487, 500, 531
  of conjecture, 388, 404
  of discussion, 140
  of existence, 20, 86, 178
  of governing, 54, 250, 451n
  of medicine, 267n
  of persuading, 381
  of speaking, 340, 355, 363

Art of living, 82, 86, 90, 92, 125,
    145n, 178, 205-206, 259,
    322-23, 424, 447-49, 485, 514,
    537, 549n
Art(s) of the self, 150, 178, 206, 257,
    316, 377, 447, 465, 517
Ascent, 71, 277, 285, 455, 475n
Ascesis, 30, 91, 211, 213, 332-33, 339-40,
    342, 351, 367, 421, 428, 429, 451,
    469, 485, 500, 522, 529, 545
Asceticism, 10-11, 30, 139, 250, 257, 321,
    416, 492
Ascetics, 416-25, 427, 431, 437, 446, 453,
    455, 462, 485
*Askēsis*, xxviii, 16, 210, 311, 315-20,
    324-27, 328n, 331-32, 371, 416, 420,
    427, 498
Ataraxy, 184, 194-95, 458
Athlete, 231, 321-24, 441, 492, 498
Attention, 10-11, 84-86, 151, 206, 221-22,
    229, 252, 286n, 308, 322, 336-51,
    372, 431, 456, 466, 493, 500,
    534, 538
Attitude, 11, 31, 56-57, 84-85, 140, 147,
    150, 163, 198, 201, 214, 299, 372-73,
    381, 384, 391, 397, 429, 431, 432,
    437, 442-43, 459, 465, 467, 481
Audition, 334-39. See also Listening
*Aufklärung*, xxvii, 487
Autarchy, 184
Awakening, 8, 216, 337

Beauty, 22n, 32-33, 58, 282, 304, 347,
    349, 403, 415
Behavior, 56-58, 111, 128, 156-57, 195,
    198, 199, 202, 274, 291, 232, 236,
    358, 530
*Bios*, 20, 447, 486-87, 489n, 531
Body, 22n, 49, 55-59, 62n, 97-99,
    107-108, 116, 122n, 162, 172,
    182-83, 209-10, 224n, 280, 284,
    335, 340, 343-45, 348, 359, 393,
    398, 426-30, 457, 492, 496, 508,
    514, 534-35, 547n
*Boēthos*. See Aid

Care, 5-7, 10, 22n, 37, 38, 54, 72, 83,
    97, 99, 108, 116, 118, 120, 145n,
    161-62, 174-78, 191, 348, 419,
    488n, 493, 523
Care of the self, xx, xxi-xxii, xxiv, 3, 4,
    6-14, 20, 30, 58-60, 66-68, 74-77,
    82-93, 96-100, 107-108, 111-13,
    116-17, 134, 177-179, 195, 448, 462,
    492, 494, 524, 533-34, 537-38,
    541-42
Cartesian, xxiv, xxv, 14, 17, 27, 68, 191,
    294, 469n, 474n
Cathartics, 173
Christian, xv, 2, 10, 11, 20n, 22n, 30, 45,
    61, 70, 81, 84, 101n, 116, 174, 191,
    208, 211-18, 225n, 235, 250, 253-58,
    268n, 299-22, 332-34, 342, 353, 363,
    391, 398, 408-409, 410n, 421-22,
    424, 446, 450, 482, 485, 488n, 492,
    503, 509, 521, 533, 535, 539, 547n
Christianity, 10, 13, 20n, 26-27, 66, 81,
    108, 120, 123n, 180-81, 185, 190,
    208, 211, 216-17, 230, 238, 250,
    255-58, 294, 327, 358, 362, 391,
    398, 399, 407-408, 411n, 420-23,
    437, 445-46, 482, 509, 511,
    527-28, 535
Church, 23n, 45, 61, 257
Citizen, 5-6, 75, 138, 173, 197, 291,
    296-98, 427, 538, 540, 541
City-state, 13, 23n, 33, 35, 36, 38, 43-44,
    51, 54, 71, 82-83, 93, 118, 174,
    176-77, 185, 192, 199, 206, 380,
    410n, 447n, 492, 493, 540
Code, 20, 156, 317, 514, 528
Community, 3, 98, 116-17, 119, 176,
    195, 197, 233, 235, 298, 364, 538,
    543, 544
Concentration, 48, 61, 67, 222, 418, 526
Concupiscence, 218, 300, 503
Conduct, 61, 154, 157, 169, 199, 236, 291,
    334, 406, 445, 484, 499, 528, 540
Confession, 355, 363-65, 370, 509-10
Confession (*confession*), 114, 156, 225n,
    390, 409, 411, 510, 547n

# Index of notions and concepts 559

Control, 61n, 102n, 123n, 134
Conversion, 15, 28, 85, 178, 181, 190, 202, 207-17, 224n, 225n, 226n, 248, 252-54, 258, 260, 289, 307, 309, 315, 317, 394-95, 522-23, 537, 540-41
Correction, 27, 93-94, 130, 212
Correspondence, 26, 76, 89, 122n, 157, 361-62, 376, 400, 407, 494, 496, 498, 504, 545
Counselor of existence, of life, 125, 143
Courage, 34, 118, 240, 291, 298, 335, 365, 427-28, 438, 495, 517, 529, 534
Culture of the self, 22n, 30, 46, 50, 76, 120-21, 179-80, 205, 210-11, 316, 318, 417, 439, 445, 447, 495-98, 502, 508, 517, 527, 532, 533, 534, 538-41
*Cura sui*, 2, 9, 491
Cynics, 8, 9, 17, 75, 150, 154, 177, 230-31, 243, 253, 259, 316, 366, 410n, 419, 420, 429, 496, 529, 532, 548n
Cyrenaic, 467

Death, 5, 6, 21n, 93, 108, 111, 142, 181, 183-84, 233, 234, 283-84, 357-59, 417-18, 442, 472, 477-80, 504-505
  moment of, 47, 111, 448, 478, 504, 505
  *See also* Meditation on death
Decipherment, 221-22, 238, 244, 253, 289, 301, 422, 434n, 499
Delight, 86, 158-59, 214, 241, 272, 495, 534
Delinquency, 229
Desire, 220, 347-48, 379, 424, 432, 520
Dietetics, 59-60, 104n, 161-62
Discontinuity, 303-305, 320, 418, 467, 488n
Discourse (true), 243, 253, 326, 333-34, 341, 345, 347, 351, 355, 360, 365, 366, 371-72, 379, 382, 384, 408-409, 416, 451n, 469, 485, 501, 510, 527
Discrimination, 445-46
Doctor, 21n, 51, 57-59, 89, 95, 97, 145, 242, 249, 267n, 328n, 365, 394n, 396, 398, 402, 535

*Dogmata*, 259, 323, 328n, 329n, 498, 528
Dream, 24n, 47-48, 62n, 480-81

Economics, 161-62
Economy, 160, 342, 547n
Education, 32, 34-36, 44, 52-53, 61n, 62n, 75, 95-96, 134, 140, 261, 341-42, 438-39, 497, 536
*Emendatio*, 212
Empire, 82, 129, 143, 150, 160, 165n, 166n, 183, 201, 206, 231, 374, 375, 381, 386, 417, 419, 426, 448, 470, 479, 488, 514
Epicurean, 13, 37, 77-78, 82, 90, 107, 113, 118, 136-37, 141-43, 146n, 152, 192-95, 217, 230, 238, 242, 253, 254, 258, 278, 374, 387, 389-91, 393n, 430, 475n, 492, 536
*Epimeleia heautou*. *See* Care of the self
*Epistrophē*, 209-11, 216-17, 224n, 495, 533
Equipment, 225n, 322-23, 325-26, 332, 350, 358, 367, 371, 416, 421, 469, 498, 527. *See also Paraskeuē*
*Erōs*, 16, 33, 37, 152, 282, 347, 348, 497
Erotics, 74, 76, 161, 162, 452n
Ethics, 109, 110, 251-52, 267-68, 355, 368, 372, 375, 429, 512, 514, 517, 520, 529-32, 540-42, 545
Ethopoetic, 237, 238, 528
*Ēthos*, xxvii, xxviii, 211, 237-38, 324, 334, 372-73, 381, 416, 469, 475n, 452
Event, xxi, 22n, 181, 183, 298, 322-26, 332, 469-71, 473, 477, 499
Examination, 200-201, 297-301, 350, 366, 417, 423, 461-63, 481-83
Examination of conscience, 11, 48, 145n, 162, 200, 345, 364, 417, 423, 463, 473, 480-84, 489n, 511, 521, 528, 547n
Exegesis, 61n, 222, 238, 244, 256-58, 279, 289, 301, 357
Exercise:
  of looking, 295, 454, 457
  of memory, 414, 461, 468
  of power, 36, 45, 157, 193, 375, 540

# INDEX OF NOTIONS AND CONCEPTS

Exercise—*continued*
  of praemeditatio, 368, 472
  of the self, 311, 359
  of thought, 260, 359, 450, 454, 459, 460, 473
  of the truth, 319
  *See also* Spiritual exercise
Existence, 12, 15, 31, 47, 86, 126-27, 143, 160, 178, 237, 262, 274, 283, 359, 362, 447-48, 511, 513-15, 520, 524, 529-31, 535, 543-44
Experience, xxvii, 156, 208-209, 216-17, 226, 352n, 404, 486, 535, 549

Flattery, 138, 148n, 158, 262, 275, 302, 335, 347-48, 373-80, 385-87, 389, 392, 396, 397
Fortress, 12, 85, 101n, 213, 325
Frankness, 157, 164, 169, 242, 366, 372, 381, 386, 399, 405, 411
Free time (*Otium*), 112, 114, 126, 151, 219, 377, 493
Freedom, 63n, 123n, 184, 225n, 233, 272, 282, 291-92, 296-97, 302-308, 324, 372, 381, 402, 411n, 424, 426, 446-47, 523, 525
Friendship, 114-15, 137-38, 146n, 152, 156, 159, 192-95, 389-90, 399, 498, 540, 544
Future, 194, 321, 463-73, 480, 481, 489n, 489, 501-502

Gaze, 49, 70, 93, 117, 213-23, 229, 235, 248, 252, 260-61, 263, 278, 279, 289-90, 294-95, 306, 308, 399, 456-57, 459, 478-79, 495, 502, 542.
  *See also* Looking
Genealogy, 188, 508, 521, 525-26, 543
Gnostics, 123n, 268n, 434n
*Gnōthi seauton*, xxi, xxii, xxiv, 3-4, 8, 14, 35, 52, 67-69, 118-19, 170-71, 173, 419, 455-56, 461-62, 491
God, gods, 3-7, 47, 56, 145n, 233-37, 240, 241, 243, 274, 341, 342, 444-45, 449, 468, 493, 498

Government:
  of oneself, 249, 250, 374, 387, 404
  of others, 33, 39, 135, 250, 374, 539
  pastoral, 267n, 543
  of the self, 252, 516, 531, 536-37, 542, 549n
Governmentality, 252, 410n, 539, 543, 547n, 548n
*Gumnazein*, 84, 101n, 356, 359, 425-26, 450, 453

Habits, 94-95, 129-31, 211, 344, 495, 534, 536
Happiness, 62n, 73, 87-88, 92, 135-36, 151, 184, 194-95, 265, 308, 310, 320, 392, 519
Hermeneutics, xxvi, 501, 503, 515
History, 3, 9-12, 14, 17-18, 22n, 59-60, 66-67, 70, 74, 76-77, 176, 179, 180, 207-209, 220, 221, 263-64, 307-309, 316, 319, 364, 449, 461-62, 508-12, 514-15, 520-26, 547
Human sciences, 188, 520
*Hupomnēmata*, 360-62, 367, 369n, 370n, 500, 528, 548n

Identity, 97, 250, 303-307, 320, 454-56, 467, 513, 541, 544
Ignorance, 35-36, 45, 93-94, 128-30, 134, 209, 224n, 254, 363
Illness, 95, 97-98, 116, 182, 197, 198, 229, 284, 349, 442, 475n, 479, 496, 504, 515
Immortality, 48, 91, 111, 142, 181, 183-84, 211, 231, 445-46, 448, 492, 497
Instant, 299, 302, 304, 305
*Instructio*, 94, 320

Joy, 109, 272, 286n, 310, 433, 478n, 488, 504
Juridification, 112
Justice, 34, 54, 63n, 71-73, 79n, 153-54, 174, 176, 200, 431-32, 513, 523

## Index of notions and concepts 561

Knowledge (*connaissance*), xxi, xxiii, xxiv, xxv, xxviii, 17, 30, 77, 130, 190, 191, 229-30, 235, 237-38, 241, 255, 317-19, 484, 487. *See also* Self-knowledge
Knowledge (*savoir*), 28-29, 171, 230, 238-39, 243, 249, 278, 318-19, 487, 527

Language, 54-55, 84, 153, 164, 297, 335, 336, 341, 342, 344, 367-68, 383, 401, 403, 415, 456
Law. *See* Right
Liberation, 24n, 94, 108, 209-10, 212, 225n, 273, 276, 278-79, 385, 460, 511, 526, 531
*Libertas*, 366, 368, 372-73, 383, 384, 391, 400, 401, 405-406
Life, 5-10, 32-33, 35-36, 75-76, 84, 86-89, 90-93, 107-14, 125-29, 131-32, 135-36, 138-43, 149, 150-51, 154, 156, 160-62, 178-79, 181-85, 197, 205, 206, 208, 211, 215, 216, 232, 233, 236, 238, 243, 247-48, 250, 261, 272, 283-85, 291, 303-305, 320-22, 361, 362, 416, 423-26, 429-32, 437-41, 445-50, 453-54, 460, 466-67, 475n, 478-81, 485-86, 493-98, 504, 527, 530, 536-37, 544
Listening, 118, 333-34, 338-52, 362, 365, 367, 403, 413-16, 500, 516, 528. *See also* Audition
*Logos*, 239, 323-27, 334-43, 348-49, 368, 375, 469, 527-58
Looking, 10-12, 15, 70, 72, 85, 202, 206, 213, 220-22, 277, 283, 295, 302, 305, 306, 335, 351, 419, 430, 443, 454-60, 464, 480, 504, 542. *See also* Gaze
Love, 239, 334-43, 348, 349, 368, 527-59

Madness, 22n, 24n, 145n, 229, 468, 512-13, 520
Marxism, 29, 524

Master, mastership, 9, 34, 37, 58, 59, 86, 92-93, 94, 98, 128-30, 141, 145n, 155, 158-59, 169, 206, 213, 221, 242, 302, 306, 348, 363, 368, 371, 373, 384-85, 389-90, 405, 408, 415, 465, 493, 496, 536
*Mathēsis*, 311, 315, 316-17, 331
Medicine, 57, 59, 60, 97-99, 104n, 107-108, 120, 126, 242, 249-50, 267, 310, 315, 328n, 340, 352n, 388, 393-94n, 398, 404, 410n, 496, 499, 511, 513, 516, 536
Meditation, xxii, 11, 23, 117, 260, 272, 294, 296, 301, 356-59, 369n, 426, 450, 453-63, 477-79, 499, 501, 504
Meditation on death, 23n, 111, 272, 359, 417-18, 477-78, 504
*Meletē*, 11, 23n, 84, 356-57, 425, 435, 454, 456, 459, 463, 477, 480, 481, 488n, 504
Memorization, 11, 88, 295, 480, 500
Memory, xxii, 48, 88, 101n, 128-29, 163, 176, 182, 226n, 280-82, 295, 325-26, 360, 403-404, 414-16, 455-56, 460-61, 464-68, 483, 500, 501
*Metanoia*, 85, 101n, 178, 211-17, 225n, 226n, 533
Method, xxii, 14, 18, 66, 77, 142, 177, 224n, 256, 293-94, 305, 309, 369, 388, 460-61
Modalization, 290, 308, 318
Model, 61, 160, 190, 216, 231, 254-59, 478, 495
Morality, 2-3, 11-14, 171, 208, 258-59, 261, 266, 344, 527, 530, 532, 535
Movement, 15, 74, 77, 78, 207, 210, 213, 214, 216, 217, 221, 248, 251, 263, 275-76, 280-83, 290, 294, 344, 345, 353n, 461, 474n, 500
Music, 48, 62n, 145n, 301, 315, 328, 335, 415, 534

Nature, 95, 171, 220-21, 223, 230-35, 238, 241-44, 259, 263-64, 266, 271, 273-79, 280, 281, 285, 310, 401

Navigation, 248-49, 267n, 404, 411n
Neo-Platonic, 76
Neo-Platonism, 74, 170, 174, 175, 186, 224n, 419-21, 434n
Norms, 188, 511, 527, 530. *See also* Right (Law); Rule

Obedience, 317, 319, 403, 424, 489n, 510, 527
Objectification, 317, 319, 333, 510, 512
Old age, 74-76, 88, 91-92, 100, 108-11, 122n, 126, 132, 146n, 262, 269, 285, 349, 448, 478, 504, 517, 533
Oneself. *See* Self
Other, others, other person, 10, 12, 35-39, 52, 59, 113, 114, 119, 128, 134, 136, 156, 140, 174-77, 180, 192, 195-99, 202, 206, 218-22, 229, 230, 233, 236-37, 249, 301, 321, 360, 379, 385, 391, 433, 441
*Otium. See* Free Time

*Paideia*, 46, 104n, 126, 239-40, 246n, 408, 517
*Paraskeuē*, 240, 320-27, 332, 350, 376, 473, 528. *See also* Equipment
*Parrhēsia*, 137, 158, 164, 170, 242, 366-68, 372-73, 379, 381-91, 396, 399, 403-407, 411n, 416, 517, 529
Passion, 97-98, 198, 267n, 310, 342, 397, 399, 433, 496
Pedagogy, 44-46, 72, 74-76, 170, 205-206, 247, 261, 408, 419, 494-95, 516, 536
Penance, 215, 263, 482, 509
Philosopher, 7, 17, 21n, 97, 135-36, 138-40, 142-43, 145, 146, 151, 153, 154, 165n, 201, 224n, 345, 350, 382, 415, 424-25, 430, 435, 441, 453
Philosophy, xix-xxiv, xxvi-xxviii, 2-3, 10-12, 15, 17, 25, 28, 31, 37, 39, 46, 51, 66, 68, 86, 87-88, 92-93, 97-99, 115, 117, 131, 135-36, 151, 154-55, 169-70, 178-79, 182, 189-92, 213-16, 239, 274, 336-38, 345, 366, 386, 426, 485, 487, 494, 509, 518, 520-27
*Phusiologia*, 238, 240-43
Piloting, 249-50, 324, 393n
Platonic, 44, 50, 54, 65, 68, 73, 74, 76, 97, 171, 172, 173, 174, 176, 191, 195, 209-11, 216-18, 254-58, 276, 280-83, 419, 459, 495, 500, 533, 534, 546
Platonism, 23n, 34, 67, 73-74, 77, 121, 170, 174, 189, 224n, 257, 419, 420, 434n, 439, 460, 518
Pleasure, 12, 23n 86, 99, 109-11, 134, 214, 220, 234, 241, 265, 273, 277, 281, 302, 304, 352, 378, 388, 430, 466, 474n, 495, 507, 514, 521, 534-35, 547n
*Pneuma*, 47, 303-304
Politics, 33-34, 44, 76, 87, 89, 126, 135, 150, 175, 203n, 252, 494, 512, 514, 517, 526, 542-44, 547, 549n
Power, 36, 157, 165n, 252, 268n, 271, 375, 508, 512, 513, 515, 540-44, 549n
Practice, 15, 17, 30, 46-49, 60, 75, 84, 87-89, 96-98, 99, 109-10, 112, 117-18, 126-27, 136-38, 141, 143, 154, 170, 182, 209-10, 214, 222, 239, 243, 297, 315-19, 339-40, 385-91, 425-26, 429-33, 447, 462, 466, 479, 481, 485, 492-97, 500-502, 511, 538
Practices of the self, xxvii, 57, 75, 82, 86-89, 91, 93, 98, 107, 109, 114-15, 117, 120, 125-27, 129, 131, 136, 149, 155-56, 161, 163-64, 169, 177, 180, 205-206, 239, 243, 258, 316-17, 331-33, 340-41, 369n, 454, 508, 512-13, 515, 517, 520, 524, 527, 529, 534-35, 543-45
*Praemeditatio malorum*, 360, 463, 468-73, 478, 501
Precept, 3-4, 13-14, 52-53, 67, 72, 79n, 118-19, 160, 172, 205, 236, 252-53, 289-91, 308, 349-50, 447, 493
Preparation, 10, 29, 48, 70, 94, 126, 211, 215, 222, 240, 320-21, 324, 326, 427, 445-46, 454, 485, 516, 527, 532, 545

# Index of notions and concepts 563

Prescription, 3, 45, 68, 112, 261, 268n, 292, 307, 350-51, 363, 459, 531
Presumption of evils. See *Praemeditatio malorum*
Prince, the, 34, 102n, 150, 151, 199, 203n, 249, 374, 377, 380-81, 392n
Prison, 182, 183, 186n, 209, 229
*Prokheiron*, 325, 329n, 357, 361, 484, 499
Psychagogy, 408
Psychoanalysis, xxv-xxvi, 29-30, 188, 525, 524
Psychology, 253
Purification, 47, 50, 173, 255, 340, 416, 480, 502, 522
Pythagorean, 48, 62n, 77, 93, 109, 123n, 136, 146n, 200, 215, 217, 316, 341, 353n, 413, 415, 480, 488n, 500
Pythagoreanism, 48, 62n, 189

Rationality, 9, 77, 196, 279-81, 324, 474n, 528
Reading, 119, 161, 163, 260, 333, 334, 351, 355-62, 369n, 370n, 372, 377, 385, 428, 508, 514, 516, 518, 528, 535, 546
Reason, 275-76, 279, 282, 297, 420, 445
Recollection, 176, 209-10, 216, 224n, 255-58, 276, 280-82, 500, 528, 533
Rectification, 130. See also Correction; *Emendatio*
Relationship to self, 84, 86, 109, 119-20, 127, 129, 135, 185, 192, 258, 265, 273, 450, 511-12, 529, 533-42, 548n
Renunciation, 23n, 185, 209, 211, 216, 225n, 250, 256-58, 267, 317, 319-20, 327, 328n, 332-33, 416, 485, 539
Representation, 132, 141, 293-94, 298, 300, 305, 312, 479
Resistance, 150, 184, 240, 252, 347, 427, 435n, 502, 526, 543-44
Retirement, 517, 521. See also Withdrawal; *Anakhōrēsis*
Return to self, 208-209, 213, 215, 230, 247-48, 250-51, 308, 315
Revelation, 24n, 120, 255, 327, 363, 408

Review of self, 171, 224n, 225n, 248, 481, 537
Revolution, 208-209, 281, 509
Rhetoric, 96, 135, 165n, 346-48, 368, 373, 381-86, 392n, 393n, 402, 406, 425, 454
Right (Law), 15, 52, 239, 240, 252, 283, 338, 341, 345, 364, 365, 390, 406, 414-15, 472, 484, 485, 522, 523
Rule, 4-5, 8, 26, 31, 71, 98, 112, 126, 149, 156, 162, 164, 247, 291, 302, 317, 340-43, 350, 388, 423-24, 429, 432, 470, 471, 480, 491, 538, 540-41

Sage, 123n, 136, 243, 283, 285, 321-22, 325, 342, 380, 392, 458-59, 511, 520, 523, 537, 541
Salvation, 23, 107, 120-21, 127, 176, 180-85, 186n, 192, 195, 250, 318, 363-64, 390-91, 416, 445, 446, 487, 513, 527, 533
Schema, 10, 207-209, 213, 216, 217, 254-57, 292, 316, 376, 439, 442, 478, 481, 535
Science, 26-29, 117, 226, 233, 245n, 309, 310, 312n, 328, 393n, 394n, 396, 519
Scout, 440-41, 451n, 516
*Securitas*, 50, 62n
Self, oneself, 3, 4, 6-14, 20, 22n, 30, 58-60, 46, 50, 66-68, 74-77, 82-93, 96-100, 107-108, 111-13, 116-17, 120-21, 134, 150, 177-180, 195, 205-206, 208-209, 210-11, 213, 215, 230, 247-48, 249, 250-52, 257, 308, 311, 315, 316, 318, 359, 374, 404, 417, 445-48, 462, 465, 492, 495-98, 502, 516, 517, 524, 527, 532-34, 536-42
Self-knowledge, xx, xxi-xxii, 3, 4, 69, 76, 82, 84, 172-73, 175, 230, 254-56, 259, 419-20, 422, 430-31, 455-56, 461, 491, 513, 523
Sensual pleasure, 378
Serenity, 184, 243, 444
Sexuality, xxi, 20n, 230, 253, 508-509, 511-15, 517, 521, 548n

## INDEX OF NOTIONS AND CONCEPTS

Silence, 183, 331, 341-43, 348, 350, 352n, 353n, 366, 368, 372, 413-14, 472, 481, 504, 508, 511, 548n
Sincerity, 138, 291, 298
Slavery of the self, 225n
Sophistic, 103n, 393n, 503
Soul:
    care of the, 88, 91, 99, 114, 115, 117, 162, 493
    errors of the, 386, 392n, 393n, 396, 410n
    exercises of the, 427
    practice of the, 99, 403, 497
    technician of the, 398, 399
Sovereignty, 16, 86, 135, 184, 200, 201, 206, 344, 372, 374, 377-78, 385, 392n, 468, 533, 540, 542, 549n
Speech, 54, 137, 242, 342, 355, 366, 372, 393n, 403, 511
Spiritual direction, guidance, 101n, 123n, 136-38, 140, 144, 156, 158, 159, 164, 201, 226n, 275, 363, 370n, 386-87, 398-99, 408, 410, 509, 510, 514
Spiritual director, guide, 61, 146, 163, 166n, 363, 397-99, 510
Spiritual exercise, 292-94, 301, 306-307, 309, 423
Spirituality, xxiii-xxv, xxviii, 10-11, 15-19, 25-30, 77-78, 178, 190-91, 257, 299, 308-311, 319, 332, 341-42, 363, 421-22, 434, 446, 503
Statement, 261, 291, 312n, 324, 510, 527
Status, 12, 18, 83, 118-19, 126, 130, 134, 142, 173, 183, 201, 247, 313n, 375, 468, 493, 541
Stoic, xxvi, 13, 37, 50, 77-78, 82, 115, 118, 151, 153, 217, 230, 283-84, 315, 322, 323, 346, 400, 426, 428-31, 438, 442-43, 445, 472, 524, 532, 541, 543
    athlete, 322
    and care of the self, 88, 113
    conception of man as a command being, 192, 195
    Cynic diatribe, 365
    eternity, 313n
    examination of conscience, 200
    examination of representations, 299, 301
    knowledge of the world and self-knowledge, 253-54, 259-60, 266
    meditation, 457, 459
    meeting, 131, 135, 143
    need to know nature, 278
    stepping back of, 276
    suspicion of oneself, 422
Stoicism, 50, 81, 89, 102, 122n, 147n, 148n, 203n, 254, 259-61, 284, 294, 306, 370n, 410n, 434n, 442-43, 460, 501, 519, 520, 526, 531, 531-33, 535, 542, 544
Structure, 13, 15-16, 18, 26, 28-29, 152, 180, 190-91, 281, 290, 326, 375, 385, 391, 447, 531
Struggle, 140, 215, 222, 226n, 231-32, 240, 265, 272, 275, 322, 361, 373, 427, 431, 444, 449, 495, 533, 535, 543-44
*Stultitia*, 130-35, 145n, 344, 353n, 465, 474n, 496
Style, 21n, 73, 338, 352n, 392, 401, 402, 415, 424, 430, 508, 513, 531, 533, 534
Subject, xx, xxii, xxiv-xxv, 2-3, 14-19, 26, 29, 30, 129-30, 157, 180, 188-92, 240, 248, 258, 291-92, 308, 310, 317-19, 327, 358, 364, 371, 385, 406-407, 409, 424, 431, 443, 457, 460-63, 511, 512, 522, 524, 538
Subjection, 212-13, 319, 460, 510-11, 526, 543
Subjectivation, xx, 20n, 61n, 214, 333-34, 351, 365-66, 369n, 372, 511, 521, 523, 526, 528, 548n
Subjectivity, xx, 2, 11, 15, 18, 129, 180, 208, 250, 319, 364, 368, 377, 378, 486, 524
Suicide, 147, 231, 285, 429, 497

Technique, 47, 49, 61n, 76, 138, 178, 242, 249, 261, 333, 338, 349, 372-73, 375,

381-82, 391, 400, 417-18, 425, 447-49, 494, 526, 544
Techniques of the self, 47-50, 61n, 62n, 65, 68, 176, 258, 417, 512-15, 517, 521, 524-26
Technology of the self, 46, 48, 50, 61n, 120, 208, 374
*Tekhnē*, xxvii, 35, 38, 51, 58, 176, 224n, 249, 339-40, 368, 372-73, 382, 387, 392n, 393n, 396, 424, 447-48, 454, 485, 486-87, 523, 524
*Tekhnē tou biou*, 86, 125, 177-78, 205, 259-60, 424, 427, 447-48, 485
Test, 299, 398, 430, 431, 433, 437, 440, 443, 446, 448, 449, 454, 469, 470, 483, 485-87
Text, 190, 255, 256, 327, 334, 363, 408
Theology, 26-27, 171, 190, 310, 313n
*Therapeuein*, 8-9, 21n, 53, 98, 105n, 225n, 272
Therapy, 9, 49, 396
Thought, xxi, xxii, 3-4, 11-13, 15, 25-29, 49, 51, 67, 71, 74, 77, 127, 130, 156, 170, 173, 181, 191, 208, 210, 216, 217, 222, 230, 250-51, 259, 291, 301, 317-19, 356-60, 367, 404-405, 418-19, 425, 433, 446, 450, 454, 459-60, 464-73, 478, 480-85, 487, 501, 503, 517, 522, 530, 532
Time, 45-46, 73, 75, 126, 131-33, 150-51, 161, 163, 185, 200, 219, 245, 263-64, 277-78, 290, 296, 301, 304, 307, 349, 350, 381, 457, 459, 467, 470, 471
Tragedy, 444, 451n
Training, 90, 93-94, 95, 125, 138-41, 160, 321-22, 414-15, 426-28, 437-41, 495-97, 501, 531
Trajectory, 74, 223, 248, 261
Tranquility, 16, 62n, 120, 184, 195, 225n, 296, 297, 343, 362, 370n, 344, 497
Transfiguration, 18, 26, 212, 216, 308, 310, 320, 417, 443

Transformation, 15-16, 26, 28, 86, 190-92, 242-43, 326-27, 408, 417, 460, 487, 522, 524, 526
Truth, xxi, xxii-xxv, 15-19, 25-30, 46-47, 76-77, 140, 178, 188-91, 242, 253-56, 260, 317-19, 332-34, 338-40, 346, 348, 350-51, 357, 362-68, 381-84, 390, 400-408, 455, 459-63, 510, 522, 528. *See also* Discourse

Veridiction, 229, 235, 362, 368, 371, 372
Vigilance, 218, 222, 438, 449, 530, 534-35, 537
Virtue, 6, 21n, 22n, 61n, 145n, 233, 234, 280, 298, 303-304, 315-16, 328n, 335, 337-38, 406-407, 426-28, 480, 491, 505

Wealth, 6-7, 33-35, 44, 52, 58, 61n, 73, 105, 277n, 429-30, 442, 491, 493, 500, 512, 539
Will, 132-33, 134, 192, 336
Wisdom, 33-34, 44, 71-72, 79n, 104n, 108, 136, 154, 155, 165n, 194-95, 207, 213-14, 226n, 234, 269n, 285, 321, 380, 401, 458, 488n
Withdrawal, 13, 47-48, 50, 67, 91, 101n, 103n, 211, 310, 418, 425, 537-38, 549n. *See also* Retirement, *Anakhōrēsis*
Work, 19, 26, 31, 103n, 114, 116, 131, 134, 161, 189, 191, 198, 200, 203n, 264, 265, 273, 275, 294, 351, 424-26, 428, 432, 433, 483, 493, 531, 539, 559n
 of the self, xxvii-xxviii, 16, 77, 120, 446, 532
World, 10-11, 89, 195, 240-43, 260-62, 265, 275-76, 279, 282-85, 290, 385, 442-43, 486-87, 524, 527, 537-38
 aristocratic, 44-45
 civilized, 119, 124n
 cultural, 93
 disengagement from the, 47

World—*continued*
  external, 47, 48, 50, 131-32, 232, 240,
    300, 322, 334, 418, 427, 442
  Greek, 20n
  Hellenic, 180
  of impurity, 181, 183
  knowledge of, 202, 232, 243, 259,
    261, 282, 289, 301, 306, 308,
    311, 315, 317
  modern, 13, 253
  other, 181, 209-210
  political, 361
  Roman, 20n, 47, 199, 317
  social, 90
  Western, 129
Writing, 119, 158, 161, 333-44, 351, 355,
    359, 362-63, 372, 377, 342, 500,
    508, 511-17